THE WORLD AND THE GREAT-POWER TRIANGLES

Center for International Studies, Massachusetts Institute of Technology

Studies in Communism, Revisionism, and Revolution (formerly Studies in International Communism),William E. Griffith, general editor

1. Albania and the Sino-Soviet Rift — William E. Griffith (1963)

2. Communism in North Vietnam — P. J. Honey (1964)

3. The Sino-Soviet Rift — William E. Griffith (1964)

4. Communism in Europe, Vol. 1 — William E. Griffith, ed. (1964)

5. Nationalism and Communism in Chile — Ernst Halperin (1965)

6. Communism in Europe, Vol. 2 — William E. Griffith, ed. (1966)

7. Viet Cong: The Organization and Techniques of the National Liberation Front of South Vietnam — Douglas Pike (1966)

8. Sino-Soviet Relations, 1964-1965 — William E. Griffith (1967)

9. The French Communist Party and the Crisis of International Communism — François Fejtö (1967)

10. The New Rumania: From People's Democracy to Socialist Republic — Stephen Fischer-Galati (1967)

11. Economic Development in Communist Rumania — John Michael Montias (1967)

12. Cuba: Castroism and Communism, 1959-1966 — Andrés Suárez (1967)

13. Unity in Diversity: Italian Communism and the Communist World — Donald L. M. Blackmer (1967)

14. Winter in Prague: Documents on Czechoslovak Communism in Crisis — Robin Alison Remington, ed. (1969)

15. The Angolan Revolution, Vol. 1: The Anatomy of an Explosion (1950-1962) — John A. Marcum (1969)

16. Radical Politics in West Bengal — Marcus F. Franda (1971)

17. The Warsaw Pact: Case Studies in Communist Conflict Resolution — Robin Alison Remington (1971)

18. The Transformation of Communist Ideology: The Yugoslav Case, 1945-1953 — A. Ross Johnson (1972)

19. Radical Politics in South Asia — Paul R. Brass and Marcus F. Franda, eds. (1973)

20. The Canal War: Four-Power Conflict in the Middle East — Lawrence L. Whetten (1974)

21. The World and the Great-Power Triangles — William E. Griffith, ed. (1975)

THE WORLD AND THE GREAT-POWER TRIANGLES

Edited by William E. Griffith

The MIT Press
Cambridge, Massachusetts, and London, England

71068

This book was typed by Evelyn Torrey, printed on Finch Title 93, and bound
in Columbia Millbank Vellum by The Colonial Press Inc. in the United States
of America.

Library of Congress Cataloging in Publication Data

Griffith, William E

    The world and the great-power triangles.

    (Studies in communism, revisionism, and revolution; 21)
    Includes bibliographical references and index.
    1. World politics—1945-   I. Title. II. Series.
D843.G772   327'.1'09047   74-31219
ISBN 0-262-07064-2

CONTENTS

Chapter 5
JAPAN AND THE GREAT-POWER TRIANGLES   271
Paul F. Langer

Chapter 6
THE DETENTE AND KOREA   321
Chong-Sik Lee

PREFACE

This collective volume is a preliminary attempt to assess the interaction of regional developments in several important areas of the world with the transition in international politics to dual mulipolarity, as expressed in the political-military and economic triangles. Some readers may wonder why the book does not include a chapter on Europe. That area will be covered in part in a book that I am now completing on the Germanies and the socialist world.

I am most grateful to the Earhart Foundation and its president, Mr. Richard Ware, for the generous financial support that made this volume possible.

William E. Griffith

Cambridge, Massachusetts
October 1, 1974

THE CONTRIBUTORS

Viktor Meier is the author of "Yugoslav Communism" in Volume I of *Communism in Europe,* edited by William E. Griffith. Author of many articles on politics in the Balkans, he was formerly Balkan correspondent for the *Neue Zürcher Zeitung.*

Arnold Hottinger is the Middle East correspondent for the *Neue Zürcher Zeitung.* He is the author of *Fellachen und Funktionare: Entwicklungswege in Nahen Osten* and many articles on Middle East affairs.

Bhabani Sen Gupta is Rockefeller Foundation Fellow for Study of International Conflict at the Research Institute on International Change, Columbia University, and the author of *Communism in India.*

Paul F. Langer is a senior staff member of The Rand Corporation, Santa Monica, California, and coauthor, with Rodger Swearingen, of *Communist Strategy in Japan.*

Chong-Sik Lee is a member of the Department of Political Science of the University of Pennsylvania and coauthor, with Robert Scalapino, of the two-volume study *Communism in Korea.*

THE WORLD AND THE GREAT-POWER TRIANGLES

Chapter 1

THE WORLD AND THE GREAT-POWER TRIANGLES

William E. Griffith

The diplomatic revolution of the early 1970s resulted from two
interacting processes of transition to tripolarity: first, from
Soviet-American bipolarity to the Sino-Soviet-U.S. political-
military triangle and, second, from a dominant U.S. world
economic position to an economic triangle composed of the
United States, Western Europe, and Japan.[1]
   The political-military triangle dominates world politics
today. Its three members earned their places in it by their
size and geographic position, temperate climate and natural
resources, population and human skills, industry and
technology, atomic capability, and national will to power.
Membership in the economic triangle has been determined by
gross national product, technology, human skills, population
control, entrepreneurial talent, labor productivity, and the
will to economic power.
   The two triangles are asymmetrical and unstable because of
the continuing rise of Soviet and Chinese military power and,
until recently, greater Western European and Japanese economic
power. Yet in spite of Soviet military gains and the decline
(until late 1973) in the American economic position and in the
will to power on the part of the American intelligentsia, the
United States remains the strongest single power, for it alone
is a member of both triangles and is thus the only political-
military and economic superpower. China, despite its
technological and military weakness and the fact that it is a
regional, not a world, power, is a member of the political-
military triangle for several reasons, including its history,
its rising power, and the Sino-Soviet split. The Sino-Soviet
split has meant that, for the U.S., only China can bring
effective pressure on Moscow in favor of Soviet-U.S. détente
and, for China, only the U.S. can effectively help to deter a
Soviet attack. Neither the Soviet Union nor China is an
economic superpower because of their autarkic economies, the
low level of their civilian technology, and their minimal
participation in international trade. Both therefore need and
want Western technology and credits.
   The major result of the diplomatic revolution has been the
intensification of international détente, caused by

successful U.S. balance-of-power politics. Sino-Soviet hostility
plus Sino-American and Soviet-American détente have enabled
Washington simultaneously to intensify détente with both China
and the Soviet Union, to its own advantage.

The Political-Military Triangle

The Soviet-American Cold War. Soviet-American hostility after
1945 was in my view structural and inevitable, because of the
power vacua in Western Europe and Japan, ideological hostility,
and Soviet political and American economic expansion.[2] Indeed,
probably only American and then Soviet atomic capabilities
prevented a Soviet-American war. Instead, after Stalin's death
in 1953 the Soviet-American conflict relationship was gradually
limited because of the existence of atomic weapons and rising
Soviet atomic power, which produced a political and military
stalemate, and later because of the Sino-Soviet split. For
geopolitical, historical, and, more recently, ideological
reasons, Russo-Chinese hostility has always been potentially
greater than Russo-American or Sino-American.
    Their limitation of their conflict relationship made
Washington and Moscow pay less attention to their allies, whose
influence in world politics was thus limited and who therefore
feared that Washington and Moscow would conclude over their
heads bilateral agreements unfavorable to their national
interests. The superpowers' alliances suffered also from the
rising economic and military power of their allies. Yet, on the
other hand, the alliances were also adversely affected by the
increasing nuclear superiority of the superpowers over their
allies, by the attractiveness to both superpowers of settling
the problems of the world themselves (in short, superpower
chauvinism), and, finally, by greater U.S. concern, for balance-
of-payments reasons, about economic competition with its allies
and trade with the Soviets and Chinese. Although alliance
tensions initially appeared between the United States and
France, they soon became much more serious between the Soviet
Union and China.
    The Kennedy and Johnson administrations gave priority,
particularly on arms control and nonproliferation issues, to
bilateral Soviet-American negotiations rather than to
discussions with allies or China. In contrast, the lower
priority that President Nixon initially gave to Soviet-U.S.
relations helped the Sino-American détente of the early 1970s,
which in turn enabled Washington to intensify Soviet-U.S.
détente. The more important cause of the Sino-American détente,
however, was Sino-Soviet hostility.

The Sino-Soviet Split. The Sino-Soviet split was probably
inevitable.[3] Its major causes were, first, historical:
traditional Russo-Chinese hostility and, in particular, forcible
Russian annexation and continued Soviet domination of some of
the Chinese Empire and thus the existence of major Chinese
territorial irredentas (the Soviet Far Eastern provinces, an
extreme eastern part of Soviet Central Asia, and the Mongolian
People's Republic) which any strong Chinese government was
bound to resent; and the multinational character of both states,
the artificiality of the border between them, and the presence
on both sides of it of the same ethnic groups (Kazakhs, Uighurs,
and Mongols). In the 1950s, the first decade in history in which
a simultaneously strong Russia and China faced each other across
common borders, these factors alone would probably sooner or
later have eroded the Sino-Soviet alliance.

Its collapse was made more certain by what is usually but, in
my view, incorrectly termed the "ideological" factor in Sino-
Soviet relations, which I prefer to call the organizational
factor: the Sino-Soviet struggle for supremacy within the
international communist and radical world. The history and
ideology of Marxism-Leninism, like that of Roman Catholicism,
require one center of power. Moreover, the orthodox of any faith
always hate heretics more than heathens. Finally, the Soviet
Communist party's domestic legitimacy rests in part on its claim
to be the recognized leader of the international communist
movement, and the maintenance of this position has always been a
significant aim of Soviet foreign policy. Although Soviet
supremacy in the communist world has been first successfully
challenged by President Tito of Yugoslavia, China's challenge
was made by the first communist party potentially equal, or
nearly so, to the CPSU, and after Stalin's death Mao Tse-tung
understandably considered himself to be the senior living
communist leader. When he challenged Soviet primacy and then
claimed communist leadership, Soviet state interests were thus
vitally involved, and pragmatic Sino-Soviet compromises on them
became far more difficult.

Controversies over organizational and state interests were
further fueled by two other asymmetries. First, the Soviet
Union and China were out of phase in economic development, for
the former was far more developed than the latter. Second,
while Stalin had killed most of the old Bolshevik
revolutionaries and had replaced them by a postrevolutionary
technocratic elite, in China Mao and his Yenan guerrilla
associates, who remained in power, were convinced that Chinese
economic underdevelopment required mobilizational, repressive
political policies if China were to move rapidly to great-power
status while maintaining revolutionary purity and enthusiasm.

In sum, the fundamental cause of the Sino-Soviet split was
the determination of China to become a superpower and thus to
be equal to the Soviet Union, and the Soviet determination to
prevent it.

The Sino-Soviet conflict was also intensified by specific
foreign-policy issues. The first was the issue of relations
with the United States: China first strongly opposed Premier
Khrushchev's policy of détente and then in the early 1970s
switched, out of anti-Soviet motives, to favoring détente with
Washington, thus provoking even greater Soviet hostility. The
second issue was that of sharp differences in policy toward
India in the context of Sino-Soviet rivalry in Asia. The third
was the Soviet refusal to continue to give China atomic aid and
its preference for a nonproliferation treaty with Washington.
Fourth, the Vietnam war and U.S. involvement in it accentuated
Sino-Soviet tensions. Finally, Sino-Soviet relations were
brought to the brink of limited war by the series of border
conflicts that culminated in 1969 on the Ussuri and in
Sinkiang.[4] The first Ussuri incident was probably initiated by
the Chinese. Sharp Soviet retaliatory attacks on the Ussuri and
later in Sinkiang were followed by what amounted to a successful
Soviet ultimatum to Peking either to cease border incidents and
begin border negotiations or to face a Soviet attack. But
simultaneously, in order to ensure an end to the incidents, and
also probably as a result of a bureaucratic compromise in Moscow
between hawks and doves on the issue of attack on negotiations
with Peking, the Soviets greatly increased their troop
deployment along the Chinese frontier, which they had begun in
the middle 1960s. By early 1974 this deployment had reached at
least 45 combat divisions,[5] around 450,000 men, with full
conventional and atomic armament. Ironically, Moscow thereby not
only achieved the ending of the border incidents and the opening
of border negotiations (so far totally unproductive) but also
drove the Chinese toward the Americans. Moscow thus made real
its own worst nightmare: a potential Sino-American coalition
against the Soviet Union.

The Sino-Soviet split decisively changed the geopolitical
situation of both powers. China was once again confronted, as
it historically had been until the 1840s, by a primary threat
from the north and west rather than from the Pacific. Russia was
for the first time confronted by a primary long-term threat from
the east. Indeed, by 1974 China had probably acquired a minimal
nuclear delivery capability over Moscow, thus making a Soviet
attack against China considerably less likely.[6] Moreover, all
four other actual or potential nuclear powers, the U.S.,

Western Europe, Japan, and China, were hostile to the Soviet
Union, and three of its neighbors, China, Japan, and Germany,
had territorial claims on it.

On the other hand, in the early 1970s Moscow improved its
position in the international communist and radical world
as compared to its rather bad showing at the 1969 Moscow multiparty meeting. General Secretary Brezhnev's willingness to
accept "competitive coexistence" with other communist parties
had begun in 1964, when, contrary to Khrushchev's policy, he
accepted the "communist neutralism" of North Vietnam and North
Korea. (Conversely, after 1964, the Chinese, who had previously
tolerated the neutralism of these countries, demanded complete
support from them.) Moscow had hoped that the 1969 international
Moscow multiparty meeting would condemn the Chinese, endorse
"normalization" in Czechoslovakia, and recognize the CPSU as the
senior communist party. When it did not, and when the Rumanians
expressed major reservations in signing the document and the
Italians refused to sign most of it, most Western observers
viewed it as a Soviet defeat. By 1973 the Soviets had obtained,
through intensive interparty diplomacy, the near-cessation of
anti-Soviet statements by parties in alliance with the CPSU and
had institutionalized interparty consultative meetings at summit
and expert levels—in short, they had begun to codify the rules
of interparty competitive coexistence.[7] They were also helped in
their dealings with the Western European communist parties by
their strategic détente policy in Europe, from which the Italian
and French communists correctly expected to gain. Yet in late
1973, for reasons difficult to understand substantively but
perhaps explicable bureaucratically, Moscow began to try to
organize an international communist party conference, presumably
to renew the previously futile pursuit of collective
excommunication of the Chinese. Just as in 1969, opposition to
an anti-Chinese policy became clear in some of the Western
European communist parties. If the Soviets were to pursue it,
it seemed doubtful that they would get any farther, or perhaps
indeed as far, as they had in 1969[8] and likely that they might
worsen their positions vis-à-vis other communist parties.

The Chinese after 1968 attempted to reactivate their ties
with other communist states and parties for several reasons: the
1968 Soviet invasion of Czechoslovakia, the 1969 end of the
Cultural Revolution, and the massive Soviet troop deployment on
the Chinese frontier. They normalized state relations with
Yugoslavia, a country they had been denouncing since 1958 as
pro-imperialist and revisionist, and they even reached a modus
vivendi with a party as revisionist as the Spanish.[9] (The
Spanish party, like the Australian, had developed strained

relations with Moscow because of the latter's support of a pro-
Soviet dissident faction within its ranks.) But China's priority
for anti-Sovietism over support of radical movements made its
new strategy rather unsuccessful in the communist and radical
world, and the Soviets profited thereby. Peking's move toward
Washington strained its relations with its still strongly anti-
U.S. ally Albania[10] and disillusioned most of its Maoist
supporters elsewhere. Peking established diplomatic relations
with conservative, anticommunist Iran, Kuwait, and Ethiopia and
therefore ceased its support for the Eritrean Liberation
Movement and the Dhofar rebellion in Oman, which the Shah was
combating. Finally, the Chinese reduced their support of the
anti-Soviet "Maoist" splinter groups that they had helped to
set up in the mid-1960s.[11]

China also increasingly activated its policies in Europe.
Immediately after the 1968 Soviet invasion of Czechoslovakia,
Peking tried to encourage Rumania and Yugoslavia to adopt anti-
Soviet and pro-Chinese policies. Brezhnev countered with
pressure on Rumania and inducements to Yugoslavia. Rumanian
President Ceauşescu consequently limited somewhat his response
to Chinese initiatives, and Marshal Tito, particularly after his
sharp turn toward domestic repression in 1971-1972, beginning
with but going far beyond the Croatian crisis,[12] moved back
toward détente with Moscow and was thus less interested in
improving relations with Peking. Chinese objectives in the
Balkans were thus far from attained, while Moscow improved its
position there.

China also tried to cultivate the Western European states and
to influence them against Moscow. In the short run, Peking was
more fearful of Moscow than of Washington and therefore
concentrated on attempting to influence Western Europe against
the Soviet Union. It hoped that in the long run Western Europe
and Japan would become stronger and more independent power
centers with which, maximally, China could ally itself against
both Moscow and Washington. Moreover, it hoped to increase its
trade with the countries of the European Economic Community,
lest it become economically dependent on Japan and the United
States, and it hoped to acquire advanced technology from all
three sources to speed its industrial and military buildup.
Like Moscow, Peking was most interested in Bonn, but West German
Chancellor Willy Brandt refused to resume diplomatic relations
with China until after he had come to terms with Moscow and East
Berlin and was unlikely to try to play the Chinese card against
the Soviets. (The Chinese would therefore prefer to see the
Christian Democratic party (CDU) in power in Bonn.) French
President Pompidou also preferred détente with Moscow to

playing an anti-Soviet game with Peking. China consequently
placed the most hope on the British, for Prime Minister Heath
had expelled over a hundred alleged Soviet spies and was opposed
to mutual balanced force reduction (MBFR) in Europe. But even
in London Peking did not get very far.

In early 1974 the Chinese continued to be very active in
Western Europe. They warned especially against Soviet-American
"superpower chauvinism" and against the Strategic Arms
Limitation Treaty (SALT), the Conference on Security and
Cooperation in Europe (CSCE), and MFBR, which in Peking's view
would make it easier for Moscow to increase its threat to China,
and they favored NATO, EEC, and a European nuclear force.[13] But
Western European military weakness, political disunity, strained
relations with the United States, and fear of Soviet power made
it unlikely that Chinese policy in Europe would bear rapid or
substantial fruit. Chinese policy in Europe, as well as the
growing (and violently anti-Soviet) Chinese activity in the
United Nations, was fully in accord with what clearly remained
the long-term Chinese motive, however much it was overshadowed
in the early 1970s by Peking's preoccupation with the Soviet
threat: to make China the leader of the underdeveloped world
(the "first intermediate zone") and of Western Europe and Japan
(the "second intermediate zone") against the two superpowers.

Meanwhile, Sino-Soviet tensions, which had declined somewhat
after 1969, rose again in late 1973, probably primarily because
of the beginning of the Soviet drive for an anti-Chinese
international communist conference and the revival in China of
some of the Cultural Revolution themes. Soviet and Chinese
polemics became more extensive and violent. Moscow accused
Peking of conspiring with the imperialists. Peking accused
Moscow of the same and of repressing intellectual and
nationalities dissidence in the Soviet Union.[14] The border
negotiations were still stalled, reportedly over Chinese demands
that the Soviets formally declare that the nineteenth-century
treaties whereby the Russian Empire annexed what is now the
Soviet Maritime Province and a small part of eastern Kazakhstan
were "unequal" and that they also agree to a mutual troop
pullback from the Sino-Soviet and Sino-Mongolian borders. In
September 1973 Chou En-lai, at the Tenth Chinese Party Congress,
listed two additional preconditions for improving Sino-Soviet
relations: that the Soviets withdraw their troops from Mongolia
and Czechoslovakia and that they return the four southern Kurile
Islands to Japan. Brezhnev's proposal for an Asian security
system was primarily intended to contain China, and almost all
East and Southeast Asian states, particularly after the Sino-
American détente, therefore showed no interest in it. Moreover,

India's move further toward the Soviet Union, inevitable after
the Sino-American détente and India's war with Pakistan in 1971,
further worsened Sino-Soviet, Sino-Indian, and U.S.-Indian
relations.[15]

The Sino-American Rapprochement. The Sino-American rapprochement
arose from a limited common interest: to deter Moscow from using
its rising political or military power against either China or
the United States. Because of the massive, menacing Soviet
military buildup on their borders, the Chinese after 1969
concentrated on maximizing deterrence against a Soviet attack.
This could be best done, Peking concluded, by domestic
stability, military mobilization, and improvement of relations
with the United States. The Chinese military buildup also
required greater inputs of Western technology, for which
improvement of relations with the United States, Japan, and
Western Europe was a precondition.
    The differences within the Chinese leadership on rapprochement
with the United States were one, but probably not the major,
factor in a power struggle between Mao and Chou En-lai, on the
one hand, and Lin Piao, on the other. (Party-army bureaucratic
rivalry and struggle over the succession to Mao were probably its
main causes.) Although Lin was very likely not pro-Soviet as
such, he perhaps felt that China should not take so strong an
anti-Soviet and pro-American line but should try to profit from
improving relations with both the U.S. and the USSR. Mao and
Chou, on the other hand, gave priority to hostility toward the
Soviet Union.[16] The reappearance of Teng Hsiao-p'ing[17] and others
purged in the Cultural Revolution further demonstrated China's
return to relative bureaucratic normalcy.
    Mao and Chou had other reasons for their rapprochement with
the United States. First, while the Soviet troop buildup
proceeded to the north and west of China, Nixon pulled the
American troops out of Vietnam to the south. The Soviet Union
thus replaced the United States as the primary military threat
to China. Indeed, Peking thereafter feared that too rapid and
extensive a U.S. military withdrawal from the Far East, and
particularly from Taiwan, would result in an independent Taiwan,
which would inevitably come under Japanese hegemony. Mao and Chou
also wanted to profit from the Sino-Soviet split, U.S.-Japanese
alliance tensions, and the Japanese cultural affinity with (and
guilt feelings toward) China. They sought a balance between
pressures from the United States and Japan and planned to use
rapprochement with the United States to reestablish Sino-Japanese
relations on Chinese terms. By so doing, they hoped to prevent

Japan from converting its technological and economic power into political-military superpower status (and thus again challenging China for hegemony in East and Southeast Asia) or from moving too close to the Soviet Union, particularly by aiding the economic development of Siberia. China also hoped to profit from rising economic tensions between Western Europe and Japan, on the one hand, and the United States, on the other, and to improve relations with all three areas and thereby become less dependent on the United States.

The motives for President Nixon's change in American policy toward China cannot be considered apart from his intensification of détente with the Soviet Union, for they were part of a consciously integrated whole. Indeed, the China policy was intended primarily to contribute to Soviet détente. The Nixon administration policy was designed to adjust to the domestic "Vietnam syndrome" of decreasing commitment to an active foreign policy, to rising Soviet power, to the opportunities of the Sino-Soviet split, and to the necessity of at least neutralizing Moscow and Peking on the Vietnam war and, if possible, getting their help to end it by a compromise peace.

Nixon therefore replaced the Kennedy-Johnson priority for bilateral, simultaneous, unlinked negotiations with the Soviet Union, especially on arms control, with a policy of overall, linked negotiations with the Soviets in order to reconstruct the American-Soviet relationship on a more stable basis. Although Nixon negotiated with Brezhnev from a weaker U.S. position, he was more successful than his predecessors because he used pressure, especially his "Chinese connection," as well as inducements and compromise.

Other factors also influenced Nixon's policy changes. The threatening technological destabilization of the arms race by ABM and MIRV made Washington (and Moscow) more anxious to limit strategic arms. The increasing gap between Soviet technology and that of the West and Japan and the 1972 Soviet need to buy grain from the United States gave Washington the trade opportunities it needed to lessen the U.S. balance-of-trade and payments deficits and also further strengthened the U.S. bargaining position.

Nixon's main reason for improving relations with China was to put pressure on the Soviet Union. He correctly calculated that the Soviets, fearful of a Sino-American alliance against them, would offer more concessions to the United States for Soviet-American détente so that Washington would at least remain neutral between Moscow and Peking—which was what Nixon intended to do anyway. U.S. détente with Moscow and Peking (and with

Moscow in large part because of Peking) was also intended by
Washington to inhibit a Soviet attack on China, which would
destabilize the international political situation and prevent
Washington from establishing a balance between Moscow and Peking.
    Nixon also favored détente with Peking because he no longer
perceived Peking to be dangerously expansionist. The 1965
replacement of Sukarno by Suharto as head of the government in
Indonesia had ended China's attempt to use Indonesia as a junior
partner in a worldwide third-world alliance against the Soviet
Union and the United States; the Cultural Revolution had turned
China inward and largely paralyzed its foreign policy; and by
1969 China so feared a Soviet attack that its policies could be
only defensive, not expansionist. Nixon's most immediate domestic
and foreign policy problem, to extricate the United States from
Vietnam, also required rapprochement with Peking and Moscow so
that both would restrain Hanoi rather than urge it on. Finally,
in the United States the fading memories of Chinese intervention
in the Korean War, the decline of anticommunist ideological
commitment, and the resultant ineffectiveness of the "China
lobby," especially vis-à-vis a conservative President, gave Nixon
freedom of action to move toward détente with Peking and Moscow.
    The Nixon-Kissinger "grand design" went further than classical
balance-of-power policy, which, they felt, required modification
because of the nuclear danger. As Nixon put it in his 1973
foreign policy message to Congress:

". . . A certain balance of power is inherent in any
international system and has its place in the one we envision.
But it is not the overriding concept of our foreign policy.
First of all, our approach reflects the realities of the nuclear
age. The classical concept of balance of power included continual
maneuvering for marginal advantages over others. In the nuclear
era this is both unrealisitic and dangerous. It is unrealistic
because when both sides possess such enormous power, small
additional increments cannot be translated into tangible
advantage or even usable political strength. And it is dangerous
because an attempt to seek tactical gains might lead to
confrontation which could be catastrophic.
    "Secondly, our approach includes the element of consensus.
All nations, adversaries and friends alike, must have a stake in
preserving the international system. They must feel that their
principles are being respected and their national interests
secured. They must, in short, see positive incentives for
keeping the peace, not just the dangers of breaking it. If
countries believe global arrangements threaten their vital
concerns, they will challenge them. If the international

environment meets their vital concerns they will work to maintain
it. Peace requires mutual accommodation as well as mutual
restraint."[18]

The Chinese achieved the primary objectives of Sino-American
détente: to improve deterrence against a Soviet attack by making
the Soviet Union more uncertain about U.S. response; to prevent,
as a result of U.S. de facto recognition that Taiwan is a part of
China, a successful Taiwanese independence movement under Japanese
hegemony; to further Chinese reentry into international politics,
particularly by permanent membership in the UN Security Council;
and to come to such terms with the United States that Japan would
be forced to accept Peking's terms for a Sino-Japanese détente—
which Prime Minister Tanaka did. The United States also achieved
its main objectives: the creation of a triangular balance of power
in which the United States, because it had better relations with
both Moscow and Peking than either had with the other, could
intensify détente with both simultaneously and thereby further
stabilize the status quo in East and Southeast Asia, Europe, and
the Middle East; to move Moscow and Peking toward restraining
rather than encouraging Hanoi and thus to contribute to a
compromise Vietnam settlement (reached later that year); and
finally, to shelve the Taiwan issue by obtaining an implicit
Chinese commitment not to change its status by force.

The first immediate result of the Sino-American détente was in
Japan. The United States seriously worsened its relations with
Japan by not consulting the Japanese before the Sino-American
rapprochement. Nixon did not consult Tokyo because he feared that
the Japanese would not keep his intentions secret and that thereby
the Sino-American rapprochement would be delayed or prevented. In
addition, he was irritated with the Japanese because of strained
Japanese-American economic relations and because of failure in
interpersonal communications. In my view his lack of consultation
was based on an incorrect analysis of the situation, for China
needed the rapprochement more than the U.S. did and would
therefore hardly have abandoned it even if Nixon had consulted the
Japanese and his intentions had become public. Japan, not China,
is the only potential third superpower, its alliance with the U.S.
is a basic necessity of U.S. national interest, and the lack of
U.S. consultation seemed to the Japanese to undermine drastically
the mutual trust that they considered a necessary component of
the alliance.

Japan also felt compelled, for internal political reasons, to
accept Peking's requirement for resumption of diplomatic
relations: breaking diplomatic relations with Taiwan. Logically,
Moscow and Tokyo should also have moved closer. But although

the Soviet Union had been proposing since 1966 that Japan
participate in the economic development of Siberia, Soviet
reluctance to return to Japan the four southern Kurile Islands
(the "Northern Territories"),[19] Soviet slowness and
bureaucratism in the economic negotiations with Japan, and
traditional Japanese fear and distrust of the Soviet Union
remained major obstacles to improvement of Soviet-Japanese
relations. The October 1973 visit of Tanaka to Moscow did not
result in major progress, and Tanaka's weakened domestic
position[20] made it uncertain how far he could profit from
developing Sino-Soviet competition with Japan. Conversely, the
initial euphoria in Japan over the resumption of Sino-Japanese
relations gave way to more sober concentration on still
unsettled problems, notably China's concern over Japan's
continuing commercial ties with Taiwan, Tokyo's desire
simultaneously to improve relations with the Soviet Union,
and potential conflict over offshore oil drilling.[21] Yet Sino-
Japanese relations had improved significantly, and both
countries could and might try to profit from a more multipolar
world. (Reportedly, Chou En-lai told a Japanese socialist
delegation in early 1973 that Japan needed its security treaty
with the U.S. and a "reasonable" military growth and that it
might need and, if so, would get Chinese as well as U.S. aid
against hostile Soviet intentions.[22] In another move to
influence Japan against the Soviet Union, he also made the
return of the four islands to Japan a precondition of Sino-
Soviet détente.)

The second immediate result of the Sino-American détente was
in Korea, where domestic developments and international détente
brought Pyongyang and Seoul in 1972 to negotiation and partial
détente. In the peninsula, Pyongyang's guerrilla subversion
against the South had failed; however, Seoul still feared
further unilateral U.S. troop withdrawals. Internationally, both
Koreas feared that they would become isolated from the major
powers, all of whom, the U.S., the USSR, and China, as well as
Japan, wanted détente in Korea as elsewhere. Thereafter progress
in Korean détente was so slow as to be hardly perceptible, but
the international factors pushing toward it remained operative.[23]

The Intensified Soviet-American Détente. The Soviet-American
détente that followed the 1962 Cuban missile crisis was
interrupted in the mid-1960s by the Vietnam war, rising Soviet
military power, Soviet gains in the Middle East, and the 1968
Soviet invasion of Czechoslovakia. Beginning in 1969, however,
Moscow resumed and indeed intensified a long-range strategic
policy of East-West détente. Soviet motives in adopting this

policy were primarily defensive, although maximal, offensive
motives were also involved. The two most important defensive
motives concerned technology and China. The increasing
technological backwardness of the Soviet Union as compared to
that of the West and Japan[24] made Moscow decide to import much
more American, Japanese, and Western European technology and
credits rather than carry out drastic economic reforms at the
cost of less political control. (In 1972 an unprecedentedly bad
Soviet grain harvest led to large purchases of U.S. wheat.)[25] A
prolonged period of East-West détente was required to achieve
these aims. Moscow was also anxious, particularly after the 1969
Ussuri incidents, to ensure peace and stability on its western
flank so it could turn its attention to the confrontation with
China.

A third defensive motive was to stabilize Soviet control in
Eastern Europe. The Soviets seemed to believe that their invasion
of Czechoslovakia had ensured stability in those states of
Eastern Europe that they deemed it essential to control and that
this stability, plus their nuclear parity with the U.S. and the
decline in the American will to power, made Western recognition
of their Eastern European sphere of influence more likely and
East-West détente less dangerous to it.[26]

Yet in 1974 it was unclear to what extent this Soviet
confidence was justified. The December 1970 Polish seacoast
risings had confronted Moscow with a choice between concessions
or possible military intervention against a nationwide Polish
insurrection. Moscow chose concessions—wisely so, it seemed
thereafter, as First Secretary Gomułka's successor, Edward Gierek,
combined a more rational technocratic approach with continued
political control and loyalty to Soviet foreign policy. Yet the
rising showed how unstable the Eastern European situation
remained. Moreover, although Brezhnev had managed, by an astute
mixture of pressure and concessions, to improve Moscow's
relations with Bucharest and Belgrade, Rumania continued to
consolidate its semi-independent, strongly nationalist position
through skillful use of Soviet-U.S. and Sino-U.S. détente.
Moreover, although Moscow was clearly pleased with Tito's 1971
crackdown on liberalism and nationalism in Croatia and on
liberalism in Serbia and elsewhere, it was clearly aware of the
probable instability and the nationalities tensions of post-Tito
Yugoslavia and of the promise and danger for Moscow in meddling
therein.[27]

The Soviets also had maximal, offensive motives, primarily in
Europe: to lower U.S. and increase Soviet influence there, notably
by diminishing the U.S. military presence in West Germany—but not
by ending it, lest it be replaced by unified, increasing Western

European and particularly West German military power; to slow
down Western European unity; and to prevent conversion of Western
European, and particularly West German, economic and technological
power into nuclear arms. (Conversely, the West wanted to
liberalize Eastern Europe while keeping Western Europe strong and
united.) The problem for Washington and Moscow in Europe was thus,
as Leo Labedz has put it, one of competitive decadence or, to use
Pierre Hassner's formulation, "Who will Finlandize whom?"[28]
   There had probably been within the Soviet leadership
differences on détente that contributed to the downgrading of
Ukranian First Secretary Shelest shortly before the Moscow
summit meeting and his subsequent removal from the Politburo.
However, his primary fault was probably insufficient repression
of Ukranian nationalism.[29]

Europe. Moscow's strategic détente policy first led to concrete
results in Soviet-West German relations. Moscow knew that East-
West détente in Europe required a German settlement. It believed
that the time was ripe to get Bonn to recognize East Germany,
thus further stabilizing Moscow's hold there, and to prevent
West German economic power from destabilizing Eastern Europe,
becoming translated into military power, or helping to develop
China. (Maximally, the Soviets probably hoped eventually to
destabilize West Germany and detach it from the United States
and the rest of Western Europe, but their minimal, defensive
goals were foremost.) The Soviet invasion of Czechoslovakia and
the coming to power in the Federal Republic of the Social
Democratic-Free Democratic coalition made Bonn decide to
recognize East Germany de facto in order to slow down the
increasing mutual isolation of the two German states and thus
maintain the "substance of the nation." Brandt and Foreign
Minister Scheel therefore abandoned the CDU policy of bringing
pressure on Moscow by dealing with Rumania and Yugoslavia and
isolating East Germany, which the invasion of Czechoslovakia had
shown to be ineffective. Instead, they decided to come to terms
first with Moscow, in order thereby to persuade Moscow to
pressure East Berlin toward détente with Bonn.
   Although the Nixon administration was only too glad to
reciprocate Moscow's strategic policy of East-West détente, it
was initially skeptical about the speed of Brandt's new West
German and Polish-West German treaties, which essentially ratified
the status quo—with both sides, however, hoping eventually to
change it. But Moscow's unexpected, substantial concessions in the
Berlin negotiations in mid-1971 (especially those concerning four-
power responsibility for access, which were made, probably not
accidentally, just when Kissinger first went to Peking) converted
Washington's skepticism into support. Moreover, Bonn successfully

made a four-power agreement on Berlin a precondition for the
ratification by the West German parliament of the Soviet-
German and the Soviet-Polish treaties. The subsequent East
German-West German Grundvertrag (Basic Treaty), which was also a
compromise giving East Germany de facto recognition but not, as
it had demanded, full diplomatic recognition in international
law, led to the admission of both German states to the United
Nations. Thereafter West German progress in Ostpolitik slowed
down, and East Berlin began again to haggle with Bonn and even
to slow down traffic on the Berlin autobahn. However, it was
unclear whether or not in the long run the rising political
polarization in West Germany and the rise of a radical left
within the West German Social Democratic party, would be rivaled
by the destabilizing effects within East Germany of more contact
with the Federal Republic and, even more, of Brezhnev's pressure
on East Berlin for concessions to Bonn, which were seen by the
East German elite to be in Soviet but not in East German
interests.[30]

The Nixon administration had also become increasingly concerned
about Senator Mansfield's drive for major unilateral American
troop cuts in West Germany. Washington tried to forestall
congressional efforts in this direction by successfully making
Soviet agreement to the Berlin settlement and to negotiations
on MBFR in Central Europe a precondition for U.S. agreement to
the CSCE, which the Soviets had long wanted in order to get
multilateral Western recognition of their hegemony in Eastern
Europe and to lower NATO and EEC cohesion and power. Finally, for
the reasons described above, Washington wanted to reach arms
limitation and trade agreements with the Soviet Union.

Nixon achieved most of his objectives during his 1972 trip to
Moscow. The SALT agreement was a compromise: the U.S. traded an
antiballistic-missile freeze (minimal ABM deployment even against
third countries) for Soviet abandonment of further SS-9
construction, that is, thermonuclear parity and "mutual assured
destruction." Although the agreement gave Moscow a significant
numerical advantage in land-based missiles and throw-weight, it
did not cover the multiple independently-targeted reentry
vehicles (MIRVs), which the U.S. had begun to deploy in 1972 and
the Soviets obtained only in 1973, or the even more accurate
maneuverable reentry vehicles (MaRVs), whose development the
United States made public in 1974. Thus the quantitative missile
race was transformed into a qualitative one, in which the U.S.
initially had the technological advantage—although for how long
was uncertain. The Soviet need for trade, technology, and U.S.
grain, plus the American need for balance-of-trade relief,
resulted in major advances in Soviet-American trade. Washington
thus made progress toward extending the Soviet long-term

commitment to détente. Far from worsening its relations with
Peking thereby, it improved them. It defused one of the most
serious potential crisis points in Soviet-U.S. relations,
Berlin. It helped to reverse Soviet policy toward Hanoi:
thereafter Moscow pressured Hanoi for a Vietnam cease-fire rather
than encouraging it to continue the war. Nixon profited
domestically, as he had from the Peking summit. Soviet-U.S.
détente temporarily defused the superpower confrontation in the
Middle East without negative consequences for the United States
such as Moscow later suffered in Egypt. Moscow agreed to begin
MBFR negotiations, although by early 1974 their results remained
uncertain and unilateral U.S. troop withdrawals from Europe
therefore more likely.
     SALT also produced new alliance problems for Washington. In
1969 President de Gaulle's departure and France's political and
economic problems had lessened Franco-American tension, and
Nixon's consultation within NATO on SALT had been relatively
effective as compared to Kennedy's and Johnson's consultation
on the test-ban and nonproliferation treaties. However, the
intensified Soviet-American détente in 1972-1973 revived Western
European suspicions of the United States.[31]
     Western Europe (and to a lesser extent Japan) became more
fearful of what De Gaulle had called Soviet-U.S. "dual
hegemony," that is, the U.S. sacrifice of Western European
interests to its détente with Moscow. Moreover, most Western
Europeans thought that the Soviets had achieved strategic
parity with the U.S., were fully prepared (as in Prague in 1968)
to use force ruthlessly, and were increasingly active in
European politics. They saw the U.S. (until 1972) as embroiled
in a "dirty war" in Vietnam, likely to pull its troops out of
Europe, and, even if not insisting on economic concessions by
EEC in return for U.S. troop presence, underestimating the
expansion of Soviet influence. They further saw the U.S. as
caught up in an enfeebling domestic crisis of authority and
stability, and beset by racial strife, a drug epidemic, and
political scandals. For many Western Europeans and Japanese the
United States had become the model for a potential future to be
feared rather than aspired to. In sum, Western Europe feared
the withdrawal of U.S. nuclear protection and the lack of
American interest in a nuclear Western Europe, while Western
Europe itself remained disunited, with its political power
increasingly limited by greater U.S. freedom of action vis-à-vis
Moscow and Peking.[32]
     During the October 1973 Middle East war, the Soviet-American
imposition of a cease-fire, the unilateral American worldwide
military alert, and Arab oil production limitations further

intensified Western European suspicions of the United States.
U.S. freedom of action again increased while Western Europe's
became less. That Western Europe was so much more dependent upon
Arab oil than was the U.S., while only Washington and Moscow had
military power and therefore political influence in the Middle
East, and that the oil production limitation and increase in
price were by early 1974 weakening Western Europe (and Japan)
economically, made Western European and Japanese frustration even
greater still.

The Soviet Union probably saw as its greatest victory at the
1972 Moscow summit Washington's recognition of strategic (and
therefore political) parity with the United States, which
fulfilled the centuries-long Russian ambition to be recognized
as equal to the West. A Sino-American alliance against the
Soviet Union became less likely. The Moscow summit opened the
road to one of the Soviet organizational goals in Europe, the
Conference on Security and Cooperation in Europe (CSCE).
Finally, it temporarily defused the superpower aspects of the
Middle East crisis, albeit, as Moscow only later realized, at
considerable cost to Soviet interests in Egypt.

Another major result of the 1972 Moscow summit meeting was the
mutual willingness to codify the rules of the Soviet-American
limited-conflict relationship so as to limit it further and make
escalation of it less likely. Soviet-U.S. détente intensified
because the positions of both countries were characterized by
paradoxical equilibria: U.S. economic power and political will
were declining, but Washington was profiting from the Sino-
Soviet dispute and was pulling ahead of Moscow in the
qualitative weapons race. The Soviet will to power continued
strong and its military power continued to rise, but the Soviet
Union continued inferior to Washington in freedom of maneuver
in foreign policy, technological sophistication, and
agricultural production.[33]

SALT II negotiations at Geneva got under way in 1973 but had
made little progress by early 1974. They centered on qualitative
issues (MIRV and MaRV) and on U.S. forward-based systems (FBS)
in Europe. Initial Soviet and U.S. positions were far apart.
Neither of the issues was amenable to easy or rapid resolution,
and FBS in particular involved U.S. relationships in Europe in a
most sensitive area: its allies' access to nuclear capability.
Moreover, the Soviets could employ MIRVs in missiles with a
heavier throw-weight than that of U.S. missiles, while at the
same time the first SALT negotiations had left the United States
numerically inferior in launchers. By early 1974, Soviet testing
of MIRV led Washington to favor more rapid U.S. deployment of
MIRVs, MaRV development, and retargeting more warheads on Soviet

military sites than on cities—i.e., from the U.S. viewpoint, to
ensure quantified if complex parity. Behind this there seemed to
be two considerations. The first was the desire to have more, and
more credible, options than a "mutual assured destruction" (MAD)
strategy,[34] which seemed, at best, credible only if the U.S. were
superior (as it no longer was). Otherwise, Moscow, with its soon-
to-be MIRVd missiles, could in theory carry out a counterforce
strike, to which the U.S. could retaliate only by a countercity
strike, thus provoking Soviet destruction of American cities.
The second consideration was that such retargeting would
compensate for the Soviet superiority in missile launchers
established by SALT I. Its proponents maintained that this new
strategy would, by making the U.S. city-avoidance strategy more
credible, make countercity strategy less likely. Its opponents
argued that it would make nuclear war less unthinkable, and
would cost more, increase pressure for ABM deployment, make a
SALT II agreement less likely, and step up the qualitative arms
race. The Soviets presumably maintained that U.S. MIRV
deployment and MaRV development were far more advanced than
their Soviet equivalents, quantitatively and qualitatively, and
that they objectively meant a counterforce strategy and a
renewed thrust toward U.S. superiority. Behind all this were two
intractable asymmetries: first, the greater difficulty of
quantifying and agreeing on strategic parity in a qualitative
missile race and, second, the U.S. technological superiority
over the Soviet Union, inevitably reflected in missile guidance
accuracy and therefore in destructive capability, especially in
a capability aimed at Soviet missile sites.[35]

The 1973 preliminary CSCE discussions in Helsinki were notable
for Rumanian recalcitrance toward the Soviets, excellent political
coordination among the EEC countries and between them and the
U.S., and a Western European and American attempt to press the
Soviets on a free East-West exchange of information. As a result,
and because the Soviet Union had already achieved most of its
immediate European objectives, Soviet interest in CSCE declined
somewhat. Working commissions on political, economic, and
cultural/informational matters began discussions in Geneva in
September 1973. The Soviet desire for CSCE institutionalization
continued to meet Western resistance, while Western hopes for
greater exchange of information were confronted by Soviet
recalcitrance, symbolized by Moscow's intensified repression of
intellectual dissidents.[36]

MBFR discussions, after a long dispute over Hungarian
participation, also began in Vienna in late 1973. The initial
Soviet proposals were for symmetrical cuts in troop strength and
the Western ones for asymmetrical cuts.[37] Moreover, while U.S.-

Western European coordination at Helsinki, as contrasted with
Soviet alliance problems there, was encouraging to the West, the
situation was different in the MBFR discussions, where the real
security issues were being discussed. (Indeed, CSCE was no longer
really about security.) There were three major asymmetries
between the U.S. and the EEC states (except France, which refused
to participate) on MBFR: first, the U.S. desire, stimulated by
domestic political pressures, for U.S. force reductions in
Europe, which contrasted with the universal Western European
desire for the maintenance of U.S. and other NATO troop levels;
second, the U.S. desire to link problems of trade, the balance of
payments, and troop deployment,[38] a linkage opposed by Western
Europe; and, third, the financial and balance-of-payments
pressure of increased petroleum cost on the EEC states, plus the
restored U.S. balance-of-payments surplus, which made U.S.-West
German negotiations and the maintenance of even the 1974 levels
of Western European defense expenditures more difficult. In
contrast, the Soviets had no problems with the other Warsaw
Pact MBFR participants, for the Rumanians and Yugoslavs were
only observers. There were also asymmetries between the Soviets
and the Western Europeans. As Robert Legvold perceptively put it:

". . . The Soviet Union dreams of converting Europe into a
sanctuary free from the dangers of political change and dedicated
to mutual economic enrichment, but refuses to see the strategic
balance in Europe as European; the West Europeans reject the
notion of a regionalization of European security but refuse to
accept the global implications of Europe's strategic balance
. . . ."[39]

   Moreover, in CSCE and MBFR negotiations the U.S. and Western
European positions became reversed. While earlier the U.S. had
been warning the Western Europeans against making too many
concessions to the Soviets, by 1972 the contrary was the case,
particularly with the British and the French. Part of this was
predictable: historically the Western Europeans have always first
urged the U.S. toward détente with the Soviet Union, only to view
it with grave alarm once it occurred, in part because the U.S.
then paid less attention to them and also because they have felt
the U.S. to be too unsophisticated in foreign affairs.

Vietnam. Sino-American and Soviet-American détente had a major
impact on the Vietnam war in spite of—or, more accurately, at
least in part because of Nixon's April 1972 mining of Haiphong
harbor and December 1972 bombing of Hanoi. Moscow probably gave
Hanoi so many tanks and other weapons in late 1971 in order to

help defeat and humiliate the United States and to decrease
Chinese influence and increase that of the Soviets in North
Vietnam. Hanoi had probably initially hoped, with Soviet approval,
to attack across the DMZ before the Nixon visit to Peking and
thereby to prevent the visit's success. This Soviet support of
Hanoi lessened Chinese support and furthered Nixon's aim of
moving Peking toward restraining North Vietnmaese policies.
The attack did not occur until April, after Nixon's successful
visit to China, a visit that further worsened Peking-Hanoi
relations. Hanoi's initial miltary successes caused Nixon to mine
Haiphong harbor. The North Vietnamese hoped that this U.S. action
would prevent or sabotage the Nixon visit to Moscow. But Moscow's
relations with Hanoi then suffered just as Peking's had before,
and the Soviets, like the Chinese, pressured Hanoi toward a
cease-fire. The Chinese and Soviet policy reversal, plus Nixon's
mining and bombing of North Vietnam and his willingness to pull
all American troops out of South Vietnam, contributed to the
compromise Vietnamese cease-fire of early 1973. The future of
Indochina remained unclear, but South Vietnam and Laos appeared
fairly stable in the short term, while the issue in Cambodia
remained in doubt. Hanoi seemed to be concentrating more on
political than on military struggle, but basically the war
continued, albeit without U.S. participation and at a lower level
of violence. In the long run, however, North Vietnam's
determination to dominate Indochina remained strong, and its
success or failure was unpredictable. In any case, the cease-fire
downgraded the impact of Indochina events on the U.S. worldwide
power position. Nixon's mining of Haiphong and bombing of Hanoi,
and Soviet and Chinese inaction in the face of these actions,
demonstrated U.S. willingness to use its superior conventional
military capability in Southeast Asia and Soviet and Chinese
unwillingness to challenge it. Thus even if Indochina did
eventually fall to Hanoi, the "domino effect" on the U.S. position
in Southeast Asia and elsewhere in the world would be not nearly
so serious.[40]

The Middle East.[41] Egypt's expulsion of the Soviet military
advisers in July 1972, a major Soviet defeat, was not caused
primarily by developments in the great-power political-military
triangle but rather by Egyptian resentment of the Soviet refusal
to provide the amount of military aid Cairo wanted for the war
with Israel and also by resentment of what Cairo saw as arrogant
Soviet treatment of Egyptians. However, Soviet inaction when
Nixon ordered Haiphong mined, which made both the Israelis and
the Egyptians think that the Soviet Union was a less reliable

ally of Egypt than the United States was of Israel, also
contributed to the expulsion. Although Moscow tried to recoup its
loss in Syria and Iraq, the instability of these countries,
together with Moscow's fear of antagonizing anti-Iraqi Iran,
limited Soviet prospects there. Indeed, immediately before the
1973 war Soviet influence in the Middle East showed some signs
of decline. Moreover, in the early 1970s the general trend in
the Arab world was toward the "Islamization" of politics, i.e.,
away from the secularized left toward the traditional or radical
right.

The trend to the political right was most evident in the rise
of Saudi Arabia, in President Sadat's rightist policies in Egypt,
in the radical rightist Colonel Qadhdhafi in Libya, and in
President Nimeiri's crushing of the leftist coup in the Sudan.
The enormous Saudi oil reserves, production, and revenues, the
first-time possibility (because of increased U.S., Western
European, and Japanese demand for Arab oil) of using the
limitation of oil production to put effective pressure, through
the United States, on Israel for evacuation of the occupied
territories, and Sadat's move (after the 1967 defeat) toward
the right and toward alliance with King Faisal combined to make
Saudi Arabia and Egypt the two leading powers in the Arab world.
This was a major regional diplomatic realignment, unfavorable to
the Soviets and potentially favorable to the U.S. Until the 1973
war, Sadat and Faisal had also improved their relations with all
other Arab states except the recalcitrant leftists (Iraq, South
Yemen) and radical rightists (Libya), so that in the war Arab
solidarity was much greater than previously. Israel, confident
in its military power and strong U.S. support, moved slowly
toward the right in foreign policy and established more
settlements in its occupied territories, confident that its
military strength and U.S. support would enable it to resist all
pressures for withdrawal from them.

Then in October 1973 came the fourth Middle Eastern war. Egypt
and Syria attacked in order to recover their dignity, avenge the
humiliation caused by previous defeats, and get back their
occupied territories. After initial Arab strategic surprise and
limited victories, the Israelis won a near-total military victory
but suffered a political defeat. Moreover, some 2,500 Israelis
were killed (a proportion of the population equivalent to 175,000
people in the U.S.). The Arabs won a political victory because
Sadat, having failed in 1972 to exploit Soviet-U.S. tensions and
having therefore expelled the Soviets, in 1973 exploited Soviet-
U.S. détente. He did so, first, by ensuring Soviet arms resupply
in spite of Soviet-U.S. détente (if Moscow had refused it would

have lost almost all its influence in the Arab world) and, second, by ensuring that the Soviets would successfully pressure the U.S. to prevent a total Egyptian defeat, and that the U.S. would do so, in order to avoid a breakdown of Soviet-American détente, to keep open the path to settlement, and to prevent the Arab oil boycott from being prolonged. The war precipitated the use of Arab oil as a political weapon and destroyed the myths of Israeli invincibility and Arab incompetence. These changes led to a recovery of Arab self-confidence and to a major questioning in Israel of prewar policies, although the Knesset election at the end of 1973 brought a significant loss for the ruling Alignment party in favor of the hawkish Likud.

In its great-power aspect, the war was significant for three main reasons. First, in spite of the (predictable) Soviet and then U.S. arms resupply to the Arabs and Israelis respectively and the brief but intense Soviet-American confrontation triggered, after the cease-fire, by Israel's cutting off the Egyptian forces east of the southern end of the Suez Canal, it did not seriously interrupt Soviet-American détente. Indeed, in my view, the détente made both superpowers more moderate in their conduct and more determined to bring about a cease-fire and move toward a settlement.[42] Second, by precipitating the use of oil as a political weapon and furthering the spiraling rise of oil prices, it made the U.S. energy crisis more severe, weakened the Western European and Japanese economic positions vis-à-vis the U.S., and worsened relations between the U.S. and its Western European and Japanese allies. (Relationships were particularly strained, when, during the war, most Western European governments chose to deny the U.S. rights to European bases rather than risk their Arab oil supply, while at the same time the U.S. carried out direct confrontation and negotiation with the Soviet Union without prior consultation with the Western Europeans.) Third, although the war initially reversed the decline of Soviet influence in the Middle East because of the Arab need for massive arms resupply, U.S. influence rose again after Washington prevented the Israelis from destroying the Egyptian Third Army and arranged the Geneva Arab-Israeli negotiations and the January 1974 Israeli-Egyptian disengagement agreement, a genuine and ingenious compromise that resulted primarily from U.S. Secretary of State Kissinger's brilliant and indefatigable personal diplomacy. (U.S. influence was likely to decline once again, however, unless some settlement was reached.) The energy crisis also intensified U.S. interest in the Persian Gulf, where Washington supported the hegemony of an increasingly powerful Iran and began to build a naval base at the Indian Ocean island of Diego Garcia,[43] all of which worked against the interests of the Soviet Union and its associates, India, Iraq, and South Yemen.

Yet as was demonstrated in late 1973 and early 1974 by the U.S. public and congressional criticism of Moscow's Middle East policies and suppression of intellectual dissidence, domestic developments in both the United States and the Soviet Union seemed to threaten the expansion of, although hardly to reverse, Soviet-U.S. détente. Brezhnev's de facto cancellation of the emigration tax on Soviet Jews, in order to appease U.S. congressional criticism and thus get most-favored-nation (MFN) treatment and U.S. credits, demonstrated again how much Moscow needed U.S. technology. But a remarkable new coalition of U.S. pressure groups against a MFN policy toward the Soviet Union had emerged, led by Senator Henry Jackson and including anti-Soviet skeptics about détente, primarily in organized labor (not in business, which favored détente), as well as in Jewish and leftist groups pushing for free Jewish emigration from the Soviet Union and enraged at Soviet persecution of such dissidents as Solzhenitsyn and Sakharov and at Soviet arming of the Arabs in the 1973 Middle East war. This coalition threatened both MFN and, far more important for Soviet-American détente, U.S. credits to finance transfer of technology to the Soviet Union. It seemed doubtful, in short, that Nixon and Kissinger could successfully carry out a policy of almost total <u>Realpolitik</u> toward the Soviet Union.[44]

The Economic Triangle
The transition from the post-World War II U.S. economic predominance in the noncommunist world to a competitive economic triangle composed of the United States, Western Europe, and Japan was the second major element in the diplomatic revolution of the early 1970s. The decline of the U.S. economic position vis-à-vis these other two economic power centers first became politically important in the late 1960s and reached its height in 1973, only to be partially reversed by the 1973 energy crisis.

Its first and most important cause was the postwar economic recovery of Western Europe and Japan. The second was the decline (until 1973) in the competitive international economic position of the United States, because of falling productivity, high labor costs, inflation (which worsened the U.S. balance of payments, primariy as a result of the Vietnam war), expenditures for U.S. troops abroad, investment abroad by U.S. multinational corporations, and until 1972 the overvaluation of the dollar.[45]

By 1970 U.S. exports remained strongly competitive only in very high technology sectors: microelectronics, computers, and agricultural products. This reduction in competitive strength led to pressure by U.S. business, labor, and agriculture for tariff protection against Japanese, Canadian, and Western European exports and for greater U.S. export and investment abroad. Except for U.S. multinational corporations, domestic support for a U.S. free trade policy declined sharply.

Yet the increasing technological gap between the Soviet Union
and China, on the one hand, and the West and Japan, on the other,
plus the decisions of Moscow and Peking to participate more
extensively in international trade, produced significant trade
and technology transfer opportunities for the United States with
respect to the Soviet Union and China. Furthermore, the bad 1972
harvest enabled the U.S. to make massive grain sales (albeit at
disadvantageous prices) to the USSR. Indeed, U.S. business and
agriculture became major supporters of trade with the communist
states. In contrast, the EEC common agricultural policy seemed
to Washington to discriminate against the sale of American
agricultural products in Western Europe, while Japanese
restrictions on foreign investment, plus the 1972 $4.2 billion
U.S. trade deficit with Japan, convinced Washington that Japan
was even less willing than the EEC to "trade fairly."
    The resultant high U.S. balance-of-trade and payments deficits
and the resultant pressure of domestic protectionism made the
U.S. inclined to cease to manage (and if necessary subsidize)
the international trade and monetary system but, rather, to
compete in it. This change of view resulted in three devaluations
of the dollar, two official and the third de facto. The result
was immediate. By 1973 the U.S. again had favorable balances of
trade and payments. (The U.S. balance of payments also improved
because of the worldwide food shortages and the key role of the
U.S. as a food exporter. The U.S. and Canada provide a larger
percentage of world grain exports than the Middle East does of
oil, and the U.S. alone accounts for 90 percent of world soybean
exports.[46]
    The U.S. tried to involve Japan in international trade and
monetary relations on the same basis as the EEC and to search
for some more nearly trilateral political and economic
relationship among all three members of the economic triangle.
But European and Japanese slowness in reaching consensus on a
response, the continuing U.S. desire to call the tune, U.S.
domestic preoccupation with the Watergate investigations, and
U.S. "negotiation without consultation" with Moscow and Peking
had by 1974 worsened the U.S.-Japan-Western Europe relationship.
    By the early 1970s a major contradiction had developed between
the economic and political-military interests of the United
States: its political-military opponents, the USSR and China, were
new and valuable trade partners, while its political-military
allies, the EEC and Japan, were increasingly its economic
competitors. Washington therefore tried to use its military
expenditures in Western Europe and Japan to gain economic
concessions in GATT and monetary negotiations, in particular to
forestall U.S. public and congressional pressure for unilateral
troop withdrawals.

The early 1970s also saw the emergence of one of the major
political and economic, domestic and foreign preoccupations of
the noncommunist world: the energy crisis.[47] It was a crisis
caused not by an overall shortage of oil but by the unreliability
and insecurity of the oil supply, and, most of all, by its cost.
If the demand trend projected in the early 1970s remains correct,
by 1980 the U.S., for example, will be dependent on Middle
Eastern oil for from 30 to 40 percent of its consumption instead
of for around 8 percent, as it was in 1972. Rising world demand
for oil, the Arab limitation of oil production and boycott of
the U.S. (in order to bring pressure on Israel) arising out of
the October 1973 Middle East war, and the 1973 quadrupling of
petroleum prices by the Organization of Petroleum Exporting
Countries (OPEC) led by early 1974 to oil shortages, the danger
of recessions, and major balance of payments problems for oil-
consuming countries. (The underpopulated Arab oil-producing
nations, notably Saudi Arabia, had convincing economic reasons
and, barring an Arab-Israeli settlement, major political ones to
limit production, but not to keep oil prices as high as they were
in early 1974. The more populous oil-producing countries, such as
Algeria and Iraq and [non-Arab] Iran, Nigeria, and Indonesia,
prefer maximum production and as high prices as possible.) The
energy crisis thus became interrelated with, and intensified by,
the Middle East military crisis and U.S. policy toward it. By
mid-1974 the Arab oil production limitation and the boycott
against the U.S. had ended. High oil prices had clearly become
the key to the energy crisis. If they were not lowered (and they
were unlikely to be lowered either substantially or soon), the
prospective capital transfer problems would put near-untenable
strains on the international monetary system.

The energy crisis was much more serious for Western Europe
and Japan than for the U.S., because costly OPEC oil constituted a
much greater percentage of their consumption than of U.S.
consumption and because they thus could not, as the U.S. could
and probably would, become largely independent of Arab oil.
Successful "recycling" of OPEC oil payments back into producing
countries, the only way to avoid the problems created by the oil
crisis, would require much more coordination than had been
achieved, or seemed likely to be, in 1974. In any case,
"recycling" would probably mean investment by OPEC states in
strong-currency areas, i.e., the U.S. and Western Germany, thus
compounding the problems. Therefore, except for West Germany
(because of its export surplus and monetary reserves), Western
Europe and Japan in early 1974 faced massive balance-of-payments
deficits vis-à-vis the OPEC countries, with probable resultant
increased inflation and, in some cases, currency devaluations,
together with tremendous strain on the international monetary

System. The U.S. economic position vis-à-vis Western Europe and
Japan began to improve again in late 1973, as demonstrated by
the rise of the dollar.

The energy crisis was even more serious for non-oil-producing
underdeveloped countries. There the much higher petroleum prices
not only produced large balance-of-payments deficits but also cut
back petroleum-based artificial fertilizer production and
therefore seemed likely to lead to massive food deficits.

India presented the clearest and most serious example of the
effect of the energy crisis, economically and politically, on
the non-oil-producing underdeveloped world. The political and
economic situation in India had been worsening in 1973, before
the October 1973 Middle East war and OPEC's quadrupling of oil
prices. Two failed monsoons, the end of the euphoria of the 1971
victory, India's failure to be internationally recognized as
predominant in the subcontinent, and Mrs. Gandhi's failure as
prime minister to carry out any decisive reforms had combined to
worsen the political and economic climate. The quadrupled price
of oil, as elsewhere in the underdeveloped world, so raised the
cost of artificial fertilizers (for which oil was required) that
Indian food production was bound to fall. Conversely,
international (and particularly U.S.) food reserves were very low.
Thus another failed monsoon in India could bring massive famine,
and in any case there would probably be a serious food shortfall.

The energy crisis and the Middle East war also had unfavorable
political results for India. Iran's increasing oil wealth and its
determination to preserve Pakistan's integrity, the Arabs'
increased cohesion and their move to the right, and King Faisal's
Islamic group policy all were unfavorable to India, which the Shah
and King Faisal saw as anti-Moslem, pro-Soviet, and tied to Moscow
and Baghdad. (Washington, whose influence in the Arab world was
rising, and in Iran was high, remained uninterested in, and even
disdainful of, Delhi.) Moreover, at the February 1974 Islamic
conference in Lahore, Pakistan and Bangladesh were reconciled,
without India's presence. (Bangladesh public opinion had been
becoming anti-Indian, and Premier Bhutto was looking for an
opportunity to establish relations with Sheikh Mujib, the
Bangladesh premier.) Finally, the Shah at the same time loaned
India $300 million to buy Iranian oil, for which India presumably
was expected eventually to pay a political price. Thus the energy
crisis, the Middle East war, and the Islamic revival, plus its
own political and economic problems, had by early 1974 deprived
India of the fruits of its 1971 victory, further increased the
power of Iran, stabilized Pakistan, and given Bangladesh some
maneuverability in foreign policy. Internationally, these
developments pleased the Chinese (allied with Pakistan and now

able to establish ties with Bangladesh), the Americans, and the Iranians and Arabs. India was the loser.

The energy crisis thus added to economic tensions between the U.S. and the EEC and Japan. In early 1974 Washington tried, with little success, to persuade both to move toward a coordinate Atlantic-Japanese position in dealing with OPEC. Both were reluctant because they did not want their relations with the Arabs to worsen as a result of what they regarded as the excessively pro-Israel U.S. Middle East policy and because many of them were making profitable barter deals (usually for arms) with oil-producing countries. The first U.S. Western European-Japanese energy conference, in February 1974, made some progress and demonstrated the rise in U.S. prestige, but France refused to join in coordinated action, thus further weakening EEC cohesion and gravely worsening Franco-American relations.[48]

The energy crisis thus revolutionized international economics, and in early 1974 it was reviving U.S. predominance in the economic triangle. The world economy was divided by it in a third way (in addition to the previous two divisions between the developed and underdeveloped and among the communist, Western/Japanese, and nonaligned countries): between energy producers and energy consumers. Moreover, for the first time in a century the terms of trade were reversed, to favor the producers of one primary product, oil, rather than those of manufactured goods, and the developed world faced a recession because of inadequate supply rather than inadequate demand. In early 1974 it seemed likely that producers of other primary products would try to follow OPEC's example. Indeed, copper, bauxite, and tin producers reportedly were already doing so; it was questionable, however, whether they would be as successful as OPEC.[49]

By 1974 the United States, even though it was in a deep domestic political crisis, had the best position in all three divisions: it led in civilian and military technology; it produced most, and could produce almost all, of its energy and most other raw materials; and it was the world's greatest exporter of food. Western Europe and Japan were far worse off. They depended technologically on the U.S., particularly on U.S.-controlled multinational corporations. They did not and could not produce anywhere near their own energy requirements and would remain largely dependent on Middle Eastern oil. They did not export food, and Japan imported it. Some of their weapons were inferior to U.S. equivalents.[50] Moreover, Western European progress toward unity and a common foreign policy, which had seemed promising in 1973, stalled on French intransigence, competition for energy sources, unilateral floating of the French franc, Anglo-German differences on regional aid, and, more

generally, on conflicting national self-interests. The EEC was able
to overcome French intransigence only by agreeing on indecision,[51]
but when, as at the February 1974 Washington energy conference, the
Western European governments had to take a stand on a major U.S.
proposal, France refused to compromise, but was unable thereby to
achieve more than its own isolation.

In early 1974 Western European and Japanese nationalism were
thus brought face to face with sudden, drastic economic
vulnerability. Most of their political classes realized that this
meant a new rise of American power and their greater dependence on
it, but some of them—understandably, from a psychological
viewpoint—were precipitated by their frustration and bitterness
into a more anti-American position. Thus in early 1974 the Western
Europeans and the Japanese were once again confronted with the
same problem that had faced the United States since the beginning
of the 1970s: the speed and extent of global economic and monetary
interdependence had "objectively" outmoded competing nationalisms,
but the very extent of this interdependence, confronting reviving
nationalisms deepened by institutional incapability to cope with
interdependence, made institutional remedies more difficult.

A basic structural problem in the U.S.-Western European
relationship tended to worsen it further. By 1974 the EEC had
reached a level of cooperation, even in foreign policy, high
enough for its members to attempt to establish a common EEC
position on the major issues of Western European-American
relations, but too low to permit the EEC, once the position was
reached, to negotiate flexibly rather than cling stubbornly to
the position agreed on with such difficulty and therefore so
nearly impossible to change.[52] At the same time, the United
States in theory wanted the EEC to take a common position but was
reluctant to eschew bilateral negotiations with the EEC states on
such issues. Moreover, it regarded many if not most such issues
as appropriate for discussion in an Atlantic, not just an EEC,
framework and saw some further issues (such as Middle East policy)
as concerning the Soviet Union and the U.S. but not in practice
the Western Europeans. These structural problems, plus French
intransigence, the British economic and political crisis, Italy's
deepening societal crisis, Brandt's weakening position in West
Germany, and President Nixon's greatly weakened authority made
intra-EEC and EEC-U.S. relations inevitably difficult.

The lack of unity and decisiveness in the Western European and
Japanese response to the October 1973 Middle East war and the
energy crisis demonstrated the political, military, and economic
impotence of both Western Europe and Japan in an area, the Middle
East, in which their economic and therefore their political
interests were more vitally involved than were those of the

United States and the Soviet Union. Their weak response destroyed
two previously prevalent myths: that Western European and Japanese
economic strength made Western Europe and Japan and that Western
Europe was well on the way to unity.[53]
    There was one other important development, more difficult to
define and analyze, in the developed noncommunist world: cultural
malaise. In the U.S., Western Europe, and even to some extent in
Japan, there was growing dissatisfaction with, and often revulsion
against, bourgeois affluence, materialism, and the "evils of
growth." These feelings ranged from such politically moderate
phenomena as "environmentalism" to such extremist ones as "Maoist"
student fanaticism. It was furthered by East-West détente: there
no longer seemed to be a dangerous enemy to unite against. It
centered in intellectual and student youth, but mass
communications transmitted it rapidly to a larger audience. From a
historical perspective, it was in part a revival of the anti-
industrial, anti-mass-culture, romantic feelings that have
recurrently characterized intellectual life in the modern
developed world. The energy crisis, the looming food crisis, the
problems of pollution, and the lack of a charismatic leader such
as President Kennedy or General de Gaulle intensified it. Although
its most extreme manifestations, the student demonstrations of the
late 1960s, seemed by 1974 a part of history, a more diffuse
malaise continued.
    In Western Europe and Japan, and perhaps most strikingly in
the U.S., this malaise was accompanied by, and was in part the
cause of, a decline in what one may term the "will to power," or,
as the "counter-culture" would say, the "will to empire," and an
increase in concentration on domestic problems instead of foreign
policy. The energy crisis showed how easily domestic problems
become intensifed by foreign ones, and it also intensified the
cultural malaise: the feeling that growth should be, whether or
not it would be, limited.
    This cultural malaise, combined with the post-Vietnam war
syndrome, contributed to U.S. public sentiment for limiting
commitments abroad. (It contrasted sharply with rising Soviet
and Chinese military power.) Yet the Nixon administration had
demonstrated that some reduction of commitments was compatible
with, and indeed furthered, continued and even rising U.S.
influence in foreign policy.

Prospects
The major potential change in the international political-military
triangle is whatever will occur in China after Mao and Chou leave
the political scene.[54] Or perhaps the change will come before
their departure: by early 1974 there were clear signs of the

revival of the Cultural Revolution themes, including xenophobia.
Although this revival of hostility seemed directed primarily
against the Soviet Union, continuing press attacks on Western
cultural figures, past and present, bode no good for Sino-U.S.
cultural exchange and perhaps foreshadow a worsening of Sino-
U.S. relations. On the other hand, the continued rise of Teng
Hsiao-p'ing might indicate that Chou En-lai's position and
policies were not yet seriously endangered. In any case, China
is again a great question mark.[55] In the past there was what one
might call a "structural détente faction" in Peking which favored
Sino-Soviet détente in order to revive Soviet military and
economic aid and to enable China to maneuver between the United
States and the Soviet Union, rather than, because of its wholly
hostile relations with Moscow, being overdependent on and
manipulated by the United States. The Soviets hope that this view
will prevail after Mao and Chou go. It may, but it will probably
not result in a major Sino-Soviet détente. In the meantime,
Washington and Peking are trying to institutionalize Sino-
American détente so as to make a future Sino-Soviet détente less
likely. However, even if Sino-Soviet relations do improve, some
degree of Sino-American détente will probably continue, for China
needs American technology even more than the Soviet Union does;
Soviet strength is so much greater than Chinese. Moreover, the
U.S. needs détente with China to help its interests in Asia and
to further its détente with the Soviet Union.

Another question is whether the Soviets will attack China.
Launching an attack was considered in Moscow in 1969-1970, but it
is now less likely because the Chinese are acquiring a minimal
nuclear deterrent capability aimed at the Soviet Union, including
Moscow. It is their contemporary equivalent of China's Great Wall.
The Soviets are more likely biding their time until Mao
disappears, in the hope that they can then interfere in the
Chinese succession struggle.

The main question for the future of Soviet-American relations
is whether Soviet-American détente has acquired a momentum of its
own, and if so to what extent, and whether it is thereby becoming
institutionalized into a "structure of stability" (Nixon) and thus
"irreversible" (Brezhnev). Such a process, in my view, has as a
precondition the institutionalization of the Sino-Soviet dispute
at a level of "neither peace nor war," a level that stabilizes
Sino-American as well as Soviet-American détente. As long as Mao
is in power, this stabilization will very likely be the case. It
follows that the possibility of a partial Sino-Soviet
rapprochement after Mao is the major single uncertainty in the
deepening of Soviet-American détente. The Soviet need for Western
technology seems likely to continue as does the Soviet and

American desire for détente in Europe and progress in arms
control. Thus even if Sino-Soviet relations improve, Soviet-
American détente might become limited but will hardly give way
to renewed cold war.[56]

The Soviet-American relationship will be largely determined
by domestic developments in both the U.S. and the USSR. In the
Soviet Union, the Great Russian ruling elite will remain far more
nationalistic than the American intelligentsia and will therefore
demonstrate a greater will to power abroad. Yet its institutions
and its ethos will increasingly lag behind the needs of a
"developed socialist society" (to use its own term), and its
desire to maintian its own power will probably preclude the
massive reforms necessary to solve the problem of this lag.
Thus the Soviet political class will for the near future continue
to see the USSR as on the rise and the U.S. as past the peak of
its power and will be determined to accelerate the rise of Soviet
power, but it will not soon bridge the widening technological gap
between it and the West and Japan. Moreover, among the great
powers the USSR has by far the greatest nationalities problem,
made more serious, ironically enough, by economic development and
education. Also, the Chinese have been actively, although
unsuccessfully, trying to subvert the national minorities in the
USSR. In contrast to the situation with the Great Russians, whose
nationalism works for the Soviet regime and against intellectual
dissent, among the Soviet nationalities both nationalism and
liberalization may combine into a potentially explosive mixture
such as developed in Croatia in 1971. Although it is most unlikely
that nationalities dissidence will come close to breaking up the
Soviet Union (however much this may be the ultimate Chinese aim),
it will increasingly preoccupy the Soviet leadership, constrain
their foreign policies, and make them even less likely to give
up their control over Eastern Europe. Finally, judging by the
past, international détente will probably cause Moscow as many
problems at home and in Eastern Europe as it will cause Washington
at home and in Western Europe. While there is no significant
evidence of a struggle within the Soviet leadership on foreign-
policy issues,[57] Brezhnev and most of his associates are in their
late sixties and will therefore soon give way to others. Whether
the succession will be smooth and what policy consequences it may
have are by definition uncertain, but the potential for policy
changes in this context seems less than in China.[58]

The prospects for Western Europe and Japan looked worse in
early 1974 than they had a year before. Soviet-American and Sino-
American cooperation, however limited, seems likely to continue,
thus limiting the freedom of action of all parties. Movement
toward Western European unity will probably be slow at best,

hindered by the competition among the EEC states for Middle
Eastern oil. Western European and Japanese balances of payments
seem likely to become negative for at least the rest of the 1970s
because of the massive capital transfers required to buy oil.
Meanwhile, the U.S. trade and monetary situation will probably
continue to improve, relative to the rest of the developed world,
since the U.S. will import less oil and will export, almost
uniquely, large amounts of food. (The Soviet Union and China are
likely to remain largely self-sufficient in oil but not in food.)

The very high 1974 prices for oil seem likely within five or
ten years so to increase the supply of petroleum and alternative
energy sources that oil prices will again fall. Even so, like the
price of many other primary products, the price of oil will
probably remain high compared to that of industrial products: a
secular change in the terms of trade. The Soviet Union will
probably try to induce Western European and Japanese investment
in Soviet oil and natural gas production as a means of decreasing
dependence on Middle East oil, and China will probably try to do
the same. Yet for the rest of the 1970s the developed world will
remain largely dependent on Arab oil. Whether or not this may lead
to an attempt by one or more power groupings among developed
countries to balance such dependence by the use, or threat of
use, of military force is unclear, but on balance such an attempt
seems unlikely, for the U.S. is not, or at least soon will not be,
so highly dependent, and Western Europe and Japan will probably
lack both unity and the will to use such military force as they
have.

Military developments also seem likely to postpone the arrival
of Western Europe or Japan at the status of superpowers. Their
political and military impotence was again revealed by Middle
Eastern developments in 1973: in an area essential to their
economies, not they, but the U.S. and the Soviet Union, were the
only significant foreign influences. Indeed, it seems more likely
than not that the Middle Eastern and energy developments in 1973
will push the Western Europeans and the Japanese more toward the
United States, despite all their complaints against Washington.

Such poor states as India seem likely to suffer drastically
from the rising prices of industrialized goods, energy, and food.
Thus much if not most of the third world will become further
devalued in the international political balance of power.

The crisis of the will to power on the part of a significant
segment of the American intelligentsia is of uncertain intensity
and duration. Although extreme racial and student strife had
largely subsided, in early 1974 the mood among the American
intelligentsia against foreign commitments remained strong.
Watergate and associated scandals crippled the Washington

administration while Nixon remained President, and their deep
scars still remain. Yet U.S. technological superiority over that
of the USSR seems likely to grow, and Washington will probably
continue to benefit, if perhaps less so after Mao's and Chou's
departure, from Sino-Soviet tension. It seems unlikely that the
Soviet Union, and far less China, will soon surmount the
technological gap between them and the Atlantic-Japanese world.
Indeed, the main U.S. problems in the near future seem likely to
be with its political allies and economic rivals, the EEC and
Japan. Whether, however, the developed noncommunist world can
surmount its disunity and the U.S. its domestic scandals and
its intelligentsia's crisis of will remain to be seen.

In any case, in 1974 one thing was clear: the "end of the cold
war," the transition from bipolar Soviet-U.S. conflict to the
interaction of the political-military and economic triangles, had
produced not only more stability but also more reengagement for
it had above all unfrozen the international situation. More
important than the intention of both East and West "to recognize
the status quo in order to change it" (as Willy Brandt put it)
was the development of triangular world politics. Détente, more
East-West trade and cultural exchange, SALT, MBFR, CSCE, the
reentry of China and Japan into active international politics,
and the rising systemic alienation and dissent in East and West—
all these seemed in early 1974 to have given rise to a confused,
complex mixture of coexistence, competition, and conflict in
East-West relations and within the communist and the developed
and underdeveloped noncommunist worlds as well. Each great
power and each alliance was trying, as Pierre Hassner put it,
to "decrease its own comparative vulnerability," and each hoped
"that the other side will be weakened or transformed by its own
inner contradictions without bringing down the whole common
structure."[59] What the outcome will be is, not surprisingly,
unclear. What is clear is that a new phase of coexistence,
competition, and conflict has begun.

Chapter 2

THE POLITICAL DYNAMICS OF THE BALKANS IN 1974

Viktor Meier

Introduction

To write about the Balkans, an area with its own regional
dynamics and potential effects on world politics, necessitates
above all the analysis of two problem areas: (1) Rumania's
attempt to end its satellite status and to obtain, in the course
of the endeavor to establish a collective European security
system, full, internationally recognized national independence,
and (2) the issue of the internal and external stability of
Yugoslavia.

These two problems derive from long-term historical processes.
In the final analysis the question is whether the principle of
national independence can further develop, or assert itself
anew, in this region, which since approximately 1800 has
successively freed itself from total domination by three great
powers, Turkey, Austria-Hungary, and Russia. And if the answer
is affirmative, the further question is whether on the basis of
this principle the Balkans can fit into the efforts for a
general relaxation and stabilization in the world, as a zone of
stability and peace. From this conception of the problem one can
also understand the great importance given at the present time
in both Rumania and Yugoslavia to the consolidation of what has
already been achieved. If the time should ever come when a
particular state of affairs in the Balkans is settled, either by
a formal or informal international political settlement or by a
collective European security system, all interested parties
would doubtless try to make the settlement coincide as far as
possible with their own goals. Rumania's behavior at the
multilateral consultations on European security in Helsinki and
Geneva served this endeavor, as does Tito's questionable attempt
to undertake a consolidation of the Party's authority in
Yugoslavia before his death. Tito's effort is based on the
frequently expressed apprehension that perhaps "somebody else"
will put Yugoslavia in order if the Yugoslavs do not do it
themselves.[1]

Rumania and Yugoslavia arrived by completely different paths
at their current position in the Balkans and in the world, but
over the years the differing positions of the two countries have
converged. This convergence represents enormous progress for

Rumania and is the result of a tough and resolute policy
followed since approximately 1963. But in the case of
Yugoslavia, this convergence represents a setback, the
consequence of domestic weakness and of the increasing
unpredictability of its leadership. In 1974 it is still
important that Rumania is a full member of the Warsaw Pact and
Council for Mutual Economic Assistance (CMEA), while Yugoslavia
is an independent socialist country and participates in CMEA
only as an observer. Rumania has been trying to limit its ties
to the USSR and the other members of the Warsaw Pact and has
decreased the CMEA share of Rumania's foreign trade to 46
percent by the end of 1972, according to President Nicolae
Ceauşescu's own statement.[2] Yugoslavia, in contrast, has been
trying to loosen its bonds to the West and to intensify its
relations with the underdeveloped countries.[3] At the same time,
President Tito, of course, has declared repeatedly and very
decidedly that Yugoslavia would not return to the "socialist
camp" and that the Eastern bloc would have to put up with the
Yugoslavs as they are.[4]

The threat for Rumania and Yugoslavia, as well as for the
principles that these two countries represent in the Balkans,
comes unequivocally and exclusively from the Soviet Union. The
threat lies in that concept of Soviet policy described by the
phrase "the Brezhnev doctrine," which has determined Soviet
policy toward the whole eastern and southeastern European region,
the so-called Middle Europe, for decades. The Soviet tendency is
to dominate this area, in which the Soviet Union has legitimate
security interests, not merely by moderate, "classical" methods
of political influence, but by integral and total political
control.

As late as the nineteenth century, Russia acted differently.
In Finland, the Baltic provinces, and Poland (i.e., even within
its own territory) Russia allowed considerable autonomy, and in
the Balkans Russia posed only as the protector, not as the
ruler, of the region's peoples. The Congress of Berlin in 1878
barred Russia's attempt completely to dominate the politics of
the Balkans by means of a Russian-protected "Great Bulgarian
Empire." Russia tolerated this limitation in the interest of
maintaining the existing world political balance, and its policy
of moderation was not changed until the reign of Nicholas II
toward the end of the nineteenth century, when centralization
and russification took the place of the previous tolerant
attitude toward the borderland areas.

In its policy toward the peoples of the border areas, the
Soviet regime basically followed the policy of Nicholas II
rather than that of Alexander I, despite an official tolerance

of nationalities. As commissar of nationalities, Stalin's actions
toward Transcaucasia, including his homeland, Georgia, were
criticized by Lenin, but they prevailed. Stalin also championed
the total, not merely the partial, domination of the Eastern
European security zone. This policy did not begin with the
conference at Yalta and the end of World War II, as is
frequently stated; it began earlier, with the signing of the
German-Soviet Pact of August 1939. This pact divided the whole
Eastern European area into two zones of influence, German and
Soviet. With brutal single-mindedness Stalin immediately
attempted to bring that part of Eastern Europe "allocated" to
him under total control. Soviet policy in the part of Poland
annexed by the Soviet Union was at least as harsh in its
denationalization efforts as the corresponding German policy
on the other side of the demarcation line. Stalin proceeded with
equal brutality in Rumania and Finland. The incidents during the
occupation of Bessarabia and Bukovina after the Soviet ultimatum
of June 26, 1940,[5] and the outbreak of the war against Finland
on November 30, 1939,[6] automatically drove Rumania and Finland
to seek in Nazi Germany the only possible guarantee for their
national existence. As soon as the first cracks appeared in the
German-Soviet alliance, both countries went over to the German
side without hesitation. German troops were initially greeted as
liberators in the Baltic states and even in large parts of the
Ukraine.

Stalin may have had concrete reasons for his security policy.
First, it was very important to him, as it was to Hitler, to
restore the territorial losses of 1918. Second, he did not
completely trust the pact with Hitler. But the practical
execution of his policy brought the Soviet Union more insecurity
than security, for it made the threatened nations in Eastern
Europe take the side of the lesser of the two evils, namely
Germany. If the Soviets occasionally claim that their total
domination of the Eastern European "security zone" is necessary
because the Soviet Union has always been threatend or attacked
from this area, one can present the counterargument that the
Soviet Union has at least partly created this real or alleged
threat itself because of its policy toward the nations of that
region.

After 1944 Stalin in principle treated Europe the same as he
had after 1939, but now his enemies were not the Nazis but the
Western allies. He pushed for total integration of the satellite
zone into the Soviet orbit of power and, certainly after 1947,
was no longer prepared to tolerate even the smallest independent
movement in this region. Here one could mention Finland as a
counterexample. It is, in fact, strange that Stalin did not

bestow the same fate on this country as on the Eastern European
satellite states. This would have been possible in 1944. The
reasons usually given for Stalin's different treatment of
Finland are as follows:[7] First, in 1944 Finland accepted a
cease-fire at a time when its exit from the war was still
strategically advantageous to the Soviets; in addition, the
Finns themselves undertook to drive the German troops from their
territory. Second, the immediate Soviet security requirements
were perhaps satisfied by the acquisition of Karelia and the
naval base of Porkkala near Helsinki. Third, and most important,
Stalin would have alarmed the Western allies and Scandinavia
regarding Soviet postwar goals, especially since it could be
assumed that Finland would have defended itself against
occupation in a fight to the finish. In 1948 Stalin did try to
force Finland to accept a friendship-and-cooperation agreement
similar to those concluded with the Eastern European satellites.
In addition, in the same year the Finnish communists attempted a
putsch. That these attempts did not succeed can be credited
primarily to the firm and tactically clever conduct of the
Finnish regime under President Paasikivi.

It seems important to point out, especially in relation to a
discussion of the Brezhnev Doctrine, that it would have been
entirely possible for the Soviet Union to safeguard its security
interests in Eastern Europe and at the same time allow its
nations their full internal autonomy. The Soviet Union would
thereby have returned to the traditions of the Russian empire
in the first two-thirds of the last century. However, everywhere
but in Finland, the Soviet Union decided in favor of total
control, and, until the present day, the Soviet Union has
scarcely moved from this position.

As a result of the Soviet decision, Rumania, which found
itself in 1944 in an especially precarious situation because it
was defeated, non-Slavic, and a Nazi satellite that did not
border on a Western state, probably had to endure the worst
conditions of oppression and exploitation of any Eastern
European country.[8] The consequence for Yugoslavia was expulsion
from the communist camp in 1948, after Tito wanted to become an
ally of the Soviet Union instead of a subject.[9] The two
countries subsequently followed completely different paths of
development, which began to converge only after 1963. Then, on
August 21, 1968, both countries suddenly saw themselves
confronted with the Soviet military occupation of a communist
country, Czechoslovakia, and the prevention of the functioning
of its legally elected state and party leadership. Moreover,
both Yugoslavia and Rumania had to admit to themselves that

probably the Soviets would not have backed away even from a
large-scale bloodbath if Czechoslovakia had shown resistance.

The Brezhnev Doctrine, justifying the Soviet action against
Czechoslovakia, was nothing new in principle; Khrushchev had
expressed a similar view after the Hungarian invasion in 1956.
However, Brezhnev's statement at the Polish Communist Party
Congress in November 1968 had far greater significance, since
not only small countries like Yugoslavia or Albania but also
the emerging world power China had in the meantime disengaged
themselves from the Moscow-dominated communist bloc. Furthermore,
Rumania had resolutely tried for five years to incorporate the
principle of national sovereignty into the Warsaw Pact. Brezhnev
stated that the Soviet Union claimed the right to intervene in a
socialist country, even by military means if necessary, whenever
external or internal enemies posed a "serious danger to the
cause of socialism" in the country and also to "the security of
the whole socialist community."[10] This fundamental declaration
of the Soviet right of intervention must have caused great
anxiety in China as well as in those Balkan states, including
Albania, intent upon independence. This tense situation in the
entire Balkan area came to a temporary end only with Brezhnev's
visit to Yugoslavia in September 1971.

It remains to be seen whether the political principles that
Yugoslavia and Rumania have elaborated during recent years can
last. The trial period has not yet ended. At the moment, the
problem in Yugoslavia is primarily domestic, while in Rumania
the problem lies in its foreign policy. But it could easily
happen that the problem in Yugoslavia will also soon become an
external one. During his visit to Yugoslavia, Brezhnev made fun
of people who talked about a "Brezhnev Doctrine," but he in no
way retracted what he had said at the Polish Party Congress in
November 1968.[11] No one knows how the Soviet Union will act in
the event of internal disorders in Yugoslavia; after all, the
country lies on the road to the Mediterranean. Moreover, there
are no definitive indications that Moscow has recognized the
independence of Rumania. Much, if not all, will depend on these
two countries' own political power and on the political
opportunities that arise. It is therefore necessary to examine
their development, their problems, and their prospects more
closely.

Internal Developments in Rumania and Yugoslavia

Rumania. In February 1963, following a conference of the CMEA
Executive Committee, a communiqué from Bucharest indicated that

differences had arisen between the Rumanians and the other
members of the Eastern bloc and that the Rumanians had no
intention of giving in meekly in settling these differences.
This announcement came as quite a surprise to the international
community. Rumania had until then been considered a loyal ally of
the Soviet Union, although some incidents, negative as well as
positive, had suggested that the Rumanian Communist party had
its own policies. But as already indicated, Rumania found itself
in an extraordinary and difficult situation in the postwar
period. The coup d'état of August 1944, undertaken on Rumanian
initiative, followed by participation in the advance of the
Soviet troops into the country, had merely gained Rumania the
return of those areas in Transylvania which Hitler had given to
Hungary and had not saved the country from a near-total loss of
sovereignty. Not until 1958 did Party Secretary Gheorghiu-Dej
succeed in obtaining the withdrawal of Soviet occupation troops.
In 1958 a new Rumanian five-year plan had been adopted, which
foresaw rapid industrialization of Rumania, based, autarkically,
on heavy industry. It seems that this plan touched off the
later differences with Moscow, because Khrushchev had ordered
his Balkan satellites to remain agricultural states and, as
later accusingly reported by the Rumanian paper Viaţa Economică,
had even thought of dividing the Balkan states into economic
zones that would not coincide with national borders.[12] Here
Rumanian nationalism came into play. The real declaration of
independence came in April 1964 with the well-known "April
resolution" of the Rumanian Central Committee.
The Tradition of Nationalism. Many segments of world public
opinion have not been able to come to terms with the phenomenon
of Rumanian nationalism. The best-known argument against the
policy of Ceauşescu is that it does not benefit the Rumanian
population. The counterexample is Hungary, which abstains from
foreign-policy experiments and in their stead offers the
population a relatively high living standard and relative
political and cultural liberalism. It is difficult to answer
these and similar arguments because the process of emancipating
Rumania has not been completed. While one can already evaluate
the result of the policy of Kádár in Hungary, one cannot do so
for Ceauşescu's policy in Rumania. The covert Western criticism of
Ceauşescu's policy very often comes from circles that can be
categorized politically as leaning toward the left. These
circles tend to disregard those analytical categories that are
still the most important in Europe, and especially in Eastern
Europe—namely, the nation and the state. Nationalism is
considered "passé" and negative. Nevertheless, it is necessary to

accept the fact that in Eastern Europe nationalism remains for the foreseeable future the most important political driving force. In the past, nationalism formed the peoples of this region into nations and states, stimulated political, economic, and cultural development, and even brought personal freedom, if one considers the conditions existing in the Balkans under the Ottoman Empire, Today, Eastern European nationalism, admittedly never free of negative elements, again operates in the spirit of national emancipation, like that existing after 1800, with the goal of enabling the various peoples to live according to their own image of themselves. Now, as then, nationalism in Eastern Europe and the Balkans is basically a creative, positive force that has not yet completed its historic mission.

The self-images that the Eastern European peoples again want to follow are different for each country. In Czechoslovakia, the country of Masaryk, the organization of the state according to the principle of democratic parliamentarianism is part of the image. In Rumania, this element is not primary; rather the national idea is the dominant one. Rumania was created from the union of three different areas—Walachia, Moldavia, and Transylvania—and each already had its own state tradition. In addition, in Transylvania, which was not joined to Rumania until 1918, the Rumanians were the weakest element of the society, as compared to the Hungarians and the Germans. Furthermore, after 1918 the country had to incorporate the quite different structure of Bessarabia. Therefore, only strong Rumanian nationalism, in conjunction with rigorous centralization of administration, could provide the connecting link and unifying force for these disparate elements. One consequence of the Rumanian situation is a certain antagonism toward minorities, especially toward the numerically strong and equally nationalistic Hungarians, but this antagonism was unavoidable and has actually resulted in a further strengthening of Rumanian national feeling. One can easily say that the beginnings of internal democracy according to the Western model were repeatedly buried in Rumania by nationalism.

It is customary in the West to consider Poland and Hungary as the countries of Eastern Europe with the most intense nationalism and, on the basis of this belief, to formulate historic parallels between these two nation. In actuality, such parallels could be better made between Poland and Rumania, with respect not only to the intensity of nationalist feeling but also to the sources of this intensity. Like Rumania, Poland was created from different, unequally developed parts and sacrificed its democratic structure for nationalistic centralism.

While after 1918 Yugoslavia always had a single leading
political force in the country, thanks to the Serbian hegemony in
the form of the Radical party or one of its later variations, the
two strong political parties qualified for political leadership
in Rumania both engaged in self-destruction—first the Liberals
party at the end of the 1920s under the "dynasty" of Brătianu
and then the National Peasant party under its leaders Iuliu
Maniu and Ion Mihalache at the beginning of the 1930s. The
moment they were unable to solve the difficult problems of their
time, they opened the way for pure nationalism. Unfortunately a
good, objective analysis of the political development of Rumania
during the interwar period is lacking; the best one available is
by Lucreţiu Patraşcanu, who was branded as a "national communist"
by the regime of Gheorghiu-Dej and executed in 1954.[13] Even
communist sources today acknowledge that the start of the new
Rumanian state after 1918 was not too bad, in spite of the
country's backwardness.[14] Substantial capital investment in
industry was carried out, and the industrial production of the
country rose 56 percent between 1923 and 1928.[15] In spite of all its
shortcomings, the agrarian reform of 1921 brought a real change
in the structure of agriculture; the size of large landed
property decreased by 66 percent.[16] Rumania gained respect on the
international scene through its work in the League of Nations
and the Little Entente, especially under Foreign Minister Nicolae
Titulescu, who was in office in 1926-1927. The world
economic crisis beginning in 1929, which severely affected first
industry and then agriculture, was in part the reason why
Rumania's internal development suddenly took an unfavorable
course. The outbreak of the crisis in 1929 finished the Liberal
party politically (it had already lost its position as the ruling
party in 1926), and a little later the agricultural depression
had the same effect on the National Peasant party, which was
first dominated and then removed from power by King Carol II.
At that time there were no foreign influences that might have
been a danger to the democratic parties. One can, therefore,
conclude that Rumania apparently did not provide fertile soil
for bourgeois democracy. The National Peasant party (which had
been created from both the old, not exclusively peasant-oriented
Rumanian National party in Transylvania, under Maniu, and the old
Peasant party of pre-1918 Rumania under Mihalache) could have
paved the way for democracy on the basis of its numerical
strength as well as its composition. That it failed was a
political tragedy for Rumania. The internal and—after 1930—also
the external weakness of the leading parties not only gave the
king the opportunity to strengthen his own political position,

but also quickly made the crown the only real recourse against
the surging extremism. A politician like Maniu, who had begun as
a protector of the rights of the "little man," finally became
part of the immediate circle of King Carol II, as the king's
adviser.

The world economic crisis caused unemployment in Rumania's
infant industry, precipitating strikes, wage disputes, and
unrest. This provided fertile soil for agitation by the small
Communist party. Railway workers were one of the most important
bases of support for the communists. The future leader Gheorghiu-
Dej won his spurs in the 1933 railroad strike in Grivița.
However, the role and political strength of the communists at
that time must not be overvalued. The Communist party had a few
clever men, among whom the already mentioned Patrașcanu stood
out intellectually. But it was not a real political power in the
country. Furthermore, the Jewish element from Bessarabia and
from the Hungarian-speaking part of Transylvania was so strongly
represented in the leadership that it was relatively easy to
accuse the communists of being an "unnational" party. Most of
its leaders subsequently emigrated to Moscow and only returned
with the Soviet troops. Ceaușescu himself, who, like Gheorghiu-
Dej, had spent the war in prison in Rumania, later repeatedly
criticized the antinational outlook of the communist leadership,[17]
especially its insistence that Rumania is a "multinational" state
and its emphasis on the right of secession for each nationality.[18]
The party was not able to free itself from this antinationalist
label before the outbreak of World War II, and of course
afterward this was for a long time even more impossible. For
this reason the Rumanian Communist party—in contrast to that of
Yugoslavia—could not gain any influence among Rumanian youth
and students before the war. Until the Soviet troops marched in,
the party remained a total outsider.

Nationalist right-wing extremism filled the political vacuum
after 1930. Here also one might ask why Rumanian nationalism
could not become stabilized along the moderate line represented
by the leading politicians rallied around the crown, by the
military and industrial circles, or by such intelligent,
personally honest persons as the historian Nicolai Iorga. There
are two reasons, of which the first was foreign influence,
especially after 1933. Perhaps Rumanians did not necessarily
see a model in German National Socialism, but they perceived the
changes in the international power relationships and were
apprehensive about Rumania's national security. They thought
that these dangers could be met by adopting organizational
structures that could give expression to Rumania's "national

strength and unity," as analogous structures were allegedly
doing elsewhere. The second reason why Rumanian nationalism
could not maintain a moderate line lies in the strong social
roots of Rumanian right-wing extremism. A book about the Iron
Guard published in Bucharest in 1971 describes quite objectively
how the aggressive ideology of the Guard, founded on national,
social, and religious myths, flourished among a landless or, at
least, land-poor rural population, namely, the agrarian
proletariat.[19] Paradoxically, the socially progressive land
reform of 1921 contributed greatly to difficulties in the
Rumanian villages. The land reform created a population of
smallholders. But because of the population density, especially
in the Old Kingdom of Rumania, the property of these
smallholders was generally not larger than three hectares, too
small to continue to support a family and its descendants. This
shortage of land led to the creation of a new rural proletariat.
Even the National Peasant party had nothing to offer to this
rural proletariat or to the agricultural laborers remaining on
the large estates. They became an easy prey to the Iron Guard,
which launched a crusade under the banner of the archangel
Michael for the "purification of the nation" from immorality,
exploitation, communism, Jews, and all kinds of other
undesirable elements. The fanaticism of this movement led to
horrible crimes, so horrible, in fact, that Rumania rid itself
of this plague in January 1941 under the dictatorship of Marshal
Antonescu. Rumania thus became the only satellite state of
National Socialist Germany which liquidated its own Nazis under
the noses of the German Nazis.

The coup d'état of August 23, 1944, took Rumania out of the
camp of the Axis powers to the side of the Allies, or, more
precisely, of the Soviet Union. Objective circumstances had
forced Rumania to the side of the Axis powers, and during the
war it was not able to follow the kind of independent political
course maintained by Finland. Nonetheless, under the regime of
Antonescu Rumania showed some signs of substantial independence.
It should be remembered that, although in August and September
1940 Rumania was forced by the Axis powers to cede northern
Transylvania to Hungary and southern Dobruja to Bulgaria, this
occurred immediately after the annexation of Bessarabia by the
Soviet Union and before Antonescu could consolidate his regime.
Rumania was isolated and had no choice but to agree to this act.
It is highly doubtful that Rumania would have complied with the
transfer demand a few months later. In any case, according to
some sources, Marshal Antonescu told Hitler personally that he
would never recognize the Vienna Award, which transferred the

territories.[20] In the spring of 1941 Rumania refused to participate in the hostilities against Yugoslavia, and also refused to annex the Banat region.[21] The liquidation of the Iron Guard has already been mentioned. Finally, Rumania maintained an independent position on the Jewish question. During the reconquest of Bessarabia and Bukovina in the summer of 1941, Rumanian troops committed major atrocities against the Jews there, who did not speak Rumanian, but spoke Yiddish or Russian, and were thus considered "foreign" Jews by the Rumanians. However, the Rumanians' "own" Jews in Rumania proper remained relatively unmolested despite nationalist extremism and pressure by Germany. In contrast, most of the Jews in northern Transylvania (which had been ceded to Hungary) were killed.[22] Thus Rumania, as weak as its political structures were, was able, under the banner of a strong nationalism, to assert itself to perhaps the greatest extent possible for a country of its size and geographic location in those difficult days.

One can draw certain parallels with the way in which Rumania tries today, under completely different premises and circumstances, to assert itself as an independent factor in the power group it was forced to join after 1944. The resolute change of allies in 1944 was an attempt to preserve its independence. The communists played a relatively small role in the coup d'état, compared to that of the king, the bourgeois politicians, and the generals. The goal of independence was not attained at that time, in spite of the 170,000 Rumanian soldiers and officers who gave their lives in combined Rumanian-Soviet military operations that ranged all the way to Prague.[23] The liberation very soon became a Soviet occupation. The communist seizure of power took place under the shield of the Soviet occupation forces, and the power struggle within the communist party was won by the group that had spent the war in the Soviet Union. Subsequently, Stalin's anti-Semitic shift in 1951-1952 enabled the "covert national communist" Gheorghiu-Dej to purge Ana Pauker and Vasile Luca,[24] the principal figures of this group. This purge was, perhaps, the first stirring of emerging national communism. At the time, of course, Gheorghiu-Dej appeared to be conducting a personal power struggle, evidenced by his move against Patrașcanu. This move later led Ceaușescu, Gheorghiu-Dej's former youth leader and political disciple, to criticize him—while fully recognizing his accomplishments—for playing personal politics.[25]

Rumania's current problems do not lie in domestic or even national conflicts. The position of Nicolae Ceaușescu, the general secretary of the party and president of the State

Council, who took over the highest party post after the death of
Gheorghiu-Dej in 1965 and the highest state office in 1967, is
practically undisputed. The few differences over concrete
economic questions which were raised at the National Party
Conference of July 19-21, 1972, cannot affect the power
relationships.[26] The same pertains to the discussions about
Rumania's cultural activity which periodically sweep the
country.[27] It is undisputable that the Rumanian official
establishment, Ceauşescu included, has adopted a rather strict
policy toward intellectuals and artists, but it is equally
demonstrable that this policy places great value on developing
Rumanian culture and increasing respect for it abroad. Clearly,
Ceauşescu himself would rather make the writers and artists his
allies in his ideologically puritanical education campaign than
suppress them. Narrow Marxist dogmatism has meant a certain loss
of creative freedom for writers and artists; on the other hand,
they are compensated by the opportunities which the primacy of
the nation in Rumanian life opens up to them.

Today, Rumania's diverse national composition is no longer a
threat, unless the issue of the Hungarian minority (8.4 percent
of the population, or approximately 1.6 million people,
according to the 1966 census) should be used by the Soviet Union
to create domestic problems for Rumania by way of Budapest. In
such a case,however, the Soviets would have to intervene in the
overall unsolved nationality problems of Eastern Europe, and
this step would result in more problems than advantages. Of
course Hungary alone might one day openly raise the issue of the
Hungarian minority in Transylvania; at present, Hungary
occasionally raises the issue indirectly. But this would mean a
general transition to a nationalist policy in Hungary. The
regime in Budapest would, without a doubt, be stopped by Moscow
from making this transition, and Hungary's self-interest would
probably be a deterrent in any case. It may be that the
treatment of the Hungarians in Transylvania occasionally gives
grounds for complaint, but in the current power constellation
even if Rumania should dissociate itself even further from the
Warsaw Pact, it does not need to fear that any foreign power
would seize upon this problem. With respect to the border issue,
it has been the policy of the Soviet Union for years to have
whatever European borders are currently in existence as
"unchangeable." The German minority in the middle Siebenbürgen
and the Banat (constituting 2 percent of the population, or
approximately 350,000 people, according to the 1966 census) is no
political problem whatever for the Rumanian state, for the
economic power that traditionally provided the basis for the

separate existence of this minority was broken by expropriation
and collectivization. The form in which the problem of the
German minority presents itself today is that a large part, and
perhaps a majority, of these Germans would like to emigrate to
the Federal Republic of Germany. Rumania is opposed to this
emigration for several reasons: first, because Rumania values
the Germans as good workers and technicians and, second, because
the Hungarians and even the Rumanians themselves might then
demand greater freedom of travel. This second reason is perhaps
the more important one. In a speech in February 1971,[28]
Ceauşescu made a few friendly gestures toward the German
minority, but in practice the policy remained the same. One can
imagine that the issue of the Rumanian Germans may become a
problem for the German Federal Republic in its relation with
Bucharest, since the Federal Republic can hardly be uninterested
in the fate of these people even though under international law
it does not have the right to represent them.

Rigid Planning in the Economy. The problems of Rumania's future
development lie in its economic policy on the one hand and its
foreign policy on the other. With respect to the economy, since
1958 Rumania has been following an intensified policy of high
capital investment and artificial limitation of consumption. In
opposition to Khrushchev's views, Rumania committed itself to
autarkic industrialization with emphasis on heavy industry. At
the Ninth Party Congress of the Communist Party of Rumania in
1965, Ceauşescu announced an increased quota of 11 percent for
capital-goods and of 10 percent for consumer-goods production
for the next planning period; the quota for capital-investment
expenditures was fixed at 28.5 percent of national income.[29]
These goals were only partially realized despite a massive
squeeze on consumption and on agriculture. In agriculture,
administrative regulations and extensive farming methods were
employed to cultivate areas sufficiently large for the country
to become self-sufficient in basic foodstuffs and eventually
even to have small surpluses. The whole system of planning was
centralized, down to the smallest detail; until 1971, individual
enterprises had hardly any freedom of action worth mentioning.
The whole Rumanian economic organization is based on the concept
of strict, rational planning, in conjunction with the best
possible technology. Technology is responsible for Rumania's
effort, begun in 1963, to enter into the strongest possible
economic relations with the West and to remove one economic
sector after another from dependence on second-class Soviet
technology and integrate it into the world market system. This
resolute effort has been successful; at the end of 1972

Ceauşescu could announce that over half of Rumania's foreign
trade was with non-CMEA countries.[30] For understandable reasons
Rumania does not value the principle of supranationality in the
international economy. Even so, it very early developed direct
relations with the Common Market. Rumania tried throughout 1972
to obtain from the Common Market the trade preferences designed
for the developing countries. The argument continually used by
the Rumanians during the negotiations and in their propaganda as
well was that a majority (even if a bare majority) of the
Rumanian labor force is still employed in agriculture. Rumania did
not, then, obtain that desired concession from the European Economic
Community, but it was accepted as a member of the International
Monetary Fund in December 1972, which made it eligible to
receive World Bank loans. Since 1970 Rumania has also been a
member of GATT.

As Montias demonstrated in 1967,[31] there are no reliable data
about the cost-return relationship in the Rumanian economy,
which in purely quantitative terms has been expanding rapidly.
It is also not known whether or not investments, especially in
the modern technology bought from the West with valuable foreign
exchange, are paying off; the productivity of this technology is
certainly lower under Rumanian conditions than in the West.
However, the economic power of Rumania should not be
underestimated. Rumania has a significant raw materials base,
especially in the petrochemical industry, and over the years it
has succeeded in building up its foreign trade to a fairly high
level both quantitatively and qualitatively. Rumania's terms of
trade appear more advantageous than those of other socialist
states. The problem is simply that the product of this already
highly developed foreign trade is reflected very little in the
living standard of the population. In a few cases, such as the
aluminum industry, one can detect serious planning errors that
burden the transportation network and the economy as a whole.
The holder of the top planning position has been changed
frequently during the last years, which doubtless indicates the
existence of serious problems.

Instead of reducing the excessive investment and growth rate
to a level tolerable by the population, Ceauşescu tried at the
National Party Conference of July 19-21, 1972, again to increase
the tempo of development; the challenge was issued to fulfill
the five-year plan in four and a half years. However, for the
first time Ceauşescu faced opposition on this issue. It was
reported that shortly before the conference, in Cluj, Premier
Ion Gheorghe Maurer had recommended that the growth rate be
slowed down rather than increased; it was further reported that

Ceauşescu had twice been in a minority in the Politburo on the
question of economic development. Individual ministerial
positions were changed even more frequently than usual during
this period. Ceauşescu himself noticeably tried to smooth over
the differences, in his concluding words at the National Party
Conference, by stating that it was not a question of using
additional resources in order to fulfill the five-year plan
sooner but only of better utilization of the resources already
committed. Nevertheless, some regions decided to adopt a longer
planning period than the four and a half years fixed.[32] The
problem of the high growth rates and the effectiveness of
investments in Rumania is not yet settled. Ceauşescu has had to
make some concessions to the population, mainly in the form of
social subsidies, and within the framework of a national
education campaign he has increasingly stressed "moral
incentives," which, as everyone knows, cost less than material
ones.

It is precisely the "moral" aspect of this campaign and the
increasing tendency of the state and party leader to champion
a moralistic puritanism which aroused some concern about
Ceauşescu's future behavior. In spite of the best
intentions, he is perhaps in danger of losing touch with
Rumanian realities and opportunities. The campaign against large-
scale and petty corruption is understandable, but it is
insufficient as the creed for a new, progressive Rumania.
Likewise, it is appreciated when the leader of the country,
between his frequent trips abroad, personally inspects the
markets of Bucharest—in the manner of Harun al-Rashid. But only
when the economy as a whole functions well will gratuities
become unnecessary and the markets filled.

From about 1970 on, Ceauşescu did not oppose in principle the
view that the Rumanian economy, which had moved from its initial
state into a complicated and differentiated stage, could not be
administered in the long run with simple, rigidly centralized
methods. Planning errors became too obvious. In Rumania, as
elsewhere, there was a search for ways to make the management of
the economy more flexible. There was little publicity about this
search, but from conversations and personal experience the
attempts may be described as follows: first, Rumanian planning
became less interested in quantity than in monetary value as the
indicator of production. This change was partly a reflection of
the belief that step by step Rumania could establish a connection
with the world monetary system. Meanwhile, however, this in no
way meant unregulated prices. Second, beginning in 1971
industrial centers were set up, occupying a place in the economic

structure between production enterprises and the ministries.
These industrial centers encompassed groups of similar
enterprises and were given powers, even in matters of foreign
trade, which had previously belonged to the ministries. Third,
within the enterprises "factory councils" and "factory
assemblies" were created in which workers, either directly or
through their representatives, could gain an insight into the
problems of the factory and make suggestions and criticisms.
Even the possibility of a "vote of no confidence" against the
director was provided for. It was apparently Ceauşescu's
intention to give a role to the labor unions in particular.
Fourth, an administrative reform increased the number of
governmental administrative organs, decentralized them, and gave
them powers of their own in order to develop their initiative. In
order to increase the initiative of local authorities, state and
party offices were often combined at the local level but, in
contrast, controls were strengthened.[33]
      All these reforms, as well as greater observance of legality
in the operation of the state machinery, were steps in the right
direction. But they did not succeed in changing the realities of
Rumanian life, the excessive centralism and bureaucratism. The
development of initiative in the factories or at the local
administrative level still leaves much to be desired. It seems
that personal initiative is simply alien to the Rumanian
tradition. On the other hand, the Rumanian leadership fears that
it may lose control in some areas. They are afraid to let the
population or local organs do anything on their own because they
may no longer be able to control it or may be forced to undo
some action taken. This consequence could be politically
"sensitive." The administrative decentralization has succeeded
the best, for there are still local traditions in the various
regions of the country which provide an administrative framework.
In contrast, little progress has been made in other areas. The
industrial centers frequently operate merely as sections of the
former ministries or, in the case of large-scale enterprises, as
extensions of management. In practice, the resulting frictions
have, paradoxically, strengthened that highest authority favoring
decentralization, namely, Ceauşescu himself. It is ironic that
the National Party Conference of July 1972 produced a Ceauşescu
personality cult reminiscent of the Stalinist period, while
Ceauşescu himself tried in his speeches to awaken individual
responsibility and initiative in his subordinates.[34]

Yugoslavia: The National Problem. Yugoslavia is more than a
multinational state; it is a multicultural state. Among its

different peoples, the Serbs, Montenegrins, and Macedonians developed under the influence of Byzantine and, later, Ottoman culture, while the Croats and Slovenes are Roman Catholic and were once under the rule of Austria-Hungary. In addition, there are numerous national and religious minorities, each of which pulls in a different direction or displays strong regionalism, as, for example the Bosnian Moslems. It follows that such a complicated entity is difficult to integrate and to govern.

Because communist centralism has prevented the manifestation of Yugoslavia's internal nationality problem, Yugoslavia's development since World War II has given the impression that the problem has been overcome. But old conflicts, which were believed by many observers to have been overcome, are again surfacing. In reality, Yugoslavia is still a state in the process of formation and has not yet found its proper constitutional form. The more time passes, the more it must be recognized that communism has not succeeded in solving the national question; the communists have been able to do scarcely more than to carry the process of nation-building a little further chronologically. As of 1974, whether they have advanced or retarded the process remains an open question.[35]

On the other hand, the view, which grew out of historical nostalgia for the Austro-Hungarian empire, that even the concept of a Yugoslav state is nothing but a "disrupter of the peace" and that Yugoslavia is one of those artifical creations of Versailles which sooner or later must again disintegrate into its "natural" components is equally untenable. The concept of a Yugoslav state has firm historical roots, which go far back with both of its principal supporters, the Serbs and the Croats. The Yugoslav state idea formed a solid component in the political and cultural development process of these two peoples. It appeared later among the two "border nations," the Slovenes and the Macedonians. Until 1917 the main political figures in Slovenia appeared to prefer a Danubian monarchy, reorganized along federal lines in accordance with the principle of national equality. Meanwhile, the Macedonians had emancipated themselves from the Bulgarian cultural and political sphere of influence around 1900. For these two border peoples there is at present no realistic alternative to membership in the Yugoslav state.

One of Yugoslavia's main problems, however, is that Serbs and Croats came to accept the concept of a Yugoslav state for completely different reasons and that neither group has accepted the concept of Yugoslavia unconditionally. The main consideration for Serbia was the state element. Shortly after the restoration of an independent Serbian principality in 1830, the leaders of the new state came to the conclusion that, in its central location in the Balkans, a Serbian state would have a chance for permanent independent existence only if it were large and strong enough to withstand the influence of all three surrounding big powers, Turkey, Russia, and Austria-Hungary. The Serbian statesman Ilija Garašanin espoused this view in 1944 in his famous Načertanje, an outline of a foreign-policy program for Serbia.[36] Garašanin recognized that the Serbs alone were not numerous enough to establish a strong and independent state in the middle of the Balkans. He therefore recommended the inclusion of the Croats and other southern Slavs and the creation of a large Slav-Serbian state, but he was of course determined that the already existing Serbian principality and its dynasty should provide the leadership. Since it was the era of legitimacy, Garašanin simultaneously used his statehood idea to justify the legitimacy of Serbia's national demands, which were aimed primarily against Austria-Hungary and as Garašanin correctly anticipated, would lead to a conflict with it. One can easily see that the Yugoslav state of 1918 largely corresponded to Garašanin's prophetic program, in its conception as well as its manner of creation.

For the Croats, the national and cultural motives, not the state idea, were predominant. The basis of Napoleon's creation of the "Illyrian provinces," with Ljubljana as the capital, was the concept of the national and cultural unity of all South Slavs. This was a modern, nationalistic idea; its premise was that Serbs, Croats, and perhaps even Slovenes were one nation in the ethnic sense. In fact, it is hardly possible to differentiate between the Serbs and the Croats on the basis of ethnic or linguistic characteristics. (The Slovenes dissociated themselves from the idea of a united South Slav nation in the first half of the nineteenth century.) Such differentiation was already impossible at the time when these two peoples emigrated to the Balkans. All attempts to classify the individual tribes as Serbs and Croats, or even to draw an ethnic dividing line between Serbs and Croats (for example, the river Cetina south of Split) are ex post facto interpretations made on the basis of state, not ethnic, boundaries. In no way can the South Slav dialects be identified as either Croation or Serbian; attempts to do so have led to absurd results. In his 1847 article "Srbi svi i svuda," the Serb Vuk Karadžić claimed the largest part of the Croats as Serbs,[37] while on the other side the nineteenth-century Croatian nationalist Ante Starčević used similar linguistic arguments to claim that the largest part of the Serbs and even the Slovenes were Croats.[38] In the present, just as in the past, one must realize that the issue of differentiation between Serbs and

Croats is exclusively one of religion or a conscious sense of group identity.[39]

It was precisely this conscious sense of group identity on which the two nationalist revival movements in Croatia focused, the Illyrian movement, which lasted until 1848, and the later Yugoslav movement of Bishop Josip Juraj Strossmayer. Both were based on the premise that an exclusively Croatian national development in the Croatian area was impossible and undesirable, in view of the mixed population (Orthodox Serbs lived primarily in the so-called military frontier zone—the Vojna Krajina), for this would result only in antagonism. The champions of the Illyrian and Yugoslav movements also believed that Croatian national "exclusiveness" would make it impossible to defend the integrity and the constitutional law of the "triune kingdom of Croatia, Slavonia, and Dalmatia" against Budapest or Vienna, especailly with respect to their unification with the Vojna Krajina and Dalmatia into the old historical union. Therefore, it is clear that the national awakening of the Croats, until well past the middle of the nineteenth century, took place in the name of Yugoslavia and not Croatia.

This Yugoslavism required, of course, a high degree of rationality and intellectual insight. Therefore it could maintain itself logically only as long as the intellectuals were the sole political and cultural representatives of the nation. When the lower segments of society in the countryside and in the cities began to emancipate themselves socially, differences in religion and origin came into play. The surfacing of these differences led to a powerful eruption, exclusively Croatian, and personified by Starčević. Starčević tried to maintain that his movement was by no means directed against the Serbs. He was, in fact, primarily concerned with the creation of a large, self-contained, united Croatia with its own constitution, independent of Budapest and Vienna, within a federalist monarchy if possible, but outside the monarchy if necessary. In practice, Starčević's ideology was based on the rejection of the "Balkanism" of the Serbs, i.e., of the South Slav concept in politics and culture. This ideology alarmed the Serbs living in Croatia and enabled the Hungarian administration, to which Croatia was subordinate, to play on the emerging Serbo-Croat differences. This situation also resulted in a new Serbo-Croat coalition between 1903 and 1906,[40] although it was a purely political one. It was led by politicians from Dalmatia, principally Frano Supilo, who later became chairman of the Yugoslav Committee in London and in 1917 negotiated the Declaration of Corfu (establishing a Yugoslav state) with the Serbian prime minister, Pašić. In contrast to the movement led by

Strossmayer, who thought primarily in cultural categories or at least visualized a Serbo-Croat coalition under "Western auspices"[41] within a federalist Danube monarchy, this coalition was in essence concerned with political action against the monarchy and with the political union of the Serbs and Croats under the leadership of Belgrade, outside the Habsburg empire.

This development clearly shows the schism in the nationalism of the Croats, between the Yugoslav movement, on the one hand, and the exclusively Croatian movement, on the other. It is clear that this schism would lead to conflicts among the Croats themselves, and it is equally understandable that these conflicts—like all family conflicts—would be carried to excess. Every time Croatian exclusiveness exalted the Croatian national idea, it had to counter the opponent in its own ranks—Croatian Yugoslavism—before it could confront the external foe. As a result, Croatian exclusiveness contained elements of exaggeration and excitability, which had expressed themselves under Starčević and his successor Dr. Frank. To this element was added a religious and mystical component arising from the merger with the fanatical Catholicism of the border areas in Bosnia and Herzegovina. All of this was combined in the Ustaša movement of World War II to produce a mystical bloodlust.

The revival of Croatian exclusivist national feeling at the time of the "national euphoria" in 1971 also showed some of this exaggeration, as, for example, in a petty insistence on linguistic and orthographic details, reminiscent of the theories of the nineteenth century. The Croatian Yugoslavists similarly were frequently guilty of exaggeration and simplification. In their blind eagerness for unification, they spurned any form of Croatian autonomy in 1918 and were thus substantially responsible for the false basis on which the first Yugoslav state was created and for its consequent collapse. The exaggerations of Croatian Yugoslavism can be summed up in the concept of "unitarianism." The representatives of this idea in the first Yugoslavia were primarily liberal Dalmatian politicans such as Ante Trumbić, but the main champions were the Serbs living in Croatia, under the leadership of Svetozar Pribičević. The attitude of the Serbs living in Croatia was understandably dictated by self-interest, but it gave the Croats the feeling that they were never the master in their own house. This feeling in turn stimulated Croatian exclusiveness. The tension subsequently exploded during the Second World War in the campaign to liquidate the Serbs living in Croatia and Bosnia.

In 1971 a repetition of this vicious circle occurred. After the Savka Dabčević-Mika Tripalo leadership was deposed, some of

the speakers (e.g., Dr. Dušan Dragosavać) who made the sharpest
attacks in the Central Committee of the Croatian Communist party
against "Croatian nationalism" were of Serbian nationality.[42]

Yet another regularity can be observed over the decades in
the interplay between the variants of Croatian nationalistic
thinking: whenever Croatia's local autonomy or rights appeared
endangered by too much interface from the Yugoslav central
government, an exclusivist nationalistic reaction would build up
in Croatia and subside again only when some kind of reasonable
balance was established between Croatian and all-Yugoslav
elements.

The first Yugoslavia, established on the basis of the Corfu
Declaration of 1917, was born under an unlucky star; for all
intents and purposes it was founded exclusively on the Serbian
conception. The Croatian unitarians, who at the time of
unification dominated the political scene in Zagreb, had
naively tried to commit Serbian Prime Minister Pašić to the
"modern" idea, proclaimed by Woodrow Wilson, that the
sovereignty of the people was indivisible. The framework of a
unitary state for the new Yugoslavia was quickly dominated by
the numerical, political, and military superiority of the Serbs.
The Peasant Party, led by Stjepan and Ante Radić, therefore
became dominant in Croatia. It was skeptical about the new state
and threatened to take Croatia out of it again. It became clear
that the political framework provided by Serbia, and the
conception of Serbian hegemony which lay behind it, could not
give the new state a sound base. Pašić himself realized this;
he tried to cooperate with Radić in order to have at least
political, if not constitutional, dualism. In Slovenia, the
People's party under Dr. Anton Korošec was the dominant power,
and the Slovenes took the side of the Serbs politically because
their local autonomy was de facto respected.

With the death of Pašić the concept of political dualism
disappeared. The assassination of leading Croatian politicians
in the Belgrade parliament (the Skupština) on June 20, 1928,
brought the country back to the beginning. The Croats wanted
autonomy in order to defend themselves against Serbian
hegemony; since this autonomy was seen in historical perspective,
it was called the Croatian "right of statehood." So that this
autonomy would not appear to be a special Croatian privilege,
the new leader of the Croatian Peasant Party, Dr. Vladko Maček,
suggested to King Alexander in 1929 a general federalization of
Yugoslavia.[43] However, the king and the Serbian circles that
supported him decided otherwise. They believed that the
establishment of a completely homogeneous, integrated Yugoslavia

would submerge all national and regional differences. This was
the goal of the dictatorship proclaimed by King Alexander on
January 6, 1930. Its policies became known as "Yugoslav
Integralism": the army as the guardian of national unity,
adoption of the new name, Yugoslavia, in place of "the Kingdom of
the Serbs, Croats, and Slovenes," and the creation of new
administrative units (banovine) whose lines were drawn across
the historical boundaries. Perhaps this attempt could have helped
to solve the nationality problem if its intentions had been
honest. But they served merely to conceal the old Serbian
hegemony, which now became even more nearly complete than before.
The only group able to maintian some political autonomy were the
Slovenes in their nationally homogeneous province (banovina) of
Drava. The Macedonians, since 1918 designated offhandedly as
South Serbs and treated as such, saw themselves further away than
ever from national independence. Croatian nationalism was
suppressed. Its extreme wing, with Dr. Ante Pavelić as its head,
looked to Germany, Italy, and Hungary for aid. It prepared for
terrorism, of which King Alexander himself became a victim in
1934. The Ustaša movement had begun.

Milan Stojadinović, the famous Yugoslav politician of the
1930s, attached little political value to the Croatian Peasant
party leader Maček and to the Croats in general.[44] He believed
that Serbian hegemony was the only possible guarantee for
Yugoslavia's existence. On the other hand, he did attempt to
defuse the Croatian question and to return to Pašić's old
conception of political dualism. By allowing the Serbian
opposition to join forces with the Croatian Peasant party for
the elections, he opened the way to even more than political
dualism; for the first time there was a voluntary integration
of political life in Yugoslavia. A real solution to the Croatian
problem slowly emerged from this atmosphere, aided by the threat
of war in Europe. The regent, Prince Paul, also must be given
credit for this development of political integration. By his
order the new prime minister, Dragiša Cvetković, signed the
so-called sporazum (settlement) on August 20, 1939, establishing
an autonomous Banovina of Croatia, which included those areas of
West Bosnia and Herzegovina in which Croats were the majority, as
well as the historical Croatian regions.

The sporazum provided special rights for the Croats, defining
Croatia apart from the Yugoslav state, which was regarded as
Serbian. It automatically made the Croats less interested in the
Yugoslav state and also placed the Slovenes in an awkward
situation. But the solution corresponded to the realiities. It
took account of the fact that, among all of Yugoslavia's

nationalities, the Croats most of all wanted constitutionally safeguarded autonomy and were prepared to go much further to get it than were the others. In spite of its imperfections, the sporazum was the politically correct solution, given the circumstances of the period; the tragedy was that there was not enough time for it to take root. The argument that the sporazum brought Yugoslavia to the edge of disintegration and was responsible for the country's sudden collapse in the April 1941 war is superficial. It ignores the putsch of the Serbian officers on March 27, 1941, organized without the knowledge of the Croat political leaders, which threw Croatia into confusion and also aroused great fears there about the position of the new regime vis-à-vis the sporazum.

In retrospect, the socialists and communists among the Yugoslav peoples had basically nothing to offer different from what the bourgeois politicians proposed to solve Yugoslavia's nationality problem. It is not surprising if the communists today are more or less in the same position as the old Yugoslavia. Perhaps, indeed, they have not even reached this stage. As long as the communists were not in power they advocated—in either a utopian or a purely opportunistic manner—the opposite of whatever the "ruling class" happened to stand for at the time with respect to the nationality question. When they came to power, they several times did the same thing King Alexander had tried in 1930, namely, to overcome the existing nationality problems by force and with an ideological leap forward. In 1968 Paul Shoup could still write (in his excellent description of communist nationality policy in Yugoslavia)[45] that as a result of Yugosavia's role in world affairs and its domestic achievements, the individual citizens of Yugoslavia had finally been induced to identify themselves as Yugoslavs abroad. In early 1974, it is doubtful if even this remains the case.

The most original theories about the nationality problem in Yugoslavia, and in the Balkans generally, proposed by the indigenous left were those of Svetozar Marković in the middle of the nineteenth century. In place of the "microimperialism" of the newly created Balkan states, Marković urged a Socialist Balkan Federation based on local and regional self-government. This idea was correct in principle even if utopian. Marković, influenced by the Russian narodniki, wanted to take the old Serbian institutions of the extended family (zadruga) and the village community as the basic units. But in his most important work on this topic, Serbia on the East,[46] even he, as a good Serbian patriot, indicated that the establishment of the Socialist Balkan Federation was only a means to safeguard the "natural" Serbian

predominance in this region more effectively than was possible
with the "Little Serbia" political conception of his bourgeois
opponents.

At the time of the Second International, around the turn of
the century, the socialists of the Yugoslav nations did not
develop any creative ideas about the nationality question. In
the territories of the Habsburg monarchy they were influenced by
Austrian Marxism, and in Serbia the socialists obediently and
naively repeated what the leaders of the international workers'
movement told them. After the establishment of the Yugoslav
state they participated in the Congress of Bukovar in 1920 under
the leadership of Sima Marković and, like the important
bourgeois leaders of the time, supported "national unity."
(Because of this position, the party history published in
Belgrade in 1963 accuses them of a "complete lack of
understanding" of the nationality problem.)[47] The reversal came
after 1929, as a result of developments in the country itself
and because the Comintern aimed to capitalize on the unsolved
nationality problem in the Balkans. Thus the Yugoslav communists
also proceeded to preach federalism, and they decentralized
their party along national lines. Under Tito's decisive
influence, the fourth National Party Conference in Ljubljana in
1934 decided to establish autonomous Croatian and Slovene
communist parties which would be federated with an all-Yugoslav
communist party, and the creation of a Macedonian party was
planned for "the very near future."[48]

It is characteristic of the political opportunism of
communist nationality policy that, in spite of this flirtation
with the fragmentation of Yugoslavia, the communists adopted a
national unity policy again in the years immediately before the
war because it offered them better opportunities at that time.
The fragmentation of Yugoslavia after April 1941 did, in fact,
create an intolerable burden for all the peoples of Yugoslavia,
and the restoration of the Yugoslav state within its old
boundaries, only now as a federation, appeared to be the
politically realistic alternative. Politically, this was an
ingenious move by Tito. It gave the communists access to all
national groups and also opened up the whole country to the
partisans for operations and supplies, while the national
resistance forces of the individual peoples, e.g., the Serbian
Chetniks, had to confine themselves to certain parts of
Yugoslavia and were thus at a disadvantage from the beginning.
The real decision in the partisan war came in the summer of 1942
in the mountains of central Croatia and western Bosnia, when, as
a result of Serbian persecution by the Croatian Ustaša, Tito's

communists were able to integrate into their ranks large numbers
of the Serbs, and to use their territory as a base. The
territory thus won, the effective freedom of movement, and the
reserves of men and supplies enabled the partisans successfully
to withstand the heavy German offensives of 1943. On November
29, 1943, in the Bosnian town of Jajce, the communists laid down
the political framework for the creation of the new state, a
"democratic, federal Yugoslavia."[49] After 1945 the new
Yugoslavia's federalism, like its democracy, existed only on
paper. It is revealing that at the end of 1970, after Tito had
recommended a basic reorganization of the state in his speech of
September 21, 1970, circles of the old partisans (even such
people as Edvard Kardelj) expressed the euphoric idea that
finally socialist Yugoslavia was returning to its origins, i.e.,
to the basic principles of Jajce, which had been suppressed for
decades by a centralized bureaucracy.[50]
    In one respect, however, Yugoslav federalism was genuine: in
the organizational structure of the Yugoslav Communist party. As
Ernst· Halperin has correctly emphasized, this was to become of
the utmost importance.[51] The party apparatus of the different
republics was in fact autonomous up to a certain point. This
autonomy enabled the individual leaders to maintain an
independent power base and even a certain amount of functional
independence from the central authority. After the economic
reforms and decentralization of 1950, political power in the
republics became increasingly combined with economic interests.
This combination then developed nationalistic overtones. (The
form in which national or territorial interests were expressed
would probably have been the same under any other regime.) This
development first became noticeable in the late 1950s in
Slovenia. The party functionaries joined the population in
opposition to the policy (issued under the slogan "Brotherhood
and Unity ") of equalizing the economic development of
Yugoslavia. The policy meant that the more developed Slovenia
had to sacrifice a substantial part of its production, and thus
its living standard, for the benefit of the underdeveloped
republics in the east and south.[52] It initiated a process in
Slovenia that at times led to a real "resentment against
Yugoslavia" and to covert particularistic tendencies. (The
official term was "tendencies of withdrawal into the boundaries
of the republic.") A climax came in the summer of 1969 in
demonstrations against the discriminatory treatment of Slovenia
in the allocation of funds for road construction. These
tendencies also found support at the managerial level. In highly
developed Slovenia, managers had greater influence than

elsewhere. They also had political backing in the government,
primarily from the president of the Executive Council of the
Republics, Stane Kavčić. After the 1969 demonstrations Kavčić
was even able to weather the strong attacks of Kardelj and his
group of Slovene party functionaries.[53] He was forced to retreat
only under the pressure of Tito's general attack on the whole
reformist wing of the party in November 1972.

The representative of the Slovene functionaries controlled by
Tito and Kardelj, Franc Popit, rejoiced at that session of the
Slovene Central Committee that the "dualism" between party and
governmental authority, as well as "opportunism" and notions
about regional cooperation with neighboring areas of Austria,
Italy, and even Bavaria, were now finally liquidated.[54]
Meanwhile, Slovenia's problem remained. The problem is that
Slovenia, which economically and culturally has reached the
Central European standard, and which has open borders, giving
all kinds of opportunities to its people to make comparisons,
must pay for its membership in Yugoslavia (and a socialist
Yugoslavia at that) with a considerable loss in living standard
and in individual opportunities for its citizens and with a loss
of freedom as well. It is difficult to predict how this state of
affairs will work out in the future. Not surprisingly, during
the 1972 political and economic reforms in Slovenia, Tito and
the Yugoslav central government emphasized the problems of the
Slovene minority in Austria and Italy, telling the Slovenes that
enemies were lurking beyond their western and northern borders,
against whom the assistance of the whole Yugoslav community was
necessary.[55]

The Croatian developments were similar, although dominated by
the traditional aspects of the Croatian problem. Basically, the
issue also was that the centralized economic leveling of
Yugoslavia was accomplished at Croatia's expense. However, a
solution was at first sought in keeping with Croatian
Yugoslavism, of which the Croatian communists, led by Vladimir
Bakarić, were the heirs. Therefore, the thesis of Bakarić and
his followers was that the Croatian problem could best be solved
if the Yugoslav economic and political system were reformed and
modernized. The ideological principles of this reform had
already been laid down; in 1950, "workers' self-government" had
been officially proclaimed as the principle of economic and
political administration. Also in the early 1950s, agricultural
collectivization had been abandoned and a market mechanism set
up. It was now necessary to translate these principles into
reality, to separate politics and economics, and to return to
the economy the resources it had acquired. These were the

general principles by which Bakarić and his followers, around
1960, justified their reform and tried to put it into practice.
At first they stressed the technical aspects, but later
increasingly the political ones as well. The Eighth Party
Congress in November 1964 brought victory to the reformers from
Zagreb and their allies.[56] Then and later, it was often thought
that now Zagreb would become the natural center of the new
"reformist" Yugoslavia. But this was not yet to be. Instead,
new, increasing opposition appeared within the ranks of the
dogmatic Yugoslav Party Control Committee, which was not crushed
politically until the downfall of the former minister of the
interior, Aleksandar Ranković, on July 1, 1966.[57] Only then could
one believe that the young, open-minded, well-educated economic
cadres that Bakarić had formed around himself in Zagreb would
now determine the future of Yugoslavia and that thereby Croatia's
position in the future Yugoslavia would also be solved.
    However, events again turned out otherwise. Quite apart from
the failure of the economic reforms to produce the anticipated
results, as so often happens in Yugoslavia, a whole series of
problems caused new difficulties and conflicts. Although
Bakarić's reforms were oriented toward all of Yugoslavia, they
were not centralist. On the contrary, their principles were
decentralization and self-management. The political units that,
because of their importance, stood to benefit first from the
decentralization of federal authority were the republics. The
paradoxical situation then arose that the dismantling of federal
authority was carried out in the name of self-government while
simultaneously (and not only in Croatia) many were perfectly
willing to accept a new republic etatism, or even to advocate it.
This situation naturally opened the way for overt nationalistic
tendencies. Soon Bakarić was confronted with a new wave of
demands in Croatia from those for whom reform had meant primarily
strengthening Croatia's independence. The Croatian reformers
applied their concepts to the cultural area as well, and almost
came to identify the concept of "self-management" with national
self-determination.[58] Bakarić moved to Belgrade in 1966 as a
member of the Presidium of the Central Committee of the League of
Communists (he was subsequently elected to the Executive Bureau
and the Presidium of the Central Party at the Ninth Congress in
1969). After his departure, a younger set of politicians, whom he
himself had sponsored, took control in Zagreb—in particular,
Professor (of economics) Savka Dabčević-Kučar (born in 1923) and
the former youth functionary Mika Tripalo (born in 1926). This
new leadership swam on a wave of increasing Croat nationalism. At
the Tenth Plenum of the Croatian Central Committee in January

1970 the leadership staged a day of reckoning with "unitarianism,"
in the course of which a petty party functionary from Dalmatia,
Zanko, served as the scapegoat for the pent-up political and
national frustrations of Croatia.

The Tenth Plenum generated the movement in Croatia which was
later described as "national euphoria." Besides transferring the
concept of self-government to the (Croat) nation, the movement
also contained other elements disquieting to the Yugoslav
communist leadership. First, Tripalo and Mme. Dabčević began to
talk more and more about a "mass movement" that marched
alongside the communist party and upheld Croatia's national
aspirations within the spirit of socialism. Second, certain
currents appeared covertly throughout Croatia which were directed
against important aspects of the communist system; thus, many in
the agricultural sector demanded the removal of the limitation on
land ownership and on the use of private workers. Likewise,
demands were made for greater freedom for private initiative in
the trade and service sectors; an important argument was that
this would create jobs for the approximately 300,000 Croats
working abroad. Third, certain forces appeared which jeopardized
the political monopoly of the communist party. One of these was
the nationalistic student movement at the university, another was
the cultural society Matica Hrvatska. At the head of the Matica's
executive committee was the respected apolitical linguist
Professor Jonke, but other personalities on the committee were
suspected of pursuing more far-reaching political goals:
Professors Djordan and Veselica, the former partisan general
Tudjman, the economist Hrvoje Šošić, the lyric poet Gotovac (who
later became the chief editor of its weekly paper, Hrvatski
Tjednik), and others. Like the leaders of the student movement,
the eleven committee members were arrested after the December
1971 purge and during 1972 were sentenced to prison terms of up
to six years.

The main motive for the Croatian movement of 1971 was the
unsolved problem of the economic-financial relations between the
Yugoslav Federation and the Croat Republic, especially the
division of foreign exchange obtained from trade, and the
distribution of assets left over from the former central banking
system and of the foreign trade companies.[59] The Croatian demands
were substantially justified but emotionalized; for example, it
was difficult to understand why Croatian circles continually
complained about the "Belgrade banks" while it took years for
them to establish a major bank in Croatia itself, as the Slovenes
had done long ago with the establishment of the Ljubljanska
Banka. Nevertheless, there was so much truth in the Croatian

complaints and demands that, one year after the purge of December
1971, they were taken up in almost identical phraseology by Tito
and other party functionaries and used against the allegedly
"technocratic" Serbian communist leadership of Marko Nikezić, who
was reproached for not having done anything to eliminate these
problems. In the fall of 1971, Zagreb students used the issue of
the foreign exchange system as occasion for a strike, during
which one of the student leaders, the erratic theology student
Čičak, imprudently made demands such as a separate army,
separate currency, and separate UN membership for Croatia. One
gained the impression that the Dabčević-Tripalo leadership was
losing control of events and that the leadership's attempt to
rationalize the Croatian movement and to keep it in step with
the communist movement had miscarried. The question arises
whether Mme. Dabčević, Tripalo, and their allies tried to ride
the nationalistic wave only to obtain support against their
opponents in the party leadership or whether they actually
wanted to inaugurate a new Croatian policy, a kind of revised
version of the peoples' movement of Stjepan Radić. In any event,
Tito intervened. At a meeting of the all-Yugoslav Executive
Bureau of the Party in Karadjordjevo he demanded the replacement
of the Croatian leadership and a radical change of course.[60] The
Croatian Central Committee fulfilled this demand on December 12,
1971, and the same evening witnessed the resurrection of pre-
World War II conditions in Zagreb's Square of the Republic:
police of Serbian nationality beat up Croatian students.
Tito's Role. Tito himself instigated the shake-up in Croatia,
which was of the utmost importance for the future development of
Yugoslavia. It initiated the retrogression in the whole process
of democratization and federalization. At Tito's personal
initiative and under his aegis, the fateful development began
which, at the time of this writing, has made Yugoslavia into a
crisis area, with consequences that cannot yet be estimated.
     To understand Tito's personal role in these developments, one
must begin by understanding that in his youth, and even until
the outbreak of the partisan war in 1941, Tito personified more
the agitator, intent upon the destruction of the status quo,
than the constructive statesman. During a large part of his life
he had been accustomed to fight against existing institutions.
During their last years older people frequently return to the
inclinations of their youth. With the first reforms of 1950, the
breakup of the party dictatorship, decentralization, and
establishment of a socialist market economy, Yugoslavia had
begun to create new institutions in politics, economics, and
society which developed their own dynamism and which were only

partly dependent on the will of the political leadership. Tito
never concerned himself very much with economic questions;
accordingly, this was the first area that slipped away from his
personal control. A broad layer of managers had entrenched
themselves in the economic enterprises. They were controlled and
even appointed by the party, but the party itself had become
decentralized. Even more important, a new generation of leaders,
molded by the requirements of a modern economy and by the need
for modern, pragmatic politics, had established themselves in
political posts. This was the so-called middle generation,
people such as Savka Dabčević and Tripalo in Croatia, Marko
Nikezić and Latinka Perović in Serbia, Stane Kavčić in Slovenia,
Krste Crvenkovski in Macedonia, and many others. All of them
were modern, flexible people who had excellent professional
qualifications, were liberal in their thinking, and showed
considerable all-Yugoslav sentiments, although their power base
was in the individual republics because of the decentralized
structure of the country. Thus by the late 1960s and early
1970s, despite the growing independence of the republics, a new,
homogeneous leadership stratus had established itself throughout
Yugoslavia. (The only exception was in the Republic of Bosnia-
Herzegovina, with its political backwardness and other special
circumstances.) The new leaders seemed capable of reaching
agreement among themselves and keeping the country together on
the basis of pragmatic reformism after Tito's departure. The
appropriate system for this leadership and these circumstances
would not have been a new centralism, personified by Tito, but
a system of consensus (the principle of dogovor), and
constitutionally it would have been more a confederation than a
federation.
    In 1970 one had the impression that Tito had come to terms
with this development; perhaps that he even approved it,
although it did not correspond to his personal inclinations and
although under the new system political weight would probably
slowly shift from the party to the state. This latter
development was quite logical. Even with the best intentions the
Yugoslavia of 1970, with its developed, complex economic and
social institutions and its market economy, could no longer be
ruled by party resolutions. The rules now required were
precisely formulated government statutes. However, communists
everywhere tend to have a certain contempt for legalism, going
back to the periods of armed struggle and of rule by force.
They maintain that legalism destroys their "revolutionary" élan,
and they generally couch their aversion to it in phrases such as
"the better is the enemy of the good." This attitude of the

Communists was also an important reason why the legal system in
Yugoslavia always lagged far behind actual development in the
constitutional field and especially in economic legislation. For
example, when solutions to the most important national political
problems were already being sought by the interrepublican
committees (medjurepublički komiteti) of the Federal Assembly in
accordance with the principle of consensus, these parliamentary
committees still had no constitutional status. This damaged their
efficiency and was perhaps a reason why such important issues as
the problem of the foreign exchange system or the problem of the
central banks could not be resolved in time.

In his speech of September 21, 1970, Tito appeared to leave
the way open for a new, reformist Yugoslavia reflecting the
tendencies outlined above.[61] He recommended constitutional reform
with the establishment of a collective presidency of the republic
(pretsedništvo) as the key element, made up proportionately from
representatives of the individual republics and the autonomous
provinces. Tito was concerned with a presidency of the state, not
of the party, and at the time it seemed entirely possible that
the future Yugoslavia would be held together by this highest
governmental organ and not by the party leadership. In this way
the federated state structure and the nationality question would
have been adequately settled. The principle of self-management
could have completed the social aspects of this political
framework. In this spirit the preparations were begun for the
large Congress of Self-Management, to be held in May 1971 in
Sarajevo.[62] A mood of joyful relief spread through Yugoslavia;
people saw the continuity of the state and its social
institutions safeguarded even for the period after Tito.

Unfortunately, things developed differently. The discussion
unleashed after Tito's speech of September 21, 1970, broke up the
planned framework. It appeared that now all the pent-up
constitutional problems were to be solved in one fell swoop, in
particular, the relationship between the federation and the
republics. Numerous proposals had the objective of giving the
republics full statehood and sovereignty. Although such
terminology had appeared earlier in the first postwar
constitution of January 31, 1946, these concepts now had a
completely different and much more concrete meaning. The alarming
thing now was that these proposals for giving sovereignty to the
republics were heard most loudly in Croatia. There they unleashed
a wave of nationalistic euphoria, and in time they raised the
mood in Croatia to a level qualitatively different from that in
the other republics. The Croatian leadership of Savka Dabčević
and Mika Tripalo did not exactly identify itself with this wave

of nationalistic euphoria, but it did recognize it as a reality.
By this action the leadership detached itself and all of Croatia
from the previously unified leadership strata. Thus in Croatia,
Yugoslavia's "weak spot" in the prewar period, a centrifugal
development was again taking place. This development aroused
fears in the other republics, especially in Bosnia and
Herzegovina, where 22 percent of the population are Croats and
which, for historical reasons, considers nationality quarrels
more dangerous than the other republics do. Slovenia also
worried about becoming isolated again, as it did under the
sporazum.

It cannot be said that Tito proceeded precipitately against
the Croatian emancipation tendencies. At a plenum of the Party
Presidium in Brioni in April 1971, he tried to smooth over the
differences, and on May 1 in Labinj he announced to the
Yugoslav population that as a result of this conference "we have
reached agreement."[63] In September 1971 Tito came to Zagreb and
again appealed to the conscience of the Croatian leadership. In
order to strengthen their stand against the nationist wave, Tito
made the rather strange public statement that he had not seen
any nationalists in Croatia.[64] This statement was inept;
nationalistic circles must have interpreted it as giving them
carte blanche for futher agitation. It can be assumed that such
actions as the strike of the Zagreb students in November 1971
were directly inspired by it. At the least the students may have
been led to believe that Tito would stand behind them just as he
had supported the Belgrade students when they staged
demonstrations in 1968.

Tito decided to act only when he knew that a solid majority
of the important politicians of the country were behind him. But
one could also feel that this party leader, over eighty years
old, was in his element when he could openly take up the battle
against those who had left the official line of his party and
searched for new directions. One could also see how much it had
offended him that his conceptions about Communist party rule
were apparently no longer shared by the majority of the party
institutions. Tito first sought support against the Croatian
leadership from the leaders of the concerned republics,
especially Bosnia and Slovenia. Since there were legitimate
arguments against the Savka Dabčević-Mika Tripalo group, the
reformist Serbian leadership could not oppose Tito's action,
although it must have clearly seen that a shake-up in Zagreb
would upset the balance in all of Yugoslavia to Serbia's
disadvantage. The shake-up and Tito's methods benefited the
doctrinaire and bureaucratic forces everywhere. These forces,

liberated from their partial banishment, surfaced and rushed to
Tito's assistance. Tito was dependent on them. In spite of the
promises that there would be no return to old methods, this is
exactly what happened. Arrests and other coercive measures in
Croatia eliminated the supporters of the previous course.

In discussing the shift back to bureaucratic and
centralist methods, we must comment on the principal political
supporters of centralism in the federal structure of Yugoslavia,
namely, the political leaders of Bosnia and Herzegovina. Moslems
are numerically stronger than the Serbs in Bosnia and
Herzegovina, while the Croats are a minority, composing 22
percent of the population. The Serbs dominate politically. The
interests of this republic, which will probably always have a
key position in Yugoslavia's political life, are three: (1) The
political elite is in agreement that no outside influences
should disturb the balance among the different nationalities.
This is the sentiment described as Bosnian regionalism, which
the Moslems represent in an especially pure form.[65]   (2) Bosnian
regionalism automatically means that the Bosnians hope for
conditions in the rest of Yugoslavia which will not create any
problems for them. This in turn means that, with respect to
Yugoslav politics, they endorse conservative and more or less
centralist policies in spite of their own regionalism. (3) In
addition, the Serbs in Bosnia, who under the Monarchy had always
dreamed of and fought for unification with Serbia, always want a
Yugoslavia that is dominated by the Serbian element so that
they can feel related to the Serbs in the Republic of Serbia.
These three elements make the Bosnian Republic a conservative
factor in the Yugoslav state, although it is not always
conservative internally, in spite of its primitive conditions.
The existence of large raw-material deposits, in part still
undeveloped, favors centralized administrative control but also
requires modern, large multiplant enterprises led be capable
managers.[66]

Tito could rely not only on the conservative republics and
dogmatic elements in general but also on two additional factors
that are likely to exert increasing influence in Yugoslavia. One
is the army, together with the security forces; the other are
the partisan veterans' associations, which before 1966 provided
an important power base for former Minister of the Interior
Rankovic. As soon as Tito first criticized the Croatian
leadership, the army and the veterans' associations in Croatia
were immediately activated. It can even be argued that they
became the advance guard in the general offensive against the
supporters of the previous course in Croatia. The army's concern
about nationalism is understandable; after all, the so-called

territorial defense units were under the control of the
republics, and in Croatia there was actually a tendency to make
something like a separate Croatian army out of them. The regular
army could not be indifferent to this.

But even more important, the majority of the officers in the
regular Yugoslav army are Serbs and Montenegrins, long-time,
primarily centralist-minded communists. With respect to the
security forces, a few months before the shake-up in Croatia, Tito
had appointed General Ivan Mišković, from Istria, as his personal
advisor on security questions and as Secretary of the Council for
State Security of the Yugoslav Presidency.[67] Mišković was a
partisan and is a reliable political general. Under his
leadership Yugoslavia's police apparatus slowly detached itself
from party control during 1971, and after the 1972 political
shake-up it again had approximately the same independent position
as it had held under Ranković. At the beginning of 1973, Mišković
could arbitrarily declare, "The battle that the League of
Communists and the responsible forces are waging, with Tito's
authorization, to remove subjective deficiencies is at the same
time a battle to limit the area in which the enemy operates."
This meant that there was to be police as well as political
repression.

The state, which after all had a remarkably developed
constitutional and legal system, could no longer provide the
framework for a return to a policy of commando and police
techniques. The reversed direction required a new activation of
the Communist party with the same sort of fighting style that it
had made its own in earlier times. Tito thus had to recentralize
and tighten the party organization. The Presidency of the
Republic, which at the end of 1970 Tito had hoped to make the
cornerstone for safeguarding his lifework, and which had been
established in mid-1971, was eclipsed. The era of dogovor
(consensus) between equal republics was over; the dictatorship of
the party was restored in all areas. Tito, who in the past two
years had let things run their course and had shown hardly any
constructive initiative, suddenly became remarkably active now
that the established structures were to be pulled down. To the
frenetic applause of old partisans, Tito talked (in Bosnia, in
December 1971) about the role of the army in the defense of
socialism, the struggle against the class enemy, the abortive
democratization, the professors who got their teachings from the
West, and the judges who clung like drunkards to legal texts.[68]
This was a renunciation of Yugoslavia's whole previous course
virtually since the sixth Party Congress in 1952.

The second conference of the League of Communists then
reorganized the party leadership structure in accordance with

Tito's wishes. The Executive Bureau of the party was reduced
from 15 members to eight and thus made more functional and
cohesive. Tito also tried to set up a three-member permanent
secretariat, but here he met with the opposition from the
Serbian party leaders who at the most were willing to accept a
secretary elected on a yearly basis. Their reasoning was that
anything else would be a return to the pre-1966 period, i.e.,
the Ranković era. Probably this was when Tito decided to settle
accounts with Serbia's party leadership as soon as possible.

At Tito's instigation the Slovene Stane Dolanc (born in 1925)
became secretary of the party's Executive Committee. Dolanc had
worked for the political administration of the army until 1960
and then had held several not very important party posts in
Slovenia. He is an example of those people who acquired power
and influence on the wave of the new centralism. He has no
personal power base in his home republic of Slovenia but,
supported by Tito's authority, has risen to the top exclusively
in the central hierarchy. He is not necessarily a dogmatist; in
Slovenia he had held quite moderate views. But he had carefully
sought to leave his connections open on all sides and had
especially kept in touch with army circles. By intelligent and
thorough work he apparently made himself indispensable to Tito.
It was Dolanc who, before a party assembly in Split on September
19, 1972, gave the signal for the new all-out offensive against
the Serbian party leadership and "liberalism" in general.[69] In
the beginning it seemed that Dolanc had rushed ahead on his own
initiative, but when Tito's critique of Serbia's party
leadership was made public on October 18, 1972,[70] it became
clear that he had only made himself Tito's spokesman. In the
following weeks and months, when Tito and various dogmatists
raged blindly against everything in Yugoslavia that had not
developed according to their own conservative conceptions,
Dolanc remained remarkably considerate and moderate. He opposed
the view that now the communists had to take everything into
their own hands again. In an interview with the Slovene
newspaper Delo at the beginning of 1973,[71] Dolanc stated that
the objective of the campaign against "anarcholiberalism and
technocracy" was to eliminate the "alienation" and the social
differences that had arisen, but that the Communist party could
no longer exercise power alone because this would reduce the
responsibility of the state and self-management organs. It can
be assumed that Dolanc will play an important role even after
Tito's departure. As a man of the central apparatus he will, no
doubt, always prefer a centralized party, but he will never have
the kind of authority Tito had, which would enable him to
disregard the leaders of the republics.

As long as Tito remains as active as he is at the moment, there will hardly be strong leadership in the republics, unless these leaders themselves join Tito's centralist-bureaucratic course. The top Serbian leaders Marko Nikezić and Latinka Perović were forced to resign a few days after Tito criticized them, in mid-October 1972, because of liberalism and favoritism toward the managerial class. These resignations brought in their wake many other resignations from the Serbian party and the central apparatus associated with the progressive tendencies represented by Nikezić. Foreign Minister Tepavac was replaced by the conservative Serbian functionary Miloš Minić, who had dropped completely out of sight for years. The former head of the General Staff and foreign minister, Koča Popović, and the party secretary of the Vojvodina, Čanandanović, resigned, and finally the head of the government in Slovenia, Kavčić, was also forced out. In this way the whole middle generation of reformist leaders, who in the late 1970s had captured the leading positions in the republics, were purged. Their places were taken by functionaries without any strong characteristics of their own, whose power came primarily from their connection with the central apparatus. These new people included Josip Vrhovec in Croatia and Franc Popit in Slovenia. Behind them, however, loomed the shadows of very old dogmatists driven out of their positions several years ago, such as Petar Stambolić and Jovan Veselinov in Serbia or Lazar Koliševski in Macedonia. In 1973 a group of old partisan fighters, with Veselinov in the background, succeeded in seizing political power in the autonomous region of the Vojvodina. This group has followed particularly radical policies. In the Serbian party, Foreign Minister Miloš Minić, who played a major role in the police apparatus in the postwar period, took over the leadership of the dogmatic elements. Whether or not there are potentially pro-Soviet forces behind these elements will become apparent only later. Sometimes it is difficult to avoid the impression that the old functionaries like to attract very young people as disciples and place them in appropriate positions, because in this way respect and a certain distance are guaranteed by age differences.

The campaign initiated by Tito in the fall of 1972 was against the Serbian ledership in particular and against "liberalism" and "technocracy" in general. It was aimed primarily at the managers, who were blamed in demagogic fashion for the bad economic situation and hence for the low living standard of the ordinary worker. It cannot be denied that management in many enterprises was unsatisfactory and that mismanagement and corruption were quite common. But it was less Tito's intention to find realistic solutions than to deflect the growing fury of the lower classes about their discriminatory treatment away from the party and to find scapegoats. These scapegoats could then also be blamed for all kinds of phenomena that threatened the supremacy of the Communist party, ranging from nationalism to independent centers of economic power that could no longer be controlled politically. The economy had become too powerful for mere party functionaries to control. Since the functionaries often had inferior qualifications, they could not master complicated economic processes, and they had to be returned to positions of authority by political pressure. The issue of technocracy in Yugoslavia is not an issue of social policy but of pure power politics, even if accompanied by other elements that often obscure this fact. Tito's action against the Serbian leadership also contained an element of personal vendetta.

Tito was once again able to assert himself against people like Nikezić, Tepavac, and Koča Popović. One of the most dangerous aspects of Yugoslav politics in 1974 was that it still appears almost impossible to oppose Tito's authority successfully. In view of the Marshal's advanced age and his present peculiar views on certain issues, it is impossible to know how this situation will finally end. The simplified speeches that Tito makes nowadays are not as important as the fact that various dogmatic or careerist people are still trying to consolidate their positions as much as possible by means of obedient conformism to the radicalism of Tito's old age and with the aid of the Marshal's authority. Once Tito's authority is removed, they would hardly hesitate to call on other authorities for assistance—the army or, as a last resort, the Soviet Union.

Nevertheless, Yugoslavia's future does not necessarily have to be viewed apocalyptically. There are still people who would like to pursue rational policies. Some of them still hold political positions; some of them, especially in Serbia, have withdrawn in such an obvious manner that they are advertising themselves as a political alternative for the future. Furthermore, there is open opposition in the Central Committee of Serbia. Here Tito had to assert himself against a majority in the highest Serbian party forum, and this majority has held in spite of the resignation of the top leadership. In Slovenia the criticized prime minister, Kavčič, was dismissed with a banquet.

The whole history of the Yugoslav nationality question and the question of the organization of the state clearly shows that Yugoslavia can exist as a functional unity only if, on the one hand, all its significant participants positively support the state but, on the other hand, each nation and each national and

social group feels at home. This requires a federal state
structure and a moderate domestic policy of compromise and
balance. After the convulsions of the war and the postwar period
it seemed that these elements had slowly appeared again by 1971.
Today, in 1974, they appear threatened. There is a strong
endeavor to disregard realities, carried on not by a movement,
but by a relatively small group led by an aging president and
loudly supported by people (for example, the new leadership
elite in the Vojvodina) who are little trusted in the other
republics. Even if this attempt is not successful for a time,
catastrophe cannot be avoided if it is continued, particularly
if, in addition, foreign policy becomes involved, as seemed to
be the case in the autumn of 1973, with the war in the Middle
East, or if the return of the Yugoslavs working in Western
Europe further sharpens internal tensions. The new constitution,
the system of delegates in the political bodies, and the changes
in the system of self-administration[72] are parts of a clear
attempt to transfer the whole discussion about the internal
problems of Yugoslavia from the nationalities arena to that of
socioeconomic, all-Yugoslav problems. This attempt also
characterized the preparation for the Tenth Party Congress,
scheduled for the spring of 1974. Behind the whole discussion
concerning social and economic themes was the attempt again to
increase the influence of the League of Communists as a
centralized party. Whether or not this attempt will succeed in
the long run will be determined partly by the internal party
power relationships and partly by whether or not the economy is
improved, income is increased, and the most obvious aspects of
social stratification are removed. At the end of 1973, however,
as in 1972, real income and investments were again declining.[73]
In any case it seems unlikely that in the long run the attempt
to keep the party organizations of the individual republics and
their leaders weak can be successful, for the League of
Yugoslav Communists is traditionally based on the independence
of the party apparatus of the republics. This tendency to allow
neither individual personalities nor the party organizations of
the republics to become too strong arises, as one could clearly
see at the end of 1973, from the attempt not to prejudice the
succession to Tito.

Foreign Policy and National Independence

Rumania. The goal of Rumanian foreign policy resolutely pursued
since 1964, is clearly the establishment of the fullest possible
national independence for the country. Rumanian policy has

pursued this goal step by step with remarkably stubborn
consistency and has never lost sight of it in spite of various
tactical shifts. Rumania's foreign policy has, of course, not
been able to alter the fact that the country is and will remain
a member of the Warsaw Pact. According to the provisions of the
Pact, the Bucharest leadership could announce its intention to
withdraw in 1974, but it is out of the question that it will do
so. Perhaps the Soviet Union arranged to hold Warsaw Pact Staff
maneuvers at the end of February 1973 on Rumanian territory[74]
in order to underline for the benefit of Rumania and the outside
world Rumania's membership in the Pact.

In the years after the April Resolution of 1964 Rumania
primarily used China as the vehicle for making its foreign
policy independent. Bucharest declared at every opportunity
that it wanted equally good relations with all socialist
countries and that the world communist movement should not be
directed from a single center.[75] Rumania did not have
particularly close relations with China at that time, if only
because of geographical distance. By proclaiming the principle
of equal relations with all socialist states, Rumania was
announcing its intention to limit its relations with the Soviet
Union. At the same time this principle allowed Rumania to defend
itself against accusations of pursuing a nationalist policy of
fragmentation and of opposing the solidarity of the socialist
camp. Rumania never intended to mediate between the Soviet Union
and China. On the contrary, Bucharest must have been interested
in the continuation of this conflict. However, it was also in
Rumania's interest that the conflict not become too acute,
because then Rumania's balancing policy would no longer be
possible. When China plunged into the Cultural Revolution,
Rumania's independent foreign policy was already so established
that it was viable without constant reference to China.

In the subsequent period, Rumania asserted its independent
views in international politics in several areas. Sometimes
these assertions expressed genuine political interest, but
occasionally Rumania's actions were simply demonstrations. The
political areas involved included the following:

1. On January 31, 1967, Rumania became the first country of the
Eastern European camp after the Soviet Union to establish
diplomatic relations with the Federal Republic of Germany.[76]
This disrupted the Soviet plan to coordinate communist policy on
the German question. At a hastily convened conference in Karlovy
Vary the satellite states had to commit themselves to proceed
only by mutual agreement vis-à-vis Bonn. Rumania's precipitate
action brought it considerable benefits, since the West German

government then wanted to establish relations in Eastern Europe wherever possible and to reward reciprocating countries with substantial economic benefits. By 1971, however, Rumania had accumulated a debt of approximately DM 1.5 billion (according to private estimates). By 1972, the debt was no longer rising, but it still has to be paid off. Ceauşescu's trip to Bonn in June 1973 had the purpose of renewing the interest of the Federal Republic in Rumania, which had lost priority in view of Bonn's policy of normalizing relations with the other socialist states as well.

2. In the Middle East wars of 1967 and 1973, Rumania, in contrast to nonaligned Yugoslavia, took an independent, indeed almost neutral, position. At the outbreak of the 1967 war Rumania refused to break relations with Israel, although the Soviet Union and all other Eastern European states, including Yugoslavia, did so. Bucharest was confronted at first with angry reactions from them, but as time went on it became clear that Rumania had gained significant advantages. It had shown the world that its independent foreign policy was serious. It had gained the gratitude of the world Jewish community and was also able to maneuver with both the Israelis and the Arabs, bringing it increased foreign-policy prestige. This diplomatic position also made Rumania interesting for American foreign policy. The invitation to Golda Meir[77] was a high point in Rumanian policy, even if very little concrete came out of it, since Rumania, as it came to realize, was too weak to mediate between the Israelis and the Arabs.

In the 1973 war Rumania tried to repeat the same tactics and again was successful. Indeed, it seemed as though Rumania's independent position was well established. Israeli Foreign Minister Eban came to Bucharest, and in December 1973 Ceauşescu went for the second time to the United States, so that Rumania was for the second time able to call its aspirations to Washington's attention.

3. During all these years Rumania tried to establish good direct relations with the United States, in part with a view toward economic assistance (especially most-favored nation treatment), and in part in the hope of obtaining, as far as possible, guarantees from the U.S. against the Soviet threat. Shortly after the invasion of Czechoslovakia by the Soviet Union and its allies, Rumania succeeded in having President Johnson publicly exhort the Soviet leadership to abstain from an invasion of Rumania. The Soviets were then obliged to expressly deny such an intention, which they had not wanted to do before.[78] Rumania tried to make itself useful as a middleman between

Washington and Hanoi, but it is not clear to what extent serious
peace feelers in the Vietnam war really passed via Bucharest.
Some communications must have been carried on this way, for
otherwise President Nixon would not have visited the Rumanian
capital in August 1969. The Rumanian leadership was disappointed
that more economic assistance did not result. The establishment
of an American Finance Institute and Rumania's admittance to the
International Monetary Fund[79] came much later, toward the end of
1972. The American Finance Institute was set up to deal with
financing Rumanian foreign trade. Rumania's membership in the
International Monetary Fund in principle gives Rumania access to
World Bank credits. It is still not clear whether and to what
extent Bucharest also was a go-between in the American-Chinese
rapprochement; in all probability Rumania's role was not
important.

4. Rumania has always had an ambivalent relationship with the
European Economic Community. On the one hand, Rumania was, of
course, very interested in active relations with the Western
European states, especially with its Latin sister-nation France
and with the economically strong Federal Republic of Germany. On
the other hand, Rumania hesitated to establish its relations
with the European Economic Community on a multinational basis
since it insisted on bilateralism vis-à-vis the Soviet Union and
the other communist countries. There were times when Rumania
tried to establish a parallel between its own position within
the Warsaw Pact and the position of France in NATO—even if
Rumania did not admit this parallel openly. During 1972 Rumania
had to search for a permanent and stable relationship with the
European Economic Community, but also tried to negotiate as much
as possible on a bilateral basis, although contact with the
organs of the Common Market in Brussels could not be avoided.
Rumania tried to obtain the EEC tariff preferences for
developing countries. It tried to prove that its economy was
still in the developing stage (this admission by a socialist
country can be considered unparalleled and was covertly
criticized by the "fraternal countries") because, in 1970, 49.3
percent of the working population was still in agriculture.[80] At
the time of this writing, the negotiations are still in progress,
and in them, strangely enough, it is France and to a lesser
extent also the Netherlands which are raising objections to
granting far-reaching concessions, out of considerations of
principle and fear of competition.

5. Emulating the example of Yugoslavia, Rumania has recently
sought to establish economic and political relations with the
underdeveloped countries of Asia and Africa. Ceauşescu made a

number of trips to these countries. This policy has made
Rumania's goals more widely known, but has not always brought
immediate advantages. Cooperation was advantageous only where
approximately equal trade was possible, as, for example, with
Iran. Ceauşescu had planned to visit Japan in 1972, but, for
unexplained reasons, the trip was postponed.

6. In recent years one of the most important spheres of
interest of Rumanian foreign policy has been cooperation in the
Balkans. The focus is on Yugoslavia. A close consultative
relationship with strong political implications has been
established with Belgrade. Its symbol is the joint power station
on the Danube at the Iron Gate, opened by Tito on May 18, 1972.
In spite of its antagonism toward the Soviet Union, Rumania has
also carefully tried to establish a satisfactory and neighborly
relationship with Bulgaria, with which it also shares a border,
essentially for security reasons. Between 1965 and 1968,
numerous regular meetings between Bulgarian and Rumanian leaders
took place. After an interruption caused by the Soviet invasion
of Czechoslovakia, the practice was resumed in 1971. The
Rumanians were very anxious to meet the Bulgarian desires for
economic cooperation, especially in the construction of a second
power station on the Danube. Rumania also tried to establish a
closer relationship with Greece, which in 1972 became noticeably
more interested in Balkan cooperation. The Greek prime minister
and regent, Papadopoulos, was repeatedly invited to visit
Bucharest. The only reason why Papadopoulos did not accept the
invitation before 1973 was that he felt his first trip abroad
should not be to a member of the Warsaw Pact.

7. The Rumanian leadership constantly attempted to mobilize
support for its views within the world communist movement.
Rumania wanted above all the recognition of the right of each
party and each country to determine its own course. These
efforts led to an informal group, in which the Spanish leader
Carillo and the Greek Koliyannis played primary roles. Although
it is significant that Rumania was also seeking support for its
independent viewpoint on this party level, the representatives
of all these communist parties who continually meet in Bucharest
can hardly provide significant political support.

It is, however, the development of the relationship with the
Soviet Union and the rest of the socialist camp which has
remained by far the most important, and simultaneously the most
sensitive, element of Rumanian policy. The conflict with the
Soviet Union has so far had two culminating points: one in
August 1968, with the Soviet invasion of Czechoslovakia, and the
other in the summer of 1971, with the unconcealed Soviet efforts

at intimidation, which did not stop until shortly before
Brezhnev's visit to Belgrade in September 1971. The Soviet
objectives were clear: if possible, to prevent Rumania from
acting independently, and to commit it to international
communist solidarity. Rumania's position in this persistent,
mostly silent struggle was and remains equally clear: to
safeguard maximum independence for Bucharest. In pursuit of this
goal internal political measures were used to make foreign
policy, e.g., the defense law of December 1971,[81] which not only
created the organization for a popular territorial defense force
but also declared that support and approval of a foreign
occupation is illegal. In accordance with their difficult
position the Rumanians must, on the one hand, act on the basis
of principle in such a way that they can always invoke a
precedent or an established norm of behavior vis-à-vis Soviet
demands. On the other hand, they also must proceed with
flexibility and abstain from any unnecessary irritation of the
Russian bear.

The principal Rumanian view about the Warsaw Pact is that it
is applicable only in Europe and then primarily against "German
revisionism." Rumania therefore refused to participate in the
occupation of Czechoslovakia and would probably not recognize
the applicability of the Warsaw Pact to China. On the basis of
its experience with the USSR, Rumania does not recognize any
right to stage Pact troop maneuvers on Rumanian soil, or to send
troops of other states to Rumania for this purpose, except on
the basis of a resolution by the Rumanian parliament. However,
Rumania approves of holding national military maneuvers with the
participation of a few (at most) liaison troops, and it also
participates in such exercises in other Warsaw Pact states.

Moreover, Rumania did not resist when the Soviet Union in the
summer of 1970—two years after the drafts had been presented—
finally demanded the signing of a new bilateral Friendship and
Mutual Assistance Treaty. The agreement was signed on July 7,
1970, by Kosygin and Maurer in Bucharest.[82] The text indicated
that the Soviets made some concessions to the Rumanians. At the
time, however, the Rumanians privately expressed the opinion
that not too much importance should be attached to these
concessions. In the final analysis, if the Soviet Union wanted to
take action against Rumania, it would not concern itself very
much with agreements. Furthermore, certain clauses in the treaty
can also be interpreted in accordance with the Soviet conception
of sovereignty and noninterference. These weaknesses of the
treaty show how little Rumania can legally safegard its
independence, which will always depend on the political
situation. Nonetheless, as a result of Rumania's insistence

on formality and principle with respect to cooperation among the Warsaw Pact states, the mechanism of command within the Eastern bloc has become more complicated for the Soviet Union. The Soviet leadership several times had to forgo passage of resolutions on political issues, and even discussion of political issues, at party summit conferences because Ceauşescu insisted that political questions be dealt with only at the governmental level, that is, within the framework of a regular meeting of the Warsaw Pact and not at the informal party level. This position also included an element of self-defense for the Rumanian leaders. Rumania achieved substantial successes in its endeavor to prevent any multi- or supranationality in CMEA integration, except for those secondary forms of multilateral cooperation in which Rumania participates on its own initiative and out of its own interest. Ever since the appearance of the well-known article in Viaţa Economica of June 1964,[83] which opposed Khrushchev's plan for creating supranational economic zones, this Rumanian line has remained unchanged. It was confirmed at the end of July 1971 in Bucharest when the CMEA Supreme Council decided to draw up a program of basic principles for economic cooperation, but expressly declared that "socialist integration is not accompanied by the establishment of supranational organs."[84]

With respect to European security, Rumania has always sought to obtain the greatest possible security for itself, primarily vis-à-vis the Soviet Union. Immediately after the preparatory consultations began in November 1972 in Helsinki, Rumania tried its utmost to push its own viewpoints:

1. Each European country should participate in the talks as a fully independent state.

2. All intergovernmental relations in Europe should be based on absolute respect for each country's independence and sovereignty.

3. Rumania should participate, as a full member, in the discussions on military security in Europe, whether in Helsinki or elsewhere.[85]

In a speech before a Central Committee Plenum of March 2, 1973,[86] Ceauşescu again reinforced this position, inter alia with respect to the Mutual Balanced Force Reduction discussions in Vienna. Rumania, he said, did not necessarily want to be able to sign all international agreements in this category, but it did want to participate in discussions concerning troop reduction and disarmament in Europe. At the same time he reaffirmed his longtime efforts toward Balkan cooperation. He said that discussions concerning a transformation of the Balkans into a zone of peace and good neighborliness, without nuclear weapons, could be carried on simultaneously with parallel discussions concerning Central Europe.

Yugoslavia. While Rumania shows how a well-planned and skillful
foreign policy can extract the maximum from a precarious
situation and attain a considerable level of security,
Yugoslavia, in contrast, shows how an excessive use of foreign
policy and an excessive craving for international recognition
can create insecurity and unnecessary complexity. Yugoslavia's
external political situation was difficult and insecure in the
years after 1948. At that time Tito very logically sought
assistance from the West. The requests for Western military
assistance and the Balkan Pact with Greece and Turkey in 1954,
which simultaneously linked Yugoslavia, through the back door,
with the Western defense system, were expressions of this policy.
As soon as the direct threat by Stalin ceased, Yugoslavia broke
away from these ties as quickly as possible and entered into a
game of international politics that attempted to play on two
pianos—that of nonalignment and that of the greatest possible
measure of communist solidarity.

The policy of nonalignment represents to some extent the
natural projection of Yugoslavia' internal policy to the sphere
of foreign policy. Nonalignment is, so to speak, the constant
effort of the state (carried on since the beginnings of the
modern Serbian state) to assert itself as an independent power
factor and to keep more or less the same distance between it and
all other power groupings. Yugoslavia followed this policy in
the interwar period as well. It considered the Little Entente
not as an act of love toward France but as an autonomous
attempt through the new nationalist organization of southeast
Europe and in conjunction with other states with the same
interests, to reestablish a balance. Even Stojadinović did not
pursue rapprochement with the Axis powers, but merely tried, at
least in his political conceptions, to reestablish the same
policy under changed conditions (changed, that is, to the
advantage of the Axis).[87]

An inner conflict between this desire for an independent
policy of keeping equal distance from all sides and an
ideologically determined need to lean on the "mother church" in
Moscow runs like a red thread through all Tito's foreign policy
after Stalin's death. Tito was always enough of a realist and a
Yugoslav patriot to insist on absolute equality and independence
in his relations with Moscow. But he was also always enough of a
communist to search for ways of cooperation with the Soviet
Union, insofar as this was possible and his fundamental
reservations could be maintained. The policy adopted by Tito in
his old age, after the Croatian events of 1971, clearly shows
the inner conflict that has always marked his political thinking.
It shows his nostalgic longing for a reunion with Moscow, even

though he never left the firm ground of reality for the sake of this secret yearning.

In the beginning, nonalignment was also directed basically toward Moscow. It was not a Yugoslav invention but originated in those states of Asia and Africa that became independent after World War II and did not want to join either of the two power groups.[88] By the beginning of the 1950s Yugoslavia had already seen the possibility of breaking out of its isolation as an independent socialist state without having to join the Western alliance. In the period from 1954 through 1958, Tito again saw his future as a member of the "socialist family," and before as well as after the 1956 Hungarian events, he thought of Khrushchev as the Soviet leader who wanted to grant Yugoslavia equality with the other communist countries.[89] These dreams ended with the Yugoslav Party Congress in Ljubljana in April 1958 and Khrushchev's bitter accusation at the Bulgarian Party Congress in June 1958.[90] Subsequently it became clear that Tito was turning to the underdeveloped countries of Asia and Africa primarily in order to win them to the cause of socialism and "anti-imperialism." Tito wanted to point out to the Soviet leaders his services to communism and thus oblige the Soviets to take Yugoslavia seriously and to readmit it, without trying to change it, into the socialist family. This goal characterized the Conference of Nonaligned States, which Yugoslavia organized in 1961 in Belgrade, and Tito's anti-Western speech at it.[91] When in October 1961 the Twenty-second Soviet Party Congress, under Khrushchev's leadership, gave the first signs of a conflict with China, Tito immediately saw a chance again for a direct rapprochement with Moscow. He even tried to retreat from internal liberalization in Yugoslavia.[92] This period lasted, however, only until 1963; then the compulsion of economic realities and pressure by the advocates of domestic liberalization became overpowering. The Eighth Party Congress in December 1964 and the removal of Ranković in June 1966 appeared to lead Yugoslavia far away from the Soviet camp and toward a genuine policy of nonalignment, coupled with close economic cooperation with the West. It appeared that nonalignment per se had now become Yugoslavia's policy. Paradoxically, it probably was concern about this policy, one of whose main supporters was Nasser, which drove Tito to a summit meeting in Moscow in the summer of 1967 when the Middle East conflict erupted.

His participation in the Moscow summit conference which was not approved by his then foreign minister, Marko Nikezić, and his signature of the joint accord of June 9, 1967, moved Tito from the camp of the nonaligned to the camp of the other

communist parties. Ceauşescu did not participate in the meeting.
From that moment on a new, disastrous linkage of Yugoslavia's
foreign policy to Moscow and the Eastern camp began which,
through many stages and vicissitudes, finally led Yugoslavia
into an uncertain, dangerous situation such as the country had
not known since 1948. On the one hand, Yugoslavia again cut
itself off politically from the West and took a hostile position
toward it, or at least toward the United States. On the other
hand, Yugoslavia again tried to participate in the affairs of
Eastern Europe. It attached greater importance than before to
being considered a socialist country. It tried to weaken Eastern
European criticism of the Yugoslav system of self-administration
and to establish independent relations with those Eastern
European states that in conjunction with developments in
Czechoslovakia, were showing emancipation tendencies similar to
those shown twelve years before, in the 1955-1966 period. Tito
visited Czechoslovakia only a few days before the Soviet
invasion.

The Soviet intervention in Prague on August 21, 1968, and the
Brezhnev Doctrine, intended as its ex post facto justification,
left Yugoslavia in almost the same situation as Rumania, a
member of the Warsaw Pact. Yugoslavia, which was supposed to be
a socialist country, now felt threatened. NATO tried to counter
the Soviet objectives, which had become unpredictable, by
proclaiming its interest in the so-called gray zones and
including Yugoslavia in this area. Tito used this occasion to
oppose the general tendency to involve Yugoslavia in the areas of
tension existing in world politics.[93] The more strongly the
Soviets insisted, before the world and the other communist
parties, on their right of intervention in "fraternal countries,"
the more a socialist Yugoslavia must have felt hemmed in.
Bulgaria in particular declared quite bluntly, with a view
toward Macedonia, that the Bulgarians would defend socialism
"everywhere."[94] The tension increased to the point where the
Belgrade newspaper Politika in June 1971[95] had to reproach the
Soviets openly for supporting Yugoslav émigrés with Cominform
tendencies and Croatian extremists.[96] In addition, Soviet and
other Warsaw Pact troops held maneuvers in Hungary and Bulgaria.[97]
At approximately the same time as Rumania, Yugoslavia also began
to seek support in Peking for the defense of its independence.[98]

Yugoslavia's entanglement in intrabloc politics and its ending
up in almost the same position as Rumania would certainly not
have happened if Tito had kept Yugoslavia's foreign policy in
1967 and 1968 free of involvements with Moscow. The partial
Yugoslav return to Moscow's political orbit was a logical

consequence of the collapse of the nonaligned bloc at the time
of the Middle East conflict in 1967. In accord with his personal
inclinations, Tito filled the vacuum by turning to the East and
was then immediately confronted with the theory of the limited
sovereignty of socialist countries.

In this rather distressing situation, Tito was of course
realistic enough to look to the West for some kind of a balance.
First, in October 1970 President Nixon visited Belgrade. This
was followed by a whole series of trips by Tito to the Western
European countries. These ostentatious visits to Western Europe
in the fall of 1970 made clear how much the Yugoslavs had
neglected this part of the world in previous years, although
economic relations with the West had become increasingly close
and the number of Yugoslavs temporarily in the West was by that
time already in the half-million range. As before, a certain
interdependence between internal and foreign policy again
appeared, since 1970 was also the year in which Tito announced
his progressive constitutional reforms.

Yugoslavia's policies were again reversed in September 1971,
when Brezhnev announced his visit to Yugoslavia. Now Tito was
seeking Soviet guarantees. In contrast to its situation at the
time of the reconciliation with Khrushchev in 1955, Yugoslavia
was no longer in a position of equality with the Soviet Union,
but instead had to grant ideological concessions that it would
never have granted previously. In his speeches Brezhnev treated
the Yugoslav system of self-administration very disparagingly,
and could not praise the Soviet system highly enough. Although
Tito obtained confirmation of the Yugoslav-Soviet accords of
1955-1956, the principles laid down there were no longer
mentioned in detail. Brezhnev made fun of people who talked
about a "doctrine of limited sovereignty of socialist countries,"
but in no way did he retract what he had said at the Polish
Party Congress in November 1968 about the right to intervene in
other communist countries. In the joint communiqué Brezhnev
recognized nonalignment only to the extent that it was directed
against "imperialism." Tito obtained no written guarantees for
Yugoslavia's security; at the most he might have obtained oral
guarantees, but no details have been made public.[99] In spite of
all this, Brezhnev tried so hard to claim the Yugoslavs as
socialist friends that Yugoslav personalities privately spoke of
a "bear hug." Brezhnev tried to interest the Yugoslavs in broad
economic cooperation and committed them in the communiqué to
favorable press reporting.

Brezhnev's visit did result in a relaxation of tension not
only in Yugoslavia but in the whole Balkan area. The Soviet

Union had decided to include the Balkans in its policy of
détente in Europe; in this sense Moscow fulfilled a Yugoslav
demand. But the relaxation of tension was a pax sovietica,
something new for Yugoslavia and in a certain sense also for the
whole southern Balkan area. It was not a question of truce or
compromise but of the inauguration of Soviet economic and
political penetration. The visit of Soviet Deputy Minister for
Economic Affairs Baibakov for several weeks in December 1971[100]
had almost the character of an inventory-taking of the Yugoslav
economy. The carefully directed establishment of concrete
economic arrangements followed. These announcements were
primarily in the form of capital development credits for the
extraction of metals and raw materials. The Soviet Union was
interested mainly in Bosnia, because development possibilities
existed there and probably because the Yugoslav Republic of
Bosnia-Herzegovina has an economy characterized by highly
developed étatism, dogmatic leadership, and an old Cominform
tradition. After the Baibakov visit, great activity by Soviet
economists and political figures could be noted in all of
Yugoslavia's republics. Besides establishing economic contacts,
the Soviets made an effort to know the interesting political
personalities in the various regions of Yugoslavia. The
communiqué of the Brezhnev visit in the fall of 1971 had opened
the way for this with the explicit formulation that contacts
between the two countries should also take place on a regional
and local basis.

It is arguable whether the objective of compromising with the
Soviet Union played a role in Tito's actions against the
Croatian leadership in December 1970. There is no concrete proof
of this, and internal political developments alone could have
justified Tito's intervention. But the whole of Yugoslav
development since the end of the war again and again presents
examples of a seemingly coincidental interdependence of domestic
and foreign policy, so that at least the possibility should not
be excluded that it was Yugoslavia's transition to the pax
sovietica that made domestic liberalization no longer necessary.
This development has since continued consistently, although
slowly and almost imperceptibly. When Tito went to Moscow in
June 1972, Izvestia reported on the "coordination" of bilateral
relations, which was denied by the Yugoslavs, but primarily by
liberal Yugoslav commentators rather than by Tito himself.[101] On
November 2, 1972, the first Yugoslav-Soviet Investment Agreement,
which committed $540 million, was concluded. This was followed by
the intensification of Yugoslavia's internal political crisis and
the purges in Serbia and Slovenia. Tito's speech in Ljubljana on

December 12, 1972,[102] was a call to the Slovenes to halt or at
least reduce friendly cooperation with the neighboring areas in
Italy and Austria. Among the leaders who had to resign in
November 1972, in the course of Tito's move against the Serbian
leadership, was Foreign Minister Tepavac̆, who came from the
Vojvodina. He was known for his advocacy of a closer
relationship with Western Europe. In addition, he had at various
times objected to having Tito and the party leaders conduct
"important" foreign policy—that dealing with the Soviet Union
and the other socialist countries—while the Foreign Ministry
was left with merely "unimportant" foreign-policy, relating to
the West and the underdeveloped countries. That such an extreme
dogmatist as Todo Kurtovic̆ from Bosnia exerted increasing
influence in the Executive Bureau of the Party on cultural and
information contacts with foreign countries also indicated a
development toward increasing isolation from the West.

These attempts to isolate itself from the West are of course
more than problematical as long as approximately one million
Yugoslaves (800,000 in Western European countries and 200,000
overseas) earn their living by temporary emigration abroad.[103]
Tito and the dogmatic elements in the Belgrade leadership
currently consider this emigration a thorn in the flesh. At the
third conference of the Yugoslav League of Communists in
December 1972, Tito opened the campaign against temporary
emigration with the argument that it weakened Yugoslavia's power
to defend itself.[104] In January the Socialist Alliance concerned
itself with the problem. The first draft resolutions contained
absurd and xenophobic proposals: for example, that qualified
workers who emigrate should repay their educational costs.[105]
These tendencies did not prevail; priority was given to the
creation of jobs in the country rather than to administrative
restrictions. There remains the question of how long this
priority will prevail. When the Yugoslav and Italian foreign
ministers met for a working session in Dubrovnik in March 1973,
Yugoslav commentators known for their liberal attitudes
noticeably stressed the existence and continuation of open
borders between the two countries, with a distinct undertone of
fear that this achievement might end.[106]

It is not clear which tendencies in Yugoslav foreign policy
will finally prevail. Tito's conduct toward the outside world
has always shown a constant back-and-forth movement. Only one
thing is certain: Yugoslavia today is much less free to make
decisions in domestic and foreign policy than it was ten or
fifteen years ago. Yugoslavia's integration into the communist
front on the Middle East issue indicated a development that

committed Yugoslavia unnecessarily in the sensitive area of the
Mediterranean. One might ask whether the country will in the
long run be capable of resisting the continued and increasingly
pressing Soviet demands for the right of transit for arms
shipments and even for bases. On the other hand, the hardening
of internal policy, not least of all the tendencies toward
national oppression in Croatia, might arouse fears within
Yugoslavia as well as among the Yugoslav emigrants and release
serious reactions. Since the end of World War II the "myth of
Yalta" persistently circulates among the Yugoslav population:
that in the event of its breakup Yugoslavia would be divided
evenly between West and East. The communists themselves played
up this theme after the coup against the Croatian nationalists
at the end of 1971.

The events of the October 1973 Middle East war highlighted an
even sharper and more dangerous aspect of these problems. In his
attempt to revitalize the policy of nonalignment and his own
leading role in it, Tito had at the September 1973 conference of
nonaligned states in Algiers taken a position of one-sided,
unconditional support of the nonaligned world, which included
the Arab states. When the war broke out in October 1973, Tito
immediately agreed to Soviet overflights airlifting arms to
Egypt.[107] The situation became particularly complicated when
around October 25 the question arose of the transport of Soviet
troops through Yugoslavia to the Mediterranean. For the sake of
Yugoslav security Tito had to reject this proposal decisively.
The extent to which strong American representations may have
contributed to this decision will become clear only in the
future. Immediately after these dramatic days Tito paid a visit
to Brezhnev in Kiev.[108] This was followed by other remarkable
intermezzos—for example, the visit of the Libyan radical leader
Qadhdhafi to Belgrade and a worsening of relations between Tito
and Egyptian President Sadat, caused, apparently, primarily
because Sadat had been quite willing to accept the good offices
of U.S. Secretary of State Kissinger and thereby from Tito's
point of view had not observed "nonalignment." The issue as of
this writing is not so much whether Tito wants to return to the
Eastern camp but rather whether a risky and increasingly radical
foreign policy, which pays little attention to the strategic
realities of the situation, may not one day bring Yugoslavia into
a situation that it can no longer master.

Extra-Balkan Influences

The Soviet Union and Bulgaria. Brezhnev's visit to Yugoslavia in
the fall of 1971 can rightly be regarded as the end—at least

temporarily—of the Soviet policy of direct threat and intimidation in the Balkans. It is equally correct to view this visit merely as a transition to a new policy of infiltration by peaceful means. This new policy was signaled by Moscow's insistence on the Soviet viewpoint in the Soviet-Yugoslav declaration signed on the occasion of this visit and was continued by the Soviets' careful but steady strengthening of their influence in Yugoslavia.

The Soviet Union détente policy has a double meaning. On the one hand the USSR gave guarantees and promises that the Yugoslavs and the Rumanians could construe as gestures of goodwill and of peaceful intentions, a welcome expansion into the Balkans of the Soviet Union's general European détente policy. On the other hand, the same gestures robbed Yugoslavia and Rumania of their defenses against an increasing Soviet influence in the Balkans. When one asked why Tito yielded to Brezhnev's wishes on so many points, Yugoslavs privately answered, almost with resignation, that in view of the détente euphoria in Europe Yugoslavia could not be left behind as a relic of the cold war.

Rumania realized the dangers of this ambivalent Soviet policy better than Yugoslavia, or at least Rumania tried to counter it better; perhaps the reason was Rumania's more precarious situation. Tito always demanded (as he did during his visit to the United States) that the problem of the Mediterranean be included in all discussions of European security.[109] He correctly recognized that a confrontation between the two power blocs in the Mediterranean would be decisive for the security of Yugoslavia and the whole Balkan area. But Yugoslavia continued its one-sided policy in the Mediterranean while Rumania actively tried to alleviate the frictions insofar as possible. Rumania acted more consistently, on the basis of the realization that the negotiations on European security, which began with the preparatory conference in Helsinki in November 1972, must be utilized to improve the security situation of the Balkan communist states. This led to demands by Ceauşescu that every country should participate in the talks in Helsinki as a sovereign and equal state and that it be recognized that the military factor was an inseparable component of all considerations about European security. When the talks on troop reduction in Europe, which began in Vienna at the end of January 1973, did not proceed as Rumania wished, the opinion was privately expressed in Bucharest that it would do no harm simply to transfer discussions about the whole military component of European security to Helsinki, although this would be anything

but agreeable to the Soviet Union. Yugoslavia did not act nearly
as decisively on all these questions.

Since the immediate postwar period, the Soviet Union has
found in Bulgaria a solid supporter of its policy of hegemony in
the Balkans. Only prior to 1948 did Tito and the Bulgarian
communist leader Georgi Dimitrov more or less try to establish
an independent communist bloc in the Balkan peninsula. Tito and
Dimitrov, not Stalin, supported the Greek communists during the
civil war. The Soviet Union was determined at that time to keep
to the agreement with the Western powers for mutual respect of
spheres of influence.[110] It was easy for Stalin to destroy the
Tito-Dimitrov alliance in 1948. First, as a defeated country
Bulgaria could not resist Soviet pressure. Second, Stalin found
support against Dimitrov's policy in the national communist wing
of the Bulgarian communist party, which disapproved of Dimitrov's
concessions to Yugoslavia on the Macedonian issue. It is ironic
that these national communist allies of Stalin, led by Traicho
Kostov, were themselves liquidated shortly thereafter.

From then on the total, almost colonial, subordination of
Bulgaria to Moscow has not changed. Without a doubt there are
historical reasons for this phenomenon; it was, after all, the
Russians who freed Bulgaria from the Turks in 1877, after
Bulgaria's uprisings had failed. It was also the Russians who,
in the peace treaty of San Stefano in 1877, encumbered Bulgaria's
new statehood with the dream of a Greater Bulgarian Empire.
Afterward this dream always hovered like a mirage above
Bulgarian political thinking and made Bulgaria a permanently
discontented state engaging in irredentist quarrels with its
neighbors and repeatedly mobilizing support from the great
powers to realize its exaggerated aspirations. It is true that
some of the Bulgarian demands had a certain historical
legitimacy, but the Bulgarians, after all, were late-comers to
the Balkans. What Bulgaria was able to attain, it gambled away
with its adventurist policy in the second Balkan War and in both
world wars, in particular with respect to access to the Aegean.
At the end of World War II Bulgaria was a totally defeated
nation that had no real national prospects. The Moscow-oriented
faction of the Bulgarian Communist party used this in the
struggle against its rivals. This faction, under Vlko Chervenkov
and Todor Zhivkov, has maintained its hold to the present day.
Zhivkov was the most aggressive communist champion of military
intervention in Czechoslovakia in 1968.[111]

The Macedonian question, settlement of which was one of the
goals of Bulgaria's irredentist policy, deserves a brief
examination. Viewed historically, Macedonia (which is primarily

the present Yugoslav Republic of Macedonia) belonged to the
Bulgarian sphere culturally, in religion, and also politically
until late in the nineteenth century. If overzealous young
historians in Skopje deny this today, they reinterpret the past
from the viewpoint of the present. The development of an
autonomous Macedonian identity did not begin until the Congress
of Berlin in 1878, which was the beginning of a different
political development in Macedonia and Bulgaria proper. After
the unsuccessful Ilinden uprising of 1903, most of the
Bulgarian supporters in Macedonia fled to Bulgaria, where they
obtained positions in the army and the state administration and
subsequently poisoned Bulgarian politics with their irredentist
terrorism and conspiracies. In the area that is today Yugoslav
Macedonia, the process of cultural and political "Macedonization"
began with a vengeance. This process suffered a serious setback
in the first Balkan War. Serbia, which since 1878 had also
engaged in propaganda activities in Macedonia and claimed
Macedonia for itself, agreed with Greece, which was then in the
grip of centralistic, hellenizing nationalism, on a border that
divided the Macedonian population. The border was drawn with the
express understanding that the population to its north would be
considered Serbs and the population south of it Greeks. By a
population exchange during the interwar period, the Slav
population in East Macedonia and Thrace was resettled in
Bulgaria. The Slavs were allowed to remain in West Macedonia
only because Yugoslavia considered them as Serbs and did not
want to see them treated as Bulgarians. Many of the Slav
Macedonians fought on the communist side in the Greek civil war
of 1946-1948 and had to leave the country afterward.

The Macedonians in Yugoslavia, who during the whole interwar
period had been treated as Serbs, were scheduled to be
transformed with equal force into Bulgarians under the
occupation after 1941. No wonder that after this they decided to
cling to the Macedonian name and identity and set about to
create a separate Macedonian nation. The Yugoslav communists
successfully utilized this predisposition. Even under communist
auspices, however, the emerging Macedonian nationalism was not
free of separatist tendencies and dreams of a Greater Macedonia,
as was shown by the attempt to establish a Macedonian
nationality in the Pirin valley of Bulgaria and by the
participation of Macedonians in the Greek civil war. At present
Bulgaria no longer recognizes any Macedonian nationality on its
soil, and the Macedonian question no longer exists for Greece.
In the future, Macedonian nationalism will have to restrict .
itself to the Yugoslav Republic of Macedonia, where it is a
purely internal problem for Yugoslavia, without effect externally.

Can the Soviet Union one day use the Macedonian issue, via
Bulgaria, to unhinge Yugoslavia from this sensitive spot near
the Mediterranean? After 1968 certain Bulgarian circles looked
quite unequivocally toward Macedonia in connection with
statements that Bulgaria must defend socialism everywhere.[112]
However, there are hardly any pro-Bulgarian circles in Macedonia.
Precisely because of its blind subordination to the Soviet Union,
Bulgaria would engage in military-political aggression only if
the Soviet Union wanted to unleash a military conflict in the
whole Mediterranean area and thereby, perhaps, a third world war.
As long as this danger does not exist, no attention need be paid
to Bulgaria. It is completely unimportant whether it is friendly
or hostile toward its Balkan neighbors. There were, of course,
periods in Bulgarian history when Bulgaria sought to escape the
Soviet influence to some degree; at times Bulgaria sought ties
with Germany and Austria. There were even some rare instances
when Bulgaria tried to maintain friendly relations with its
neighbors in the Balkans: e.g., under Stamboliski and his
Agrarians after the First World War, and then again in the early
1930s under the officer group Zveno. During the past few years
(under Foreign Minister Ivan Bashev, mysteriously killed in an
accident in 1971) Bulgaria has given the impression of a certain
openness toward Balkan neighbors which was not merely compliance
with Moscow's wishes. This period has now ended. However, in
spite of different political views, Bulgaria has so far
abstained from any polemic directed against its northern
neighbor, Rumania.

The case of Bulgaria is the best illustration of the
impediment to Soviet hegemonic policy in the Balkans and to its
attempt to push forward through this area to the Mediterranean,
in accordance with the historical pattern of the nineteenth
century. Only thirty kilometers separate the Bulgarian border
from the Aegean Sea, but the border between the two alliances is
so rigid and fixed here that the Soviet Union could think about
crossing this space only in a general war. Greece and Turkey are
still with the NATO camp, and a general U.S. retreat from the
Mediterranean would have to take place before there can be a
change in the situation. The forward position of such a
completely subservient yet potentially aggressive Bulgaria
operates to consolidate this rigid border and creates a serious
handicap for Soviet policy in the Balkans.

On the other hand the Soviet Union appears to have serious
expectations in the long run about Yugoslavia. A Soviet success
in Yugoslavia would of course also mean the end of Rumania's
policy of independence and would probably result in internal and

external reactions of panic in Italy. The United States would be
faced with an extremely serious strategic problem.

Soviet intentions can be assessed to some extent by the
interest of the USSR in direct inquiry into the internal
conditions of Yugoslavia and, connected with this, by slow,
patient infiltration accompanied by exploitation of internal
conflicts. However, the Soviet Union is also trying to expand
its influence in the Balkans in a larger, international
framework. Unofficial sources have repeatedly stated that when
Tito visited the Soviet Union in June 1972, shortly after
President Nixon's trip to Moscow, the Soviet leaders dangled the
prospects of future U.S-Soviet cooperation before the Marshal's
eyes, with the unspoken challenge to draw his own conclusions
and to incorporate himself into this wider framework. Since this
wider framework generally includes the presumption of a
continuing dismantling of American positions in the Mediterranean
and in Europe generally, it can be assumed that the Soviet
leaders confronted Tito with this prospect as well. At the time
of this writing it is not clear whether, or to what extent, Tito
drew certain conclusions from this for his foreign policy.
Politically important circles in Yugoslavia always tend to
overestimate the direct effect of international factors on
Yugoslavia, just as they have always overestimated Yugoslavia's
international role. Meanwhile, signs of American lack of interest
in Europe and the Mediterranean will always operate to draw
Belgrade closer to the Soviet Union.

At the preparatory talks on Mutual Balanced Force Reductions
in Europe, which began in January 1973 in Vienna under rather
confused circumstances, the outline of an even more far-reaching
Soviet plan to gain influence in the Balkans appeared. During
the first week of the conference the Soviet Union suddenly posed
the problem of participation by Hungary. It then became
increasingly clear that the Soviet intent was to remove Hungary,
where Soviet troops are stationed, from the Central European
area, which was to be dealt with first in the talks on force
reduction, and to place it in the Mediterranean-Balkan area. If
this Soviet conception prevails, then the Balkan area, if not
the Mediterranean in general, would in a certain sense become
the object of strategic negotiations or of an agreement between
the U.S. and the USSR. Because of the inclusion of Hungary in
this zone the Soviet Union would have a stronger position there
than it has now.[113]

The Balkans and China. Shortly after the Hungarian revolution of
1956, Communist China emerged as a political factor in the
Balkans for the first time. This first appearance by China was in

no way directed against the Soviet Union or Soviet hegemony. On
the contrary, during his visit to Poland and Hungary in January
1967 Chou En-lai attempted to such an extent to get the Eastern
European communists again to recognize Soviet hegemony that an
important American political scientist spoke about the "Maoist
reconstruction of the center."[114] It seemed as if the Chinese
were blaming all the difficulties in the satellite area on the
collapse of the strict discipline of Stalinism.

In the beginning of 1960 the first Sino-Soviet differences
became visible, and, strangely enough, they coincided with
serious differences between the Soviet Union and Albania, which
erupted much more violently than the differences between
Moscow and Peking.[115] At the Twenty-second Communist Party
Congress in Moscow in October 1961, Khrushchev publicly
denounced the Albanians, shortly afterward broke diplomatic
relations with Albania, and subsequently excluded Albania from
the Warsaw Pact and CMEA de facto. This little isolated country
on the Adriatic then became the only real political and
ideological ally of China and has remained so until the present
day.

Albania won national autonomy even later than Bulgaria. In
fact, it was able to form itself into a nation only with the
greatest difficulty even after it won independence after the
first Balkan War in 1913. At the time Albania could not have
achieved independence on its own, because a unified national
will was only in the process of developing. The creation of the
Albanian state was attributable to the successful efforts of
Austria-Hungary and Italy to prevent Serbia's gaining a foothold
on the Adriatic coast.[116] Even then about half of the total area
settled by Albanians remained outside the new Albanian state and
remains excluded to the present day. The areas thus excluded are
primarily the Kossovo-Metohija in Yugoslavia and several
neighboring areas of the Yugoslav republics of Macedonia and
Montenegro. Beginning with their incorporation into the Serbian
state and continuing through the whole interwar period, these
areas were exposed to strong pressures for denationalization,
which did not succeed only because conditions were too primitive
and the natural vitality of the Albanian population too strong.
Since most of the Albanians in Yugoslavia supported their own
nationalist movements during the Second World War and fought
against Tito's partisans, Belgrade in fact continued to suppress
the Albanians, in spite of formal equality, at least until 1966,
when Ranković was deposed. Only since then has it been possible
to speak of a national Albanian identity within Yugoslavia.

Greece also practiced a policy of denationalization against
the Albanians. In Greece, however, common membership in the Greek
Orthodox church served in some respects as a natural bridge to
Hellenism. Only the Albanians of Islamic faith suffered real
oppression, but the last of these were driven across the border
into Albania by the nationalistic Greek resistance organization
EDES during the Second World War.

The reasons why the Albanians had not been able to form a
united and functional nation earlier were, first, the topographic
fragmentation of the areas they settled and, second, their
fragmentation into three large religious groups (actually four,
if the Moslem sect of the Bektashi is considered a separate
group). Furthermore, each area had a mixed religious composition.
The population of the present Albanian state is 65 percent
Islamic, 21 percent Orthodox, and 10 percent Catholic.[117]
Because of the wildness and inaccessibility of much of Albania,
the tribal system has remained almost unchanged to the present.
The ruthless suppression or, more correctly, "elimination" of
religion since 1967 has its ideological roots in nationalism as
well as communism. It is the reaction against the nation's
previous fragmentation and lack of unity. According to official
propaganda the only acceptable religion for an Albanian is
"Albanianism," i.e., national consciousness. In fact,
segmentation into tribes and their internal consolidation by
such means as blood feuds impeded the establishment of a
homogeneous national consciousness far more than religion did.
There were, and still are, many Albanian tribes of mixed
religion. Another factor doubtless was the partially strong
identification of the Moslem population with the Ottoman Empire.
The collapse of the Ottoman Empire placed the Moslem Albanians in
a position of isolation and hostile defensiveness, in which they
basically remain to this day. This Moslem isolation is a factor
in all of Albania's politics, although the elite generally comes
from the Orthodox population.

Albania's policies in the whole postwar period have been
marked by fear of the intentions of its neighbors and enforced
self-isolation. Until 1948 Albania had a close allegiance with
Yugoslavia, which had clearly been imposed by Tito and basically
was supported with real conviction by only a small part of the
Albanian communist leadership. In 1948 Enver Hoxha used the
break between Moscow and Belgrade to get rid of the Yugoslav
tutelage overnight and to seek the direct protection of the more
remote Moscow. However, the Albanians soon began to display
mistrust of the Soviets. When the reconciliation between Tito
and Khrushchev became a reality in 1955 and when Khrushchev even

found a few friendly words for Greek interests in the Balkans, an
alarm signal sounded for Tirana. Moscow-Belgrade-Athens
cooperation was the worst thing the Albanians could imagine. It
was thus only logical that Enver Hoxha greedily seized the
opportunity when he saw the first signs of friction in the
Moscow-Peking relationship and immediately sought the even more
remote Peking as his major ally and protector. This precipitate
action created a situation in which the Soviets always attacked
the Albanians when their real object was China, and the Chinese
criticized the Yugoslavs when they really meant Khrushchev. The
two Balkan states did not cease serving as whipping boys until
the outbreak of the open Sino-Soviet conflict after 1962.

    This background for Albania's dependence on China must be
understood in order to interpret the current state of the Peking-
Tirana partnership correctly. The two countries did not get
together because of common ideological viewpoints, although a
certain radicalism united them, but primarily because of power
politics. China represented the only suitable protector for
Albania, because there was no danger that one day China would
try to become its master. For China, on the other hand, Albania
was a base for political propaganda and political influence in
the European-African hemisphere. Peking could use Albania to
broadcast its radio propaganda to the communist parties in
Eastern Europe, the Maoist groups in the West, and the developing
countries in Africa and the Arab world. This propaganda was
continued even when China had lost almost all interest in the
outside world as a consequence of the Cultural Revolution. In
addition, the Albanians were in the UN and could also render
useful services to the Chinese there.

    Chinese influence in the Balkans, however, had little in
common with the Maoist propaganda emanating from Tirana. In the
case of Rumania after 1964 it was exclusively a question of
Realpolitik; even Premier Chou En-lai apparently did not gauge
this fact properly during his visit to Bucharest in June 1966.
After the end of the Cultural Revolution in 1969, the character
of Maoist China changed completely. Ideological radicalism and
ideological loyalty no longer were primary. The emphasis shifted
to a realistic foreign policy that would earn China its deserved
status as a third or fourth world power. Peking stepped on the
international stage with the claim to be the protector of the
small and medium-sized powers in the world against the
imperialism of the two superpowers. Although not always so
expressed, this was without a doubt directed more against Moscow
than against the United States, since China and the Soviet Union
shared a disputed border. The Soviet invasion of Czechoslovakia

contributed to China's return to world politics with this anti-
Soviet thesis. It must have been extremely disturbing for China
when the Soviet Union declared its right to intervene militarily
at will in any socialist state. President Nixon's visit to China
followed in 1972. The occupation of Czechoslovakia and the
subsequent Chinese feeling of being threatened may also have
acted as a catalyst in the Sino-American rapprochement. Thus the
principles of the original revolutionary Maoism were finally
discarded. China did not stop all assistance to the Maoist
groups in different parts of the world without a good reason.

The second concrete manifestation of Chinese policy in the
Balkans occurred in 1971. This time its anti-Soviet character
was clear, as China supported the aspirations for independence
of the Balkan peoples led by Rumania and Yugoslavia. Ceauşescu
visited China in June 1971 and combined his trip with a renewed
rejection of an "international communist center." In exchange,
the Rumanian leader received barely disguised Chinese offers of
assistance against an "imperialist attack." In the final
communiqué the Chinese explicitly declared that Rumania "had
resisted imperialist pressure with total determination and
thus achieved significant victories in the battle for the
maintenance of national independence and sovereignty."[118]
While in Moscow on his return trip, Ceauşescu was criticized by
Kosygin for his visit to China. Shortly afterward a Yugoslav
delegation led by Foreign Minister Tepavac went to Peking and
received a similar Chinese endorsement.[119] The earlier long
ideological quarrel between Peking and Belgrade was completely
forgotten.

Viewed politically, Chinese support of strivings toward
independence in the Balkans was extremely useful, when the
Soviet Union was staging maneuvers in Hungary and Bulgaria and
again exerting pressure for political and economic integration
of the Eastern block. However, this usefulness must not be
overestimated. Chou En-lai himself made this clear when he
quoted a Chinese proverb in an interview with a Yugoslav
newspaper: "Water that is far away does not put out the fire."[120]
But Chinese support of the independence aspirations of the Balkan
and other Eastern European peoples should not be looked at only
from the military viewpoint and then dismissed as negligible.
China could suddenly cause a great deal of trouble for the Soviet
Union if the Soviets should again undertake military aggression.
China could mobilize the countries of the third world against the
Soviet Union and transform the UN into a political instrument
against the Soviets, quite apart from its direct opportunities in
Mongolia or Indochina. It is unlikely that Chinese influence
alone could deter the Soviet Union from an action like the

invasion of Czechoslovakia. But it is a factor that the Soviets
must take into account. Together with other factors, the factor
of China can certainly be an effective deterrent.

Peking's ally Albania has not emulated the surprising speed
of changes in Chinese policy. This is perfectly natural and is
due not so much to some special stubbornness of the Albanians as
to the fact that it is much easier for a big power to execute
political shifts without loss of face than it is for a small
state. After the Soviet intervention in Prague in 1968, Albania
abandoned its hostile attitude toward Yugoslavia in the interest
of a united defense of independence in the Balkans. But so far
Albania has been unwilling to participate in the rapprochement
with the United States. In his speech to the Sixth Albanian
Party Congress in November 1971, Enver Hoxha emphasized
(probably with a side glance at Peking) the continued necessity
of the two-front war: "It is not possible to use one imperialism
in order to oppose the other."[121] But in practice Albania has
already begun a policy of relative openness. The Maoist radio
broadcasts are being continued, but they find hardly an echo and
do not bother anyone; in time these broadcasts will adapt
themselves to the new conditions. Tirana's propaganda will then
no doubt project the Chinese influence in the direction it has
taken since the Cultural Revolution, namely, the political
strengthening of the concept of national independence in the
Balkans against Soviet hegemonic ambitions.

The Western Influence. The essential points about the importance
of a continuation of Western and, especially, American influence
in the Balkans and the Mediterranean have already been covered
in the examination of Soviet objectives. Neither Yugoslavia nor
Rumania considers this influence to be a negative one,[122] but
desires its continuation and regards it as an essential base for
their independence policy. The West, with the U.S. at the head,
can no longer consider the Mediterranean as mare nostrum, as it
did in 1958. After the Middle East conflict in 1967 it even
appeared for a time that genuine parity of strength and
influence with the Soviet Union would be established in the
Mediterranean. As of 1974, it is clear that the United States
still is the kingpin in Mediterranean politics. The Arab
countries themselves, especially Egypt, have recognized that
they can realize their political goals vis-à-vis Israel only
with U.S. intercession and assistance, and never with Soviet
support alone. This realization automatically relegates the
Soviet Union to second place.

Only the United States now personifies Western influence in
the Mediterranean and the Balkan area. The Western European

members of NATO and the European community in general have
practically no importance, except perhaps economically. This
has been the case ever since the United States took the place of
Great Britain as guarantor for Greece and Turkey by means of the
Truman Doctrine in 1947. The abortive Suez adventure of 1956
merely confirmed it. At the moment there is no change in sight.
Before the European nations reemerge as power factors in the
Mediterranean there must be an unbearable situation, perhaps
created by the radicalism and terrorist activities of certain
North African states such as Libya or Algeria, similar to the
piracy of North African states of an earlier era, or by the
energy crisis.

Accordingly, until the 1974 Cyprus crisis, the two NATO
countries of the Mediterranean, Greece and Turkey, focused their
foreign policy primarily on direct relationships with the United
States and considered Europe important only economically. Greece
even gave first priority to the American orientation in the
economic field; during all monetary crises Greece allowed its
currency to fluctuate with the dollar. It would be an
oversimplification, especially in the case of Greece, to explain
the American orientation merely as the instinct for self-
preservation of a dictatorial regime that saw as its mainstay
the strategic interest of the U.S. in stability in the
Mediterranean area and in the use of Greek military bases. The
pro-American orientation of Greece existed earlier, and will
probably recur, although it is too early to tell. It is founded
on geopolitical realities, i.e., the strength of the potential
aggressors in the north and their geographic proximity. Similar
factors operate in the case of Turkey, which controls the
strategically important straits and knows the Soviet drive for
access to the Mediterranean. In addition, relations with the
U.S. in all sectors intensified enormously during the last
twenty years, especially in Greece; one need only point to the
approximately million and a half Greeks in the U.S. and the
role of their ethnic organizations as bridges. Until the 1974
Cyprus crisis the danger of anti-American feeling was greater in
Turkey because the national character is less open and the
conditions more complicated. But in spite of all agitations, the
basic lines of domestic and foreign policy are so firmly drawn
in Turkey that it will be difficult to upset them.

The weak point at which the Soviet Union is most likely to
make a breakthrough to the Mediterranean is certainly Yugoslavia.
The West has every reason to wish that Yugoslavia continue to
exist in its present form—independent, unified, strong, and
nonaligned. But if this unified Yugoslavia should go over to
the Soviet sphere of influence, then Western interest in

Yugoslavia's unity probably would disappear quickly. Perhaps this chain of reasoning is why Croatian émigré circles conjure up Soviet interest in their aspirations; the apparent aim is to awaken a similar interest in the West.

Any direct or indirect Western concern about keeping the "Western" areas of Yugoslavia in the West's political sphere while leaving the "Eastern" areas to the Soviets, according to the 50:50 formula of Yalta, in the event of Yugoslavia's collapse would be extremely dangerous and questionable from the political point of view. The location of the "Western" and "Eastern" areas in Yugoslavia is not as easy to determine as it appears and could lead to tragic misunderstandings. The West, and its leader, the United States, has every interest in supporting the continued existence of Yugoslavia as a strong, internally secure, and above all nonaligned state. Among the Yugoslav population itself there is the belief, which an interested party has eagerly tried to foment, that the West would no longer react as quickly as ten years ago to serious Soviet pressure on Yugoslavia or even to a Soviet military attack. This opinion should periodically be countered, in particular by the United States.

The question arises of whether the emerging Soviet-American efforts at compromise in world politics make the approach sketched above obsolete; i.e., in the final analysis, what is the difference if the Soviets are given direct access to the Mediterranean and a genuine partnership is established with them in this area? The only answer is that at the present time such a point of view is completely alien to the whole Balkan and Mediterranean area. Until now the Soviet Union itself has done nothing in this area to indicate that it has any other objective than to increase its influence and its area of control under all circumstances. If the Soviets move toward this objective, the United States would have to expect political reactions in the Western European states, especially Italy, as well as in Greece and Turkey. Passive observation by the United States in the event of a Soviet takeover in Yugoslavia would be viewed as capitulation.

The final question is whether a regional organization can be created in the Balkan area which would give stability and would make the Balkans independent of the two international power blocs. On the basis of history the answer must be negative, until proved otherwise. There have been several attempts to establish an alliance between the Balkan states. The first, led by the Serbian Prince Mihailo in 1858-1867, ended with the murder of its initiator. The second attempt was more serious: the alliance of Balkan states in 1912 for the expulsion of Turkey from the Balkan

peninsula. After their prey had been finished off, the victors
quarreled, with the result that in the First World War the front
went right through the Balkans. The Little Entente and the
Balkan Entente of 1934, new attempts of cooperation in the
Balkan area during the interwar period, also miscarried. The
efforts of individual Balkan states toward mutual cooperation in
the period after the Second World War were equally shortlived,
even under communist governments.

The reason for the lack of cohesion among the Balkan states
perhaps does not lie in the reciprocal quarrels of these
countries; with mutual goodwill these could be bridged. The main
problem is that each of the Balkan countries has a different
political orientation, and its special problems with the
neighbors outside the Balkans, especially the big powers, and
would lose rather than gain security if it joined with one or
several of its small Balkan neighbors into an alliance. For
example, the problems that Rumania has with the Soviet Union are
different from Greece's problems with the Soviet Union; and
what, in the final analysis, could Yugoslavia do for Turkey?
These were exactly the reasons why the Balkan Entente of 1934
was a failure from the beginning as an instrument for joint
defense.[123] There are enough difficulties already in holding the
two western Balkan states, Greece and Turkey, to a common line
in NATO.

This analysis does not mean that it would be impossible to
neutralize certain internal conflicts and establish friendly and
neighborly cooperation in the Balkans. The Rumanian proposal for
a meeting of the prime ministers of the Balkan countries has
been lying on the table since 1957; it was later supplemented by
a proposal for a nuclear-free zone.[124] In the spring of 1973
Ceauşescu again appealed for cooperation in the Balkans.[125] But
the response was always meager. For example, Greece today takes
the view (confirmed in unofficial talks in Athens) that during
the period of negotiations on European security a nuclear-free
zone in the Balkans would be meaningless. Furthermore, Greece is
not yet sufficiently assured of the friendly intentions of its
northern neighbors, including the Soviet Union, that it would be
willing to give up any freedom of decision in the strategic
area. Moreover, Bucharest never wants to commit itself when
asked how "Balkan cooperation" is visualized in concrete terms.
One attempt of Ceauşescu to make this more concrete, in the
summer of 1973, had unfortunate results. At a meeting with Tito
in July at Brioni, Ceauşescu, taking up the theme of his speech
in the March 1973 Central Committee plenum reportedly proposed
a "system of peace" in the Balkans to be guaranteed jointly by

the United States and the Soviet Union. The Yugoslavs were reportedly not at all interested in this, for they feared a new Yalta in the Balkans.[126] The visit to Athens that Ceauşescu had planned in November 1973 had to be canceled because of the new military coup in Greece.

In view of the fact that Soviet objectives have remained unchanged in principle, the powerful presence of the United States in the Mediterranean and in Western Europe will continue to be the most important guarantee for security, independence, and balance in the Balkan peninsula. Other factors supplementing the U.S. presence, such as efforts with respect to European security, or the interest of China in the area, can be viewed as positive developments, but can never be decisive.

Chapter 3

THE GREAT POWERS AND THE MIDDLE EAST

Arnold Hottinger

A Regional Subsystem

Few areas of the globe can be called a regional subsystem with
as much justification as the Middle East. The Arab-speaking core
of the region brings this out most clearly. An event in any Arab
country from Morocco to Iraq and South Yemen will echo in all
the other Arab countries many times stronger than in any non-
Arab state, even an adjoining one. The Arab countries are
normally involved with one another much more intensely than with
the outside world. In this context, Israel should be viewed as a
part of the Arab world; the Arab countries tend to view and to
treat it as a Palestinian irredenta that awaits liberation.

Language is the strongest bond of the Arab "community of
fate," but religion, common history, and participation in the
same civilization count as well. The Arab world in itself can
be divided for convenience into two groups. The first is an
inner group constituted by the two great river states, Egypt
and Iraq, plus the countries linking the two: Jordan, Syria,
Lebanon, and Palestine-Israel. The second is a circle of
outlying regions: the Arabian peninsula and the Persian Gulf,
the Sudan, and North Africa. A further tier, outside this
double-layered Arab nucleus, is constituted by the countries of
Muslim civilization and history but non-Arab languages: Turkey,
Iran, Afghanistan, Pakistan, and even farther, Indonesia and
India.

The inner core of the Arab states is the crucible of Arab
politics. Rivalry is frequent between the two river states,
Iraq and Egypt. Most of the time the countries between them,
geographically ill-defined and all merging into the open desert,
are pawns in this rivalry. Lebanon, Syria, Jordan, and
Palestine have been at times attracted to the Nile valley, and
at other times, but on the whole more rarely, have been under
the influence of Mesopotamia. These countries can be combined
in different constellations against one another, or they can
float in equilibrium between Iraq and Egypt, preserving their
independence.

Arabia has its most populous part in the South, the Yemen,
isolated from the rest of the Arab world by the deserts of the

Arabian peninsula. The Maghreb, comprising the states of
Morocco, Algeria, and Tunisia, is linked to the inner core of
Arab states by the large desert country of Libya and is thus
rather separate from the center. For the Sudan the cataracts of
the Nile have always served as an isolating barrier. The outer
layer of the Arab countries thus usually remains outside the
political fray, except when one of the central states—the
strongest of which is usually Egypt—reaches out to conquer, or
is (exceptionally) conquered by, one of the outlying states.

The rise of Israel, in the very center of the Arab regional
subsystem, is seen by the Arabs as abnormal and disruptive.
Basically, the cultural differences between Israel and the Arabs
have made Israel unacceptable to the subsystem. In terms of
power, these cultural differences (above all, that Israel
belongs to the modern technological and scientific world, while
the Arab states do not, or do so only marginally) have meant
that Israel, since its foundation as an independent state, has
been able to remain politically an outsider, even though
geographically it is at the center, and to defend itself
successfully every time it has been challenged. Thus, in terms
of political emotions, Israel's position as an outsider, from
the inception of the state under colonial rule up to the
present day, has made it unacceptable to the Arabs. It is viewed
by them as a symbol of foreign rule over "Arab" territory. They
have thus attacked it as the last, or at least the most visible,
survival of colonialism, once supreme in nearly all the Arab
lands.

The Arabs' desire for Arab unity and the emotional appeal of
that idea must be explained in terms of common language, shared
civilization, and related historical experiences. But these
feelings probably would not have reached the peak of passion
that they did in certain moments (e.g., in the 1956 Suez crisis
and thereafter), and might reach again, were it not for a
deeply felt need of the Arabs to differentiate themselves from,
and to stand up to, the outside world, particularly Europe and
the United States, whose presence in the Middle East has weighed
on the Arab world economically, culturally, politically, and
militarily from Napoleon's expedition to Egypt to the present
day. The center, "occupied" by Israel, is viewed by the Arabs as
part and parcel of this same "colonialist" force.

Arab nationalism, historically an ideological import from
Europe via the Balkans and Turkey, is ambivalent in the area

even today.* It exists in each Arab state and is strongest in
those that possess a long-standing separate entity, such as
Egypt, Lebanon, and Morocco. Nationalism also characterizes
the "Arab nation" as a whole. Its pan-Arab variety has never been
realized and will always encounter severe obstacles, arising out
of the self-interest of the existing institutions and power
structures and their beneficiaries in the various Arab states.
Such beneficiaries are rarely willing to lose their positions
for the sake of pan-Arab state mergers. But the pan-Arab ideal
retains its attractiveness for most Arabs (apart from religious
and ethnic minorities, who tend to dislike it strongly) because
of its chiliastic content.[1] The Arab urge to stand up to the
pressures of the outside world (engendered by "alien," modern,
technological civilization and symbolized largely by Israel and
"colonialism-imperialism") is so great, and these oppressive
pressures are felt so much, that it is instinctively assumed
that only "all Arabs together" will generate sufficient
counterpressure and thus reach the pan-Arab millennium.

    Even though pan-Arabism may perhaps never achieve any
permanent mergers of Arab states (the only one seriously
attempted in the past, between Syria and Egypt, lasted only
from 1958 to 1961), it is still an important political force,
because any appeal to Arab unity is certain to strike a
responsive chord in most Arab hearts. It can thus serve as a
rallying cry to mobilize people, even though in the end it may
well not be institutionalized. Pan-Arabism is thus the hoped-for
countervailing force against Zionism, colonialism, and
imperialism—which Arabs see and feel as three aspects of one
and the same thing: an alien force that intends to thrust itself
on the Arabs and deprive them of their very identity.

    Arab nationalism in its more chiliastic manifestations is
intimately connected with the challenges with which the Arabs
feel confronted, essentially the more recent versions of
European or Western civilization. The fact that this Western

---

* Arabs call this ideology wataniya (patriotism) when it applies
to individual states or regions and qaumiya (nationalism) when
it applies to the "Arab nation," i.e., all Arabic-speaking
territories. When they speak of "nationalists," they nearly
always mean people believing in one Arab nation, i.e., pan-
Arabists.

civilization has grown out of European Christianity and that
European Christendom has been a rival and an intimate enemy of
Islam (and specifically Arab Islam in many instances) for some
twelve centuries is certainly relevant to the outlook of Arab
nationalism. The more recent Arab colonial past has brought
added bitterness to the old confrontation, and the bitterness
has continued because, in Arab eyes, Israel is an extension of
the Western colonial presence in their lands.

This Arab resentment has a religious as well as a political
dimension. For the Arabs, Islam, which differentiates much less
between the "world of Caesar" and the "world of Our Father in
Heaven" than does Christianity, ought to rule the world, because
it is superior to the tolerated but inferior religions of
Christianity and Judaism. If it does not so rule, there must be
something radically wrong with the Muslims and with their way of
life.

Some recent evidence suggests that not only Western
imperialism, with its Christian, colonial background, is felt as
a menace by the Arabs, but atheistic Soviet communism as well.
Religious and traditional circles have always been hostile to
communism, but only after President Sadat took over in Egypt,
after the death of Gamal Abdel Nasser, did Egyptian officials
become concerned about the alien qualities of Russian atheism.
In part this hostility was caused by increased contacts between
Soviet instructors and their Arab military pupils, which
produced a feeling that the Russians, although "enemies of our
enemies," were also an essentially alien and menacing force
just, or nearly, as much as the "colonializing" Westerners.

Three Decades of Arab Politics
Arab politics since independence can be divided into three
decades, the third of which is not yet over. The first ten years
after the Second World War (1946-1956) were a period of the
consolidation and extension of the independence won at the end
of the war or, in a few cases, earlier. (Iraq became partially
independent in 1932, Egypt officially in 1936.) They were also
marked by the first lost war against the emerging state of
Israel (1948-1949) and the aftertaste of failure which led to a
succession of disturbances and coups d'état in Syria, Egypt,
Jordan, and Iraq. This period was ended by Abdel Nasser's
nationalizing the Suez Canal, the ensuing Suez war of October
1956, and the enforced withdrawal, as the Arabs saw it, of the
belligerents (France, Great Britain, Israel) under U.S. and
Russian pressure, which left Nasser in a position of apparent
strength and pan-Arab popularity.

The second decade (1956-1967) was dominated by the
personality of Abdel Nasser and by his policies. In this period
Nasser attempted to unify the Arabs, using differing policies
and tactics ranging from subversion to voluntary collaboration
with existing governments. In the Maghreb only in this second
decade was independence from France achieved. This delay was due
principally to the "settler" nature of French colonialism,
especially in Algeria, which made a long, bloody, cruel
guerrilla war (1954-1962) inevitable. This decade also saw the
short-lived unity between Syria and Egypt (1958-1961), the
revolution and resultant radicalization of politics in Iraq
(1958), and the inconclusive civil war in the Yemen (1962-1967),
which involved a large Egyptian expeditionary force.

Arab socialism was launched in Egypt, Syria, and Algeria
(after the civil war and, more realistically, after the
overthrow of Algerian President Ben Bella by Boumédienne in
Algeria in 1965), as well as in part in Iraq. Arab socialism
tried to harness economics and institutions to development
policies. Externally it gave an added dimension to the inter-
Arab struggle and polemics, for it contributed to the division
between "progressive" (but poor) and "conservative" (but mostly
oil-rich) countries. The conservative regimes feared that they
would be overthrown by their progressive neighbors, who were
masters at propaganda, and they found themselves periodically in
real danger.

Toward the end of this second period, the Palestinian
refugees, who had become disenchanted with Nasser's pan-Arabism
and disillusioned about its ability to succeed against Israel,
decided to take things into their own hands by forming guerrilla
bands to infiltrate Israel. They thus contributed decisively to
a series of Arab (and Soviet) miscalculations that led to the
Six-Day War (1967) against Israel and to the occupation of
Egyptian, Jordanian, and Syrian territory by the victorious
Israelis. Other important factors leading to the war were Syrian
overconfidence in the fortifications of the Golan Heights;
Nasser's impatience with a number of failures in Egyptian
development and foreign policy during the preceding years and
his attempt to recoup his diminished stature by one grand
gamble (the march into Sinai of the Egyptian army and the
closing of the Straits of Tiran); and, finally, Soviet
miscalculations and misinformation about their Arab allies.[2]

The first half of the third decade has been spent thus far in
ineffectual Arab efforts to erase the consequences of "the
setback," as their defeat was called by the Arabs in the first
years that followed it. The Egyptian and Syrian armies were

rebuilt with Soviet, and the Jordanian with U.S., aid. The
fedayeen, the Palestinian guerrillas, began feverish activities,
principally political, in Jordan, Syria, Lebanon, and the
Israeli-occupied Gaza Strip. But they were militarily
unsuccessful against Israel and did not achieve the political
mobilization of most of the occupied territories. They were
crushed in Amman (1970) and in the rest of Jordan (1971) by the
Jordanian regular army, because they had challenged and
threatened the authority of the Jordanian state.

Inter-Arab struggles, a principal feature of the preceding
decade, became dormant after the Six-Day War, because Nasser
(and, after his death in 1971, his successor Sadat) gave
priority to the struggle against Israel and obtained financial
and political backing from the conservative oil states in
exchange for ending propagandistic and subversive attacks
against them.

Military coups brought "Nasserite" military regimes to power
in some peripheral Arab states: the Sudan (Nimeiry in 1968)
and Libya (Qadhdhafi in 1969). But after a narrowly defeated
communist takeover in Khartoum in 1971, Nimeiry adopted a
Sudanese rather than a pan-Arab policy and was thus able to end
the civil war in the south, which had been going on
intermittently ever since 1955, a year before the Sudan's
independence.

Qadhdhafi for his part tried to take on Nasser's mantle of
pan-Arab leadership and to become the main architect of new
Arab unification attempts, such as the Syria-Egypt-Libya
federation of 1971 and a project for complete union with Egypt
that was scheduled to be achieved by September 1973.

A new radical state emerged in 1967 in South Yemen (capital:
Aden) out of a protracted independence struggle with Great
Britain, while (North) Yemen (capital: San'a) ended its civil
war by compromise after Egyptian withdrawal and was ruled
thereafter by a moderate regime of former republicans mixed with
former monarchists.

The emirates of the Gulf, previously protectorates of Great
Britain, also became independent in 1971. Two of them became
separate states, Bahrain and Qatar, while the five of the
Trucial States formed the Federation of the Arab Emirates. Oman
emerged from isolation after Qabus, the son of the previous
sultan, overthrew his father. But the civil war in Dhofar
(Western Oman) against insurgents, abetted by the Aden regime,
continued and remained a potential menace for all the Gulf
states.

Iraq also became a potential menace for the other oil
countries, Saudi Arabia, Kuwait, and Iran, nearly all of whose
oil fields were close to the Gulf, after the 1968 coup in
Baghdad produced a radical Baath regime. But Iraq found itself
isolated in the Arab world after the Six-Day War and drew
progressively closer to the Soviet Union.

In Syria a milder variant of Baathism developed, hostile to
its "brother" regime in Iraq and obliged to follow more prudent
policies because of the closeness of superior Israeli forces to
its capital, Damascus.

Lebanon had its difficulties between fedayeen attacks from
its territories on Israel and Israeli retaliations against
Lebanon. These difficulties came to a provisional end in the
summer of 1972 with the fedayeen promising for the time being
not to use Lebanese territory for future actions.

Each of the three postindependence periods of Arab politics
ended in frustration. In Arab eyes, complete and true
independence of the "Arab nation" was not achieved after the
first decade, because the "occupation" of Palestine by Israel
continued and the Israelis in 1948 even expanded farther into
the neighboring countries. There were also other irredenta:
Algeria, with her cruel guerrilla war; Aden, a British colony;
and the Gulf states under British rule. Moreover, the economic
interests of foreigners loomed large and came to be seen by the
Arabs as part of the neocolonialist structure working in
alliance with international capitalism and reaction in order to
impose the will of the foreigners on the Arabs.

The second decade ended in failure as well. There had been
successes in the independence struggle: Morocco, Tunisia, Sudan
(1956); Algeria (1962); Aden (1967). Some spectacular
achievements in the fight against neocolonialism had occurred:
the unity between Syria and Egypt (1958); the Iraqi revolution,
which overthrew the royal regime (1958); the popular-front
government in Jordan (1958)—all of which were connected with
the diplomatic victory of Nasser after the Suez defeat of 1956.
But Arab socialism proved to be at best a limited blessing in
Egypt, Syria, Iraq, and the Sudan. Iraq never entered into a
real union with Syria or with Egypt. The Egyptian-Syrian union
broke down. The conservative royal regimes managed to survive
crises in Morocco (war with Algeria, 1964), Saudi Arabia
(attempts at overthrow by Egypt between 1962 and 1965), and
Jordan (numerous attempted coups, the most important in 1957).
The moderates in Tunisia and Lebanon also survived their

difficulties with Nasserite and Baathi radicalism (civil war in
Lebanon in 1958, and polemics, spiced with an occasional murder
plot, between Nasser and President Bourguiba of Tunisia between
1965 and 1967). The Yemen war remained inconclusive,
notwithstanding both the large Egyptian army engaged in it and
Soviet aid to Egypt and to the Yemeni republicans. Israel
managed to survive and to build up its army and its economy.

The Arab defeat in the Six-Day War, triggered essentially by
the desire of Nasser to end his frustrations and disappointments
by one grand, successful strike, caused the bitterest
frustration of all. This further deepened during five years of
promises to liberate the Israeli-occupied territories "soon."

If politics is the art of the possible, Arab radical
politicians have proved ineffective, because they have regularly
set their own policy aims at a level higher than they proved
able to attain. In the case of Egypt, though, it must be
admitted that its bad internal situation led to very ambitious
foreign policy aims. Egypt seems to have very little chance
indeed, given its present demographic, educational, and
economic circumstances, to achieve successful internal
development. Population growth is enormous, crippling, and so
far not successfully checked. The agricultural area of the
country is limited to the Nile valley, and irrigation by Nile
water cannot be greatly extended. Egyptian agriculture, already
of a very high quality, leaves little room for growth by
improved methods. Even the Aswan Dam has given at best temporary
relief. The escape route of industrialization, assiduously
pursued by Nasser's regime, has not been really successful, for
it has brought a severe shortage of foreign currency, caused by
difficulty in exporting industrial products and by increased
demands for imports of machinery, technology, raw materials, and
consumer goods for the new working class. Escape into an
adventurist foreign policy must thus have appeared to Nasser as
the best possible gamble, all the more tempting because the
conservative, oil-rich, underpopulated countries of the Arab
world, close neighbors of Egypt, appeared to be so susceptible
to the attraction of Arab nationalism and Arab socialism.

Even an activist policy against Israel, which in itself does
not promise material rewards for Egypt even if it were
successful, can be justified by any Egyptian government, on the
grounds of the increase in prestige that any success against
Israel would bring to Cairo in the eyes of the whole Arab world.
The possible rewards in terms of Arab unification or closer Arab
collaboration might be high indeed. But an activist policy, in
order to bring Egypt relief, ought to be successful. If it

fails, as it did at least until 1973, it only brings increased
burdens.

In the career of Abdel Nasser a cyclical movement can be
detected, swinging from emphasis on Egyptian development
(wataniya)to pan-Arab activism (qaumiya) and back. This movement
is best explained if one assumes a certain awareness on the part
of Nasser, perhaps partly subliminal, that for Egypt alone it
would be extremely difficult to develop toward self-sustaining
growth, and that therefore Egypt needs to use foreign policy to
obtain increased foreign advantages—at worst, increased
financial aid and, at best, pan-Arab coups and possible mergers
of richer Arab countries with Egypt.

If Egypt's and the Palestinian refugees' needs thus
justified their adventurist, activist foreign policies, for most
other Arab countries that participated in the pan-Arab movement,
principally Syria, Iraq, and, most recently, Libya, no such
justification is apparent. The overwhelming appeal to them of
the qaumi ideals can be explained only by their deep resentment
of and humiliation by the material success and freqently
undeniable superiority of the threefold monster of Zionism,
colonialism, and neocolonialism and by the consequent deeply
felt need to unite against it and thus overcome it.

The Russian Connection

The USSR and Egypt under Nasser. The relationship between the
great powers and the Arab states must be understood within the
context of the complex network of inter-Arab and anti-Israeli
policies outlined above. Arabs see inter-Arab and anti-Israeli
policy as their primary interest and try to make their
relations with the great powers serve that primary interest.
Given the general anti-European and anti-Western orientation of
radical Arab nationalism, which is due to the colonial heritage
and to the protecting role the West plays toward Israel, it was
probably unavoidable that the Soviet Union would gain
considerable influence in the Arab world, much more so than in
Turkey and Iran, who have no grievances comparable to the Arab
resentment against Israel-Palestine and whose colonial
experiences include some clashes with imperial Russia. The
Soviets were rather slow to exploit the opening the Arab
situation offered them. They remained outside of the region
after the first Arab-Israeli war, and only six years later, at
the initiative of Nasser and through the mediation of Chou En-
lai,[3] did they enter Arab politics, by selling arms to Egypt
in May 1955.

The Soviet Union had previously attempted to gain footholds
in Turkey (1945) and in Iran (1945-1946). Their demands on
Turkey, "rectification of the northeastern borders and bases on
the straits,"[4] were checked by the Truman Doctrine in 1947 and
by Turkey's joining NATO in February 1952. In Iran the Russians
were forced to withdraw in 1946 under U.S. pressure and were at
the same time outsmarted by Qawam as-Saltaneh, who promised them
an oil concession and a joint Iranian-Russian oil company if
they would withdraw from the northern provinces of Iran that
they had occupied during the war. Iranian troops were moved into
those northern areas with American approval and British backing.
A new Iranian Assembly was elected in 1947 and refused to ratify
the Russian oil agreement in October of the same year.

As for Nasser, the first appreciation by Moscow of his regime
had been negative. The Soviets had been aware of the links
between the Free Officers movement and the American Central
Intelligence Agency,[5] and the hanging of two strike leaders in
Kfar ad-Dawar in August 1952 by the officers' junta, apparently
against the will of Amer and Nasser,[6] had seemed to confirm
Moscow's judgment. At that time, the Soviets called the Free
Officers "fascist military adventurists."[7] But this appreciation
had to be revised after Nasser rejected American and British
invitations to join the Baghdad Pact and after he had become
instrumental in keeping Jordan, Syria, Saudi Arabia, and
Lebanon out of it as well and had started a furious propaganda
campaign against Iraq, which had joined the Pact in February
1955.

Nasser came into conflict with the United States, toward
which he had at first been friendly, over the Baghdad Pact issue.
The retaliatory attack of Israel on Gaza in February 1955 (which
killed thirty-seven soldiers and nine civilians) made it urgent
for him to obtain more arms. The retaliation had occurred
because eight months previously the Egyptians had authorized
fedayeen raids into Israel. Nasser requested arms from Paris and
from Washington. The Americans told him to join the Baghdad Pact
first, and the French told him to stop aiding the Algerian
rebels. The Soviets finally sold him the arms. Soviet contact
was made first by the Soviet ambassador in Cairo on May 18, 1955.
Later the Russians preferred to work via Prague "in order not to
disturb the Geneva spirit" (as Mohammed Hassanain Heikal has
written). Also according to Heikal, on May 22 Nasser told the
U.S. ambassador that he had a Soviet arms offer. "He still would
have preferred Western arms," Heikal wrote. But American
Secretary of State Dulles thought Nasser was bluffing. When the
negotiations in Prague started and the Israelis and the

Americans heard of them, Washington said it was ready to talk
arms, but it was then too late. The U.S. attitude was seen in
Cairo as a maneuver to delay the Prague negotiations. The price
of the first Soviet-Egyptian arms deal, according to Heikal, was
$80 million, payable in twelve years.[8] Finally, Heikal went on,
in the face of the activity of the CIA in Cairo, Nasser made a
public announcement on the occasion of an exhibition of army
photographs in Cairo on September 27, 1955; and when Dulles then
sent Kermit Roosevelt and later George Allen to Cairo with
"menaces," Nasser refused to receive such "ultimata," and the
emissaries kept Dulles' written messages in their pockets.

Also according to Heikal, when Bulganin and Khrushchev visited
London in April 1956, Eden asked them to stop arms deliveries to
all countries in the Middle East. The Russians agreed if the
stoppage would be general and imposed by the UN. (Eden could not
consent to this because of his Baghdad Pact commitments, as the
Soviet leaders undoubtedly knew.) Nasser was informed by the
Soviets of these conversations. They troubled him, and he decided
to recognize Peking. He reasoned that in case a UN embargo should
be established, Communist China, which did not belong to the UN,
could continue to send Soviet arms to Egypt.[9]

In retaliation, Dulles "permitted" the French to supply Israel
with Mystère airplanes, in the framework of the tripartite
declaration of France, Britain, and the U.S. in favor of an arms
balance in the Middle East and existing frontiers. Nasser
thereupon demanded MIG 17s from Russia instead of the MIG 15s he
had first been promised.

After reconsideration, Dulles attempted to tie Egypt
economically to the U.S. by agreeing to help finance the Aswan
High Dam. But later, irritated by Nasser's high-handedness,[*] he
changed his mind again and canceled his promise on the pretext
that Egypt's economy could not support such a large project.
Nasser, who allegedly had advance knowledge of the step Dulles
would take (according to Heikal through secret Baghdad Pact
documents brought to him by an Iraqi minister),[10] retaliated by
nationalizing the Suez Canal.

Heikal tells another significant story: when the Suez

----

* Jon Kimche, The Second Arab Awakening (London: Weidenfeld and
Nicolson, 1970), p. 115, claims that Nasser had committed
himself at the time of the Russian arms deal to having the dam
built with Soviet help, and that he provoked Dulles into taking
back his offer for the benefit of his associates in the junta
and the Arab world. But Kimche cites no sources for this
statement.

intervention began, Syrian President Kuwatli was visiting Moscow.
He heard of the British air raids on Cairo as he entered the
Kremlin conference room. He thereupon deviated from the agenda
and asked the Soviets to intervene in Egypt. In the presence of
Bulganin and Khrushchev, Marshal Zhukov opened a map in front of
Kuwatli and asked him, "How can we intervene?" The Soviets tried
to calm Kuwatli and to convince him that military intervention
was impossible and that therefore political action, together
with steps in the UN, was the proper course. Kuwatli reportedly
nearly wept from fury and despair.[11]

Propagandistically and diplomatically, the Soviets went all
out for Egypt during the Suez crisis. But it is well known that
they also kept their ties to the West and that they were careful
to make their veiled nuclear threats only after it had become
clear that the U.S. refused to support the actions taken by
Britain, France, and Israel.[12] To the Arabs, however, the U.S.
seemed to speak with many voices during the war. The Egyptian
communists managed to make political capital out of the Soviet
threats. "They thought that they could use these for a political
offensive," Heikal writes,[13] and some had to be arrested. Nasser
himself noted that the Russians had taken 36 hours to announce
their support for his nationalization of the canal.[14]

For a short time after the Suez crisis, Nasser considered the
U.S. and the USSR friends of Egypt. But this did not last long.
The Eisenhower Doctrine, proclaimed on January 5, 1957, provided
a new focus for anti-U.S. propaganda. Washington's idea of
"filling a vacuum" in the Middle East was offensive to Arab
pride. The crisis in Jordan in April 1957, in which the
Americans intervened to help King Hussein against his Arab
nationalist opponents, was seen in Cairo as the first
application of the Eisenhower Doctrine. It caused violent
outbursts of anti-American propaganda from Cairo, Damascus, and
Moscow, and it ended all Egyptian notions of gratitude for the
U.S. aid during the Suez crisis.

An attempt to change the balance of power toward the right in
Syria, which had closely aligned itself with the Soviets, was
undertaken by Baghdad Pact and U.S. agents. (The details of this
operation were published by Baghdad after the Iraqi revolution
of 1958). It failed and was followed by purges of Syrian
parliamentarians and officers of the right and the pro-Western
wings. The replacement of the moderate chief of staff, Tawfiq
Nizam ad-Din, by the procommunist Afif al-Bizri on August 9 was
a decisive step. Khaled al-Azm, a rich former prime minister (in
1939, under the Vichy regime), who intended to become president

of Syria with Soviet help, became one of the most important
figures in the Syrian rapprochement with the USSR.[15]
    American and Baghdad Pact pressure on Syria gave the Soviets
the opportunity to start a propaganda campaign. Soviet maneuvers
were held close to Turkey and Marshal Rokossovsky threatened
that Turkey would be attacked if it took any action against
Syria. But in October the crisis suddenly evaporated, perhaps in
connection with Khrushchev's purge of Marshal Zhukov.[16]
    A similar pattern of events could be observed in the next
crisis. The U.S. was at first reluctant to intervene in the
Lebanese civil struggle of the spring and summer of 1958, even
though the government of Lebanon appealed to the Eisenhower
Doctrine and spoke of "massive intervention" by Syria. But the
revolution in Iraq (July 14, 1958) made the U.S. change its
policy. There followed a U.S. landing in Lebanon, a U.S. airlift
from Germany to Adana (Turkey), and a British airlift into
Jordan. The Soviets started maneuvers again on their southern
border, and Nasser flew to Moscow and then to Damascus.[17] He
ordered mobilization in Egypt to help the Iraqi revolution. The
crisis finally subsided when it became clear to the U.S. special
envoy in the Middle East at the time, Robert Murphy, that the
Iraqi revolution under its leader Qassem was not going to join
Iraq to Nasser's Egypt and would thus not really upset the
traditional equilibrium in the region, even if Iraq left the
Baghdad Pact, thereafter renamed CENTO.
    The Iraqi revolution led to the first major clash between
Nasser and the Soviets. Qassem used the Iraqi Communist party as
a counterweight to the pan-Arab nationalists who worked for
union with the United Arab Republic (i.e., Syria and Egypt, at
that time united). Qassem had Aref, his vice-president and the
leader of the nationalists, arrested and condemned to death but
not executed. There were uprisings against Qassem by nationalist
officers (such as Shawaf in Mosul in the spring of 1959), and
the communists helped in their bloody suppression. At the end, a
kind of gang war developed between the nationalists (qaumiyun
and Baathi) and the communists in Baghdad.
    In Syria the communist party, illegal at the time because
Nasser had insisted on the dissolution of all parties before
agreeing to the union with Syria, came out in favor of the Iraqi
communists and of Qassem and against the union of Egypt and
Syria. These Syrian communists were imprisoned and persecuted.
Some died under torture. Nasser also struck at the communists in
Egypt.
    The Soviets had agreed toward the end of 1958 to aid Egypt in
building the High Dam. This decision had marked a new stage in

their involvement in Arab politics. At that time they must have
had hopes of fostering communism via the local communist parties
in Iraq and Syria and of maintaining their political influence
in Egypt. After the Iraqi revolution and the unification of
Syria and Egypt, the Middle East must have begun to look to them
like a major area of opportunity in a world that offered few
other opportunities for extending their influence. But the
persecution of the communists in Syria and Egypt and Nasser's
violent attacks against Qassem and his communist "agents"
required a Soviet reply. This was given by Khrushchev at the
Twentieth Party Congress in Moscow. He attacked Nasser personally
and called him "a hot-headed young man." Heikal cites interviews
between Nasser and the Soviet ambassador of that period. Nasser
is said to have declared, "You [Soviets] must decide if you want
to collaborate with the Arab people as a whole or with only a
minority of isolated communist parties."[18] A lengthy and bitter
exchange of letters followed. Khrushchev insisted on the
importance of Soviet aid. Nasser replied:

"At Suez we were alone. The Soviet 'ultimatum' to the West came
after nine days of fighting and without previous knowledge by
us. We could have lost our nerve and surrendered after three or
four days, or a week, or even on the morning of the day on
which you published your warning."[19]

But the bridges were never destroyed entirely. Nasser could
not expect the West to take over the task of building the dam
from the Russians. Instability in Iraq and the personal
instability of Qassem must have shown Moscow that it would be
more prudent to rely on two strongpoints in the Middle East,
Iraq and Egypt. In fact, in 1960 Qassem himself liquidated the
Iraqi Communist party by licensing an unorthodox communist
splinter group as the officially recognized party in Iraq. He
also began using the arms Moscow had provided for his war against
the Kurdish minority in the north, a move that cannot have been
to Moscow's liking.

Egyptian-American relations improved, basically because after
the failure of the Eisenhower Doctrine the Americans gave up
their attempts to build pacts in the Arab world. The importance
of such alliances was declining anyway because of overall
strategic developments. The U.S. nuclear deterrent now could be
located in nuclear submarines.[20] A new political concept emerged.
Washington began to aim at helping Nasser make the Egyptian
revolution and Arab socialism a success. If he succeeded, the
Soviets would be denied deeper penetration into Egypt. The

Kennedy administration sent huge shipments of agricultural
surpluses to Egypt, and President Kennedy exchanged personal
letters with Nasser.[21]
    But Arab socialism was not sufficiently successful to permit
Nasser to concentrate exclusively on developments in Egypt. Or
perhaps Nasser's own character prevented such concentration. He
was too much involved in Arab politics. The breakup of the UAR
in September 1961 meant an enormous loss of prestige for him.*
He threw himself into the new adventure of the Yemen civil war
(at the end of 1962) in the hope of recovering his Arab
influence and, initially, perhaps to trigger a revolution in
Saudi Arabia as well. There, however, he came into direct
conflict with American interests, especially those of Aramco.
His interference in the Congo crisis was also strongly disliked
by Washington. The Yemen war at the same time made him more
dependent than ever on Soviet military aid. In return he showed
himself willing to aid Soviet foreign policy in both Africa and
the rest of the world. Internally, after the breakaway of Syria,
Egypt embarked on a resolutely "socialist" course. At first
Washington was not frightened off by this. But gradually U.S.-
Egyptian relations became cooler, and eventually food-surplus
aid was reduced and in the end discontinued.
    The Soviets for their part were forced to improve their
relations with Egypt as their hopes were disappointed in Syria
and Iraq. In both countries, coups (1961 in Damascus, 1963 in
Baghdad) swept into power regimes more firmly anticommunist than
that of Nasser. A "bourgeois" democracy was set up in Damascus,
and the nationalistic Baath, by now bitterly opposed to the
communists in Baghdad, took over in Iraq.

----

* A real or imagined communist danger for Syria had played an
important role in the formation of the UAR in 1958. The
communists, in collaboration with the rich and ambitious Khaled
al-Azm (the only significant rival of President Kuwatli) had
made considerable progress in Syria during 1957. One of the
arguments of the officers who flew to Cairo on January 8, 1958,
and offered "unity" to Nasser was that Syria was in danger of
becoming communist. See Patrick Seale, The Struggle for Syria
(London: Oxford University Press, 1965), pp. 315 ff. The Syrian
communists became the chief object of the dictator Sarraj's
sadistic persecution during the "unity" period, but after
secession (1961) Nasser changed his alliances. He blamed the
"reactionaries" for the separation, went all out for Arab
Socialism, and sought an alliance with the communists internally
and externally.

It was certainly no accident that in this period, after the
failure of the communist parties in Syria and in Iraq to gain
power, the Soviet theoreticians developed new theories,
essentially designed to justify collaboration between third-
world state parties and the local communists. In the third
world, the theoreticians discovered, there existed "states of
national democracy."[22] A "direct road to socialism" was, with
the help of the Soviet Union, possible in such countries, if the
"national democratic regime" was "progressive," e.g., instituting
an agrarian reform, nationalizing the banks and "monopolies,"
especially Western ones, and supporting Soviet foreign policy.
Such regimes the communists were justified in joining, either
individually or, preferably, as an allied party in a common
"national front." Their role was to act within the "revolutionary
democracies" (as the "national democracies" later came to be
called) as friends and counselors. The flexibility of the new
theory becomes clear when the theory is contrasted with classical
Marxist doctrine, according to which in the underdeveloped world
a bourgeois revolution has to take place before a socialist
revolution becomes possible.

Before Khrushchev's visit to Egypt in May 1964 to inaugurate
the first stage of the High Dam, the local communists were freed
from prisons and internment camps. Many were put in charge of
state publications. They were made to join first a new communist
party and then the state party, the Arab Socialist Union (ASU).

Khrushchev had sharp discussions with Abdussalem Aref of Iraq,
Ben Bella of Algeria, and Abdel Nasser about the importance of
class solidarity versus "national" (pan-Arab) solidarity. From
then on the phrase "Arab unity" was used in joint Soviet-Egyptian
statements, and Nasser felt that he had made some headway against
Khrushchev on this issue.[23]

After Khrushchev's fall the new Soviet leaders assured Nasser
of their continued support. They had little choice, for their
investment in Egypt had grown so large that they had to continue
it. Nasser was in a similar position; he could not afford to
break with Moscow. The Yemen war also helped to freeze the
situation. There is also now new evidence that from 1964 onward
the army was more in the hands of Amer than in those of Nasser
himself.[24] This meant that, partly for the sake of "victory" in
the Yemen and partly for an even better life for the officers,
the military establishment under Amer made increasing demands on
the civilian part of the government, which had remained under
Nasser. The Egyptian economic situation also grew steadily
worse.[25] For the first time Nasser saw himself seriously
challenged by Arab nationalists more radical than himself, both
by the "neo-Baath" (also called the "left Baath"), which had come

to power in Syria by a coup in 1963 and a coup within the coup in
1966 and by the emerging fedayeen of the Fatah. Even the
Jordanians managed to taunt Nasser about hiding behind the UN
troops in the Sinai. Nasser's Arab prestige had fallen quite low.
He also developed a phobia about the Americans, who he thought
intended to bring about his fall by deliberately fostering
trouble for him, just as, he believed, they had done to Ben
Bella, Nkrumah, and Sukarno.

The most detailed analysis of the events leading to the
outbreak of the 1967 Six-Day War is by Nadav Safran.[26] Probably
the Soviets knew that they were feeding false information to
Nasser when they warned him of enormous Israeli troop
concentrations on the Syrian border. Probably Nasser knew that
the Soviets knew that it was false. Moscow, however, wanted
Nasser to protect Syria by a show of force. Syria, now decidedly
to the left of Nasser (particularly since the coup of February
1966) and with two communists in the government, was important
to the Soviets as their new hope in the Middle East, which had
by now become rather costly to them. Nasser obliged the Soviets
because he wanted to profit from the fact that this time it was
the Soviets themselves who encouraged his aggressiveness. But he
was driven too far by his own momentum: demanding the withdrawal
of the UN force, closing the Straits of Tiran, and uniting the
Arab countries (Jordan and Iraq) around himself. He finally
decided that war had become highly probable, but he wanted the
Israelis to strike first in order to keep the U.S. out of the
war.

After the war, Cairo gave priority to eliminating the traces
of the setback. This meant in practice trying to regain the
occupied territories by diplomacy or by force, or by a judicious
use of both. Nasser did resign for a moment and named Zakhariya
Muhieddin as his successor. Muhieddin could conceivably have
followed another policy, less popular but perhaps more realistic,
which would have given priority to the development of Egypt. But
popular demonstrations occurred, at least partially fostered by
Muhieddin's rivals for power, who were based on the state party
and had a stake in collaboration with the USSR: Ali Sabri,
Sha'rawi Gum'a, and their friends. Nasser quickly took advantage
of the popular protest movements and proclaimed that he would
stay on after all. This meant that the military establishment
had to carry the blame for the defeat. Marshal Amer, his main
associates, and the security chiefs were purged, as they largely
deserved to be. For the new military buildup and for
indispensable economic aid, Egypt became more dependent than
ever on the Soviet Union.

But at the same time there was a marked easing off of the
internal organizational and propagandistic drive toward both
Arab and "scientific" (i.e., Marxist-Leninist) socialism. This
was partly because socialism was blamed by the people for
Egypt's troubles, which Nasser took into account, but probably
also because Nasser saw little point in doing the Soviets'
propaganda work in Egypt himself. So Islam was again permitted
to come to the fore. All efforts to prove that Islam and
socialism were really one and the same thing, or at least not
incompatible (a line that before the war had been quite strong),
ceased suddenly. A large part of the procommunist literature
disappeared from the newsstands. Since the Soviets had gained
such a powerful position in Egypt and had become the main prop
of the regime, Nasser saw little point in persuading the
Egyptians to accept their ideological and political positions.
If the Egyptians ceased being Muslim and Arab and became
procommunist, "modern," and "progressive" in outlook and in
internal organization, there would be really little need for
the Soviet Union to keep Nasser and his regime as an
intermediary between itself and the Egyptians. Instead they
might seek to govern Egypt more directly, in satellite fashion,
through their own hommes de confiance. Thus the more Muslim and
Arab the Egyptians remained, the more indispensable Nasser's
charisma was to Moscow.

In the military field Nasser's war of attrition and the
Israeli response (March 1969 to August 1970) led to a growing
involvement of the Soviet Union. The most spectacular step
forward was the installation of Soviet ground-to-air missiles
(SAM 3) with the sophisticated radar equipment needed for their
operation. The installations were manned at least initially by
Soviet military technicians. The missiles arrived after, and
because of, Israeli "deep penetration" air raids on military
targets close to Cairo and in the Delta in the winter and spring
of 1970.* Nasser made a secret trip to Moscow (January 22, 1970)
to convince the Soviets that Egypt had to be protected more
effectively.[27] The Soviets agreed to protect the Nile valley.
During the spring of 1970 numerous SAM 3 sites were established
around Cairo, Alexandria, Aswan, and elsewhere. But a strip 47
kilometers wide along the canal on the Egyptian side was left
"open" for the Egyptians alone to defend. Thus the Soviets

---

* In particular, the raids on Inshass, February 8; Khanka,
February 12, killing 68, and wounding 98 workers; Cairo West,
February 27; and Salahiye, April 8, killing 30 school children.

attempted to keep themselves out of any direct confrontation
with Israel, and indeed they succeeded, with a few exceptions,*
in staying out of the fighting. The Soviets flew operational
missions over the Delta and the Nile valley, thus completing the
new defensive network provided by their SAM 3s. It soon became
apparent that their flights combined surveillance of Egypt with
shadowing the U.S. Sixth Fleet, thus giving to their
Mediterranean Eskadra the air protection it had not had before
because of its lack of aircraft carriers. Probably this use of
their own planes and pilots (with Egyptian markings), operating
from airports guarded by Soviet troops, was the quid pro quo
allowed them by Nasser in exchange for their protective air
defense network.

After March the Israelis limited their air actions to the
strip left open by the Russians, but intensified their ground-
based bombardment there to such a degree as to cause
considerable losses and serious concern to the Egyptian army.[28]

In late June 1970 Nasser went again to Moscow. (His trip[June
29-July 16] was extended because he spent part of the time in a
sanatorium being treated for heart trouble). Before going he had
talked optimistically about the growing strength of the Egyptian
army.[29] He had some reason to do so. The days of Israeli "deep
penetration" had passed. But if he did ask the Soviets to help
the Egyptians cross the canal, they must have discouraged him
strongly, for shortly after his return he decided that he would
accept U.S. Secretary of State Rogers's "peace plan." This meant
in practice an Egyptian-Israeli armistice of ninety days, later
extended several times, finally formally "terminated" by Sadat,
but in fact in force until the October 1973 war. His decision to
accept this cease-fire, it is said in Cairo, was the only major
decision after the Six-Day War that Nasser took alone, not
collectively with his closest associates.

In the following month, on September 28, 1970, Nasser died.
As long as he lived, his personal relations with the Soviet
Union were by far the most important link between Moscow and the
Arabs. This was so not because the Soviets had not tried to
forge other links, both institutional and with other
personalities and other Arab states. It was simply because of

---

* In June 1970 five planes piloted by Russians were downed over
the canal. This loss was admitted by Heikal in al-Ahram, August
11, 1972. Israel had announced on April 29 that the Soviets were
flying operational missions over the Nile valley.

Nasser's immense influence in the Arab world and also because of
his long political career, which guaranteed a certain stability.
Soviet collaboration with Iraq and with Syria had proved
disappointing because of the political instability of both
countries.

Syria, Iraq, and the USSR. In Iraq the 1958 revolution had
seemed to offer an important opportunity to Moscow, so much so
that Baghdad for a short while had become its chief Middle
Eastern interest, much to the wrath of Cairo. But the
opportunity soon passed. Qassem used the Iraqi communists only
as long as he needed them as a counterwieght against the
nationalists. After that he used the pretext of licensing
political parties to recognize a splinter group as the Iraqi
Communist party and to force the real communists underground.
After Qassem's fall in 1963, his successors continued to
persecute the Iraqi communists.

In Syria there was a first, hopeful honeymoon between Moscow
and the republican regime between the 1956 Suez War and the
unification with Egypt. The moderate and bourgeois political
forces in the government and in the army had been eliminated by
the radical nationalists (Baathists and Nasserites) and by the
procommunists. But the unification with Egypt put a stop to the
freedom of action that the communists and their friends had
enjoyed.

After the separation from Egypt and the subsequent fall of
the parliamentary regime in 1963, a limited friendship developed
between the Soviets and the Baathists led by Amin al-Hafez. But
this friendship was difficult for the Soviet Union to exploit,
because Nasser and the Syrian Baathists were declared enemies,
while the Iraqi Baath, at that time in power in Baghdad and
close to its brethren in Damascus, was actually persecuting the
Iraqi communists and was consequently labeled fascist by the
Soviet press.

Then the situation changed again. The Baath fell in Iraq
(November 1963), and General Abdussalem Aref took power. Aref
disliked the communists and the Soviets, while Khrushchev, who
had met Aref at Aswan shortly after Aref had ordered the hanging
of two communists in Baghdad, called him "a goat" when talking
to Nasser.[30] In Syria the left Baath wing of Salah Jedid took
power in 1966. This Baath faction was influenced by Marxist
ideas and moved quite close to Moscow, but it was unstable. The
Soviets tried with some success to reconcile it and Nasser, and
at their insistence a defense agreement was signed between Syria
and Egypt in December 1966. The Soviets promised the Syrians at

that time to build their high dam on the Euphrates. The veteran
leader of Syrian communism, Khaled Bakdash, returned from exile.
But the Syrian leaders were not only militant socialists. They
came predominantly from the Alawite minority, which harbored a
deep resentment against the Sunni bourgeoisie of the cities who
had long kept the Alawite "rurals" under their thumb. They were
also fervent partisans of the Palestinian guerrillas and planned
to use Syria as the rear base for the "popular war" against
Israel which the Palestinians were to unleash by infiltrating
Israel via Jordan, Lebanon, and the Golan Heights (at that time
the Syrian province of Quneitra). As suggested above, it seems
probable that the desire to protect Damascus from Israeli
retaliation caused the Soviets to give the Egyptians false
information about Israeli troop concentrations on the Syrian
border and thus to encourage them to begin the chain of events
that led to the Six Day War.*

Finally, in November 1970, after the Six Day War, there was
a new shift in power in Damascus. Defense Minister Hafez al-Azad
took over as president, after having imprisoned the previous
party secretary, Salah Jedid, and the previous president, Nur
ad-Din al-Atassi. Many confrontations had already taken place
between Asad and the leftist Baath leaders. Their disputes had
turned principally on the question of responsibility for the
1967 defeat, but the problem of Soviet involvement in Syria also
had played a role. Asad had criticized the excessive reliance of
the leftist group on Moscow.

Asad himself, when in power, did not break with the Soviets.
He needed them for arms supplies, economic aid (the Euphrates
dam was under construction), and diplomatic support. However,
he did downgrade Soviet–Syrian relations somewhat, inter alia
by seizing the opportunity (in April 1971) to join a federation
with the anticommunist Qadhdhafi of Libya and the conservative
Sadat of Egypt.

----

* The Sixth National Convention of the Baath in 1963 called for
"recruiting Palestinian Arabs as the first weapon in the
liberation of Palestine" and the "establishment of a Palestine
Liberation Front," which "must be kept out of disputes among
the Arab states." See Kamel S. Abu Jaber, The Arab Baath
Socialist Party (Syracuse, N.Y.: Syracuse University Press,
1966), p. 164. The Eighth Congress (1965) spoke of a "people's
liberation war" as the "secure way for the return of the
Palestinians." See Horst Mahr, Die Baath Partei, Porträt einer

The final downfall of Jedid, Atassi, and their leftist friends
was the result of a gamble that failed. While in September 1970
the fighting between King Hussein's army in Jordan and the
fedayeen was in progress, the left-wing group sent 200 Syrian
tanks, disguised as Palestinian tanks, into Jordan to help the
fedayeen. They had come close to Irbid on September 22, but they
were forced to retreat by a combination of Jordanian resistance
and big-power maneuvering that made it clear to Damascus that
there would be no air cover available for the tanks in case
of likely Israeli military intervention, backed by the U.S.
Sixth Fleet. The Syrians had overstepped the limit to which the
Soviets were willing or able to protect their protégés; their
tanks brought them defeat, and the planners of the enterprise
lost their own positions in Syria shortly thereafter.

In the meantime the situation in Iraq was becoming once more
favorable to the Soviets. There the "national" (i.e., pan-Arab)
Baath took power by a coup in July 1968 and gradually moved
closer to the Soviet Union. The Iraqi Baathists were—and still
are—rivals and enemies of their Syrian neighbors.* At first
there were conflicts between the Baathists and communist
militants. But with the emergence of Saddam Hussein al-Takriti
as the Baathist leader and the strong man behind President
al-Bakr, a gradual rapprochement was achieved with the local
communists and the Soviet Union.

The Baath regime in Iraq was isolated. It took a critical
line toward Egypt and tried to outbid in militancy all other

----

panarabischen Bewegung (Munich: Beiheft 13 der Zweimonatsschrift
Politische Studien, Gunter Olzog Verlag, 1971), p. 159.

* The rivalry between the Iraqi Baathists and Syria goes back to
interparty struggles. The coup of February 1966 in Damascus
directed against the "national" Baath (Aflaq, Bitar, Amin
al-Hafez, Aissami, and others) was carried through by
"regionals," Salah Jedid and his friends, with the help of the
then air force commander Hafez al-Asad. The "nationals" lost
power in Damascus and never regained it. But a similar group of
"nationals" came to power in Baghdad as a result of the coup of
July 1968. Their party friends from Syria came to Baghdad and
formed there the national command (i.e., the pan-Arab
leadership) of the party. Those national Baath leaders who had
fled to Iraq (Hafez, Aflaq, Aissami) were condemned to death in
Damascus in absentia on August 3, 1971. The trial lasted ten
months; the 99 persons who were tried were accused of having
plotted against the Damascus regime.

Arabs, particularly its Syrian rival regime, which found itself
hemmed in by the lost war and the proximity of the Israelis. For
Baghdad, far away, it was much easier to play an extremist role.
But this posture was not appreciated by Nasser and his successor
or by Damascus.

Thus Baghdad moved toward the USSR in order to find at least
one friend. There were things the Iraqis could do for the
Russians. They could give them access to Iraqi oil, and they
could do what the Egyptians and the Syrians so far had refused
to do: grant a legal existence to the Communist party. They did
both.

The oil deal came first. On August 30, 1970, an executive
agreement was signed between Iraq and the Soviet Technoexport.
An agreement in principle had been reached previously, in 1969.
It concerned Rumailah North, an oilfield discovered by the
foreign-owned Iraqi Petroleum Company (IPC) but "nationalized"
by Qassem in 1961 along with other IPC concession areas where no
actual oil production was going on. Subsequently Rumailah North
had been the subject of many legal battles and attempts at
compromise. By the new agreement this oilfield, close to Basra,
was to be brought into production by the Iraqi National Oil
Company with the help of Soviet technicians and material. Moscow
was to be paid in crude oil. Later several more economic deals
were concluded by which the Russians were to be paid in "Iraqi
produce," which meant mainly crude oil.

A political deal was more difficult to achieve. The Iraqi
communists were deeply split. Moscow brought them into line, and
the Bakr regime managed to suppress the remaining dissidents.
The most spectacular of these had been Aziz al-Hadj, who in 1967
after a long career in the Soviet-sponsored peace campaign had
tried to start a "peasant revolt" in the swamps of the south. He
was captured and subsequently appeared on television in April
1969, declaring himself ready to join the Baath party. The
Kurdish question had to be solved as well, because many of the
Iraqi communists are Kurds, and the party had long called for
Kurdish autonomy. Finally, with Soviet help, in March 1970 an
agreement was reached with the Kurds providing "local autonomy"
for them. (It has as yet not been fully implemented.)

This political deal set the stage for a political
reorganization of the Iraqi regime, announced after long debate
on November 15, 1971. The CP, the KDP (the Kurdish Democratic
Party, dominated by Mullah Mustafa Barzani, the Kurdish leader),
and the Iraqi Baath were to form a National Front. This meant
that the communists and the Kurds would have legal parties, even
though the Baath would be dominant. The Baath reserved to itself

the indoctrination of the army and the domination of the
decision-making Revolutionary Council. Communists and Kurds were
admitted into the government.

To Moscow all this was important because it meant that for
the first time a "revolutionary" Arab regime had recognized the
communist party and shown itself ready to collaborate with it.
Moscow hoped by this arrangement to use the CP to influence and
steer the Baath "majority."[31]

The same arrangement, with slight variations reflecting the
local situation, was achieved in Syria in April 1972.[32] A
National Front was formed there also, led by the Syrian Baath,
with the communists, along with one "Nasserite" and two
"socialist" groups, as the junior members. Moscow had to work
hard to heal a CP split resulting from a rebellion of younger,
more nationalist (and anti-Israeli) party leaders against the
veteran Khaled Bakdash. In Syria also the CP was intended by
Moscow to become the channel through which the policies of the
Baath government were to be influenced and managed. Things did
not go too well at the beginning. One document containing a
Soviet critique of a draft political program of the Syrian CP
leaked out. It was published by a Beirut paper inimical to Asad
and caused a considerable stir among nationalist politicians, who
were shocked by the antiextremist Soviet views on such things as
the Palestinian question and the fedayeen movement.* An Egyptian
state party document made use of this critique to attack the
Soviet Union after the expulsion of the Soviet experts.[33]

In this context of the new National Fronts, it has to be kept

----

* Ar-Rayah, June 26, 1972. The document said, e.g., "Do not talk
of 'liquidating Israel,' only of 'struggling against Zionism.'
Not to 'ignore the Palestine cause' but also not to treat it as
'a primary issue.' Not 'too much emphasis on the armed struggle,'
to the exclusion of other solutions. 'Liquidating Zionist
institutions' means to liquidate Israel; we should either remain
silent or take a clear proletarian attitude. It is said that the
resistance movement is a movement of the masses; this is not
true. We either say that it should be a movement of the masses
or remain silent. Is it beneficial to say that everything is all
right? Isn't it better to work to transform the Palestinian
movement into a movement of the masses?" English text: Journal
of Palestine Studies, vol. 2, no. 1 (Autumn 1972), pp. 187-212.
Ar-Rayah expresses the opinions of the Jedid group of Baathists.

in mind that the Egyptian communists had joined Nasser's state
party (the ASU) "as individuals," after having "voluntarily"
dissolved their communist party. (Meanwhile, the Soviets were
supporting an exile Algerian communist party, the Socialist
Vanguard of Algeria, illegal inside the country.) Ever since
Khrushchev had agreed with Nasser to dissolve the Egyptian
Communist party and to allow communists to join the state
party, the other progressive Arab regimes on good terms with
Moscow had wanted a similar arrangement. But Moscow could not
grant it without endangering all communist parties in the
"national democracies" of the third world. The concession made
to Moscow by Baghdad and later by Damascus, to legalize their
CPs and accept their representatives in the government, was
therefore important, for it repaired the consequences of the
mistake committed by the "impetuous" Khrushchev in the case of
the Egyptians.*

The new National Front in Iraq published a political program,
one of whose main planks was "complete liberation of the
national oil resources from domination and exploitation by
foreign interests." Another point, for the future, was "to
fight against the attempts of imperialist circles and their
instrument, the Shah of Iran, to eliminate the Arab nature of
the Persian Gulf and to appropriate certain parts of it."

In fact, half a year after the political reorganization in
Iraq, which meant in fact a harmonization of interests between
the Baath regime and the Soviet Union, the IPC was nationalized
(June 3, 1972). Relations between the IPC and the governments
of Iraq had been strained since the time of Qassem, who in 1961
had unilaterally taken back 99 percent of the concessional area
of the company. The break came over a dispute about production
of the Kirkuk field. The IPC had reduced its output there
because, according to the company, a price differential
negotiated the year before made Kirkuk production too expensive
for the 1972 market. The price differential for so-called
Mediterranean oil (i.e., oil that does not have to travel around
Africa to reach the European market even when the Suez Canal is
closed) had become excessively large because freighter rates had

----

* The minority of Egyptian communists under Hussein Ara who
refused to dissolve their party were arrested and tried in Cairo
in 1965. The Soviets called them political adventurers corrupted
by Maoism. See Michel Salomon, _Méditerranée Rouge_ (Paris:
Laffont, 1970), p. 198.

gone down since the year before. Kirkuk oil was delivered to the
Mediterranean via the IPC pipeline to Baniyas (Syria) and
Tripoli (Lebanon). The Mediterranean differential had been
calculated on the basis of the earlier freight rates. Baghdad
did not want to give up or to reduce the differential. The
company refused to keep its production on the previous level or
to let the state buy, or produce itself, the difference in
amount, as Baghdad had proposed.

There is little doubt, however, that the dispute gave the
government a welcome occasion to nationalize the IPC, as it had
planned to do beforehand. Only the IPC at Kirkuk, not the
subsidiary companies at Basra and Mosul, was nationalized. This
meant that marketing the oil, now incumbent on the government,
would not be quite so difficult because of IPC opposition.
Shortly before nationalization was decreed, Saddam Hussein
at-Takriti had gone to Moscow (February 8, 1972), and a
fifteen-year treaty of permanent friendship and cooperation
between Iraq and the Soviet Union had been signed on April 9,
1972. It was closely modeled on the Soviet-Egyptian treaty of
May 27, 1971, and seems to have been Hussein's idea at least as
much as the Soviets'. Its main clause declares that both
countries denounce imperialism and colonialism in all their
manifestations and underline their determination to fight
against imperialism, Zionism, and the like. The treaty, like
its Egyptian model, provides for regular consultations and
"defense cooperation."

The nationalization of the IPC, seven days after the treaty
had been concluded, made clear that Hussein's policy had been to
give the Soviet Union a maximum of guarantees, and thus to
demonstrate the Iraqi will to collaborate in order to obtain
political and, if needed, economic backing by the Soviets at
the moment of nationalization. Soviet political backing was
forthcoming immediately in a _Pravda_ article praising this
"important blow against the monopolies."[34] Immediately before
nationalization, Iraqi Foreign Minister Abdel Baqi had arrived
in Moscow and was received at the airport by the Soviet
minister of petroleum production. But as of early 1974 the
Soviet Union has not done much more to aid Iraq than to permit
some of its satellites to buy Iraqi oil.

The Soviets like to make barter deals with Iraq, trading
Soviet technical exports and services for Iraqi crude oil. One
example is an agreement made in the summer of 1971, consisting
of a Soviet credit of 200 million rubles for building a
refinery at Mosul, a pipeline between Basra and Baghdad, and
two generating plants, all to be paid in "Iraqi produce," i.e.,

crude oil. Iraq has a great deal of crude oil in its possession.
The nationalized IPC at Kirkuk produced about 55 million tons in
1971 (and its two subsidiary companies, not yet nationalized,
another 30 million). Rumailah North produced, with Soviet aid,
about 18 million tons in 1972. Of this the Soviets took one
million tons and, in 1973 and afterward, two million tons.

The French IPC partner, CFP, has been granted special
treatment by Iraq because of the French political attitude
toward Israel. CFP agreed to buy 15 million tons of oil a
year for ten years, at a price considered too high by
international standards. The Mediterranean differential, at
which the IPC had balked, was maintained. But even this
agreement left Iraq with over 50 million tons to be sold, in the
face of opposition by the international companies, which
threatened legal action if sales were made before an agreement
about compensation was reached (as it later was). Sales
contracts were concluded with Balkan countries and with Italy,
Spain, Brazil, East Germany, and others. Baghdad maintains that
it need sell only about 30 million tons to make a profit,
because after nationalization the previous profits of the
company fall to Iraq. But the prices of oil sold so far have
been kept secret. There has been an added complication about the
IPC pipeline. Baghdad asked Damascus to nationalize the Syrian
stretch of it and Damascus complied, but shortly afterward a
quarrel broke out about transit dues. Iraq maintained that the
Syrians wanted to double them, while the Syrians said that they
were asking only for what was their due.[*] Lebanon, where one of
the pipeline terminals is situated, refused to nationalize its
part of the line and the Tripoli terminal, leaving only the
Syrian branch of the terminal at Baniyas working. A legal
formula to keep the Tripoli branch in business will have to be
worked out. The total capacity of the Lebanese line is about 55
million tons.

The Organization of Petroleum Exporting Countries (OPEC),
which has followed a policy of keeping oil prices high, is

----

[*] The dispute with Syria was settled in January 1973. Syria
obtained an increase in transit fees from 340 to 600 million
Syrian pounds. See an-Nahar, Jan. 20, 1973. A solution of the
conflict with IPC was announced on February 28, 1973. The BBC
stated that IPC had agreed to pay all outstanding Iraqi claims
and was to be compensated with 15 million tons of crude oil.

somewhat disturbed by the possibility that the Iraqi oil might
be dumped on the market, either directly or indirectly via
Moscow (if the Soviets would buy Iraqi oil and sell their own,
say, in Europe) and thus lower prices.[35] Nevertheless, the Arab
OPEC (OAPEC) approved the Iraqi nationalization and even granted
Iraq a three-month emergency credit of £53.9 million (and £6.8
million to Syria) in order to tide those countries over any
emergency caused by the nationalization. But this action does
not preclude the possibility that certain OPEC members, such as
Iran and Saudi Arabia, would be willing to increase their
international convertible currency reserves at the expense of
Iraq. By encouraging the Iraqi nationalization, the Soviets
created a difficult dilemma for the West. If the oil companies
were to punish Iraq by boycotting its nationalized oil, they
would risk driving the country into economic dependence on the
Soviet Union. Iraqi sources have maintained that the Soviets
hinted at the possibility of taking Iraqi oil and, making an
exception in this case, paying for part of it (perhaps 50
percent) in hard currencies. This has not happened so far, and
it would probably occur only for a short period in an emergency.
And even then the other half of the payment would have to be
taken in Soviet goods and services. In the past, oil income in
Iraq (1971: £370 million; 1970: £210 million) has provided 52
percent of the state budget and 71 percent of the development
budget. Oil exports have represented 83 percent of all Iraqi
exports. The dependence of the country on its oil exports needs
no further elucidation.

If, on the other hand, the oil companies did not react
against the nationalization, they would be virtually asking to
be nationalized in the rest of the Arab world. Moscow probably
counts on the rapaciousness of the oil monopolies to drive Iraq
wholly, or at least a good deal of the way, into the Soviet
economic embrace.

Saddan Hussein al-Takriti, who is no doubt the architect of
the Iraqi oil policy, would perhaps not mind too much being
embraced by the Soviets, even though it is clear that he counts
on the French to keep at least one Western door open as well. He
visited Paris in June 1972, shortly after the nationalization
and made it very clear that Iraq was willing to offer special
treatment to France. He wanted the French, he said, not only as
economic partners but as allies.

Hussein's oil policy is primarily based on political, not on
economic, motives. He wants his country to demonstrate to the
Arab world how oil can be used as a political weapon. If the
others would follow his lead, countries having good relations

with Israel could be starved of oil. They would have to import
it via the USSR or via France at a price differential as
prohibitive as possible, while countries hostile to Israel could
be "associated" with the Arab producers in the oil business.

Hussein is certainly not so naive as to believe that the
other oil producers will automatically follow his lead. But he
probably calculates that the example he is trying to set will
eventually influence the Arab military in places such as Saudi
Arabia and the Gulf states, so as to bring about coups and
changes of regime. He is not in any hurry. One should not forget
that the Baath has pan-Arab ambitions. The Iraqi Baath is
protecting and maintaining the "historical" founders of the
party, Aflaq, Aissami, Amin al-Hafez, and others in Baghdad,
where they form the "national" leadership.[36] Today the Iraqi
Baath is internationally isolated. But Hussein calculates, no
doubt, that many a regime closer to the Israeli frontiers will
come to grief sooner or later, and he believes that at the end
he and his policies will prevail.* His calculations might come
true if there is no peace with Israel, as seems probable, if
Arab bitterness continues to rise, and if the present regime in
Iraq manages to survive.

In many respects Qadhdhafi is in a position parallel to that
of Saddam Hussein. He is waiting on the political right and
geographic western wing of the Arab core region, just as Saddam
waits on the left and in the Arab east, for the succession to
Arab leadership after the central leaders, King Hussein, Sadat,
Asad, and others, fail. The Libyan leader has repeatedly shown
that he is aware of his competitor on the eastern fringe, by

---

* During the short-lived left-wing coup in the Sudan in July 1971
the Iraqis were the first to ask Khartoum to accept a
congratulatory delegation from Baghdad. But the Hashem al-'Ata'
regime delayed their arrival because it wanted first to receive
the Egyptian delegation sent by Sadat. This was on July 19; the
Iraqis were given permission to come on July 22, after the two
Egyptian scouts sent by Sadat had been there. But their airplane
crashed over Saudi Arabia, and some party dignataries were killed.
The episode showed the urgency Baghdad felt to get back in step
with some Arab regime. In 1969, when Qadhdhafi took over in Libya,
there had been similar attempts by Baghdad to get "in" first. Cf.
Fuad Matar, The Communist Party in the Sudan: Did They Kill It or
Did It Commit Suicide? [al-hizb ash-Shiyu'i as Sudani naharuh am
intahar] (Beirut: Dar an-Nahar li-n-nashr, 1971), pp. 65ff.

publicly criticizing the Iraqi policies of "voluntary
dependence" on the Soviets.

The USSR and Egypt after Nasser. After the death of Nasser Egypt
was still the major channel of Soviet influence in the Arab
world and the country in which Soviet investment was by far the
heaviest. A Soviet delegation headed by Premier Kosygin hurried
to Cairo as soon as Nasser died.[37] Moscow must have known all
about Nasser's illness, since Soviet doctors had treated him,
but his death seems to have come sooner than they had foreseen.
Before conferring with Sadat, whom Nasser, shortly before his
death, had named the only first vice-president, and with the
full leadership, Kosygin met with Sami Sharaf, Sha'rawi Gum'a,
and Ali Sabri. Sami Sharaf had been the chief of the services of
the presidency, supervising as such Nasser's own intelligence
services. He was thus the chief depository of Nasser's secrets.
Gum'a was minister of the interior and thus chief of all
civilian police. Ali Sabri was at the time a marshal in the air
force and the chief Egyptian partner of the Soviet air force
specialists who collaborated in the Egyptian war effort. But his
political importance came perhaps more from the fact that in
previous years (before Nasser had decided in August 1969 to
discredit him, ostensibly over a customs affair, and to
downgrade his position)[38] he had built up the apparatus of the
state party, the ASU. Many of its leaders and permanent
functionaries were his clients and political creatures.
    The Soviet-Egyptian talks were secret, but journalists
learned that Kosygin asked everyone he met, "What are you going
to do now?"[39] He is said to have expressed the Soviet desire
that Nasser's political line continue and that his successor not
be someone of the political right who might compromise the
socialist achievements of Egypt.
    This expression was generally interpreted as a Soviet veto
against Abdel Latif al-Baghdadi and Zakhariya Muhieddin, the two
most outstanding remaining Free Officers, old companions of
Nasser who had been forced out of political life by him years
before. But Sadat thought that the Soviets could be alluding to
himself, chiefly because he had heard talk that Moscow would not
like as chief of the socialist state a personality who had been
in the past secretary-general of an Islamic congress. Sadat was
made provisional president by the chief dignitaries of the
Nasser regime. The formal reason was that Nasser himself had
appointed Sadat first vice-president and had thus singled him
out as his successor. But politically, probably the fact that
Sadat was a neutral and not a strong candidate was of greater

importance. Sadat did not possess a great deal of personal
prestige and had no personal power base. The leading Nasserites
seem to have thought that he would be a president under whom
they would continue to wield power—it was fashionable at the
time to speak of a troika that would lead Egypt—and that
perhaps eventually one of them would emerge as the absolute
ruler.

Vinogradov then became Soviet ambassador to Cairo, and Sadat
clashed with him from the beginning. The Lebanese journalist
Fuad Matar, who carefully collected all the revealing Cairo
rumors and political gossip, tells us that after the presentation
of his credentials the Soviet ambassador told some of the
Egyptian communists that he was surprised to hear Sadat speak of
"my people" instead of "the people of Egypt" or "of the UAR" (as
Egypt was still called officially). In fact, Sadat had said, "I
assure you, in the name of my people, that we will never forget
the noble stance of the Soviet Union at our side." Vinogradov
liked to walk around in the populous old quarters of Cairo,
a habit that intrigued and troubled the Egyptians, the more so
because, as some communists commented, "He wants to come to know
the dark sides of Egypt as well, not only the clean parts."

The Soviet ambassador's criticism of the Egyptian press, in
an interview in Rose al-Yusef, was also criticized. When in this
interview he spoke of "true Arab unity," Egyptians asked, "What
would the Russians say if our ambassador gave advice to the
USSR?" Vinogradov also told some journalists that the war must
be "really prepared" and that the domestic front seemed not to
be ready in some respects.

Ponomarev, the Soviet Central Committee specialist on
nonruling communist parties, was even more disliked by Sadat.
He repeatedly spoke of religion, which he thought stood in the
way of Egypt's progress. At a seminar at the official Cairo
newspaper al-Ahram on January 5, 1970, Soviet writers and
political scientists spoke of the shortcomings of Egypt as
they saw them. Matar gives a long list of Soviet assertions and
complaints: the public sector is weak and disorganized; in
agriculture the private sector is still predominant; foreign
capital still plays a role; socialism is not studied in the
schools and is even attacked; socialism is not taught in the
army; there is too much illiteracy; Arab writers misunderstand
the USSR entirely; religion and socialism do not clash, and it
is capitalist propaganda to say they do; patience is needed to
cope with the present situation, and impatience with "neither
peace nor war" will not help; Soviet Jews dislike Zionism and
only a very few want to go to Israel; the Soviets are not

against Arab unity, but they question whether or not an Arab
nation exists; the USSR helps the Palestinians but they ought to
unite; Vietnam succeeded against colonialism because there was a
profound social and economic transformation there.[40]

The Soviets also considered the "war of attrition" not to be
to Egypt's advantage as long as it was fought on Egyptian
territory, and not in the Sinai or in Israel. The most important
subject of controversy was arms. According to the Soviets, what
the Egyptians needed were not so much new and better arms but
rather the creation of a society ready for war on the civilian
as well as on the military side. Instead, they said, the
Egyptians wanted all the modern arms that they had ever heard
mentioned or that the Israelis had obtained from the Americans.
They had, indeed, gone so far as to ask for the MIG 25, which
was still on the drawing board.

The Egyptians, they continued, envisaged the future war with
Israel as a long-drawn-out affair in which their numerical
superiority could eventually be brought to bear. But the Soviets
assumed that such a war would never occur; rather, there would
be quick raids and sudden strikes by the Israelis. From the
very beginning the Soviets saw their role as a political one.
Nasser had called them in to impress the Americans by their
presence in Egypt. They had agreed to play this role because of
the political gains it could bring them. Consequently, the
Egyptians felt, the Soviet specialists were training the
Egyptians for a war that the Soviets believed would not take
place. There was no common goal such as had existed when the
High Dam was built.

One of the early instances of a significant Soviet-Egyptian
friction occurred when Sadat, in a speech at Tanta on January 4,
1971, said that Nasser had brought the Soviets to Egypt because
the Egyptian soldiers would have needed eight months to learn
how to handle the SAM 3 missiles and there had been no time for
that. Six Soviets, he added, had lost their lives at Dahshur in
the service of Egypt. This mention of the six Soviet soldiers
killed in Egypt, presumably while the missiles were being
installed, had to be eliminated from a second version of the
speech put out by the official Egyptian news agency MENA. Matar
concludes that this revised version was issued after an
intervention by the Soviet ambassador, who reacted quickly to
Sadat's attempt to depict the Soviets as militarily involved.

On December 20, Ali Sabri was received in Moscow with very
great honors, and the three principal Soviet leaders
participated in all discussions with him and his delegation.
This warm welcome made Sadat suspicious.[41] When on February 13,

1971, Soviet chief of state Podgorny came to inaugurate the High
Dam, Sadat was disappointed, for he had wanted Brezhnev. At the
dam site a stone was unveiled; the inscription mentioned Nasser
and Sadat but no Soviets. The visit of a Soviet destroyer,
announced previously, did not take place. And in a speech in
Podgorny's presence, Sadat said that the battle was essentially
a struggle for the liberation of the "national will" of the
Egyptians.

On February 5 the six-month Israeli-Egyptian armistice
accepted by Nasser (as outlined in the Rogers plan) was due to
expire. After warlike declarations by several Egyptian
dignitaries, Sadat decided to prolong the armistice for another
month. At the same time he proposed a "partial solution" that
would open the canal, but only on the condition that this move
would be considered a first step toward a total evacuation of
the occupied territories. An interview Sadat granted to
Newsweek indicated the full extent of the concessions he was
willing to make.[42] Before the month's prolongation had expired,
Sadat decided to make a secret trip to Moscow (March 1, 1971).
He told about it on Egyptian television on March 7, saying that
political efforts toward settlement would go on, even though the
armistice had ended. Later it became known that he had talked
for nine hours in Moscow without any results.[43]

Shortly after this the Ali Sabri affair broke. It was
basically internal in character: it can best be seen as the
liquidation of Abdel Nasser's establishment in favor of Sadat's.
The Soviets were indirectly implicated because they wanted to
preserve Nasser's political line and because Ali Sabri had been
more in their confidence than Nasser himself.*

The affair began with an attempt by Ali Sabri to stir up
criticism against the proposal by Sadat, Qadhdhafi, and Asad to
federate their countries. He attacked the project in the ASU
executive committee. Sadat convened the Central Committee and
attacked Ali Sabri on April 25. Sadat felt forced to revise the
federation project in one important respect: decisions of the
proposed High Presidential Council composed of the three
presidents would be binding only if unanimous and not, as

---

* The Soviets relied on Ali Sabri because his dislike of the
U.S. was public knowledge in Egypt. This antagonism seems to have
gone back to Secretary of State Dulles's time, when Ali Sabri was
involved in the arms negotiations in Washington.

planned and already published, if approved only by a majority.
Sabri argued, correctly, that if the latter were the case, the
two smaller states, Libya and Syria, could force Egypt to accept
decisions against its will. In a second Central Committee
session on April 29, the revised project was unanimously
accepted. Sadat dismissed Ali Sabri on May 2 after declaring in
a public speech on May 1 that he would not tolerate any "centers
of power."[44]

The arrival in Egypt of U.S. Secretary of State Rogers three
days later produced speculation that Sabri had been "sacrificed"
to Rogers. But the two events were not directly connected, as
the continuation of the Sabri affair demonstrated. On May 13
Sadat suddenly dismissed Interior Minister Sha'rawi Gum'a. The
reason (not published at the time) seems to have been that the
organizational committee of the ASU, of which Gum'a was
chairman, had printed and prepared for distribution a report
that criticized Sadat's method of dismissing Ali Sabri. Shortly
after the dismissal of Gum'a was announced, Cairo Radio
announced on its late evening newscast that five ministers and
three members of the ASU executive committee had resigned. Sadat
either had not been told of these resignations in advance or,
according to another version, had been told only minutes before
the news was broadcast. Those who resigned included Sharaf, the
minister of state; Fawzi, the war minister and army commander;
Faiq, the information minister; and Zayed and Sa'id, ministers
of housing and electricity. The three resigning members of the
ASU executive committee were Abu Nur, Shuqair, and Daoud. Sadat,
surprised by their move, took it as a threat to his own position.
Reacting quickly, he named a new minister of war and army
commander, General Muhammed Sadek, who had been chief of staff
and an interim information minister. During the night about
fifty arrests were made. There was no public reaction. On May 11
and 12, 1971, Sadat held conferences with the officers at army
headquarters at Cairo and at Inshass, an air force base, and
gained their confidence. General Sadek, still chief of staff,
was with him and must have been instrumental in arranging the
meetings. It seems that in these discussions General Fawzi was
accused by Sadat of disloyalty. In any case, the direct contacts
between Sadat and the officers deprived Fawzi of his power to
act. Presumably the various police organizations still in the
hands of the dissident ministers dared do nothing when they saw
that the army supported Sadat.

An official accusation was leveled against the dissidents,
stating that Ali Sabri and his associates had planned a coup
against Sadat. Sabri and his supporters were later tried and

received long prison sentences, but the alleged coup was not
proved to everyone's satisfaction.[45] It is certain, however,
that there had been discontent among the principal lieutenants
of the Nasser regime, such as Sabri, Gum'a, Sharaf, and Fawzi.[46]
At the very least they had expected to participate collectively
in the direction of the country. But Sadat saw himself as the
president, wielding near-absolute power just as Nasser had.

The visit of Rogers intervened between the two acts of the
Ali Sabri affair, the dismissal of Sabri and that of Gum'a. It
brought no permanent results. Sadat was ready to fulfill UN
Security Council Resolution 242, at least according to the Arab
interpretation of that ambiguous document, negotiating peace
with Israel in return for the evacuation of all occupied
territories and recognition of the rights of the Palestinians.
According to Sadat, Rogers told him that there was nothing else
that he was expected to do and that he would soon hear from the
Americans. But he never heard.[47] Later, Sadat clearly came to
believe that he had been taken in by U.S. diplomacy. He
suspected that Rogers's aim had been to prolong the cease-fire
and at the same time to block any outcome contrary to Israel's
wishes. He was therefore bitter.

The Ali Sabri affair and the Rogers visit made Moscow feel
less secure than ever with its new partner, Sadat, who, the
Soviets feared, would sell them out to the Americans. This was
why Podgorny was again sent to Cairo, this time to obtain a
written treaty. He arrived on May 25, 1971, and immediately
started negotiations. He is said to have told Sadat that Nasser
had repeatedly offered the Soviets a treaty but they had refused.
Now, however, the treaty had become indispensable.[48] Sadat was
surprised but signed a treaty on the evening of May 27. The
negotiations were so brief that it seems probable that Podgorny
had brought a draft of the treaty with him. When the signing was
announced, Egypt, both military and civilian, was reportedly in
a state of "depression and sorrow" (hâlat wujûn).[49] In a later
speech on June 2, Sadat managed to justify the treaty, telling
the Egyptians that Egypt had wanted the treaty and pointing to
paragraph 8 ("please consider carefully every expression and
each point"), which spoke of military cooperation in training
and arms deliveries. Sadat added that the treaty had been made
because war (the Egyptians always use the term ma'raka—the
battle) was inevitable.

But in fact it was clear that the Soviets had wanted the
treaty more than the Egyptians did. They cannot have believed
that the Egyptians would feel especially bound just because they
had signed a piece of paper. But the treaty gave the Soviets the

right to ask for consultations with the Egyptians every time they saw peace endangered and on all other issues that mattered to the two countries (section 7). It also obliged both Egypt and the USSR not to enter into any alliance directed against the other or contrary to the other's interests (sections 9 and 10).

Probably the effect that the treaty would have on the U.S., on the world at large, and perhaps even on China was as important to the Soviets as its possible influence on the Egyptians. It served to emphasize to the U.S. and all other countries that the USSR was rightfully in the Nile valley. The Egyptians themselves certified this right by the treaty. It could thus be used as a possible bargaining counter in negotiations with Washington.

But perhaps the Soviets underestimated how ugly the word treaty sounded to the Egyptians and the Arabs in general. As a result of the later phases of colonial history, the word still means to most Arabs an unequal treaty that they are forced to conclude, rather than an undertaking that they enter into in their own interest. Nasser's fight against the Baghdad Pact had been over the same question. But the Soviets had to make their own mistakes.

Sudanese Intermezzo. The next major development affecting Egyptian-Soviet relations was the coup of Hashem al-'Ata' in the Sudan on July 19, 1971, and the countercoup four days later, which brought Nimeiry back to power. This coup was so closely associated with the communists that, had it succeeded, it would have meant a virtual communist government in the Sudan. Nimeiry's government itself had been considerably to the left of Sadat's. But now, if the coup's leaders had remained in power, Sadat would have had a communist neighbor in one of the two countries bordering on Egypt. The Soviets immediately insisted that Sadat recognize the new regime. He temporized, saying that he was not sure that the revolutionaries were firmly established and that he would not hesitate to recognize them as soon as he had convinced himself of their staying power. He even sent two Egyptian "Marxists" (as the communists preferred to be called) Ahmed Hamrush and Ahmed Fuad, on a fact-finding mission to Khartoum. Ponamorev, who happened to be in Cairo at the time conducting conversations with the ASU and celebrating the anniversary of the July 23 revolution, felt that the new regime in Khartoum would gain stability if Sadat would recognize it. Sadat, however, held to the position that he would recognize it only if it appeared to be permanent.

In the meantime Sadat and Qadhdhafi collaborated with Nimeiry's defense minister, Hassan Khaled Abbas, who had been in Yugoslavia during the coup, to bring down the new left-wing

regime. Abbas came to Cairo in a private plane. He conferred
with Sadek, the Egyptian war minister, and then went on to
Tripoli. From there he called on the Sudanese by Libyan radio to
rise against the coup. The countercoup took place on July 23,
executed by tanks that appear to have come from the officers'
academy established by the Egyptians at Jebel al-Awliya near
Khartoum. Some sources affirmed that the tanks were driven by
Egyptian officers.[50] Another story was that a part of the
Sudanese brigade stationed on the Suez Canal was flown to
Khartoum. These troops seem in fact to have been moved, but it
was tanks, not infantry, which liquidated the coup of al-'Ata'.

After the return of Nimeiry to power, a hunt for communists
started in the Sudan. The Soviets asked Sadat to intervene to
save the life of the leader of the Sudanese communists, Abdel
Khaleq Mahjub, and his associates. Sadat is said to have
telephoned Nimeiry, and the Soviets are credited with having
obtained a recording of their radio-telephone conversation. In
it, according to the story, Sadat told Nimeiry simply that he
was under pressure by the Soviets to save the life of the
ringleaders and other communists. This information served, of
course, only to accelerate their execution.[51] Mahjub and other
civilians, including Shafi' Ahmed ash-Shaikh, a union leader,
and Joseph Gareng, the previous minister for the South, were
hanged. The military responsible for the coup were shot, as
were Babakr an-Nur and Faruq Hamad Allah. These last two had
previously been dismissed from Nimeiry's officers' junta, were
in London at the time of the coup, and then tried to return by
BOAC to Khartoum. Their plane was forced down on Qadhdhafi's
orders at Benghazi on July 22; they were taken prisoner and
handed over to Nimeiry by way of Egypt.

A fuller account of the coup in Khartoum goes as follows:
Nimeiry had come to power on May 25, 1969, by a coup. He stood
at the head of a coalition of nationalist and leftist officers.
Some of the leftists were declared communists, others were
secret ones. Following Nimeiry's coup the Sudanese communists
split. One group, the "May people," stayed with Nimeiry in the
government and in the revolutionary council. The best known of
these were Faruq Abu Issa, Mu'awiya Ibrahim, Ahmed Suleiman,
and Joseph Gareng, all of whom became ministers. All four publicly
opposed the other group, led by the CP general secretary, Abdel
Khaleq Mahjub. But after the July 1971 coup it came to light
that Gareng maintained secret contacts with the Mahjub
communists and had kept them informed of happenings in the
revolutionary junta and in the government. He was hanged for his
"treachery."

The 1969 split among the communists was over the issue of
participation in the Nimeiry government. At first Nimeiry, then
modeling his policies on those of Nasser, tried to make the
Sudanese communists do what Nasser had forced those in Egypt to
do, to dissolve their party and join the regime. Mahjub had
refused, pointing out that the Sudanese party was much better
organized and more numerous than were the Egyptian communists.[52]
He maintained that Nimeiry's regime was not a revolution and not
a mass movement. The other faction, the May people, used the new
doctrine of the "democractic road to socialism" to justify
participation in the regime of Nimeiry.

Three important members of Nimeiry's revolutionary council
who had kept up relations with the Mahjub communist group,
Babakr an-Nur, Faruq Hamad Allah, and Hashem al-'Ata', were
dismissed by Nimeiry on November 16, 1970. With them about
thirteen active officers were also purged from the army. All of
Khartoum knew that Nimeiry had got rid of them because of their
links with the communists.

But there were other communist officers whose links with the
CP were not known. The most important of these was Othman al-Haj
Hussein. He was very close to Nimeiry and managed to become the
commander of the "palace guard," which included tank units and
was in charge of the security of the revolutionary council.

Mahjub, the communist leader, was arrested when his friends
were dismissed from the revolutionary command council and was
imprisoned in a military camp. But he escaped on June 20, 1971,
and the security forces searched for him frantically and
unsuccessfully for 19 days. All during this time he was hidden
on the grounds of the "palace" itself (the former British
residency) as a guest of the guard commander, Hussein.

On July 19 the coup occurred. Nimeiry and the other
principal members of his revolutionary command council were
taken prisoner by soldiers of the guard. Khartoum Radio was
occupied. The parachutists and tank forces stationed in Khartoum
surrendered, through the efforts of officers who belonged to the
conspiracy. But in retrospect, it is clear that the communist
officers were much too confident of their popularity and mass
support. They openly declared that they were communist or
procommunist. Hashem al-'Ata' was to become president, and
Babakr an-Nur, at the time absent in London, was to become prime
minister. The conspirators were surprised that only the
communists and a few communist-led trade unions came into the
streets to demonstrate in their favor. If they had judged their
own popularity realistically they would have concealed their
communist ties until they had consolidated their power. But they

had obviously come to believe their own propaganda, which had so
often called the communists the party of the masses of the
people.

As mentioned earlier, the military force that gave the
countercoup its power probably came from the Jebel al-Awliya.
This military academy had been established by the Egyptians
after the Six-Day War, in order to have a military training
ground beyond the reach of the Israeli air force of that period.
The officers there—all the instructors were Egyptian—could
have received their orders directly from Cairo. In a speech made
shortly after the July events in the Sudan, Sadat did not
conceal the fact that Egypt and Libya had intervened. He said
that the federation "had been born with teeth." But how exactly
the intervention had come about will be difficult to discover,
for since then relations between Egypt and the Sudan have
deteriorated sharply, and both countries have at present an
interest in remaining vague about the intervention that saved
Nimeiry in 1971.

The coup made Nimeiry aware of the dangers of associating too
closely with the communists. Clearly the coup would not have
been possible if the Nimeiry regime had not begun as an intimate
and unsuspecting mixture of nationalists, left-wingers, fellow-
travelers, and hard-core communists. This mixture gave the
communists their chance to infiltrate the army, the ministry of
the interior, the security services, and so on. Only some of
the infiltrators were known communists; others, officers, had
kept their political allegiance hidden. Hamad Allah, one of the
expelled Revolutionary Command Council (RCC) members and one of
the leaders of the putsch, had previously been minister of the
interior.

Such political innocence ended with the coup. Nimeiry
selected new associates. He gradually got rid of not only the
communists and the leftists but also the pro-Egyptian and pro-
Arab nationalists, such as the defense minister, Khaled Abbas,
who had been instrumental in liquidating the coup. Under the
influence of the new foreign minister, Mansur Khaled, an
African policy was begun. Before, there had been only an Arab
one. The African policy was designed to lead to reconciliation
with the southern rebels, and it did so. Thus the Sudan's
greatest problem, which had plagued it since before
independence, was at least provisionally solved.

Growing Egyptian Difficulties with the USSR. After the events in
the Sudan, relations between Egypt and the Soviet Union became
distinctly cool. The Soviets started a campaign of recrimination

after the executions at Khartoum. The executive committee of the
general union of Egyptian workers, an Egyptian state institution,
declared itself shocked by the "bloody events in fraternal Sudan."
TASS promptly picked up the statement. At the same time (August
2, 1971), a communiqué of a meeting of communist party chiefs in
the Crimea spoke of their "deep concern about the terror used
against the Sudanese CP and other democratic institutions."
Sadat reacted by having the program of Cairo Radio interrupted
to announce the opposition of Egypt "to all kinds of interference
in the interior affairs of fraternal Sudan." He also ordered the
arrest of Ibrahim Saad and house arrest for Khaled Muhieddin,
both well-known Egyptian Marxists, because he suspected that
they were behind the communiqué of the Egyptian trade-union
organization.[53]

A new Egyptian visit to Moscow, on October 11-13, 1971,
exhibited signs of outward cordiality; Sadek and Soviet Defense
Minister Marshal Grechko embraced. The conversations lasted
much longer than had been planned, and there was apparently some
kind of reconciliation. The joint statement mentioned for the
first time that both countries condemned anticommunism and it
spoke of Egypt's will to build a new life on the basis of
socialism and to take advantage of the rich experience of the
Soviet Union and the other socialist countries.[54]

The rejection of anticommunism angered Nimeiry, but probably
these concessions were made by Sadat in exchange for promises
of more Soviet arms. However, as Sadat explained later, the
Soviet promises were not fulfilled. Sadat was thus in a
difficult position because he had promised on July 9, 1971, and
later repeated many times that 1971 would be the "year of
decision" (i.e., of decisive action against Israel). Now that
the year was approaching its end, there was no decision.
Retrospectively, and in view of subsequent explanations, it
seems probable that this promise had originally been made
because of secret American promises or encouragement that "soon"
there would be an American political initiative along the lines
of the Rogers plan. But this initiative failed to materialize.

In October Sadat felt forced to turn back to the Soviets. He
probably explained his predicament to them and obtained
promises of "offensive weapons." But still the arms did not
arrive. As the end of the year approached, Moscow used the war
on the Indian subcontinent as an excuse, declaring that the
offensive weapons destined for Egypt had to be sent to India
instead. It even seems that an airlift from the USSR to India
used airports in Upper Egypt for refueling. Some Egyptian
airports were under exclusive Soviet control; more specifically,

it was reported that there were "six airbases and four ports in
varying degrees under Soviet control, operated by 10,000 to
15,000 men."[55] The Egyptians were deeply disturbed that the
Indian war seemed to take precedence in Moscow over theirs. The
added complication that their closest Arab ally, Qadhdhafi,
sided passionately with the Pakistanis (principally because of
Muslim solidarity), while the Indians obtained part of "their"
arms via Egypt, increased Egyptian concern.

On January 13, 1972, Sadat felt forced to explain to the
Egyptians why he had not kept his often-repeated promise. This
was his famous "fog" speech, so named because of its references
to both figurative and literal fogs—and perhaps because of the
fogginess of its reasoning. Sadat said that on July 9, 1967, an
Israeli armored brigade moved to cross the canal. The Egyptian
command decided to resist them. Egyptian bombers were in the air
for two hours, but thick fog covered the area. The command
communicated with Nasser, who took it on himself to stop the
operation. He thought that the Israeli brigade came only to
reinforce their positions on the canal bank, while the army
command feared that they would cross. Then Sadat continued:

"In the last days of November 1971 the situation was exactly the
same. In October 1971 I convoked the highest council of the
armed forces. After studying the military and the political
situations it was decided to act before the end of 1971. October
went by and everything functioned according to plan. In the
first days of December the armed forces were waiting for the
signal to start. But there was a fog, because a fight developed
between two friendly countries, India and Pakistan. This
occupied the attention of the whole world and developed into a
struggle between the big powers. [Egypt did not want to get
involved] so that at the last moment I said to Marshal Sadek:
Wait, we have to revise our calculations!"

Sadat clarified his point only after his expulsion of the
Soviet advisers. He said that the Soviets had agreed with him on
a fixed time schedule for handing over the arms, but they did not
keep their promises, even though they had a second copy of the
schedule with them. "So I was forced to talk of the fog and to
take everything on myself."[56]

The fog speech caused student riots in Cairo that began on
January 19, 1972. The students assembled at first in the main
hall of the University of Cairo, called Abdel Nasser Hall. They
wanted answers to the following questions: How can it be said
that we were about to start a war in December, but the interior

front was not ready? What is the meaning of the excuse called
"fog"? Although there is information among the students that
Soviet aid is limited at this time, you (Sadat and the
government) say that there are conversations at a high level—
what are those conversations? If the U.S. is our enemy, why were
no decisions taken to damage their interests in Egypt and in the
Arab world?[57] The students also presented a list of 15 demands of
a more extremist nature. It began, "Rejecting a political
solution of the Middle East crisis and annulling the acceptance
by Egypt of the Security Council resolution of November 22, 1967"
and went on to demand, "rejection of the Rogers plan and
annullment of the Egyptian initiative to reopen the Suez Canal."

On January 24 the students occupied Midan at-Tahrir, the main
square of Cairo. Police armed with sticks and tear-gas grenades
tried to dislodge them several times, but in vain. One of the
reasons the students gave for their action was that the press,
radio, and television had nearly ignored their movement. The
following day (January 25) Sadat declared that the old political
parties and foreigners had been stirring up the students. The
same day a three-week university vacation began.

A new Egyptian trip to Moscow was planned for February 2.
Sadat prepared the way for it by telling soldiers and officers
whom he visited shortly before at Aswan that he would decide
"zero hour" after his return from Moscow. He went without any
military staff. This meant that he would not ask for new arms
but would rather insist on the fulfillment of his old demands.
When Sadat came back, al-Ahram wrote that the visit had been a
great success. But there was no more talk of "zero hour."

A national ASU congress was held February 16–18. Sadat made a
speech and answered questions. By the end it had become clear
that the Soviets had not given their approval to beginning the
war.[58] After the explanations to the Egyptians there were
explanations to the West, again via Newsweek. This time Sadat
even said that Egypt would go to the negotiating table if UN
mediator Jarring thought it possible to bring about the
fulfillment of the UN resolution. But Israel would first have to
answer Jarring's letter of February 8, 1971, about evacuating
the occupied territories. In the Egyptian press, however, this
point was obscured.

There was a new, initially secret Egyptian visit to Moscow on April
27, preceded by a new series of warlike speeches. Sadat also
promised on April 25, the Prophet's birthday, that by the next
Prophet's birthday, in 1973, a "decisive victory" would be
achieved. But Brezhnev was sick, and the visit was short. It
became clear later that above all Sadat wanted assurances from

the Soviets that they would not come to an agreement on the
Middle East with the U.S. over his head.[59] The future Nixon-
Brezhnev summit (scheduled for May 1972) was on his mind.
Although the visit was short, it was apparently friendly. A
statement was published at its conclusion which said for the
first time that Egypt had "every right to use all kinds of means
to regain the territories usurped by Israel." (the Russian
version said "other means").[60]

On the home front there had been disturbing developments. On
April 4, 1972, a memorandum had been sent to Sadat signed by
Abdel Latif al-Baghdadi, Kamal ad-Din Hussein, and eight other
retired officers associated with the Nasser regime. The best
known of the others were Marshal Abu-el-1'Izz and Salah
Dessouqi. Baghdadi, who had left Nasser's government in 1964,
was still considered, together with Zakhariya Muhieddin, the
most outstanding personality of all the Free Officers after
Nasser. (But Muhieddin was more feared and disliked by his
contemporaries.) The memorandum called for a return to a policy
of independence and neutralism toward the big powers and
proposed to form a national front of "all national personalities
known for their devotion to Egypt and to the revolution of July
23 [1952], for their courageous views and for their
decisiveness."[61] Of the Soviets the memorandum said: "The U.S.,
one of the big powers, gives to Israel all the power and might
that permits it to continue its aggression and induce it to
more. The Soviet Union, the other big power, gives us help that
has not been sufficient until today to liberate our land and to
recover our rights." It emphasized that five years had passed
since the 1967 war. It said that the authors did not want to
destroy Egyptian-Soviet friendship, for Egypt needed friends.

"What we want [the memorandum continued], is that the
relationship with the USSR returns to the level that is natural
and safe between a recently independent country vitally
concerned with its independence and one of the big powers whose
strategy is not free (because of its doctrine and of its
interests) from the desire to extend its influence. [Egypt
should] return to the secure zone between the two big powers, or
between several big powers. . . . Overstepping the limits of this
zone has no doubt been one of the reasons for the present
misfortunes. . . . There is nothing wrong with the policy of an
alliance with the devil, except if it is, or ends, to his
advantage. It will necessarily end so if his ally is not his
equal and not capable of driving him off."

It appears that the Baghdadi memorandum was circulated among friends of the authors and politicians in general until it became so well known that Sadat felt compelled to take a position on it.[62] He did this in a major speech on May 14, 1972, in which he mentioned the memorandum, together with an earlier and less significant one of 1970, and declared that there could be "no activity outside the constitutional institutions." The doors of policy discussion, he said, were open to everyone. Open dialogue was desirable, but competitive maneuvering was not. This was an unmistakable warning, and no further memoranda were circulated. Nevertheless, three months later Sadat himself was doing what the memorandum asked for, even though perhaps not in a way that the authors would have approved.

From the evidence of conversations in Cairo, it seems likely that General Sadek and his chief of staff, Shazli, played major roles in the expulsion of the Soviet military advisers. It must have been friction inside the army, which build up gradually until it caused the final step. Sadat on one occasion strongly denied that he was under pressure by the army. But he no doubt had to make this denial to safeguard his position as head of state. All evidence points to the probability that Sadek really was the man who caused the break. Matar cites a speech Sadek is said to have made to a meeting of officers, and Cairo was full of anecdotes about clashes between the Russians and Egyptian officers months before the break occurred.

Basically the army was angry because the Soviets did not furnish the arms the Egyptians judged necessary to renew the war against Israel. All kinds of personal frictions were also important. The Egyptian officers tended to rationalize their resentment by raising the question of whether or not the Soviets had an interest in making the situation of "no war and no peace" last as long as possible. After all, it gave them a reason to stay on in Egypt without risk and even to be paid good money by the Egyptians. It was no secret to anyone in the army that the air and sea "facilities" (not "bases," the Soviets insisted) partly under the Soviets' control were of great strategic value to them.

The substance of the remarks Sadek is reported to have made to the officers expresses the Egyptian hostility toward the Russians.[63] They contained passages such as these:

"The Soviets give Egypt nothing of decisive importance. The aid they give us is not even sufficient to liberate the Sinai. We have no factories for shells, so if we started to fight, the shells would not suffice for ten days. The Soviet Union asks us for bases in Marsa Matruh and another one in az-Za'faran [on the Red Sea]. This is a strange request."

Continuing, Sadek reportedly banged his fist on the table and said:

"As long as I am minister of war, the Soviets will not get one base in Egypt. I swear this on my military honor. If the Soviets enter Matruh and establish a base there, we will never be able to get them out. If it is difficult for us to get Israel out of the Sinai, and it is a small state, what will it be like with the Soviet Union, which is one of the big powers?

"The Soviet Union is selling us arms at black-market prices. Tanks whose price in the world market is £ 25,000 are sold for over £ 44,000 by the Soviet Union. The Russians complained a lot about Qadhdhafi and his stand against them. We asked him to ease his attacks so they would not use his attitude as a pretext to deny us what we want. Qadhdhafi understood us and said he would be ready to send a delegation to Moscow to buy arms from them. In fact, a delegation under Jallud went to Moscow and started negotiations with responsible people there. The latter, it seemed to us, were distinguished by their excuses and complications. For our information the Libyan brethren sent us the prices quoted to them by the Soviets. We found that they were multiples of world prices. So the arms transaction with Libya was not concluded. The Libyan brethren were to pay the price in cash. I told them, after having studied the prices and the situation, that it would be better to cancel the transaction and that the best solution would be to buy the arms, of which we have few in our forces, in the West.

"Moreover, the Russians proposed to us officially that Egyptian pilots take over the training of Syrian pilots. This would mean that our pilots would have gone to Syria while there is a lack of pilots at the Egyptian front. The Russians maintain that there should be unification in this respect. But we don't accept this argument because training is their task.

"I talked to you about the bases. I want to tell you that Tito warned us not to give bases to the Russians. Tito received Grechko before he [Grechko] had talked to us about bases. Grechko had come to see Tito to find out if there was a chance to obtain bases in the Adriatic. Tito refused, and he did not forget to ask on that occasion: 'And what are you doing about Egypt? Are you studying their needs?'"

Matar comments, "So it was natural that Sadek entered the
opposition [against the Russians] and Sadat forced the situation
to blow up; and he did blow it up!" He quotes Sadat as having
said on one occasion to a restricted audience, "The decision [to
expel the Soviet advisers] was taken by two people: I am one,
and I think you know the other." The other, of course, was
Sadek.[64]

The Soviets realized before the break occurred that it was
the Egyptian military that really mattered. Sadek had not
accompanied Sadat on his last two trips to Moscow. He had
reasoned that it was useless to do so, since the military needs
of Egypt had been presented to Moscow and promises to meet
these needs had been made in October.[65] Relations between him
and the Soviets were not good in any case. When Sadat returned
from his February visit to Moscow he brought back Soviet
promises that they would help Egypt to manufacture the MIG 21.
But when on February 18, 1971, Grechko visited Cairo, Sadek
surprised him by saying that Egypt did not need any such
factories. (Sadek was also minister of military supplies and war
industries.) Grechko is reported to have replied that the
factories had been agreed upon with President Sadat.

Grechko returned to Cairo on May 15. An air show was held in
which, according to press releases, a new kind of fighter was
flown, said to be capable of flying at more than 2,000 miles per
hour and at an altitude of 16 miles. This news electrified the
Egyptians because they thought that the famous MIG 23 had
finally arrived.[66] But Qadhdhafi told the Lebanese newspaper
an-Nahar in an interview on June 1, 1972, that it was all
propaganda and that Grechko had taken his airplane back to
Moscow.[67] Later events proved this to be correct. During this
second visit relations between Grechko and his host Sadek were
so cool that the papers had difficulty in finding a picture in
which Sadek did not frown.[68] He had good reason to frown, for he
must have known that the first press releases about the new
airplane were only propaganda.

In order to alleviate tensions Sadek was invited to Moscow.
He went for a week (June 7-14) and got red-carpet treatment. He
was present at maneuvers and saw many Soviet generals.[69] After
his return to Cairo on June 14 he publicly praised the Soviets
and Soviet-Egyptian collaboration: "I don't want to give any
details, but I do say that this visit was important and
successful."

As the Soviet-U.S. summit approached, al-Ahram held a seminar
about what Arab diplomacy should do (or ought to have done)
about it. Among the participants were two high officials (and
former press spokesmen) of the ministry of foreign affairs,

Ismail Fahmi and Tahsin Bashir. They were outspoken in their
evaluation of the limited benefits Egypt could, in their view,
obtain from alliance with Moscow—so much so that for a short
time they were dismissed from the positions they held and sent
on leave by the foreign minister, Murad Ghaleb.[70]
Fahmi said it would be best if

". . .the Vietnam problem and the Middle East question could be
put at the same level. If there is a role the Soviets can play
in Vietnam to help the Americans, America also must play a role
to help the Soviets in the Middle East. Not that the two states
want to end the Middle East struggle from one day to the other;
I don't believe this. I am on the contrary convinced that the
two states desire what is called the state of neither war nor
peace in the Middle East.
    "The Middle East is for the Soviet Union priority number
three and for the U.S. priority number four, while Vietnam for
both of them is priority number one. I must have enough
political courage to tell this to the Soviets: Vietnam matters a
lot, but the Middle East for me is a question of life and death.
If we do not accomplish [a linkage between Vietnam and the
Middle East], and our estimate of the Brezhnev-Nixon meeting
indicates that we will not . . . ., then we must revise the basic
policy we are following.
    "The reasons for the immobility of the Middle East crisis are
the two big powers. It will not be possible to reactivate it
except with their help. If the Soviet Union today is not in a
position to ensure that Egypt first and the Arab world later
reach the stage of confrontation and are enabled to reject the
politics of 'no war and no peace,' then it has made a big
mistake in its calculations. I think the Soviets know this after
their long experience with Egypt and the Arab world."

Fahmi then went on to postulate a dialogue with the Soviet Union
"of a new and special kind, free from threats."

    Bashir was even more direct:

"Recent Soviet moves made clear that their policy in the Middle
East is defensive and that the Americans have the upper hand.
The big question is: What will cause the Soviets to change their
attitude and to accept risks for the sake of our interest? Or,
what can we give to the Soviet Union [to achieve this]? If we
are not in a position to give additional benefits to the Soviets
in order to change the balance, the other possibility would be
to exert friendly pressure as soon as the Soviet Union takes a
stand as a spectator."

There were also some left-wing intellectuals in the seminar who thought that Egypt could give more to the Soviet Union, that it could come closer in its internal policies and institutions to the Soviet model. But any realist would doubt whether this would have the desired effect of making the Soviets "accept risks for the sake of [Egyptian] interests." It might well have achieved the contrary. The Soviets could have decided that since they already had control of Egypt, why take risks?

One of the most significant things about the seminar was that Heikal decided to publish its proceedings in his paper. It seems likely that he was aware of the way the tide was running when he did this. He also took up the defense of the two high functionaries, who were punished by the foreign minister. The Cairo diplomatic world knew that these sanctions were not going to last long in any case. In the end it was the foreign minister who lost his job.

Heikal continued his offensive by publishing a series of long weekend articles about "neither peace nor war." In those articles he asked the delicate question of who was "guilty" of the "crime" of perpetuating that situation. "The Israelis" was one predictable answer, filling one page of the paper; "the Americans" were guilty as well, as a second long article explained a week later; "and the Russians?" asked a third one. This last article did not come to any clear conclusion, but it did suggest a number of arguments about why the Soviets, too, could be assigned part of the guilt, at least by "certain people" who tried to suggest that the Russians might have an interest in prolonging the status quo.

It was in this context that the Brezhnev-Nixon summit meeting occurred. After it Sadat sent a list of seven questions to Moscow, concerning summit discussions of the Middle East. The list must have included questions such as: Will there be a change in the Middle East after the summit? If not, are the Soviets going to do anything about the situation? Will they change their attitude on the arms question?

According to his own account Sadat received an answer to his questions on July 6, which was translated and read to him on the next day. The Soviet reply was not responsive. It contained three parts. In the first, several vague promises were given about what the Russians would do for Egypt. The second contained complaints about the "anti-Soviet" campaigns going on in the Egyptian army and in the press, especially in Heikal's articles. The third section spoke about the Soviet concept of war and the wars the Soviet Union had gone through. Sadat, who was waiting for concrete replies to his concrete questions, at first could not believe that this was all that the letter contained.

Sadat later declared that at that moment he made the decision to expel the Soviet advisers. The decision was communicated to the Soviet ambassador the next day, July 8.[71] As Sadat expressed it in a speech on July 24, the moment for "an objective stand toward the ally" had arrived. (His expression, waqfa maudû'iya ma'a-s-sadîq, is difficult to translate exactly because of the ambiguous quality of the preposition ma'a [toward, with] which implies a cordial "hand in hand" as well as a more antagonistic "face to face" position.) The formula is the most precise expression Sadat has ever given publicly to whatever position it was he wanted to maintain with the Soviets. Al-Ahram made it its main headline when the break was announced on July 19, 1972: "An objective stand toward [in front of, with] the friend grants to each his right."

A week after receiving the unsatisfactory answer from the Soviets, Sadat sent his prime minister, Aziz Sidki, to Moscow, accompanied by a primarily economic ministerial delegation. This delegation was, as later became clear, a hedge against the possibility that at the last minute a positive result would come of the conference and that it would then become important to prevent reports of the real meaning of the negotiations from reaching the outside world. Sidki, according to Sadat's later account, was to put two demands to the Soviets, and if they rejected them he was to announce Sadat's decision to send home the Soviet military experts. The twofold ultimatum was this: the promised arms must be delivered to Egypt immediately, especially the MIG 23s and ground-to-ground rockets, and, second, all Soviet sites and facilities in Egypt (they were not officially called bases) must be put under Egyptian command.[72] The Egyptian delegation had orders to avoid all private discussions and to negotiate only in plenary sessions. (Thus Mamduh Salem, the interior minister, who was in the party, could supervise Sidki, as a friend of the Soviets.)

The Soviets replied that the arms question was open to further discussion, but that agreement on the second demand was out of the question. Accordingly Sidki asked for the withdrawal of the advisers. He proposed a Soviet-Egyptian announcement that both countries had agreed that the tasks of the advisers had been accomplished and that they would be leaving Egypt. But the Soviets rejected this proposal. If the Egyptians wanted the advisers removed, that was their decision, and if they wanted to make an announcement about it, that was up to them as well. Sidki cut short his visit after eight hours of talks and returned to Cairo on July 14.

Sadat announced his decision to the ASU executive committee
on July 18. The July 19 Cairo newspapers printed only a small
part of his one-and-a-half-hour speech. An executive committee
statement was published either completely or in excerpts. It
contained a short résumé of the Soviet-Egyptian negotiations, a
historical review of relations between the two countries, and a
long quotation from Sadat's speech in which he praised the
Soviets for all they had done for the Egyptians. After this the
statement briefly mentioned the divergence of views, arising
from the fact that the USSR was a big power with its own
strategic interest, "while we have part of our territory under
occupation and our principal aim on the Arab and Egyptian level
is to end this aggression." The statement mentioned Sadat's
explanation to the executive committee that the Soviets had
promised certain arms but had not delivered them "on time." It
cited the president as saying: "After we obtained the Soviet
explanation of the talks between Nixon and the Soviet leaders,
we felt the need, in the light of all the things mentioned
above, to take a stand in front of our friends." Sadat warned of
hysteria. He announced that on July 17 the Soviet advisers had
begun to leave and that Egyptian troops had already taken over
all Soviet installations in Egypt. Conversations about future
relations "and how to make them more effective" had already
begun, the statement said. Now principles had to be found on
which friendship could be based. "The battle" would be the task
of the Egyptian soldiers, and it would not be delayed by the
departure of the Soviets. Sadat had the full approval of the
executive committee, the statement concluded.
  Sadat said much more to the executive committee, and later to
a closed meeting of journalists and finally to the Central
Committee itself on July 24. Even though the speeches were not
all public and printed in the press, many of their main points
became known. Matar has noted a number of them, such as the
following:

"There was much distrust between the Egyptian and the Soviet
leadership, ever since the time of Nasser. Because of this,
Nasser had charged Murad Ghaleb, then ambassador to Moscow, to
consult the Soviets about signing a treaty in order to reassure
them. The Soviets refused, backing up his leadership and
assuring him of their confidence. But the Soviets sent Podgorny
to Cairo after what happened with the 'breakaway children' (i.e.,
Ali Sabri and his group). He brought a draft treaty with him,
already prepared in Russian and Arabic. Thus the Soviets made
clear that they did not trust me [Sadat]. But in order to calm

them, I said to Mahmud Riad [then the foreign minister]: 'All right, go ahead with the thing!'"73

Sadat was asked by one Central Committee member, "Do you expect that the Soviets will do anything in response to our decision?" He answered, "I will keep my own account and return one measure with ten!" Sadat also said:

"The breakaway children tried to make the Soviets believe that I wanted to undo the Egyptian-Soviet friendship and that they alone had it in their hands to preserve the relationship. As if it were a friendship belonging to them and not to the whole country."

He claimed that the Soviets did not want to keep their promises for arms and that they had agreed with him on a time schedule giving the dates for delivery and the kinds of arms that were wanted. He went on to say: "But they did not stick to it. . . . So I was forced to talk of the fog and to take everything on myself."

He was asked by one of the members of the Central Committee how he would act if the battle broke out. He said that Egypt would fight in a certain way if the arms were delivered, but if their requests were not fulfilled they would fight in a different way.

He hinted in his speech before the Central Committee that the Soviets wanted neither war nor his regime, nor himself as president. "This is the way they work. If this were not the case, why do they delay the fulfillment of our demands?"

He also said that Grechko came "on an information mission" to Cairo before the U.S.-USSR summit meeting in Moscow. The Soviets were afraid that the summit might raise many questions, doubts, and "initiatives" among their Arab friends. So they sent Grechko, who, as a military man, would have a good "cover." (This was the visit during which the new Soviet fighter was demonstrated.) Sadat said he knew that the visit was all just a cover for an information mission. However, he concluded, he trusted Grechko and at the end of the visit told him a few frank truths.

The sequence of events as described here leaves two questions open: Why did the Soviets reject a friendly joint communiqué such as Sidki had proposed, and what lay behind the Egyptian timing of the operation? Only speculative answers can be given. Matar thinks that the Soviets wanted no responsibility for the expulsion of their advisers and its possible consequences. They thus refused to act as if their expulsion had been jointly agreed upon. Matar argues later that the Soviets had wanted to get their experts out of Egypt anyway, because they felt that they were overextended. They were thus secretly glad when Sadat took it upon himself to expel them. His two theories are obviously linked. Matar goes on to speculate that the Russians had already agreed with the Americans to reduce their presence in Egypt, in return for some quid pro quo granted to them by the U.S. This view also is logically linked with Matar's preceding assumptions.

However, it is difficult to see what responsibility the Soviets would have shouldered if they had agreed to publish a joint statement. In fact, a TASS statement on July 19 said (incorrectly) that the Soviet experts had returned home by mutual agreement. It seems more probable that the Soviets tried to bluff and failed. They thought that the Egyptians might not dare expel the advisers unilaterally. Perhaps they had some reason to think so, for it seems that Cairo had made similar threats previously but had not gone through with them. It has also been reported that the Soviets had previously offered to take their advisers back. If this was so, it was possibly also only bluff, and the Egyptians had then asked Moscow to prolong their presence.

If one assumes that Moscow tried a bluff, one also has to assume that they really would have liked to stay on, and one must therefore conclude that their removal had not been "sold" to Washington. This seems much more likely than the opposite proposition. Even so, it is quite possible that, once expelled, the Soviets began to seek the brighter side of the picture. After all, they were now safe from the dangers of overinvolvement. They were free to give more aid to Iraq, who had oil to pay for it, who did not have Israel as an immediate neighbor and would consequently cause fewer military difficulties, and who could in the future serve as a springboard for such splendid prizes as Kuwait, "Arabistan" (i.e., Iranian Khuzhistan), and the Persian Gulf states and their oil fields.

As for timing, it was clear to all observers that a much more reasonable time for the Egyptian move would have been after the U.S. elections and, if possible, after a Vietnam settlement. Then Washington might have been ready to pay for Egypt's expulsion of the Russians by giving some kind of assurances or undertaking some step toward a peace settlement in accord with Egyptian

ideas.* It was obvious that at the time the move did take place
the Egyptians could not expect any real quid pro quo from
Washington.**

That the expulsion of the advisers nevertheless took place in
July can be explained only by the impatience and pressure of the
Egyptian military. They seem to have transmitted their sense of
urgency to Sadat, but by what means is not clear. Certainly
there was much talk in Cairo about the resentment of the
officers, and also about the danger that the Soviets would
remain permanently, if they were not removed at once. There must
have been considerable misgivings among the higher officers
about their loss of control of Soviet comings and goings, for
the Soviets had their own airports guarded by their own soldiers
and closed to even the very highest military officers of Egypt.

The Nixon-Brezhnev meeting probably played a minor role,
compared to that of the military tensions, even though there is
no reason to doubt Sadat when he describes the summit meeting as
the final drop of water that caused the barrel to overflow. The
Soviets had used the summit to stave off Egyptian demands,

---

* Heikal seems to have thought so; see his article written after
the expulsion of the Russians (al-Ahram, July 28, 1972) in which
he explains that he had expected a move against the advisers,
but at a later time, perhaps toward the beginning of 1973.

** There is some evidence that Egyptian diplomacy hoped for help
from Europe. A diplomatic initiative was started toward Britain,
France, Germany, and others. Arms negotiations also took place,
in particular in London. But all this was ruined by the action
of the fedayeen at the Munich Olympics. In any case, the role of
Europe was too secondary to the Egyptians to have motivated a
step as important as the expulsion of the advisers.

There was also considerable speculation about the role the
Saudi defense minister, Sultan, could have played. He passed
through Cairo on June 7 after his visit in Washington. It was
assumed that he could have brought a message or even some kind
of guarantee from Nixon assuring Sadat that the Americans would
step in once the Soviets stepped out. But if Sadat's decision was
taken early in July, as all information agrees, it could not have
been Sultan who motivated it. There would have been at least
some checking of his reports by the Egyptian diplomats in
Washington before any steps were decided upon.

complaints, and requests for information and for action. When it
went by without anything decisive having happened and when,
moreover, the Soviets appeared reluctant to give Sadat any real
information about it, it became the last straw.

The Soviets left quietly, with no fuss at all. Their secret
equipment went with them. In Alexandria they were said to have
taken to their ships even the beds and barracks furnishings of
their soldiers. The SU 11 planes flew out, and the MIG 23s were
said to have been taken apart and loaded on transport planes.
For more than two weeks, as midnight approached, the departure
lounge of the civilian airport in Cairo would suddenly fill
with Russian men and women. There were only normal customs
checks, with no special precautions,* a few last drinks, and
then Aeroflot would announce over the loudspeaker the departure
of one of its regular flights to Moscow.

Partial Soviet-Egyptian Reconciliation. The high-level Soviet-
Egyptian contacts desired by Sadat at the time of the expulsion
of the Soviet advisers did not materialize immediately. On the
contrary, the Soviet ambassador to Cairo and the Egyptian
ambassador to Moscow were each called home for consultations.
There is little doubt that the Soviets calculated that they
would improve their negotiating position by staying away for a
while. They never stopped supplying such necessities as spare
parts, as they assured any questioner, but it was obvious that
they slowed down delivery of them drastically. Thus the effect
was much the same.

Egypt held arms conversations with Great Britain, and Sadek
made a long trip to Czechoslovakia to try to buy arms. There
were also triangular negotiations between Qadhdhafi, the
Egyptians, and different European arms sources. The Egyptian
military could not have seriously hoped that these sources
could fill the gap the Soviets had left, but presumably they
hoped other suppliers would reduce it at least to a tolerable
size.

---

* It was well known that the Soviets like to buy gold or gold
jewelry in the bazaar of Cairo, presumably with the portion of
their locally paid salaries they had not used, and to take the
gold to Russia. As any Armenian knows, it is profitable to
smuggle gold into the USSR (where it is used for traditional
jewelry in the Soviet Asian republics) and to "reexport"
platinum. There were some scandals about gold being taken out
through the Cairo airport before the expulsions.

A polemic developed between Egyptian and Soviet news media.
On the whole, the Egyptians were the more aggressive, while the
Soviets remained controlled and subdued. The Soviet media
recalled the virtues of Abdel Nasser, spoke of the great
benefits in Soviet military and economic aid which Egypt had
received, and reminded the Egyptians and the world at large of
the very severe losses the USSR had suffered in the Six-Day War.
The Egyptians went further: Ihasan Abdel Qaddus, a special
friend of Sadat, distinguished himself in long articles in the
official newspaper Akhbar al-Yaum, in which he declared that the
Soviets had not conformed to the spirit of the Soviet-Egyptian
treaty when they withheld from Egypt the arms that were the only
realistic means of regaining the occupied territories. In fact,
he wrote, the treaty had assured Egypt of "sufficient arms" to
recover the lost lands. Moreover, Abdel Qaddus wrote, the
arrangement between the USSR and the U.S., resulting from the
summit, although not exactly a pact directed against the
interests of Egypt (such as the treaty forbade), was something
quite close to it.[74]
   The left-wing writers in the Egyptian press had a difficult
time. They usually took the line that there were in fact
divergencies of interest between Egypt and the USSR, but that
the friendship between the two countries was more important and
their relationship ought to gain by being on a new footing.
Heikal, for one, began to write about the importance of the
Soviet relationship. He made it quite clear that in his view
Egypt needed the Soviet partner, even though he permitted
himself a few sharp side attacks, as, for example, when he wrote
that the Soviets had no airplane equivalent to the U.S. Phantom
and that the Israeli pilots were in any event better than the
Soviet ones (al-Ahram, August 18), or when he maintained in the
same article that the Americans had agreed with the Soviets to
let the Soviet Jews emigrate to Israel and admitted that the
Egyptians had made a mistake when they had omitted to question
the Soviets more persistently about their emigration policies
regarding Soviet Jews.
   But by October 1972 it had become clear that Egypt had no
alternative but to improve relations with the Soviets again.
Heikal wrote on October 13 that it was very important to repair
the relationship, and Sadat announced to the parliament on
October 15 that Prime Minister Sidki would go to Moscow. He
spoke of the need to preserve the "strategic friendship" between
the two countries. Sidki left the next day and stayed in Moscow
two days. He brought back a promise that the three Soviet
leaders would visit Cairo, but no time was fixed. That the visit

had been important became clear when on October 27, the Egyptian
minister of war and army commander, General Sadek, was suddenly
dismissed from his position. Abdel Qaddus wrote two days later
in Akhbar al-Yaum that the general had been dismissed for
failing to execute certain orders of President Sadat.

The Soviet embassy in Cairo came to life again. A limited
number of military technicians arrived, bringing with them a
limited number (apparently sixty) of low-altitude SAM 6 missiles,
urgently needed to close holes in the Egyptian defense system.[75]

According to Cairo rumors, Sadek had refused to go along with
the changes in Egyptian policy. Two explanations were given for
his alleged insubordination. One was that he had refused to
accompany Sidki on his mission to Moscow and had ordered his
subordinate Hassan Abdel Qader not to go either. He had
reportedly even refused to give Sidki a new list of military
requirements. When Sidki came back, he and Sadek clashed. Sadek
reportedly reproached him for failing to come back with the
famous MIG 23 and ground-to-ground missiles, which in Sadek's
eyes had become the decisive symbols of Soviet-Egyptian
cooperation. He continued to want either these or nothing. Sidki,
primarily in charge of economic development, must have been
aware of the need for collaboration with the Soviets in the
economic field. For this reason also any rapprochement would
have been welcomed by him.

According to another report, Sadat said, in one of the closed
sessions in which the dismissal was explained, that he had
ordered Sadek to be ready for an attack on the Israelis by
November 15, but that Sadek had refused. The sources of this
report usually added that it was probably not true; Sadat only
wanted to enhance his position in the eyes of the Egyptian
state and party leaders and to paint Sadek as weak and
indecisive. Whatever the truth of such reports, it was fairly
clear that Sadek had not agreed with the new policy toward
Moscow and that he had clashed at least with Sidki, and
possibly also with Sadat, on this issue. One can also assume
that his very rigidity weakened Sadek's support in the army.
When it became clear how much the Soviet exodus had weakened
the army, Sadek must have been blamed by at least some of the
officers. His rigid refusal to collaborate with the USSR must
have antagonized more. Probably Sadat selected this moment to
strike down his army commander who, hailed as the hero of the
Soviet expulsion, had become more popular than Sadat himself
with the army and with right-wing civilians.

Sadat's prestige in Egypt had risen sharply with the
expulsion of the Soviets. But his "Canossa" back to Moscow made

him appear to most Egyptians as a man who did not know what he
wanted. Their suspicion grew that all he was really interested
in was to remain president for as long as possible. There were
new reports of disturbances in the army and rumors of attempted
coups, foiled while still in the planning stage. The arrest of
twenty-four air force officers, allegedly for disrespectful
utterances in a conversation with the president, was officially
confirmed.[76] Twelve of the officers were held for investigation.

New evidence published in 1974 indicates that Sadek in fact had
disobeyed orders by Sadat. These were said to have been that the
Egyptian army had to be ready for action on November 15, 1972. But
in a session of the Highest Military Council of Egypt on October
24 it appeared that nothing was ready. The army chief and some
generals excused themselves on the grounds that certain kinds of
arms were lacking. Certain army chiefs did not even know about the
decision of Sadat to have everything ready for war by November 15.
This led to the dismissal of Sadek on October 28. As revealed in
the important book by Musa Sabri, Documents of the October War (in
Arabic)(Cairo: al-Maktab al-Masri al-Hadith li-Ttaba's wan-Nashr,
1974, pp. 15 ff.), the timing had been established with an eye to
the U.S. presidential elections of that year. (The book presents
an account given by Sadat himself and publishes a verbatim record
of the session of the Highest Military Council. This study had
been concluded long before it appeared.)

The American Connection: Israel and Its Partner
Unlike the Arabs, who had serious friction with their superpower
partner, the Israelis have so far successfully managed their
relations with their partner, the United States. It has been
easier for them. They won the 1967 war and needed less shoring up
than the Arabs. They had no technological and military problems
comparable to those of the Arabs and consequently no need to bring
into Israel great numbers of American instructors and technicians.
They held the occupied territories and needed no American help to
defend them, while the Arabs wanted Soviet support to regain them.

The positions of the superpowers were also different. The
Russians were on the offensive, pursuing strategic aims in the
Mediterranean and the Middle East which did not entirely
coincide with those of the Arabs. The Americans in the Middle
East were on the defensive. The Israelis were their most
reliable and efficient friends and partners there. As long as
Israel withstood Arab and Soviet pressure, the U.S. position in
the Middle East would not be entirely lost. Thus the Israelis
were an asset for the U.S. defensive position, while the Arabs
turned out to be something of an embarrassment to the Soviet
political-strategic offensive.

U.S. policy itself had been shifting, largely as a result of overengagement and defeat in Vietnam, from "policing the world" and "making it safe for democracy" to "selective involvement,"[77] for which Israel, because of its own military efficiency, was an ideal place. In the Middle East itself American policy before the Six-Day War had emphasized "stability," i.e., preserving the existing frontiers and cease-fire lines, because peace had come to appear as an impossible aim. The Six-Day War had proved that there could be no real stability without peace. Consequently, U.S. emphasis was again on achieving it. Paradoxically, the occupied territories were seen by the Americans as a means to exert pressure toward peace. Consequently, the U.S. was willing to help Israel to keep the occupied territories until peace could be achieved. But with the passage of time these territories and the additional military, although not political, security they gave Israel, as well as the sacrifices made to keep them, led Israel to prefer more and more to keep them rather than to give priority to any Arab peace offer that might be forthcoming if the territories were returned.

Just as the MIG 23 assumed a symbolic value in the relationship of the Arabs with their Soviet partners, the Phantom became symbolic in Israeli-American relations. Immediately after the war the Johnson administration decided to withhold provisionally the Phantoms that Israel had requested (although some A-4s ordered before the war were delivered in 1968).

The arms situation was "kept under review" in Washington. This was a hint to the Soviets that their arms deliveries to the Egyptians would be taken into consideration before new arms would be supplied to Israel. But the whole concept of arms "balance" was complicated by the human factor. What on paper might look like a balance meant in reality a considerable superiority for the Israelis, because they could use their weapons so much more efficiently. It was also unclear whether all the Arab countries were to be included in the balance or only the "front line" countries, Egypt and Syria, or only Egypt. The Soviets tended to send arms to Egypt in part to serve their own military purposes, such as air reconnaissance of the Sixth Fleet or indirect help to African friends and clients (e.g., Egyptian war planes were helping in the Nigerian war against Biafra). Should such arms also be included in the balance? Israeli diplomacy was able to play on all these factors in order to induce Washington to give "protection" to Israel, which in fact assured great Israeli superiority.

The decisive breakthrough for the Israelis was probably the delivery of Phantoms.[78] Negotiations about them were opened by the Johnson administration at the end of 1968 and officially concluded only on December 27, 1969, under Nixon. But Israeli pilots had trained on the Phantoms before the negotiations were concluded, so they were able to use them as soon as they were handed over.

The military and diplomatic developments of 1969 helped the Israelis. Nasser opened the "war of attrition" on April 1, 1969. Israeli casualties on the canal front totaled seventy during July. Israel, always very sensitive to casualties, began massive air attacks on the Egyptian canal positions on July 20, plus commando raids on the southern flank of the canal front. These efforts were stepped up during the last three months of 1969. The Israelis destroyed almost all the Egyptian SAM batteries and thus gained air supremacy over all of Egypt.

Peace negotiations made no progress. On October 8 the Egyptians spoke officially about possible indirect negotiations, but later indicated that Israeli withdrawal from the cease-fire line was a precondition for them.[79] An American peace initiative (the first Rogers plan) of October 28 was rejected by the Israelis, the Soviets, and the Arabs. The Arabs did so primarily because the military situation had evolved to their disadvantage on the canal front and Cairo did not want to negotiate from a position of weakness. That the Soviets and the Arabs had also rejected the Rogers initiative kept the Israelis from having to suffer the consequences of American disappointment.[80]

As soon as the Israelis had obtained their Phantoms, they used them for raids into the interior of Egypt, the so-called deep penetration raids. These raids had an effect opposite to the one intended. Instead of forcing the Egyptians to observe the cease-fire (Dayan: "There will be no limits to military objectives within the UAR until Cairo respects the cease-fire," New York Times, January 25, 1970) or to bring Nasser down (which was perhaps the maximum objective of the operation), the raids caused Nasser to make his secret trip to Moscow (January 22, 1970) and to arrange for SAM 3 missiles to be installed and initially manned by Soviet crews.

These consequences meant an important escalation of the war. But even this proved to be to the advantage of the Israelis. The Soviet presence in Egypt rapidly increased, with Soviet personnel not only as instructors but also as active participants. From that moment on the Israeli-American relationship was cemented by the simple fact that the Soviets had taken up positions on the

Egyptian front. The U.S. did not want American personnel to take
up counterpositions in Israel, and there was no need for them to
do so, for the Israelis were ready to do their own fighting. But
Washington was all the more interested in preserving Israeli
superiority. By March the Soviet deliveries of new arms to
Egypt, principally SAM 3s and all the air and ground electronic
equipment needed for their operation, were in full swing. In
April there was evidence that Soviet-piloted planes were flying
defense missions over the Delta and the Nile valley. Israeli
deep penetration raids thereupon ceased. Twenty SAM 3 sites had
been set up west of the canal, reportedly Soviet-manned. In May
1970 the Egyptians built SAM sites inside the canal zone but
made little progress against Israeli air attacks until in June
the Soviets took over the batteries and gradually edged them
toward the canal. It was reported that "devastating attacks by
the Israeli Air Force, approaching the scale of the U.S. raids
in Southeast Asia, blunted but did not halt the gradual
buildup."[81] While Nasser again went to Moscow (June 29) and
decided to accept the Rogers peace plan, the Soviets moved up
their SAM 3s (during the night of June 29-30), took an Israeli
Phantom raid by surprise, and shot down two planes. The SAM 3
defenses were consolidated parallel to the canal, but about 30
miles were left open for the Egyptians to defend. In July the
Israelis lost three more Phantoms. They had their revenge on
July 30 by shooting down four MIG 21s piloted by Soviets,[*]
which they had "baited" and trapped in an ambush. Kutakhov, the
commander of the Soviet air forces in Egypt, left Cairo for
Moscow immediately after this clash.

On July 31, Israeli Prime Minister Meir accepted the ninety-
day cease-fire proposed by Rogers, and it went into effect on
August 7. The Soviets and the Egyptians immediately thereafter
moved their missiles closer to the canal, even though Cairo had
signed a standstill agreement in this respect, which the U.S.
had guaranteed. They thus gained a military advantage, for

----

* According to Heikal, who said he had the story from Nasser
himself, five, not four, Russian MIGs were downed. See Fuad
Matar, Nasserite Russia and Egyptian Egypt, citing p. 41, Aug.
11, 1972: "I remember well [Heikal wrote]; the telephone
sounded in my office. It was Abdel Nasser who spoke. He said
immediately, 'Something strange has happened. Five airplanes
with their Russian pilots have been shot down. Sometimes I have
wronged our pilots and I wonder, did I depress their fighting
spirit? —Now I am sure that they have a really difficult task.'"

theoretically missiles close to the canal could challenge
Israeli air supremacy on its eastern, Israeli-held side and
could thus be an important factor if a crossing should be
attempted. But at the same time this open violation of the
agreement by the Soviets and their Egyptian protégés again
reinforced the Israeli-American relationship. Three weeks of
strong Israeli-American tension followed (August 13-September 1),
until the Americans admitted that the Soviet-Egyptian side had in
fact broken the armistice agreement. Thereafter Washington
supplied the Israelis with electronic countermeasure devices
(ECM) against the missiles and generally became very willing to
shore up further the Israeli defenses. The armistice having
begun, the Israelis could explain to the Americans with a
considerable degree of truth that the clearer it was made to the
Egyptians that the Israelis were militarily superior, the longer
the armistice would last. The Israelis no doubt emphasized as
well the need for the Americans to match the Soviet military
buildup in Egypt, which went on after the cease-fire and reached
its peak toward the end of 1970. Even before the armistice had
begun, U.S. arms "started pouring into Israel in such vast
quantities that the Minister of Defense was amazed, and this
profusion of arms induced Israel to agree to the initiative."[82]

The death of Nasser and the Egyptian-Soviet treaty of May 27,
1971, must have once more given Israeli diplomats the opportunity
to insist on the need for the U.S. to counterbalance the close
Moscow-Cairo relationship by giving Israel the means to resist
Soviet pressure.[83] The treaty could be presented to Washington as
an indication that Egypt had permanently entered the Soviet
sphere of influence and that there was little that could be done
by the U.S. to regain influence on the Nile. Thus, the argument
went, it was that much more important to preserve U.S. influence
in Israel and to keep Soviet influence in the Middle East hemmed
in by the menace of Israeli military power.

On the diplomatic front the August 1970 Egyptian violation of
the armistice terms enabled the Israelis to refuse to participate
in the talks with UN mediator Jarring, scheduled to start
immediately after the cease-fire. Finally, on December 30, 1970,
the Israelis agreed to participate in the talks, but Israeli
spokesmen made it clear before they did that they had obtained
from Washington, as Eban put it on November 19, "an American
promise not to press U.S. ideas of a territorial settlement."
Mrs. Meir hinted at similar American military and diplomatic
assurances in a Knesset speech.[84] The American assurances gave
the Israelis a basis on which to withstand any pressure to commit
themselves to withdrawl before a peace agreement had been

negotiated and before the definition of "secure borders" and all
that the phrase implied had been arrived at by negotiation.
    The Jarring talks broke down over these issues. Nor did
Rogers's visit to the Middle East in May 1971 overcame the
obstacle. The focus of the negotiations was shifted toward a
"partial solution," but the basic contradictions remained.
Israel wanted a canal agreement including a permanent cease-fire
and no passage of Egyptian troops across the canal, i.e., a
durable "provisional" solution. Egypt wanted a canal agreement
as only the first stage of an overall settlement, including
passage of Egyptian troops across the canal and an Israeli
commitment to complete withdrawal from all occupied Egyptian
territory according to a fixed time schedule.
    According to the Israeli analyst Dan Margalit:

"At the end of 1971 Israel was swamped with infuriating
documents, like the 'Bergus document' and the 'proposal for
proximity talks.' The obscurity in regard to supplies of
Phantoms, the technical innovations of which Israel was not
always informed, resulted in many cables being exchanged between
the Israeli and the American Foreign Ministries. . . .
    "When did the change take place? When did the United States
start to withdraw from the Rogers plan? What did Golda Meir
promise Nixon in 1971?
    "Some people say that the turning point came during the Prime
Minister's talks with the President, the content of which
remained a secret. Some say that the knell of election year had
rung for Israel. In any case the formula of 'elucidations' that
Israel made the United States agree to at the beginning of 1972,
and the character of the summit talks in Moscow, as briefly
reported to Israel by the Americans, gave Israel a long spell of
political tranquility, and the Phantoms were no longer linked
with political concessions.
    "The fundamental question, whether all these efforts will come
to nothing two months after the Presidential elections, remains
unanswered."[85]

    After the reelection of President Nixon, relations between
Israel and the U.S. became even more cordial. A self-
congratulatory appraisal about how well the Israelis had managed
their relations with the U.S., by Yoel Marks, appeared in Haaretz
on March 7, 1973.[86] The author saw Mrs. Meir's trip to
Washington from February 26 to March 11, 1973, as a success. The
same, he thought, could be said of developments in the relations
between the two countries. The Israelis made clear to the

Americans that "there is not going to be another Vietnam; . . .
no American blood will be shed here." Markus thought that the
Israelis convinced the Americans that a strong Israel was the
best guarantee for "the Arabs' despairing of armed struggle" and
consequently of the peace being preserved. A third argument,
also successfully put over, was that a strong Israel was "really
a safeguard of American interests in the area, the first line of
defense for American interests in the Mediterranean basin." The
author concluded that Israel had been able "in certain fields to
merge [its] interests with American interests" and had come to
understand the Americans better and learned to deal with them.

One can only guess at the reasons that kept the U.S. so
passive before the war of October 1973. The cease-fire seemed
solid. The Russians appeared to regress rather than to progress,
at least in Egypt. The coming oil troubles were realized too
late. Generally, among all the urgent problems facing the U.S.
the Middle East did not seem the most pressing. The approach of
détente and superpower diplomacy led to concentration of
attention on the global level. It was assumed that the minor
troubles of minor states might work themselves out as long as
the superpowers could be won over to a general détente and thus
would not encourage their clients to become overtruculent. This
proved true in a way, but the "working out" included a war.

A New War in the Middle East
Egyptian relations with the Soviet Union after the expulsion
of the Soviet military advisers, up to the summer of 1973 when
the final decision must have been taken to begin another war
against Israel, were characterized by growing awareness on the
Egyptian side of the importance of the policy of détente and
economic collaboration that had started between the two
superpowers. The evolution of Egyptian thinking can be seen from
the two speeches Sadat made on the anniversary of the Egyptian
revolution in July 1972 and in July 1973. In the 1972 speech,[87]
made immediately after the expulsion of the Soviet advisers,
Sadat contrasted the American-Israeli relationship with the
Soviet-Egyptian one:

"Our disagreement with the USSR arises from the fact that the
U.S. does not content itself with fulfilling its engagements
toward Israel; it overfulfills them. In the framework of our
friendship with the USSR I do not ask them to do as the U.S.
does for Israel. I do not ask them for what Israel asks from the
U.S. Sixty percent of the investments in Israel come from the
U.S., and Americans have the same capitalist system as the state

of the Zionists. As for us, our system is not that of the USSR;
ours is an alliance of the working forces of the people, while
the USSR has the Marxist system, which we do not adopt. But the
disagreement that opposes us to the USSR as to a friend lies in
this: given the attitude taken by the U.S. toward our enemy, the
crisis cannot be solved as long as the USSR continues to adopt
its overcircumspect attitude."[88]
   In 1972 Sadat was unhappy with the Russians because, as he
saw it, they did not give him as much aid as the Americans gave
the Israelis. Consequently he felt that they were of little use
to him in overcoming the Israelis. He seemed to suspect that the
lukewarm attitude of the Russians went back to the Egyptians'
refusal to "adopt the same system" as the USSR.
   In 1973 his analysis had changed. In his speech of July 1973,[89]
he mentioned Egypt's extreme concern over the Soviet-American
détente. This concern, he said, was the reason for the journey
of Hafez Ismail, the presidential adviser for security, and Ahmed
Ismail, the minister of defense, to Moscow in February 1973. "We
wanted to know what was happening." One of the problems with the
Soviet Union, he continued, was the "international détente of
which I have just spoken." He underlined this concern:

"We are not against international détente or that the United
States and the Soviet Union should get together or that the
specter of war should completely disappear from the world. We
are certainly not against this. But we live in an extremely
sensitive area where the two are present. What would our
attitude be if the two should adopt one single view in one way
or another? What would our interests be?"

   Sadat made haste to assure his audience that Moscow had
promised "continued support for and backing of our cause and
that détente would not affect a larger circle [i.e.,] one
affecting the Soviet support for our cause and our attitude."
   A few minutes later he pointed clearly to the dilemma that
confronted the USSR in connection with détente:

". . . we believe that if the détente makes the Soviet Union
abandon the national liberation movements, it will harm the
Soviet Union and in fact isolate it. That is what our Soviet
friends are fully aware of."[90]

Unmentioned but present in such considerations were the Chinese.
   Sadat's 1973 speech culminated in a recommendation that the
Egyptian Central Committee and People's Assembly, before whose
joint session the speech was made, meet again to discuss the new

international situation. Three days later, in a speech before
the students of Alexandria University, Sadat said:

"We have seen a blockade carried out by enemies. We have also
seen a blockade carried out by friends. . . . Today we know our
way in the light of the variables we see around us. We see
ourselves besieged from every side and an understanding, nay an
embrace, between the big powers. We shall never surrender. . . .
No surrender, however hard and long the battle may be."[91]

   Even in 1972 Sadat had been aware that the Middle East
problem might look different according to whether the point of
view was that of the USSR or of Egypt. He made that point in the
speech cited earlier:

"I was always convinced that the USSR stood on our side,
politically, economically, and militarily. But our evaluations
of the situation could be different, because the Soviet Union is
a big power with its commitments and responsibilities, its
strategy, and its special way of envisaging things. On our side
we have our problems, our strategy, our calculations. The Middle
East problem is not necessarily the primary problem for the USSR,
but for me the occupation of our territories is the most vital
problem."[92]

By 1973 his understanding had broadened into awareness that
there was a mutual "embrace" of the two superpowers, a blockade
by enemies and by friends.
   As to the answer to the question about what to do in the
changed international circumstances, most people seem to have
misunderstood Sadat. (The writer does not exclude himself.)
Looking back, it seems evident that Sadat was preparing for "the
battle." But at the time few people thought so—few among the
Egyptians, few among the Israelis, and perhaps even fewer among
outside observers.* Sadat had so many times said that the battle

---

* Eric Rouleau, "La guerre d'Octobre ou la diplomatie du canon.
I. La chance de ne pas être cru," Le Monde, Nov. 24, 1973. Also,
for an example of reporting before the war, see Irene Beeson,
"The Egyptian Dilemma," Observer Foreign News Service (London,
1973), as reprinted in Journal of Palestine Studies, vol. 3, no.
1 (Autumn 1973), pp. 185-186: ". . . No peace no war . . . no
change in position of political and military inferiority . . .

was imminent that in the end no one took him at his word. He
must have realized this and thereupon began using this
misunderstanding as camouflage. He continued to speak of the
impending battle until the last few days before the war broke
out. He said that he did not need even to mention it anymore as
it had become "axiomatic." Simultaneously, in secret he
coordinated military plans with Syria; he informed the fedayeen
of the coming war;[93] and the Soviet Ambassadors in Cairo and
Damascus were told of it.[94] It is not clear whether Faisal knew
the scheduled date of the attack. It seems probable that
Qadhdhafi, as he complained later, was not told of it, nor
Hussein either. Qadhdhafi must, however, have known of the
general plan for war; he disapproved of it heartily and said so

---

no stability . . . armed and political confrontations have all
been against other Arabs . . . internally Arab regimes have
fought a political war of attrition against radical nationalist,
leftist, liberals and any group which calls for serious planning
and action to get the area out of the rut. . . . Internationally,
most Arab regimes have wooed the U.S., although still describing
Washington as 'enemy number one'; the Soviet Union, the 'faithful
friend of the Arabs' . . . is kept at arm's length. . . . The
sixth anniversary of the Israeli occupation of Sinai was
celebrated in silence and apparent normality. Egypt is in the
third month of the 'phase of total confrontation' which Sadat
declared when he recently reshuffled the Cabinet for the fifth
time in two months and gave himself absolute power as Prime
Minister and 'Military Governor-General.' Coming after the 1971
'year of decision,' the 1972 'year of inevitable battle' and
sundry intervening alerts and decisions to mobilize for the
battle, the new 'phase' failed even to inspire traditional
Egyptian political wit. . . . The Egyptians believe his latest
phase of threats and sabre rattling is merely another display to
convince the U.S. to move, a dramatic backcloth for the debate
in the UN Security Council. There is talk of 'oil war.' . . .
Those Egyptians who are deeply concerned by the state of
unpreparedness of the country and unconcern of the ruling class
argue that if Sadat decides to 'cause an explosion,' he will not
be initiating a war of liberation, but playing his last card—a
desperate move that will force the U.S. and the great powers to
intervene and impose a separate settlement on Egypt and
Israel."

in public on several occasions.[95] The general war plan, as
worked out between Egypt and Syria under Egyptian inspiration,
must have been from the beginning one of a limited war, aimed at
reactivating the diplomatic struggle for a settlement in accord
with the wishes of the Egyptians. The two superpowers were to
realize that their "embrace" could be disturbed by the Arabs as
long as the Middle East problem remained unsolved.

Another consequence of the new international situation and
its realization by Sadat and his collaborators was the need to
give renewed emphasis to Arab collaboration. If Egypt could no
longer rely absolutely on Russian help in a war against Israel
because of U.S.-Soviet détente, it was all the more urgent for
Egypt to obtain maximum backing from the other Arab countries.
Sadat understood that the policy of Nasser could not serve his
present needs. Nasser's Arab policy had consisted in appealing
to the people of the Arab nations over the heads of their
governments, summoning them to an Arab nationalist revolution
under the leadership of Egypt. This policy had led to strong
resentment on the part of the governments affected and, in
time, to considerable fear of Egyptian subversion in nearly all
Arab countries.

Sadat changed all that. He took care to reconcile himself
with all the governments attacked by Nasser: he visited the
Maghreb, Saudi Arabia, Kuwait, and Iran, and return visits were
made by the leaders of these states. Everywhere he offered
assurances that the days of Egyptian interference in the
internal affairs of the other Arab states were over. In the case
of Syria and Libya a closer relationship matured in the shape of
the Arab Federation of the three countries. Later, under
pressure from Qadhdhafi, a union with Libya was projected. Only
with Iraq did it prove difficult for Sadat to form closer links.
Jordan had to remain an outsider because of the Jordanian
treatment of the fedayeen in 1970 and 1971.

The new Egyptian policy of inter-Arab collaboration (instead
of attempts at subversion and domination) began to bear fruit
when Faisal gradually overcame his distrust of Egypt and began
to collaborate economically and later politically with Sadat.

This development coincided with the growing consumption of
Arab petroleum in Europe and in the United States. In 1970 the
Libyans demonstrated that the market had become a seller's one.
They were able to reduce their production, in order to conserve
their reserves, and to increase their prices. The foreign-owned
companies operating in Libya had to accept this Libyan move
because they needed the oil. At the end of 1970 all the OPEC

countries called for tax increases and achieved about half of
their initial demands in the Tehran negotiations with the oil
companies in February 1971. Again the oil companies had to give
in because they needed the oil. The Arab threats that the oil
supply would be cut off or reduced achieved the desired effect.

An Arab oil congress at Algiers in May and June 1972
criticized OPEC for having been too soft on the companies. The
idea of participation (partial host government ownership) took
hold, and long-drawn-out negotiations resulted from OPEC's
demand for it. By the end of 1972 an agreement had been reached
at Riyadh making all the oil-producing countries part owners of
the oil companies, with a 25 percent share immediately and a 51
percent share by 1982, but some OPEC countries soon disregarded
it. Algeria had already nationalized 51 percent of its oil
production. Iran then demanded complete ownership immediately
and obtained it in return for guaranteed sales of oil to the
companies. Iraq nationalized the Kirkuk oil field "successfully."
Thereupon Libya demanded 51 percent participation immediately and
got it by nationalization in September 1973. It became clear that
the company negotiators were condemned to start negotiating new
contracts as soon as they had finished making the concessions
necessary to achieve the previous one.

In this general atmosphere of the growing power of the oil-
producing countries, Faisal allowed himself to be gradually
persuaded that he could use his oil as a political weapon without
sacrificing his financial interests. Saudi Arabia was earning
about as much money as it could profitably use. If it increased
its production substantially, the resulting revenue would have to
be invested in some fashion. Given the worldwide inflation and
the increasing price of oil, it was most economic for the Saudis
to keep production from increasing too rapidly and to preserve
significant quantities of their oil underground.[96]

Faisal and his officials reasoned that if they should act
contrary to their economic self-interest in order to oblige the
consumer countries in Europe and America, they could expect
something in exchange for their kindness. This "something," they
first hinted and later said more and more clearly, ought to be
political. The countries profiting from their oil ought to
pursue a political line friendly to them or, at the very least,
not excessively friendly to their enemy, Israel. If their
consumers should continue to aid Israel, the Saudis would see
themselves obliged to follow their own economic interest,
forbidding a rapid rise in production or even reducing their
output. This policy had been thought out in Saudi oil circles
and seemed to enjoy the approval of King Faisal in the months

before the war broke out. Measures to slow the increase in
production, or even to reduce current output, had not yet been
taken, but the stage of discreet warnings had been reached: "If
the U.S. does not begin to show a more even-handed policy we
cannot maintain our growth in production."[97] Faisal's position
has always been strategic for any oil boycott because he
controls the biggest proved oil reserves of any country. His
tentative support for the use of oil as a weapon before the war
was later transformed, by the war itself, into limitation of
production and an oil embargo directed against the United States.

   Meanwhile, in Egypt, relations with the Soviets remained
"frozen" until February 1973. On January 24 Sadat had met Soviet
Ambassador Vinogradov for the first time since the expulsion of
the Soviet advisers. (Vinogradov had returned from Moscow in
November.) After the visit of Hafez Ismail and Ahmed Ismail to
Moscow in February, relations improved further, and the flow of
Soviet military equipment began again. Hafez Ismail became the
principal negotiator with the Russians. President Asad of Syria
also worked to improve Soviet-Egyptian relations. In July Sadat
said that Soviet arms supplies were not "fully satisfactory" but
added: "But that is that, and we should not lose our friend
whatever his aid is to us." In fact, as the war came to show,
considerable amounts of Soviet military equipment continued
flowing into Egypt.

   It is probable that the Soviets continued to counsel caution
to their Arab friends. To the Soviets, the primary purpose of
the arms was to give weight to Egyptian insistence that the
occupied territories be liberated. They seem to have seen the
actual effort to recover the territories as a diplomatic rather
than a military operation. The Egyptians agreed to one last
diplomatic effort, at a meeting of the Security Council
scheduled for June. Egyptian Foreign Minister Zaygat clearly
stated that this would be the last effort, saying, "If the
avenue of international diplomacy is closed, we will employ
violence."[98] But no one took him seriously. The debate took
place from June 6 to June 15; it was adjourned and resumed on
July 20. It ended on July 26 when the U.S. vetoed the resolution
that would have expressed the concern of the Council about
Israel's lack of cooperation with UN mediator Jarring. Shortly
after this the date for the October war must have been fixed by
the Syrians and the Egyptians.[99]

   The first military moves of the October war took place on
September 1, but because these were disguised as maneuvers, very
few people realized that a war was impending. There is no
evidence that the Soviets were among these few. According to

Eric Rouleau of <u>Le Monde</u>, the Soviet ambassadors in Cairo and
Damascus were told about the war by the two heads of state only
on October 3. The Soviets evacuated their nationals and began
deliveries of arms by air to Cairo and Damascus. The
Palestinians were told "about 10 days in advance," according to
the radical fedayeen leader Nayef Hawatmeh.[100] According to
Rouleau they had already been told in August that a war was near
and had been asked what their attitude would be toward a peace
conference after the war.[101]

The events of the war will not be chronicled here. Both
superpowers accepted their predicted roles, i.e., each supplied
arms to its protégé. Through artificial-satellite communication,
they were able to follow developments closely, without having to
rely entirely on information from their clients.

The Soviet airlift began first. When the U.S. began its
effort on October 14, American spokesmen maintained that the
Soviets had already delivered 4,000 tons of armaments to Cairo
and Damascus had flown about 280 transport missions.[102] The
Soviet flights were via Yugoslavia and the Mediterranean. The
U.S. airlift, which started just a week after the war had begun,
went on for the rest of the war and thereafter. Both superpowers
felt obliged to continue the airlifts because they could not
abandon their protégés, particularly as long as the other
superpower went on supplying the opposite side.

On the other hand, both were clearly aware that the airlifts
were dangerous for both. Kosygin was in Cairo from October 16 to
October 19, talking to Sadat. We know about these conversations
only from Sadat's later claim that he had received "guarantees"
from the Soviets. He cited specifically his October 16-19
conversations with Kosygin and also a message received from
Brezhnev on October 21. October 21 was the day on which
Kissinger arrived in Moscow to negotiate with Brezhnev. The
message could easily have been in connection with that visit,
either to reassure the Egyptians before it took place or to
inform them about the agreements with Kissinger. Sadat mentioned
the Soviet "guarantees" in order to explain to other Arabs, Asad
in particular, why he concluded the armistice of October 22. One
can assume that the Soviet "guarantees" consisted of some kind
of assurance that Egypt would be able to obtain its war aims
even if the war were stopped at the then indecisive stage. Even
after the armistice the Soviets continued supplying arms to
Egypt and Syria and the Americans to Israel. During the war from
October 17 to October 19, the Arab oil ministers met in Kuwait
and decided to apply the oil weapon, an embargo against the U.S.
and Holland and a reduction of shipments to all other countries,

initially 10 percent and thereafter 5 percent each month, as
long as the Israelis remained in the occupied territories.*
     When, notwithstanding the armistice, the war continued after
October 22, and the Israelis made rapid progress toward
completely encircling the Egyptian Third Army on the southern
end of the canal, a Soviet-American confrontation occurred. This
happened after the Egyptians had called on the UN for Soviet and
American troops to police the armistice. The Americans had
refused to provide troops, but the Soviets had replied
ambiguously that the Egyptians were justified in making this
demand. Messages were sent from Moscow to Washington whose
precise content was not divulged; they were, however,
characterized as "brutal" by Senator Jackson. Perhaps the
Soviets threatened to send soldiers or "volunteers" to the
canal. There also seems to have been some suspicion in
Washington that the Soviets were mobilizing troops—according to
some reports, seven parachute divisions—near the Black Sea.
During the night of October 23-24 Nixon ordered a worldwide
"stage three" alert of all U.S. forces. After this alert was
relaxed came a return to détente. Washington and Moscow agreed
to exclude all permanent Security Council members (including
themselves) from the UN peace-keeping force, and Finnish
soldiers were brought from Cyprus as an advance UN unit. The
Israelis, having achieved their aim of surrounding the Egyptian
Third Army, observed a second UN cease-fire proclaimed on
October 24. On October 26 Brezhnev made a peace speech in
Moscow, calling for immediate negotiations. Peace, he said, was
"irreversible."
     The precise chronology of all these events remains obscure.
Different U.S. officials, among them President Nixon himself,
have spoken in vague and contradictory terms about them.
Suspicion was even voiced that the whole crisis could have been
exaggerated by President Nixon to repair his prestige or to
distract attention from his Watergate troubles.[103]

---

* According to information collected in Kuwait, Faisal had
originally intended to proceed gently and gradually against the
U.S. But he became indignant immediately before the meeting in
Kuwait at what he felt was U.S. treachery, when it was announced
that President Nixon had asked Congress for $2.2 billion for
arms aid to Israel. Only shortly before, the U.S. was said to
have given the Saudi foreign minister, Saqqaf, assurances of a
future even-handed policy in the Middle East.

From that crisis (or quasi-crisis) on, the going was fairly smooth as far as the Americans and Russians were concerned. It fell to Kissinger to work most actively for a settlement. He appeared to establish a basis of confidence with the Egyptians, but his dealings with the Syrians were less successful. It might seem surprising that the Soviets were willing to let Kissinger try to construct a Middle East peace almost alone, without their assistance, but they had reasons for this attitude. After the war it was truer than ever before that only the Americans could exert effective pressure on the Israelis. Perhaps an agreement between Kissinger and Brezhnev had been reached to the effect that the Israelis had to give way in the occupied territories, and it consequently became the task of the American to try to make them do it. As for parallel pressure on the Egptians and the other Arabs, both participants and nonparticipants in the war, the more the Soviets kept in the background in the negotiations, the less they would be obliged to exert pressure on their allies and the more they could hope that the Americans would be obliged to exert pressure themselves and make themselves disliked in the process.

Moscow did invite representatives of the fedayeen to visit the Soviet Union and tried to convince them to form a government-in-exile, which the Soviets promised they would recognize as the only representative of the Palestinians.[104] They explained that it would be best for the Palestinians to participate in the coming Middle East peace conference in Geneva. There were exploratory talks about the possibility of a "mini-Palestinian state" on the occupied West Bank of the Jordan. But the Palestinians were split on these issues. A considerable part of the more moderate leadership of Fatah were willing to participate in the conference if they were invited. The extremists and a considerable part of the rank and file of the fedayeen were against giving up their strategic aims as they had been defined so far: a "democratic" Palestinian state in which Arabs and Jews could live as equal citizens and which would mean the destruction of the existing "Zionist" state. To them negotiation meant principally to recognize the existence and legitimacy of that Zionist state. After some postponements and many consultations among themselves and with the Arab states, a Palestinian delegation went to Moscow, but their conversations had no conclusive results. Their leadership seemed inclined to consider that a new, more gradualistic strategy might be necessary, but there was still no unanimity about it. The Egyptians exerted pressure in this direction, as did the Soviets, but they were not successful.[105]

In general, the Soviet attitude toward the Arab states after
the war changed little from what it had been before. It could be
defined as political support, economic aid, and arms aid, but at
the same time counsels of caution and insistence that a
political solution to the problems of the Arabs should be
attempted and could be obtained. This position was conditioned
by Russian overriding interest in superpower collaboration; it
was calculated to avoid clashes with the U.S. as far as possible
without relinquishing too much of the interests and influence in
the Middle East which the Soviets had acquired during the
previous eighteen years.

The Egyptian attitude toward the Soviets had changed before
the 1973 war broke out. This change was due to the full
realization by the Egyptians of the extent and consequences of
Soviet-American détente. It took place between 1972 and 1973,
after the expulsion of the Soviet military advisers in Egypt. At
the time of the expulsion itself the Egyptians tended to analyze
their relations with the USSR preponderantly in terms of right
versus left in ideology and policies. They suspected that they
did not obtain enough Soviet help because they were not
sufficiently in harmony with Soviet policy and ideology. But
even then they suspected that the Soviets preferred détente with
the U.S. to military collaboration with Egypt. In the course of
the redefinition of the relations between Egypt and the Soviet
Union after the expulsion, the previous suspicion became a near-
certainty. This shift brought about a revision of Egyptian
political strategy.

Contrary to the observations and speculations of nearly all
observers, Egypt, faced by these realities, did not renounce its
political aims, namely, recovery of all the occupied territories
and reestablishment of the "legitimate rights" of the
Palestinians. It sought new policies to reach them. These
policies included building up the army, closer collaboration
with the other Arab states, and continued use of as much Soviet
support as possible. All this was done while the ultimate
Egyptian aim, to wage another war against Israel, was kept in
the background, hidden by means of the device itself, at first
accidental and later intentional, of talking about it so much
that any credibility it ever had tended to disappear.

The war against Israel was designed by Sadat from the
beginning to lead to a diplomatic solution of the Israeli
question. It aimed to convince the two superpowers that in their
own interests they could not ignore that question. Egypt's other
aims were to lift Egyptian morale and deflate Israeli pride as
far as possible. The military behavior of the Egyptians and what

we know of the military plans made at the outset of the war make
it clear that regaining the lost territory was not an immediate
aim of the Egyptian attack. This, it was hoped, would be
achieved by diplomatic means, once the two superpowers were
convinced that the situation existing from 1967 to 1973 could
not be preserved indefinitely without their own bilateral
détente being compromised.

The Chinese Connection
If no lasting solution to the Palestine conflict is reached,
as seems likely, a slow but steady increase of Chinese influence
in the Middle East is to be expected. This will come less
through material aid in the military and economic fields than
through political and ideological influence. If it is clear that
neither the Soviets nor the Americans are going to help the
Arabs get what they see as their rights, the Arabs, and
particularly Arab youth and the intellectuals, will turn toward
the Chinese. They will expect not material help from them but,
rather, a new ideology of which, happily for the Chinese, the
idea of self-help is an important ingredient. The Chinese have
always been careful to make it clear to their friends that they
have to help themselves; even ideologically, they have to evolve
their own special road of "peoples' revolution." China will
give them some aid, but it does not claim, as the Soviets have
done (perhaps a bit too confidently), that their help can be
decisive for the breakthrough to socialism. This breakthrough
has to be accomplished by the people concerned and by their own
revolution. The Soviet promise of building socialism with the
help of the socialist camp has, in the eyes of the Arabs, proved
a failure. At least the Soviets have not been able to deliver
the socialism the Arabs want. And the reasons impeding this
delivery are, in the eyes of the Arabs, the Soviets' own big-
power preoccupations, including a measure of cooperation with
the U.S.
     Chinese aid has been present in the Middle East for some
time. Its conditions have been more generous than Soviet or
Western ones. Chinese loans bear either no interest or very
little, and repayment can be very prolonged. But these loans
have been much smaller than the Soviet or Western ones. Between
1954 and 1971 Egypt obtained economic aid from the Soviet Union
in the amount of $1,845 million and from China, $85 million.
Iraq obtained in aid from the USSR $775 million and from China
$40 million. Syria received $450 million from the USSR and only
$15 million from China. For the Sudan the figures were $215

million and $80 million, and for Algeria, $515 and $50 million.*
In March 1972 the Russians agreed to lend Egypt $195 million for
rural electrification (a follow-up to the High Dam project) and
for constructing several factories. There were also loans from
Rumania and Hungary of $100 million and $12 million. After the
expulsion of the Soviet military advisers, China offered Egypt a
loan of $84 million (no interest, repayable in 20 years) to
build eight factories in Egypt, including textile plants and
steel mills.[106] (The projects or merchandise offered by the
Chinese have not always been satisfactory to the Arabs. In the
years before the Cultural Revolution, for instance, Chinese
credits granted Syria were not used because no worthwhile goods
or services were available.

In the Sudan, Chinese-Sudanese relations did not suffer when
Soviet-Sudanese relations became strained after the unsuccessful
procommunist coup in the summer of 1971; on the contrary, they
became more cordial. Defense Minister Abbas, one of the main
authors of the countercoup that saved Nimeiry, visited Peking
shortly after the events, was received with much praise, and
obtained another credit of $40 million, added to the $40 million
granted to Khartoum before. After the coup, Nimeiry liked to
contrast the "self-seeking" Russians with the "disinterested"
Chinese.[107] Similarly, the Chinese are said to be well liked in
Yemen (North), while the Soviets are not.[108] The reasons in both
cases seem to be that the Soviets intend to "educate" their
counterparts or even the government officials involved in their
projects. This causes friction. The Chinese come into other
countries as self-contained units, paying their own experts,
bringing their own supplies and sometimes their own laborers,

---

* Neue Zürcher Zeitung, Jan. 8, 1972; see Sevinc Carlson, "The
Chinese Intrusion," The New Middle East, no. 27 (Dec. 1970), p.
35, which presents interesting information about Chou and Nasser
in 1965: "During Chou's third trip to Cairo serious negotiations
took place between him and Nasser. Among the points of agreement
reached were the conditions that Communist China would abstain
from activities in the Arab world that would be harmful to the
interest of the UAR, and that the UAR would abstain from taking
sides in the Sino-Soviet conflict. Chou made a statement of the
points the Chinese had agreed to, before he left Cairo.

"Two months later, President Nasser made a trip to Moscow. He
obtained a promise of the acceleration of the construction of the
Aswan Dam as well as other aid in return for a promise to back
the USSR candidature in the coming conference in Algeria. . . .
What was evident was that he had not abided by his agreement with
Chou." (No sources for this report are given.)

and thus avoiding friction. This may well be a paradoxical
consequence of their ideological attitudes: the Chinese do not
expect any help from the "bourgeois" regimes they aid, so from
the start they rely on themselves, while the Russians want to
teach those regimes (which they consider "progressive
nationalists") in order to accelerate their advance toward
socialism.

The "New Left" in Aden. There are two Arab regions in which the
Chinese style and doctrines play a leading role today and which
are of interest because of the implications their development
might have for the future of the Middle East: the People's
Republic of Yemen (South Yemen) and the rebellion in Dhofar. It
is no accident that many of the radical Arab students and
intellectuals, who used to be admirers first of Nasser and then
of the fedayeen, only to become disillusioned with both, today
turn to those two regions in their search of "real" people's
socialism.

The regime in South Yemen emerged from a guerrilla war, urban
and tribal, against the British in 1967. The war in the
mountains behind Aden and in some of the industrial settlements
outside the city was waged by tribal forces gathered together in
the National Liberation Front (NLF). The city of Aden also had
its own liberation front, FLOSY, which enjoyed the support of
Nasser and those Egyptians stationed in Yemen at that time. The
two organizations competed for power and finally came to armed
hostilities. FLOSY proved the weaker, notwithstanding Egyptian
support; the reasons are still being discussed today. According
to the sympathizers of FLOSY, it was defeated principally
because the British carried on an all-out war against it,
secretly aiding the NLF in order to split the liberation fronts.
According to the NLF, the need to rely on themselves, without
any petit bourgeois outside help, forced the NLF to become so
tough and independent that eventually it proved superior to
FLOSY. Another important factor was no doubt the tribal
composition of the so-called Federal Army at the time of the
transition to independence. The army and the police threw their
weight in favor of the "rural" NLF and against the "urbanized"
FLOSY at the moment of independence (November 30, 1967).

That the NLF came to power despite Nasser's opposition made
it natural that the new South Yemen regime should consider Nasser
and the Arab nationalists as petit bourgeois elements and decided
to build "true socialism" on a Marxist-Leninist basis.

In 1969 an internal revolution inside the NLF brought down
the moderate president, Qahtan ash-Sha'bi, and his political

friends and brought to power the radical wing. This wing, under
Abdel Fattah Ismail, al-Khamiri, Rubai'a Ali, and others,
already had won an ideological victory in March 1968 at the
party congress at Zinjibar. There the radical "popular" line was
formulated, agreed to by the party, and later put into practice:

"All the power to the people; people's councils in every valley
and village; elections limited to peasants and workers; a
politically conscious popular militia formed by the peasants
and workers; agricultural collectives formed and directed by the
peasants themselves; industries managed by the workers in the
framework of a planned economy."[109]

But the army, which disliked such radicalism, arrested the left-
wing leaders on March 20, 1968, and forced Sha'bi to move to the
right. The leftist leaders went into the mountains or into
exile. A reconciliation and then new struggles followed,
frequently connected with sometimes violent changes in the
command of the army and the police. Finally Sha'bi was
overthrown by the left wing and was arrested on June 22, 1969.
    Thereupon the theories of Zinjibar began to be put into
practice. In this process the crucial importance to the regime
of the small, NLF-controlled "peasant revolt" emerged. It is
said that the first such revolt happened spontaneously in the
region of Lahej. The local police put its leaders into prison.
An agricultural reform had been decreed, and the revolting
peasants had tried to expropriate the holdings of landowners who
possessed less than the legally admitted maximum of land. But
President Rubai'a Ali proclaimed that the peasants were right
and that the police were infected with bourgeois ideology. So
the peasants obtained the land, the police went to prison, and
the land was expropriated notwithstanding the land-reform law.
"The land is not given, it has to be taken" became a slogan, and
peasant rebellions were instigated by the NLF party leaders in
all regions. The new landowners had to band together into
cooperatives or, in a few cases, state farms. These rebellions,
abetted by the regime, became its trademark. They served also as
patterns for the takeover by the workers of small enterprises,
such as fishing boats and hotels. The aim of the regime seems to
have been to awaken the initiative of the farmers and workers
and to enlist their enthusiasm and hoped-for creativity for the
"revolution." Most of the former bourgeois proprieters went to
prison, at least for a time. Others, principally from Aden, left
for foreign countries or for North Yemen.
    Both the Soviets and the Chinese took an interest in the new

regime. The Chinese had helped the NLF during its struggles
against the British, the Egyptians, and the "bourgeois
nationalists" of FLOSY. Then the Chinese and Soviets began to
wage a propaganda war in Aden against each other, unimpeded by
the presence of capitalist powers. The Soviets (and the East
Germans, who took considerable interest in the country)
criticized some of the "adventurist" policies of the NLF. Some
of the Soviet development projects stopped. The most important
of these, the road to Mukalla, was taken over by the Chinese.
But the Chinese did not replace the Soviets everywhere. Finally,
under Soviet pressure a new split in the NLF seemed imminent.
The Soviet candidate for leadership, Abdulla Badeeb, the minister
of education, declared that the NLF should be dissolved and the
communists should take over (even though, according to Eric
Rouleau of Le Monde, there were not more than fifty of them).
Rubai'a Ali decided on November 30, 1970, to enlarge the NLF by
admitting the communists (who agreed to dissolve their own party)
and the Baathists, as well as some "petit bourgeois" elements.
At the death of Nasser, large, spontaneous demonstrations took
place in Aden, despite the official ideology painting Nasser as a
petit bourgeois exploiter.

The economy had suffered greatly from the closing of the Suez
Canal and from the policies of the regime. The regime's economic
plan foresaw for 1970 a national income of $120 million, 40
percent less than the national income of the last year before
independence. It seems likely, moreover, that the plan was not
fulfilled.

There was also strong military pressure from Saudi Arabia.
The Saudis financed tribal armies that made incursions into South
Yemen during almost every Ramadan since 1968 to wage holy war
against the "atheists" of Aden. Exiles from South Yemen and the
border tribes, militarily inactive since the Yemen civil war,
furnished the manpower. Nevertheless, South Yemen has so far
withstood all attacks. The NLF is officially neutral in the Sino-
Soviet dispute. But it is clear that, although the Soviets are
indispensable to them economically and militarily, at least as
long as things remain as difficult as they have been, the Yemens
like the Chinese better personally and ideologically.

Aden has become the chief base for the Soviet naval and
fishing fleets in the Indian Ocean. The crews fly from Aden to
the USSR for rest periods while the ships stay in the Indian
Ocean, using Aden as a base.

In February 1972, sixty-five Northern Yemeni tribal chiefs
were killed by the Southern Yemenis on the border, close to
Beihan, a strategic corner where South Yemen, Yemen, and Saudi

Arabia join. The NLF declared that it had won a battle. But the
story told by their enemies seems the more likely one. This
report maintains that the sixty-five tribal leaders were called
to a meeting under a flag of truce and then were machine-gunned
by the Southerners. This version is more likely because of the
number of chiefs which both parties said had been killed. Among
the victims was Naji al-Ghader, the most important sheikh of the
Yemeni southeast region. He had played an important role in the
civil war and possessed direct and special links with King
Faisal. The indignant tribes demanded revenge.

    At the same time the exiles from South Yemen took action.
They also obtained arms and financial help from the Saudis and,
it was reported, from Qadhdhafi as well. The former chief
leaders of FLOSY were living in San'a and one, Abdulla al-Asnaj,
was even a minister in the northern government. (Some of the
southern ministers and party chiefs, conversely, are from the
North, like Abdel Fattah Ismail himself.) Ex-officers of the
South Yemen army, many of them by now refugees in the North, led
the exile forces. A war ensued during the summer of 1972. San'a
profited from the occasion by occupying the island of Kamaran,
which is close to North Yemen but had been administered by Aden
since British times. Surprisingly, the war was ended in October
1972 by the agreement, arrived at under the auspices of the Arab
League and Qadhdhafi, of both Yemens to unite. Probably both
parties hoped to profit from the agreement: the North by ending
the war and extending its influence into the South; the South
by avoiding an invasion attempt and hoping to infiltrate the
North politically. Hostilities in fact ceased, and talks about
realizing the unification agreed upon on paper have begun. But
so far the most important result of the agreement has been a
change of government in San'a resulting from the resignation of
Prime Minister Muhsin al-'Aini. Al-'Aini, considered a
"progressive" technocrat, was one of the chief architects of
the unity agreement. He came under pressure from the army and
the tribal council (Majles Shura) and was replaced at the end
of 1972 by Abdullah al-Hujari, considered a conservative and
close to the Saudis. The army and the tribal chiefs had hoped
for a "good" war with Saudi money and disliked the political
risks inherent in the unity plan. Nevertheless, officially,
unity remains the aim of both these widely divergent regimes.
The Northern Yemenis like to add that it must come, if not by
peace then by war.

    In the context of the struggle for influence between the
Chinese and the Soviets in Yemen, the "unity" project can be
seen as another step in the Soviet direction. It means

watering down, under pressure of the need to survive, the
revolutionary doctrine of the NLF to a more bourgeois and less
adventurist mixture, somewhat more in harmony with the
surrounding realities and, no doubt, with the general attitude
of the Southern Arabian population.

Rebellion in Oman. The Dhofar rebellion against the Sultan of
Muscat and Oman, of whose territory Dhofar is the extreme
western part, began in 1964 as a rebellion by the tribesmen who
live in the Qara mountains behind the plain of Salala. They
speak a language of their own, Shahri, of ancient Arabian
(Himyaritic) origin but incomprehensible to Arabic speakers.
The Qara mountains have tropical vegetation, monsoon rains, and
deep gorges with great caves, but almost no roads. The only
road through the region leads from Salala to Thamrit up through
the mountains and into the desert behind, on the way to Oman.
This road was the scene of the first attacks by the Qara
tribesmen.[110] In 1966 an attempt was made on the life of Sultan
Said bin Taimur by Qara troops who tried to shoot him during a
parade. Some Pakistani officers serving in the sultan's army lost
their lives, but the sultan escaped.

The tribal rebellion took on a nationalist and pro-Nasser
coloration as a result of the implantation of Arab nationalist
ideas. These ideas came to the Dhofar region through Qara
tribesmen who had emigrated to the Gulf sheikhdoms. Also, groups
of rebels who had been associated with the movement of Imam
Ghaleb of Nazwa, which had obtained Arab support after 1957,
decided after the defeat of the Imam to continue their struggle
in the region of Dhofar, which is geographically well-suited to
partisan war. The movement took on the name of the Dhofar
Liberation Front (DLF) and collaborated closely with the NLF of
South Yemen, at that time not yet in power and still fighting
the British.[111]

After the independence of South Yemen, the front obtained
aid from that side of the frontier and opened a liaison office
in Aden. A DLF congress at Himrin in 1968 criticized the
weaknesses of the previous movement, due in part, it declared,
to the

". . . presence of bourgeois forces in the leadership of the
Arab National Democratic Liberation movement, who because of
their class basis and ideology pursue policies of hesitation and
compromise, striving above all to save the interests and
privileges of their class."[112]

The movement elected a new leadership and elaborated a new
national charter. It changed its name from the Dhofar Liberation
Front to the People's Front for the Liberation of the Occupied
Arab Gulf (PFLOAG) and mapped out a strategy "for the whole of
the occupied Arab Gulf by linking the struggle in Dhofar with
the mass struggle in the Gulf—this being the final destiny of
the revolution in Dhofar." Ideologically, "scientific socialism"
(i.e., Marxism-Leninism) was adopted, "which constitutes the
historic doctrine that guides the struggles of the poor masses
for the eradication of colonialism, imperialism, the
bourgeoisie, and feudalism."

In this period Chinese arms, Chinese-trained military
leaders, and apparently also some Chinese instructors joined the
PFLOAG guerrillas via Aden and the sixth province of South Yemen.
The movement set up supply bases on South Yemeni territory at
Hauf, as well as training camps for the guerrillas in the sixth
province.[113]

The French journalist Viennot, having studied the PFLOAG
literature at the Hauf base camp, concluded that its ideology
was neither Chinese nor Soviet but closer to that of Cuba and
Che Guevara. He saw a strong ideological link with Hawatmeh's
People's Democratic Front for the Liberation of Palestine
(PDFLP), the most extreme leftist Palestinian movement.
Officially PFLOAG, like the South Yemeni NLF, has refused to
take a position on the Sino-Soviet dispute. In fact there is
little doubt that it is closer to the Chinese in theory and
military practice than to the Soviets. (However, the Chinese in
1972 withdrew their support to PFLOAG as a result of their
rapprochement with Iran.) Presumably, the Dhofar movement feels that
it must take help from any quarter willing to give it. In the
party literature studied by guerrilla recruits a whole section
concerns the bourgeois immorality of positive neutralism and
nonalignment, considered to be an opportunist policy because it
refuses to choose between the imperialist-capitalist and the
socialist camps. But neutrality in the Sino-Soviet struggle
seems to be seen in a different light.[114]

On June 12, 1970, the so-called National Democratic Front for
the Liberation of Oman and the Arab Gulf (NDFLOAG)[115] launched
three attacks against the garrisons at Jebel Akhdar, inside Oman
proper, much closer to the oil fields and the Gulf. But a number
of leaders were arrested in Matrah (the twin city of Muscat),
and documents and stocks of arms were seized. According to a
PFLOAG spokesman, this was partly the fault of the militants
themselves, who had refused to leave Matrah for the mountains.
The identity of the new front, NDFLOAG, was obscure. According

to Viennot it originated from a split in the MNA (Movement of
Arab Nationalists or, in Arabic, Haraka) in the Gulf. The
"Marxist-Leninist" elements are said to have left the MNA.
Rouleau of Le Monde was told in 1971 by Graham, the British
general in charge of pacification in Oman,[116] that the NDFLOAG
was formed by pro-Soviet communists. This is quite likely. The
movement seemed to the general more dangerous than that of
Dhofar.

It was probably because of the outbreak in Oman itself and
the deteriorating position in Dhofar, where only the capital of
Salala, ringed by barbed wire, remained firmly in the hands of
the sultan, that the British decided discreetly to remove Sultan
bin Taimur and to replace him by his son Qabus, who had been
kept prisoner by his father. Bin Taimur's authoritarian methods
had not proved successful against the Qara guerrillas. The
replacement operation was carried out on July 23, 1970. Bin
Taimur, slightly wounded, left Salala for London, and his son
began a new and more liberal regime in Oman and in Dhofar. One
of the first concerns of Qabus was to establish new relations
with the Qara tribesmen, the popular base of the PFLOAG
rebellion. They were promised amnesty, social-development
programs, schools, hospitals, and employment in the sultan's
army. (Schools, except for one palace school, had been
prohibited under Bin Taimur, as had possessing or even listening
to a radio, talking for more than fifteen minutes in public,
wearing shoes or glasses, smoking, uttering the word
"revolution," playing football, riding a bicycle, leaving the
country, and going out at night without a lamp.)

Qabus began radio broadcasts to explain the "new deal" to the
Qara and to accuse the PFLOAG leaders of atheism. Initially he
had some success. On the "eastern front" a rising against the
PFLOAG was attempted on September 12, 1970, but this was crushed
by the guerrillas.[117] Sources not unsympathetic to the new sultan
admit that, after some initial desertions, the Front imposed
death sentences on people suspected of treason and forbade the
Qara to go to Salala and to other government-held towns.[118]

Talks between PFLOAG and NDFLOAG, held on December 2, 1970,
did not lead to the unification of the two fronts, perhaps
because NDFLOAG was (and continues to be) tied too closely to
the Soviets. Instead, the two organizations called on

". . . all the national forces in Oman and the Arabian Gulf to
group in a broad national front to eliminate the colonial
presence and to end the rule of the feudal families, establish
progressive national rule, and realize all the accomplishments
required at this stage."[119]

It is no doubt significant that the communiqué of the two fronts contained no attacks against the "bourgeoisie" and the "petite bourgeoisie"; when PFLOAG speaks for itself such attacks are never omitted.

According to PFLOAG and NDFLOAG, the "reactionaries," principally the Saudis, aim at founding a separate state in Hadhramaut and the Mahri region, thus cutting off Aden from Dhofar. PFLOAG and NDFLOAG see this as the strategic aim of the different armed expeditions financed by the Saudis so far.[120] Such a strategy would probably be more promising than the attempt to conquer and pacify the Qara people in their mountains and gorges, which appears to be a nearly impossible task, given the troops that the sultan has (perhaps 6,000 men overall) and the PFLOCAG sanctuaries on the other side of the frontier.[121] Moreover, the war eats up a considerable amount of the sultan's oil income.

The promises of Qabus and the relaxation of the tyrannical rules of the old sultan have caused a wave of hopeful expectations in Oman proper. If these are not fulfilled to a reasonable extent because revenues are used for the war, there will be danger of discontent and rebellion in Oman and in Muscat itself. Riots and strikes have occurred already. More "conspirators" have been arrested recently, and more arms caches have been found.* According to Rouleau, something like a

----

* The arrested are said to number 77; their arrest took place in December 1972 and seems to have been due to an attempt by PFLOAG to infiltrate Oman proper. According to The Economist, arms were smuggled from South Yemen to the harbor of Sur. The Economist speculated that the attempt of PFLOAG to extend its operations might have been due to a rebuff that the Black September movement is said to have given to a request for aid by PFLOAG. But this is probably to exaggerate the importance of that rather shadowy terrorist group. See "Oman: Embarrassing the Money Lenders," The Economist, April 21, 1973.

See also the major journalistic accounts of the situation in Oman in an-Nahar, March 19, 20, and 21, 1973, and in L'Orient-Le Jour, April 6, 7, and 8, 1973. The an-Nahar articles (by Riad ar-Rayes) concentrate on the complex tensions between Oman and Abu Dhabi and describe the change of orientation of Oman politics "away from the sea and toward the desert." This change includes closer collaboration with Saudi Arabia, Jordan (for military training), and Iran. In an interview (March 20 in al-Nahar) Sultan Qabus admitted that the Iranians give Oman

prerevolutionary situation already exists in Muscat.[122] According
to The Economist, the sultan spent over 20 million of his 55
million of oil royalties on arms alone in 1971.[123] In 1972, BAC

---

military aid and that there are "some airplanes." This was
confirmed in a vague way by Iranian Prime Minister Hoveyda in
London on April 13. Correspondents estimated that there might be
about 400 specialized Iranian troops in Dhofar. According to
Rayes, "All Salala knows" that Chinese aid to the revolutionaries
was reduced, and that the Russians took over. There is also a
training mission of Dhofar revolutionaries in Russia. According
to Rayes, troop strength in Dhofar is as follows: 10,000 men in
the Oman army (there were only 3,000 in 1970); about 250 British
officers on loan, 50 or more of whom are affiliated with the
Oman army; 100 retired Pakistani officers; some Indian navy
officers for coastal patrols. Efforts are being made to
"arabicize" the army; there are some Omani officers; Fahd Bin
Taimur is assistant defense secretary; the secretary of defense
is a British colonel, H. Oldman. A defense council has been
established. Sixteen hundred Dhofaris, split off from the
revolutionaries, are said to collaborate with the Oman army as
scouts. About 60 percent of the Oman army are still Beluch
soldiers.

Edouard Saab, of L'Orient-Le Jour, who has been with the
revolutionaries, was principally impressed by their poverty. It
seemed so great to him that the help they receive from China and
Russia cannot be important.

On June 20, the result of the trial of the 77 PFLOAG people
captured in December 1972 was announced in Muscat. Ten were
originally condemned to death, but nine of these were
subsequently sentenced to prison for life; 23 others were given
life prison sentences; 24 others were given prison terms ranging
from one to twelve years. Six women received sentences of six
months; one woman was given a sentence of one year. Three more of
the accused were acquitted, and ten remain unaccounted for. The
tribunal found that the accused were members of PFLOAG, some of
whom had been trained outside of Oman in the use of arms "which
other countries had sent to Oman" (an-Nahar, June 22, 1973).
Also, in Bahrain a "worker" received a prison sentence of eight
years because he had hidden arms in the wall of his house
(Muhammed Jaber al-Ansari in al-Hawadith [Beirut], June 8, 1973,
p. 23). The author thought that perhaps this was the first of
more trials because there has been news about cells of PFLOAG
being discovered in Bahrain and in the Federation of Arab
Emirates.

Strikemaster planes, piloted by British expatriates, bombed gun positions on the Yemeni side of the border. Protests from Aden followed. In 1972 about seventy officers and fifteen NCOs of the British army were seconded to the sultan's forces. In addition, an unspecified number of expatriate "mercenaries" joined the government forces.[124] More recently, and particularly after the Shah sent Iranian commando troops and helicopters to Dhofar, the rebellion has suffered some defeats.

A tentative lesson can be drawn from these rather obscure and still inconclusive developments in the southern part of Arabia: If there should be further Arab exasperation and political frustration (as is bound to develop if there is no solution to the Palestine conflict), the possibility that the Arab "new left" will gain ground has to be taken into account. How successful it will be cannot be predicted. Its first clashes with the "nationalist" regimes were in the 1972 student troubles in Cairo. If frustration mounts, the regimes are bound to grow weaker and the protest movements stronger. It is inside the protest movements that the "new left" will find its chance. It is no accident that a large proportion of the student slogans used in the 1972 demonstrations in Cairo and repeated one year later were "people's war" slogans.[125] The protest movement has by no means only one ideological position. All activists, from Muslim fundamentalists through the different shades of nationalists and socialists to the communists and groups to the left of them, find their place in it. But as all other political forces lose credibility by being unable to lead the Arabs out of their present position of no peace and no war, the new left is bound to gain influence. As a way out, it offers a slogan and a policy, "people's war," which, being untried, at least does not bear the stigma of failure. The "people's war" policy can even claim that it has been successful against the Americans in Vietnam. It has the added attraction of appearing to be a policy of the East imposing itself on a West that is resented as an arrogant and provocative menace. A people's war in the desert cannot of course, be the same as one in the jungle. It will have to evolve its own methods. Urban guerrilla war might be one such method, with the aim of impressing Arab officers and gradually infiltrating Arab armies, then bringing down the governments, and eventually establishing that Middle Eastern North Vietnam which has been for some years the dream of the Arab new left.

The Chinese could help in a limited, discreet fashion. One can see from the Gulf events that the Soviets would feel bound to enter the picture as soon as any movement became important enough, just as they did in Aden. Moreover, in the years in

which the Palestinian movement looked as if it could succeed
politically, the Soviets had the Arab communist parties form
their own guerrilla group, although never a very effective one.
A complex Sino-Soviet struggle inside the Arab new left would be
one result of such a development. The Arab new left itself would
almost certainly try to avoid taking sides in such a struggle,
in order to profit from both.

Such a new left movement would very probably have to replace
the Arab regimes, or some of them, before it could make any
significant gains against Israel. Quite possibly, the oil
countries could become the main aim of its attack. They are much
more vulnerable than Israel. Drives against the oil countries
could be justified ideologically by pointing to the importance
of Arab oil to world capitalism and the need to harm the
imperialists in order to punish them for their aid to Israel.
Both China and the USSR would try to profit from an oil crisis
in the West or Japan. They could attempt to become well-paid
middlemen in the sale of Arab oil, disposing of part of it and
keeping another part for their own use.

But with political conditions as they are today in the Arab
oil countries, such developments would require a previous
overthrow of the present conservative oil regimes by the Arab
new left, a possibility still very much in the future. But the
first signs of this future are becoming apparent in the mood of
the Arab students today. "They think in class categories and
explain everything by the concept of imperialism," said one Arab
professor, himself an Arab nationalist. Perhaps it can also be
taken as a sign of this future that Chou En-lai has promised to
give more attention to the Middle East, "now that the Vietnam
question has been solved."[126]

Chapter 4

SOUTH ASIA AND THE GREAT POWERS

Bhabani Sen Gupta

In the last days of March 1971 the India-Pakistan subcontinent was caught in a major upheaval while a spring thunderstorm was about to occur in the sphere of international relations. An acute political crisis in Pakistan was immediately transformed into a serious crisis between Pakistan and India. At no time did it suck in the three major powers of the world, the Soviet Union, the United States, and China, but great-power involvement transported another local conflict to the level of global strategic considerations of the major actors of the world system. The events of 1971 would probably not have culminated in tearing Pakistan into the two sovereign nations of Pakistan and Bangladesh had not the spring thunderstorm finally transformed the postwar bipolar world into an emerging tripolar or multipolar balance of power. The changed relationships among the major powers undoubtedly facilitated the redrawing of the political map of South Asia. The new political map of the subcontinent, in its turn, helped clarify the changing pattern of great-power relationships.

An electric change in the core relationship of an international system must necessarily be felt in all of its subsystems. The trauma of the Sino-American rapprochement ran through all the limbs of the world body politic, but in South Asia alone it interacted with an entirely new local convulsion. Unlike the actors in the Vietnam war and the Middle East conflict, those on the subcontinent were given no time to absorb the meaning of the great transformation in superpower relations. The reaction patterns of the three conflict zones to the great change were therefore basically different. While the North Vietnamese were afraid of a Sino-American deal made behind their back, and the Egyptians of a Soviet-American agreement injurious to vital Arab interests, for India, the principal actor in the South Asian drama, it was the double shock of the collapse of a favorable system of great-power relationships and the emergence of another that it regarded as hostile to Indian interests. For ten years and more, the Indian ruling elite had been sustained by what they had perceived to be parallel actions by the United States and the USSR in Asia to contain Chinese

power and influence. In the summer of 1971 this Soviet-U.S.
convergence suddenly collapsed. In its place, as Indians saw it,
there developed a Sino-American convergence of interests for the
containment of Soviet power and influence. The convulsion in the
subcontinent brought about an instant polariziation of
superpower interests. The United States and China were seen by
Indians to be standing by Pakistan, and the USSR to be
supporting India and Bangladesh.

In evaluating the impact of the changing pattern of great-
power relationships on the conflict-prone region of South Asia,
we must, then, bear in mind that here is an unanticipated
mingling of two traumas, one local, the other global. The grim
realities of the local trauma shaped the actors' perceptions of
the global changes. These perceptions were shaped not
necessarily by the realities of the new great-power
relationships, but by the local elites' images of those
realities. Elite groups, however, are seldom assailed by
Cartesian doubt; to them there is little or no difference
between the real world and their own ideas about it.

The primary factor shaping the foreign-policy behavior of the
smaller nations almost always is the realities of domestic
politics; except for the two superpowers, the foreign policy of
any member of the international community is hardly an
autonomous pursuit of the state apparatus. On the subcontinent
it was the internal politics of Pakistan and India that in the
main determined the course of events during 1970-1972 (as in
the previous periods). However, Pakistan and India are two
physically contiguous, if psychologically distant, neighbors.
Their internal politics mesh at a hundred points. Indeed India
has been, and continues to be, Pakistan's number one internal
problem, and Pakistan India's at least number two.[*]

In 1971 the political crisis in East Pakistan drove millions
of refugees to seek shelter in India, thus creating for the
Indian government an economic, political, and social problem of
tremendous magnitude. Many among the Indian elites saw in the
conflict between the two wings of Pakistan a welcome opportunity
to cut Pakistan down to a size at which it could no longer be a

---

[*] India's number one problem is India itself. Even after the
Sino-Indian border war of 1962, India's security posture
remained primarily pointed at Pakistan. Pakistan casts its
shadow on India's domestic politics and affects the Indian
psyche in a way that China cannot.

serious competitor of India, or an enemy to be afraid of. From
the beginning of the East Pakistan crisis, therefore, opinion-
makers in India built up systematic pressure on the government
to act on behalf of the Bangladesh movement. No government could
have survived in New Delhi if it had taken a neutral, hands-off
attitude to the political upheaval in East Pakistan. The
Pakistani military crackdown on the Awami League and the East
Bengal autonomy movement drove thousands of rebel political
actors to seek refuge in India and operate from Indian
territory. Soon the rudiments of a partisan force were allowed to
operate from the Indian side of the border. By granting the
partisans sanctuary, India committed itself to the emergence of
Bangladesh. As the political crisis deepened and the freedom
struggle intensified in the latter half of 1971, there
developed, in New Delhi's perception, a security threat of far-
reaching implications, affecting the entire eastern flank of
the Indian Union. What was unacceptable to the leaders of the
Indian government was not only the triumph of the military
regime in East Pakistan but also the passing of the leadership
of the resistance movement to groups and factions more radical
and less liberal-democratic than the Awami League. Such a
development might have established linkages between the radical
communist movements in West Bengal and radical groups across the
border, posing a serious threat to the Indian political system.*
The events of 1971, then, showed how closely linked are the
internal politics of two neighboring states, and how easily the
internal affairs of one impinge on the internal affairs of the
other.

South Asia's Strategic Disunity
One of the striking features of South Asia since the withdrawal
of British imperial power is its lack of strategic

----

* This was one of the main political factors that weighed with
the Indian government in 1971 and influenced its decision-
making. See Chanchal Sarkar, "Explaining India's Stance,"
Hindustan Standard (Calcutta), June 24, 1971. Sarkar wrote,
"Perhaps there is more substance in the argument that, if the
Awami League leadership of Bangladesh is allowed to wither, then
the new leadership will be of extreme elements, many of whom
already profess allegiance to Chairman Mao Tse-tung and that the
radicalization of Bangladesh could be very unsettling for the
rest of South East Asia.

unity. During the imperial period the strategic unity of the
region had rested on Britain's predominant political position,
its control of the seas, and the strong Indian army that could
protect Burma and Afghanistan as well as project its force into
the Middle East and Southeast Asia. All this changed in 1947.
The empire's final offspring, certainly not its noblest, was the
partition of the subcontinent into India and Pakistan. At the
core of the never-ending tensions in the region lay the deep,
inbred antagonism between the two states. Afghanistan's leaning
toward India and the Soviet Union sprang from its territorial
claims on Pakistan, while the neutrality of Ceylon and Burma was
to a large extent motivated by fear of Indian (and Chinese)
domination. Nepal remained India's exclusive sphere of influence
until the late fifties when China met India in that Himalayan
retreat to compete for influence and power. Although India was
the central power in the region, it did not try to establish
security accords, nor could it compose differences with its
principal neighbors. The existence of the two strong communist
powers to the north of the subcontinent drew the attention of
the United States to South Asia during the cold-war period, and
Pakistan, by signing a military pact with the United States in
1954, struck a strategic posture entirely different from
India's. Although the American arms supply to Pakistan created a
major security problem for India, Nehru was able to counter it
by forging strong political links with the two communist
neighbors, without accelerating India's defense expenditure.[1]
In general, during the fifties Pakistan looked upon its alliance
with the West as a security guarantee against India, and India
regarded its close political relations with the USSR as a
safeguard against any joint Pakistan-Western anti-India move at
the United Nations with regard to Kashmir.

This scenario changed in the sixties. The Sino-Indian
conflict accomplished two contradictory things simultaneously.
It exposed more sharply than ever before the strategic disunity
of the region. It also imposed on it some promise of strategic
symmetry. The border crisis with China spiraled India's defense
expenditure upward; after the debacle of the border war of 1962,
defense became India's first priority.[2] American military aid to
bolster India's anti-China defense brought into the open the
tenuousness of Pakistan's strategic linkage with the United
States. In Pakistani perception, the two superpowers were now
working together to strengthen its principal enemy, India.
Pakistan could turn with assurance only to China for help. In
1963, Zulfikar Ali Bhutto, then Pakistan's foreign minister,
asserted that "the largest power in Asia" would come to his

country's rescue if it were attacked by India.[3]

The strategic symmetry came from parallel Soviet and American aid to build up India as a countervailing power in Asia vis-à-vis China. The United States, with British collaboration, tried at the same time and failed to nudge India to work out a settlement of the Kashmir problem with Pakistan. India responded reluctantly to the Anglo-U.S. pressure, but soon found justification for abandoning its conciliatory efforts when China concluded a border agreement with Pakistan conferring tentative sanction on Pakistan's occupation of two-thirds of the state of Jammu and Kashmir.[4] Although India refused to permit the establishment of U.S.-controlled bases on its territory, Nehru, according to the then American ambassador in New Delhi, Chester Bowles, agreed to "support a genuine effort by [the U.S.] Government to negotiate a political settlement that could end the fighting in Southeast Asia [Vietnam]" as well as to "negotiate a ceiling of military expenditure with Pakistan."[5]

A major American initiative in South Asia, however, did not come. On the contrary, after the assassination of President Kennedy, the United States apparently lost interest in India on the political and developmental planes. Increasing involvement in the Vietnam war led to a general American disengagement from the uncommitted nations of the third world in terms of economic aid. By the mid-sixties, anxiety to avoid a direct military conflict with the Chinese over the Vietnam war evidently persuaded President Johnson to lower America's anti-China profile in South Asia also. Washington found it wiser to concede to Moscow the primary diplomatic and strategic role in South Asia because of the Soviets' larger stakes in containing China and because of India's relative political unimportance to the United States. India turned to the Soviet Union and got everything it had asked from the United States and more. What pleased the Indians most was that the United States was no longer committed to tilt toward Pakistan. American neutrality during the India-Pakistan war of 1965 hurt Pakistan more than India and widened the divide between the two erstwhile allies. The Soviets quickly took advantage of the new situation to bring about the Tashkent accord between the two neighbors of the subcontinent.

It was now for Moscow to try to accomplish what had eluded Washington's grasp in the fifties and early sixties. Moscow moved steadily to improve relations with Pakistan, assuring India that a Soviet presence in the neighboring country would contribute to peace and stability on the subcontinent. Nevertheless, when the Soviets began to supply military aid to

Pakistan in 1968, the Indians reacted in much the same way as
the Pakistanis had done to the supply of American arms to India
in 1963.[6] There was, however, an important difference between
the two situations. Moscow did not lose interest in India.
Indeed, the conflict with China enhanced India's importance to
the Soviet Union, which remained heavily tilted toward New Delhi
while improving its relations with Pakistan. The Soviets
continued to extend substantial defense and development
assistance to India and came forward to help build India's own
infrastructure of defense industry.[7] In 1968, undaunted by
adverse Indian reaction to Soviet military aid to Pakistan,
Premier Kosygin, while on a visit to Rawalpindi, proposed an
economic collaboration conference, with Russian participation,
of the countries of South Asia and the Near East (Turkey, Iran,
Afghanistan, Pakistan, India, and Nepal). The Afghan government
was willing to host the conference, which, however, fell
through, largely because of Pakistan's strong opposition.[8] A
year later, Leonid Brezhnev launched a major anti-Chinese
initiative in Asia by announcing his concept of an Asian
collective security system that had prevailed in most of Asia
since the fifties.[9] As the sixties came to an end, the Soviet
Union had clearly assumed the initiative to draw South Asia and
much of Southeast Asia within its global strategic orbit. The
American perception was otherwise:

"The subcontinent retains its high strategic importance and can
still make a substantial contribution to the security of
southern and eastern Asia. It also remains the point of greatest
long-run potential danger for stability in Asia. The antagonism
aroused in both India and Pakistan toward the United States
during 1965—because of its military aid to the rival side and
its failure to use its alleged capacity to make this enemy yield
the essential concessions—indicates the frustrating complexity
of American security problems in this vital region."[10]

India's Role in South Asia
If the acuteness of the crises of South Asia have so far remained
somewhat muted, it is because in this region, unlike in
Southeast Asia and West Asia (and of course in Europe), the
superpowers have avoided a direct confrontation. They have
engaged in shadow-conflicts, with the United States and China
operating their strategies, at different times, through
Pakistan, and the Soviet Union operating through India. The
subcontinent has, however, experienced twelve military actions
in twenty-four years, half of them within the geographic

frontiers of India or of Pakistan, the rest involving the two
countries or India and China.* This high salience of armed
actions and conflicts in relation to the politics of the
subcontinent would suggest that there were serious tensions and
imbalances built into the "arrangement" that in 1947 partitioned
the empire into the two mutually hostile states of India and
Pakistan.[11]

Some of the imbalances stood in the way of nation-building
and were removed by military action after the politics of
pressure and persuasion failed. These include the Indian "police
action" against the princely state of Hyderabad and the
Pakistani measures to subdue the ruler of Kalat. The interstate
conflicts, whether between Pakistan and India or between India
and China, afflicted the subcontinent's political climate with
an overdose of mutual fear, suspicion, hatred, and rejection.
Within the subcontinent coexist, far from peacefully, warring
ideologies and religions; a multiplicity of cultures, races,
nationalities, and languages; neonationalist states informed by
power aspirations; ancient traditions and taboos exposed to
modern catalysts of science and technology; areas whose
political status is either in dispute or indeterminate; and long
frontiers, sometimes irrational and undemarcated, quickened to
life by clashing nationalist claims. Relations between Pakistan
and India have been bedeviled by a cosmic clash of values and
principles. Nowhere in Asia has the process of nation-building
been unattended by internal or interstate war. The peculiarity
in South Asia is that while the conflicts have been many, they
have been contained more or less regionally. The tensions have
thus remained undiffused and have been driven into the nerves of
governments and peoples. These tensions culminated in the
intermeshing conflicts of 1971. These conflicts ended the
"arrangement" of 1947.

----

* The twelve military actions are these: the India-Pakistan war
in Kashmir, 1948; Indian military action against the Nagas and
the Mizo tribesmen; Indian police action against the princely
state of Hyderabad; Indian military action against the
Portuguese in Goa; Pakistani military action against tribesmen
on the northwest frontier and against the ruler of Kalat; the
Sino-Indian border war of 1962; the India-Pakistan clash at the
Rann of Kutch in 1965; the India-Pakistan war of 1965; Pakistani
military action in East Pakistan in 1971; the India-Pakistan war
of 1971.

The history of the subcontinent since 1947 centers on the basic contradiction of the "arrangement," namely, India's determination to be counted in the world as a major power, together with the severe restraints imposed on this determination by the creation of the Islamic state of Pakistan. Put another way, it is the history of Indian persistence to bend in its favor the balance of power that grew out of the 1947 "arrangement." This balance of power rested on the British imperial concept of parity between India and Pakistan, a concept that stemmed from the imperial policy of treating the Indian national Congress and the Muslim League as two coequal political forces. This British theory of parity was later adopted by the United States.

India's nonalignment prevented it from joining the collective security system of the United States; lack of resources made it impossible for India to assemble a security system of its own. Nevertheless, before nonalignment was elevated to a doctrine, India had taken a series of strategic, power-political measures to alter the balance of power that had been imposed on the subcontinent. By military intervention it safeguarded the accession of Kashmir to the Indian Union and was able to hold the Vale of Kashmir against the invaders from Pakistan. In 1950 Nehru unilaterally brought Nepal within India's security area and a year later intervened successfully in the power struggle between the Nepalese king and the hereditary feudal lords known as Ranas. The security measures against the Naga insurgents were designed to prevent the defection of extramural nationalities peopling the strategically important but politically soft eastern and northeastern frontier regions. The initial Indian opposition to the victory in Tibet by the Chinese communists was accompanied by rapid extension of the Indian administration, albeit in a token manner, up to the MacMahan Line in the northeast. The final agreement with the Chinese on Tibet left India with substantial rewards. In return for recognition of Chinese sovereignty over Tibet, India obtained Peking's explicit recognition of its special relationship with Nepal, Sikkim, and Bhutan and of its interest in peaceful social change in Tibet itself.[12]

Since the mid-fifties, India's effort to establish itself as the dominant power in South Asia began to meet with obstacles both within and without. In 1954 the United States reinforced the British doctrine of parity by drawing Pakistan into its interlocking chain of anticommunist military alliances. India, as noted, turned to the Soviet Union and China for political and developmental support to counter Pakistan's growing military

strength. Nation-building in the subcontinent from then on had
to proceed parallel to competitive influence-building by the
superpowers. In fact, even in the mid-fifties India was caught
in this influence-building competition not merely between
Washington and Moscow but also between Moscow and Peking. In the
cold-war rivalry between Washington and Moscow, nonalignment did
enable India to acquire a certain measure of independence in
decision-making and a good measure of developmental assistance
from both power blocs. India was, however, unable to derive any
such advantage from the Sino-Soviet cold war, simply because in
this India was not nonaligned;[13] indeed, it could not be in view
of the hostilities that broke out along the Sino-Indian border.
Since the early sixties India has not had an autonomous China
policy. If Sino-Soviet relations continue to be as bad as they
are and Indian security assurances from the USSR therefore
remain credible, India cannot at the same time attempt to
normalize relations with Peking on terms that would satisfy the
rulers of China. India's security posture is therefore unusually
sensitive to Sino-Soviet and Sino-U.S. relations. It is the lack
of autonomy in its China policy that makes India highly
apprehensive about any realignment in great-power relationships
in which the United States and China may adopt an anti-Soviet,
and therefore anti-Indian, posture. The situation would be
equally unpalatable for India if a détente were to develop
between Moscow and Peking. An Indian foreign-policy expert
rightly affirmed in the late sixties that the ideal situation
for India was to be on friendly terms with both the United
States and the USSR, while Pakistan remained an ally of Peking.[14]

India's "Stability of Stagnation"
The principal obstacle to India's growth as a major power
lies within the country: it is India's massive poverty and slow
pace of development. India's decision-makers, while speaking to
the world, project a picture of the world's largest democracy
with enormous development potential. However, when they turn
inward to face problems of national order and political
management, the country becomes "vast," its citizens "the
toiling, teeming masses," its society "turbulent and threatened."
The leaders of the independence movement set about the near-
impossible task of developing and modernizing an essentially
change-resistant society and without giving compulsion a
strategic role in the rigorous enforcement of obligations.[15]
Broadly speaking, the fundamental contradiction in India today
is the contradiction between the political system of
parliamentary democracy and the inequalities and stratifications

resulting from democratic planning. Gunnar Myrdal has argued
that because India moved so slowly toward fundamental change, it
lost its ability to make the necessary structural
transformations conducive to growth. India's political stability
is a "stability of stagnation"; the government has remained
stable at the cost of development.[16]
    At the end of two decades of democratic planning, India
remains the world's poorest nation, with roughly one-half of its
547 million people living in abject poverty and earning not more
than four dollars a month. A recent study of Indian poverty
sponsored by the Ford Foundation observes:

"During the past decade, the per capita private consumer
expenditure increased by less than half per cent per annum.
Moreover, the small gains have not been equitably distributed
among all sections of the population. The condition of the
bottom 20 per cent urban poor has definitely deteriorated, and
for another 20 per cent of the urban population, it has remained
more or less stagnant. Thus, while the character of rural
poverty has remained the same as before, the character of urban
poverty has deepened further."[17]

    It is not that the economy has not made any advance, but
that whatever advance has taken place has been highly uneven
from period to period and region to region, and has been
neutralized by the growth in the population. Moreover, the bulk
of the gains seem to have been siphoned off by a relatively
small segment of the society. Thus, during the decade of 1960-
1970, the national income at constant prices (1960-1961 = 100)
increased to 142.5, but because of the parallel increase in
population, per capita income, once again at constant prices,
has shown only a slight increase of 14.1 percent over the
decade. Between 1961 and 1965 the general index of industrial
growth went up by 10.8 percent a year. But from 1966 to 1970 the
growth rate tumbled to 3.4 percent. In the first half of the
sixties the proportion of the national income from large and
small industries had reached 15.1 percent. It declined to 13.2
percent in the latter half of the decade—a process, indeed, of
deindustrialization.[18]
    Much has been made of the so-called green revolution in
recent years, but the new technology has hardly touched three-
fourths of Indian agriculture, and its impact is felt only on
the output of food grains, mainly wheat. A noted Indian
economist has asked the question, "What precisely therefore has
been the achievement of the new technology? On what lies the
claim for pride and glory we have been apportioning to the green

revolution during recent years?" His own answer:

"The sustained increase in food production . . . is 15 million
tons between 1964-65 and 1972-73, and almost entirely made up of
the rise in the output of wheat. Beyond wheat, apart from
scrappy results here and there, it is almost one unrelieved area
of darkness. Equally noteworthy is the other fact that the
average annual rate of growth of food production at 1.8 percent
during these eight years is less than half of what was attained
in the [pre-green revolution] period between 1950-51 and 1964-
65."[19]

The stability of the Indian political system despite the slow
pace of development has been, by and large, the result of the
convergence of two systems, the system of parliamentary
democracy and the system of the Congress party as the party of
consensus and balance. The Congress party has been the umbrella
under which the major factions of the Indian bourgeoisie have
operated together in a broad consensus. Most of the opposition
factions also have been operating just outside the umbrella,
more or less as part of the Congress party system; only the
communists have a stable and differentiated support base of
their own.[20] The Congress party has thus played the role of the
government party as well as that of the main opposition party
within its dominant one-party-plus system. The mobilization-
recruitment-linkage drive of the Congress party enabled it to
draw large segments of the emerging middle class, industrial
workers, and the peasantry into the twin system of party and
government. Monopoly of government power made a wide
distribution of patronage possible. At the state and district
levels, the implements of power were shared among the main
factions through established social institutions. The castes
were thus politically activated, lending strength to the
functional structure of the system.[21]
The quiescence of the countryside was maintained mainly
through the political linkages established between the ruling
Congress party and the landowning community; here stability was
largely the result of the slow pace of change in the agrarian
sector. While no sections of the rural population were entirely
deprived of the benefits of development, the bulk of the new
resources created by community development—irrigation, power,
rural credit societies, industrial cooperatives, and rural
electrification—accrued to the new kulaks. They manned the new
institutions of political power in the villages, ranging from
the panchayat (village council) to the zila parishad (district
council). It was among these rising village leaders that the
ruling party sought new recruits.[22]

If the stability of the Indian political system has been the product of the convergence of politics and party, the decay of one cannot but lead to the decay of the other. In other words, for the continued survival of the political system, continued survival of the Congress system of consensus and balance may also be essential. A threat to the Indian political system therefore developed in 1967 when the Congress party lost control of the government in as many as eight states in the fourth general election. The debacle has to be ascribed to the sudden shrinkage of the economy since 1964-1965 and a serious recession, followed by two years of severe drought and famine conditions in large parts of the country. The rewards at the command of the Congress party also shrank, making factional competition and conflicts highly attritional. The crisis in the economy became a political crisis. The defections from the party during the 1967-1969 period were clearly attributable to unsatisfied demands for patronage and power from various sections in the states. Leaders of defecting groups became chief ministers while almost every defecting member claimed a ministerial post. The defeat of the Congress party changed the role of the opposition factions as pressure groups. They now joined together in eight states to form non-Congress coalitions. Thus ended the first phase of India's postindependence politics.

The collapse of the Congress system led to a series of political developments of some significance for the next phase of Indian politics. Most of the non-Congress coalitions in the states failed to introduce any fundamental change in the socioeconomic fields, confirming thereby that they had no autonomous role to play in the political system and that they were nothing but suburban extensions of the Congress system. However, in two states, Kerala (on the southwest coast) and West Bengal, and one Union-administered territory, Tripura (in eastern India), leftist coalitions were dominated by the Communist Party of India (Marxist). These coalition governments sought to bring about some structural change in agrarian relations by encouraging the poor and landless peasantry to seize land vested in the government under the "land reforms" of the fifties but undistributed to the landless peasants, as well as land illegally possessed by landlords in excess of the ceilings imposed by the land-reform legislations. The decision of the West Bengal united-front government not to give police support to the landlords in the "legitimate" struggle of the land-hungry peasants created a law-and-order situation of unprecedented magnitude and seriously threatened to upset the twenty-year social balance in the countryside. An already

polarized political climate in West Bengal was further
complicated by the activities of a newly created Maoist
communist group, the Communist party of India (Marxist-
Leninist). These activities first took the form of armed
peasant guerrilla action in small selected areas and then, when
these guerrilla groups were flushed out by the security forces,
of urban guerrilla activity in the Calcutta metropolitan area.
Although conflicts among India's three communist factions (the
third being the Moscow-oriented CPI) seriously weakened the
leftist movement in West Bengal, an entirely new element was
introduced into Indian politics by, first, efforts of the CPI(M)
to build an extensive peasant-supported base in the countryside
around programs of controlled militancy and, second, the
eruption of peasant guerrilla groups in several widely
scattered parts of the country. For the first time the
traditional quiescence of the village appeared to yield to
organized militant movements. Vast multitudes of the rural
proletariat began to exert class pressure on a political system
ill-prepared to face it.[23]
    The crisis soon affected the Congress party leadership as
well as the government led by Indira Gandhi. One section of the
leadership wanted to move a little to the right and sought to
remove Mrs. Gandhi from the prime ministership. She, on her
part, moved a little to the left and staged a coup against the
rival group. The Congress party split into two in the autumn of
1969, and Mrs. Gandhi's government was reduced to a minority in
parliament. She could now continue in power only with the
support of the leftist groups in the Lok Sabha (the lower house
of parliament) including the communists. Faced with the problem
of survival, Mrs. Gandhi shifted her own faction, the ruling
Congress, to the left by nationalizing fourteen large Indian
banks and by bringing in legislation depriving the former
rulers of the princely states of their privy purses, allowances
that had been granted by the government while integrating these
states into the Indian Union. Taking tactical advantage of the
popularity of these actions, the prime minister dissolved the
Lok Sabha and held midterm parliamentary elections in March
1971; midterm elections were also held simultaneously for the
state assemblies of Madras, Orissa, and West Bengal. Mrs.
Gandhi's Congress party won a more than two-thirds majority in
the Lok Sabha (350 out of 515 seats) and in West Bengal emerged
as the second largest party, after the CPI(M). The immediate
result of the impressive victory of the ruling Congress party
was that in several states—Uttar Pradesh, Mysore, Gujarat, and
Andhra Pradesh—Congress legislators who had either joined the

rival Congress faction or had defected from Mrs. Gandhi's
hurried back to the ruling party. Thus, on the surface, this
party looked almost the same as it had been before.

The 1971 parliamentary elections were remarkable not because
they revealed massive popular support for Indira Gandhi and her
party (which secured only 3 percent more votes than the
undivided Congress party had received in 1967) but because the
voters in large numbers shifted their support from the
opposition factions and also because they restored, at least at
the national level, the position of the ruling Congress party as
the party of national consensus and balance.[24] An Indian
political scientist, Rajni Kothari, saw for the 1970s the
emergence of two "competitive coalitions" of rightist and
leftist parties, "both sharing in the larger consensus of the
system, and providing the electorate with alternative teams to
choose from." The task that faced the "elite at the center of
the system" was "to turn the new opportunity of adopting the
democractic consensus to a new institutional framework." If the
elite failed in this task, it was likely to be swept away by
another tendency, "the tendency of a polarization of extremes
around the appeal of a sectarian and revivalist right on the one
hand and the doctrinaire militancy of the left on the other."
The alternatives Kothari saw for India in the next decade were a
polarization of the extremes and a "polarization of the center,
which assimilates other divisions around a structure of
alternatives while still sharing the basic consensus of the
system."[25]

It took Indira Gandhi and her party another year to restore
the supremacy of the Congress system in the management of the
Indian political order. In this she was helped by the political
crisis in Pakistan, the independence movement in its eastern
wing, the birth of Bangladesh after the India-Pakistan war of
December 1971, and, last but by no means the least, the great
realignment in relations among the major world powers. Before we
get into this latest aspect of Indian politics, however, we must
first look at what was happening in Pakistan and at Pakistan's
role in the affairs of South Asia.

Pakistan's Structural Imbalance
The political crisis that overtook Pakistan in 1970-1971 and
led finally to its disintegration was inherent in the structural
imbalance with which it was born in 1947. Geography was against
it. The two parts of Pakistan were separated from each other by
eleven hundred miles of Indian territory. The two parts were
also separated by language, race, culture, historical experience,

and economic disparities.[26] To weld a nation out of such
divergent elements in the context of an insurmountable
geographical problem would have foiled the world's greatest
political talent. The rulers of Pakistan, who belonged by and
large to the Urdu-speaking northern Indian Muslim aristocracy
that had spearheaded the Muslim League movement, depended
exclusively on two instruments to galvanize a nation. These were
Islam and fear of India.

Born out of the Muslim League leadership's hatred for and
suspicion of the Hindus who dominated the population of
undivided India, Pakistan from the beginning aspired to an
autonomous role in South Asia to curb Indian power. Given time
and patience, Pakistan might have played this role somewhat
effectively by mobilizing the other smaller units of the region
who, for one reason or another, were apprehensive of India.
Within a year or so of Pakistan's creation, however, the country
got into a military conflict with India in Kashmir and into a
territorial dispute with Afghanistan over the Pushtoon-inhabited
tribal region between the two countries. The rulers of Pakistan
turned toward the Arab world in search of an Islamic identity.
Hostility toward India, a much stronger and more united power,
made seeking external support almost unavoidable. It is
signficant that Moscow's attention fell upon Pakistan long
before it fell upon India. In 1951, the Pakistani prime
minister, Liaquat Ali Khan, received an invitation to visit the
USSR, but went instead to Washington in search of economic and
defense support. To qualify for this support, Pakistan adopted a
superficially anticommunist posture. When it signed a military
pact with the United States, its leaders made no secret of their
perception that India, not the USSR or China, was the real
enemy. American military and economic aid did not, however,
solve the basic problem of Pakistan's security. It did not
enable Pakistan to get Kashmir. However, to the extent that it
gave the leaders of Pakistan a strong measure of self-confidence,
American aid probably contributed to the maintenance of Indian-
Pakistani peace for eighteen years.[27]

Pakistan's stability and economic development were achieved
during the fifties and the sixties at the cost of the evolution
of a viable political system that could grapple with its
congenital structural problem. In fact, tension between the two
wings surfaced within months of the birth of the new state. In
February 1948, an East Pakistani member of the constituent
assembly moved a resolution that Bengali, along with Urdu, be
used in the assembly proceedings. This brought forth an

immediate retort from Prime Minister Liaquat Ali Khan: "Pakistan is a Muslim nation. . . . It is necessary for a nation to have one language and the language can only be Urdu and no other language." This attempt to identify Pakistani nationalism with a single language, Urdu, rested on such flimsy grounds that it was bound to prove unproductive. The 1951 census of Pakistan showed that 54.6 percent of its population spoke Bengali and lived in the eastern wing, while Urdu was the language of only 7.2 percent of the population. The 1951 census figures reinforced East Pakistan's Bengali subnationalism. In January, Prime Minister K. Nazimmuddin, an East Pakistani who did not speak Bengali, declared while on a visit to Dacca, the provincial capital, that Urdu would be the sole official language of Pakistan. Within a month, strong agitation on the language issue built up in East Pakistan, spearheaded by the students of Dacca University. A number of students were killed when the police fired on a mob on February 20.

The language issue immediately dominated the politics of East Pakistan. In the first general election in the country in 1954, the Muslim League was completely routed in East Pakistan. It won a mere ten seats in the legislature, while a coalition of opposition factions, dominated by the Awami League, captured 223 of the 237 Muslim seats.* The coalition, which called itself the United Front, had fought the election on the basis of a twenty-one point program. Its economic clauses had a mildly socialistic accent; for example, it proposed both nationalization of the jute industry, the mainstay of the province's economy and controlled from the beginning by West Pakistani interests, and land reform. The program emphasized, first, East Pakistan's autonomy in a federal system in which the central government was to control only foreign affairs, defense, and currency and, second, the recognition of Bengali as a state language on a par with Urdu.

In the next four years the political gap between the two wings widened, in spite of the fact that of Pakistan's four short-term prime ministers two came from the eastern wing. What made bridging of the gulf difficult was the consolidation of

---

* While the "parental" Muslim League collapsed in Pakistan within seven years of the country's birth, in India the "parental" Congress party suffered its first major electoral reverses twenty years after independence, but recaptured its dominance of the political system in five years.

political and economic power in the hands of the bureaucracy,
the military, and a relative handful of feudal-industrial
magnates who drew their support mainly from the landed gentry
and urban rich of Punjab and Sind. East Pakistan's share of
political and economic power was negligible. The interest groups
and factions in West Pakistan who controlled the apparatus of
power saw in parliamentary democracy the main source of
political strength of the emerging elite of East Pakistan.
Behind the facade of parliamentary rule, control over the system
was steadily usurped by the military-bureaucratic complex, until
in 1958 two generals, Iskander Mirza and Ayub Khan, staged a
coup and seized power in the name of the army and the people.

Field Marshal Ayub Khan gave Pakistan a decade of stability
and development. Instead of imposing direct military rule, he
built a new power structure around 80,000 "Basic Democrats"—
kulaks and capitalists, divided equally between the two wings.
These "Basic Democrats," elected on the basis of a limited
franchise, were to form the electoral college for the
presidency as well as the national and provincial assemblies
provided for in the new constitution that Ayub Khan "gave"
Pakistan in 1962. The Ayub regime, however, lacked popular
support in East Pakistan. In the first national assembly
elected in 1962, the group supporting the government had only
78 seats in a house of 156, the opposition had 60 seats, and the
rest of the members were "independent." The bulk of the
government supporters came from West Pakistan, the bulk of the
opposition from the East. In the second national assembly,
elected in 1965, the government had a majority of 130, but
almost all of the 17 opposition members once again came from
East Pakistan. In the presidential election of 1965, the
opposition candidate, Fatima Jinnah, received 27 percent of the
votes of the "Basic Democrats" in West Pakistan and 47 percent
in East Pakistan.[28]

Ayub Khan did make an attempt to repair the gross political
and economic disparities that had grown between the two wings.
Not merely by giving each wing 40,000 "Basic Democrats" but
also by providing for equal representation in the national
assembly, he recognized the eastern wing's political equality
with the western wing. At the same time, by uniting the four
linguistically and ethnically different western provinces into a
single administrative unit ("One Unit"), he also gave the East
Pakistanis the feeling that all of West Pakistan had "ganged up"
against them. Ayub Khan substantially expanded the eastern
wing's share of the development budget and sought to increase
the East Pakistani presence in the civil service and the

defense forces. But he held the Bengali-speaking Muslims of East
Pakistan in contempt and was never capable of fathoming the
depth of their sense of deprivation.[29]

East Pakistan's sense of deprivation and alienation became
deeper and sharper as a result of the India-Pakistan war of 1965.
The war brought home the utter defenselessness of East Pakistan
in a war with India. The Indian government, too, by not taking
any military action against the province, treated it for all
practical purposes as a separate entity. The war ended trade
between the two neighbors. Since whatever trade had existed was
between East Pakistan and India, its cessation hit the economy
of the eastern wing. The ban imposed by the Pakistan government
on the flow of books from West Bengal to East Bengal as well as
on the broadcasting of the music of Rabindranath Tagore from the
Dacca station of Radio Pakistan sharpened the Bengali Muslims'
resentment. The autonomy movement received an impetus from the
combined impact of all these and other consequences of the war.
In February 1966, the Awami League's famous "Six Point" program
was put forward by its leader, Sheikh Mujibur Rahman, at a
meeting of the opposition leaders in Lahore. The Awami League
asked for a new constitution providing for a federation in which
the center would control only defense and foreign affairs and
for a parliamentary form of government with the legislature
directly elected on the basis of adult franchise. It demanded
separate currencies for the two wings, or one currency subject
to statutory safeguards against the flight of capital from the
eastern wing, as well as the self-sufficiency of East Pakistan
in defense matters and the location of the federal naval
headquarters in the eastern wing.

Mujibur Rahman and most of the leadership of the Awami League
were arrested on May 6, 1966, under the Defense of Pakistan
Rules. It took the government nearly two years to put Rahman and
34 others, including some Bengali members of the civil service
and the armed forces, on trial for treason against Pakistan in
conspiracy with elements in India.[30] By this time the struggle
in East Pakistan had begun to take on aspects of a national
movement: all the political factions except the Muslim League
took up the demand for autonomy and asserted the East Bengalis'
right to "honorable existence" either within or outside Pakistan.
In the spring of 1968 Ayub's serious illness raised the question
of political succession. In November a full-scale agitation was
launched in the urban areas of West Pakistan for restoration of
parliamentary rule. The agitation was led by the students, but
the leadership soon passed to Zulfikar Ali Bhutto. Leadership of
the anti-Ayub Khan movement in 1968 became Bhutto's great

political asset in Pakistan's turbulent politics in 1970-1971.

When Ayub Khan recovered from his illness and returned to the task of government, he made major political concessions. He announced in February 1969 that he would not seek another term as president and that there would soon be a restoration of parliamentary democracy based on universal adult franchise. He convened a round-table conference of political party leaders in March. The conference decided that a new national assembly, to be elected on the basis of universal adult franchise and with equal representation for both wings, would decide such questions as provincial autonomy, dissolution of the "One Unit" in West Pakistan, and representation of the various provinces in the national legislature in case the "One Unit" was dissolved. While these decisions were acceptable to most of the factions in West Pakistan (though not to Bhutto, whose Pakistan People's party did not attend the round-table conference), they were rejected by most of the groups in East Pakistan, including the Awami League. Mujibur Rahman accused the West Pakistan opposition leaders of betraying the cause of East Pakistan: once the president had met their main demand for restoration of parliamentary democracy, he complained, they turned their backs on East Pakistan's principal demand for effective autonomy. The virtual collapse of the decisions of the round-table conference triggered a fresh wave of agitation in East Pakistan. Spearheaded once again by the students of Dacca and other cities, the movement this time spread to the villages and turned violent. Thousands of East Bengali Muslims attacked hundreds of West Pakistanis and killed many of them. The rural areas in northern Bengal were up in arms. According to one account, "In North Bengal the peasants stopped all payments due to the government and some villages elected People's Courts to try the local 'evil gentry.'"[31] These areas were the support bases of the National Awami party of Maulana Abdul Hamid Bhashani, the octogenarian peasant leader who combined a Maoist approach to the peasantry with militant Bengali nationalism and who had tried, not without some success, to wrest the leadership of the autonomy movement in 1966-1969 from Mujibur Rahman.

On March 25, 1969, Ayub Khan bowed out of the Pakistani political scene. He handed over power to the commander-in-chief of the army, General A. M. Yahya Khan.

During the decade of Ayub Khan's rule, Pakistan had seen considerable economic development and substantial achievements in foreign policy. In the sixties, Pakistan loosened its ties with the United States without forfeiting its claim to American economic and military aid and the affection of the U.S.

administration, which saw Pakistan as an old and trustworthy
ally. At the same time, it developed friendly relations with
both the USSR and China. New technology brought about
agricultural prosperity. The pace of industrial development
increased with the help of private foreign investment and aid
received from the three major world powers. The 1965 war with
India was unproductive in the sense that Pakistan failed to
sever Kashmir's links with India. But Ayub did not lose the war,
although the Tashkent agreement did come as a disappointment to
many of his countrymen. The man who in 1959 had offered India a
joint defense plan against China was getting sizable quantities
of military equipment from China, the Soviet Union, and the
United States when his regime collapsed ten years later.

Ironically, Pakistan's success in development widened the
division between its two wings. Since most development took
place in West Pakistan, a colonial-type economic relationship
grew up between the two wings. Although East Pakistan was the
home of nearly 55 percent of Pakistan's population, its share of
the average annual national budget of Rs. 6,000 million was only
25 percent— 10 percent of the expenditure on defense and 15
percent of the civil expenditure. Of the country's entire
exports during 1958-1968, East Pakistan accounted for 59 percent
and West Pakistan for 41 percent. But East Pakistan's share of
the total imports came to only 30 percent, as against West
Pakistan's 70 percent. During the five years between 1964 and
1969, West Pakistan exported Rs. 5,292 million worth of goods
to the eastern wing and imported goods valued at Rs. 3,174
million. East Pakistan's share of development project funds
averaged 23 percent, while West Pakistan's was 77 percent. The
bulk of the development aid received from the United States, the
USSR, and China went to the western wing. In Pakistan's civil
service, 84 percent of the civil servants came from the West and
a mere 16 percent from the East; in the foreign service, the
East's share of jobs was only 15 percent. In education, health
services, urbanization, and transportation, the eastern wing
lagged far behind. "Economic experts have evidence that in 1959
an average East Pakistani was 20% worse off than another in the
West. In 1968, he was 40% worse off than his brother in West
Pakistan."32

Two Tidal Waves
With Ayub Khan's exit, General Yahya Khan took over the
government of Pakistan. He declared martial law and appointed
himself chief martial-law administrator. For the first time the

army was openly and visibly in control of the country, and yet
Yahya Khan realized that it could not maintain that control
because the country was far too turbulent. He therefore made it
clear that he was heading only an interim regime and that his
main task was to create "conditions conducive to the
establishment of a constitutional government." He stood by the
concessions made by the former president about adult franchise
and parliamentary government, and if he had to suspend all
political activity, it was only "till tempers cooled down."[33]

After an extensive tour of the two wings of Pakistan, Yahya
Khan announced on November 28, 1969, that elections to a
constituent-cum-national assembly would be held on October 5,
1970, on the basis of one-man-one-vote, thus conceding the
eastern wing's claim to majority representation. The new
assembly, Yahya Khan added, would determine the question of
provincial autonomy. Meanwhile, he dissolved the "One Unit" in
West Pakistan, restoring the four provinces of Punjab, Sind,
Baluchistan, and the Northwest Frontier, each of which was now
to have, once again, its own provincial legislature. He accepted
the principle of "maximum autonomy" of each of the two wings of
Pakistan "so long as it does not impair the national integrity
and solidarity of the country." Yahya Khan also announced his
decision to lift the ban on political activity after January
1970. At the same time he made it clear in a Legal Framework
Order (LFO) that any constitutional document passed by the
national assembly would come into force only when authenticated
by the president; if authentication was refused, the national
assembly would be dissolved. LFO also included a number of
substantive provisions to be included in the constitution, the
most important of which related to the unity and integrity of
Pakistan.[34]

Yahya Khan and his advisers clearly foresaw an elected
national assembly in which no political party, whether from the
East or the West, would enjoy an absolute majority. His chief
constitutional adviser, Professor G. W. Choudhuri, stated on
September 10, 1970, that "there is no likelihood of any one
single party emerging either from West or East Pakistan" and
that "there is no question of East Pakistan members forming one
single group in confrontation—if that comes, then the state has
come an end."[35]

This, however, was exactly what happened. The Awami League in
East Pakistan had its rivals, the most influential being the
National Awami party of Maulana Bhashani. Both Bhashani and
Mujibur Rahman found much in the presidential orders that was
objectionable, and both now tried to mobilize public opinion in

support of the "national" demand for autonomy based on the Six
Points. While Bhashani's party decided to boycott the election,
the Awami League used the occasion for a massive demonstration
of East Pakistan's priorities. In this the party was helped by
a natural calamity that hit large portions of the province's
coastal areas. On November 12, 1970, a cyclone and a tidal wave,
the likes of which even perennially cyclone-prone East Pakistan
had not experienced before in living memory, laid waste a huge
area and killed an estimated one million people.

The government in Islamabad failed to rush relief operations
to the devastated areas, and the efforts of the East Pakistan
provincial government were far too inadequate to measure up to
the calamity. In fact, the tragedy drew more sympathy and help
from abroad than from those in power in the country. The
Financial Times of London reported, "In the most dramatic and
momentous form, the failure or inability of the Center to
respond quickly, demonstrably and efficiently to the east wing's
needs has confirmed the entire argument of Bengali separatism."[36]

Mujibur Rahman, after a tour of the affected areas, issued a
sharp indictment of the central authorities:

"While we have a substantial army stationed in West Pakistan, it
is left to British Marines to bury our dead in Patuakhali. While
we have army helicopters sitting in West Pakistan, we have to
wait for helicopters to come for relief operations from across
the earth. . . . All powers vest in the Central Government and
its bureacrats. It is they whom I accuse today of criminal
neglect and discrimination against Bangladesh."

He further declared, evidently with an eye on the coming
elections,

"Power must be won by the people, whether it be through
elections, or if elections are aborted, through the strength of
an awakened people. . . . The urge of the people of Bangladesh
for autonomy cannot be denied. Bangladesh will give its verdict
at the polls. . . . If the polls are frustrated, the people of
Bangladesh will owe it to the million who have died to make the
supreme sacrifice of another million lives, if need be, so that
we can live as a free people and so that Bangladesh can be the
master of its own destiny."[37]

When the elections were held on December 7, 1970 (after a
three-month postponement), the Awami League won not only all but
two seats in the provincial assembly but also a clear, absolute

majority (167 out of 313 seats) in the national assembly.
Zulfikar Ali Bhutto's Pakistan People's party, with 88 seats,
emerged as the majority party in West Pakistan. Most of its
election gains were, however, in Punjab and Sind; its presence
in the legislative assembles of Baluchistan and the Northwest
Frontier Province was negligible.[38]

From Confrontation to Conflict

The elections dangerously polarized the political crisis
between the two wings. There were now three principal actors:
the Awami League and its leader, Sheikh Mujibur Rahman, the
People's party led by Zulfikar Ali Bhutto, and the group of
generals represented by President Yahya Khan.[*] Bhutto had fallen
out with Ayub Khan, had played a major role in his exit, and
was leading West Pakistan's popular movement for the replacement
of military rule with a representative form of government. But
he had significant linkages with the armed forces since his
party's stronghold was Punjab and among its supporters were many
middle-ranking officers of the army.[39] More important was that
both the PPP and the army belonged to West Pakistan and had
shared perceptions and preferences. Both, for instance, wished
to see a united Pakistan ruled from a strong and viable center
in a federal system that would correct the gross imbalance that
had been permitted to develop between the two wings, without
giving the eastern wing an opportunity so to mutilate the center
that it became thoroughly impotent to stand up to the strong
enemy, India. In the triangular confrontation that dominated the
politics of Pakistan between December 1970 and March 1971, the
PPP and the military in effect acted together, first, to bend
the Awami League to an acceptable compromise and, finally, when

---

[*] In one of his first statements after the election, Bhutto said
that the constitution could be framed only by a consensus of the
two major political parties and President Yahya Khan (The
Pakistan Times [Lahore], Dec. 22, 1970). "The army occupied the
most pivotal place in this Awami League-army-PPP triangle.
Because of the impending showdown between the two major
political parties, the army seemed to hold the balance to
Pakistan's constitutional future" (Mohammed Ayoob and K.
Subrahmanyan, The Liberation War [New Delhi: S. Chand, 1972],
pp. 99-100). According to Mascarenhas, six generals formed the
inner circle of the decision-making apparatus in Pakistan
(Anthony Mascarenhas, The Rape of Bangla Desh [New Delhi: Vikas,
1971], pp. 83-84).

this effort failed, to break it by force.

The Awami League since 1966 had championed East Pakistan's autonomy. Although it had a national image and a national role— its one-time leader H. S. Suhrawardy, had been Pakistan's prime minister for more than a year—its self-image as well as its image in West Pakistan was predominantly that of the "national" party of the East. Surprised by its unexpected electoral success, the party's main dilemma was how to project itself as the premier political party of all Pakistan, without relenting on its demand for eastern autonomy. The electorate's verdict entitled the Awami League to rule Pakistan and to write its constitution, but the League's supporters belonged exclusively to the East; how could Mujibur Rahman now persuade the people of the West that their future was safe in the League's hands?[40] The very immensity of the victory made Rahman a prisoner of the event; he could hardly compromise on his Six Points. His position was made all the more difficult by Maulana Bhashani, who interpreted the election verdict as a vote for East Pakistan's independence.[41]

In his first statement issued after the election, Rahman predictably declared, "There can be no constitution except one which is based on the Six Points programme." In subsequent statements and speeches he emphasized that the Awami League had emerged as "the absolute majority party not only in Bangladesh but also in the whole country. So the right to rule the country is ours."[42] In the beginning he asserted the right of his party members in the newly elected national assembly to frame a constitution of their own choice: "We want to frame a constitution and we shall frame it on the basis of the Six Point programme. Those who would accept it, let them accept, and those who won't, let them not accept it."[43] When President Yahya Khan announced that the national assembly would convene in Dacca on March 3, 1971, and Bhutto declared that the PPP members would not attend it unless there was a previous understanding with the Awami League on the basic framework of the constitution, Mujib made a tactical move of some political significance. He offered to negotiate with West Pakistan groups other than the PPP, conceding that while the Awami League would not compromise on the Six Points insofar as East Pakistan was concerned, it would not force the program on the Western provinces, who would be free to delegate to the center as much power as they considered it fit to delegate.[44] This tactical move enabled Rahman to gain the support of the non-PPP factions. Two of these factions were the largest groups in the provincial assembles of Baluchistan and the Northwest Frontier Province.

Rahman's gain, however, was more than neutralized by the closer
ties this brought about between the PPP and the military
leadership.

    Bhutto's position was strategically stronger than Rahman's.
He overcame his tactical weakness by adopting a posture of
militant intransigence and by moving close to the group of
generals. He had a shrewd understanding of their weakness. They
had no mandate from the people to continue to rule Pakistan, and
they had lost most of their linkages with the political
elements. It was in their interest that Pakistan remained
united, for West Pakistan alone might not be able to support the
existing military machine. The generals had no faith in the east
wing's loyalty to Pakistan; most of them strongly suspected that
Mujibur Rahman's "maximum autonomy" would be only an interim
step toward complete independence and that he enjoyed the
support of powerful political elements in India, if not that of
the Indian government. The generals, Bhutto accurately
calculated, needed him at least as much as he needed them. In
the final act of the drama they had to swim or sink together.

    Bhutto asserted that the election had produced "two
majorities," one in each of the two wings. Each had a mandate
from the people to give Pakistan a new direction at home and
abroad. The PPP therefore could not be treated as a minority
party that would sit with the opposition in the national
assembly while the Awami League ruled and wrote the constitution
of Pakistan. "The authority at the center will have to be shared
between the Awami League and the People's Party to enable them
to execute the mandate given to them by the people."* The two
parties' socioeconomic programs had a great deal in common; both
stood against "capitalist-feudal exploitation" of the poor. It
was this "capitalist-feudal exploitation" that had reduced East
Pakistan to the status of a colony of the West. If Pakistan had

----

* Pakistan Times, Dec. 22, 1970. Bhutto came out with some
ingenuous political concepts. He questioned the right of the
majority to govern Pakistan, claimed that a minority could be as
important as a majority, and insisted that the majority had no
right to write a constitution. He was apparently drawing upon
the political experience, concepts, and tactics of the Muslim
League before 1947. The majority-minority parity formula of the
Muslim League worked only because the British backed it; in
Pakistan in 1971, Bhutto's formula had the backing of the
army.

to write a new federal constitution, it could be framed only "with the mutual agreement of the two main political parties of the country."[45] Bhutto visited Dacca for three days at the end of January, 1971, but his talks with Rahman merely sharpened the lines of division. Their relations were further exacerbated by an incident that was to have a far-reaching impact on coming events. At the beginning of February, two Muslims whom Bhutto described as "two young Kashmiri freedom fighters" hijacked an Indian Airlines plane from Srinagar to Lahore. Bhutto immediately met the hijackers at Lahore airport and endorsed them when they blew up the aircraft.[46] In retaliation New Delhi banned Pakistani overflights, thus denying Rawalpindi the shortest air route to East Pakistan. Bhutto exploited the psychological fallout of the incident, which enhanced for many West Pakistanis the importance of a united Pakistan with a strong center if Pakistan were to befriend the Kashmiris. Mujibur Rahman, on the other hand, saw in the incident a "conspiracy" to "subvert" the national assembly and the political process initiated by the December election.[47]

That the gulf between the two leaders had widened became evident in Bhutto's declaration at Peshawar on February 15 that he and the PPP would not attend the national assembly if it were to meet in Dacca on March 3 "only to endorse the constitution which had already been prepared by the Awami League."[48] He was willing to accept two of the Awami League's Six Points, but he would never accept a "two-subject" center. (Later Bhutto accepted four of the Six Points, but insisted that the center must have full control of Pakistan's foreign trade and aid if it were to conduct foreign policy effectively. Rahman equally stubbornly refused to yield foreign trade and aid to the center, arguing that the center had used these as instruments of East Pakistan's "colonial" exploitation.)[49] Bhutto insinuated that the life of the PPP members might be in danger if they went to Dacca to attend the national assembly, and he even warned that those members of the assembly from West Pakistan who went to Dacca might be "liquidated."* On March 1 Bhutto gave President

----

* After the aircraft incident and the banning of Pakistani overflights by India, Bhutto insinuated that linkages existed between India and the Awami League. He said that if PPP members went to Dacca for the national assembly session, their lives would be in "double jeopardy." The assembly would be a "slaughter house," he added (Dawn, Feb. 18, 1971).

Yahya Khan two alternatives: to postpone the national assembly
or to remove the 120-day time limit for the assembly to frame
the constitution.[50] The same day the president announced an
indefinite postponement of the assembly session, pleading that,
in view of the "political confrontation between the leaders of
East Pakistan and those of the West," it had become "imperative"
to give them time to come to a "reasonable understanding."[51]
    Apparently, postponement of the national assembly was the
result of major decisions taken by the group of generals on how
to deal with the intransigence of the Awami League. Immediately
after the election President Yahya Khan had assured his
countrymen that the end of military rule was in sight and that
power would soon be transferred to the people.[52] He visited
Dacca on January 14, 1971, and had "very good discussions" with
Rahman, whom he publicly described as Pakistan's "future prime
minister."[53] He refrained from any public intervention in the
Bhutto-Rahman confrontation for nearly a month. On February 12
Yahya Khan conferred with Bhutto at Rawalpindi before announcing
that the national assembly would meet in Dacca on March 3; it is
reasonable to speculate that Bhutto told him that his party
would boycott the session in the absence of a previous
understanding with the Awami League on the main principles of
the constitution. Did Yahya Khan, then, deliberately convene the
assembly in order to escalate the conflict between Bhutto and
Rahman? Bhutto is reported to have boasted at a cocktail party
the same evening that the "powers that be" had decided that he,
not Mujibur Rahman, would be prime minister.[54] On February 21
Yahya Khan dismissed his civilian cabinet (formed in August
1969) and presided over a three-day meeting of military
governors, martial-law administrators, and the chiefs of the air
force and the navy. At this meeting, according to one account,
the decision to postpone the national assembly was finalized.[55]
The military governor of East Pakistan, Admiral S. M. Khan, and
the martial-law administrator, Lieutenant General Shahizada
Yaqub, reportedly opposed the postponement which, they warned,
would create an "unmanageable situation."[56] Both men were
removed from their posts on March 2. In his March announcement
Yahya Khan made it clear that there could be no constitution
unless "both East and West Pakistan have an adequate sense of
participation" in its making. He regarded the confrontation
between Bhutto and Rahman as a confrontation between the two
wings, thereby bestowing official confirmation on Bhutto's
claim that he was the undisputed leader of the West. And he did
this at a time when thirty-six non-PPP members of the national
assembly from West Pakistan had already arrived in Dacca for the

national assembly session, and others were getting ready to
leave home.[57]

Apparently the generals had decided in February on a forceful
showdown with the Awami League. As David Loshak of the Daily
Telegraph (London) reported,

"Early in 1971, it gradually grew more difficult to book seats
on the daily Pakistan International Airways flights from Karachi
to Dacca. . . . President Yahya Khan was putting his contingency
plan, long ready, into operation. Steadily, beginning with a
trickle, a stream of reinforcement which was to become a
torrent, began to flow towards East Pakistan. The soldiers wore
'civvies' and so attracted no attention. About 20,000 West
Pakistani troops were already stationed in the eastern wing. As
the reinforcements flowed across, senior officers scrupulously
planned the complex logistics of supplying and equipping what
was to become an occupying army of initially 35,000-40,000 and
then to grow to 60,000 men from a sailing distance of 3,000
miles. It was calculated that it would take about two months to
get the army into a state of full readiness. Unknown to any but
the topmost generals in President Yahya Khan's innermost circle,
the civil war which was the sole alternative to a return to
civilian rule, had begun."[58]

The Fateful Days of March
There is little doubt that in postponing the national
assembly session President Yahya Khan once again obliged Bhutto;
at any rate, he did not consult Rahman. The postponement placed
Rahman in a predicament. A political leader of moderate, middle-
of-the-road persuasion, he was still looking for a solution to
the political crisis within the framework of a federal or
confederal Pakistan. The aroused and frustrated people of East
Pakistan on the other hand were pressing for more radical
measures. Sporadic armed clashes between the army and knots of
infuriated people broke out at several places; a few lives were
lost.[59] On March 3, 1971, Rahman ordered a four-day shutdown of
normal activity in the province from 6:00 in the morning until
2:00 in the afternoon. The entire government machinery was
paralyzed, and the public response to the strike was most
impressive.* In a speech on March 3 Rahman advanced an idea that

----

* The People, March 2, 1971. On March 1 Rahman announced a six-
day "complete strike" throughout East Pakistan, which he
declared on the following day would continue until the people of

a little later was to cost him a great deal. In a reference to
the West Pakistani leaders, he declared, "If you do not want to
frame one constitution, let us frame our own constitution and
you frame your own. Then let us see if we can live together as
brothers."[60] He refused to attend a round-table conference fixed
by Yahya Khan for March 10, describing it as a "cruel joke" when
unarmed people were being killed and maimed by the military in
East Pakistan.[61] He fixed March 7 as the date of an important
announcement to be made at a mass rally in Dacca. There was
widespread expectation among his followers, and apprehension in
the government, that he would declare the independence of
Bangladesh. The continued, yet orderly, paralysis of normal
political and economic life, except for what was permitted in
the "directives" systematically issued by Rahman, had apparently
confirmed in the public mind the Awami League's claim that it
alone was the source of real and effective power in East
Pakistan.[62]

Faced with the massive, unmistakable demonstration of
Rahman's hold on the population of the province, Yahya Khan beat
a tactical retreat. On March 5 the army was ordered back to
barracks.[63] The following day the president, after a five-hour
"secret" meeting with Bhutto in Rawalpindi, announced that the
national assembly would meet in Dacca on March 25. He combined
this apparent concession to Rahman with certain measures in the
opposite direction. One was the appointment of Lieutenant
General Tikka Khan, known for his ruthlessness, as East
Pakistan's governor and martial-law administrator.[64] The second
was an order to the army to "use the absolutely minimum force
required" to maintain the integrity and security of Pakistan.

March 7 was a crucial day for Rahman's leadership of the
tidal wave of nationalism that was now overtaking East Pakistan.

Bangladesh had "realized their emancipation." When a
correspondent asked if he would proclaim unilateral independence,
his reply was, "You wait." The strike was joined by the vast
majority of civil servants, white-collar workers, industrial
workers, and others, and life throughout the province came to a
standstill. What was even more indicative of the popularity of
the autonomy movement was that banks and institutions such as
hospitals were "allowed" to function by Rahman for limited,
specified periods; no transfer of currency to West Pakistan was
"permitted." For reports of the effectiveness of this
unparalleled civil-disobedience movement, see Dawn, March 8, 10,
and 16, 1971, and Pakistan Times, March 11, 1971.

He was evidently under considerable pressure from the hard-
liners within his party, from the students, and from the general
public to go over the precipice and declare independence. At a
marathon nine-hour meeting of the executive committee of the
Awami League, Rahman overpowered the hard-liners. According to
David Loshak, he insisted that East Pakistan would gain nothing
from secession except bloodshed and torment, and he argued that
the Awami League's mandate was "not for independence but
autonomy."[65] He announced that his party would join the national
assembly session, but only if four conditions were met,
including the lifting of martial law and the return of the
troops to barracks.[66] To prevent the political confrontation
from developing into a civil war, he urged the president to
implement immediately a seven-point program to restore normal
life in the province; the national assembly, he argued, could
not function in "an atmosphere of terror."[67] He warned his
people that a minority party in West Pakistan was conspiring
with "certain forces" to deprive them of their constitutional
rights, ordered a continued shutdown of all normal activity,
and, as a sop to the hard-liners, asserted that "our struggle
this time is a struggle for independence."[68]

In West Pakistan, Bhutto, isolated from the minority parties
whose leaders were now anxious to work with the Awami League,
moved even closer to the president. For the first time he
explicitly identified the armed forces as one of the three
principal parties to the political problem which, he emphasized,
could be resolved only on the basis of an accord among the
three.[69] Picking up and subtly modifying Rahman's March 3
suggestion, Bhutto declared that if power had to be transferred
to the elected representatives of the people, it should be
transferred separately and simultaneously to the two majority
parties of West and East Pakistan.[70]

Yahya Khan flew into Dacca on March 15 with a clutch of
generals, most of whom stayed out of sight at a military base
while the president conducted negotiations with Rahman and other
political leaders. There are several accounts of what took place
in these negotiations, which lasted ten days. At a very early
stage the president and Rahman reached "broad agreement" on a
plan put forward by the Rahman for an interim arrangement to
replace military rule with popular government. As Yahya Khan
himself put it, the plan provided for presidential proclamations
withdrawing martial law and setting up provincial governments
headed by the leaders of the two majority parties. The national
assembly was _ab initio_ to sit as two committees, each composed
of members of one wing. At a later stage the two committees

would sit together to work out a federal or confederal
arrangement. Yahya Khan stated that he was prepared to agree in
principle to this plan, to which Bhutto too had apparently given
his consent. Objections came from the leaders of the minority
parties, who were afraid that the plan might lead to the
restoration of "One Unit" in West Pakistan. The president did
not appear to attach much importance to the misgivings of the
minority party leaders until March 24. On that day the advisers
to Rahman and the president all but finalized the draft
agreement, and Rahman waited in his house for a call from the
President's camp for a final session where the draft was to be
approved and the agreement signed and released to the press. The
Agence France Presse put out a report on March 24, quoting an
"impeccable source" as saying that President Yahya Khan was to
proclaim within twenty-four hours virtual autonomy for
Bangladesh under a new Pakistan confederation.*
   The final call never came. The president flew back to
Rawalpindi, and the army moved into action in and around Dacca.
Mujibur Rahman was arrested at his residence and flown to West
Pakistan. During the night of March 25-26, Yahya Khan, in a
broadcast, denounced Rahman as a traitor and an enemy of

---

* For details of the complex and deceptive process of the
"negotiations," see Bangladesh Documents, pp. 237-277. Of
particular interest are the roles played by Bhutto and leaders
of the minority groups in the national assembly. In March the
minority leaders rallied round the Awami League; their main
target of attack was Bhutto. They rejected Bhutto's concept of
"two Pakistans." They were afraid of PPP and Punjabi domination
of West Pakistan and were strongly against the revival of "One
Unit" (Dawn, March 16, 1971). Even the president of the
"Council" Muslim League, one of the two factions into which the
party broke during the Ayub Khan period, rejected the concept
of two majority parties (ibid., March 17, 1971). Leaders of
three minority factions, including the National Awami League
and the Jamait-i-Ulema-i-Islam, the majority parties in the
Northwest Frontier Province and Baluchistan respectively, formed
a joint group during the Dacca "negotiations" and had separate
talks with both Mujibur Rahman and President Yahya Khan. Leaders
of these two factions issued a statement on March 25:

"If Mr. Bhutto is not prepared to accept the Awami League's
overall majority in the National Assembly, because it is based
on one province, he can hardly expect that his less decisive

Pakistan: "He has attacked the solidarity and integrity of this
country—this crime will not go unpunished." Yahya Khan banned
all political activity throughout Pakistan and suppressed the
Awami League more severely than the other political parties: "As
for the Awami League, it is completely banned as a political
party." He imposed complete press censorship and proclaimed, "I
have ordered [the armed forces] to fully restore the authority
of the Government."[71] This was a gross understatement of the
orders actually given to the army, which was apparently
ordered to wipe out all vestiges of East Bengali resistance. The
mood of the senior army officers was ominous. A report in The
Sunday Times included this quotation: "We are determined to
cleanse East Pakistan once and for all of the threat of
secession, even if it means the killing of two million people
and ruling the province as a colony for 30 years."[72]

The officers were as good as their word. Several eyewitness
accounts report how they set about their task: one of them by
then U.S. Senator William B. Saxbe,

"My wife and I watched from our roof the night of March 23 as
tanks rolled out of the Cantonment, illuminated by the flares
and the red glow of fires as the city was shelled by artillery,
and mortars were fired into crowded slums and bazaars. After
two days of loud explosions and the continual clatter of machine
guns, we took advantage of a break in the curfew to drive

----

victory in the Punjab and Sind entitles him to speak on behalf
of all the provinces of West Pakistan, which no longer exists as
one entity. . . . Let it be understood that the One Unit scheme,
against which the smaller provinces of West Pakistan struggled
for 14 years, cannot be revived under any circumstances" (ibid.,
March 21 and 23, 1971; Morning News [Karachi], March 25, 1971).

On March 22, Bhutto said that the various parties to the
"negotiations" were examining "the broad agreement reached
between the President and the Awami League"; he described it as
an "interim arrangement." He met Rahman and Yahya Khan
separately a number of times. Two days later Bhutto told
reporters that the talks were making progress. On March 25,
however, he spoke of a "new development" as having occurred on
March 24, which had made it necessary for him to meet the
president. What the Awami League was demanding, he said, was
"more than autonomy." It was "bordering on sovereignty" (Dawn,
March 23 and 25, 1971).

through the city. Driving past streams of refugees, we saw
burned-out shacks of families living by the railroad tracks. . .
. A Bengali friend living close by had watched the army set fire
to the hovels, and, as the families ran out, he saw them shot
down 'like dogs'. . . . In the old city we walked through the
remains of Nayer Bazaar, where Moslem and Hindu wood cutters had
worked, now only a tangle of iron and sheet and smouldering
ruins. . . . On the 29th we stood at Ramna Kali Bari, an ancient
Hindu village of about 250 people in the center of Dacca-Ramna
Race Course, and witnessed the stacks of machine-gunned, burning
remains of men, women and children butchered in the early
morning hours of March 29. . . .

"At the university area on the 29th, we walked through Jagannath
Hall and Iqbal Hall, two of the student dormitories at Dacca
University shelled by army tanks. All inmates were slaughtered.
. . . The two ensuing weeks have documented the planned killing
of much of the intellectual community, including the majority
of professors of Dacca University.

    "In Gulshan, one of the suburban areas of Dacca, where we
lived, we witnessed the disarming of the East Pakistan Rifles,
stationed in the Children's Park across the street, the army
looting the food supplies from the market nearby, and finally
the execution of several [of the East Pakistan Rifles] as they
were forced by Punjabi soldiers onto a truck to be 'taken away.'
The mass execution of several thousands of Bengali policemen
and East Pakistan Rifles is already documented. We also
witnessed from a neighbour's house army personnel fire three
shots across Gulshan Lake at several little boys who were
swimming. . . ."[73]

The Proclaiming of Bangladesh
Leaders of the Awami League proclaimed a "sovereign people's
republic of Bangladesh" on April 10, 1971, with Mujibur Rahman as
president and Tajuddin Ahmed as prime minister. The seat of the
"government" was Mujibnagar, a village "within a mile" of an
outpost of the Indian Border Security Force in West Bengal.[74]
In East Pakistan, groups of people rose spontaneously to resist
the military, while a few thousand men of the police force and
East Pakistan Rifles formed the nucleus of the Mukti Bahini
(Liberation Army). This force, aided by students and other
youths, met the Pakistan army in set-piece engagements and
suffered heavy casualties. Within two weeks the Pakistan army
had spread out to all of the major towns of the province; by
the end of April, its strength had risen to some 50,000 men.

The Indian government made two major decisions within days of the military crackdown in East Pakistan; these in effect committed it to the eventual emergence of a Bangladesh within or outside Pakistan. The terrorized refugees were allowed by the Border Security Force to come to India, and the mauled remnants of the Bengali personnel of the East Pakistan Rifles and the police were allowed sanctuary in India for regrouping, as were members of the Bangladesh "government" and thousands of the Bengali elite, who were the first to flee East Pakistan. Indian armed forces and paramilitary formations took up the task of training the new recruits to the Mukti Bahini. Two streams of training were undertaken. One was for those personnel who were later to operate under the control and supervision of the Mukti Bahini in coordination with the Indian army and paramilitary forces. The second stream of general weapons training was for the political cadres of the Awami League who operated within East Pakistan on their own initiative. Because of the Indian army's limited capacity for training, inexperience in partisan warfare, and reluctance to part with weapons, the training program never was very extensive, and the first trained personnel were not available for actual operations before August.[75]

The Indian press was flooded with exceedingly romanticized accounts of the exploits of the Mukti Bahini. In purely military terms, however, its achievements were limited during the first six months of the "occupation." What was astonishing, however, was the unbroken will for freedom of the broad masses of the population despite the systematic, cold-blooded brutalities of the Pakistani army. Partisan warfare never involved the peasantry, nor did the Awami League leaders and the Indian authorities intend to build up a peasant guerrilla force. The Mukti Bahini did not acquire the dimensions of a revolutionary army. Loyalty to the Awami League was a rigid requirement for an aspirant partisan to receive military training in India. The political cadres of the Awami League who operated within East Pakistan became more radical than the leaders who were running the Bangladesh "government" in Calcutta, and the Mukti Bahini as a whole was more radical at the end of the liberation war than in the first week of April. Its overwhelming ideological passion (like that of the Bengali elite) was nationalism, symbolized by the emerging nation's charismatic leader, Mujibur Rahman.[76]

India's Role in the Crisis
The crucial role in the unfolding drama belonged necessarily to India. If the uncertainties of Indian politics in

March encouraged the Pakistan government to unleash the military
in East Pakistan and restrained Rahman from openly opting for
independence, in April Mrs. Gandhi was in a position to deal
with the civil war across the border with a firm sense of
direction. That she committed herself and her government to
Bangladesh became quite evident in her speeches, in the
resolution she introduced in parliament, in the formation of the
provisional government on Indian soil, in opening the Indian
borders to the refugees, in keeping them in camps and treating
them differently from the refugees who had been coming into
India from East Pakistan almost ceaselessly since the partition,
in her repeated assertions that the refugees must return in
safety and honor, in training and arming the partisans, and in
her orders to the Border Security Force to extend such
assistance as lay within its resources to the resistance within
East Pakistan. Indian commitment to Bangladesh, however, did not
necessarily mean commitment to East Pakistan's independence.
What it certainly meant was a political settlement acceptable
to the Awami League and, more precisely, to Mujibur Rahman.[77] In
the resolution that Mrs. Gandhi introduced in parliament on
March 31 and that was passed unanimously amid thunderous
applause, India's sympathy and support were extended to the East
Bengalis for "their struggle for a democratic way of life."[78]
When the flow of refugees passed the three million mark in May
and some 60,000 were still coming in each day, Mrs. Gandi
developed her strategic perception of the crisis. "What was
claimed to be an internal problem of Pakistan has also become an
internal problem of India," she asserted on May 24. "Pakistan
cannot be allowed to seek a solution of its political and other
problems at the expense of India. . . ." Two days later, she was
even more explicit: "It is a problem that threatens the peace
and security of India, and indeed of South-East Asia . . . . We
are not concerned merely with the legal aspects of this
situation. We are concerned with one thing and one thing only—
our national interest and security, and naturally that of the
heroic people of Bangladesh."[79]

   Mrs. Gandhi resisted the swelling pressure of public opinion
to extend recognition to the Bangladesh "government," but gave
the "government" the hospitality it needed to function as such.
Throughout the crisis she was able to maintain skillful control
of public-opinion pressure, which she needed to justify
strategic responses to the military-political situation across
the border, but which she could not afford to allow to reach
such a pitch as to dictate major policy decisions. She
unleashed an unprecedented spurt of diplomatic activity to
persuade the international community, especially the two

superpowers, to put effective pressure on the rulers of Pakistan
to come to an agreement with Mujibur Rahman. On May 25 she
spelled out the threefold objective of India's massive
diplomatic effort. First, she was trying to build up "the
requisite pressure" on Pakistan to create conditions that would
stop the further inflow of refugees to India. Second, she was
endeavoring to impress upon the major powers that conditions
must be created so that the refugees could return to Bangladesh.
Third, she was trying to make it clear to the world that India
would not accept the refugees as a permanent burden. She wanted
all military and economic aid to Pakistan to stop, since such
aid could only prolong the conflict without in any way ensuring
Pakistan's victory and would thus increase the suffering of the
people of Bangladesh. The success of her diplomacy depended on
the superpowers' response and, more precisely, on the response
of the U.S. government. Mrs. Gandhi pressed Washington for "a
forthright and clear expression of disapproval" of the road
Yahya Khan was taking and for stopping military and economic aid
to Pakistan.[80] The refusal of the Nixon administration to do
either placed New Delhi in a serious predicament.

The period from April through June turned out to be rather
barren for Mrs. Gandhi's diplomatic offensive. The prime
minister had committed herself to Bangladesh, but was anxious to
act only within the diplomatic norms. The Soviet Union alone had
publicly deplored the developments in East Pakistan and had
urged Yahya Khan to resolve the crisis by a political settlement
with its elected representatives.[81] While Moscow's open
intervention in the domestic political developments in Pakistan
was most pleasing to the Indians, establishing as it did a
shared Soviet-Indian perspective on the crisis, the USSR
remained firmly committed to the integrity of Pakistan and was
anxious not to lose whatever presence it had been able to build
there since 1968. It was, at any rate, not in a position to put
effective pressure on Pakistan's rulers. Peking's message to
Yahya, issued and made public nine days after the message of the
Soviet president, implicitly took note of the political crisis.
However, it not only recognized Pakistan's exclusive right to
deal with a domestic problem but also promised its ally its
support in the event of Indian "aggression."[82] The Nixon
administration exhibited some concern about the plight of the
refugees and made some relief available. In July it sent a
private communication to Yahya Khan pleading for restraint and
efforts toward a political settlement, though not necessarily
with Rahman. Whatever international indignation over the
ruthless brutalities of the military in East Pakistan found

expression came almost exclusively from the advanced countries
of Europe and from intellectuals and students in North America.
In the Afro-Asian community, where India once counted for so
much, no significant voice was raised in protest, nor was there
any readiness to question Pakistan's sovereign right to deal
with a domestic political crisis. In Indian perception, the
world was turning Nelson's blind eye to a situation that was
posing an increasingly intolerable threat to the vital national
interests of India.

Between June and early August the Pakistan government
appeared to have captured what to India was a dangerous
strategic initiative in the eastern wing. The army extended its
control to all of the districts, and though the partisan forces
were still active here and there, the absence of any Indian
military move in support of the Bangladesh movement apparently
was taken by Yahya Khan as evidence of Mrs. Gandhi's
predicament.

The three major external powers were acting separately for a
common objective: to persuade Yahya Khan to bring about a
political settlement in East Pakistan.[83] The United States
government, with British support, was working to install UN
personnel on both sides of the border to supervise refugee
relief operations. In India, this move was regarded with the
greatest suspicion. For India, the centerpiece of the scenario
was the unresolved political conflict between Pakistan and
Bangladesh, which posed a serious threat to its vital national
interests. India saw in the move to install a UN presence on
both sides of the border a "sinister design" to transform the
crisis into one directly between Pakistan and India, to equate
the two, and, in the process, to bring to international light
whatever linkages existed between the Mukti Bahini and the
Bangladesh movement on the one hand and India on the other.[84]

In a broadcast on June 28 Yahya Khan blamed the trouble in
the eastern wing on the "collusion" among Awami League
extremists, rebels, and "our hostile neighbor," and affirmed
that "all major sabotage activities" were being conducted "by
Indian infiltrators in the name of the secessionists." Having
thus openly and clearly accused India of clandestine military
intervention in East Pakistan, the president announced political
measures to defuse the crisis. He would appoint a group of
experts to frame a new constitution for Pakistan, federal in
character and ensuring "real autonomy" for the provinces. A
number of Awami League members of the national and provincial
assemblies would be disqualified for treason, and by-elections
would be held to fill the vacancies. While political activity would
continue to be banned, the elected members of the national assembly

would continue to be allowed to sit as independent members when
it assembled on December 27. Meanwhile, measures were being
taken to set up a civilian administration in East Pakistan.*
About this time the Indian foreign minister returned almost
empty-handed from an extensive diplomatic mission to Moscow,
Bonn, Paris, Ottawa, Washington, and London. There was a strong
impression in India that Pakistan was successfully coordinating
its policies with the United States and other friendly
governments, including China.** As a columnist of The Times of
India wrote:

"Pakistan has carried out the first part of its plan fairly
successfully. Most governments have subscribed to its view that
the international community has no right to insist on a
particular kind of political settlement in East Bengal because
this falls within Pakistan's internal jurisdiction. Gradually
even those capitals which at one stage took the view that the
seven million refugees in India will not go back unless there is
a political settlement between the ruling military elite and the

----

* Yahya Khan visited East Pakistan in early August to prepare
the ground for the establishment of a civilian regime. An
Associated Press report said that the president's new
constitution would curb both the Awami League and the Pakistan
People's Party; no party would be considered to be a national
organization unless it had a minimum representation in the
national assembly from both wings. On August 7, 72 Awami League
members were removed from their national assembly seats, while 88
were allowed to retain theirs. This obvious move to split the
party caused considerable alarm in India (Northern India Patrika
[Allahabad], Aug. 4, 1971; Sunday Standard, Aug. 8, 1971).

** In July, reports appeared in the Indian press that Pakistan
was getting arms from both the U.S. and the USSR. The Soviet
ambassador assured the Indian Foreign Office that no arms had
been given to Pakistan since the beginning of military action in
East Bengal. In Washington, Senator Church alleged that $35
million worth of military supplies to Pakistan were still in the
pipeline. New Delhi told the U.S. government that continued arms
aid to Pakistan "amounts to an intervention on the side of the
military in West Pakistan against the people of Bangladesh" (The
Times of India, July 7 and 13, 1971).

elected representatives of the people in East Bengal are
beginning to endorse the Yahya Khan regime's stand that the mere
presence of UN teams on both sides of the border will suffice."*

The Sino-American Breakthrough

The startling events of July 1971 in the sphere of great-
power relations had an immediate and profound impact on the
crisis in the subcontinent. Henry Kissinger made a brief halt in
New Delhi on his way to Rawalpindi, but this only confirmed the
Indian government's fear that Washington did not intend to exert
any strong pressure on Yahya Khan for a political settlement
with the Awami League.[85] What shocked the Indians in the next
few days was not the news of Kissinger's secret visit to Peking,
but the fact that the visit was made from West Pakistan with the
help of Yahya Khan's government. This immediately planted in the
Indian mind the image of Sino-American convergence in Asia and a
Pakistan-China-U.S. axis. Peking's invitation to President Nixon
to visit China, issued at his own request, fitted in Indian
perception into the pattern of Sino-U.S. support to Pakistan in
managing the crisis in its eastern wing. Indian commentators now
linked the Bangladesh issue with the "power struggle of the
great powers in the Indian Ocean and the Persian Gulf region,"
as well as with the Soviet-U.S. competition for strategic
superiority.

----

* Girilal Jain, "Yahya's Threat of War," The Times of India,
July 28, 1971. Also, "International Climate Favourable to
Pakistan," Deccan Chronicle (Bangalore), Aug. 3. 1971. Toward
the end of August, Yahya Khan, interviewed by a correspondent of
Le Figaro, declared that "if the Indians imagine that they can
take a part of my territory without provoking a war, they will
commit a grave error. . . ." He was evidently referring to
reports in some Indian newspapers that the government might
"liberate" a certain area in East Pakistan to send the refugees
back. Yahya Khan spoke disparagingly of Indira Gandhi: "She does
not like my guts. But that does not bother me because she is
neither a woman nor a statesman by wanting to be both. She does
not have the qualities of her father. If I have to meet her,
I'll say, 'Shut up, woman! Leave me alone and let my refugees
come back.'" Of Rahman he said, "He was very brilliant and sure
of himself in public. But in front of me he was but a little
cat" (Dilip Padgaonkar, "Yahya's Outburst Against India," The
Times of India, Sept. 1, 1971).

In Indian perception, the United States anticipated that the
Soviet Union was about to emerge as the world's leading military
power. If the Soviets could bring China under control, the
Indian view went on, either by military force or political
means, Soviet hegemony over the entire Eurasian landmass would
be unquestioned. Thus both for the United States and for China
there was a compelling need to contain the might of the USSR.
This was what President Nixon had initiated, and for the time
being at least the U.S. would join with China to block Soviet
power expansion. If in the sixties Washington had tacitly
recognized the primacy of Soviet interests in South Asia and
allowed Moscow to assume the role of conflict-manager in the
subcontinent, in the seventies it would cooperate with China to
restrain Russian influence and power. For this the U.S. might
very well sacrifice some of its regional interests in order to
advance its global interests; hence Nixon's assurance that the
U.S. would respect China's legitimate interests in Southeast
Asia. The Nixon Doctrine implied that in the post-Vietnam U.S.
strategies for Asia, military force would act not as the
centerpiece but only as the backdrop. Inherent in this strategy
was, in Indian perception, a readiness to make strategic use of
the Sino-Soviet conflict to contain Soviet power and influence
in Asia. Since, in South Asia, Pakistan was the ally of China
and India was that of the USSR, the United States would
naturally incline toward Rawalpindi under the compulsion of its
new strategy, even apart from Nixon's personal affection for the
military regime and the Pentagon's strong and old linkages with
the Pakistani military establishment.[86] The mainstream of Indian
perception of the new Sino-American "collusion" against the
Soviet Union was summed up by Professor Sisir Gupta:

"As the crisis in Bangladesh was deepening, America's global
policies were undergoing some significant changes. During the
mid-1960's, the major concern of the United States was to
improve its relations with the Soviet Union and to discover in
the need for countering China an area of Soviet-American
agreement. However, by the late 1970's, the United States
appeared to be taking a dim view of the vast expansion of Soviet
power and influence during the years of their mutual accord. The
open military conflict between China and the Soviet Union along
the Ussuri river underlined to Washington the new opportunities
of countering Soviet power through improvement of relations with
China. The occasion for this occurred during the Bangladesh
crisis when Dr. Kissinger visited Peking in July 1971. To pave
the ground for a successful attempt to improve Sino-American

relations, Washington had to demonstrate that its South Asia
policy was by no means being conducted with the primary object
of securing a Soviet-American accord. This was particularly
important because Peking had for long accused the two
superpowers of colluding in the subcontinent and strengthening
India vis-à-vis its smaller neighbors."[87]

The image of the United States and China jointly helping
Pakistan to reverse the political process in East Pakistan
produced immediate action in India. It made the government
turn to the USSR more closely than ever before. The opinion-
makers reinforced the government's leaning on the USSR by
putting forward the view that Moscow needed India to meet the
Sino-U.S. collusion as much as India needed the Soviets and that
all India had to do to gain its strategic objective in
Bangladesh was to seize the initiative and act as a major power,
in which case Moscow would have little option but to give it the
support it might need.[88]

The Indian-Soviet Treaty
Moscow's perception of the changing pattern of Sino-U.S.
relations was not basically different from India's. In an
articile in _Pravda_, Georgii A. Arbatov, director of the USSR
Academy of Sciences' Institute on the U.S., analyzed the
diverse forces that persuaded President Nixon radically to
reverse his country's two-decades-old China policy. Among these
forces, Arbatov identified progressive and liberal elements who
had always wanted better relations with China as well as "rabid
baiters" of the Soviet Union, who had been attracted by Peking's
anti-Sovietism and who would have liked to use China to
undermine the power and influence of the USSR. Arbatov
visualized two diverse directions in which American policy could
move with regard to the USSR. The U.S. could combine steps
toward improving relations with China "with a turn toward a more
constructive position" on issues that stood between it and
Moscow. "But there are grounds to expect that events will develop
in another direction, in which U.S. policy will remain unchanged
except for relations with China, and its course will, as before,
be the main obstacle in eliminating sharp international
conflicts."[89]
While Arbatov reserved "definite conclusions" on the "future
of American-Chinese relations," the Soviet leaders appeared to
have made up their minds to direct the main thrust of their
policy in Asia at isolating and containing Chinese power and
influence during the transitional phase in Sino-U.S. relations.

An article in Pravda toward the end of July betrayed Soviet fear
of even a limited Sino-U.S. accord to serve the two powers'
parallel interests vis-à-vis Moscow. "It should be clear,"
Pravda warned, "that all plans to use the contacts between
Peking and Washington for some sort of pressure on the Soviet
Union and the states of the socialist commonwealth are only the
result of the loss of an understanding of reality." The article
anticipated a Sino-American "political combination" against the
USSR and its East European allies. To counter such a
combination it suggested a Soviet initiative to woo a string of
middle-level powers, notably Japan in Asia and West Germany in
Europe, keeping options open at the same time to work with the
U.S. to resolve specific issues of major conflict.*

  Nixon's China diplomacy, then, intensified the conflict
between Moscow and Peking. South Asia was the first region to
reflect the intensification. In the summer and autumn of 1971,
Soviet media made it clear that Moscow regarded the "Maoist
clique" as its principal adversary, just as Peking perceived the
"social-imperialist" leaders of the CPSU as its number one
enemy. The principal theme of a torrent of anti-China polemics
from the USSR was that Maoist China was an arrogant,
expansionist power at whose hands neither the territorial
integrity nor the political stability of Asian nations was or
could be safe.[90]

  It was this mirror image in India and the Soviet Union of an

----

* The Soviet stance toward China hardened sharply after the
Ninth Congress of the CCP, which in Moscow's perception heralded
the final defeat of the pro-Soviet elements in the Chinese party.
Kommunist (March 1969) printed a long article on Mao's China,
setting forth a formidable list of charges against the "Maoist
clique," the gravest of them being that the Maoists were
"stepping up their subversive activities against the socialist
countries" and were trying to set up "illegal groups" to head
"the struggle of the people" against the Communist party
leaderships and that Peking's ultimate objective was to unleash
a "clash between the USSR and the socialist countries on the one
hand and the forces of imperialism on the other." The article
conceded that "the CPR's return to the path of scientific
socialism will be a complicated and difficult process, attended
by all sorts of unexpected occurences." Moscow and its allies
must therefore be ready for a long and difficult struggle
against "the theory and practice of militant Maoism."

approaching Sino-U.S. accord, together with Yahya Khan's
boastful declaration in July that, in a war with India,
"Pakistan will not be alone" that brought about the Indian-
Soviet treaty of peace and friendship on August 9, 1971. The
treaty ended India's isolation and at the same time refurbished
Mrs. Gandhi's socialist image to her countrymen.

In signing the treaty New Delhi and Moscow entered into a
coalition in which collaboration for the attainment of shared
objectives did not preclude effort by each to influence the
other for the pursuit of its own strategic interests.* India's
minister for external affairs, Swaran Singh, when presenting the
treaty for the Lok Sabha's approval, saw "a rapidly changing and
dynamic picture" in the configuration of world forces, and
declared that the treaty would "act as a deterrent to any powers
that may have aggressive designs on our territorial integrity

---

* Of the twelve Articles of the Treaty, Articles 9 and 10 are
related to security. "In the event of either Party being
subjected to an attack or a threat thereof, the High Contracting
Parties shall immediately enter into mutual consultations in
order to remove such threat and to take appropriate effective
steps to ensure peace and the security of their countries"
(Article 9). "Each High Contracting Party solemnly declares that
it shall not enter into any obligation, secret or public, with
one or more States, which is incompatible with this Treaty. Each
High Contracting Party further declares that no obligation
exists, nor shall any obligation be entered into, between itself
and any other State or States, which might cause military damage
to the other Party" (Article 10). The Indian-Soviet treaty
differs substantially from the Soviet-UAR treaty of May 27, 1971.
The latter treaty provides for cooperation at the political level
"to create the necessary conditions for safeguarding and
maintaining the development of their two peoples' social and
economic gains" (Articles 2, 6). The Soviet-UAR treaty is more
ideologically oriented and commits Cairo to certain socioeconomic
policies and programs. It provides for elaborate military
collaboration (Article 7) and almost commits the USSR to come to
Egypt's defense in the event of war: "In the event of the
emergence of circumstances which, according to the view of both
parties, constitute a threat to or a violation of peace, they
will contact each other immediately with a view to coordinating
their stand to remove the arising threat or to restore peace"
(Article 8).

and sovereignty."[91] The security aspects of the treaty made the profoundest impression on the Indian elite. As the Financial Express put it, "In the present context of strained relations with Pakistan, and the possibility of armed clash between the two countries and the likelihood of Chinese intervention in support of Pakistan, the assurance of military support from the Soviet Union is of no small significance."[92]

It soon became clear, however, that Indian and Soviet strategic objectives in East Pakistan were not the same in the fall of 1971. The question that assailed many Indians was whether the treaty would enable the USSR to use India for its global strategic purposes rather than enabling India to use the Soviets for its regional strategic objectives. To most Indians it appeared that the Soviets were opposed to any action that might lead to Pakistan's dismemberment and that they still sought a political solution within the state structure of Pakistan. Indian analysts urged their government to take advantage of the treaty to pursue the country's own national interests. An Indian expert in strategic affairs speculated that current developments in Sino-U.S. relations would "result in a strategic stand-off between the United States and China on the one hand and the Soviet Union on the other, thereby restoring to India the full initiative in the subcontinent."[93] The task for India was only to use that initiative.

In early September, the Soviet embassy in New Delhi took the unusual measure of printing as an advertisement in a mass-circulation English daily what was undoubtedly intended to be an authoritative interpretation of the treaty. The 6,000-word document devoted one-half of the wordage to detail what the Soviet Union had already done to strengthen the economic, defense, and cultural base of the Indian democracy and how Indian-Soviet collaboration within the framework of the treaty would further accelerate India's social transformation. In dealing with the international implications of the treaty, the document played down its security aspects. The treaty was not a military alliance, it did not draw India into a military bloc, and therefore it did not injure or limit India's policy of nonalignment. Nor did it herald the launching of a Soviet drive for collective security in Asia:

"Does the treaty represent the first link in the chain visualized in the so-called 'Brezhnev Plan' for the collective security in Asia, as claimed by some vociferous pseudo-political pundits in the West? Political analysts   [in Moscow] are of the view that an attempt to put the treaty as a component of a grand Soviet strategy design in Asia is nothing but a striving to turn the

treaty, an act of peace, into a scarecrow. Those who make such
claims only reveal their reactionary outlook and their aversion
to peace and stability and progressive social change in Asia. In
fact, the treaty has a much more modest objective. It aims to
give juridical concretization to a manifold relationship between
the two countries and peoples that has long since become an
established fact of contemporary international life, a
relationship to which the Soviet people are used to refer as
traditional."[94]

Between August and October the Soviet and Indian leaders were
each apparently trying to win over the other. Indians noted with
chagrin the Soviet reluctance to use the word "Bangladesh" in
any official document. In early October the Indian government
appeared to have made a major concession to the Soviet point of
view. Swaran Singh announced at the meeting of the All-India
Congress Committee, the policy-making caucus of the ruling
Congress party, that a political solution of the East Bengal
crisis between the Pakistan government and the Awami League
would be acceptable to India even if it were within the
framework of United Pakistan.

October, however, saw a sharp rise in tension between India
and Pakistan. Both governments moved troops toward the border.
The air smelled of war. With the monsoon over in East Pakistan,
the partisan forces increased their activity and apparently
succeeded in inflicting considerable damage on vital
communication lines and military installations. In a broadcast
on October 12, Yahya Khan spoke of an all-out war, which led to
immediate high-level conferences in New Delhi. What perturbed
Delhi more was the appointment of a civilian governor in East
Pakistan and Yahya Khan's attempt, with U.S. assistance, to wean
away a faction of the Awami League leadership.[95] Soviet deputy
foreign minister Firyubin paid an extended visit to New Delhi.
While he was reported to have entirely approved of the defensive
measures taken by the Indian government, he also urged caution
and restraint.[96] Then came Mrs. Gandhi's trip to Moscow, where
she held extensive conversations with the Soviet leaders, during
which the two countries evidently agreed on the crucial question
of Indian intervention in East Bengal. Mrs. Gandhi, who was
scheduled to undertake a tour of Western capitals, including
Washington, in November, reportedly told the Soviet leaders that
she would give them two to three months to persuade Islamabad to
negotiate a political solution with the Awami League. In return,
she apparently got an assurance that the Soviets would back her
fully if she were compelled to act in East Pakistan. A
knowledgeable Indian correspondent located in Moscow summed up
the results of the Prime Minister's visit:

"In the first place the Soviet side has stopped conveying the impression of ambiguity [on the Pakistan issue] which it did before Mrs. Gandhi's visit to Moscow. In the second place, the Soviet side, in spite of its known and strongly expressed preference for peace, has accepted the idea that, if unavoidable, India can take very firm steps in East Bengal without being concerned about Soviet support at any level—political, economic or otherwise."[97]

In November Mrs. Gandhi returned from her tour of Western capitals quite convinced that India would not get American cooperation to bring about a political settlement acceptable to it and the Awami League. The partisan army in East Bengal was now receiving increasing logistical support from India. The prime minister ordered the Indian army to move inside East Pakistan territory to silence the forward Pakistani positions from where the troops had been firing across the border. The Soviet Union moved toward supporting India in this situation of escalating tension. On November 9, a visiting Soviet dignitary, V. Kudryatsev, described the struggle in East Bengal as "a national liberation movement with an element of civil war in it."[98] Six days later Kudryatsev declared that in the event of a war between India and Pakistan or any other country the Soviet Union would play the role it played in the Vietnam war.[99] Meanwhile, Pravda in a series of articles blamed Pakistan for the increasing tension, counseled it to build good-neigborly relations with India, and defended the Indian government against the accusation that it was about to attack Pakistan, taking advantage of that country's weakness.[100] Toward the end of November the Soviet ambassador to Pakistan, Rodionov, met Yahya Khan to convey his government's "demand" that Yahya Khan come to a political settlement with the Awami League and desist from escalating the crisis in the subcontinent.[101] Almost simultaneously the Soviet ambassador to India, Nikolai Pegov, saw Mrs. Gandhi to assure her of Moscow's support should the United States raise the India-Pakistan issue in the Security Council.[102] On December 1 the joint Soviet-Bulgarian communiqué issued at the end of Kosygin's visit to Sofia mentioned the tension in the subcontinent, thereby indicating that Moscow had begun to enlist the support of the East European countries for its line of action.[103] On December 3 Pravda carried Mrs. Gandhi's remark that the withdrawal of Pakistani troops from East Bengal would create conditions for the return of the refugees who had taken shelter in India.

The India-Pakistan War

Full-scale fighting between Pakistan and India broke out on December 3, 1971.[104] Two days later the Soviet government warned all nations to keep away from involvement in the conflict. In a statement issued through Tass, it identified as the cause of the conflict Pakistan's refusal to accept the eastern wing's demand for autonomy with the elected representatives of the people and declared that "in the face of the military threat now overhanging Hindustan, the Soviet Government comes out for the speediest ending of the bloodshed and for a political settlement in East Pakistan on the basis of respect for the lawful rights and interests of its people."[105] In the Security Council, the USSR vetoed three resolutions backed by the United States and China calling for a cease-fire and withdrawal of troops, and it fully supported the Indian position. It also backed a Polish resolution that could very well have been drafted in New Delhi.* On December 18 the Soviet government issued another statement welcoming India's unilateral offer of a cease-fire on the western front after the surrender of the Pakistani forces in East Bengal and warning the nations once again not to take any steps that could "impede normalization of the situation in the subcontinent."[106] Both Soviet statements implied that South Asia's close geographical proximity to the USSR and its importance for the security of the Soviet state made it a Soviet sphere of influence.

It was reported in the Indian press that Moscow had asked New Delhi to conclude the military operations in East Bengal within

----

* New York Times, Dec. 6-8, 1971. The Security Council sessions dramatized the Sino-Soviet rivalry with regard to the subcontinent and illustrated how it got mixed up with the strategic antagonism between the two communist powers. Henry Tanner reported in the New York Times, "The two powers came to the Council with diametrically opposed tactics. The Soviet Union was committed to support for India and China for Pakistan. But almost immediately the exchanges turned to the basic aspects of the ideological and national conflict between the two Communist regimes." At one stage of the debate, the Chinese delegate asked the Soviet representative for a categorical assurance that there would be no Soviet intervention in Sinkiang should China move in support of Pakistan. No such assurance was forthcoming.

a week.* Apparently the Soviets were afraid that prolongation of
the war beyond a week might lead to intervention by the United
States or China or both. In the second week of the war the U.S.
ordered a task force of the Seventh Fleet, including the nuclear
carrier Enterprise, into the Bay of Bengal. The Soviet
government dispatched to New Delhi a five-man delegation headed
by the first deputy foreign minister, Vassily Kuznetsov, who
remained in the Indian capital until the end of the war, holding
daily consultations with Indian officials. Mrs. Gandhi on her
part sent D. P. Dhar, chief architect of the Indian-Soviet treaty,
to Moscow for close liaison with the Soviet leaders. Thus was
ensured the closest coordination between the two countries
during the most crucial phase of the fourteen-day war.

The Soviet decision to move naval units into the Bay of
Bengal, which was conveyed to the Indian government on December
15, illustrated more vividly than anything else the changes that
had occurred since 1965 in the big-power position of the USSR.

----

* The Statesman, Dec. 12. Reports in the Indian press suggest
that Moscow proposed sending a high-level official to New Delhi
to coordinate the two countries' strategies, but Mrs. Gandhi
wanted an Indian official of comparable status to be
simultaneously located in the Soviet capital. Soviet impatience
with the slow pace of the Indian advance in East Pakistan was
evidently coupled with anxiety lest the Indians carry the war
into West Pakistan once Bangladesh was liberated. Apparently
Mrs. Gandhi had already given the Soviet leaders to understand
that she would accept a cease-fire after the liberation of
Bangladesh if Pakistan did the same (The Times of India, Dec.
12).

First Deputy Foreign Minister Vassily Kuznetsov, after his
arrival in New Delhi on December 12, told Indian officials that
the Kremlin was "impatient with the Indian armed forces for
their inability to liberate Bangladesh within the ten-day time-
frame mentioned before the outbreak of hostilities." Kuznetsov
pointed out that Soviet opposition to a cease-fire became "more
untenable the longer the war goes on in the East. . . ."

The Washington Post reported that "Kuznetsov delayed his
scheduled return to Moscow because he was awaiting special
instructions from Leonid Brezhnev. . . regarding India's request
that the Soviet Union sign a defense agreement with the
Bangladesh government after Soviet recognition of Bangladesh"
(Jack Anderson in the Washington Post, Dec. 21, 1971).

The U.S. administration decided on its show of naval power
apparently more out of angry despair than in accordance with a
well-laid-out design to intervene in the conflict. The "Anderson
Papers" reveal that even in the first week of December, the
White House had reconciled itself to the emergence of
Bangladesh. However, it was highly apprenhensive that after the
fall of East Bengal India would carry the war deep into West
Pakistan and "make Pakistan defenseless." As Kissinger outlined
the Presidential perception, "What we may be witnessing is a
situation wherein a country, India, equipped and supported by
the Soviets, may be turning half of Pakistan into an impotent
state and the other half into a vassal."[*] The news of the
movement of the Seventh Fleet task force delayed Kuznetsov's
scheduled departure from New Delhi. The Indian government
reacted to the U.S. move with quiet self-confidence. Jack
Anderson claimed that Moscow assured New Delhi that "it would
not allow the Seventh Fleet to intervene in Bangladesh" and that
it would "open a diversionary action in Sinkiang" in case the
Chinese attacked India across the Himalayas."[**]

----

[*] New York Times, Dec. 16, 1972. Jack Anderson said that the
secret White House papers dealing with the two-week war made it
clear that the task force was sent into Indian waters as a "show
of force." The naval deployment was intended (1) to compel India
to divert both ships and planes to shadow the task force, (2) to
weaken India's blockade against East Pakistan, (3) possibly to
divert the Indian aircraft carrier Vikrant from its military
mission, and (4) to force India to keep planes on defense alert,
thus reducing their operations against Pakistani ground troops.
"The evacuation of American citizens was strictly a secondary
mission, adopted more as the justification than the reason for
the naval force" (Washington Post, Dec. 31, 1971).
    Anderson also reported that after President Nixon ordered
the Seventh Fleet to send a task force into Indian waters, plans
were made to "arrange provocative leaks in such places as
Djakarta, Manila, and Singapore of the task force's approach. By
the time the ships had assembled in the Malacca Strait, both the
Indians and Soviets were well aware they were on the way" (ibid.,
December 21, 1971).

[**] According to Anderson, Soviet Ambassador Pegov told the
Indian government that "a Soviet fleet is now in the Indian Ocean
and the Soviet Union will not allow the Seventh Fleet to
intervene." He also "promised" on December 13 that the Soviet

Vessels of the Soviet Pacific fleet steamed through the Strait
of Malacca three days after the U.S. task force led by the
Enterprise. The unilateral Indian cease-fire on December 16 and
its acceptance by Yahya Khan rendered the U.S. show of force
ineffective. President Nixon, however, claimed that he had
sought and obtained Soviet cooperation in inducing India not to
carry the war into West Pakistan after the collapse of East
Bengal. Indians, on the other hand, maintained that they held
the entire decision-making initiative during the war and that
"at no stage [had] the Soviet Union intervened themselves or on
behalf of anyone else to tell us to do one thing or another or
refrain from doing one thing or another."*
     Whether the cease-fire offer was entirely an Indian
initiative or the result of Indian-Soviet consultation, it was a
triumph of Soviet diplomacy in South Asia. Nixon in fact helped
Moscow by telling the world that the Soviet leaders had been
partly responsible for the survival of West Pakistan. Moscow
sent a cordial message of greetings to Zulfikar Ali Bhutto on

----

Union "would open a diversionary action" against the Chinese if
Peking took any adventurist move." Anderson claimed he was
quoting from CIA reports to the White House (Washington Post,
Jan. 10, 1972).

* The Times of India, Dec. 19, 1971. See also The Statesman,
Dec. 28, 1971. Mr. Nixon gave the Soviet Union "credit" for
"restraint after East Pakistan went down to get the cease-fire
that stopped what would inevitably have been the conquest of
West Pakistan as well." He was evidently trying to salvage the
image of some parallel superpower interests in the South Asian
region. The Soviets no doubt did not want India to conquer West
Pakistan, but there is no reason to believe that Mrs. Gandhi had
any such intention. What the Soviets perhaps feared was that the
prime minister might be under strong pressure of public opinion
to pursue the war even after the fall of Dacca. According to the
CIA, as reported by Anderson, Pegov told the Indian government,
"If India should decide to take Kashmir, the Soviet Union would
not interfere. But India would have to accomplish this objective
within the shortest possible time" (Washington Post, Jan. 18,
1971). It should be added, however, that CIA reports, as quoted
by Anderson, sometimes proved to be quite different from the
originals, and it is therefore difficult to assess their
credibility.

his appointment as Pakistan's president and offered friendly
assistance to the new regime. At the same time, Moscow moved
fast to consolidate its influence in the newly born state of
Bangladesh.

A New Subcontinent
The unexpectedly quick collapse of the Pakistani army in East
Bengal resulted in the emergence of a new subcontinent. India
won a decisive victory at a relatively low cost; its gain was
most impressive.[107] In Pakistan, which now comprised only the
four western provinces and where the GNP was reduced by one-half
and the population to 65 million, the military junta handed over
power to Zulfikar Ali Bhutto, who could rule only with popular
consent. East Pakistan now became fully and finally the People's
Republic of Bangladesh. Thus an immediate political fallout of
the December war was that the entire subcontinent was brought
within the symmetrical framework of representative government.
This in itself was no small gain for India, which now emerged as
unquestionably the dominant power in South Asia.* India had
accomplished what not even a great power had been able to do
during the postwar period: it had successfully intervened with
military force on behalf of a political movement against the
established regime in a sovereign country. The birth of
Bangladesh removed what most Indians had seen as the fundamental
root of tension in the subcontinent: the state system that had
been created by the 1947 "arrangement." The Indian elite now saw
new possibilities of reshaping intraregional politics. Opinion-
makers in India were convinced that New Delhi's relations with
the world community would be determined by the latter's
readiness to recognize the new realities in South Asia or, more
precisely, the primacy of India in that region.
    India's claim to primacy stemmed not merely from its military
victory. Within three months of that event, Mrs. Gandhi's
government ordered mid-term elections to eight state
legislatures, all of which the ruling Congress party won by
overwhelming majorities. By electoral arrangements with the pro-
Soviet CPI, it was able to rout not only the rightest parties
but also the CPI(M), which was reduced in the new West Bengal
assembly to a mere 14 seats as against the 103 it had won in the

----

* Many Indians saw in the Indian victory a triumph of the
country's democratic form of government (Ayoob and Subrahmanyan,
Liberation War, pp. 270-277). Mrs. Gandhi herself heralded it as
a "victory of ideas."

1971 elections.*

The Congress "system" thus almost fully restored after a lapse of five years, Mrs. Gandhi proceeded to strengthen the center's power over the states.[108] Political stability and military success combined to generate expectations that India would soon be able to restructure interstate relations in the subcontinent and thus oblige the great powers to recognize India as one of the world's principal independent centers of decision-making and therefore worthy of consideration as an equal partner in the emerging global balance of power.

"By virtue of her size, population, strategic location, basic economic progress and further potentialities, and to some extent her military development, India also occupies a crucial position in Asian politics. The powers have not yet conceded this role to India. A few years ago India was looked upon as the sick man of Asia by some countries, and the association of India with Asian cooperation schemes was considered something of a liability. The political consolidation of India under Indira Gandhi, the success we have achieved on the agricultural front by eliminating dependence on food from the outside, the realization in the world of the industrial progress we have made, the decisive and brilliant victory of Indian arms over Pakistan, the emergence of Bangladesh as a secular, democratic, friendly neighbour and the dwindling of Pakistan as a middling Islamic State—all these have demonstrated the fact that India is the principal power in South Asia and that she cannot be ignored by the superpowers or China or Japan or the countries of Southeast Asia and West Asia."[109]

The challenge to India's claim to be counted as a major power, however, persisted throughout 1972. It came both from within the subcontinent and outside. The primary task of India's foreign policy was to bring Pakistan within India's coveted pattern of

----

* The Marxists and their leftist allies charged the government with "wholesale rigging of an entire election" and boycotted the West Bengal legislative assembly. That unfair practices took place on a large scale is generally acknowledged by most impartial sources; the extent of the "rigging" remains unknown in the absence of reliable evidence. A recent study in Bengali undertaken by "An Impartial Journalist" concludes that "rigging" took place in some seventy constituencies.

subcontinental good neighborliness and to persuade the major
powers that instead of intervening in South Asian affairs to
promote their respective global strategic interests they should
help India to bring about a stable order in the region. The
success of this policy depended mainly on three factors:
convincing developmental progress within India, Pakistan's
readiness to live in peace and friendliness with India and
Bangladesh, and the growth of an "inner balance of power" in
Asia around China, Japan, and India, in which the United States
and the Soviet Union would play a peripheral role from the
global point of view and refrain from intervening directly in
Asian affairs.[110]

With respect to none of these factors were the realities in
1972 moving in India's favor. While Mrs. Gandhi's supremacy
remained unquestioned, her party was soon beset by the same
factional squabbles that had robbed the undivided Congress
party of much of its dynamism in the sixties. In fact, by the
end of 1972 Mrs. Gandhi's Congress party looked very much like
the party before the split, except for her own unchallengeable
and towering leadership.[111] Indeed, the supremacy of Mrs. Gandhi
symbolized the weakness of the new structure of political power.
It lacked an inner balance. During the period of Nehru, there
was no threat to him as prime minister, yet in his cabinet there
were a number of coequals, while at the head of most of the
state governments stood leaders firmly resting on their own
political bases. Since 1971, however, as Ashoka Mehta, a former
planning minister put it, "no one can expect to be in the
cabinet in his own right. Here is a shift from 'Prime
Ministerial Government' to a near-Presidential regime."[112] In
the states, the chief ministers held their positions "more as
trusted representatives of the Prime Minister than as spokesman
of the States in their own right. The source of their power is
obvious: it is the confidence of the Prime Minister."[113] The
weakness of the chief ministers put a premium on factional
infighting and reduced the states' ability or will to
concentrate on development. The gap between promise and
performance continued to widen, and the radicalism of 1969
seemed to be largely spent by the end of 1972. The land reforms
attempted in 1972, for example, once again failed to bring
about a fundamental transformation of agrarian relationships.[114]

The cost of the 1971 crisis began to be felt in 1972 in the
shape of alarmingly rising prices and an unusually high pace of
inflation. Inadequate rainfall created scarcity conditions in
several parts of the country and forced the government to import
1.5 million tons of food grains to strengthen heavily depleted

reserves. Industry failed to make any perceptible progress. The
rising cost of living led to large-scale urban unrest, involving
workers, teachers, and government employees, and violence and
disorder invaded many of the university campuses. By the end of
the year, Mrs. Gandhi's once-inspiring "Remove Poverty" slogan
began to ring hollow in many formerly responsive minds. India
appeared to be back to the syndrome of "stability at the cost of
development."[115]

Bhutto's Problems in Pakistan

In Pakistan Zulfikar Ali Bhutto was faced with the unenviable
problem of putting a defeated and truncated nation back on its
feet. As noted earlier, he was invited by Yahya Khan to take
over as president and chief martial-law administrator; the
military junta evidently regarded him as the only political
leader who could steer Pakistan through the transition from
military to civilian rule. Bhutto was in New York pleading
Pakistan's case at the Security Council when the Pakistani army
in East Bengal surrendered and Yahya Khan accepted the
unilateral cease-fire announced by Indira Gandhi. After a
hurried visit to Washington, where he had a meeting with
President Nixon, Bhutto returned to a Pakistan that was
suffering the trauma of defeat: "It is as if the entire nation
had pulled a blanket over its head to avoid seeing or being
seen."[116] If Bhutto had to do a lot of tightrope-walking and
indulge in bland contradictions, it was because of the highly
confused and depressed character of Pakistan's domestic politics
after the December defeat. His first action as president was to
retire as many as 30 senior officers of the armed forces, yet he
could not put them on trial or even disgrace them too much
because of his strong ties with the army. He wanted in Pakistan
a "democracy of the people which no future dictator can end." In
January 1972 he ordered his law minister to prepare the draft of
a constitution. Yet he refused to repeal martial law, which he
claimed was necessary to deal with the waves of unrest that
still rocked the country.* He was willing to begin talks with

----

* Pakistan was threatened with a near-civil war in 1972. The
basic cause of tension and conflict was the defeat, but there
was little objective, dispassionate discussion of it in the
press. The defeat aggravated the regional imbalances and ethnic
conflicts in Pakistan. In his bid to enforce the authority of
the central government, Bhutto came into conflict with the
leaders of the Northwest Frontier Province and Baluchistan,

India, Bhutto told a press conference in Lahore on December 30,
1971, if "India changes its present policy toward Pakistan," but
at the same time he had to reckon with the deep-rooted fear and
hatred of India among his countrymen, especially among the
Punjabis, who constituted the strongest support base of his
party. For the same reason his attitude to Bangladesh had to be
extremely ambivalent. He had released Mujibur Rahman in the hope
that the two would be able to arrive at some kind of an
understanding so that he could tell his countrymen that Pakistan
had not lost everything in the war. When he found that his hope
could not be realized, Bhutto took refuge in a cluster of
contradictory postures. In quick succession, he would describe
the Bangladesh phenomenon as a "passing phase," express the hope
that "Muslim Bengal" would one day return to Pakistan, plead
with his countrymen to recognize the "new realities" of the
subcontinent, and assert that he would recognize Bangladesh only
if Rahman agreed first to meet with him. Bhutto apparently
shared, or pretended to share, "the average Punjabi's sentiments
on Bangladesh and the unrealistic belief that Bangladesh is
merely occupied by India and would return to the Pakistani fold
if given the chance."[117]
     Bhutto's political difficulties stemmed also from the
regional imbalance and antagonism inherent in the ethnic
structure of West Pakistan. In the past, the three minority
provinces of Sind, Baluchistan, and the Northwest Frontier had
always looked on the 75 million Bengalis in the distant eastern
wing as a political counterbalance to offset the immediate
threat of Punjabi dominance. With that counterbalance gone, the
fears of the 20 million inhabitants of these provinces naturally
sharpened. The situation was made all the more difficult for
Bhutto by the fact that the PPP had little following in
Baluchistan and the NWFP; of the ruling party's 86 deputies in
the national assembly all but 20 had been returned from Punjab.
Bhutto had, then, to devise a political system that would allay

---

where his party lacked a support base. The minority parties
wanted provincial autonomy and a settlement with India and
Bangladesh. Opposition leaders frequently threatened to start
another "Bangladesh" in one or the other of the minority
provinces. See the New York Times, Feb. 27, 1972; The Times, Aug.
22, 1972, and the monthly News Review on South Asia, published by
the Institute for Defense Studies and Analyses, New Delhi (Feb.-
Sept. 1972).

the fears of the minority provinces and yet assure the 45
million Punjabis that they would not be threatened by the
dictates of a possible alliance of Sind, Baluchistan, and the
NWFP.[118] Anti-Urdu (i.e., anti-Punjabi) riots broke out in Sind
and Baluchistan in the spring and summer of 1972, and although
Bhutto did not have much difficulty in putting them down, they were
a warning of the kind of political problems he would have to
face.*

Within the subcontinent, Bhutto's strategy was to deal with
India without recognizing Bangladesh. He told an Indian editor
in March, "East Pakistan is literally 1,000 miles away. There is
no chance of East and West Pakistan going to war. But here our
armies are confronting each other. The situation can get out of
hand. There is the question of disengagement and prisoners of
war."[119] India was waiting for Pakistan to take the initiative
for talks leading to normalization of relations; the only
condition that Mrs. Gandhi had laid down immediately after the
cease-fire was that the talks must be bilateral, with no third-
party presence or good offices. Bhutto repeatedly affirmed his
desire for "peace with honor," offered to travel to Delhi "any
time" to meet Mrs. Gandhi in order to substitutute the
confrontation of the past with "reconciliation" in the future,
and even suggested that the two countries put the Kashmir
question in cold storage and work for normalization of
diplomatic, economic, and cultural relations. At the same time
he announced his determination to rebuild the Pakistan army as
the "finest military machine in Asia," looked for arms from
whatever sources he could get them, refused to recognize
Bangladesh, and insisted that there must not be a Nuremberg-type
trial of Pakistani war criminals by the authorities in Dacca.[120]

The initiative for India-Pakistan talks came from Moscow. In
February 1972 the Soviet Union sounded India out on how far it
was prepared to go to accommodate Bhutto on the prisoners-of-war
question. According to a knowledgeable source, the Soviet deputy
foreign minister, Firyubin, told the Indian ambassador that

----

* Agreement with the minority parties providing for restoration
of representative government in all of the four provinces was
reached in March, and martial law was lifted on August 14
(Pakistan Times, March 6-9, 1972). However, an armed rebellion
by tribesmen broke out in Baluchistan in January 1973, and
direct central rule was imposed on this province and the NWFP in
February.

Bhutto had informed Moscow through the Soviet embassy that he
was under great pressure from "rightist forces" to get the
90,000 prisoners of war released. Firyubin advised the Indian
envoy that it was not in India's interest that Pakistan be
weakened. Moscow had some leverage with Pakistan and would like
to retain it. A long stalemate in the subcontinent would
embolden China, which might egg Pakistan on to another
confrontation.[121]

This Soviet initiative, coupled with reports that Bhutto had
succeeded in replenishing most of Pakistan's war losses with
help from China, the United States, Iran, Saudi Arabia, and
Turkey, was presumably among the factors that induced Mrs.
Gandhi to write to Bhutto in March, proposing a meeting of
special emissaries to prepare the ground for talks between the
two leaders. Bhutto agreed. The question then was whether
Bangladesh would join the summit meeting. Bhutto wanted India to
repatriate the war prisoners as part of a deal between New Delhi
and Rawalpindi. The Bangladesh government, on the other hand,
made it clear that India must not settle any issue with Pakistan
that involved Dacca without the new republic's participation in
the talks.[122] D. P. Dhar, who had played a crucial diplomatic
role during the 1971 crisis, was appointed by Mrs. Gandhi as the
Indian envoy for talks with Pakistan. Dhar went to Dacca to talk
to Rahman, and the Bangladesh foreign minister came to New Delhi
for discussions with Mrs. Gandhi. It became quite clear that
Bangladesh participation in the summit meeting could not be
brought about. The envoys of India and Pakistan, however, met at
Muree, near Rawalpindi, on April 26 and decided that the
Pakistan president and the Indian prime minister would meet in
New Delhi toward the end of May or at the beginning of June.
After some intervening doubts and misgivings the two finally met
at Simla on July 2 and signed the Simla Agreement. The agreement
pledged the two countries to "put an end to the conflict and
confrontation that have hitherto marred their relations and work
for the promotion of a friendly and harmonious relationship and
the establishment of durable peace in the subcontinent." The
measure of the difficulty of moving firmly toward this happy
direction was that it took the two governments four months of
negotiations simply to draw a new control line in Kashmir.*

----

* For reports on the Simla summit, see Nayar, Distant Neighbors,
pp. 212-243. For a highly negative appraisal of the Simla
summit, see G. S. Ghargava, Success or Surrender? (New Delhi:

Bangladesh: Problems of Nation-Building
The year 1972 ended with Pakistan still not turning toward India
but, rather, turning away. In Bangladesh, even before the first
year of building a new nation ended, polarization began to
emerge between the Awami League and its opponents on the
question of turning too much toward India.

As already noted, Mujibur Rahman was released from prison by
Bhutto on January 8 on the basis of an understanding that the
Bangladesh leader would maintain some kind of a link between his
country and Pakistan. Returning to Dacca on March 10 (after a
brief halt in New Delhi, where he received a hero's welcome),
Rahman declared that Bangladesh had broken with Pakistan once
and for all and that no link was any longer possible.[123] The
logic of the liberation struggle and the December war cemented
Bangladesh's friendship with India, and Rahman began the task of
nation-building with massive help from Delhi.

His problems were tremendous. Pakistani rule and the gruesome
events of 1971 had left Bangladesh with a ravaged psyche and a
desolate landscape: 3 million people killed, 30 million homeless,
nearly five million houses razed, 565 bridges blown up, 1,139
schools and colleges destroyed, a good portion of the cream of
the intellectuals slaughtered, and almost every second able-

Sterling, 1972).
At Simla, India pressed Pakistan to accept the principle of
"bilateralism" in resolving disputes and differences between the
two countries. The Indian objective was to eliminate the twenty-
four-year UN presence in Kashmir. The new line of control, India
insisted, replaced the old UN-supervised cease-fire line; it had
to be maintained jointly by India and Pakistan. The Indian
position regarding the old cease-fire line and the UN presence
was not acceptable to Pakistan. Negotiations for drawing the new
line of control took four months to complete. Agreement was
reached in December 1972, and India began to withdraw its forces
from Pakistani territory. The Simla accord, however, produced
hostile reactions among groups in both countries; the outbreak
of riots in Sind and other places in Pakistan in July and August
compelled Bhutto to harden his stand on reconciliation with
India. See Bhargava for interesting accounts of debates on the
Simla accord in the Indian Lok Sabha and the Pakistan national
assembly. For details of the agreement and repercussions in
Pakistan and India, see also News Review on South Asia (Aug.,
Sept., and Oct. 1972).

bodied man in possession of arms.[124] The liberation struggle had
radicalized much of the urban population, especially the youth,
and differences in outlook and life-style had grown between
those Awami League leaders who had functioned on Indian
territory and those who had borne the brunt of partisan warfare
from within East Pakistan.[125] "Collaborators" and "pro-
Pakistanis" presented a particularly sticky problem. Twenty-
eight percent of the electorate had voted against the Awami
League in the December 1970 election, and those who had
supported the rightist parties were suspected of being
sympathetic to Pakistan.[126] The leftist elements had rallied
round Rahman during the liberation struggle, and they pledged
him their support when he returned to Bangladesh. Rahman's
greatest asset was his charisma. This got him the support of
the middle class, a newly developed social entity. The leftism
of this middle class was largely superficial. It had done pretty
well during the last decade, and although it now felt deprived
of much of its recent affluence, an Indian journalist reported
in January that "this prosperous middle class will go along with
the dominant political force and its administrative apparatus,
and try to make the best of the existing situation. . . . There
has been no radical change in its outlook, and it is by no means
prepared for a drastic change in its life-style."[127]

Within twenty-four hours of his return to Dacca, Rahman gave
up the presidency of Bangladesh and took over as prime minister
in a cabinet system of government whose framework was laid down
in a Provisional Constitutional Order. He declared that
Bangladesh would build a socialist society within a democratic
form of government; its foreign policy would be guided by the
principle of neutrality and peaceful coexistence. His government
nationalized banking and insurance, brought a large portion of
foreign trade under state control, froze salaries at $140 per
month, and announced its intention to fix maximum family
landholdings at 33 acres as against the prevailing ceiling of
125 acres.[128]

Although Bangladesh was described by an American official as
"an international bread basket case," the republic began its first
year with more external assistance than many of the third-world
countries had at the beginning of their independence. India
strained its limited resources to help with money (including
foreign exchange), food grains, crude oil, and technical and
administrative personnel, including experts in planning and
industrial management. The Indian federal budget provided for
Rs. 200 crore (about $650 million) for aid to Bangladesh, the
bulk of which was given within the first six months of 1972. The

Indian army stayed on at Dacca's request until the middle of
March and was withdrawn only after the Bangladesh government
raised eight regiments as the nucleus of its own army.

The socialist countries led by the Soviet Union built up a
rapid presence. By March the Soviet embassy staff had expanded
to ninety. Many of the Russians spoke fluent Bengali. The
Soviets signed a three-year trade pact with Bangladesh providing
for yearly trade worth $435 million and committed $39 million to
finance Soviet-aided projects. They gave a squadron of MIG
fighter planes, a small fleet of transport aircraft, helicopters,
and cargo ships. Moscow agreed to train Bangladesh air force
pilots. A twenty-unit floating Soviet task force was set up in
the strategic Bay of Bengal to clear the ports of Chittagong and
Chalna of sunken ships and mines. Bangladesh signed trade
agreements with Poland, East Germany, Hungary, Yugoslavia, and
Czechoslovakia. Mujibur Rahman's first visit as prime minister
outside the subcontinent was to the USSR.[129]

Rahman, of course, took special care to strengthen
Bangladesh-Indian friendship. In February he paid a four-day
visit to India, and the communiqué issued after his discussions
with Indira Gandhi announced their decision to give "practical
shape" to the "legitimate and deeply-felt aspirations of the
common peoples of the two countries."[130] In March came the
India-Bangladesh treaty of friendship, cooperation, and peace,
reportedly to the annoyance of the Soviet Union, which wanted to
conclude a similar treaty with Dacca. Three of the twelve
articles of the twenty-five-year treaty related to security. The
two countries each pledged not to enter into or participate in
any military alliance directed against the other. They pledged
not to commit acts of aggression against each other. In case
either country was attacked or threatened with attack, it was
agreed that they would immediately consult in order to take
effective measures to eliminate the threat.[131]

"Implicit in the pact [wrote an Indian analyst] is a recognition
on the part of Bangladesh that it is an integral part of what
the Russians prefer to call the Hindustan peninsula and that its
future well-being depends on the preservation and strengthening
of the age-old bond with India, which the recent war with
Pakistan has revived. . . . Judging by the past it is not an
altogether unreasonable inference that the United States may
wish to persuade the new state to dissociate itself from [India]
and seek fulfillment in collaboration with other countries of
South East Asia, especially Indonesia and Malayasia with whom it
shares common religious ties."[132]

The United States government was quicker to extend economic aid to Bangladesh than it had been to realize the intensity of the liberation movement of 1971. In February the Senate voted $250 million for refugee relief in Bangladesh. (An American relief program had been operating there even in 1971). Diplomatic recognition of Bangladesh came on April 4. By June the United States had given $267.5 million in credits and grants. By the end of 1972, Bangladesh had the largest American economic aid program outside countries militarily allied with the United States. Modest but not negligible aid came also from Britain and Canada, while the UN was running a $100 million refugee-relief operation.

Nevertheless, the first year of nation-building could not end on a note of national confidence in goals shared by the different segments of the population. For this the flabbiness of the government was mostly responsible. The country lacked experienced personnel to run the nationalized industries and other establishments. The bureaucracy, crippled by the forced retention of a large number of senior Bengali civil servants in Pakistan, lacked dedication and dynamism. Large-scale smuggling across the India-Bangladesh border very largely defeated the trade agreement signed between the two countries in February. Soaring prices, scarcity of food grains, failure of the government equitably and effectively to distribute scarce daily necessities of life such as cloth, sugar, edible oil, and salt, and corruption and nepotism created considerable discontent in urban as well as rural areas. These problems were made worse by the style in which the new regime functioned. Far too much decision-making was left to Rahman, who conducted himself more as a benevolent patriarch than an efficent, down-to-earth prime minister. An Indian correspondent visiting Bangladesh in April found that the "change in the character of the state" was hardly "reflected in life of the people." A member of the Bangladesh cabinet told this journalist, "The Awami League is not a party but a movement, which includes people of many different political persuasions. It is futile therefore to expect too much cohesion in it. For one thing, the rewards of power have exacerbated personal frictions. For another, the youthful cadres have become radicalized in the course of the liberation struggle."[133]

Political polarization began in April, when Rahman was criticized publicly for the first time since Bangladesh gained independence by the ninety-two-year-old leader of the National Awami party, Maulana Bhashani. As The Indian Express reported, "The progressives of Bangladesh, who under the leadership of

Maulana Bhashani had joined with fanatical communal parties of
the right in running down the India-Bangladesh treaty, have now
made a common cause with petty traders and businessmen to demand
scrapping of the trade pact between the two nations."[134] Also in
May, the Dacca University students' union, which had spearheaded
the anti-Pakistan movement, split into pro- and anti-Rahman
groups, and the Students' League, affiliated with the Awami
League, which had controlled the union for many years, was
routed by procommunist students in a keenly fought election.[135]
A faction of the Students' League and the labor organization of
the Awami League joined to ask Rahman to form a "revolutionary
government" and demanded a constitution guaranteeing "full
socialism." In August, 19 leftist groups formed an "action body"
against the government under Bhashani's leadership, while on
September 3 Bhashani led a procession of 5,000 "hunger marchers"
to the constituent assembly in Dacca, demanding an all-party
government to replace Awami League rule.[136] In November the
radical student factions of Dacca University joined hands with
Bhashani to demand a "truly revolutionary constitution." By the
end of the year Bhashani formed a "united front" of several
radical groups to oppose the Awami League in the first general
election scheduled for March 1973, under the constitution
adopted by the constituent assembly. These radical elements,
Bhashani particularly, now became stridently anti-Indian in
their rhetoric; they rejected Indian "socialism" and were afraid
of Indian domination of the Bangladesh economy. Bhashani even
asked the Indian state of West Bengal to secede from the Indian
Union and join Bangladesh in an independent Bengali-speaking
state. Faced with this challenge from the extreme left, Rahman
appeared first to move closer to the pro-Moscow Bangladesh
Communist party and the like-minded National Awami party led by
Professor Muzaffar Ahmed. His relations with these two leftist
groups changed, however, when in January 1973 they opposed his
bid to improve relations with the United States. The police
opened fire in January on an anti-U.S. demonstration near the
USIS library in Dacca, killing two students. This incident
immediately led to a countrywide strike called by all the
leftist groups. Rahman took up the challenge and swung into a
political offensive against the entire left. His followers
raided the Dacca offices of the Bangladesh Communist party and
of the pro-Moscow faction led by Muzaffar Ahmed. At a mass rally
in Dacca Rahman declared that he would not allow Bangladesh to
be dominated by "one great power."

The first general election in Bangladesh, held on March 7,
exposed the basic weaknesses of the left. The leftist groups

failed to unite against the Awami League. It became evident that
they had no mass base and that their support came mainly from
sections of the urban middle class, youth, and organized trade
unions. The pro-Moscow groups, including the Bangladesh
Communist party, were forced to oppose the Awami League whereas
their official tactical line had been to work with Rahman's
party. The Awami League won a stunning landslide victory,
capturing all but 9 of the 300 seats in the national assembly.
The only areas where its candidates fared badly were the hill
tracts in Chittagong near the border with Burma, inhabited by
tribals. The victory immediately led to a marked improvement in
the "law and order" situation in Dacca and enabled Rahman to
shift pro-Moscow Abdus Samad Khan from the Foreign Office to the
agriculture department and to give the foreign affairs portfolio
to his close and trusted aide, Kamal Hossain, a product of
Cambridge University. Kamal Hossain, as law minister, had been
instrumental in drafting the constitution of Bangladesh and
getting it adopted by the national assembly and also in
preparing the legal framework for the trial of "war criminals."
Within six weeks of the formation of the new government, certain
shifts in Dacca's foreign-policy action and behavior became
noticeable. While friendship with India remained the
"inescapable compulsion" of Bangladesh foreign policy—as Kamal
Hossain said shortly before the March election—there was now a
calculated attempt not to play up the relationship and to
practice rhetorical reticence when referring to it in public. An
element of hard bargaining also entered the process of India-
Bangladesh cooperation. Dacca made a positive response to Mrs.
Gandhi's initiative in April to break the deadlock in the
negotiations with Pakistan, but it apparently refused to go all
the way with New Delhi. On April 17, 1973, the two governments
jointly offered to repatriate all but some 200 Pakistani war
prisoners if Pakistan simultaneously returned the Bengalis and
took back the Urdu-speaking Bihari Muslims of Bangladesh, most
of whom had collaborated with the Pakistani regime in 1971 and
had been labeled "pro-Pakistanis." While Bangladesh thus made a
major concession in the joint offer, no longer insisting on
recognition by Pakistan as a precondition for settling the POW
question, its insistence on going ahead with the trial of "war
criminals" and on an exchange of the Bengalis and Biharis did
not make Bhutto's acceptance of the "package" very easy. April
thus passed without a positive Pakistani response.

The March election gave Rahman a massive popular mandate to
reconstruct Bangladesh in the light of the declared objectives
of the Awami League. Whatever challenge there exists to his

leadership and to the dominant one-party system comes from
disenchanted urban youth and sections of the middle class. Of
greater potential danger is the sizable quantity of arms still
retained by groups that profess leftist ideologies. Immediately
after the election the government gave these groups ten days to
return these arms, but apparently the ultimatum did not produce
the expected results.[137] Meanwhile, Rahman's objective seems to
be to develop a balanced relationship with the two superpowers
and, eventually, friendly relations with China. His principal
foreign-policy problem is how to maintain close ties with India
and at the same time demonstrate to elite groups that friendship
is not another name for subservience.

South Asia and the Great Powers

South Asia in 1973, then, is not exactly an Indian pasture.
India's primacy is still unrecognized by Pakistan, and in
Bangladesh also the Awami League leadership's pro-Indian stance
is beginning to be matched by popular resentment and fear of
India's eminence in the subcontinent. As a regional subsystem,
therefore, South Asia remains unstable; its instability stems
primarily from the drift and scale of the internal politics of
the political units and of relations among them. This
instability exposes South Asia to the power politics of the
great powers, to their rivalries and their competition for
influence and power.

South Asia's close physical proximity to the Soviet Union and
China has inevitably drawn it into the Sino-Soviet cold war. As
long as the two communist giants could stand together, South
Asia had remained one of the areas where the United States and
the Soviet Union faced each other in their global competition
for influence-building. Neither of the superpowers nor China,
however, has had an autonomous strategy for South Asia, and far
less have they had one for India, despite its size, population,
potential resources, and strategic location. For each, the
importance of South Asia and of its individual political units
is measured by the region's relevance to its global rival or
rivals. This has lent a strong element of uncertainty (or
flexibility) to the South Asian strategy of each of the three
great powers. If Soviet strategy has been much more stable than
American and Chinese, it is because the Russian leaders
anticipated problems with China even in the mid-fifties and
decided to build up India as a counterweight to China, even
during the zenith of Sino-Soviet amity.

The Role of the United States

The South Asia strategy of the United States has passed through

two postwar phases of great-power rivalry to arrive at a third.
During the fifties, the main thrust of U.S. strategy was to
involve as many nations as possible in military pacts designed
to contain Soviet-Chinese power. In the sixties the United
States generally worked with the USSR in South Asia to contain
the influence and power of China. In the seventies the U.S.
remains as interested as before in containing both the Soviets
and China, but considers the USSR stronger and therefore more
necessary to be contained. It is now in a position to make use
of the Sino-Soviet antagonism to contain the Soviets as well as
China. The compulsions that gave birth to the Nixon Doctrine—
failure of American force to create a "free" Asia and exhaustion
of America's moral and material resources—rule out a high U.S.
profile in South and Southeast Asia in the foreseeable future,
mainly because of the region's relative unimportance to the
somewhat lowered strategic objectives of American global
policies. If the United States can afford to play only a
marginal role in South and Southeast Asian affairs, reserving
its resources for the more important areas such as Europe, the
Middle East, and the Pacific north of the China Sea, it is only
common sense that this role be played in conjunction with its
stable and temporary allies against its stable and temporary
antagonists. The great realignment in relations among the major
powers places at the disposal of American policymakers a
considerable amount of flexibility, more in South and Southeast
Asia (where Sino-Soviet antagonism is most acute and Japan is
rapidly rising as a rival of both China and the USSR) than in
the Middle East and the Persian Gulf region where there is
virtually no Chinese presence. President Nixon, in his foreign-
policy report to Congress in February 1972, ruled out competing
with the Soviet Union for influence in India. A low profile U.S.
role in South Asia can be played with effect only if it is
deployed to shore up gains where the Soviet presence is weak or
problematical.

This was the principal logic behind Nixon's "tilt" toward
Pakistan during the subcontinent's 1971 crisis. The White House
had four alternative, though not mutually exclusive, strategies
that it could pursue. It could exercise effective pressure on
Yahya Khan to release Mujibur Rahman and come to a political
settlement with him and his party. It could work with the USSR
for a settlement acceptable to Pakistan, Bangladesh, and India.
It could openly or tacitly permit India a limited intervention
in Bangladesh and thereby force Parkistan to come to a
settlement with Rahman. And, finally, it could lean on China and
play a marginal autonomous role of its own to prevent an

unacceptable expansion of Soviet influence. Nixon tried the
first two alternatives in the summer and autumn of 1971 without
much conviction and with little or no success. The third
alternative apparently was not considered at all. The pressure
on Yahya Khan was not strong enough, and it missed the crucial
point of the crisis, namely, that a viable solution could be
worked out only with Rahman and his colleagues. Working with the
Soviet Union was inhibited by the Nixon approach to China; South
Asia being a sore point in the Sino-Indian conflict, it was
neither possible nor desirable to reconcile the strategic
interests of the two communist giants in that region. Neither
Nixon nor Kissinger apparently expected the Pakistani army in
Bangladesh to collapse in two weeks. Such was the measure of
their understanding of the depth and intensity of the liberation
struggle and of the political isolation of the Pakistani
occupation army. After the cease-fire, Nixon apparently decided
to make use of the Sino-Soviet antagonism to contain the
Soviets as far as possible. This at any rate was the impression
that his actions firmly planted in the minds of Indians. They
found evidence of Nixon's intentions in his administration's
blaming India for the December war, in the continued suspension
of economic aid, in the inclusion in the Nixon-Chou En-lai
communiqué of a paragraph outlining the Chinese position on the
India-Pakistan conflict and on the question of Kashmir's self-
determination, in the near-shutdown of USAID in India, and in
the lukewarm attitude of the U.S. government to the admission of
Bangladesh to the United Nations.

After Nixon's visit to China, Indians perceived a sharp swing
in U.S. policy in Asia. It had been Japan-centered until then;
now it was to be China-centered. A leading analyst articulated
the widely shared fear that "from the one extreme of unremitting
and senseless hostility to China, the United States may swing to
the other extreme of ignoring the legitimate interests of
others."[138] Indira Gandhi herself complained in an article in
Foreign Affairs that no American administration during the
postwar period had been willing to concede to India the right to
make its own independent decisions when these were at variance
with American perspectives.[139] Indian correspondents in
Washington reported an "ugly, anti-Indian mood" in the White
House and warned that India, and indeed the entire subcontinent,
was low on the U.S. scale of priorities and that with Nixon in
the White House for a second term no basic change in America's
attitude toward India could be expected.* They also warned their

----

* K. Subrahmanyan, who attended the 14th Annual Conference of

countrymen that America was weary of foreign aid and that
Nixon's cutting of it would be injurious to Indian interests.[140]
The stoppage of economic aid and the near-certainty that no aid
would be forthcoming even in 1972-1973 sharpened India's
sensitivity about the PL-480 surplus grain agreement. In the
fall the Indian finance minister, Y. B. Chavan, met with several
U.S. officials in Washington, including Secretary of State
William Rogers, but received no indication that American policy
toward India would change.[*]

Mrs. Gandhi hit back without being able to hurt Nixon very

---

the International Institute of Strategic Studies in Ste. Adèle,
Québec in October 1972, found a "vast communication gap" between
U.S. (and Western) strategic thinkers and their Indian
colleagues. In a report on the conference he wrote, "For most of
the establishments of the Western countries and Japan, the Cold
War is not yet over. Only its methodology has changed. The
Soviet Union still continues to be the major adversary. They
still discuss Soviet penetration and policies in Asia and
security threats to Japan and Southeast Asia without specifying
from whom though making it explicit that the threat is no longer
from China. . . . The framework, perceptions and value systems
of Western strategic establishments are as different from ours
today as they were during the days of Nehru. However, till
recently, the Westerners found an overwhelming majority of our
elite echoing their views. Now some Indians have started
articulating their own world views and perceptions and these do
not always get across in view of the vast communication gap that
exists between this country and the Western world" (Hindustan
Times, Oct. 19, 1972).

* In August Mrs. Gandhi remarked that India was quite willing to
patch up its relations with the United States, but the Nixon
administration showed no desire to do so (The Times of India,
Aug. 13, 1972). In September, Finance Minister Chavan, on a
visit to Washington, offered to sign a treaty of friendship with
the U.S. At a reception at the residence of the Indian
ambassador to celebrate the silver jubilee of India's
independence, the U.S. government was represented by the acting
secretary of state, John Irwin; Dr. Kissinger had accepted the
invitation but did not turn up. After Chavan's return, the
Congress party president, S. D. Sharma, said that no improvement
was expected in Indian-U.S. relations (ibid., Sept. 27, 1972;
Patriot, Sept. 28, 1972).

much. She upgraded India's relations with North Vietnam and
appointed an ambassador to Hanoi. The government of India for
the first time took up a clearly anti-U.S. position on the
Vietnam war. Mrs. Gandhi also extended diplomatic recognition to
the German Democratic Republic. Her government refused visas to
several thousand American scholars, particularly those who were
to use PL-480 rupee funds. Mrs. Gandhi also publicly accused the
CIA of fomenting and supporting civil disorders and separatist
movements in India.*

When all this brought Indian-U.S. relations to an all-time
low,[141] a thaw suddenly took place, immediately after Nixon's
reelection to the presidency. By April 1973 it was possible to
speculate on the drift and scale of Indian-American relations
during the seventies. U.S. policy for the subcontinent,
explained Daniel Patrick Moynihan, the new American ambassador
in New Delhi, rested on three major postulates: recognition of
changed realities, including the emergence of Bangladesh as a
sovereign republic; determination to withhold lethal weapons
from the three countries; and keenness to build "realistic and
pragmatic new relations with India based on mutual interests."
The difficulties besetting the building of "new relations"
between the U.S. and India had been dramatized only a few days
before the Moynihan statement by the announcement in Washington
that Pakistan would be allowed to buy 300 armored cars worth $13
million and $1.1 million worth of spare parts, parachutes, and
reconditioned aircraft engines, for which orders had been placed
and a down payment made before the war of 1971. Although the
announcement committed Washington not to sell lethal weapons to
the subcontinent once the "earlier blocks" had been cleared, New
Delhi was "dismayed" by the "resumption" of American military
aid to Pakistan. Foreign Minister Swaran Singh told an incensed
Lok Sabha that the U.S. decision would "aggravate India's
security problem," strengthen the military in Pakistan, and
retard the process of bilateral settlement of India-Pakistan
issues envisaged in the Simla Agreement. India was, however,
somewhat mollified by the U.S. refusal to sell B-57 bombers
and F-104 interceptors to Pakistan, by the release of $87.6

----

* The CIA cry was raised first by the Congress party president
in September. Mrs. Gandhi said in October that the CIA had
increased its activity in India and "we must continue our
vigilance" (Hindustan Times, Sept. 27, 1972; The Times of India,
Oct. 14, 1972).

in aid to India (frozen during the 1971 war) to buy farm
equipment, and by an agreement that talks would begin soon to
decide on the disposal of the huge accumulation of Rs. 3,200
crore ($3.2 billion) in U.S. credits resulting from the sale of
PL-480 grains against payment in Indian currency.[142]
    For the next few years India and the United States will have
to reconcile themselves to a relationship that is very low-key
compared to relations during the fifties and sixties. In his
foreign-policy report of February 1972, Nixon asked India to
work out a "balanced relationship" with the great powers; an
India tilted too heavily toward the USSR, he implied, would be a
cause of U.S. concern. The "imbalance" of India's relations with
the superpowers stems primarily from the low priority accorded
to India in President Nixon's grand design to build a
"generation of peace" on the basis of a multipolar global
balance of power. While the United States would like to balance
India with Pakistan and Bangladesh, India wants to be balanced
with China and Japan in recognition of its dominant position in
South Asia. The United States has invested over $8 billion in
India's development but is clearly unwilling or unable to give it
significant aid any longer; the country that helped India raise
ten mountain divisions to defend the frontiers against China is
not likely to contribute meaningfully to further augmentation of
India's defense capability. A vacuum will therefore exist in
Indian-U.S. relations in the coming years and will continue to
be exploited by the Soviet Union. Anti-Sovietism has disappeared
even in the traditionally pro-American political parties in
India, such as the Jan Sangh and Swatantra.

The Role of China
The Chinese perception of India and the subcontinent is dimmer
than the American. For Peking, the subcontinent, or most of it,
has fallen under the Soviet shadow; India is virtually a Soviet
satellite. This perception developed during the latter period of
the 1971 crisis and was confirmed by the Indian military
intervention in Bangladesh. For an authoritative expression of
China's perspective of the crisis and the war, we have to turn
to the statement issued by the Peking government on December 16,
1971. "A large-scale war of aggression against Pakistan," it
affirmed, "was brazenly launched by the Indian Government on
November 21, 1971, with the active encouragement and energetic
support of the Government of the Soviet Union." By rejecting the
UN General Assembly's resolution of December 7 calling for an
immediate cease-fire and withdrawal of armed forces to their
respective sides of the Indian-Pakistan border, the Indian

"expansionists" exposed their true ambition to create "a greater Indian empire." They wanted "not only to swallow up East Pakistan but also to destroy Pakistan as a whole." Indian expansionism posed a threat to all of India's neighbors.

The Chinese government categorically rejected India's right to intervene in the internal turmoil in Pakistan. "Many countries in the world have nationality problems. . . but these are the internal affairs of the respective countries, which can be solved only by their own governments and peoples, and in which no foreign country has the right to interfere." India itself had very complex nationality problems: "How would India react if other countries should deal with India in the same way that India is today dealing with Pakistan and use armed force against India?" India's concern for the self-determination of the Bangladesh people rang hollow in view of its indifference to the Kashmiri people's right to determine their own affairs. "The Indian Government has single-handedly manufactured a so-called 'Bangladesh' and inserted it into East Pakistan." The Bangladesh government was a "puppet regime" that could hardly exist "without the protection of Indian bayonets." In that sense, "it is totally the same stuff as the so-called 'Manchukuo' of the thirties and forties, which was under the aegis of Japanese militarism."

The Chinese indictment of the Soviet Union, "the back-stage manager of the Indian expansionists," was no less vigorous:

"For many years, the Soviet Government has been energetically fostering the Indian reactionaries and abetting India in its outward expansion. In last August the Soviet Union and India signed the treaty . . . which in substance was a treaty of military alliance. They claimed that this treaty was not directed against any country, but actually it is precisely under their joint conspiracy that the subversion, interference and aggression against Pakistan have been intensified. Since the outbreak of the war of aggression, the Soviet Union has stepped up its efforts in pouring a steady stream of arms and equipment into India. . . . What makes people particularly indignant is that the representative of the Soviet Government in the UN Security Council should have time and again used the veto to obstruct the ceasefire and troop withdrawal which are desired by the overwhelming majority of countries and peoples all over the world. . . . The purpose of the Soviet Government . . . is further to strengthen its control over India and thereby proceed to contend with the other superpower for hegemony in the whole of the South Asian subcontinent and the Indian Ocean and at the same time bolster India and turn it into a sub-superpower on the South Asian subcontinent as its assistant and partner in committing aggression against Asia. The present sudden invasion of Pakistan by India with the support of the Soviet Union is precisely a repetition on the South Asian subcontinent of the 1968 Soviet invasion of Czechoslovakia. The acts of the Soviet Government have once again revealed its hideous features as social-imperialism and its expansionist ambition."[143]

The Chinese perception of the events in the subcontinent came as a disappointment to India. Since the autumn of 1969 a thaw had seemed to be slowly setting in in Sino-Indian relations, frozen since the 1962 border conflict. Chinese media had stopped advertising the exploits of Maoist groups in India and supporting the CPI(M-L). On May 1, 1970, Mao Tse-tung sought out the Indian chargé d'affaires at the May Day function in Peking, shook hands with him, and made some laudatory remarks about India. This immediately generated hopes in India that Peking's policy would change. In the next few months diplomatic contacts took place between the two countries in Rangoon, Cairo, Katmandu, and Moscow. The three meetings in Moscow between the Chinese and Indian ambassadors in March and April 1971 could not have taken place without the knowledge and tacit approval of the Soviet government. At all these meetings, steps to be taken to normalize Sino-Indian relations were reportedly discussed.*
Mrs. Gandhi herself affirmed publicly on a number of occasions that India would like to live in peace and amity with China. The crisis in Pakistan enhanced in Indian eyes the importance of Chinese friendship or at least neutrality; even

----

* In early September the Indian envoy in Peking, B. Mishra, was recalled to New Delhi for consultations. The Times of India reported on September 4, "There are reasons to believe that Mr. Mishra left Peking soon after he was assured that the Chinese Government would be interested in having a dialogue on the bilateral issues with India." That Peking should have made this gesture immediately after the conclusion of the Indian-Soviet treaty was considered significant. "According to informed sources, the signing of the treaty might perhaps have promoted Peking to have an early dialogue with India." India was invited to the Afro-Asian table tennis tournament in Peking in November; the team included at least one senior official of the foreign office. It became clear, however, that progress of normalization of relations would be long and difficult.

the right-wing parties urged the government to try to improve relations with Peking. There was no longer any insistence that India must not speak with China until the Chinese vacated or had been thrown out of the "Indian territories" they had occupied along the border in 1962.*

Up to the end of March 1971 Chinese media took no notice of the crisis in Pakistan. In April, however, Chou En-lai sent a message to Yahya Khan making two points: he advised the Pakistan president to isolate the "handful" of secessionists but settle with the broad masses of the people in East Bengal; and he assured Pakistan of Chinese support in the event of Indian aggression.[144] The Chinese stance did not unduly discourage the Indian mind. Efforts to improve relations continued. Peking refrained from commenting on the Indian-Soviet treaty for several weeks after it was signed. Soon after the signing, Mrs. Gandhi wrote to Chou En-lai to explain the Indian position on the crisis in Pakistan and to assure him that the treaty was not aimed against any country. In October Han Suyin, the Belgian-born author and confidante of the Chinese prime minister, arrived in New Delhi from Peking; in a newspaper article she reported the view on Sino-Indian relations of "a certain [Chinese] official whose position and words command attention." This official, whom many Indians took to be Chou En-lai himself, said that China hoped that "India will not become a pawn in the play of superpower politics." China wanted India and Pakistan to settle their own problems and disputes between themselves. "The break-up of Pakistan can do India no good. The intrusion,

----

*"The border question, it appears, has not figured in any details in the probings so far, and may not be a substantive point of discussion in the initial stages, if and when contacts are resumed" (The Statesman, Sept. 1, 1971). Indian analysts showed a certain understanding of the Chinese fears and suspicions. The Hindustan Times wrote in an editorial on September 1 that "there is equal reason for the Government of India to signal Peking that the Indo-Soviet treaty is not to be regarded as anti-Chinese." Girilal Jain wrote that the Chinese "cannot but be haunted by the fear that if Soviet power comes to be established in the Indian Ocean and the Himalayas, India may reopen the question of Tibet" (The Times of India, Sept. 1, 1971). See also A. Appadorai, "China's Foreign Policy," Indian Express, Nov. 25, 1971; Swaran Singh's statement in Amrita Bazar Patrika, July 23, 1971; and Ajit Bhattacharjea, "Ten Years After Thag La," The Times of India, Oct. 21, 1972.

under any pretext whatever, of any so-called great power in what
concerns these two states alone can do harm to India herself."
The Indian-Soviet treaty was India's business. China, however,
was not unaware of its military clauses, which put India in a
"position of inferiority."

"What it amounts to is this: That at the moment the USSR has got
troops stationed on certain borders, poised in what may be
construed as a threatening attitude. India was not informed of
these troop movements, yet by this treaty India's agreement to
these troop concentrations has been tacitly given. This already
places India in the position of agreeing to a situation created
after the fait accompli. This position of inferiority should
perhaps worry the Indian people. It certainly does not worry the
Chinese. . . . We have had our experience in the past and we
hope that the Indian people will not be made use of."[145]

If the Chinese government intended to convey a message to
India, the Han Suyin article conveyed it quite clearly. In 1969
the Indian government had endorsed the Soviet position on the
Sino-Soviet clashes on the Ussuri River. Soviet support for
India in its border problem with China and Indian support for
the USSR in its border troubles with China had meshed the two
inner-Asian frontiers politically and even strategically. China
wanted India to extricate itself from involvement in the Sino-
Soviet border problem, to assert by deeds its independence from
the USSR. What the Chinese feared was Soviet use of India and
the subcontinent to "encircle" China. Chou En-lai wanted India
to stand up, like China, against the two superpowers' bid to
control and manage the destiny of the entire world.

This was precisely what India was not in a position to do.
Apart from its economic and defense dependence on the
superpowers, India in 1971 was committed to a Bangladesh within
or outside Pakistan, and it needed the support of at least one
of the superpowers, which could be only the USSR. The Chinese,
in the meantime, extended military and economic support to the
Pakistan government; many of the weapons used to suppress the
Bangladesh movement were of Chinese make. During the Ayub Khan
period, China had built up a presence in East Pakistan while the
Soviet presence was limited mostly to the western wing. Unlike
any high-ranking Soviet leader, Liu Shao-chi, Chou En-lai, and
Chen Yi had visited Dacca, and Mao reportedly had asked Bhashani
in 1968 not to work against the government of Rawalpindi until
China had been able to bring Pakistan securely under its
influence. The Bangladesh movement, therefore, cut across
Chinese strategy for Pakistan and the subcontinent, which,

broadly, was to build up its presence in Pakistan to counter the
Soviet presence in India. The Chinese, then, had reason to
view with concern an Indian-Soviet initiative that might break
up Pakistan and significantly alter the balance of power in the
subcontinent in India's favor. China's stance toward India
hardened in November when Indian troops began to penetrate East
Pakistan and move against the forward positions of the Pakistani
army. At no stage, however, did Peking promise Pakistan military
intervention. Peking was probably deterred by the Indian-Soviet
treaty and the ugly mood of the Russian leaders. Armed
intervention across the Himalayan passes in the winter of 1971
would have been a most difficult enterprise and less certain of
success than it had been nine years earlier. One reason why
India delayed intervention in Bangladesh was certainly that it
waited for the mountain passes to be closed by snow.
Nevertheless, China (like the United States) might have
intervened if India had carried the war into West Pakistan and
Pakistan-controlled portions of Kashmir. The war would then have
been prolonged and the Chinese could have struck in Kashmir.[146]

After the December war Peking made no response to Indian
overtures for normal relations. The annual report of the Indian
external affairs ministry for 1971-1972 said that for "quite
some time" there were hopes of a favorable response from China
but that China's attitude in the recent events had resulted in a
"temporary setback."

In 1972 Pakistan had friendly relations with each of the
three great powers, but China was perhaps the centerpiece of its
external relations. Bhutto was not just indulging in one of his
rhetorical flourishes when he declared at a reception honoring a
visiting Chinese dignitary that Pakistan would not build up
relations with any nation, including the Soviet Union, if this
had to be done at the cost of friendship with China. Indeed, in
1972 Bhutto had received from China much more than he had from
either of the superpowers. Within a month of taking over as
president he had paid a two-day visit to Peking with a fifty-
seven-member delegation including the three service chiefs. He
sought a treaty of friendship, apparently to counter the Indian-
Soviet treaty, but did not get it. He did, however, get
assurances of continued military aid and substantial economic
and trade support. Four Chinese loans were converted into grants,
repayment of a 1970 loan was deferred for twenty years, and more
grants and loans were promised on similar terms.[147] The Chinese
leaders showed a sympathetic understanding of Pakistan's
priorities and problems in the subcontinent. The joint
communiqué issued after Bhutto's talks with Chou En-lai

condemned India's "naked aggression" but had not a word of blame
for the Soviet Union. The prescription it offered for return of
normalcy to the subcontinent may give us an insight into
Peking's preferences. India must withdraw from territories
occupied during the war, restore the 1948 cease-fire line in
Kashmir, repatriate Pakistani war prisoners, and withdraw its
troops from Bangladesh so that future relations between "the two
parts of Pakistan" could be decided through negotiations between
"elected leaders of the people" without "foreign intimidation
and influence."[148] Later in the year Bhutto told an Indian
editor that once India had returned the POWs and vacated
occupied territory, China would be interested in improving
relations with it.[149]

At Bhutto's request China vetoed on August 25 a four-power
resolution in the Security Council recommending the admission of
Bangladesh to the UN.* Three days later Chiao Kuan-hua, the
Chinese vice foreign minister, arrived in the Pakistan capital on
a two-day visit at the same time Pakistani and Indian officials
were meeting in New Delhi in an effort to break the deadlock on
drawing the new line of control in Kashmir.[150] China's position
on Bangladesh somewhat softened in late 1972, but the year ended
with no indication that Peking would recognize Dacca without a
signal from Rawalpindi.[151] In the main the Chinese seemed to
have succeeded in their South Asia policy objective. New Delhi
realized that Soviet pressure alone was not enough to persuade
Pakistan to recognize Bangladesh and enable India to return the
war prisoners. "As India sees it," reported the political
correspondent of The Hindu, "the chances of a settlement with
Pakistan will depend to a large extent on China's readiness to
normalize its relations with the other two countries of the
subcontinent. The crux of the problem therefore is how to ease
the continuing Sino-Indian tensions before hoping for better
relations with Pakistan."[152]

The Role of the USSR
After the December war and the birth of Bangladesh the Soviet
Union bent its foreign-policy resources to bring about
symmetrical relationships among the three partners of the

----

* The veto was used to defeat a joint Indian-British-Yugoslav
resolution recommending the admission of Bangladesh. China asked
for postponement of consideration of the matter pending "complete
withdrawal" of Indian armed forces and return of the Pakistani
POWs.

subcontinent. If earlier in 1971 Soviet media had blamed
Pakistan for the upheaval in East Bengal, from December onward
the principal target of Soviet verbal onslaughts was China. The
strongest indictment of Peking came in the columns of Pravda on
December 28. "An enormous share of the responsibility for the
conflict rests with the Chinese leaders," it affirmed: Pakistan
would not have launched its military operations against India
"if it had not been aware of instigating support from outside."
This support was "considerable," and it came from the U.S. as well
as China. Since the war, China had been following "an openly hostile
course against India." It was trying its best to discredit India in
the third world; it refused to normalize relations with India and
settle the border problem; it was interfering in India's internal
affairs by supporting the various Maoist groups; and indeed it was
engaged in isolating India by fomenting anti-Indian sentiments and
actions in Nepal, Burma, Ceylon, and Pakistan. The conflict in the
subcontinent had clearly demonstrated that the Peking leaders were
pursuing "a great-power social-chauvinist course which not
infrequently unites them and American imperialism."[153]

Soviet efforts were now directed at preventing Pakistan's
leaning too much on China and the United States. The Soviets
greeted Bhutto immediately after he took over as Pakistan's
president and invited him to visit Moscow. Bhutto, on his own
part, was anxious to go to Peking and Moscow (he had already met
with Nixon) before he formulated his strategies for the
subcontinent. The Times correspondent in Rawalpindi wrote, "The
Russians are playing an important part as intermediaries between
Pakistan and India, and Bhutto is apparently hoping that they
will have a moderating influence on Delhi's negotiating
position."[154]

Bhutto's visit to Moscow came off in February, after his
return from Peking. He received assurances of economic support
and was urged to recognize Bangladesh, which would pave the way
for an amicable settlement of the aftermath of the war. Kosygin,
who conducted most of the discussions on the Soviet side, also
urged Bhutto to respond positively to the Soviet move to build a
collective Asian security system. Bhutto told an Indian editor
that he had opposed the Soviet move.[155] The Soviets, however,
were pleased with Pakistan's withdrawal from the British
Commonwealth and from SEATO, and they were not bothered by
Pakistan's continued membership in CENTO because they had
already taken a mellower view of this regional cooperation
organization and had been engaged in building positive relations
with its two other principal partners, Turkey and Iran. After
Bhutto sent a message to Kosygin explaining that domestic

developments had made it impossible for him to recognize
Bangladesh immediately, Moscow nudged New Delhi to hold an
India-Pakistan summit meeting and welcomed the Simla accord.
Meanwhile, Soviet economic aid to Pakistan was resumed, work
began on Soviet-aided projects, including a steel plant near
Karachi, and a cultural agreement was concluded in August. On
the occasion of the 25th anniversary of Pakistan's independence,
a joint message from Podgorny and Kosygin noted "with
satisfaction that friendly relations are developing between the
Soviet Union and Pakistan."

Through these relations were not developing as fast as the
Soviets would have liked them to, at the end of 1972 Moscow was
not without hope that Pakistan would sooner rather than later
have to recognize Bangladesh and turn increasingly to the USSR
for trade and aid. A Moscow Radio broadcast to Asia on September
30 claimed that the three countries of the subcontinent, as well
as Afghanistan, Iran, and Nepal, had been showing interest in
"setting up regional cooperation with Soviet participation," and
on October 2 a broadcast commended Moscow's economic relations
with India, Afghanistan, and Iraq as an example to other Asian
countries. On October 12 a fifteen-year economic and technical
cooperation agreement concluded in Moscow between the USSR and
Iran during the Shah's visit put forward the idea of regional
cooperation in economic matters, trade, and transport. A Moscow
Radio commentary claimed that Iran's experience of collaborating
with the USSR and Eastern Europe had convinced the Iranians that in
the future "most" of their trade and economic relations should be
with these countries—a prospect no doubt also intended for
Pakistan.

Meanwhile, the Indian and Soviet economies were closely tied
in 1972 in line with Article 6 of the Indian-Soviet treaty. A
trade protocol signed in May envisaged the volume of trade in
1972-1973 to reach the figure of Rs. 500 crore ($666 million), a
30 percent increase over 1970. The Indian trade minister, L. N. Misra,
told his Soviet couterpart that structural changes would be made
in foreign trade, placing much greater reliance on trade with the
socialist camp and the third world. On September 19 an agreement
was reached to set up an intergovernmental commission on
Economic, Scientific, and Technical Cooperation; its first
meeting was held in February 1973. The agreement stipulated that
each country would take into account the needs of the other's
economy when formulating national plans, and one of the
commission's tasks would be to supervise the implementation of
joint enterprises. Another agreement concluded on October 2
provided for joint research and exchange of documentation on

technology, as well as periodic meetings to draw up "specific programs of cooperation." The Soviets also agreed to help India expand its merchant marine and its space, nuclear-energy, and development programs.[156]

The Soviets shifted to the advocacy of joint schemes in which they would take part of the output since their previous aid projects proved in several cases too large for the needs of the Indian market, and major idle capacities of these projects had made them uneconomic and had provoked public criticism. Economic collaboration of such magnitude, however, raised several complex problems. The Soviets pressed India for long-term integration of the two economies. They argued that large-scale export of capital goods to India required matching imports if an intolerable trade imbalance was to be avoided and if shortages of capital and consumer goods in the USSR were to be alleviated. Negotiations on dovetailing the two economies were proceeding in December. The two countries were grappling with problems such as the pricing of goods, and "much hard bargaining was going on."[157]

In the realm of the supply of major military weapons to the subcontinent, the Soviets have acquired a vast lead over the U.S. and China. Since 1965 the USSR has supplied 65 percent of the total arms trade in the subcontinent, as against a mere one-half percent supplied by the United States. In 1971 Egypt and India received 80 percent of the Soviets' major weapons exports to the third world, while 65 percent of America's exports to the third world went to the Middle East, with the bulk of that going to Israel and Iran. According to the Stockholm International Peace Research Institute:

"India is the second largest third world recipient of Soviet arms, and the only country outside the Warsaw Pact which has licensed manufacture of the MIG-21, its Atoll missiles and the engine. Licensed production appears to be progressing, and the first airframe with Indian-made components was completed in 1970. The current plan involves the production of 300 aircraft from 1970 onwards to equip fifteen squadrons. From 1973 India will also produce the latest export version—the MIG-21M—used, for example, by Soviet Air Force units in Egypt in 1970. By 1971 India had received a large number of Su-7 fighter-bombers as well as SAM-2 and SAM-3 missiles. Large deliveries of tanks, including the PT-76 amphibious tank were made during 1970-71. Politically, the massive military supplies to India manifested the presence of the USSR on the subcontinent, and this was formalized by the Treaty of Peace, Friendship and Cooperation.
. . .

"The East Pakistani conflict brought the Soviet Union and
India closer together. . . . Spare parts for MIG-21 and Su-7
aircraft were delivered during October-November, followed by
freighters whose cargoes reportedly included S-A missiles, tanks
and armoured personnel carriers."[158]

In comparison, American and Chinese arms deliveries were much
smaller.

"The partial embargo on [U.S.] arms deliveries to Pakistan, in
operation since 1965, was temporarily lifted in 1970. In October
1970, Pakistan ordered seven Canberra bombers, six Starfighters
and 300 armoured personnel carriers under MAP. However, in April
1971 deliveries were halted retroactive to 25 March. On 8
November the U.S. Government announced that orders for arms
worth $3.6 million destined for Pakistan, held in the Department
of Defense stocks or licensed before 25 March, were cancelled.
In the meantime, some deliveries, consisting mostly of spare
parts, had been made. The 1965 embargo on India was never
lifted."[159]

China's exports of arms to Pakistan during 1970-1971 consisted
about exclusively of tanks. "By 1970 Pakistan reportedly
possessed about five squadrons equipped with MIG-19s, and in 1971
Pakistani sources reported that China had begun deliveries of as
many as 400 fighter and bomber aircraft."[160] Reports in the
Indian press said that China also helped Pakistan in 1971 to
equip two freshly raised divisions, while the United States
persuaded Jordan, Iran, Turkey, and Libya to deliver aircraft and
other equipment. During 1972-1973 Pakistan seemed to be getting
regular arms deliveries from Iran, where the Shah announced a
huge arms buildup with $1.5 billion worth of purchases from the
United States.
    The closeness of Indian-Soviet relations could not but raise
doubts and misgivings in the minds of some Indians. However, the
government, and Mrs. Gandhi particularly, insisted that close
collaboration with Moscow did not inhibit India's independent
decision-making.* Relations between the two countries continued

----

* At the intellectual level, two kinds of fear were articulated
even in 1972 about the scale of Indian-Soviet relations. Sisir
Gupta, representing one line of apprehension, warned the Russians
against dividing the subcontinent with the U.S. and China into
spheres of influence. "Sino-U.S. Détente and India," India

to expand. A combination of international developments increased
rather than diminished India's dependence on the USSR for the
strategic demands of its economy and security. It was the Soviet
Union, and not the United States or Canada, India's traditional
grain suppliers, which came to Mrs. Gandhi's rescue when near-
famine conditions threatened to sweep through vast parts of the
country in the fall of 1972. When the world energy crisis
sharply worsened the Indian economic crisis in 1973, the Soviets
emerged as the only power willing to supply India with large
quantities of fertilizer, kerosene, and crude oil, as well as
massive renewed assistance for oil exploration.[*]

This was the outcome of Leonid Brezhnev's five-day official
visit to Delhi in November 1973, which according to the Soviet
leader brought about a further "qualitative" improvement in
Indian-Soviet friendship and enabled the two governments jointly
to plan long-term economic collaboration through the principle
of the "international division of labor." A significant event of
the visit was Brezhnev's separate series of meetings with the
president of the ruling Congress party and a delegation of the
CPI. The CPSU was now clearly trying to establish collaborative
linkages with the principal political institution of the Indian
national bourgeoisie.[**] An immediate outcome of the visit was

----

Quarterly, Vol. 27, no. 3 (New Delhi, July-Sept. 1971), pp. 179-
184. G. D. Deshingkar, representing the second line, warned
India against getting too deeply involved in the Sino-Soviet
conflict ("Indian Security after Bangladesh," Economic and
Political Weekly, Annual number, vol. 7, nos. 5-7 (Feb. 1972),
pp. 225-231.

Mrs. Gandhi affirmed in a speech welcoming Brezhnev that the
main thing about the Indian-Soviet treaty of peace and
friendship was that "in all these years Soviet leaders have
never put pressure on us, never dictated conditions to us, never
imposed their will on us" (Pravda, Nov. 28, 1973). See also
Indian and Foreign Review (New Delhi, Dec. 1 and 15, 1973).

* Under a trade agreement signed during Brezhnev's visit, Moscow
agreed to deliver 325,000 tons of fertilizer to India on rupee
payment. For a critical view of the trade agreement, see N.J.N.,
"The Strings Are Very Much There," The Statesman, Dec. 18, 1973.

** For a full report on the visit, see Pravda and Izvestia, Nov.
28 and Dec. 1, 1973. The Soviet leader met with the Congress
party chief, S. D. Sharma, and during the conversation, "some

the electoral pact concluded between the Congress party and the
CPI to campaign in state-level elections in Orissa and Uttar
Pradesh, the latter being Mrs. Gandhi's home state. The pact
enabled the CPI to quadruple its seats in the Uttar Pradesh
assembly and more than double them in Orissa; more important,
the Congress party had to rely on the CPI votes in order to form
stable governments in both states. From its vantage position in
three states (the third being Kerala), the CPI hoped that it
could press forward for a national coalition with the ruling
party after the parliamentary election scheduled for 1976.*
    The Brezhnev visit, nevertheless, was probably not an
unmitigated success. The Soviet friendship strategy aims at
establishing what Talcott Parsons has called a "genuine
consensus at a certain level of values" between the CPSU and the
"left and democratic forces" in third-world countries. The
rising scale of the relationship with the Soviets, with no other
external relationship to balance it, appeared to divide the
Indian national bourgeoisie, and the impact of this divisiveness
could be seen even in Mrs. Gandhi's own party. Her dilemma in
1973-1974 was that while she needed Soviet friendship not only
for the Indian economy and for defense but also to refurbish her
own image as a progressive prime minister, she could not afford
to close the door on all possibilities of a balancing
relationship with the United States or China or both. During
Brezhnev's visit Mrs. Gandhi resisted his pressure for a formal

----

questions relating to the maintenance of ties and close contacts
between the CPSU and the INC were also discussed" (_Pravda,_ Nov.
29, 1973). The CPSU has been building formal contacts and ties
with the ruling political parties in Iraq, Syria, and Egypt.
Unlike the treaties the Soviets have signed with Iraq and Egypt,
the Indian-Soviet treaty does not provide for interparty contacts
and consultations. Linkages between the CPSU and the Cogress
party are, thus, posttreaty developments.
    Brezhnev's meeting with a CPI team took place in Delhi on
November 27 and was reported in _Pravda_ the following day. This
was the second meeting between leaders of the two parties in two
years. For a detailed and politically meaningful report of the
June 1972 meeting in Moscow, see _Pravda,_ June 30, 1972. It
outlines the broad political strategy to be pursued by the CPI
with regard to the ruling Congress party.

* Mrs. Gandhi's party won the Uttar Pradesh election by a narrow
margin and lost the Orissa election, also by a narrow margin. In

endorsement of the Soviet proposal for a collective Asian
security system.* This was partly because of the oncoming
agreement with the United States for the disposal of the rupee
funds accumulated by the U.S. through the sale of grain under
PL-480. The conclusion of this agreement in February 1974
considerably eased Indian-U.S. relations, but almost immediately
these relations came under a fresh cloud following the American
decision to build a full-fledged naval base on the island of
Diego Garcia in the Indian Ocean. Mrs. Gandhi described the U.S.
action as a "threat to our security." Once again Indian
perception of the U.S. naval role in the Indian Ocean largely
corresponded with the perception of the Soviet Union.[161]

Conclusion
At the mid-seventies, India is clearly not riding the wave of
history in South Asia. American economic aid has shrunk to

----

both, it will have to rely on CPI support to form a stable
government. For the CPI assessment of the election result, see
New Age (New Delhi) March 3, 1974.

* The joint communiqué issued after the talks mainly stressed
how the Indian-Soviet treaty had helped strengthen friendship
between the two countries. All that was said with reference to
Asian security was that: "This treaty has become one of the most
important factors in strengthening peace and stability in Asia
and throughout the world. . . . The Soviet Union and India
reaffirmed that they attach special importance to the broad
development of mutually advantageous cooperation and the
strengthening of peace and stability in Asia, based on the joint
efforts of all states in this largest and most populous part of
the world. The Soviet Union and India have agreed on the need to
promote the creation of conditions in which peoples can live in
an atmosphere of peace and good-neighborliness. . ." Pravda,
Dec. 1, 1973).
     The Politburo of the CPSU, in a review of Brezhnev's visit,
noted "with satisfaction the positive results of the broad
exchange of opinions on Asian problems. . . . The Soviet Union,
two-thirds of whose territory lies in Asia, and India, a major
Asian state, are deeply interested in the preservation of peace
and stability in that region, based on the joint efforts of
Asian states" (ibid., Dec. 4, 1973).

almost nothing; relations with China remain practically frozen.
The euphoria of 1972 died with its offspring of great
expectations, leaving the intellectual community in a mood of
unprecedented gloom and despair, if only because it felt
grievously let down by the prime minister. Successive years of
drought brought widespread hunger to large areas, and the
government was unable to implement socioeconomic measures
directed against the vested interests of the rural rich.
Inflation, runaway prices, black-marketing, and corruption
conspired to create a bleak prospect for the stillborn Fifth
Five-Year Plan. On top of all this, the world energy crisis
erupted in 1973, multiplying at one stroke the cost of oil
imports by about 300 percent. The government's prebudget report
on the national economy in February 1974 spoke of the "worst
economic crisis since independence" and promised no prospects of
an early recovery.[162]

Nor did developments in the subcontinent correspond to
India's expectations. As a result of a tripartite agreement in
1973 India began to repatriate the Pakistani war prisoners
while Pakistan started the repatriation of the Bengalis detained
as hostages. The future of the Biharis living in Bangladesh
remained largely uncertain.[163] However, Mrs. Gandhi failed to
obtain what Bangladesh needed most: diplomatic recognition by
Pakistan. When this recognition finally came in February 1974,
it came in a manner that could hardly lift the hearts of the
Indians. They had to bear with the spectacle of Sheikh Mujibur
Rahman attending the pan-Islamic conference in Lahore, the
success of which was undoubtedly a feather in Bhutto's
diplomatic cap. Relations between India and Bangladesh remained
officially friendly, but there was little left of Bangladesh's
postliberation warmth for its big neighbor. After Rahman's visit
to Lahore, Indians realized that Bangladesh was in a position to
normalize relations with Pakistan without New Delhi's help, and
although they looked forward with somewhat muted hopes to a
tripartite summit leading to normalization of relations in the
subcontinent, they were no longer certain that this desirable
course would add up entirely in India's favor.[164]

What surprised and somewhat stunned the Indians was Bhutto's
political and diplomatic success. He had been able to weather
the political storms in Baluchistan and the Northwest Frontier
Province with a mixture of political suppression and political
concessions; the army had made no bid to usurp power; Pakistan
had been given a new constitution; and representative
institutions had continued to grow in a society where they had
remained suppressed for a decade and a half. Bhutto was on

friendly terms with each of the world's three great powers. Thus
it was Pakistan rather than India that seemed to have wrested
advantages from the realignment in great-power relationships
since the summer of 1971. Moreover, Bhutto had succeeded in
strengthening Pakistan's friendship with the Shah of Iran, who
had publicly committed himself to its territorial integrity and
political stability. Indeed, Pakistan's cordial relations with
China, Iran, and the rulers of the oil-rich sheikhdoms of the
Arab world contrasted sharply with India's relatively barren
relations with most countries outside the Soviet bloc.[*]
    The politics of the subcontinent, internal as well as
international, continues to derive much of its dynamics from the
rivalries of the great powers that have characterized the entire
postwar period. When the subcontinent was thrown into the crisis
of 1971, the great-power rivalries passed into a period of
major, if slow, transformation. The war of December changed the
political map of the subcontinent, but it has not, as of early
1974, made the relations of the powers symmetrical. Nor has it
mellowed great-power rivalry with regard to the subcontinent; if
anything, it has made the subcontinent a major issue in the
solidified Sino-Soviet conflict. India seems to have lost a
historical opportunity to establish itself firmly as South
Asia's predominant power. Its stature in much of Asia is likely
to be further diminished as a result of its economic problems
and also because of the vast rise in the military and economic
power of China and Iran.
    The nations of the subcontinent, like other third-world
countries, share a common dilemma. While they can ill afford to

----

[*] Much of Indian diplomacy in 1973 was devoted to improving
relationships with Iran. These efforts met with some success
when the Shah announced in February 1974 that his government
would sell oil to India on credit and extend to Delhi a loan of
$300 million to develop iron-ore mining. While this will
certainly lessen the intolerable burden of paying for oil
imports with 40 percent of India's entire export earnings, the
back of the problems remains unbroken. Ninety percent of India's
imports of 17 million tons of oil comes from Iran. The Arab
suppliers have so far shown no concern for India's distress
despite Delhi's firm support for the Arabs in their conflict
with Israel. India is clearly not in a position to loosen the
Shah's commitments to Pakistan. In fact, the Shah has all the
leverage against India, India almost none against the Shah.

absorb the trauma of great-power antagonisms and conflicts, they
wish at the same time to profit from them, as indeed they often
do. The cold war enabled India and like-minded countries to
project the doctrine of nonalignment, which stemmed basically
from their desire, and need, to cultivate the friendship of both
power blocs. Likewise, the Sino-Soviet conflict enabled India to
gain from the massive friendship of the USSR, and Pakistan to
gain from China's. Yet neither seems to be strong enough to
withstand the tremors of this conflict. And the drift and scale
of the Sino-Soviet conflict are likely to have the most profound
impact on the subcontinent during the seventies.

It is toward the Persian Gulf region that the center of
conflict appears to be shifting in the mid-seventies. The
American stance has already shifted there from Southeast and
South Asia. Pakistan has begun to assert a new identity as a
Persian Gulf power with the generous assistance of the Shah of
Iran. Close to Pakistan, the Shah is constructing the largest
naval base on the Indian Ocean. He is expected to cooperate with
the U.S. navy to contain the Soviet naval presence in the Indian
Ocean. India cannot view without apprehension the prospect of a
major conflict building up in the Gulf region. Indians watched
with extreme uneasiness Pakistan's close and growing ties with
Iran, Iran's cordial relations with the United States, and
Peking's eagerness to move closer to the Shah. (But the Shah's
1974 $300 million loan to India to buy his oil allayed many of
their fears.) Precisely because both India and Pakistan have
entangled themselves with great-power rivalries in much of Asia,
the infant republic of Bangladesh will strive to balance its
relationship with New Delhi and Rawalpindi and to be on friendly
relations with the United States, the Soviet Union, and China.[165]

It should be instructive to watch how rivalries, competitions,
and conflicts among the great powers influence and shape the
dynamics of political and social change within the subcontinent.
The events of 1971 confirmed that the frontiers of the new
nations are only as permanent as is the capability of their
rulers to keep their domains together. Pakistan was an extreme
case of geographical absurdity, but political dissidence
covering large ethnic areas exists in many of the third-world
countries. The events of 1971 also showed that military
intervention in national interests beyond the frontiers of a
nation-state is not the exclusive prerogative of the great
powers. The course of history since 1971 has also confirmed that
for the new nations war is too expensive and uncertain an "other
means" for the continuation of politics and that each war whets
the appetite of the military machine that already consumes the

bulk of meager resources. The upheavals and uncertainties in
Asia stem primarily from the great social imbalance triggered by
the process of modernization and social change. In the
subcontinent, one-sixth of humanity struggles to get away from
the ancient world of poverty and stagnation.

This struggle has so far been joined by only a small fraction
of the population. But vast numbers are being drawn into the
process of participation with the passage of time, and the
tentative sociopolitical systems are being continuously tested
for their ability to meet and control the expectations and
demands of swelling and maddeningly multiplying multitudes. In
such a volatile milieu, stability can only be chimerical; the
future will certainly be more convulsive than the past. The
rivalries and conflicts among the great powers often act as
catalysts for change. They mingle with countless native tensions
and conflicts, and they render the twists and turns of history
all the more unpredictable.

Chapter 5

JAPAN AND THE GREAT-POWER TRIANGLES

Paul F. Langer

Is Japan today a great power? Certainly not, if we associate
with that term a large and sophisticated military establishment
capable of defending the country against external attack.
Politically? Perhaps in some world areas—primarily East Asia.
But even there Japan's qualifications are debatable, for until
now the Japanese have made very little use of their leverage to
influence the course of events in that region. Yet the Japan of
the 1970s is being described with increasing frequency as one of
the five big powers, together with the United States, the USSR,
China, and Western Europe—powers which, in the view of some,
are capable of assuring world stability by balancing one
another. If Western analysts place Japan in that select company
of nations (the Japanese themselves are rather hesitant about
making such claims), it is obviously because of the phenomenal
growth and the impressive dimensions of Japan's economy. By
1974, Japan's gross national product had eclipsed the GNP of all
countries but the United States and the USSR, and it was well on
its way toward catching up with that of the latter.*
   Japan's economic achievement during the past two decades has
no precedent in world history. Yet it is questionable whether
the impressive scale of Japan's economy is in itself sufficient
reason to rank Japan among the great powers. After all, power is
measured by its effect. Power among nations is reflected by its
impact on international affairs. To be felt, power must be
exerted. However, postwar Japan has proved most reluctant to use
its power except in the defense of narrowly conceived economic
interests. To date, Japan remains a very low-key presence in

---

* The GNP of the USSR is estimated to be about 60 percent of
that of the United States (which now exceeds $1 trillion), and
that of Japan (with half the population of the two superpowers),
about 35 percent. However, while the growth rates of the three
countries have fluctuated substantially during the past decade,
Japanese economic growth has been markedly more rapid than that
of either the United States or the USSR. Despite the
difficulties faced by Japan because of its lack of resources,
this trend is expected to continue during the 1970s.

world affairs, apparently satisfied with playing a minor
political role not at all proportional to its economic muscle.
As a result, when a Japanese prime minister speaks, his voice is
not heard around the world, and his views are rarely reported in
the world press. How many people outside Japan can recall the
name of Japan's prime minister or that of his predecessor?

Yet in a sense, the Japanese are engaged in a historic
experiment seeking to achieve great-power status through
economic growth and trade, without the backup of a commensurate
military apparatus. The outcome of this experiment ought to have
significance well beyond Japan, particularly in an age when
doubts are being raised in some quarters about the continued
relevance of military power in international relations among the
larger nations.

But at this point it is by no means clear whether the
Japanese will continue along the road they have followed since
their defeat in World War II. The growing visibility and
influence in Japanese politics of the Seirankai, a small group
of young politicians opposed to Prime Minister Tanaka's
"unprincipled" foreign policy (especially with regard to
abandoning Taiwan), are only two of several pieces of evidence
suggesting that Japanese policy is in flux. Many foreign
analysts and some of their Japanese colleagues, perhaps more
influenced by precedents than by the available evidence, wonder
whether Japan will not soon be compelled to act more
independently, as traditional great powers have always acted.
Such a course could lead to the development of much greater
military strength, including nuclear weapons.

It is precisely this uncertainty regarding the future course
of Japanese policy that in the 1970s adds a new dimension to the
importance of Japan. It is not only Japan's economic power but
also its unused power potential that makes Japan of such central
concern today. A Japan that should decide to build great
military power and to project that power abroad might indeed
become the world's third superpower—if adverse foreign
reactions (Chinese? Soviet? perhaps even American?) were not to
prevent the achievement of such a goal (requiring at least a
decade)—and in the process might set off worlwide repercussions.
But even a Japan that decided merely to play a more active role
on the international scene, translating its economic muscle into
political influence, could produce major changes in the present
balance of forces, at least in the Far East.

The Japanese will not make their decisions in isolation from
the world. Certainly the policies of the three major Far Eastern
powers—the United States, the USSR, and China—will impinge
strongly and directly on the formulation of Japanese policies.

We are dealing here not only with a number of bilateral relationships, but with a complex interplay of many forces. With respect to the effect on Japan of changing relations within the great-power triangles, two major factors deserve special attention: the continuing Sino-Soviet conflict and the ongoing adjustment of American relations with both big communist powers.

The combined impact of these events is being felt in Japan at a particularly critical time. Today, the three major powers' interests are converging on Japan with unprecedented intensity, propelling it onto the world stage as a more active participant, compelling it to make policy choices calling for greater responsibility and commitments. But Japan is also in a transitional stage with regard to the balance of its internal, domestic forces, as the value system and the objectives that have dominated Japanese policies for two decades are now being widely questioned. And these developments are occurring at a moment when new problems—such as the energy crisis—are confronting Japan.

Japan's significance once lay in its being a key component of the U.S. posture in the Far East, very much under American sway and firmly committed to the support of American policy positions. Chinese and Soviet influences were felt only weakly in Japan. This is no longer the situation. Japan is becoming a more independent force in world affairs, and its policy decisions no longer inevitably coincide with those of the United States. In the 1970s, Japan, the only important country where American, Soviet, and Chinese interests intersect, has gained enormously in significance vis-à-vis all three powers. It is impossible for any of them to ignore Japan, just as it is impossible for Japan not to react to the three powers' pressures.

The outcome of this interaction will be a major factor— perhaps the critical factor—in determining the future of Asia in the next decade. But it would be a mistake to attempt to analyze Japan's interplay with the great-power triangles while disregarding trends in Japan's domestic context and Japan's changing conception of the outside world. It will be necessary, therefore, to touch on some of the characteristics of Japan as it emerged from World War II and has evolved since.*

----

* The following discussion of the Japanese domestic context is a distillation of the author's own research and of the many excellent studies of Japan published in Japan and in the West during the past two decades. No attempt will be made to document each statement, except where the author's views are in

Japan's Domestic Environment

The Psychological Climate. In more than a thousand years of
recorded history, the Japanese had not experienced surrender of
the home islands to a foreign enemy—until 1945 when Allied
occupation forces landed in Japan. Military defeat was therefore
a traumatic experience for the Japanese people, especially since
it marked the culmination of a single-minded national effort of
nearly a decade to mobilize at great sacrifice the entire
population for the war. The year 1945 constitutes a temporal
dividing line in modern Japan's development, as well as the
point of departure for a critical reappraisal of national goals
and values, of the nation's institutions, and of the
individual's relationship to the state. Under the guidance of
the occupation forces—largely American in composition—postwar
Japan underwent a remodeling of its political, legal, and social
order. At the same time, the war and its aftermath also had a
far-reaching influence on the Japanese people's perception of
their world role.

There is room for disagreement as to how enduring these
changes, psychological and institutional, will prove to be.
There can be no question, however, that in important respects
Japan in the 1970s is indeed a very different country from that
which emerged from the war in 1945. The traditional, complete
subordination of the individual to the state and to the concept
of a national mission has given way to an unprecedented stress
on the rights of the individual and his personal goals, thereby
placing clear limits on the government's ability to command
Japan's resources for the execution of national policy. In line
with the democratic reforms of the postsurrender years,
government has become everyone's business and has grown much
more responsive to the will of the electorate. Further, legal
and political reforms, reinforced by strongly antimilitaristic
trends among broad strata of the population, have eliminated the
once-predominant influence of the Japanese military over
national policy.

----

conspicuous conflict with those of the majority of other
students of Japanese affairs. In the case of quotations or of
similar direct references calling for footnoting, Japanese
sources have been used only when adequate English-language
documentation or translations were not available. (Unless
otherwise indicated, translations from the Japanese are the
author's.)

Modern Japan's unbroken record of victorious wars and foreign conquests was possible only because of the Japanese people's extraordinary discipline, their belief in the intrinsic superiority of Japan, and their faith in their nation's mission. The collapse of the Japanese military effort in World War II and the immense material destruction and loss of human lives with which the Japanese people paid for that failure of national policy have substantially eroded the psychological foundation on which that policy had been built. Thus, postwar Japan's psychological climate favors a national policy that is the reverse of that of prewar times. In the past, domestic welfare had to take second place to Japan's international concerns. Now, the stress is on the betterment of the social order within Japan. The mood of the postwar Japanese militates strongly against any commitment abroad—alliances, regional arrangements, and the like—which might give rise to military involvement, or even to political confrontation or friction, with foreign nations. The external role of Japan tends to be limited by domestic pressures to a strict minimum, and that minimum further limited to economic activities. For the moment at least, Japanese ambitions remain inward-directed.

Underlying these postwar trends is a widespread abhorrence of military solutions to the problem of national security. Since the supreme effort, material and human, made during the war by the Japanese armed forces in the end only made the catastrophe more severe, the Japanese have been cured—if not permanently, at least for some time to come—of any desire to take the road to military power. Only a direct, patent, and serious threat to their national existence could abruptly change this attitude.

Furthermore, from lofty ideological and nationalistic mystical concerns, the Japanese have turned toward the enjoyment of material things. For the past two decades, they have been indulging in a spree to satisfy long-suppressed material aspirations. The austere life and the haughty disdain of the samurai for financial gain and physical comfort no longer characterize the Japanese life-style, nor is the government in a position to reimpose such principles on the people. Popular attitudes discourage an active—which is to say, an expensive—foreign policy. Such attitudes and moods must now, in contrast to prewar times, be taken into account by the government in formulating national policy.

Taken together, these and other changes in the Japanese outlook produce a certain aloofness from involvement in developments abroad. But countervailing forces are at work which prevent such attitudes from degenerating into pure isolationism.

A major conclusion drawn by the Japanese from their wartime experience was that they had been ill-informed about the strength of their adversaries and that it was important for the new Japan to learn from foreign experience. Confidence in Japan's ability to compete in a world dominated by Western nations endowed with greater material resources and superior technology was severely shaken by the military defeat and the Japanese people's massive exposure to the American occupying forces during the late 1940s. Self-confidence gradually returned as the Japanese economy rose from the ruins of the 1940s, recovered during the 1950s, and took off during the 1960s. But even today, despite the economic might of Japan, the country's leaders and the general public have no doubt that Japan stands to benefit from intensified contacts with other nations, particularly the advanced nations of the West. For that matter, for the first time in Japan's history, large numbers of ordinary Japanese are going abroad, and not in uniform— seeing for themselves and in the process inevitably shedding some of their traditional insularity. Meanwhile, the steady growth of Japanese foreign trade has created a firm and material foundation for an intensive Japanese concern with developments abroad. There is hardly a Japanese alive, certainly none in a responsible position, who is not aware that virtually all of his country's energy resources and industrial raw materials as well as much of his food are now coming from abroad. The worldwide energy crisis that began to affect Japan in late 1973 has strongly impressed this point on every Japanese.* Resurgence of national pride and heightened national consciousness (even among the political left) are thus balanced by the recognition that Japan's welfare is intimately linked to the course of world events.

The Power Structure. Japan is no longer ruled in the name of the emperor, but in the name of the people. A majority of the elected representatives making up the Diet designate the prime minister, who sets national policy within the limits prescribed by the postwar democratic constitution. For the past two decades, i.e., ever since Japan regained its independence, the country has been ruled by conservative elements, gathered since 1955 into a single political organization, the Liberal

----

* It is estimated that the weighted average of Japan's dependence on imports for ten major basic commodities stood at 90 percent in 1970 and will rise to 93 percent in 1975.

Democratic party (LDP).[1] The president of this majority party
concurrently serves as prime minister and as the nation's top
policymaker.

The LDP's uninterrupted hold on power has given Japan a
degree of political stability quite unusual in Asia. But by
barring the opposition from participating in government, the LDP
has prevented their evolution into a responsible political
force. The decay that tends to set in when a party is
semipermanently entrenched in power has not spared the LDP.
There has been a gradual erosion of the party's electoral
strength so that its hold on power has become shaky.* The
political consequences of this trend may not become fully
apparent for some time (and meanwhile the trend could, of course,
be reversed), since the electoral system of postwar Japan
operates in such a way as to assure the ruling party of a safe
majority in the Diet even though it no longer represents a clear
majority of the electorate. Nonetheless, the steady decline in
the party's popular vote is of increasing concern to its
leaders, making them more responsive to opposition pressures,
especially when these appear to reflect popular trends and
aspirations. This applies, for example, to the growing desire of
the Japanese people to reduce dependence on the United States
and more actively to promote relations with the communist
nations. In that sense, Japan today is entering a transitional
era characterized by a reappraisal of past policies.

Certain inherent weaknesses in the makeup of the ruling party
also have a strong effect on its domestic and foreign policies.
In theory, the party is a single organization. In practice, it
is a gathering of factions without sharply defined ideological
outlook. It is loosely held together by shared, vaguely
conservative views (and opposition to Marxism and communism) and
by a desire to hold on to political power. The LDP has never
been a tightly organized political action group. Its leader, who
is serving concurrently as prime minister, is permitted to
remain as party president for only a limited number of terms. As

----

* In 1958, the LDP took 57.8 percent of the vote; in 1960, 57.6
percent; in 1963, 54.7 percent; in 1967, 49.5 percent; and in
1969, 47.6 percent. In the most recent national elections
(December 1972), the LDP garnered only 46.9 percent of the total
vote. Even when we add to this the 5.1 percent polled by the
Independents, who are in fact conservatives and support the LDP,
the government party now commands a bare majority of the popular
vote.

<u>primus inter pares</u> among the chiefs of the party factions (often
numbering more than ten) which in loose association—and in
constant rivalry—makes up the majority, his position is rarely
stable enough to enable him to impose his will and preferred
policy when the party's views are not unified. Such situations
occur not infrequently as controversial issues are seized upon
as weapons in the internecine struggle for succession to the
party presidency. The prime minister, his executive assistants,
and the other prominent personalities in the party therefore
spend much of their time and energy in attempts to forge a party
consensus through compromise. These conditions severely limit
the party head's ability to lead with determination. They also
slow down the decision-making process in party and government.
   In contrast to the Japanese Communist party (JCP), which
commands a much smaller share of the political vote, the Liberal
Democratic party (like most other Japanese political
organizations) operates on an exceedingly weak infrastructure.
The party has a head (or rather heads—the faction leaders), but
only weak limbs. In a sense, the organization consists almost
entirely of the Diet members affiliated with the LDP and of
their staff. Policy is made at party headquarters in Tokyo and
within the multitude of party committees staffed by Diet members,
but with very little input from below since the LDP lacks
organizational cohesion and a solid popular foundation.
   The Japanese government's policy is primarily the result of
the direct interplay of three elements, linked by tangible and
intangible bonds and engaged in a continuous round of mutual
consultation: the LDP, of course; the bureaucracy (i.e., the
higher-echelon civil servants); and the business community (i.e.,
the top managers of Japan's big industrial and financial
institutions).*
   These three principal elements of the Japanese power structure

----

* The LDP by no means neglects the interests of its rural
constituents, since much of the party's electoral strength is in
the areas outside the big cities. However, the rural interest
groups are not sufficiently important in the economy as a whole
or sufficiently well organized to compete as pressure groups with
the big financial and industrial companies. They are therefore
less important in the formulation of national policy, except
where their interests are directly involved, as is the case with
regard to import policy for agricultural commodities or price
supports for agricultural products.

operate in an intimate relationship, coordinating their policies
and acting in cooperative fashion. Although not wholly free of
conflicting interests, these three groups always seek to
harmonize their views before the government submits any
legislation to the Diet for approval or makes important
decisions affecting Japan's domestic or foreign policies.
      Communications between the LDP politicians who (in theory)
determine policy and the business elite are very close. No major
decision is made by either side without consulting the other
when such matters as foreign trade or other economic aspects of
national policy are concerned. But the same statement also
applies, if to a lesser extent, to other national policies,
including the sensitive subjects of foreign relations and
defense.* It has been calculated that the Japanese prime
minister averages one meeting a day with representatives of the
business world. A similar educational background (Tokyo
University) and shared conservative convictions create a
predisposition for cooperation between big business, government,

----

* An important role in coordinating trade and other economic
policies, as well as foreign-relations positions between the
various interested parties, is played by LDP committees that
have their counterpart in the business world. A key party in the
formulation of LDP policy is given to the Policy Affairs
Research Council (Seimu Chosakai), often referred to as the
Policy Board. The Council studies all significant policy issues
and drafts relevant legislation. For administrative purposes,
the Council is divided into fifteen divisions—counterparts of
the cabinet ministries and other major government agencies—and
some sixty special committees and commissions, all of them
staffed by LDP Diet members. Especially relevant to foreign
policy are the following divisions and committees: foreign
relations and national defense divisions, and special committees
on foreign affairs, economic affairs, national security, foreign
aid, military-base problems, northern territories, and
international cultural relations. The key figures of Japan's
business world are normally consulted by the prime minister and
his cabinet ministers on all important national and international
policy issues. In addition, the influence of the business world
on foreign affairs and foreign economic policy is primarily
exercised through the leading business organization, Keidanran
(Federation of Economic Organization), in which the principal
industrial and financial institutions participate and which has
its own committees and study groups as points of contact with

and the ruling party. But other, more concrete considerations
favor such a relationship. Because of the organizational
weakness of the LDP previously alluded to, its leaders and
candidates cannot expect to be successful at the polls without
ample donations from corporations and other economic interest
groups.* Moreover, the existing ties between the ruling party
and the business community are constantly being renewed, as
businessmen enter politics and join the ranks of the party
leaders.** The upper echelons of the government bureaucracy are
also tied in closely with the party establishment. In theory,
the ruling party, through its various committees, determines
policy for government officials to implement. But only the
bureaucrats command the necessary data, traning, and experience
on which policy formulation must be based. Hence, party
committees by necessity rely heavily on the advice of the
specialists in the government, and new legislation is almost
always first drafted by the bureaucracy rather than by party
officials.***

----

the government bureaucracy and the ruling party. These
committees include the following (all of them headed by
important business leaders): general policy, economic affairs,
foreign affairs, energy problems, foreign investments,
international finance, foreign trade, export regulation,
economic cooperation, Africa, Iran, the Atlantic Institute,
Indonesia, Japan-Thailand, overseas resource development, and
overseas minerals development, as well as several other
committees touching peripherally on foreign relations.

* Some thirty large cooperations reportedly paid into LDP
coffers 5.6 billion yen (then over $18 million) for use in the
1969 general elections. Even larger amounts were reported to
have flowed from the business community into party coffers in
connection with subsequent election campaigns. Business
contributions to the LDP in 1973, for example, were estimated
at $80 million. Much of this support goes directly to party
factions, enlisting the support of particular groups within
the LDP in furthering specific policies favored by economic
interest groups, and thus increasing the potential leverage of
business circles in the formulation of policy.

** Usually one-third of the LDP's Diet delegation is composed of
men who are active in business or who are former businessmen.

*** In matters of foreign trade and economic policy, experts

Cooperation between the government bureaucracy and the ruling
party is also encouraged by other considerations. Career
government officials, especially at the policymaking levels of
the hierarchy, depend for promotion to high position on good
relations with the political leaders. At the very top, the two
power pyramids fuse: every cabinet member is a high-ranking
party official, and the prime minister, as previously mentioned,
is the party president. These ties are continuously being
strengthened by the influx of former bureaucrats into the ruling
party, as evidenced by the fact that at any given time 25 to 40
percent of the LDP's Diet delegation is made up of former
bureaucrats. Thus, with a few exceptions (the present government
leader, Kakuei Tanaka, being one of them), the prime ministers
of postwar Japan have been chosen from the ranks of the most
able former civil servants: Yoshida (1946-1947 and again in
1948-1954), Ashida (1948), Kishi (1957-1960), Ikeda (1960-1964),
amd most recently Sato (1964-1972).

Ties between the government bureacracy and the business
community are just as intimate, for Japanese business operates
under various forms of administrative guidance in such matters
as exports and imports, foreign investment, licensing
arrangements, business connections with foreign firms, and the
like. Japanese business can more easily accept such
restrictions when its representatives participate in the
shaping of relevant policies and regulations, indirectly through
their influence in the political world and directly through
their presence on scores of government advisory committees
involved at every step in making policy. Bonds between the two

----

whose advice is sought by the party come mostly from the
Ministry of International Trade and Industry (MITI) the
Ministry of Finance (the most powerful agency of the government),
and the Economic Planning Board. The information-gathering agency
of the Japanese government, the Cabinet Research Office, also
plays a role, if an indirect one, in the interagency consultation
process. On issues more clearly within the realm of foreign
affairs, the Foreign Ministry plays an important role.
Nonetheless, here too economic agencies of the government also
exert a decisive influence, since the economic aspects tend to be
central to Japanese foreign policy. Generally speaking, the
Foreign Ministry views problems from the vantage point of their
effect on international relations and is inclined toward close
cooperation with the United States, whereas the economic agencies
place greater stress on the interests of the domestic producer
and on considerations of financial responsibility.

communities are cemented by similarities in outlook, by school
ties, and often by intermarriage. They are reinforced by the
realization on the part of the government official who must
retire while still in his prime (normally by age 55) that large
industrial and financial institutions can offer attractive
opportunities to the highly trained and experienced bureaucrat
after he leaves government service.

Japanese Decision-Making and Foreign Policy. Decision-making in
Japan is characterized by a search for consensus within a system
that lays great stress on the principle of cooperation through
mutual compromise.[2] In resolving conflicts, both within and
outside of the power structure, there is a tendency to avoid at
virtually any cost the application of superior power to obtain
one's ends. The formulation of policy and its implementation are
normally preceded in Japan by a slow process of mutual
adjustment of conflicting interests, leading eventually to a
compromise acceptable to all parties concerned. It is only
natural that such compromise tends to be vague, especially when
judged by Western standards. Precise, hence also inflexible,
formulations are shunned. This does not mean, however, that
there is no agreement on the basic features of the solution—
allowing substantial leeway for future readjustments in the
light of changing realities. (The Japanese language is
particularly suitable for formulations that are vague yet
meaningful.)
    This approach can be an advantage in dealing with foreign-
policy issues, as evidenced by the way in which the knotty
problem of Taiwan was handled in the Sino-Japanese declaration
of September 29, 1972 (which will be discussed below). But it
can also give rise to serious misunderstandings, as was the case
with regard to the settlement of the textile problem that soured
U.S.-Japanese relations in the early 1970s, partly because the
two sides were not in agreement as to what exactly had been
agreed upon. From the Japanese point of view, the desire of the
Western negotiator to press for precise definitions of the
terms of an agreement is counterproductive because of the
rigidity it imposes on the two parties' positions. It is
resented as contributing to an unnecessary aggravation of the
problem at issue rather than to a smoothing over of existing
difficulties. On the other hand, the Japanese approach often
strikes the other party as suspiciously vague, ambiguous, and
evasive.
    A number of important consequences for Japan's domestic and
foreign policies flow from this Japanese attitude toward

solving conflicts of interest. In the first place, the constant
search for compromise and the assignment of insoluble
differences to a more propitious time minimize internal shocks
and disruptions that might otherwise occur if the party in power
were inclined to impose its will outright. The extraordinary
stability of the Japanese social and political order owes much
to this factor. Second, the Japanese process of conflict
resolution is a long-drawn-out, time-consuming one. It does not
lend itself to sudden, surprise decisions and abrupt policy
changes like the ones that have, for example, marked recent U.S.
policy and unpleasantly shocked the Japanese. Third, the
Japanese policymaker thus favors a succession of small
incremental changes and policy readjustments (through a
reinterpretation of existing agreements, where possible) in
matters both of domestic and of foreign policy. He is unlikely
to go out on a limb and will be disinclined to act until he has
protected his position through wide-ranging consultation.
Finally, it is only natural that such conditions do not favor
anticipatory action. Faced with problems still in their initial
stage, Japanese policy tends to be reactive until shocks or
serious pressures convince at least a broad segment of the power
elite that action must now be taken. (This was the case, for
example, in 1972 when the sudden American approach to Peking
made it clear that Japan had to made a determined and official
move toward rapprochement with the Chinese People's Republic.)
   The application of the consensus principle to the settlement
of internal differences marks the policymaking process in the
faction-ridden ruling Liberal Democratic party. But it is also
reflected in the majority party's dealings with forces of the
political opposition. Here, however, it encounters serious
obstacles, since a wide gulf separates the two camps, especially
with regard to foreign and defense policies. Nevertheless, and
despite the appearance of extreme hostility, the pattern of
government-opposition relations is not one of noncommunication.
Simple practical considerations make it advisable that the
Japanese government not ignore the opposition forces. These
forces are not, after all, a negligible portion of the
electorate, numbering as they do close to half the voters.*

----

* The party lineup in the more important of the two houses making
up the Diet, the House of Representatives, in late 1973 was as
follows: Liberal Democratic party (the ruling party), 279;
Japanese Socialist party (JSP), 118; Japanese Communist party
(JCP), and affiliates, 40; Komeito (Clean Government Party), 29;

Their trouble-making potential is enhanced by their control of
the administration of Japan's major metropolitan centers
(including the capital, Tokyo), where they can easily mobilize
large numbers of supporters for street demonstrations and other
extraparliamentary actions. They also dominate the labor unions,
particularly those of the workers in government administration,
services, and corporations. Hence, they are in a position to
paralyze public transportation, as they did in the spring of
1973, and other key services. The political opposition can count,
moreover, on the strong support of the mass media, especially the
press, which tends to be extremely influential as well as highly
critical of the government.* Furthermore, the academic and
intellectual community is largely outside the orbit of the
government party's influence.

But these facts alone do not sufficiently explain the extreme
care with which the Japanese government handles the political
opposition. After all, the LDP does have a mandate from the
people. But it is simply not in postwar Japan's pattern of
behavior to force a decision, until an all-out and convincing
effort has been made by the government leaders to bridge
existing differences with the opposition and to give the
opposition ample opportunity to state its views. To avoid adverse
public reaction, the government must never exercise what the
Japanese term the "dictatorship of the majority." Considering the
irreconcilable policies advocated by the government and the
opposition, there is therefore a surprising amount of behind-the-
scenes bargaining and compromise between the two parties.

Caution in the handling of the political opposition is also
dictated by the factional makeup of the ruling party, which when

---

Democratic Socialist party (DSP), 20; Independents, 1;
vacancies, 4. In terms of percentage of the popular vote, the
distribution in the 1972 elections was as follows: LDP, 46.9;
JSP, 21.9; JCP, 10.5; Komeito, 8.5; DSP, 7.0; Independents, 5.1;
other, 0.3. On the eve of the 1974 elections, the less
influential House of Councillors showed the following
composition: LDP, 135; JSP, 60; Komeito, 23; DSP, 11; JCP, 10;
Niin Club, 4; Independents, 2; vacancies, 6.

* Japan is a nation of insatiable readers absorbing the contents
of vast numbers of newspapers, magazines, and books. The
Japanese are also avid viewers of television. All the media
report in much detail on foreign developments and especially on
the United States.

confronted with problems tends to lose its unity and engage in intensive infighting. Such was the case, for example, in 1960 when the Kishi government was forced to resign not only because of the frantic opposition activity against the adoption of the U.S.-Japanese security pact, but also because elements within the LDP thought this a good opportunity to unseat their leader. Fear of such repercussions—i.e., of a merging of opposition and factional troubles—is also one important reason why the Japanese government decided in 1970 to bypass a formal argument over the future of the security pact and allowed it to be extended automatically from year to year, a solution requiring no action by or prolonged debate in the Diet. Similarly, in late 1973, Prime Minister Tanaka, faced with mounting difficulties within and outside his party because of an alarming rate of inflation and threats of energy shortages, invited his rival, Takeo Fukuda, an advocate of stable economic growth and of conservative foreign policies, to assume a key position in the cabinet so as to prevent the opposition forces from playing on internal discord within the LDP.

Yet it is legitimate to ask how the government can hope to escape confrontations with the opposition when positions of the two sides on foreign and national-security policies are diametrically opposed. The government and the LDP continue to view the close and special relationship with the United States as the key to Japan's security and prosperity. The opposition seeks to loosen the existing ties, especially insofar as they involve defense relations, and to build a new foreign policy on "friendship with all nations," preferably cemented by a security guarantee for Japan by the major powers, communist and noncommunist. The government argues that the so-called Self-Defense Forces are constitutional, and it wishes gradually to develop a military potential sufficient to provide at least against nonnuclear attacks. Meanwhile, it insists that the security pact with the United States remains essential to Japan and that American bases there are necessary as deterrents against potential aggressors. The opposition, on the other hand, argues that the Japanese defense forces have been created in violation of the "Peace Constitution" and demands their abolition. It rejects the security pact with the United States and prefers to put its faith in disarmament and the peaceful intentions of Japan's neighbors, while actively working toward the complete elimination of American bases from Japan.

Even on the much less sensitive issue of Japan's nonmilitary regional relations with particular governments (e.g., South Korea, South Vietnam, and Taiwan), the positions of the government and the opposition parties remain far apart.

Thus, ironically, in a system in which consensus and
cooperation are writ large, the Japanese find themselves unable
to achieve unified views on foreign and national-security
policies. This failure to achieve unity, rather than any
disagreement on domestic policies, has in fact been the central
issue in Japan for the past two decades. Since much of the
difference of views is deeply rooted in the Marxist beliefs of
the two major opposition parties, which see the world in terms
of a capitalist-versus-socialist dichotomy, there is in the
final analysis not much that the conservative government can do
to achieve a national consensus on foreign policy.

Considering the domestic constraints, the Japanese leadership
understandably sees little benefit in assuming a more active
international role unless forced to do so by major adverse
developments in Japan's international environment. In the
present circumstances, therefore, the politically least
troublesome way of coping with the internal divisions of the
nation is for the government to abide by the three mutually
reinforcing policy principles inherited from the immediate
postwar period, particularly since this strategy has proved its
worth during two decades of growing Japanese prosperity and
sustained peace. The first principle might be termed "leaning to
one side"—i.e., to the side of the United States. It is
difficult to exaggerate the role the United States has played in
Japan ever since the war and the tremendous influence this has
had on Japanese foreign, defense, and domestic policy. It was
largely American military force that ended Imperial Japan's
expansion and started the process of postwar change in Japan. It
was an American occupation force that guided the political and
economic reconstruction of Japan and produced the formal
framework within which Japan has been developing during the past
twenty-five years. U.S. power, through American bases and
security arrangements, at first made it unnecessary for postwar
Japan to rebuild a major military force and then, at the time of
the Korean War, started Japan on the road to limited rearmament.
American values, views, practices, and preoccupations have
entered Japan along with vast numbers of American military men,
administrators, businessmen, and tourists. The reverse flow
began with a trickle, after Japan regained its sovereignty in
1952. By now it constitutes a vast stream, with Japanese
visitors to the United States outnumbering those coming from all
countries outside the Western Hemisphere. Commercial exchanges
with the United States have increased phenomenally, constituting
today the most conspicuous material tie between the two nations.

As a result, the American impact on postwar Japan has been
profound (for evidence one need only examine the language of
contemporary Japan). Hence, the relationship with the United
States in all its diversity remains to this day at the core of
Japan's foreign and defense policy. It constitutes the most
important legacy of Japan's lost war. Japan's special
relationship to the United States—with Japan content to follow
the course of American policy—is a major reason why Japan, with
all its economic power, has remained inactive in world affairs.

The second principle of postwar Japan's strategy, again a
direct legacy of the war, is its reliance on nonmilitary
instruments to deal with international problems. Already,
constitutional provisions (Article 9) preclude the legal
development of any military force having an offensive potential.*
Neither does the ruling political party command the necessary
two-thirds majority of its leaders wish to take such a step, so
long as the American alliance provides protection against
external threats. Moreover, the last war generated intensely
pacifist sentiments among the Japanese people, making them
profoundly hostile to rearmament, nuclear weapons, and military
involvement abroad. Evidence suggests that these attitudes
persist essentially unchanged, and that this is particularly
true of the postwar generation (even though this group is
credited with also harboring increasingly nationalist
sentiments.** Since Japan's policy-makers and the general public

----

* Although there can be no doubt about the general intent of the
so-called Peace Constitution, there is no unanimity in Japan
regarding the precise limitations it imposes on the government
with respect to the maintenance of military forces. The leftist
opposition interprets Article 9 narrowly, as prohibiting any
kind of armament, including that intended for purely defensive
purposes. A succession of Japanese governments have asserted that
the constitution does not rule out a defensive force, equipped
and structured strictly for the defense of the home islands.
However, it has firmly pledged not to send any Japanese forces
abroad and not to build or introduce nuclear weapons. For a
detailed discussion of these issues, see Paul F. Langer, Japanese
National Security Policy: Domestic Determinants (Santa Monica,
Calif.: The Rand Corporation, 1972), R-1030.

** Supporting evidence for this conclusion can be found in
numerous public-opinion surveys, both official and private,

can see no immediate external threat on Japan's horizon, and
since reliance on the military might of the United States has
been so eminently successful in keeping Japan out of conflicts,
there is little incentive to depart from a strategy of "wisdom
rather than arms."

A third factor, once again a legacy of the war, is Japan's
drastically changed material circumstances. The colonial empire
is gone, and with it any hope of making Japanese industry even
halfway independent of foreign supplies. Japan's dependence on
foreign energy sources, especially oil, is greater than that of
any other major industrial nation, and prospects are that this
dependence will continue during the years ahead.* This
consideration has operated as a powerful incentive for the
Japanese to maintain an international environment free of
fiction that might interfere with Japan's vital foreign trade or
the security of its overseas supply lines. Hence, friendship
with all nations is not merely a slogan that meets the
aspirations of the Japanese people, but also a practical
necessity. During the long years of the cold war that pitted the
United States, Japan's sponsor, against the communist powers,
and despite the turmoil in much of Asia during the 1950s and
1960s, Japan's strategy has been remarkably successful in
maintaining the country's position of noninvolvement in
international conflicts without seriously impairing its
relations with the major powers.

----

conducted in recent years. See, for example, the survey
undertaken by the Shakai Kodo Kenkyujo (Social Behavior Research
Institute) in March 1970 and reported in Shukan Asahi (Asahi
Weekly), one of Japan's largest weeklies, on March 27, 1970; the
government-sponsored poll reported in Chosa Geppo (Monthly
Survey Report), February 1972; and another government poll, the
results of which were made public in the Japanese government
publication Seron Chosa (Public Opinion Survey), February 1972.

* Japan's dependence on foreign oil supplies is close to 100
percent, and such imports ran in 1973 at a daily average of 5.4
million barrels. In 1970, oil imports constituted about 12
percent of Japan's total imports. The rising price of oil since
then may triple this figure by the end of 1974. (Imported oil
cost Japan $6.6 billion in 1973, and the Japanese estimate that
this item will increase to $18 billion in 1974.) In 1973, the
Arab countries—primarily Saudi Arabia, Kuwait, and Abu Dhabi—

Past policies served Japan well even when they failed to be
psychologically satisfying to a nation distinguished by
extraordinary energy and pride. But in the last several years,
the international environment of Japan has undergone marked
changes. Circumstances have arisen that place in doubt the
continued validity of the principles on which a succession of
postwar Japanese governments have been acting in international
affairs. In the first place, Japan's American alliance is at
least temporarily in disarray, so much so that many Japanese
wonder whether the two nations are not once more destined to
become antagonists. Next, a new order in the Far East appears to
be emerging as a result of the American detente with China and
China's continued tense confrontation with the Soviet Union.
Obviously, the triangular relationship of the three great powers
is in flux, and the effect of these uncertainties is
increasingly being registered in Japan, which no longer can rely
on American support and guidance as completely as in the past.
In turn, the changes in Japan's international environment are
stimulating the debate in Japan regarding the country's future
role. Thus, both Japan itself and the context in which it is
placed are in a state of transition.

Japan and the United States in an Era of Transition
For the past quarter of a century, the weight of the United
States in its relationship with Japan has been overwhelming.
Japanese policy has consistently taken its cue from that of the
United States, particularly when relations with the communist
powers were involved. To mention but one example, when Japan
concluded a peace treaty with the Nationalist regime on Taiwan,
thereby implicitly recognizing the latter's claim to being the
true representative of China, it was with considerable
reluctance and only because American policy demanded such a
step. During the nearly three decades since the end of World War
II, U.S. policy toward Japan has undergone a number of changes
reflecting the evolution of American strategy and changes in
world conditions. These policy shifts were the result of
American rather than Japanese initiatives.

---

accounted for 45.4 percent of Japanese oil imports; Iran
provided 35.5 percent, and Indonesia most of the rest. These
figures will explain why Japan is so vulnerable to the Arab
nations' pressure in matters of Japan's Middle East policy.

There are a number of reasons for Japan's reactive role in its
relations with the United States.[3] Japan's defeat in World War II
was largely a defeat by American forces. The Allied military
occupation of Japan, which lasted until Japan regained its
sovereignty in 1952, was almost wholly an American military
occupation, with the United States assuming responsibility for
reconstructing Japan, for reordering its political and economic
systems, and for representing it in international affairs. The
American decision not to withdraw its military forces from
Japan, even after conclusion of a peace treaty, and to make Japan
a cornerstone in U.S. Far Eastern strategy during the years of
the cold war against the Soviet Union and China further tended to
increase the American weight in Japanese policies and decision.
There was also, of course, the enormous discrepancy in military
and economic strength between the two alliance partners, as well
as America's vastly more intensive involvement and greater
leverage in world affairs. Japan's reappearance on the world
scene was a gradual one—largely limited, even in the 1960s, to
commercial exchanges. Then, too, there was the conviction on
both sides of the Pacific that the Japanese needed the United
States much more than the United States needed Japan; the result
was a superior American bargaining position. Finally, the
dependent and subordinate part played by Japan for two decades
after the war was in a way sought by the Japanese, who were
knowingly, if temporarily, abdicating a world role in order to
gain time to heal the wounds inflicted by the war, to restructure
their political and social systems, and to rebuild their economy.
  A number of shifts occurred in American policy toward Japan
during the 1940s, 1950s, and 1960s. Each shift modified Japan's
place in American strategy and had an impact on Japanese
domestic affairs. During the first phase, from Japan's surrender
until 1948, the United States viewed Japan as the former enemy
who was to be disarmed and "democratized." This was the era of
the American-inspired Peace Constitution, with its abnegation of
war as an instrument of national policy, of the breakup of the
zaibatsu concerns, of the purge of former militarists, and of
many other reforms that had the wholehearted support of Japanese
liberals and even of most elements on the political left.
  As the cold war heated up, Japan's role in American strategy
changed from that of an ex-enemy to that of a new ally. The
following decade witnessed a number of significant developments
in American-Japanese relations. Japan signed a peace treaty with
the United States (September 8, 1951)—but not with the Soviet
Union—and concluded at the same time a security treaty allowing
American forces to remain on bases in Japan and to use them

virtually without restriction in carrying out U.S. strategy in
Korea and elsewhere in the Far East. Okinawa remained under
American control as a military strong point vital to the defense
of Korea and important to any U.S. military action along the
periphery of China. The Japanese were encouraged to abandon
destabilizing social and economic reforms and to rebuild their
military forces within certain limits and along strictly
defensive lines.

This shift in American policy was momentous in its impact on
Japan's policies, internal and external. By strengthening the
conservative forces in Japanese society, it brought about an
alienation from the United States of the Japanese political left,
much of the intellectual community, and the mass media heavily
influenced by them. While the United States won friends among
Japanese conservatives, it lost friends at the opposite end of
the political spectrum where neutralist beliefs were dominant.
The shift in Japan's function tended to center the resulting
internal power struggle on the role of the United States in
Japan, where it has remained ever since. It produced a split
between those who supported and those who opposed the American
alliance, the presence of U.S. forces and bases in Japan, and
Japan's alignment alongside the United States in the cold war
against the communist powers. The Korean War solidified the
opposing positions. To most Japanese people, it demonstrated
that they lived on the edge of a dangerous world and that the
American presence could indeed guarantee their security, for
Japan furnished bases for U.S. military operations in the war,
but suffered no damage itself. But to other Japanese—a minority,
but a rather substantial one—it provided evidence of the
dangerous course that the American alliance spelled for Japan.
To them, it proved that close military and political ties with
the United States would inevitably lead to the remilitarization
of their country and to its involvement in conflicts not of
Japan's choosing. They were particularly worried that the new
relationship with the United States would condemn Japan to
isolation from China and other parts of the socialist world.

Another phase in American-Japanese relations began in the
late 1950s and lasted until quite recently. It is symbolized by
the conclusion of the Treaty of Mutual Cooperation and Security
(signed in January 1960), which was a first if modest attempt to
take note of the growing strength of postwar Japan. The new
treaty placed the alliance on a more nearly equal basis by
eliminating the U.S. role in maintaining Japanese internal order,
by obliging the United States to resist external attack against
Japan, and by making the use of American military bases more

susceptible to Japanese influence.* Hope was held out for the
eventual return of Okinawa to Japan, a step that was actually
carried out in 1972. The softer line assumed by the United
States in its dealing with Japan during the 1960s was evidence
of American recognition of the growing strength and power
potential of Japan, and of the realization that Japanese national
pride and sensitivity deserved more attention.**
For two decades, the two nations took each other for granted.
The United States assumed the lead and Japan followed more or
less voluntarily, adjusting its interpretation of the national
interest to that of its American partner. It has been obvious to
most observers on both sides of the Pacific that the changes that
over the years have transformed both Japan and the United States,
as well as the international environment, would eventually also
force a reexamination of a bilateral relationship whose pattern
was set in the early postwar period.
A quarter of a century now separates the Japanese from the
traumatic experiences of defeat. Their economy has grown with
phenomenal speed. The Japanese people's self-confidence, too,
has grown, though not at the pace of the economy. But
increasingly, Japanese national pride and sensitivities, cutting
across domestic political divisions, required that Japan play a
role in the world more commensurate with its economic strength.
The Japanese now find it psychologically difficult to maintain a
dependent and exclusive relationship with the United States. The
problem is that while the Japanese seek greater autonomy and
increasingly object to their subordinate position within the
American alliance, to some actions of their American ally, and
to the minor part they play in world affairs, they are by no
means agreed on the alternatives open to them and on the scope
and nature of the responsibilities they are willing to shoulder
in the future.

---

* In separately exchanged notes the United States also agreed to
consult the Japanese government before making any major changes
in deployment to and use of American bases in Japan. Also major
equipment changes (e.g., nuclear weapons) were to be the subject
of prior consultation between the two parties.

** These conclusions were not unrelated to the upheavals that
occurred in Japan in 1960, when fear for the security of
President Eisenhower, who was scheduled to visit Japan, resulted
in the cancellation of the trip. Another consequence of this
crisis was an intensified American effort to explain U.S. policy
and to listen more carefully to Japanese views.

But the pressures for change in the U.S.-Japanese
relationship are not merely reflections of the transformation of
Japan into an economic giant and of the growing distance from
the war. They also reflect a changing Japanese image of the
United States and its policies, as well as sharp conflicts of
economic interest between the two countries.

The rather exaggerated image of American power, influence,
and wisdom which predominated in Japan after the war has been
severely eroded over the years.* So has the image of a
benevolent American partner, profoundly concerned about Japan's
welfare, a product largely of American occupation policy, which
was indeed distinguished for its benevolence, and of the
generous American aid offered for the economic reconstruction of
Japan. One notes also a changing Japanese assessment of U.S.
power to influence world developments. A decline is seen in the
ability of the United States to order its affairs at home and to
control developments abroad. The United States is viewed as
beset by social and economic problems that will require careful
and prolonged attention and will absorb American energy and
resources to an unprecedented degree. Weakened by mounting
problems at home, the United States now confronts a world in
which the Soviet Union has attained equal military strength and
where the influence of other nations is more and more felt. The
Vietnam war, which was viewed with ambivalence even by the
Japanese conservatives, who consistently support American
policies, had its share in tarnishing the American image.
Japanese confidence in the wisdom with which the United States
allocates its resources in the global conflict with the Soviet
Union was reduced, raising doubts about American priorities.
(This was the effect of American policy on conservative elements
in Japan; the impact on opposition groups, and particularly on
the mass media, was even more sharply adverse.) The decline in
American popularity since 1965, as registered by Japanese
opinion surveys, is thus attributable to a composite of factors.**

----

* The following observations are based on an extensive study of
the Japanese news media, on public-opinion surveys, on
interviews with leading Japanese, and on a wide reading in
Japanese literature, undertaken in connection with the author's
long-range study of the evolution of Japan's image of the
outside world.

** The results of public-opinion surveys should be used with
caution. Nevertheless, they are significant, at least in the
Japanese case, in pointing to certain distinct trends. For one

More recently, the "Nixon Doctrine," its meaning and
motivation, and its subsequent gradual implementation in Asia
have been the subject of much speculation in Japan. Two messages
have come through very clearly, both of them disturbing to
Japan. The new U.S. policy is read as foreshadowing substantial
decreases in the American military presence and in American
commitments in the Far East. It is also interpreted as demanding
greater military and economic efforts on the part of nations
allied with the United States if the alliance relationship is to
remain acceptable to American policymakers. Questions raised for
the Japanese by these messages can be subsumed under three
headings: American intentions, American credibility, and
American expectations with regard to Japan.

Japanese concerns on all three scores are heightened by a
realization that the foundations of the Japanese alliance with
the United States are shallow. Nothing in the history of
American-Japanese relations inspires the Japanese with great
confidence in the permanence of the alliance, for during the
past century the two nations have several times vacillated

----

thing, Japanese surveys are generally conducted with extremely
sophisticated methodologies. They are also undertaken by so many
organizations (government agencies, newspapers, public-opinion
research institutes) that their results can be cross-checked for
consistency. Some surveys have been asking the same questions of
random samples of informants on a regular monthly or quarterly
basis. The best-known of these is the Jiji (news agency) monthly
survey. It clearly shows that American popularity has declined
in the past several years (coinciding first with the U.S.
involvement in Vietnam and subsequently with the growing U.S.-
Japanese friction over economic issues), sinking to a position
second to Switzerland's and not much ahead of that of the more
important Western European nations. The October 1973 survey, for
example, asked respondents to list up to three nations they
liked or disliked. Switzerland ranked first, being liked by 34.0
percent of the respondents, while the United States was liked by
21.9 percent and France by 20.8 percent. Switzerland was
disliked by 0.2 percent and Western European nations by 1 to 2
percent, whereas the United States was mentioned as disliked by
10.3 percent. Correspondingly, 13.2 percent liked China, but
only 3.1 percent the Soviet Union; 6.1 percent disliked China,
but 26.7 percent the Soviet Union. These figures are taken from
Seron Chosa, December 1973, p. 113.

rapidly between hostility and friendship. More important perhaps
is that even if the alliance rests on a solid foundation of
shared (though not identical) economic and security interests,
it lacks one extremely important dimension for attenuating and
resolving conflicts of interests. That dimension is the
cultural-psychological one.*

Despite a quarter of a century of broad and generally
friendly contacts between Japanese and Americans, the gulf
between the two countries remains immeasurably wider than that
between the United States and Europe. History, race, language,
and any number of other areas where American and Japanese
societies lack commonality work to widen the great distance
between the two countries. Even the closer intermeshing of the
two economies has so far had little effect in bridging the
existing communications gap. The two societies continue to
differ in their patterns of behavior, in their decision-making
processes, and in many other important respects. Nor are these
differences well recognized in the two nations' dealing with
each other.

Japanese suspicions of American intentions have been
nourished by many events of recent years and months. The very
vagueness of the Nixion Doctrine has allowed the Japanese to
place varying interpretations on the motivations behind it. The
recent abrupt shift of American policy toward China deeply shook
the Japanese, not so much because of the resulting rapprochement
but because the shift suggested a lack of American willingness
to consult with Japan and explain American intentions.

----

* Until recently, attempts to bridge the cultural gap between
the two peoples were almost entirely financed by the United
States. The so-called Nixon shocks suffered by Japan in 1972 had
the effect of finally convincing the Japanese government and
prominent civic leaders that Japan should play a more positive
role in such matters. One result was the establishment of the
Japan Foundation, which is to be provided with substantial
financial resources for the promotion of cultural relations with
other nations and especially the United States. A recent
Japanese government grant of $10 million to leading American
universities engaged in the study of Japan is another
consequence of this new awareness on the part of the Japanese
leadership.

Consequently, the question being raised in frustration and anger is whether Japan still plays the vital role in American Far Eastern policy which it thought it played during the past two decades. The world of bipolarity was a comfortable one for Japan. The meaning of multipolarity and of the now popular notion of a balance of power is unclear to the Japanese, as is the role they are supposed to play in such a structure. Certainly it is a cause for confusion and anxiety among Japanese policymakers. Looking beyond Japan itself, they are not reassured by what they see. They wonder whether the American military presence can continue to be relied upon in other parts of Asia, particularly on the Korean peninsula where Japan's security interests are deeply engaged. Are these areas to be left to their own devices? Is the United States perhaps striking a bargain with Peking to the detriment of Japan? Can Japan become an integral part of Washington's suggested trilateral structure when Europe displays little interest in admitting Japan and even the United States seems at times reluctant to treat Japan as an equal partner? These are some of the questions raised in the Japanese mind by the changing political configuration of the Far East, as set in motion by a readjustment of relations within the great-power political-military triangle.

But even where these doubts have been largely quieted by American assurances and renewed guarantees of continued interest in Asia, circumstances themselves seem to raise questions about the American commitment—i.e., about the capacity of the United States to spread its protective umbrella over Asia. In turn, these lead back to the question regarding the future role expected of Japan by the United States. Is Japan, loosed from its American ties, to assume responsibilities in Asia until now shouldered by the United States, in the expectation that U.S. and Japanese interests will continue to coincide substantially— thus relieving the United States of a burden without detrimental effects on the U.S. position? Or is Japan merely expected to play a more active role in international affairs, using its newly acquired and enormous economic potential for political ends in the interest of both the United States and Japan? Or does the United States expect Japan to rearm and take on military responsibilities earlier borne by the United States? If so, can such a posture be limited to conventional armaments? And what about legal and political domestic constraints on such a course, constraints that can be anticipated to defeat any government so long as there is no convincing external threat on the Japanese horizon? At the same time these questions are being raised, the fear persists that the United States has drastically shifted its policies and that in American eyes Japan has once more become an antagonist rather than an ally. Japanese press reports from the United States do nothing to allay this fear, as the Japanese reader is regaled with accounts of an alleged revival of anti-Japanese sentiments in the United States and particularly among a sector of the American business community and among labor. The results of public-opinion surveys commissioned in the United States by the Japanese mass media and given wide publicity in Japan have reinforced the impression that the American leadership as well as the general public harbor great hostility toward the Japanese.

The U.S. decision not to consult with Japan regarding the planned change in American China policy is seen as only the first of many U.S. moves demonstrating that the United States intends to ignore Japan and the sensitivities of the Japanese people. One consequence of such interpretations has been a growing coolness toward the United States on the part of many of the ruling Japanese conservatives. Evidently, it no longer pays for a Japanese politician to be too closely identified with the United States. At least that is the conclusion that emerges from the analysis by Japanese news commentators of the 1972 defeat of Takeo Fukuda by Kakuei Tanaka in the contest for the prime ministership. The news analysts see Fukuda's reputation of being a strong supporter of a policy of intimate cooperation with the United States as one important reason for this defeat.

Doubts about the future of the American-Japanese alliance are exacerbated by economic conflict between the two nations. It is here that the foundation of the alliance was thought to be firmest. For many years, both sides preserved a faith in the commonality of their economic interests and in the harmonizing effect of economic interdependence. That easy faith is long gone. Japan's GNP has grown immensely over the years. The level of prosperity in Japan is now such that the Japanese have attained, and may soon outpace, Western European standards. It is not surprising then that the United States has concluded that it cannot behave toward the newly emerging Japanese economic giant as it behaved for many years toward the economic weakling that was Japan during the 1950s. But force of habit and lack of confidence, as well as an understandable desire to cling to benefits acquired, makes Japanese policymakers extremely reluctant to readjust the economic relationship, except at a very gentle pace. As U.S. commitments abroad increased during the 1960s, American irritation grew, and with it came pressures on Japan to open up its markets, drop its many restrictive

regulations, and become a more active donor in foreign aid.
Until the mid-1960s the balance of trade between the two
countries had generally favored the United States. In 1965, the
balance tipped in favor of the Japanese; surpluses occurred and
continued to build at a slow pace. Then, in the 1970s, the gap
widened dramatically. By 1972, the major share of the U.S.
foreign-trade deficit was accounted for by Japan.*

It was not appreciated in Tokyo that Japan had been
benefiting for too many years from exceptionally generous terms
of trade with regard to the yen/dollar exchange rate and that an
array of Japanese protectionist restrictions on imports from the
United States rules out any substantial improvement in the U.S.-
Japanese balance of payments with Japan. Or if this was
recognized in Tokyo, the Japanese government nevertheless
hesitated to respond to U.S. requests for corrective action.
Japanese barriers to American imports and to investment
liberalization were only slowly dismantled and then only as the
result of persistent and strong U.S. pressures. When Japan's
trade surplus with the United States assumed disturbing
dimensions, the Japanese government at first failed to offer
more than token gestures to reverse or halt the trend. This
situation inevitably produced a change in U.S. strategy toward
Japan. Enormous pressure was successfully brought to bear on
Tokyo to revalue the yen upward, to rescind investment controls
on foreign capital, and to remove the existing protective
barriers against American imports.

The intensity and abruptness of American countermeasures
(including surcharges imposed on Japan and a revaluation of the

----

* U.S. and Japanese official statistics show that until 1965 the
U.S. surplus in trade with Japan never exceeded a few hundred
million dollars. In that year, Japan for the first time had a
surplus, amounting to somewhat over $300 million. Although in
the late 1960s Japanese excess earnings mounted to about $1
billion in some years, the level in 1970 was about $400 million.
The dramatic upward push of Japanese exports to the United
States started in 1971 with a trade gap of more than $2.5
billion, growing to $4.1 billion in 1972, as imports from Japan
exceeded $9 billion and U.S. exports to Japan amounted to $5
billion. Since 1961, Japan has been second most important
trading partner of the United States, next to Canada, accounting
now for about one-seventh of all U.S. foreign trade. The
importance of the American trade is even greater for Japan, as
it constitutes about one-third of Japan's foreign trade.

yen), beginning in 1971, startled the Japanese, unaccustomed to
such behavior on the part of the United States. The shock was
the greater in that these measures coincided with the Sino-
American rapprochement, which was equally startling to Tokyo.
Nor had the long-drawn-out argument over Japanese textile
exports to the United States and its difficult settlement helped
to improve the atmosphere between Japan and the United States.

In 1973, the long overdue readjustment of economic relations
between Japan and the United States was proceeding at full speed
in response to sustained American pressure. As a result, the
trade gap was shrinking substantially, thereby minimizing if not
entirely removing a major area of friction between the two
countries. But meanwhile new problems were appearing on the
horizon. A policy of high economic growth had stoked
inflationary pressures in Japan, raising prices at an annual
rate of nearly 20 percent and swallowing up an ever-growing
share of the world's scarce raw materials. The developing energy
crisis, exacerbated by the restrictive policies of the Middle
East nations, created a perfect setting for U.S.-Japanese
competition and misunderstandings. A seemingly desperate supply
situation was driving resource-poor Japan into making hastily
negotiated bilateral deals with the oil-producing nations while
the comparatively oil-rich United States could afford to take
the long-range view and call for cooperation rather than
competition among the consumer nations, for multilateralism
rather than bilateralism.

How these unprecedented problems will be resolved and how
their solution will affect the U.S.-Japanese relationship can
only be surmised. At this early stage, one can only point to
certain developments that may suggest the direction of future
events. It seems probable—and most responsible Japanese share
this view—that the era of high economic growth has now come to
an end in Japan. The objective of stable but moderate economic
growth has now all but officially been accepted by Japan's power
elite. Not only will such a new policy greatly reduce the
unsettling appetite of the Japanese production machine and
thereby reduce the international tensions that result from it,
but it will also reflect a more basic change in Japan's value
system away from quantitative goals and toward greater stress on
improving the quality of life—trends that are also apparent on
the American side of the Pacific. In the years ahead, therefore,
one might expect less abrupt changes in the American-Japanese
economic balance and a resulting softening of the economic
confrontation, providing a context more propitious for mutual
efforts to reestablish a cooperative relationship in the economic

sphere as in others. Moreover, on the Japanese side, recent
events have produced an acute awareness of the weakness on which
Japan's prosperity rests and a commensurate positive reappraisal
of American strength. This process has convinced the Japanese
leadership of the vital importance for Japan of maintaining and
developing a working relationship with the United States even
while continued efforts are made to diversify Japan's
international relations. Also on the American side, there is
evidence that Japan's key role in assuring peace and stability
in Asia is once more being appreciated. The need is being
recognized for correcting the dangerous impression created in
Japan that American policy is now favoring China to the
detriment of U.S. relations with Japan. But these essentially
favorable conditions for a return to a more cooperative
relationship between Tokyo and Washington will be affected in an
important way by the relationship of the two powers with the two
other sides of the Asian quadrilateral, China and the USSR.

Japan and China—Rivalry or Cooperation?

In the past two decades, the Japanese have published literally
hundreds of books and thousands of articles concerned with the
"China problem" in all its aspects, and the flood continues. In
these writings the authors have sought to clarify Japan's
relationship to China and to help the reader define his own
position vis-à-vis that country. In reading these interpretations
and in examining Japanese public-opinion polls regarding
attitudes toward China, one is struck by the ambivalence with
which the Japanese appear to view their Chinese neighbors. This
is reflected in the frequent use of paired antonyms to describe
the Japanese reaction: "love-hate" is a favorite, along with
"respect-contempt."*

Japan's China syndrome can probably be explained as a result
of the protracted, intense, and varied interaction between two
peoples separated geographically by a narrow expanse of water,
but by a wide gulf in their world view, national characteristics,
and behavior. A thousand years of contacts prior to Japan's
emergence as a modern power left a deep Chinese imprint on
Japanese language, literature, art, though, and civilization
without ever completely overwhelming them. The Japanese people

----

* "Love-hate" is used, for example, by Professor Shinkichi Etō,
the Manchuria-born specialist on contemporary China, widely
acknowledged to be the authority in his field.

to this day are well aware of the debt they owe Chinese civilization and are taught to respect China for it. When they refer to the Chinese as "half-brothers," or when the older generation of Japanese talk about dōbun-dōshu (same script, same race), they are thinking of the past.

But the more recent past has added another element to the Japanese image of China. In modern times, the roles of the two nations have been reversed. Japan has demonstrated to China how an Asian country can modernize and behave internationally like the Western powers and be successful at it. But this role as an expanding power has been played by the Japanese at the expense of China. The past century in the Far East was marked by armed Japanese intrusions into Chinese territory, the dismemberment of China by occupying Japanese armies, and Japanese attempts to impose its rule on China and the rest of Asia under the label of the Co-Prosperity Sphere. The war in the Pacific that ended so disastrously for Japan was merely the last chapter in a succession of violent Sino-Japanese interactions in which Japan was the aggressor and China the victim. It is only natural that from the Chinese viewpoint—communist or noncommunist—Japan must be regarded as a potential threat. For the Japanese, on the other hand, the residue of the past century consists of feelings of guilt alongside feelings of superior strength.

The advent of a communist regime in Peking in 1949 added still another element to the already complex Japanese reactions to China. One might have expected that the Japanese response would follow lines of ideological commitment—i.e., pro- and anti-communist lines. But this expectation would be an oversimplification. Widespread sympathy for a China that had suffered so long from foreign interventions—much of the time at Japanese hands—moderated the views of those Japanese who were otherwise antagonistic to communism. Guilt feelings were also mixed with an Asia-centered (and by implication anti-Western) nationalism and sentimentalism that had been common among the prewar generation and had once expressed itself in the concept of the Asian Co-Prosperity Sphere. This nationalism was at the same time a natural reaction to the high visibility and extraordinary influence of the United States in Japan. China, both that of Taipei and that of Peking, benefited from such sentiments. The Chinese communist regime was thus received in Japan with greater sympathy than its communist complexion might have led one to expect. Also, very practical considerations made it desirable, in the view of conservative circles in Japan, to establish some kind of communication with Peking. These considerations were, of course, economic ones.

Confronted with the problem of how to cope with the two
Chinas, Japan in 1951 understandably thought that it had little
choice. If Japan was to regain its sovereignty it had to follow
the American lead in all important matters. As a nation under
American military occupation and an important element in the
American cold-war strategy, Japan saw no alternative to signing
a peace treaty with Taiwan even though it would have preferred
to leave the issue open until a more opportune time.

The treaty with the Chinese Nationalists did not prevent the
Japanese government from making approaches to Peking with regard
to the opening of trade channels. The Japanese motive was
primarily an economic one, but political considerations also
entered in. Long before the United States abandoned its
containment strategy toward China, the Japanese leadership
appears to have concluded that a China in isolation would be a
greater danger to stability in Asia than a China participating
in world affairs. Commercial exchanges with Peking—implying
neither political recognition nor political ties—were thought
to be both beneficial to the Japanese economy and useful for
keeping channels of communication open. If Peking agreed to such
informal contacts with Japan despite the prominent Japanese role
in the American containment strategy and Japan's continued
recognition of Taiwan, it was not only for purely economic
reasons, but because economic relations promised to be an
effective means of exerting influence on Japanese policy.

In a massive and sustained political campaign, Peking
mobilized all sympathetic forces on the Japanese domestic scene
and all those groups interested, for political or material
reasons, in developing a better relationship with China. These
Chinese efforts, of course, enlisted the support of the
opposition parties—the Communist, Socialist, and Democratic
Socialist parties and the Komeito—who were ideologically
leaning toward Peking or simply convinced that the China issue
provided an effective weapon against the ruling conservative
party. Trade proved to be helpful to Peking as a means of
attracting diversified backing in Japan and lending recognition
to sympathetic supporters. A useful role in this effort was
played by the "friendly companies," small trading firms that had
subscribed to Peking's claims to being the legitimate Chinese
government. Such companies were often politically close to the
socialists and communists—until the latter had a serious
falling out with Peking in 1967, a situation that continues to
this day. On the eve of the resumption of Sino-Japanese
relations, the share of the "friendly" firms in trade with China
was about 90 percent. Since total commerical exchanges between

the two countries amounted in 1972 to about $1.1 billion, the leverage obtained in this way was not negligible.

Perhaps equally effective was the 10 percent share of trade conducted through the so-called Memorandum Trade Offices in Peking and Tokyo, for it provided the Chinese with semiofficial channels into the strongholds of Japanese big business as well as into the ruling party itself. After some experimentation, Peking had come to the conclusion that by rallying to its support all opposition parties, together with the many groups and individuals sympathetic to the Chinese cause (e.g., labor, intellectuals, the press), it could keep the China question alive as a key issue in the domestic political struggle and in this way create difficulties for the Japanese government. But the conclusion could not be escaped that in order to bring about policy changes in Japan it was essential to establish contacts with the ruling party and to gain leverage within the conservative camp. The Memorandum trade was one element of such a strategy, since it involved the larger and politically more influential Japanese business firms and groups close to the ruling party. The difficult annual trade negotiations provided an opportunity to exert pressure on the Japanese power structure via the business community by imposing conditions on trade which implicitly worked to undermine the Nationalist regime's position. An important role in that respect was played by Chou En-lai's so-called "four conditions," which stipulated that Peking would not deal with Japanese firms involved in Taiwan or South Korea or with the "American imperialists" in Indochina.

The makeup of the ruling Liberal Democratic party, its pronounced factional tendencies, and the consequent instability of the party's power structure have been discussed earlier. Through the Memorandum trade, through an invitational diplomacy, through press and propaganda channels, and in a variety of other ways, Peking has played on these internal weaknesses in Japan, magnifying the existing intraparty differences over Japan's policy toward Taipei and Peking. Despite the Japanese government's strenuous efforts to keep economic relations and politics separate, or at least to minimize their interconnection, Peking increasingly succeeded during the 1960s in joining them and in making their interplay work in its favor.

It has at times been argued that Japan, with its prevailing antiwar mood, its constitutional prohibitions against offensive weaponry, and its various other domestic constraints on the remilitarization of the islands, cannot possibly be regarded by Peking as a threat. But the decision makers' threat perceptions must also take account of a potential enemy's intentions and his options for action. With a GNP several times that of China, a technology vastly superior to that of its neighbor, and a proven capacity to marshal its resources in an effective and disciplined way, Japan cannot simply be ignored. But what creates a semipermanent threat in the eyes of Peking is China's historical experience with Japanese aggression. Throughout the 1930s and 1940s, substantial portions of Chinese territory were under Japanese military occupation. Mao Tse-tung and his associates conducted their struggle for power in a context of Chinese resistance against Japan. The close working relationship between "Japanese imperialism" and "American imperialism" (two of the principal officially designated enemies of Peking) in Korea, Taiwan, and elsewhere did nothing to soften the image of a Japanese threat. The use of American bases and industrial facilities for the conduct of war in Korea and later in Indochina could not but remind Peking of Japan's strategic position in Asia and of this position's potential for hostile employment against Chinese interests.

The Chinese initially tended to view the Japanese threat as a component of the threat to China posed by the United States. But, beginning in the mid-1960s, one could notice a growing tendency on the part of the Peking leaders to treat Japan as a separate though still hostile entity in the American-sponsored containment of China. This trend became most apparent after Japanese Prime Minister Sato, in November 1969, in a joint communiqué with President Nixon, pointed to the vital role of Korea and Taiwan in Japan's security—precisely those areas that, next to the Soviet border regions, are Peking's most sensitive spots. In line with Premier Chou En-lai's prescription that dangers must be opposed when they are in the budding stage, Chinese leverage in Japan was directed increasingly toward curbing any Japanese desire to rearm. When, subsequently, it became clear that the United States was to reduce its military presence in the Far East, the potential danger posed by a Japan acting independently from the United States appears to have assumed greater importance. A Japan no longer controlled by the United States might develop into the nucleus of a new anti-Chinese coalition with Taiwan and Korea, or its international isolation might stimulate Japan's return to reliance on military force and perhaps a rapprochement with the Soviet Union. Such speculations, farfetched as they may seem with reference to a Japan where antimilitaristic sentiments continue strong, might well have been important considerations in bringing about a shift of Chinese policy toward Tokyo, resulting in the September

1972 agreement to resume diplomatic relations and marking the
beginning of a Sino-Japanese détente.

Ever since the buildup of tensions between China and the
USSR, Chinese concern about U.S. and Soviet intentions has
enlarged to include fear of a prominent Soviet role in Japan.
Much of the leverage gained by Peking, as described above, has
since been used to curb and (where possible) eliminate Soviet
influence in Japan. As a result, most of the procommunist groups
of the Japanese left have split into pro-Moscow and pro-Peking
wings, while the Japanese Communist party, exposed to
contradictory Soviet and Chinese pulls, has chosen to adopt an
independent stance.[4] Peking has also repeatedly lent official
and vocal support to Japanese territorial claims in the Kurile
Islands, now held by the Soviet Union. Chinese leaders
(including Chou En-lai and Teng Hsiao-p'ing) have gone so far as
to declare that China and Japan share the same threat from the
north, i.e., from the Soviet Union. They have signaled their
displeasure at Soviet attempts to involve Japanese business
interests in the development of natural resources in Soviet
Siberia, including a proposal to build a giant oil pipeline
along the Sino-Soviet border, to be financed with credits
extended by Japan.

High among Peking's other objectives in Japan has always
been the goal of alienating Tokyo from Taipei, of discouraging
the Japanese government from developing an important stake in
Taiwan's future. Peking has made little headway with regard to
the economic aspects of Japan's ties with Taiwan. Japanese-
Taiwanese trade developed in healthy fashion over the years and
stayed well ahead of commercial exchanges between Japan and
China. In 1970, for example, Taiwan was Japan's third of fourth
largest market, while China ranked eleventh. By 1972, Taiwan's
trade with Japan amounted to some $1.4 billion, topping its
rival's trade by a substantial margin. But one should perhaps
not attribute too much importance to these figures. It is true
that Peking was unable to impede commercial transactions between
Japan and Taiwan in any substantial way. It did succeed, however,
in making Japanese investors more cautious and in forcing some
of them to shift their trading emphasis away from Taiwan. More
important, the Chinese campaign to win friends among the
conservatives while mobilizing its sympathizers for political
action had considerable effect on the Japanese domestic scene.
It split the Liberal Democratic party into pro-Peking and pro-
Taipei wings and forced its leaders, ideologically inclined
toward Taipei, to behave in a more circumspect and even-handed
fashion in matters of China policy. It created within Japan a

mood extremely favorable to a normalization of relations with Peking.

By the early 1970s, it was no longer a question of whether such a step should be taken, but rather of when and on what terms. In analyzing the Japanese political scene on the eve of the Sino-American rapprochement, one cannot escape the conclusion that Peking had been able to reserve the balance in Japan in its favor. Conditions for normalization of Sino-Japanese relations were ripe if the Chinese leaders were only willing not to press for a complete cutting of Japan's economic ties with Taiwan. The U.S. decision to embark on a new China policy, surprising as it was to Japanese policy-makers, found Japan thus ready to follow suit.

Peking and Tokyo agree on the historic significance of the Sino-Japanese communiqué establishing diplomatic relations between the two countries, which Premier Chou En-lai and Prime Minister Tanaka signed in Peking on September 29, 1972. With this agreement China and Japan entered a new era. Ambassadors were exchanged in 1973. In April of that same year, Tokyo-born Liao Cheng-chih, president of the China-Japan Friendship Association and an important associate of Premier Chou, arrived at Tokyo's Haneda airport, heading a fifty-five member goodwill mission, to tour Japan for a full month. At the same time, Japan was financially rewarded for its policy shift. Its trade with China almost doubled in 1973.[*] Already China's leading trading partner before the Sino-Japanese agreement, Japan was able to raise its share in China's trade to something like 25 percent (which, however, still constitutes only about 2 percent of Japan's total trade). A trade agreement, signed in January 1974, has eliminated the politically inspired structure of Sino-Japanese trade which gave preference to certain pro-Chinese firms and has placed economic transactions on a solid official basis. Mao Tse-tung himself has provided the Chinese imprimatur on the new cordial relationship by granting, in January 1974, an extended television interview to Japan's Foreign Minister Ohira. Chinese goodwill—as well as Peking's attempts to undermine Soviet efforts for Japanese participation in the development of Siberia—has also been reflected in the Chinese promise to export some 1.5 million tons of crude oil to Japan in 1974.

----

[*] Preliminary figures indicate that Sino-Japanese trade in 1973 reached the $2 billion level (as against $1.1 billion in the previous year). However, Japan's trade with mainland China still lags by about 10 percent behind Japan's economic transactions with rival Taiwan.

Admittedly this amount represents only 1 percent of Japanese oil consumption, but it raises Japanese hopes for a favored position in Chinese plans to expand oil production substantially during the coming years. Similarly, Peking has been willing to play down the potential conflict arising from competing Chinese and Japanese claims to the Senkaku Islands, which are thought to be located near undersea oil deposits. Even a Japanese agreement with South Korea suggesting the possibility of joint oil exploration in waters also claimed by Peking has elicited no more than a firm Chinese protest. For the moment, at least, détente is the key word in Sino-Japanese relations.

The change in Japan's policy toward China was so abrupt—or at least it so appeared to those not attuned to the subtle subsurface changes in Japan—that it inevitably produced resistance in circles whose members for ideological or political reasons were reluctant to turn away from Taiwan. In that context, there was for a while much discussion in Tokyo about whether or not the Sino-Japanese agreement constituted a good bargain for Japan. Some criticism is still being voiced among the most conservative elements of the LDP (such as the young politicians of the Seirankai) regarding the haste with which the Japanese government responded to Chinese overtures. But it is now generally agreed that the Sino-Japanese understanding was inevitable under the prevailing international conditions and that each party appears to have gained its immediate objectives without having paid an undue price.

What in fact are Japan's objectives with regard to Peking? In the first place, Japan desires a relationship of coexistence— though not necessarily of cooperation—with China rather than a confrontation. This is so for reasons of domestic Japanese policy, but also because such a relationship fits into the general pattern of Japan's postwar world view and maximizes its assets—i.e., its economic advantage. That goal appears to have been attained. But in the end, the nature of the Sino-Japanese relationship will hinge not only on whether the atmosphere has been cleared between the two capitals, but also on the way in which important issues affecting both nations' interests are handled. There is really only one such issue of immediate importance, the question of Taiwan. The solution, as incorporated in the Sino-Japanese agreement, is in line with the previously described way in which Japanese society prefers to handle conflict situations. While Peking "reaffirms that Taiwan is an inalienable part of the territory of the People's Republic of China," the government of Japan merely states that it "fully understands and respects this stand of the government of China."

The formula is thus sufficiently vague to allow for
reinterpretations and adjustments in an uncertain future very
much dependent on U.S. policies. In that sense, Peking has
clearly retreated from its tough position with regard to Japan,
but it has thereby gained full recognition as the sole
government of China. What matters to Peking is the political
aspect of the question, rather than its economic dimensions,
which matter to Japan. Thus the compromise with regard to Taiwan
gives both parties what presently is most important to them:
Peking gains its political objective, while Tokyo is allowed to
benefit for the time being from continued economic ties with
Taiwan. But it is already becoming clear that political and
economic considerations cannot always be so easily separated.
The deadlock over the Sino-Japanese civil aviation agreement,
i.e., over the appropriate way of handling Japan's air
communications with Taiwan, and the resulting political
repercussions in Tokyo during the first months of 1974 were a
case in point.*
    From Peking's viewpoint, two other important issues enter
into its determination of a Japan strategy: the question of
Japan's rearmament and the future of the Soviet-Japanese
relationship. Developments in the Japanese domestic scene
already make it obvious that one of the immediate effects of the
1972 agreement creating the conditions for détente has been to
impede Japanese plans to build up its defense capabilities.
While this effect may be welcome in Peking, it also, in light of
the deterioration of U.S.-Japanese relations, evokes the danger
that Japanese isolation will stimulate nationalistic and perhaps
militaristic sentiments in Japan. This may explain why Peking no
longer seems bent on driving a wedge between Japan and the
United States. Chinese objections to Japan's security pact have
been quietly dropped, and Peking has even tacitly endorsed the

----

* China insists that it will not allow Taiwan's planes flying
into Japan to appear on the field side by side with its own and
that it cannot permit them to display the Nationalist flag,
since Taiwan is part of China and not an independent state, as
Japan, it is asserted, has acknowledged in the 1972 Sino-Japanese
declaration. But pro-Taiwan and nationalist circles in Japan
object to any further weakening of the Republic of China's claims
to legitimacy, which compliance with Peking's demands would imply.
In early 1974, intensive efforts were therefore under way within
the LDP to find a formula that would meet the requirements of all
interested parties.

U.S. military presence in Japan. Japanese defense ties with the United States, which is now on friendly terms with Peking, must be preferable, from the Chinese viewpoint, to a Japan that might be driven into rearmament by a lack of security.

Japan and the Soviet Union—Conflicting Pulls

One glance at the results of Japanese public-opinion polls will suffice to show that the Soviet Union has an image problem in Japan. Nor is this a recent phenomenon. Ever since polls were introduced to determine the relative public standing of various nations important to Japan, the USSR (along with Korea) has proved to be most unpopular.* Other indicators also suggest that the Japanese image of the Soviet neighbor is a rather unfavorable one and that this holds both for the general public and for Japan's elite.

There are many reasons for this phenomenon, rooted for the most part in the history of the two peoples' relations as well as in their cultural and racial differences. In all these respects the Soviet Union finds itself in a most unfavorable position when compared with its Chinese rival. The Soviet Union did not have a good press even in prewar times. Events during World War II and subsequently did little to improve the Soviet image. Soviet armies overran the Japanese forces stationed in Manchuria during the closing days of the war despite the nonaggression pact concluded earlier between the two countries. Hundreds of thousands of Japanese military personnel and civilians were carried away into Soviet labor camps, returning to Japan only years later with tales of having suffered great hardships. Meanwhile, the Soviet Union seized territories to the north of Japan, including some that in the Japanese (and U.S.) view had never been meant by the Allies to go to the USSR. Soviet attempts to occupy and adminster Hokkaidō, the northern part of Japan, after the surrender were frustrated by American opposition, but they increased the Japanese fear of Soviet designs on Japan.

The hostile atmosphere that has persisted between the two countries for several decades was intensified by the emergence

---

* Thus, the survey undertaken in October 1973 which asked the respondents to list "liked" and "disliked" nations, resulted in (from the Soviet viewpoint) discouraging findings. (For details, see page 294.) Soviet policy obviously faces difficult conditions in Japan.

of the USSR as a far from benevolent superpower, armed with
nuclear weapons, and apparently not reluctant to use its
superior might wherever American protection did not come into
play. The Soviet invasion of Czechoslovakia shocked Japan and
accentuated the image of Soviet brute force ruthlessly applied.
(One cannot help but be struck by the constrast with the rather
mild Japanese reaction to Chinese intervention in Tibet, even
though Tibet might have been assumed to be closer to Japanese
hearts than Czechoslovakia.) Soviet pressures on Japan throughout
the postwar decades have done nothing to diminish Japanese
uneasiness about Soviet intentions. Soviet reconnaissance
flights regularly skirt the periphery of Japan, and Soviet
patrol boats seize Japanese fishing craft and carry the crews to
Siberian internment for violation of what the Soviets insist are
the territorial waters of the USSR. Japanese negotiations with
the Soviet Union have generally followed a pattern of wrangling,
sustained Soviet pressures, and bureaucratic delays (e.g., the
annual "one-hundred-day" fishing talks).

But, little by little, Soviet policy toward Japan has added
the use of the carrot to that of the stick. The Soviets may have
found the Japanese left—the Socialists and the Communists—
useful in attempts to disrupt the U.S.-Japanese alliance, but
gradually Moscow, like Peking, has come to understand that to
affect Japanese policy it is necessary to gain leverage within
Japan's establishment. The consistently poor image of the Soviet
Union must also have been of concern. The application of
pressure against Japan could not fail to reinforce that image
and thus prove counterproductive by intensifying Japan's need to
rely on the United States. Furthermore, a hard line no longer
fitted in well with Soviet coexistence policies. Finally, the
Sino-Soviet conflict played an important role in moving the
Soviet Union toward a more flexible position that might
forestall a Sino-Japanese rapprochement by improving Moscow's
relations with Japan.

In the propaganda broadcasts emanating from Moscow and Peking
and in the tenor of their press, one might not have detected
much difference during the 1950s between the two communist
powers' objectives. Both lashed out against "American
imperialism" and against related Japanese support (i.e., the
security pact and the provision by Japan of base facilities for
U.S. forces), and both cautioned the Japanese against a revival
of militarism. But that was not the entire picture. Both Moscow
and Peking had been shut out by American diplomacy from
concluding a peace treaty with Japan. Rather than make common
cause with Peking, as suggested by the Sino-Soviet alliance
concluded in 1950 and aimed against Japan, Moscow as early as

the mid-1950s decided to go its separate way with regard to
Japanese policy, concluding, in 1956, a separate agreement
ending the state of war. (No peace treaty has been concluded as
yet, because of the unresolved territorial problem.)
Ambassadors were exchanged between Tokyo and Moscow, while
Peking was still fighting for Japanese diplomatic recognition.
Moscow and Peking were no longer allies, but were pursuing
their interests separately and often with a view to damaging
the other's position in Japan.

Against this background, it is understandable that the Soviet
Union decided to emphasize in dealings with Japan the
development of economic ties. In that way, it could be expected
that Japan's self-interests—or at least the interests of the
powerful business community—could be mobilized for an
improvement of relations with the Soviet Union. A political
payoff could be expected eventually, drawing Japan closer to
Moscow and further away from Washington and, for that matter,
from Peking.

In neither respect has this Soviet policy been very
successful. The reasons are both clear and diverse. First, there
is the unfavorable Soviet image already alluded to, which will
take a long time to change. In the case of China, cultural,
racial, and historic factors work in favor of nonhostile
communication, as was evidenced during China's Cultural
Revolution. Although the Japanese were shocked by its excesses
and as uncertain about its motivations and objectives as
everyone else, they reacted with impressive restraint. Excesses
in Soviet behavior have never met with such tolerance on the
part of the Japanese. To this day, there is something cold,
hostile, and remote in the Soviet-Japanese relationship which
necessarily colors their contacts. In competing with American
and now increasingly also with Chinese influence, Moscow has
recognized that it must make greater efforts to improve its
press in Japan. Some positive results have been chalked up over
the past few years, which are reflected in the slow decline in
the number of those who express dislike for the Soviet Union.
The undercurrent of fear and distrust, however, remains. That
the Japanese Self-Defense Forces are deployed against a thrust
by the Soviet Union can be explained by the military realities
of the situation around Japan; but it also suits the mood of
the Japanese, to whom the most convincing potential enemy is
the USSR.

Commercial exchanges between the two nations have steadily
grown, it is true, surpassing the level of Japanese trade with
Peking in 1972, and in that year for the first time exceeding

$1 billion in two-way exchange.* Hence, Japanese business
interests are beginning to develop a stake in relations with
the Soviet Union. But the great expectations that Soviet
approaches to Japan have periodically raised in Tokyo have yet
to materialize.

The two economies are in many ways more complementary than
are those of China and Japan. The Soviet Union has large
quantities of oil, timber, coal, natural gas, and the minerals
that Japanese industry needs. Japan's efficient production
apparatus can in turn provide the Soviet Union with
technologically superior equipment and with all the items that
one of the world's most advanced consumer-goods industries can
produce. There is also the geographic factor. The proximity of
Japan to the vast, underpopulated, and still only partly
exploited regions of the Soviet Far East is a powerful
attraction for Japanese business circles. It must also be clear
in Moscow that to develop those areas (far from Soviet and other
economic centers but close to a hostile China) no country is in
a better position than Japan. That is a consideration that works
in Japan's favor at the same time that it arouses suspicion in
the Soviet Union, where the invasion of Japanese armies in
precisely those areas during the early days of the Bolshevik
regime is still remembered. Then there is the obstacle of
financing the gigantic cooperative projects—"projects on a
continental scale," as the Soviets call them—that both sides
have been dreaming about, so far with such little effort.**

Japan is understandably reluctant to commit the necessary
vast resources in view of the uncertainties posed by Soviet
policies toward Japan and the dangers inherent in the Sino-
Soviet conflict. That conflict casts its shadow over Sino-
Japanese relations. In a way, it provides Japan with added
leverage in both communist capitals, where it is realized that
Japan's enormous economic potential could make a dramatic
difference in Chinese development. The attraction of Siberian

----

* Soviet trade with Japan amounted to $630 million in 1969; $822
million in 1970; close to $900 million in 1971; and $1,098
million in 1972 (almost equaling Japan's China trade during that
last year). For the 1971-1975 period a total trade volume of
$5.2 billion is anticipated.

** Firm agreements have been reached only on Japanese
participation in the construction of a new harbor at Wrangel on
the Sea of Japan and in the exploitation of timber resources.

ventures for Japanese capital is great, but so are the roadblocks and the risks.* For Japan to commit billions of dollars in Siberia might mean arousing renewed hostility in Peking.

Long-range Japanese investments in the USSR could be justified only if they were both very profitable and politically safe. It is not clear at this point that the proposed projects, first suggested in 1962 by Khrushchev, are either. There is fear in Tokyo that conditions imposed by the Soviet Union may make the projects less attractive than they at first appeared.** As to the political risk, Japan would feel much reassured if the United States were to participate sufficiently to have a stake in these ventures and so would the government in Peking. None of these problems has as yet been fully studied or resolved. As a result, agreements on some smaller Japanese projects have been signed with the Soviet Union, but the major ones remain in posse: development of the vast, low-sulfur oil resources of Tyumen in western Siberia, of the natural gas and coking coal in Yakutia, of the copper in Udokan, and of the coal in the Maritime Provinces.***

----

* Kiichi Saeki, president of the Nomura Institute of Technology and Economics and a respected commentator on Japanese national security policies, examines the history of Japan's negotiations with the USSR regarding joint exploitation of Siberian resources and weighs the considerations involved from the Japanese viewpoint in his excellent article "Toward Japanese Cooperation in Siberian Development," Problems of Communism vol. 21, no. 3 (May-June 1972), pp. 1-11. He foresees slow but steady progress rather than any dramatic breakthroughs in Japan's economic relations with the USSR.

** For example, in 1973 the Soviet Union indicated that Japanese assistance in the development of the Tyumen oil fields could be rewarded with exports to Japan of only 25 million tons of crude as against the 40 million tons that initially had appeared to be available. This reduction led some Japanese to conclude that the tightening international energy situation had convinced the Soviet Union that it should attempt to develop its oil fields without foreign participation.

*** The Tyumen project is the most attractive from the Japanese point of view because it would help to ease Japan's energy problem. This project of vast size would, however, require

 With the intensification of the Sino-Soviet conflict, Japan
has become the object of a tug-of-war between Moscow and Peking.
In that contest, the psychological-political advantages clearly
lie with Peking. * But Moscow may have an edge with regard to
the economic dimension of the three-way relationship. Japan has
managed to become the biggest trading partner of the Soviet
Union as well as of China (not to mention trade with Taiwan).
But there is fear in Japan that, with growing hostility between
Moscow and Peking, Japan will find it increasingly difficult to
play a neutral role and maintain good relations with both its
big neighbors.
 Certainly Japan is trying hard not to give offense to either
of the two communist powers, while remaining within the shelter
of its American alliance. Thus, Brezhnev's offers of a
collective security system in Asia—which, notwithstanding
Soviet denials, would be directed against China—have fallen on
deaf ears in Japan. One of the reasons for this negative
Japanese response is unrelated to China: the pact would
reaffirm the territorial borders of the signatories, and the
Japanese government is unwilling to abandon its historic claims
to the four northern islands now under Soviet control.** This is

----

Japanese credits of about $1 billion for the construction of a
4,000-mile oil pipeline to Nakhodka on the Japan Sea. The Soviet
Union would repay Japan through the sale of crude oil.

* In an interview with Time in the spring of 1973 (published in
Time, May 7, 1973, p. 35), Prime Minister Tanaka gave his
estimate of Japan's relations with the three major powers in
these terms: "Relations with China will become important, but
relations with the U.S. come first. The Japanese attitude toward
China has been split around 50-50 pro and con closer relations.
When it comes to the Soviet Union, the pros are only 10% of our
people. In the case of the U.S., I would say that about 70% are
supporters of the U.S."

** These islands can be divided into two groups. The first
consists of tiny islands northwest of Hokkaidō, the Habomai
group, and Shikotan Island. The Japanese consider them an
integral part of Japan and insist that they had never been
under other than Japanese domination until seized by the
Soviets in the wake of Japan's defeat. The Soviets have offered
to return these islands as a gesture of goodwill once a peace
treaty has been concluded, but it is not clear whether that

something of a test case for Soviet-Japanese relations, one by
which the intensity of a Soviet desire to establish closer
relations with Japan might be measured. Without Soviet
concessions on the territorial question, it will not be easy to
go beyond the present state of Soviet-Japanese relations,
characterized by mutual distrust mitigated only by mutual
economic interests.

Soviet reactions to recent changes in U.S. and Japanese
policy toward Peking might serve as an indicator of future
Soviet strategy. When the sudden U.S. approach to China stunned
the Japanese leadership and drove a wedge between Japan and the
United States, Moscow immediately responded to the opportunity.
One could notice a perceptible softening of the Soviet line
toward Japan. Foreign Minister Gromyko came to Tokyo for a
friendly visit, and there were indications that the Soviet Union
might be prepared to reconsider the territorial issue within the
framework of peace-treaty negotiations with Japan. Whether
Moscow then thought that Japan's dismay and feeling of
isolation could rupture the American-Japanese alliance is
unclear. Certainly, the situation seemed propitious for Soviet
efforts to draw Japan somewhat further from the United States as
well as from China.

But then it was the turn of the Soviet Union to be shocked by
new developments among the three Pacific powers. Japan rapidly
seized the chance to normalize its relations with China and at
the summit signed an agreement to that effect with Peking,
leaving Moscow with feelings of disappointment and rebuff. One
might have expected that, in view of Japan's improved leverage,
the Soviet Union would have become more conciliatory toward
Japan so as to prevent too close an association with Peking.
Initially at least, Japan's détente with China seems to have had

---

offer still stands. The other islands are Etorofu and Kunashiri
islands, forming the southernmost part of the Kurile Islands,
ceded by Japan in the San Francisco Peace Treaty of 1951 (which
the Soviets refused to sign). In the Japanese (and U.S.) view,
disposition of these islands remains to be determined. A more
important argument on the Japanese side is that the two islands
are not part of the Kuriles but historically have been part of
Japan proper. This contention is rejected by the Soviet side.
Etorofu and Kunashiri have considerably more military
significance than do the Habomais and Shikotan.

the contrary effect on Moscow. Japan's territorial claims were
rejected as "pointless and absurd," the Japanese were cautioned
against allowing themselves to be drawn into a net of U.S.-
Chinese collusion, and Soviet attacks against Japanese
militarism and Japanese foreign policy were revived.

Since then, the Soviet leaders appear to have had second
thoughts. When in 1973 Prime Minister Tanaka suggested a visit
to the Soviet Union to get talks on a peace treaty moving again,
Brezhnev promptly and positively responded to the Japanese
initiative. In the fall of the same year, the Japanese leader
was therefore able to visit Moscow, but the results must have
been disappointing to both parties. Neither side appears to
have made a major concession on the territorial issue, although
a softening of the Soviet position was read by some into the
statement issued after the conference.* As a result of this
deadlock, Japan's economic involvement in the development of
Siberian resources has been slowed down and, as of early 1974, a
peace treaty between Japan and the USSR still seemed some time
off. Neither Moscow nor Tokyo appears to be ready to make major
concessions. In the absence of such concessions, a full
normalization of their relations will require considerable time,
unless changes in the international situation force either Japan
or the Soviet Union to modify its stand.

----

* It should be noted, however, that the statement issued in
Moscow on October 10, 1973, at the conclusion of Tanaka's talks
with the Soviet leaders contains this passage (here quoted from
the English-language Tass report of that day): "Realizing that
settlement of outstanding questions, a leftover since the time
of the second world war and the signing of a peace treaty will
make a contribution to the establishment of genuinely good-
neighborly and friendly relations between the two countries, the
[two] sides held talks on questions pertaining to the content of
a peace treaty." It is evident that this passage refers to the
territorial issue. This appears to be the first time that the
Soviet Union has officially conceded that this question has not
been definitively settled by Soviet occupation of the contested
islands. One could read into this statement therefore that the
Soviet government is now prepared to negotiate the issue and in
the future to make some concessions to Japan in order to
regularize its relations with Tokyo before Peking succeeds in
drawing Japan into the Chinese orbit. The major obstacle on the
Soviet side in settling the territorial question appears to be
the fear that any Soviet compromise in dealing with Japan might

Japan's Future and the Big Three

Until recently, Japan's position among the major Far Eastern
powers seemed fixed and quasi-permanent: the American alliance
formed the anchor of Japanese foreign policy, and relations with
the two communist nations were essentially determined by that
fact. Japan appeared content to follow the U.S. lead and entrust
its national security and interests to American protection.
However, from the late 1960s on, even Japanese supporters of
such a policy—i.e., the majority of the Japanese nation—were
beginning to complain that Japan lacked a foreign policy of its
own.

In actual fact, postwar Japan has not been without national
goals or a national strategy. The problem is that today this
strategy no longer seems to fill the psychological needs of the
Japanese people. Noticeable pressures within Japan question
whether economic growth can ever be a proper national goal and
whether Japan's potential to affect world events should not be
more actively employed than is possible under conditions of
total dependence on American direction. Such sentiments,
however, need not necessarily lead to accelerated rearmament.

These changes in Japan's perception of its national purpose
are occurring at a time when the foundations of the American
alliance have become shaky, at least in the minds of the
Japanese. They also occur at a juncture in history when American
initiatives are profoundly altering the context in which Japan
has been operating quietly and successfully for the past twenty
years. Hence, Japan stands today at the confluence of two
currents. At home there is a search for new and psychologically
more satisfying national goals, a search marked by self-doubts,
uneasiness, and hesitations. On the international scene, but
particularly in the Far East where demands on Japan are
greatest, the situation is in extreme flux, as all three Pacific
powers reappraise their interrelationship as well as their
policies toward Japan.

The world around Japan is now rapidly changing. Peking and
Washington are drawing closer, while China and the Soviet Union
are drawing further apart. The two superpowers—the United
States and the Soviet Union—are redefining their relationships
through a step-by-step de-escalation of tensions. All three
major powers are gradually withdrawing from the Indochinese
conflict, and the two Koreas, on Japan's doorstep, are beginning,

---

embolden other nations bordering the USSR—including China—to
press for territorial readjustments.

if only intermittently, to talk to each other. The ideological
factor appears no longer to dominate policy, as presumed allies
are turning into potential antagonists and adversaries into
potential allies.

Japan is of course affected by this new state of affairs,
often described as "multipolarity" (can there be more than two
poles?), and is affected also in other ways. There are now great
powers of various kinds, classified by their functioning on the
economic, military, or political level. Only the United States
simultaneously predominates in all these realms. It is
characteristic of the fluidity of the situation that a nation
need no longer operate on all three planes in the same fashion.
It is possible, as the case of Japan and the United States
demonstrates, to maintain close defense ties while engaging in
confrontation on the economic level. The questions arises,
particularly in Japan, of how long such economic dissonances can
be sustained before they disrupt the military-political
relationship. What is Japan to make of these circumstances, and
how is it to respond to them in the years ahead?

At this time, Soviet economic assets with respect to Japan—
and also its superior military might—are canceled out by
negative factors militating against a close relationship. It can
be assumed that any attempt to translate intensified economic
relations between the two countries into more intimate political
ties would cause adverse reactions, in both the United States
and in China (quite aside from the fact that the Japanese scene
offers obstacles against such a trend). Even if Japan's American
alliance should be weakened further and eventually reach the
point at which its credibility was in serious doubt, the
Japanese would be more likely to move toward an independent
stance, politically and eventually militarily, than to seek
alignment with the USSR.

The Sino-Soviet conflict, should it continue (as it probably
will), is certain to have an important bearing on how far Japan
would be prepared to move toward cooperation with the USSR, even
in the strictly economic realm. The eventual profit in the
proposed development projects in the Soviet Union is too
uncertain and the political risk too large to provide compelling
reasons for bold Japanese steps taken without regard for Chinese
reactions and the presence or absence of American support.
Limited and gradual improvement of relations with the Soviet
Union, always with an eye to their effect on Japan's
relationship with the other major Pacific powers, would seem to
be the course dictated by the logic of Japan's situation vis-à-
vis the Big Three of the political-military triangle.

Chinese concern about the possibility of a military revival
in Japan (unlikely to be as urgent a consideration in Moscow),
as well as the economic factor, create in Peking favorable
conditions for promotion of a détente with Japan. These
conditions are rendered even more favorable by the Chinese
desire to preempt the Soviet Union in Japan. On the Japanese
side, too, primarily for economic but also for political reasons,
the mood for Sino-Japanese cooperation is likely to continue to
be essentially positive. But serious questions arise as to
whether relations between China and Japan will be as smooth as
the 1972 summit meeting between Chou and Tanaka might have
suggested. Japan is reluctant to take any steps that would
seriously provoke the Soviet Union or that could be interpreted
in Washington as attempts to undercut the American position. The
euphoria following the normalization of Peking-Tokyo relations
has temporarily blurred the realization that Chinese and
Japanese interests will in the long run require a difficult
adjustment if they are not to generate friction and
confrontation. This is as true with regard to a conflict over
leadership in Asia generally as it is with respect to the
contending influences of the two powers in Southeast Asia and on
the Korean peninsula, not to mention the unresolved question of
Taiwan, the potentially troublesome territorial dispute over the
Senkaku Islands and other reputedly oil-rich offshore areas, and
the fact—sometimes overlooked in Japan—that the political
philosophies of the two governments are so far removed from each
other. Hence, in relations with the two communist nations, it
seems logical for Japan to pursue its global goal of relaxation
of tension without aligning itself with either of them and
without weakening further its special relationship with the
United States.
      That relationship constitutes the central question for Japan's
future. Should this relationship be ruptured, Japan might turn
toward unarmed neutralism—a highly unlikely choice—or, somewhat
more likely, it might seek to meet its security problem through
the buildup of an independent force, perhaps including nuclear
weapons. At present, domestic opposition to such a move is
prohibitive, but the passage of a few years, intensified external
pressures against Japan, and a feeling of international isolation
could gradually remove the existing psychological obstacles to
remilitarization. Such a course could have a strongly adverse
effect on Japan's relations with all three Pacific powers, since
to all of them a reassembled Japanese military apparatus could
appear as a threat to their interests and security. In view of
such potentially dangerous external reactions to a Japanese

decision to build independent military strength, it would be logical for Japan to emphasize the defensive nature of its buildup, at least in the initial stage of any massive rearmament.

On the other hand, the basic interests of both the United States and Japan—including that of preventing Soviet hegemony in the Pacific—inhibit their assuming wholly antagonistic positions. In fact, for political as well as for strategic reasons and, presumably, in the long run, also for economic reasons, it is difficult to imagine any rationale recommending that the United States voluntarily abandon its close association with Japan. The incentives for Japan to maintain its American ties are even more compelling. On both sides it is likely, therefore, that the dangers inherent in prolonged economic confrontation will become sufficiently apparent to bring about a resolution of the pending issues. Developments of the past year certainly point in that direction. Out of such a give-and-take, protracted and difficult as, no doubt, it will continue to be, it is logical to assume that a new relationship will emerge, providing the Japanese with greater independence from the United States, politically and eventually also militarily, as well as with greater responsibility in the use of their economic power in Asia. Increasingly, then, Japan will become an independent factor in the relations of the Pacific powers, but one that will not normally operate against the interests of the United States.

That such a development is logical, however, does not mean that it can be counted on to occur. Precedent should caution against such an easy assumption. During the past century, American-Japanese relations have oscillated rapidly between conflict and cooperation. The two countries are so different in so many respects and so far from being fully appreciative of these differences—and of their policy significance—that the risk of accumulating misunderstandings in dangerous proportions always exists. A mutual and sustained effort would therefore have to be assumed if the American-Japanese alliance is to continue to be a central fact in shaping the future of the Pacific area.

Chapter 6

THE DÉTENTE AND KOREA

Chong-Sik Lee

That the 1971 "Ping-Pong diplomacy" and the subsequent détente between the United States and the Chinese People's Republic would affect the behavior of the two belligerent states on the Korean peninsula was a foregone conclusion. For a number of reasons, the two states have been particularly susceptible to environmental influences, and the détente, which for all practical purposes ended the era of the cold war, could not but affect the Korean peninsula. Among these reasons are that the Democratic People's Republic of Korea (DPRK) and the Republic of Korea (ROK) are the by-products of the cold war; that Korea as a whole is a small area with limited material resources; that the level of scientific and technological development of the two Koreas is still in the "developing" category, while both states have very high aspirations for economic and other development; and that the two-decade-old belligerency heavily taxed their human and material resources. For these reasons, the two states have been obliged to depend upon the support and aid of their allies for both economic development and defense. The drastic turnabout of the attitudes and actions of their respective allies, therefore, could not fail to impress the leaders of the two states.

One must not, however, attribute all the actions of these leaders to environmental influences, in spite of the countries' high degree of susceptibility to environmental changes and the magnitude of the changes that have occurred around them. During their two and a half decades of separate existence, each of the two states (or the two political systems) has developed its own ethos, structures, and problems. It has been demonstrated time and again that the leaders of these systems have their own convictions, aims, and perspectives and that they have not always been willing to let the external environmental forces dictate their actions. Indeed, at times, these leaders have displayed tendencies to pursue their own goals even when these manifestly injured the effectiveness of their systems.

Analysis of the policies of these two states therefore requires understanding of the environmental changes and the leaders' perception of these changes, as well as understanding of the

internal needs and problems of each system. An underlying
assumption, of course, is that the leaders of each system are
intent on enhancing the interest of their own system for either
altruistic or selfish reasons. Even if we advance the rather
far-fetched supposition that the leaders of these systems are
ultimately interested in dissolving the two systems for the sake
of creating a larger whole, their basic motive, which is to
enhance the strength and power of the group to which they belong,
will not diminish.

Before we proceed to analyze their motives, however, we must
briefly survey the events on the Korean peninsula in the wake
of the dramatic shifts in the international arena.

The Korean Reaction to Détente: An Overview

The swirl of events in the international arena was triggered by
President Nixon's usage of the official designation of the
People's Republic of China (PRC) on February 25, 1971.
Subsequently, on March 15, American restrictions on travel to
China were lifted, and, on April 10 the American table-tennis
team landed in China. On July 15, President Nixon made the
dramatic announcement of Presidential Adviser Kissinger's visit
to China and his acceptance of an invitation for Premier Chou
En-lai to visit Peking. On October 25 the PRC was seated in the
United Nations, and in February 1972, Nixon made his epochal
visit to the forbidden land.

On the surface, at least, the Koreans seemed to follow Nixon's
July 15 announcement without demur. Within a month of Nixon's
announcement, on August 12, the South Korean Red Cross,
obviously acting on the initiative of the government, proposed
a meeting with its North Korean counterpart to discuss the
problems of Korea's divided families: how to locate missing
relatives, inform them of one another's condition, and arrange
for reunions. A preliminary meeting to be held in Geneva before
the end of October was suggested. The North Korean response was
almost immediate. Two days later, the North Korean Red Cross,
officially responding via Pyongyang Radio, proposed that
preliminary talks take place in September at Panmunjom and
indicated that on August 20 its representatives would deliver an
official letter at that site to South Korean Red Cross
representatives. On that date, a four-minute meeting ensued, the
first bilateral contact in the troubled history of a divided
Korea carried out solely by North and South Koreans. Millions of
Koreans greeted the event as though the walls between the two
societies had been removed, and it was indeed an event of

historical dimensions.* Other Red Cross meetings followed, and on
June 16, 1972, after ten months of negotiations, both sides
agreed on the agenda for future discussions.

On the heels of the Red Cross agreement came a more dramatic
announcement of a political agreement between the two Koreas.[1] On
July 4, the two governments simultaneously released a joint North
and South Korean communiqué disclosing that high-level
discussions had taken place in Pyongyang and Seoul and that a
number of significant understandings and agreements had been
reached. The communiqué said that Yi Hu-rak, the director of the
South Korean Central Intelligence Agency, had visited Pyongyang
from May 2 to May 5 to hold talks with Kim Yŏng-ju, the director
of the Organization and Guidance Department of the Korean
Workers' party (KWP). Kim, incidentally, is the only surviving
younger brother of Premier Kim Il-sŏng. In 1974 he ranked
sixth in the 172-member Central Committee and was one of the ten
members of the Secretariat headed by his brother and a member of
the fifteen-member Political Committee (Politburo). North Korea,
in turn, delegated Pak Sŏng-ch'ŏl, fourth-ranking Central
Committee member, second deputy premier, and director of the
International Department of the KWP. Pak had been with the
premier ever since the Manchurian guerrilla days and had served
as a lieutenant general in the army, as ambassador to Bulgaria,
as minister of foreign affairs, and so on. He was also a member

----

* It might be noted in passing that face-to-face meetings
between representatives of North and South Korea had occurred
twice earlier, on both occasions under the aegis of the
International Olympic Committee. The first of these meetings
took place in Lausanne, Switzerland, in January 1963, with an
IOC representative presiding. The IOC had approved North Korea's
membership in the Olympic association and had recommended the
organization of a combined North-South team for the 1964 Tokyo
Olympic Games. While agreement was reached in Lausanne that the
folksong "Arirang" would be used instead of a national anthem,
other issues, such as the question of a national flag, remained
unresolved, and it was agreed to solicit IOC advice. North Korea
then proposed a second meeting, which took place in Hong Kong in
May 1963. It proved impossible to reach any agreement on a wide
range of issues, however, and negotiations were broken off. For
the above, see Robert A. Scalapino and Chong-Sik Lee, Communism
in Korea (Berkeley and Los Angeles: University of California
Press, 1972), p. 677.

of the Politburo. The highest-ranking leaders in the two
capitals, Premier Kim Il-sŏng in the North and President Pak
Chŏng-hui in the South, saw the emissaries. The announcement
said that "the two sides in these talks had frank and open-
hearted exchanges of views, and made great progress in promoting
mutual understanding."

A word count of the joint communiqué reveals where the main
concern of the Korean leaders lay. In the 500-word communiqué
the basic theme of mitigating tension, misunderstanding, and
mistrust was repeated four times. Note the following statements:

"In the course of the talks, the two sides [have engaged] in an
effort to remove the misunderstandings and mistrust and mitigate
increased tensions that have arisen between the South and the
North as a result of long separation. . . .

"Unification shall be achieved through peaceful means, and not
through the use of force against each other. . . .

"In order to ease tensions and foster an atmosphere of mutual
trust. . . , the two sides have agreed not to slander or defame
each other, not to undertake armed provocations whether on a
large or small scale, and to take positive measures to prevent
inadvertent military incidents. . . .

"The two sides, in order to restore severed national ties,
promote mutual understanding and to expedite independent
peaceful unification, have agreed to carry out various exchanges
in many fields. . . .

"The two sides [wish to] prevent the outbreak of unexpected
military incidents, and to deal directly, promptly and
accurately with problems arising between the South and the
North. . . ."[2]

The basic aim of the two sides, then, can be seen as
reduction of tension and creation of an atmosphere in which
peaceful coexistence is possible. To this end, both sides agreed
not to undertake military provocations, but to engage in
exchanges, cooperate positively to bring about the early success
of the Red Cross talks, install a direct telephone line, and
create a South-North Coordinating Committee. They also affirmed
the desire for unification that "shall be achieved through
independent Korean efforts" using peaceful means, "transcending
differences in ideas, ideologies, and systems."[3]

The inspiration for the Korean joint communiqué is not
difficult to find. One need only read the following paragraphs
from the joint communiqué of February 28, 1972, issued by
President Nixon and Premier Chou En-lai:

"The U.S. side stated: Peace in Asia and peace in the world
requires efforts both to reduce immediate tensions and to
eliminate the basic causes of conflict. . . . The United States
believes that the effort to reduce tensions is served by
improving communication between countries that have different
ideologies so as to lessen the risks of confrontation through
accident, miscalculation or misunderstanding. Countries should
treat each other with mutual respect and be willing to compete
peacefully, letting performance be the ultimate judge. No
country should claim infallibility and each country should be
prepared to re-examine its own attitudes for the common good.

"There are essential differences between China and the United
States in their social systems and foreign policies. However,
the two sides agreed that countries, regardless of their social
systems, should conduct their relations on the principles of
respect for the sovereignty and territorial integrity of all
states, nonaggression against other states, noninterference in
the internal affairs of other states, equality and mutual
benefit, and peaceful coexistence. International disputes should
be settled on this basis, without resorting to the use of threat
of force. The United States and the People's Republic of China
are prepared to apply these principles to their mutual relations."[4]

Thus one finds a close parallel between the Korean and
Shanghai communiqués and may draw the conclusion that the
similarities are not coincidental. Later, we shall discuss the
influence and roles of China and the United States on Korean
developments. It is necessary at this point to discuss the
significance and implications of the Korean communiqué.

The Nature of the Confrontation in Korea

Although the timing of the Sino-American rapprochement and the
manner in which it was reached caught the world by surprise, the
change in American policy toward China had been anticipated for
quite some time. The United States had begun to modify its
stance toward the PRC as early as the regime of Secretary of
State Dean Rusk, and the trend had become unmistakable. Of
course, the turnabout in Chinese policies toward the United
States was much more sudden, but at least the Chinese had been

willing to engage in conversations with the Americans in Geneva
since August 1955, had made overtures by lifting the ban on
American newsmen entering China in August 1956, and had engaged
in bilateral talks in Warsaw since September 1958.[5]

In contrast, the separation between the two parts of Korea
had been complete and the attitude each had toward the other had
involved much more than foreign policy or diplomatic recognition.
In fact, it entailed constitutional and legal issues of grave
magnitude for both sides. Article 3 of the ROK constitution
states, for example, that "the territory of the Republic of
Korea consists of the Korean peninsula and its accessory
islands." Thus the ROK claims sovereignty over the entire
peninsula, and therefore, by definition, the communist regime in
the North is an antistate and treasonous organization. In fact,
according to the Law on State Security adopted in June 1960 and
amended in September 1962, Premier Kim Il-sŏng had been
sentenced to death or life imprisonment. Article 1 of the law
states:

"Those who have formed organizations or groups for the purpose
of usurping the title of the government or to cause rebellion
against the state shall be punished according to the following
classifications: (1) The chieftain shall be executed or
sentenced to life imprisonment; (2) officers or those engaged in
leadership duties shall be executed or sentenced to life
imprisonment, the minimum being five years of hard labor; (3)
all others shall be sentenced to hard labor with a maximum of
seven years."

The anticommunist law adopted in July 1961 and amended three
times since then makes it a state crime "to meet, communicate,
or otherwise establish liaison" with an antistate organization,
and those convicted under the law are subject to hard labor for
up to seven years (Article 5). Any accomplice to the crime is
subject to hard labor for up to ten years (Article 7), and those
knowing of the existence of such a scheme and not informing the
investigative and intelligence authorities are also subject to
hard labor for up to ten years (Articles 8 and 9). The president
himself is immune from criminal prosection (as Article 82
exempts him from all criminal prosecution except for internal
rebellion or external invasion), but even the discussion of
establishing liaison with the DPRK by any other individuals
entails the risk of severe punishment.

Although the constitution of the DPRK does not contain a

clause defining the territorial boundaries,* the DPRK has also
claimed sovereignty over the entire peninsula ever since the
state's founding in 1948. For example, the first Supreme
People's Assembly (SPA) elected in 1948 included 360 members
supposedly elected by the constituency south of the 38th
parallel and only 212 members elected from the north. (This
practice was abandoned after the second SPA election held in
1957.) The North Korean position vis-à-vis the South Korean
government has been much more flexible than that of the South
toward the North. On June 19, 1950, just a week before the
outbreak of the Korean war, for example, the SPA sent a message
to the South Korean National Assembly proposing the merger of
the two legislative bodies into a unified legislature.[6] The
North Korean representative at the Geneva Conference of April-
June 1954 also introduced a resolution that referred to "the
Republic of Korea" along with the DPRK. In practice, however,
the leaders of the South have consistently been branded national
traitors by the North, thus rendering meaningless whatever de
facto recognition was given to the ROK.

Thus the 1972 announcement of high-level talks and resultant
agreements raised many thorny and controversial questions in
the ROK National Assembly. Did it mean that the ROK government
was willing to recognize the DPRK de facto? Did it mean that the
government was willing to accept the notion of two Koreas? Did
not CIA Director Yi Hu-rak violate the existing laws? Premier
Kim Chŏng-p'il answered all these questions at the National
Assembly in the negative, but not all his listeners were
convinced. In any event, the nature of questions raised in the
wake of the July 4 announcement showed the magnitude of the step
taken by the North and South Korean leaders in the summer of
1972.

The July 4 announcement was all the more startling because
the initial reaction of the two governments to the U.S.-Chinese
détente was far from one of equanimity, in spite of the opening
of the Red Cross talks. Both states had been unprepared for such
a sharp turnabout in Sino-American relations, and they were far
from being ready to follow the new course.

----

* The only constitutional provisions that reflect the DPRK's
claim to the entire peninsula are Article 7 ("In the areas of
Korea where land reform has not yet been implemented, it will be
carried out on the dates determined by the Supreme People's
Assembly") and Article 103 ("The capital of the DPRK shall be
Seoul").

The North Korean Reaction: A Closer View

Neither the DPRK or the ROK seems to have had an inkling of what
was happening when the American table-tennis team was invited to
China. According to at least one account, the Chinese and North
Korean teams at the Nagoya World Table Tennis Championship
matches were not on very friendly terms. While the Chinese team
refused to play the South Vietnamese and Cambodian teams, it did
play a match against the South Korean team. On the other hand,
the DPRK team played against the very teams the Chinese refused
to compete with. The officials at the championships could not
draw any meaningful conclusions, but they felt that something
was amiss between the North Korean and the Chinese teams.[7] The
North Korean press all but ignored the China visit of the
American team which began on April 10, although the news of the
visit reverberated around the world.

The North Korean reactions to Nixon's announcement of July
15, 1971, in which he indicated his acceptance of Chou's
invitation to visit China, were also very slow in coming. When
they did come, initial reactions were muted, and there were no
signs of approval. Thus, the Nodong Sinmun editorial of July 21,
1971, which expressed the KWP's official policy, warned the
Chinese to maintain "the position of principle" for the sake of
solidifying the unity of international revolutionary forces
because, at that juncture, "the imperialist aggressive forces
headed by American imperialists are carrying out an
antirevolutionary offensive and are engaged in a malicious plot
to internally disintegrate the revolutionary forces."[8] On the
following day, Kim Il-sŏng delivered a fairly long speech at a
banquet given in honor of Prince Sihanouk of Cambodia, who had
arrived just that day from Peking for a three-week visit, but
the premier made no mention of Nixon's announced trip. The most
specfic reference to the Peking-Washington détente in the
premier's speech was his describing the American imperialists'
"conciliatory and deceptive maneuvers to put a noose of
neocolonialism around Cambodia" before they allegedly "concocted
the reactionary coup d'état and following it perpetrated the
burglarous armed invasion" and so on. On the other hand, the
premier's attack on "American imperialists" was as vitriolic as
ever: "The invariable nature of the U.S. imperialists and their
brutal and ferocious true color" were those of "the most heinous
and crafty aggressors and plunderers of the modern times, who
are running riot wielding an olive branch in one hand and a
bayonet in the other."

After thus analyzing the nature of "American imperialists"
and their "uncontrollable serious political and economic crisis"

and "contradictions within the American ruling circles," the premier defined the tasks confronting North Korea and its allies:

"The present time is the time of struggle in which a fierce life-and-death struggle is waged between the new emerging forces including the socialist forces and national liberation movement and the outmoded and moribund imperialist reactionary forces headed by U.S. imperialism. . . . If the peoples of the Asian countries making revolution, with the support of the revolutionary peoples of the world, join in dealing blows at and exerting pressure to bear upon U.S. imperialism, it will be driven out of Asia in the end."[9]

The premier's analysis therefore required continuous struggle on the part of the North Koreans, rather than falling into "the trap of the imperialists' "conciliatory and deceptive maneuvers."

It took the North Korean regime two more weeks to arrive at an official reaction to the Nixon announcement. There is no way of knowing what took place behind the scenes between Peking, Pyongyang, and Moscow during the interval, but obviously, the decision was not an easy one for the leaders in Pyongyang. It is also quite plausible that Prince Sihanouk served as an intermediary between Peking and Pyongyang, as one commentator has suggested,[10] when Sihanouk had been a resident-guest of Peking, he very likely would have been given extensive briefings by the Chinese leaders before his departure for Pyongyang. Since there was a strong possibility that the Peking-Washington détente would adversely affect the fate of Prince Sihanouk himself, there is an equally strong chance that the North Korean leaders listened to what he had to say.

In any event, the North Korean leaders decided that they should not uncritically emulate the Chinese line. While the importance of China as a North Korean ally cannot be minimized,[11] North Korea was not prepared to antagonize the Russians by welcoming the sudden change in the Chinese attitude toward the United States. The North Korean leaders therefore decided to reaffirm their independent stance. Major newspapers of North Korea were caused to publish on August 5 a long article entitled "Let Us Thoroughly Arm Ourselves With the Chuch'e Idea of Our Party," which took up the first three pages of each paper. The basic theme of chuch'e (self-identity and self-reliance) had been expounded time and again since 1955, but the timing and the manner of publication of the article left little doubt about the intent of the leaders. A few paragraphs from the long article will suffice to convey the central message:

"A communist can discharge his duty to the end only by adhering to the independent stand of solving all problems arising in revolution and construction independently and using his own brains. . . .

"Needless to say, revolution in each country develops in relationship with the world revolution and enjoys the support of the international revolutionary forces. . . . But the main thing here is the internal factor and support and encouragement from the outside play no more than secondary role. . . .

"Only when parties of the working class and communists not only creatively apply the Marxist-Leninist theory to the requirements of revolutionary practice from the standpoint of chuch'e but also develop it constantly, can they correctly solve new theoretical and practical problems and lead the revolutionary cause of the working class to victory. . . ."[12]

Having thus set forth the basic line of policy, Premier Kim Il-sŏng articulated the government's attitude toward the Nixon visit at a mass rally held in Pyongyang in honor of Sihanouk on the following day. Basically the position entailed two elements: that Nixon's visit represented a clear victory for the Chinese people and that the imperialists must be decisively overcome. This two-pronged position approved the Chinese invitation to Nixon while insisting on Chinese maintenance of the basic "revolutionary principles." While the premier did not voice any criticism of the Chinese leaders, it is clear that he was not very pleased with the Chinese action either. His misgivings will become clearer if we examine his speech more closely.

Kim Il-sŏng's premise was that American imperialism was confronted with a great crisis, both within and without. A rising antiwar and antigovernment movement, economic stagnation and inflation, increase in unemployment, and a worsening trade balance were noted. Social unrest was increasing and becoming serious, according to Kim Il-sŏng, and contradictions within the ruling strata had reached an extreme. The strategic weaknesses of American imperialism that had dispersed and deployed its aggressive forces around the world were becoming more and more exposed, and competition among imperialist powers for markets and power was sharpening. American imperialism was being defeated repeatedly in Indochina and elsewhere.[13]

What should be done in these circumstances? Kim Il-sŏng's answer was clear:

"The present situation demands that all the revolutionary countries of the world and the peoples of the struggling nations solidly unite, and inflict more forceful blows against the imperialists, who are confused and treading the declining road, so that the last breath of the imperialists be cut off."

There could be no compromise for Kim Il-song:

"The experience of history has shown that the aggressive nature of imperialism does not change even if it has been emasculated. Imperialists would never voluntarily withdraw from their position. The more they are driven to the corner, the more they will cling to the 'two-faced strategy' of waving an olive branch on the one hand and a rifle and sword on the other, presenting the sign board of 'peace' while engaging in aggression and war in a more wily fashion."

Therefore the premier argued again,

". . . we must always heighten our vigilance against the 'two-faced strategy' which is the desperate gasping effort of the enemy, smash any and all of their intrigues, and thoroughly bury the dying imperialism."

The premier then specifically addressed himself to the relationship between the Koreans and the Chinese:

"The Korean and Chinese peoples have always fought shoulder to shoulder in identical steps in their united front against American imperialists and their running dogs, and through actual life, they have experienced that their fate could not be separated. Today, when American imperialism and Japanese militarists have joined together to openly engage in aggression and war, the Korean and Chinese peoples have consolidated all preparations to face jointly as revolutionary comrades and blood brothers any aggression from the enemy just as they had fought together in the same trench and shared life and death, hardship and pleasures, leading to the victory in the past."

The premier recalled that very recently the parties and governments of China and Korea had exchanged delegations and held mass meetings in both capitals and elsewhere to celebrate the tenth anniversary of the treaties of friendship, cooperation, and mutual assistance. Through these events, they had demonstrated to the world the firm determination of the two peoples to "oppose American imperialism and Japanese militarism, to fight together to the end, and win" (emphasis added).

In short, American imperialists were faltering, and hence this was the time to exert more militant pressure. The Chinese had pledged only very recently to fight against the enemy to the end; this pledge should not be broken.

Of course the premier was not opposed to the prevention of war in Asia, reduction of tension, and the attainment of peace. But attainment of peace in Asia did not necessitate compromise by the "revolutionary camp." The premier asserted,

"We argue strongly that in order to prevent war in Asia, eliminate tension, and attain true peace, American imperialist aggressors must withdraw from South Korea, Taiwan, Indochina, Japan, and all areas of Asia in which they have stepped in, stop the maneuver of arming the followers and the puppets to 'Let Asians fight among themselves,' stop the American and Japanese reactionaries' oppression of national liberation struggles of other peoples, stop interference in the domestic politics of other peoples, and let the peoples themselves solve their own problems with their own hands."

In other words, only the complete surrender of the imperialists would bring peace.

Thus the premier was not in a mood to accept with equanimity the trend toward détente. But how should he, his party, and his state react to the announced visit of Nixon? Should the Chinese be denounced as revisionists? Were the Chinese in fact following the Soviet precedent? Or was this simply a tactical move on the part of the Chinese? Undoubtedly, much probing and many deliberations took place behind the scenes. The Chinese must have gone to great lengths to reassure the North Koreans that the Chinese attitude on crucial issues involving the DPRK and other Asian communists had not changed and would remain constant. In any event, the North Korean decision was to endorse the initial moves of the Chinese, interpreting President Nixon's willingness to travel to China as a sign of American defeat. Certainly the fact that the American leader was going to be visiting the Chinese leaders rather than vice versa made it easier for the North Koreans to accept whatever assurances the Chinese provided.

The North Korean leader declared in the presence of Sihanouk that Nixon was going to visit Peking with a white flag just as the American imperialist aggressors had appeared at Panmunjom with a white flag, having been defeated in the Korean war. This

proved to him that the crumbling process of imperialism had
taken place with extraordinary tempo during his lifetime.
Nixon's China visit was not a march of the victor but the trip
of the defeated, and it was a reflection of the fate of American
imperialism, similar to the sun setting behind the western
mountain. This was the great victory of the Chinese people and
of the revolutionary peoples of the world. These statements were
followed by further praises of the Chinese party mixed with
admonitions: that the Chinese Communist party (CCP) and the
Chinese people had a long and glorious tradition of anti-
imperial revolutionary struggle; that they had had abundant
experience of struggle in smashing the enemy's deceiving
strategies with revolutionary principle; that the CCP was a
refined and fortified party; that the People's Republic of China
was the most trustworthy pillar of Asian anti-imperial
revolutionary forces fighting frontally against imperialist
aggression and war policy headed by American imperialism and
standing firmly on the principle of proletarian internationalism;
that the PRC government had proclaimed its intention firmly to
uphold its revolutionary principles without change in the future
and to provide continuous and positive support to the fighting
revolutionary peoples. From these statements, we can surmise the
extent of Chinese concern and the kind of reassurances that the
Chinese had provided the North Koreans.

It should be noted that the two-pronged policy of North Korea
required very few departures by Pyongyang from its previous
stands on the United States and South Korea. Within the framework
of the premier's August 6 statement, North Korea could continue
its unflinching stand against "American imperialism," while
waiting for international events to unfold. Meanwhile North Korea
could contact its two principal allies and other powers concerned,
formulating policies that would be most beneficial to its cause.

Thus, in spite of Peking's muting its attacks on the United
States, the Pyongyang regime continued to issue vitriolic
statements on "American imperialism and the Pak Chŏng-hui clique."
As might be expected, the Nodong Sinmun editorial of August 9,
"Historical Current Cannot Be Countered," was almost a word-for-
word echo of the premier's August 6 speech. The only noticeably
new items in that editorial were the mention of Stalin (twice) in
an analogy between President Nixon's proposed visit and American
recognition of the Soviet Union in 1933, insistence on the
alleged American effort to renew the aggressive war in Korea, and
a call for heightening "revolutionary vigilance to counter any
provocations of the enemy." The evidence provided for the
American war aim was the importation of a great quantity

of armaments into South Korea, completion of an
air and water transportation system, strengthening and
modernization of the South Korean army, and the continued
military provocations against the North. On August 15, on the
anniversary of national liberation, the same organ repeated the
call for the withdrawal of foreign (American) troops from Korea
and the unification of Korea by the Koreans themselves according
to "democratic principles." At the same time, the editorial
again denounced American imperialism and the "Pak Chŏng-hui
clique" by saying that "whatever methods they use, American
imperialism and its running dog, the Pak Chŏng-hui clique,
cannot block the future of the Korean people in their efforts
for independent and peaceful unification." Similar but even
stronger language was used against the two archenemies by the
same paper on August 26 and 27. On September 9, First Vice-
Premier Kim Il delivered a major speech commemorating the
twenty-third anniversary of the founding of the DPRK, but there
was no sign of letup in the rhetorical attack. American
imperialism was still the prime enemy of the South Korean
revolution, and Kim Il still called for an anti-imperialist and
anti-American united front of Korea, China, Vietnam, and other
Asian peoples.[14]

There was a familiar ring to the North Korean public
pronouncements at this point. One recalls similar statements
directed against Premier Khrushchev in the 1961-1962 period:
praise mixed with a strong admonition to treat "American
imperialism" with the utmost seriousness and severity. At the
same time, whatever the course of future international relations,
Pyongyang must regard the present era with uncertainty and some
trepidation, given the recent history of its relations with both
Moscow and Peking. Big-power diplomacy, communist or
noncommunist, evokes unpleasant images. This was one reason why
Washington and Peking publicly announced that they would
restrict discussions during President Nixon's visit to matters
concerned with their bilateral relations.

The DPRK and the People's Republic of China. As we have seen,
the Chinese leaders clearly perceived the need to allay the
suspicions and misgivings of the Korean communists and went to
great lengths to reassure the North Koreans about the essential
consistency of Chinese policy. The Chinese were not prepared to
let Sino-Korean relations revert to the low ebb of the pre-April
1970 period. Thus, the New China News Agency and Radio Peking
reported the full text of Premier Kim Il-sŏng's August 6 speech
on the following day and during the month of August no fewer

than three substantial North Korean delegations were welcomed in China. An economic delegation headed by Vice-Premier Chŏng Chun-t'aek visited Peking between August 8 and 16 and signed an agreement on economic cooperation on August 15, "with a view to further strengthening the militant friendship sealed in blood between the peoples of China and Korea and continuously developing the relations of mutual aid and cooperation."[15] At a banquet given in honor of the Koreans, Chinese Vice-Premier Li Hsien-nien assured the Koreans that "the Chinese people will always unite with the fraternal Korean people, the three peoples of Indochina, and the people of other Asian countries and fight to the end to completely smash the schemes of aggression of the United States and Japanese reactionaries." The Chinese must have been satisfied to hear Chŏng Chun-t'aek say on August 16, at another banquet,

"We have gained a clear understanding of the firm stand and strong determination of the Government of the People's Republic of China and the Chinese people to uphold the revolutionary principles in the struggle against imperialism and U.S. imperialism and actively support the people of the world in their struggle for freedom, liberation, national independence and socialism (emphasis added)."[16]

The economic delegation was followed by a delegation of Korean journalists led by the director of the Korean Central News Agency. Finally, on August 18 a military delegation headed by the North Korean chief of staff and Politburo member, O Chin-u, and including the commander of the North Korean air force arrived in China and was given a royal welcome, including tours, mass rallies, receptions, and banquets. The Chinese were effusive in praising the North Koreans, attacking the American imperialists and Japanese militarists, and pledging support for the DPRK position on unification and other matters.[17] On September 7 Huang Yung-sheng, chief of the general staff of the Chinese People's Liberation Army, and O Chin-u signed an agreement in Peking whereby the PRC agreed to provide the DPRK with "military aid gratis."[18]

The Chinese pursuit of North Korean friendship did not stop there. On September 9, on the occasion of the twenty-third anniversary of the founding of the DPRK, Jenmin Jihpao [People's Daily] printed a long editorial entitled "The Korean People Advance With Great Strides on the Road of Victory," extending the "warmest festive congratulations and the highest military salute." Full-column articles on Korea were published, and

celebration meetings were held in a commune near Peking and in
various plants in Shanghai. What must have been most reassuring
to the North Korean leadership, however, were such paragraphs as
the following in the Jenmin Jihpao editorial:

"Pounded heavily by the revolutionary struggles of the people of
various countries, the Nixon administration is beset with
difficulties at home and abroad and finds itself in a
predicament. . . .

"The Chinese people will, as always, resolutely support the
Korean people in their struggle against aggression by U.S.
imperialism and Japanese militarism and for the unification of
their fatherland, and will unite firmly together with the Korean
people in the joint struggle to defeat the U.S. aggressors and
all their running dogs."

One could argue, of course, that the Chinese would have
issued statements antagonistic to the Nixon administration in
any event and that they would have courted the friendship and
support of the DPRK in the late summer of 1971 even if Premier
Kim Il-sŏng had not taken the stand he had taken. But it is
probably more accurate to say that the Chinese leaders were
surprised by the unflinching stance of North Korea and quickly
moved to allay the fears and misgivings of an ally who could
become a source of international embarrassment, which in turn
might even affect the delicate power balance within the Chinese
leadership. It is plausible to argue also that the unstable
power relationship among the Chinese leaders as well as the
delicate position of North Korea in the Sino-Soviet conflict
allowed North Korea to exert more influence on the Chinese than
its size and strength would indicate. All this, of course, would
"prove" the intensity of the desire of certain Chinese leaders
to bring the Sino-American détente to fruition.
    The amicable relationship between the PRC and the DPRK
continued in the subsequent months. Exchange of cultural,
women's, sports, and youth groups continued, and in October 1972
the two regimes signed an agreement on a Sino-Korean geological
survey and economic and technical cooperation.[19] In late October
Premier Kim Il-sŏng was reported to have paid an unofficial one-
day visit to Peking.[20] In December 1972, Chinese Foreign
Minister Chi Pen-fei visited Pyongyang to solidify the
friendship, and in February 1973 the North Korean foreign
minister, Hŏ Tam, paid a return visit.

Gradual Change in the North Korean Stance. Meanwhile, the North
Korean leaders continued to study the alternatives open to them.
The intensive contacts with the Chinese leadership evidently had
some effect on the North Koreans, who began to see certain
advantages in the moderating international environment. By
September 25, when the premier granted an interview to Motoo
Gotō, the managing editor of Asahi Shimbun, at least one major
decision had been made. When he was asked for his opinions on
the changing international situation as it affected Asia, Kim
Il-sŏng replied that "as a result of the China visit by
President Nixon, the international situation will move in the
direction of easing tensions, albeit temporarily." He also
stated that easing of tensions is a good thing, and that "when
the trend is toward the easing of tensions, [he had] no
intentions of pursuing policies which go against the current
situation." He added that "in line with such a situation, we are
presently studying foreign policy with comrades."
    This did not mean, however, that North Korea was going to
follow the Chinese line automatically. Kim Il-sŏng added, "How
U.S.-China relations will change has no direct relation to us"
and "We intend to see what attitude the United States takes
toward us." To his mind, it was "important that American troops
should be withdrawn from South Korea. No matter what the
relations between the U.S. and China are, we cannot be friendly
with the United States. We will consider an independent foreign
policy without any relation to U.S.-China ties and other Asian
policies of the United States."[21]
    An interesting aspect of this important interview is that the
text of the interview was not released to the North Korean mass
media. The text can be found neither in the party's daily organ,
Nodong Sinmun [Workers' Daily], nor in its monthly organ Kŭlloja
[The Worker], which normally publish important pronouncements
and speeches of the premier. The readers of these publications
could not know that a major shift in foreign policy had taken
place at the highest level. Thus on October 4, Mme. Kim Il-sŏng
(Kim Sŏng-ae), head of the Korean Women's General League,
denounced "fascist warmonger-madman Nixon, who is pretending to
have abandoned the policy of aggression and war by howling about
the transition from the age of confrontation to the age of
negotiation." She declared that this was nothing but an
atrocious and sly intrigue to implement the ambition to commit
aggression against nations more effectively.[22] On December 10,
Yŏm T'ae-jun, the head of the Korean General Federation of Trade
Unions, also called for "more intensified struggle of the Asian

nations engaged in revolution and their peoples against American
imperialists who are in confusion and declining in power."23 In
the same speech, Yŏm alluded to the "recovery of its legal
position by the PRC at the United Nations," calling it evidence
of the might of the PRC and its heightened international status,
but he made no mention of the Nixon trip. In fact, North Korean
publications made no reference of the trip after Mme. Kim Il-
sŏng's speech of October.

The new year did not bring any noticeable change in the North
Korean attitude as far as the United States was concerned. The
New Year's speech of the premier spoke of the victory of the
revolutionary peoples of Asia in their fight against American
imperialism and Japanese militarism, the stagnation of the Nixon
Doctrine as a result of "firm solidarity in the anti-imperial
and anti-American struggle of our people and the people of China,
Indochina, Japan, and elsewhere in Asia" and the "heightening of
the international position of the Chinese People's Republic
which is our fraternal ally." Attacks agaīnt the "reactionaries,"
"military gangsters," "the South Korean puppet clique," and so on,
were as vitriolic as ever, and "the signboard of peace hoisted by
American imperialism" was still denounced as "a smoke screen to
deceive the people." President Nixon was denounced as "the most
heinous and sly rascal." The premier pledged that North Korea
would "solidly unite with the Chinese, Indochinese, Japanese, and
other Asian peoples to deploy a strong united struggle against
the American and Japanese imperialists and their running dogs."
January 11 in his response to questions asked by the reporters
of the Tokyo newspaper Yomiuri Shimbun. In the widely publicized
statement, Kim reaffirmed the unchanged evil, aggressive, and
sly nature of American imperialism, stressed the need to
heighten vigilance against its aggression and provocations of
war, and called for more intensive struggle against it.24

The North Korean Proposal to South Korea

In contrast to his continued hard line toward the United States,
Kim Il-sŏng's answers to queries from the Yomiuri reporters
contained a proposal made to the South Korean government which
can be interpreted as an indication of the second shift in North
Korean policy. What was needed to reduce the tension in Korea,
the premier argued, was to "change the truce agreement into a
peace treaty." Further, the premier argued that "on the condition
that American imperialist aggressive forces have been withdrawn
from South Korea," armed forces in North and South Korea should
be greatly reduced. Also, in order to intensify contacts and
ties and to solve the problem of uniting the fatherland,

political talks should be initiated. He also reiterated the
North Korean willingness to talk to any political party or
individuals from South Korea concerning matters related to
unification. (He had presented this last point in his speech of
August 6, 1971.)

The Nodong Sinmun editorial of January 18 was exclusively
devoted to Kim Il-sŏng's proposal to South Korea. It is
significant that the North Korean premier revealed two important
shifts in North Korean policies in his answers to queries from
Japanese reporters. Clearly, North Korea was aiming at wider
international publicity, hoping to place South Korea on the
defensive.

North Korea and Japan. Indeed, there were signs that North Korea
decided to capitalize on the new atmosphere to bring about a
change in the Japanese attitude toward the Korean problem. It is
quite possible that, in the course of the numerous, lengthy
discussions between key Chinese and North Korean officials that
took place in both Peking and Pyongyang, mutually agreed-upon,
coordinated approaches had been effected, particularly with
respect to policies toward Japan. At the beginning of 1972 an
intensified North Korean campaign was launched to change past
Japanese official policies and expand Japan-DPRK relations
without sacrificing any basic North Korean positions.

Thus, Pyongyang hailed the creation of a Japanese League for
the Promotion of Japanese-Korean Friendship, a group claiming to
have a roster of 234 upper-and lower-house members, with Chūji
Kuno, a Liberal Democratic party man, as provisional chairman.
In late January 1972 a delegation from this group, headed by
Kuno, visited North Korea, and on January 23 a trade agreement
was signed by this group and the North Korean Committee for the
Promotion of International Trade. An economic link similar in
type to that existing between the People's Republic of China and
Japan had been fashioned. A month later, moreover, it was
announced that a Korea-Japan Export and Import Corporation would
soon be established to, facilitate trade and economic intercourse.
Negotiations proceeded briskly, and the amount of trade in 1972
reached $140 million, approximately 90 percent more than that of
the previous year, and trade in 1973 was $172 million, an
increase of 23 percent over that of 1972.[25]   Export items
to North Korea included a urea fertilizer plant, an ammonia
plant, dump trucks and passenger automobiles, thermal and
steam power generators, passenger and freight cars, refrigeration
and dehydration facilities for marine products, animal-feed
plants, television and radio plants, hosiery plants, and

ball-point-pen plants.

Obviously, the importation of these items will have a great
impact on the North Korean economy, and North Korea is
understandably eager to increase the rate of import from Japan.
Had the South Korean government not exerted strong pressures
upon some of the major Japanese industrial firms, the growth
rate of Japan-North Korean trade would have been much higher.
The Mitsubishi Company, the giant Japanese industrial-economic
combine, for example, stopped negotiations with North Korea on
the export of cement and steel plants, both to accomodate the
desires of the South Korean government and because of
nonavailability of credit from the Export-Import Bank in
December 1972. Citing Mitsubishi's trade record with the PRC and
recalling a statement of a high official of the Mitsubishi
combine that "even if we miss the [China] bus now, we can always
catch up with it in a jet," a Japanese reporter predicted that
improvement of the political atmosphere would quickly reverse
the situation.[26]

The visit of the Diet members, accompanied by a large retinue
of newspaper, radio, and television reporters, clearly carried
with it the imagery of the forthcoming Nixon trip to China. In
addition, in February the North Koreans had their Olympic team
meet with such sympathetic Japanese visitors as Mayor Ryokichi
Minobe of Tokyo, various important figures of the media, and
other prominent Japanese. This was "Ping-Pong diplomacy," North
Korean style. The Japanese government later announced that it
was seriously considering the issuance of visas to North Korean
dancing troupes and economic missions, although in May the
Japanese government denied a visa to Kang Ryang-uk, vice-
chairman of the Presidium of the Supreme People's Assembly, who
had been invited by Mayor Minobe.[27]

Via the Japanese mass media, the North Korean premier also
launched a diplomatic offensive aiming at the "normalization" of
relations with Japan. In response to questions submitted by
Yomiuri Shimbun, Kim Il-sŏng asserted that "the poor relations
between Japan and [North] Korea represent a very abnormal
situation," the responsibility for which rested entirely with
the Japanese government. "We have always wanted close ties," he
stated. What was required to achieve these? The Japanese
government should abandon its hostile policies toward the DPRK,
abrogate the South Korea-Japan treaty of 1965, stop "reinvading"
South Korea, and "renounce the foolish act of trying to make
Koreans fight Koreans by instigating the South Korean puppets."

Fortunately, in Kim's view, "an extensive campaign" was
under way among Japanese progressive circles for the

establishment of good-neighbor relations. "If the Korean and
Japanese people jointly struggle," he asserted, "diplomatic
relations between our two countries will be possible. Meanwhile,
we are ready to have more visits of personages as far as
possible and to undertake wide-scale trade and intercourse in
the economic and cultural fields."

At the same time, Kim made it clear that North Korea intended
to abandon none of its basic positions on current issues. For
example, the struggle to enable Koreans living in Japan to have
a "national education" taught in the Korean language by
(communist) Koreans, funded from Pyongyang, and separate from
Japanese training would continue. Also, Pyongyang would
vigorously oppose "the immoral policy" of forcing Korean
residents in Japan to apply for "permanent residence" status and
accept Republic of Korea nationality. "But," added Kim, "even if
they accept ROK nationality, they will give active support to
the DPRK just as the South Korean people unanimously support us
today."

Because of these policies and others, the government of Prime
Minister Satō continued to come under Kim's savage attack. Only
a few Asians like Satō were "stupid" enough to support the Nixon
Doctrine, Kim proclaimed. And in a broader vein he alleged,
"Under American aegis, the Japanese militarists have turned into
dangerous forces of aggression in Asia with the backing of
American imperialism. This is a hard fact." Japanese
"militarists" were "invading other countries, subordinating them
economically and through intensified ideological and cultural
infiltration."

The central objective was to establish an economic and
cultural beachhead in Japan, penetrating Japanese domestic
politics, building a united front against the "reactionaries,"
and at the same time creating tensions between Japan and the
South Korean government. This diplomatic offensive showed some
definite parallels with the new Chinese foreign policy and
caused a mixture of interest, uncertainty, and apprehension in
official Japanese circles. It has continued to have considerable
impact on Japanese political leaders. While it would have been
unthinkable for Japanese to talk about the "normalization" of
relations with North Korea even as late as 1970, the possibility
of such a development is no longer remote. On September 7, 1972,
the North Koreans exerted further pressure on the Japanese
government by easing the conditions for the normalization of the
Japanese-North Korean relationship. Second Vice-Premier Pak
Sŏng-ch'ŏl told visiting Japanese reporters that the new
Japanese government under Prime Minister Tanaka should cease the

past policy of hostility toward North Korea and establish a
policy of treating the two Koreas on equal terms. He withdrew
the previous condition that Japan abrogate the 1965 treaty with
the ROK and emphasized that there are many nations maintaining
relationships with both Koreas.[28] The shift in the North Korean
line was duly noted by the Japanese government, which was not,
however, willing to jeopardize the relationship with the ROK
government by responding favorably to the North Korean overture.

North Korea in Search of Wider International Support. The
diplomatic and propaganda offensive against Japan was
accompanied by massive diplomatic overtures to communist nations
and other selected nations in the Middle East and Africa. Thus,
a delegation headed by the Second Vice-Premier Pak Sŏng-ch'ŏl
visited Cuba, Poland, and Hungary between February 10 and March
2, 1972. Foreign Minister Hŏ Tam's delegation also left
Pyongyang on February 10 to visit Rumania, Czechoslovakia, and
East Germany before arriving in Moscow on February 22. He
returned to Pyongyang on March 2 after paying a short visit to
Yugoslavia, the first high-level visit to that country from the
DPRK. (The DPRK and Yugoslavia had agreed to exchange
ambassadorial missions in September 1971.) A third delegation,
headed by Vice-Premier Chŏng Chun-t'aek, visited the Sudan,
Syria, Iraq, Egypt, and Bulgaria, and a fourth group, headed by
the vice-chairman of the Presidium of the Supreme People's
Assembly, Kang Ryang-uk, visited Mali, Kenya, Sierra Leone,
Mauritania, and Mongolia. A fifth group, led by Finance Minister
Kim Kyŏng-ryŏn, visited Yemen, Somalia, Tanzania, Burundi, and
Zambia. A sixth group, under Vice-Minister of Foreign Affairs
Kim Yŏng-t'aek, visited Burma, Indonesia (for ten days), and
Singapore. A seventh delegation, under the chairman of the
Central Broadcasting Commission, consisted of parliamentarians
(members of the Supreme People's Assembly) who visited Finland
and Sweden.
    From the joint communiqués and "joint informations" issued at
the end of these visits, one can surmise the general intent
behind the massive offensive. One common element in all joint
pronouncements was a paragraph that can be found in the
communiqué issued in Moscow:

"The Soviet side again declared the Soviet Union's complete
support for the policy pursued by the DPRK to attain Korea's
peaceful unification by the Korean people themselves on a
democratic basis and without any outside interferences after
making the troops of the U.S. aggressors withdraw from South

Korea. The Soviet Union expressed full support for and
solidarity with the new constructive proposals of the DPRK
Government aimed at eliminating tensions in Korea, including the
proposals for the signing of a peace treaty and the holding of
political talks between North and South Korea."[29]

Thus, the North Korean delegations appear to have been
dispatched to explain the new line of policy first announced to
the Yomiuri reporters on January 11. The North Koreans were
clearly intent on creating a peaceful image abroad and on
enlisting the support of their East European allies and some of
the neutralist countries in implementing the new course. It is
significant that Indonesia was included in the itinerary of one
of the delegations, for the relationship between Indonesia and
the DPRK had been virtually terminated in 1966. It is also
noteworthy that Albania, the closest ally of the Chinese
People's Republic in Eastern Europe, was omitted from the list.

The DPRK maintained diplomatic relations with most of the
countries to which the delegations were dispatched, and hence
one could ask why such missions were necessary. Could not
ordinary diplomatic channels have been used if all that was
involved was to explain the newly adopted policy? Perhaps the
answer can be found in the magnitude of the policy change. As
indicated earlier, North Korea had pursued a belligerent course
against the South, sending out armed guerrillas and
assassination teams and calling for revolts. North Korean-
trained guerrillas turned up in Mexico, Ceylon, and other
places, creating a distinctive image of North Korea as the most
radical nation in the world. North Korea also had joined the
Chinese in vehemently attacking various communist countries as
revisionists, thereby alienating most of them. Therefore, it
would have required much more than a diplomatic note from the
ambassadors-in-residence to convince foreign nations that North
Korea was indeed altering its stance toward South Korea and that
Pyongyang wanted to join the broader community of nations. It is
also quite probable that the North Korean delegations strove to
explain the "independent" character of the DPRK's new policy by
differentiating it from that pursued by the Chinese. The
sympathy and support of communist and other nations appeared to
the DPRK to be essential particularly because, in the wake of
the PRC's victory at the United Nations, the Korean communists
began to see the utility of United Nations membership in
heightening their international prestige and in broadening
contacts abroad.

It was not surprising, therefore, that the North Korean
regime contacted United Nations Secretary-General Kurt Waldheim

in late March while he was in Vienna, asking him to serve as a
secret intermediary in their dealings with South Korea.
According to Waldheim's subsequent disclosures, the North Korean
delegates passed on to him their positions on the various
issues, reviewed the contacts they had already had with South
Korea, and made a number of suggestions. These suggestions,
according to Waldheim, were passed on to South Korea.[30] It is
reasonable to assume that the North Korean delegates stressed
Kim Il-sŏng's January 11 statement regarding a peace treaty
between the two Koreas as well as the need for political talks.
The use of the secretary-general as an intermediary was an
excellent maneuver for North Korea in that it could serve as an
indication of North Korea's conciliatory attitude toward the
United Nations, while at the same time placing South Korea on
the defensive. By involving the secretary-general, the North
Korean regime also underscored the seriousness of its desire to
deal with the South Koreans.

North Korea's diplomatic offensive produced excellent results.
In March 1973 five Scandinavian countries decided to recognize
and establish diplomatic relations with the DPRK. On April 28
the International Parliamentary Union admitted the DPRK by a
vote of 57 to 28 with 20 abstentions. On May 17 the DPRK was
accepted as a member of the World Health Organization by a vote
of 66 to 41 with 22 abstentions. These developments measurably
increased the DPRK's position in the international arena.

North Korea and the Soviet Union. But were these diplomatic
missions simply aimed at explaining the new North Korean
position and winning the sympathy of other countries? The fact
that Albania was excluded from the thirty-nation itinerary
certainly justifies a suspicion that there was an ulterior
motive. Foreign Minister Hŏ Tam's visit to the Soviet Union in
February precisely coincided with President Nixon's visit to
Peking. Was this merely a coincidence? Or was this a subtle
North Korean warning to the Chinese not to push matters too far
too fast lest they lose the support of the DPRK? Or was this an
attempt on the Soviets' part to lure the North Koreans away from
the Chinese side? These questions come to mind particularly in
view of the Soviet hostility toward the Nixon visit to Peking.[31]

The fact that Hŏ Tam discussed the Nixon visit with Brezhnev,
Gromyko, and others is clear from the joint communiqué issued on
February 26. The communiqué said, among other things, that

"during the talks, which passed in the atmosphere of mutual
understanding and cordial friendship, the two sides discussed

the questions of bilateral relations between the USSR and DPRK
and had an exchange of views on a number of topical
international problems."

The two sides also

"noted with satisfaction that Korean-Soviet relations have
steadily been developed and strengthened on the basis of the
treaty of friendship, cooperation, and mutual assistance. They
reaffirmed their intentions to exert unceasingly all efforts to
further expand and strengthen the fraternal friendship and all-
around cooperation between the DPRK and the Soviet Union in the
political, economic, scientific, technical, cultural and other
fields on the basis of the principles of Marxism-Leninism and
proletarian internationalism."

Concerning "a series of urgent international problems," the
communique said:

"The two sides confirmed their strong resolve to continue
struggling consistently to strengthen unity and increase the
might of the socialist countries, to insure the stable peace and
security in Asia, Europe, and other areas of the world, and to
oppose imperialism, colonialism, and neocolonialism."[32]

Whatever hint the North Koreans intended to give Peking by
the timing of Hŏ Tam's Moscow visit, it is clear from the
communiqué that North Korea was following an independent course.
While the PRC was still feuding with Moscow on a variety of
points, Pyongyang was promising to "exert unceasingly all
efforts to further expand and strengthen the fraternal friendship
and all-around cooperation." While the DPRK was not in full
agreement with the Soviet Union, it was strongly resolved to
"continue struggling consistently to strengthen unity" on a
series of urgent international problems.
If one reflects on the past relationship between the DPRK and
the Soviet Union, the content of the communiqué itself does not
come as a surprise. Even while North Korea was involved in harsh
polemics directed against the Soviet Union between 1962 and 1965,
trade between the two countries steadily increased, although
Soviet imports from North Korea decreased slightly between 1963
and 1964.[33] After the political demise of Khrushchev in late
1964, however, the North Koreans began to veer away from the
Chinese, and the relationship with the Soviets was "normalized."
The new leaders in the Soviet Union were more conciliatory

toward the Koreans, as evidenced by Kosygin's Pyongyang visit of
February 1965. While the Soviet Union needed to win friends and
neutralize enemies, the Koreans needed parts, replacements, and
supplies in both the economic and the military fields. The North
Koreans were also concerned that year about the establishment of
formal ties between the ROK and Japan, which opened up enormous
possibilities of economic development for South Korea, as well
as about the escalation of the war in Indochina. Because of the
escalation, the North Korean leaders could not rule out the
possibility of again engaging the Americans and South Koreans in
a costly war, and therefore reconciliation with the Russians
became absolutely essential.[34] Only the Russians could supply
the advanced modern weapons North Korea needed.

After the Kosygin visit the Soviet Union quickly resumed the
supply of military and economic aid. Thus Moscow Radio reported
on March 31, 1965, that an agreement had been signed between the
USSR and the DPRK which "provided assistance for the further
strengthening of the defensive potential of the DPRK."[35] In June
1966 the Russians agreed to assist North Korea in enlarging an
iron and steel mill and in building a thermal power station, an
oil refinery, and other industrial installations. The Soviet
Union also announced at the same time its decision to
"considerably increase" Soviet-North Korean trade during 1967-
1970.[36] This promise was kept, and Soviet exports to North Korea
more than tripled between 1967 and 1971, increasing from 99.3
million rubles in 1967 to 207.0 million rubles in 1970, and to
330.1 million rubles in 1971. Meanwhile, Soviet imports from
North Korea increased more slowly, from 97.2 million rubles in
1967 to 128.9 million rubles in 1970. (This last total was
adjusted in 1971 to 122.3 million rubles). Imports declined
slightly in 1971 to 122.2 million rubles. One must assume that
the discrepancies between exports and imports are covered by the
long-term, low-interest loans from the Soviet Union (normally
covering twelve years at an interest of 2 percent per annum. The
sharpest increase in Soviet exports was shown in the category of
machinery and equipment, which rose from 16.9 million rubles in
1967 to 42.5 million rubles in 1968, 89.4 million rubles in 1970,
and to 100.4 million rubles in 1971,* indicating the economic
priorities established by the North Korean leadership.

----

* It should be noted, however, that Soviet exports of "machinery
and equipment" in 1965 and 1966 were higher than in 1967: in 1965,
this category totaled 26.2 million rubles and in 1966, 26.5
million rubles (Radio Moscow, March 31, 1965, cited in R. O.

A Soviet commentator asserted in December 1971, "At present, some thirty large industrial projects and other projects are under construction in the DPRK with Soviet assistance. Among them are new workshops at the Kim Ch'aek steel mill, one of the biggest industrial plants in the DPRK, a big oil refinery at Unggi, and the second stage of the construction project at the Pukch'ŏng thermopower plant."*

Freedman, Economic Warfare, pp. 142-147). The data on 1970 are drawn from Vneshniaia Torgovlia SSSR za 1970 (Moscow: Mezhdunarodnye Otnosheniia, 1971), p. 235, and for 1971, ibid., 1972 edition, pp. 248 and 251. The 1971 edition changed the category "machinery and equipment" to include "means of transportation." With the new classification, the figure for 1970 was revised to 90.0 million rubles, an increase of 618,000 rubles.

* Nikolayev, "The Ties of Fraternal Friendship and Cooperation Between the USSR and the DPRK," Moscow Radio (in Korean), Dec. 13, 1971. Nikolayev's commentary of August 13, 1971, was more revealing of the then current Soviet attitude toward the DPRK. The Russians were undoubtedly aware that the North Korean regime had been playing down the role of the Soviet Union in the liberation of Korea during the last decade, and, most likely, this had irritated them. In any event, Nikolayev declared on the eve of the 26th anniversary of Korea's liberation that "the liberation was brought to Korea by the heroic Soviet soldiers and the daring Korean patriots who fought alongside them. Twenty-six years have passed since then. Those who visit Pyongyang can never fail to notice two monuments standing tall in Moranbong. One of them was erected immediately after the liberation of Korea. Inscribed in gold thereon are the following words of appreciation in both Korean and Russian: 'Everlasting glory to the Soviet soldiers who liberated the Korean people.'"
  In the same commentary, Nikolayev emphasized the role of Soviet economic assistance in the development of the North Korean economy. He said: "For example, over 50 major industrial establishments have been built in people's Korea with Soviet technical assistance since the liberation. Over 20 large enterprises, including power plants, collieries, and textile mills, currently under construction with the participation of Soviet technical personnel, will go into operation before long. Among these are new facilities at the Ch'ŏng-jin steel works, the

It seems probable that the détente between Peking and
Washington increased North Korea's bargaining power in Moscow.
Thus Moscow Radio on December 3, 1971 (broadcasting in Korean to
Korea) reported that "the USSR and the DPRK have reaffirmed
their desires to further promote their economic cooperation on
the basis of fraternal assistance" and that the conference of
the USSR-DPRK Commission on Economic, Scientific, and
Technological Affairs would discuss matters of Soviet assistance
to the DPRK in building industrial projects. It added that
twenty-eight industrial plants were scheduled to be built in the
DPRK with Soviet assistance over a period of five years from
1971 through 1975. Sino-Soviet competition was continuing.*

Thus, in the interest of drawing the DPRK closer to their
side in the Sino-Soviet dispute, the Soviets increased their aid
to and trade with the DPRK. The DPRK, on the other hand, began
in 1965 to modify its stance against "revisionism," calling
instead for a broad united front of the socialist nations
against "American imperialism" in southeast Asia. Unlike the
Chinese in their relations with the Soviet Union, the North
Koreans were willing to bury the hatchet, at least temporarily,
for the sake of attaining the common goal of defeating the
Americans in Indochina as well as of modernizing their armaments
and industries. However, North Korea could never return to the
days before 1956 when it "leaned on" the Soviet Union. It

----

first petroleum-processing plant of the DPRK at Unggi, and the
Pyongyang battery factory. In the past few years alone, the
volume of trade between the two countries has roughly doubled.
Taking into account the needs of the rapidly developing economy
of fraternal Korea, the Soviet Union is presently supplying
completed goods and raw materials needed by the republic. The
Soviet Union exports, for instance, precision gauges, complex
equipment, and coke, which is vitally necessary for the
metallurgical industry." In light of this comment, it is
noteworthy that both the Western and Japanese reporters visiting
North Korean plants are constantly told that all the machinery
was built in Korea.

* On May 25, 1972, a South Korean news agency, Haptong T'ongshin,
citing "military sources," reported that the North Koreans
reinforced their armament with "Frog 7" ground-to-ground missiles,
with a maximum firing range of 40 kilometers, and T-55 tanks
equipped with cannons of more than 100 mm, all from the Soviet
Union. Since North Korea has been receiving arms from the Soviet
Union for a long time, one cannot attribute any particular
political significance to this report.

insisted upon a new relationship based on "complete
independence," equality, and the mutual interest of both parties
and permitting disagreement on a wide range of fundamental
questions. Soviet-Korean relations were no longer based on
implicit trust and effusive sentiments, and one could detect
elements of volatility, uncertainty, and precariousness. Except
during the period of the Cultural Revolution, furthermore, the
North Korean leaders consistently manifested their affinity with
the Chinese on many fundamental issues that divided the
international communist camp, while the post-1965 Soviet-Korean
relationship was based more on pragmatic interests. Therefore,
there is a strong chance that Moscow requested that Hŏ Tam's
visit coincide with Nixon's visit to Peking in order to diminish,
by whatever small portion, the luster of Peking's coup in
establishing a "normal" relationship with the United States. For
their own part, the leaders of the DPRK may have found it
congenial to schedule Hŏ Tam's visit at that time to reassert
their independence in foreign policy, which could serve as a
subtle warning to the PRC.

North Korea and the Nixon Visit. The supposition that the DPRK
had misgivings about the Washington-Peking détente up to the
minute of Nixon's arrival in Peking is supported in part by the
DPRK's coolness toward the historic journey. On February 11,
ten days before Nixon's arrival in Peking, Pyongyang Radio
scored President Nixon's foreign-policy message:

"Nixon, the notorious boss of war, submitted to Congress on
February 9 a 'foreign policy message' giving an outline of the
direction of this year's aggressive foreign policy of U.S.
imperialism. . . . Nixon the rascal revealed to the full the
invariable insidious intention of U.S. imperialism to reverse
by 'strength' behind the smokescreen of 'peace' the trend of the
time developing to its disadvantage in Asia and the rest of the
world. . . .

"Nixon, the crafty and sly rascal, croaked in the 'message' that
1972 will be a so-called watershed towards peace and blew the
trumpet that the United States will maintain 'balance of forces'
with big countries to build an edifice of peace and strengthen
'cooperative relations' with the 'allies,' opening a 'new page
of history.'

"The outbursts of Nixon the rascal on the so-called 'balance of
forces' and 'cooperative relations' showed in all its nakedness
the sinister scheme of his clique to shun confrontation with the
big countries and seek temporary 'reconciliation' with them and

to destroy one by one small and divided revolutionary socialist
countries and national liberation forces by whipping together
all the imperialist aggressor forces and reactionary forces
bound to the war chariot of U.S. imperialism."

The broadcast concluded by repeating North Korea's warning to
China:

"Nixon's 'foreign policy message' enables the world
revolutionary people to clearly see through the aggressive
nature of U.S. imperialism wearing the mask of 'peace' and
demands of them to vehemently smash all the schemes of U.S.
imperialism through an uncompromising, staunch struggle, not
harbouring any illusion about it."[37]

On the day of Nixon's arrival in Peking on February 21, on
the same day that Premier Chou En-lai was host to Nixon at a
banquet and told the audience, "I have the pleasure on behalf of
Chairman Mao Tse-tung and the Chinese government to extend our
welcome to President Nixon," Pyongyang Radio released another
blast to the effect that "Nixon, the boss of the U.S.
imperialists, had to take his scheduled trip abroad, holding a
white flag. . . . The fact that Nixon once again has been
humiliated on the way to his pilgrimage is really spectacular."
Nixon allegedly "stopped over in Hawaii on his way to Peking and
issued an order not to receive any telephone calls while staying
at a villa overlooking the Pacific Ocean, taking a rest alone to
ease his headache. . . ." The conclusion was clear to the
commentator:

"The blow Nixon sustained this time nakedly reveals the pitiful
situation of the U.S. imperialists, who have been beaten from
within and without and are tightly cornered. What is clear right
here is that there is only one way—the road of ruin destined by
the trend of history—which the U.S. imperialists can follow, no
matter how they reveal their deceptive peace strategy."[38]

With this blast, the mass media in North Korea fell silent
about President Nixon's visit. On February 28 Pyongyang Radio
dutifully transmitted without comment a report from the New
China News Agency concerning the joint communique issued on the
same day in Shanghai, but this was followed by two more barrages
against "Nixon, the war chieftain of U.S. imperialism," on the
following day.[39]

Pyongyang's official reaction to the Shanghai communiqué was

made known on March 4, in the form of an editorial in <u>Nodong</u>
<u>Sinmun</u>. Read against the background of North Korea's previous
statements, the editorial reveals a sense of relief that the
Chinese had not abandoned "revolutionary principles" as well as
revealing North Korea's decision to moderate its future policies
in accordance with the guidelines set forth in the Shanghai
communiqué. Contrary to Kim Il-sŏng's August 6 speech, the
editorial did not raise the cry to "heighten vigilance" against
the imperialists' intrigues nor did it demand that the "last
breath of the imperialists be cut off." President Nixon was no
longer depicted as "the most heinous and sly rascal," although
North Korea was not yet ready to absolve U.S. imperialism of the
sin of aggression.

The Shanghai communiqué revealed signs of Chinese sensitivity
to North Korea's anxieties, and for this the North Koreans
openly expressed their gratitude to the Chinese. Thus the
editorial commented,

"Especially in the communiqué China resolutely supported again
the 8-point program for the peaceful reunification of Korea put
forward by the Government of the Democratic Republic of Korea on
April 12, 1971, and the demand of the government of our republic
for the abolition of the 'U.N. Commission for the Unification
and Rehabilitation of Korea.' <u>This is a powerful support of the</u>
<u>fraternal Chinese people to our people in their just cause for</u>
<u>driving the U.S. imperialist aggressors out of South Korea and</u>
<u>achieving the independent, peaceful reunification of the country</u>
(emphasis added)."[40]

As to the overall Chinese stand on "revolutionary principles,"
the editorial was equally laudatory: "The Chinese side
maintained its consistent revolutionary principle and expressed
it with clarity." The distinct impression one gathers is that
the format of the Shanghai communiqué, in which both sides
expressed their respective stands on various matters, saved the
day for the Chinese as far as the North Koreans were concerned.
It followed as a matter of course that the Nixon visit was
interpreted as a sign of the "complete bankruptcy" of the U.S.
imperialists' "hostile policy against China" and as "a great
victory of the Chinese people."

The March 4 editorial did not renew the call to smash
American imperialism to its last breath and thereby
significantly moderated Kim Il-sŏng's initial policy enunciated
on August 6, 1971, but the North Koreans were still not willing
to accept the position of the United States as it was presented

in the Shanghai communiqué. Thus, after referring to the U.S.
position in the communiqué, the editorial stated, "If the
'stand' of the U.S. side which was expressed in all these
honeyed words is backed up by actual deeds, no one will take
issue with it." From the North Korean point of view, however,
American "troops of aggression" were occupying other countries
and committing acts of aggression and war provocation against
peoples of other countries. Specifically, the North Koreans
wanted the American troops withdrawn from Korea. "Along with
this," the editorial demanded, "all the resolutions of the
'United Nations' on the 'Korean question' for justifying U.S.
imperialism's aggression on Korea should be revoked and the
'U.N. Commission for the Unification and Rehabilitation of
Korea,' a tool of U.S. imperialism for aggression on Korea, be
dissolved forthwith." Contrary to the Shanghai communiqué and
various statements of President Nixon in China, the editorial
argued that "the U.S. side showed its intention to maintain the
present policy of aggression in the part of the joint communiqué
manifesting its stand on the foreign policy."

The prescribed remedy, however, lacked the acerbity of the
past. The concluding sentence of the editorial was this:

"The Korean people will vigorously fight on against the policies
of aggression and war of the U.S. imperialists and Japanese
militarists and for achieving the independent, peaceful
unification of the country, uniting with the revolutionary
peoples of the world (emphasis added)."

It should be noted that there is a considerable distance between
fighting against "the policies of aggression and war of American
imperialists" and smashing American imperialism to its last
breath.

Indeed, the North Korean decision to follow the Chinese line
of moderating the stand against "American imperialists" was
quickly put into high gear in early March. During the first
week of March, American correspondents in Tokyo were told that
personnel exchanges between North Korea and the United States
might be possible even while American troops were still in South
Korea. In an interview with the New York Times correspondent in
Tokyo, John M. Lee, the North Korean spokesman in Tokyo, Kim
Pyŏng-sik, stated that "the time has come for North Korea to
normalize its relations with the United States," although he
reaffirmed the position that "normalization" would not be
possible until the American forces were withdrawn.[41] Selig
Harrison, head of the Tokyo bureau of the Washington Post, also

had an interview with a North Korean spokesman in Tokyo soon after the Nixon visit to China and was told, "It is time for an end to the confrontation between our two countries" and that visits by American "writers, personalities in the arts, newsmen, politicians and businessmen will create conditions favorable for the withdrawal of the U.S. armed forces from South Korea."[42] These overtures received an immediate response from Secretary of State William P. Rogers, who stated at a press conference on March 7 that the United States had "a general willingness to improve relations with all countries, and that would include North Korea."[43] These interactions were soon followed by the visit to North Korea in May and June by three American correspondents representing the New York Times and the Washington Post. Professor Jerome Cohen of Harvard University was permitted to visit North Korea with his family in June. A Canadian correspondent, Mark Gayn, was also invited to North Korea to tour a number of places. These visitors were treated with the utmost courtesy and were accorded interviews with Premier Kim Il-sŏng, although their movements were much more restricted than the customary practice in China.

A number of hypotheses can be advanced to explain the sudden moderation, if not reversal, of North Korea's attitude toward the United States. First, the North Koreans must have seen from the Shanghai communique that establishing nonhostile contacts with the United States did not necessitate selling out their "revolutionary principles." On the contrary, the Nixon visit brought about unprecedented worldwide exposure and publicity to China, changing almost overnight the truculent or otherwise unfavorable image of China that the masses of the West had held. The establishment of amicable relations with the United States advanced China's international position vis-à-vis not only the Soviet Union but also Japan, not to mention the relationship with Taiwan. Undoubtedly the North Korean leaders hoped that similar benefits would accrue to them if they moderated their stand toward the United States. As Kim Pyŏng-sik asserted, the withdrawal of the U.S. troops from South Korea was one of the objectives. But even if this was still a distant hope, the improvement of relations with the United States by North Korea would shake the confidence of the South Korean leaders, particularly in connnection with the United States' support of South Korea's defense, and this would enormously enhance the future bargaining power of North Korea in dealing with the South. In any event, North Korea had much to gain from improved relations with the United States while very little risk was involved.

North Korean Reaction: A Summary. North Korea's reaction to the
Peking-Washington détente up until March 1972 can be summarized
as follows: The North Koreans were unprepared to receive the
July 15 announcement of President Nixon's acceptance of Premier
Chou En-lai's invitation to visit China and they greeted the
news with uncertainty, suspicion, and obduracy. The North Korean
leaders were soon persuaded to approve China's move, but they
still had misgivings about the Chinese action. The North Koreans
were not willing to abandon their hard line against the United
States and continued to call for smashing the imperialists. By
January 1972, however, the North Koreans had decided to utilize
the new atmosphere to gain maximum advantage. A worldwide
diplomatic offensive was launched to create a peaceful image; it
concentrated on Japan, the Soviet Union, and other sympathetic
nations both within and outside the communist camp. A peace
offensive was also launched against South Korea in January,
seeking support from diverse sources including the Secretary-
General of the United Nations. Finally, in March, perhaps as a
result of canvassing the opinions of some thirty foreign
nations, North Korea decided to soften its attitude toward the
United States. These diplomatic offensives culminated in a
positive response from the Republic of Korea government in South
Korea, which decided to send an emissary in May to open high-
level political talks.

The benefits that accrued to North Korea through these moves
were enormous. It was not the first time that Premier Kim Il-
sŏng had advocated North-South meetings or the reduction of
armed forces on the Korean peninsula, but because of the timing
and because of the scale and intensity of the North Koreans'
effort to publicize their case, their proposal was accorded much
more credence by the world than ever before. It could be said,
in fact, that world opinion welcomed the mellowing of the
attitude and behavior of North Korea, which had been regarded as
the most intransigent, most unpredictable, and most isolated
communist regime in the world (and hence the likelihood of
another military conflict erupting on the Korean peninsula had
been regarded as very strong). By March 1972, at least the North
Korean leaders were definitely aiming at changing this image,
and there is little doubt that they succeeded in this goal. The
chances of the DPRK's being accepted as a member of the
international community were enhanced tremendously, and North
Korea began reaping economic benefits.

Another aim that the DPRK pursued consistently during the
last two decades has been the increase of its international
prestige. Strong efforts were directed toward the emergent

nations in Africa and Middle East and considerable results were
attained. But these efforts were consistently hampered by the
aggressive and intransigent image North Korea projected. The
changed image of North Korea, however, began to have its effects
on various nations, making the work of North Korean diplomats
much easier than ever before.

All these North Korean actions, however, cannot be separated
from the context of the Korean peninsula where the ROK is poised
against the DPRK. In the past, the communists in the North
consistently advocated the need, and indeed the inevitability,
of a communist revolution in the South. Hence all actions by the
North Korean communists must be measured by their effects on the
South. What effects did these moves have on South Korea?

In the context of the fierce and often violent rivalry, any
improvement in North Korea's power or prestige affected the ROK
in an adverse manner. But, as discussed above, one of the
specific aims of the DPRK was to create tension, if not
alienation, between the ROK and its allies, particularly the
United States. To what extent did the North Korean efforts
succeed on this point? Before this question can be answered,
the South Korean reaction to the Sino-American détente must be
examined.

The South Korean Reaction
If the initial North Korean reaction to the Sino-American
détente can be characterized as unmitigated suspicion followed
by grudging concession, the South Korean reaction was swift and
accommodating, although the South Korean leaders were also
troubled by a sense of uncertainty about the swirl of change in
international politics. Since the enunciation of the Nixon
Doctrine in July 1969 the South Korean leaders had been hard put
to fathom the implications of the new United States policy for
the Korean peninsula. It was clear, of course, that the United
States was intent on reducing its commitment to South Korea, but
where would the United States draw the line? How fast would the
Nixon administration proceed with the withdrawal of the United
States troops from Korea? At what level of conflict between
North and South Korea—if at any level— would the United States
see it fit to commit its military power against the enemy, as
provided in the Mutual Defense Treaty of 1954? To what extent,
and with what speed, would the United States assist the
modernization of the ROK armed forces? Answers to these
questions of magnitude were vital to the South Korean policy-
makers because the South Korean reliance on the United States

was absolute and the challenge from the North was perceived to
be imminent.

While the South Korean leaders anxiously sought authoritative
and credible answers to these questions and negotiated with the
United States government to modify some of the American
decisions, one of the major premises of the new American policy
became clear: that the United States was intent on reducing its
Asian commitments and that this would be possible only if the
prevailing level of tension in Asia were substantially reduced.
The United States was to take a series of actions—including the
withdrawal of some 20,000 troops from Korea in 1970—to bring
about the thaw, and its allies would be expected to redirect
their efforts to usher in an era of accommodation replacing the
one of confrontation.

In the tense atmosphere of the Korean peninsula at the end of
1960s, the talk of thaw had a sense of unreality. The North
Koreans had seized an American intelligence ship, the USS
Pueblo, in January 1968; they had continually dispatched
commando troops and other armed agents southward on suicidal
missions; and they had shot down an American reconnaissance
plane.

South Korean intelligence continued to report the imminence
of an all-out assault from North Korea in 1970 or 1971. While
Foreign Minister Hŏ Tam of the DPRK did present an eight-point
program for "peaceful unification" on April 12, 1971, his
proviso that negotiation would be carried out and collaboration
would be brought about "when people's power is established in
South Korea or patriotic-minded new figures assume power after
the withdrawal of the U.S. imperialists and the downfall of
traitor Pak Chŏng-hui effectively canceled any hope of a thaw
on the Korean peninsula.

In short, the South Korean leaders were caught in a vise
between the extremely belligerent state across the truce line and
the strong current of Sino-American détente. If the sudden change
in the structure of international relations in East Asia provided
new challenges and opportunities to such great powers as the
United States, the Soviet Union, China, and Japan—and one could
also add the DPRK—the fluid new environment presented enormous
challenges and risks to South Korea, whose policy options had
been greatly constricted by its traditional and extraordinary
dependence on the United States and by its rigid anticommunist
ethos. Unlike the DPRK, the ROK government was not in a position
to exploit the hostile relationship between the two big allies.
Unlike the leaders of North Korea, who had the advantage of an
intensely mobilized and monolithic political system that

permitted them to adjust to environmental needs without any fear
of disrupting the ongoing operation of the system, the South
Korean leaders had been obliged to calculate carefully the
effect of their actions upon the quasi-open political system in
the South as well as upon their two close allies, the United
States and Japan. Never before in the history of the Republic of
Korea had its leaders been called upon to exhibit such dexterity
and skill in coordinating foreign policies with domestic
politics.

It was in this situation that the South Korean leadership
announced their desire to bring about peace and called upon the
North Koreans to renounce force. South Korean President Pak
Chŏng-hui had in fact addressed himself to this subject on
August 15, 1970, before there was any inkling of the Sino-
American détente. He had stated,

"Any approach toward unification by peaceful means is not
feasible without the easing of tensions. Therefore, such an
approach should be preceded above all by an unequivocal
expression of attitude by the North Korean Communists assuring
the easing of tensions and its implementation. Accordingly, the
North Korean Communists should desist forthwith from
perpetrating all sorts of military provocations including the
dispatch of armed agents into the South and make an
announcement publicly that they renounce henceforth the so-
called policies of theirs of communizing the whole of Korea by
force and overthrowing the Republic of Korea by means of violent
revolution, and prove their sincerity by deeds."[44]

If the North Korean leaders accepted this prerequisite, the
president would be "prepared to suggest epochal and more
realistic measures."

On July 1, 1971, in his inaugural address as a third-term
president of the republic, Pak Chŏng-hui acknowledged the "mood
of thaw between East and West" as well as the rapprochement
between the United States and China and expressed his hope that
the new developments would lead to a reduction of tension in
Asia. He also reiterated the point he had made before that only
the "anachronistic and fanatic revolutionary dogmatism" of the
communists was preventing him from taking actions that would
presumably reduce tension on the peninsula. Aside from the
stress placed on the "prerequisite," he seemed inclined to be
flexible.[45]

Flexibility and independence indeed became the two key
concepts for South Korea's foreign policy, and these themes were

stressed time and again by Premier Kim Chŏng-p'il. On July 1, at
the inaugural ceremony, the premier asserted that "a correct
stand must be taken according to international currents."[46] He
reiterated the same points on July 6 at a briefing given to the
Democratic Republican party members of the National Assembly.[47]
On August 6 the premier again told a plenary session of the
National Assembly that "while we must not be oversensitive to
surface phenomena of the international current, we must not be
isolated by going contrary to the current. . . . We must be
prudent but, at the same time, take a positive and flexible
stance seeking national interest."[48]

These statements of principle were quickly translated into
policy, although the initial steps taken were very cautious and
exploratory. Thus on May 31 the president instructed his
ministers to investigate the possibility of lifting restrictions
on foreign ships and travelers who had been to communist
countries just prior to calling at Korean ports. The existing
law had prohibited any ship from calling at Korean ports within
three months after it had been to a communist port, and any
traveler that had visited "hostile communist countries" had
been required to obtain special permission before applying for a
Korean visa. (All restrictions were lifted as of June 3 except
on travelers who had visited North Korea.)[49] The government then
announced on July 16 that the possiblities of trade with Eastern
European countries were being actively explored.[50] It was clear
that South Korea's initial moves were to be directed toward
Eastern Europe. On August 6 the foreign minister announced at
the National Assembly that "in order further to isolate North
Korea internationally, the government has adopted policies to
establish trade relations with Eastern European nations and
positive measures have been taken for this purpose." He added
further, "We shall take a flexible posture toward [all]
countries that do not take a hostile attitude toward us."[51] The
foreign minister's avoidance of the phrase "hostile communist
countries," which had designated North Korea, communist China,
North Vietnam, and Cuba, was construed by the press as an
expression of the willingness of the ROK government to establish
contacts with the Chinese communist regime.

While the Soviet Union and the Eastern European countries did
not pose a serious problem for the ROK government, communist
China and its rapid rapprochement with the United States did
present one of major proportions. As the foreign minister
revealed at the National Assembly, the ROK government distinctly
felt the possibility that the Sino-American détente would
placate the aggressiveness of North Korea. But the Chinese

government had supported the North Korean regime on many
important issues affecting South Korea, even to the extent of
providing certain ports on the Shantung peninsula for North
Korean espionage operations directed against the South.[52]
"Would Peking abandon its hostile attitude toward the ROK in the
event that the détente was actually brought to fruition?" was a
question very much on the minds of the South Korean leaders, who
were not at all certain of the North Korean reaction to the
Sino-American détente. In other words, the South Korean leaders
were not certain that their North Korean counterparts would
follow the overall trend toward the relaxation of tension,
despite some of the statements issuing from Pyongyang.

Since the ROK government had adopted the basic principle of
riding the international current toward relaxation, its overall
strategy called for a dual policy of approaching North Korea as
well as its own allies. Thus the ROK foreign minister revealed
on August 6 that his government's flexible diplomacy included
some compromise with North Korea. This was indicated in his
answer to questions posed by National Assembly members regarding
the invitation extended to North Korean delegates by the United
Nations. The ROK government's position had been that the North
Korean delegates should not be allowed to attend United Nations
sessions until they recognized the legitimacy of the United
Nations actions vis-à-vis Korea. But the ROK government, after
consulting allied nations, was now willing to "modify the
language."[53] Even though the foreign minister did not elucidate
the extent of the change, this was the first expression of South
Korea's willingness to retreat from its previous adamant
positions.

It appears in retrospect, however, that the ROK government
had decided to approach the North Korean leadership a few weeks
before Seoul's foreign minister hinted at a change in the policy
toward North Korea. A government spokesman had emphasized on
July 19, four days after Nixon's historic announcement of his
acceptance of Premier Chou's invitation, that the diplomacy of
South Korea should not be that of following others and that the
government would seek solutions to the problems of the Korean
peninsula from an independent position.[54] The spokesman did not
reveal the content of this "independent diplomacy," but
circumstantial evidence leads to the conclusion that a direct
approach to the North Korean leadership had been decided upon.
This supposition was reinforced by the expression of strong
concern from Seoul, after President Nixon's announcement, that
the United States might conclude agreements with China regarding
Korea which might be contrary to the interest of the Koreans.[55]

The likelihood that the United States would "sell out Korea" was considered very remote, but even the thought of such a possibility would have been enough to catapult the South Korean leaders into action. Furthermore, the South Korean leaders needed an opportunity to assure the people of South Korea as well as the world that the ROK government was not simply following international events.

Given the intense hostility between the two parts of Korea during the past quarter-century, however, it would have been impossible for South Korea to call for political negotiations with the North. The North Koreans had not responded to earlier calls from the South to renounce the use of force, and hence any further political proposal emanating from the South would have been interpreted as a sign of weakness. Kim Il-sŏng's statement of August 6 at the Pyongyang rally welcoming Prince Sihanouk ("the Chiang Kai-shek clique and the South Korean puppet clique are raising a hue and cry, overcome with great uneasiness and fear" at the Sino-American détente) reduced the South Korean options even further.

It was under these circumstances that the president of the South Korean Red Cross issued, on August 12, his highly publicized statement calling for a meeting of the delegates from the two Red Cross societies to discuss the ways and means of locating and facilitating meetings of separated families in North and South Korea. Although the Red Cross president, Ch'oe Tu-sŏn, stressed the humanitarian nature of his pronouncement, its political significance escaped no one. The fact that he referred to "North Korea" rather than as customary, the "North Korean puppet" in his statement was seen as further evidence that the South Korean proposal was serious.

The use of the Red Cross as an avenue of approach to the North Korean leadership was highly appropriate for many reasons. By raising an issue that directly affected an estimated ten million people in Korea, or approximately 20 percent of the total population, the South Korean government significantly gained in popularity. By utilizing an ostensibly nongovernmental agency, the South Korean government minimized the chance of further estrangement and frontal confrontation with the North Korean leaders while at the same time maximizing the opportunity for a North-South encounter. In other words, rejection of the South Korean Red Cross proposal would not necessarily have been interpreted as an affront to the South Korean government, and the acceptance of the proposal commit the North to the legitimacy of the South Korean political leadership, or vice versa. If in fact the proposal led to a face-to-face encounter

with the North Koreans, it would provide an opportunity for the
political leaders in both Koreas to assess one another and learn
how to deal with one another in a peaceful manner. Initial
contacts having been established, the leaders of each regime
could observe and analyze the international currents at a more
leisurely pace and explore the strategies that suited them best.

The North Korean leaders evidently found no fault in the
proposal, and a favorable reply was delivered by radio two days
later. The site of the meeting was quickly agreed upon, and the
year-long preparatory meetings got under way at Panmunjom.

The opening of the Red Cross talks was undoubtedly a giant
step forward in the postwar history of Korea, but it did not
bring about an immediate change in the attitudes of the South
and North Korean leaders toward one another. On August 31 the
South Korean foreign minister, Kim Yŏng-sik, stated that the
"purely humanitarian" Red Cross talks did constitute the first
step toward political solutions, but that at a time when the
North Koreans were continuing to dispatch armed guerillas to the
South to engage in aggressive acts it was totally inconceivable
to move into a second stage of engaging in nonpolitical
exchanges, material, personal, or cultural. Political
negotiations leading to the settlement of the issues of
unification were regarded by the foreign minister as the third
and final stage of the solution of "the Korean problem."

On October 1, at the twenty-third anniversary celebration of
the founding of the ROK army, President Pak made a somewhat
hawkish speech directed at both North Korea and the citizens of
the South. He stressed that there was no sign whatsoever that
the "North Korean puppets" had abandoned their strategy of
militarily unifying Korea; on the contrary, the communists,
while engaging in a peace offensive, were increasing their
military preparations. He warned against the easygoing mood in
the South and called for further consolidation of the armed
forces and the heightening of the anticommunist spirit. At the
same time, the president called on the North Korean communists
to abandon their aggressive policy and react positively to his
repeated appeal to relax tensions on the peninsula.[56] In short,
until the North Korean communists ceased all hostile acts, the
South Korean leader was not willing to take any further action.

Even though there was no positive response from Pyongyang to
the South Korean demand that the North cease hostile actions,
ROK policy toward North Korea continued to evolve. On November 1
the ROK minister of unification announced that henceforth the
government would attempt to induce the North to change its
aggressive nature by abandoning the traditional ROK policy of

isolating the North Korean regime.[57] This was a tacit
admission by the ROK government that its past policies toward
the North had been counterproductive and that it was itself
responsible, at least in part, for the heightened tension on the
peninsula, a concession of major significance that eventually
paved the way for future dialogue with the North.

That conciliatory gestures toward North Korea by South
Korea's cabinet ministers occurred along with strongly
denunciatory pronouncements by the president suggested, however,
that the ROK government was still groping for an appropriate
policy to surmount the severest crisis in foreign policy it had
ever faced. Like its North Korean counterpart, the South Korean
leadership was not persuaded that the détente between Washington
and Peking would mitigate the hostility and aggressiveness of
its opponent on the Korean peninsula. On the contrary, the South
Korean leaders believed that the North Korean regime was
consolidating its military posture and that there was imminent
danger of another all-out assault against the South.[58] To the
chagrin of the South Korean leadership, the United States did
not share this view. While recognizing the high level of DPRK
military preparedness, the United States minimized North Korea's
capability for an all-out war[59] and strongly urged the ROK
government to initiate negotiations with the DPRK in order to
reduce tensions on the peninsula.[60] The ROK government's
conciliatory posture of November 1, as represented by the
unification minister's pronouncement, can therefore be regarded
as a concession to the United States.

Nevertheless, fear and suspicion persisted on the part of the
South Korean leadership. Even by December the South Korean
assessment of North Korean motives had not changed. President
Pak, proclaiming a state of national emergency on December 6,
noted that, contrary to the peace-oriented trend in the
international arena, tension on the Korean peninsula had
increased. Furthermore, foreign and domestic developments after
the initiation of the Washington-Peking détente had been such,
the president announced, that the Republic of Korea was now
"faced with a grave crisis." He noted in particular that the
admission of the PRC into the United Nations was likely to have
an adverse effect on the ROK, in view of the close ties between
China and North Korea, and that the heated debates in the
United States Congress on foreign aid clearly indicated further
need for South Korean self-reliance in security matters, which
would add a considerable burden to South Korea's already
strained economy. Japan was also moving closer to the PRC and
North Korea, clearly showing that "no one feels as profoundly as

we—who have actually experienced it—the acuteness of the
danger of communism in Asia." On the domestic side, President
Pak was particularly critical of the "easygoing and illusory mood"
that equated the thaw in international politics with one on the
Korean peninsula. He charged that "self-styled intellectuals"
and "self-seeking politicians" were engaged in irresponsible
discussions on national security matters, which led to
bewilderment and the lowering of morale among the populace.[61]

The prescribed remedy was spelled out in the Law on National
Emergency adopted by the National Assembly on December 27.[62] The
law retroactively granted the president the right to proclaim a
state of national emergency and also gave him unilateral,
absolute power to control, regulate, and mobilize the people and
the economy. His new powers included the right to regulate the
press and restrict or prohibit assemblies and demonstrations.
Journalists and other intellectuals were quickly intimidated and
opposition politicians muzzled.

While President Pak's declaration of emergency was
interpreted by some as a warning to the United States that the
fate of the Koreans should not be settled by the big powers
without the participation and consent of the Koreans themselves,
South Korea's foreign policy showed no visible change during the
next few months. The ROK government responded favorably to the
Shanghai communiqué of February 28, noting in particular the
statement that the United States would maintain its close ties
with and support for the Republic of Korea and would support
efforts of that country to seek relaxation of tension and
increased communication on the Korean peninsula.[63] As to North
Korea, South Korean Foreign Minister Kim Yŏng-sik issued four
demands on February 12 calling for North Korean actions rather
than propaganda efforts. The South Korean demands included the
dismantling of fortifications and withdrawal of troops from the
demilitarized zone, discontinuance of dispatching armed agents
to South Korea, return of the hijacked Korean Airlines plane and
its crew and passengers, and abandonment of the strategy of
unifying the peninsula by force. (These points were reiterated
by the foreign minister on March 15 and by the president on
March 30.) The ROK government repeatedly stressed the
discrepancy between the words and deeds of the DPRK and refused
to take the North Koreans' public statements seriously. The
South Korean view, as expressed by Premier Kim Chŏng-p'il on
February 28, was that North Korea was not likely to abandon its
militancy and ferocity for some time to come and that South
Korea needed to increase its military preparedness.[64]

On March 25, however, the vice-president of the ROK Red Cross

reported that he had had unofficial contacts with the
representatives of the DPRK Red Cross at Vienna, where both
groups were attending an international Red Cross meeting. He
said that the North Korean delegates had actively sought the
contacts (presumably through United Nations Secretary-General
Waldheim). Evidently some frank remarks were exchanged at these
meetings, and the South Korean delegation found the discussions
positive. The contacts at Vienna eventually led to the
dramatic, high-level secret visits between Pyongyang and Seoul
that preceded the July 4 announcement.

Two circumstantial pieces of evidence indicate that the ROK
government maintained close contacts with its principal ally,
the United States, while the secret talks were being held in
Pyongyang and Seoul. On April 24 Assistant Secretary of State
Marshall Green, without referring to the circumstances that
necessitated his pronouncement, announced to baffled reporters
that the United States would support all ROK efforts at
relaxing tensions on the Korean peninsula.[65] On April 26
President Nixon granted an interview to the South Korean
foreign minister in Washington and reaffirmed his overall
understanding and support of the South Korean positions on
defense and foreign relations.[66] Yi Hu-rak's historic visit to
Pyongyang took place a few days later, on May 2. It may have
been coincidental, but at the U.S.-ROK Joint Security Conference
at Colorado Springs, which was attended by Defense Secretary
Melvin Laird and Defense Minister Yu Ch'ae-hung and was concluded
on June 27, just a week before the July 4 announcement, the
United States reaffirmed its pledge to provide "speedy and
effective" assistance to South Korea in the event of external
attack and agreed that modernization of the Korean armed forces
was essential for the security of Korea.[67]

The North-South Negotiations

The joint announcement of July 4, 1972, was certainly an
auspicious beginning for the future relations between the two
Koreas, but progress after the announcement was very slow.
Considering the nature of the confrontation between the two
systems during the preceding twenty-five years, however, every
agreement that the leaders of the two regimes were able to bring
about during the ensuing months must be regarded as something
extraordinary, rather than as a matter to be taken for granted.
Even if the leaders of the two regimes were determined to find
common ground they were far apart in idiosyncrasies,
assumptions, and, indeed, style of life. It was to take more
than several months for the representatives of both sides to
adjust to one another.

The glaring discrepancy in assumptions became clear within
hours after the joint communiqué was read to the mass media in
the respective capitals. The "first principle" in the joint
communiqué stated that "unification shall be achieved through
independent Korean efforts without being subject to external
imposition or interference," but it became clear that the two
parties attached different meanings to the wording. Yi Hu-rak,
for example, stated at a news conference that South Korea would
"welcome" a United Nations role in unifying Korea through the
supervision of all-Korea elections, since the UN could not be
considered a "bad foreign force." And, as noted, the UN had
already played a role, albeit unofficially, and there were
strong indications that North Korea was now aiming at UN
membership.

The North Korean emphasis was using this clause to get the
United States out of South Korea. Pak Sŏng-ch'ŏl declared in a
Pyongyang news conference that a primary objective in working
toward unification was "to remove outside influences," adding
that "the U.S. imperialists must no longer meddle in the
domestic affairs of our country" and that "they must withdraw
[their troops from South Korea] at once." On the other hand,
the South Koreans, in order to negotiate with the communists
from strength, stressed the need for the continued presence of
U.S. forces.

Later, in mid-September, when the second session of the Red
Cross meetings was held in Seoul, the North Koreans dismayed and
angered the South Korean populace by repeating adulatory phrases
about Kim Il-sŏng at an open session televised throughout South
Korea. At the same time they openly expressed irritation at
South Korean reporting, which tended to focus on the North
Korean delegates' mannerisms, informal utterances, and other
trivialities. Facing North Korean protests, and seeing the
prospect of agreements diminishing, Yi Hu-rak sent an open
letter to the South Korean journalists on September 28 chiding
them for their "commercial journalism" and requesting them to
take a broader perspective in reporting. While these incidents
did not affect overall progress in the negotiations, they
reflected the different patterns of sociopolitical development
in the two parts of the Korean peninsula.[68]

The signing of the joint communiqué did not mean that the two
regimes would cease all forms of competition or would
automatically come to a mutual understanding. For example, a
fierce competition developed at the United Nations over the
issue of removing the mantle of the United Nations from the U.S.
forces in Korea and dissolving the United Nations Commission for

the Unification and Rehabilitation of Korea (UNCURK). Since
neither Korea was a member of the United Nations, a group of
countries headed by China and Algeria strove to place on the
General Assembly agenda an item dealing with the issue. They
argued that the withdrawal of the U.S. and all other foreign
forces "occupying South Korea under the flag of the UN" would
contribute to peaceful reunification of Korea. South Korea's
allies insisted, however, that since talks were already under
way between the two Koreas, an acrimonious debate in the United
Nations at this time would hinder reunification rather than help
it. In the end, the General Assembly rejected the proposal by a
decisive vote of 70 to 35 with 21 abstentions.[69] While
theoretically neither North or South Korea was involved in the
contest, the developments at the UN hardened the atmosphere
between them.*

That the joint communiqué was still a fragile instrument for
alleviating tension was revealed by an exchange that took place
in early October. ROK President Pak reportedly made the
following statements on October 1 on the occasion of the South
Korean Armed Forces Day and at a reception at his residence on
the following day:

"We have witnessed first hand what the North Korean Communists
are really like, and I believe we have clearly perceived
suitable measures to deal with them. . . .

"We have neither front lines nor rear areas since the Communists
adopted the strategy of so-called 'revolutionary liberation' by
means of either military provocation or a deceptive peace
offensive. . . .

----

* On May 17, 1973, North Korea was admitted to the World Health
Organization, a specialized agency of the United Nations, and
thus won the right to send permanent observers to the United
Nations. On November 14, DPRK Deputy Foreign Minister Yi Chŏng-
mok delivered his first speech at the General Assembly's
Political Committee, demanding the dissolution of the UN military
command in South Korea, abolition of and the withdrawal of the
U.S. forces. After some debate, the 28th General Assembly reached
a compromise whereby UNCURK was dissolved and the two Koreas were
encouraged to negotiate on their own.

"[The] North Korean Communists' intention in promoting the
current South-North Red Cross talks seemed to be different from
ours. . . .

"The underlying intent of the North Korean Communists [is] to
relax the will of the South Korean people and slacken their
alertness in a scheme to resume infiltration since their direct
armed provocation proved to be futile."[70]

These remarks addressed to the South Korean armed forces were
obviously not intended to please the North Koreans, and the
reaction from Pyongyang was vicious in tone. Perhaps the defeat
at the United Nations had put the North Korean leadership in an
irascible mood. In any event, the (North) Korean Central News
Agency attacked the South Korean leader without reserve on
October 5. President Pak was called a "traitor and a running dog
of the American and Japanese imperialists." He and his "fascist
hangmen" were also accused of trying to hamper the development
of national unification.[71] Obviously the agreement reported in
the joint communiqué "not to slander or defame each other" was
disregarded in this instance.

If these developments emphasized the precarious nature of the
relationship between the two regimes, later developments also
demonstrated the strength of the forces that propelled the two
regimes to seek an accord. Under normal circumstances the North
Korean statement of October 5 would have led to a prolonged
break in negotiations, but such was not the case. Yi Hu-rak of
South Korea met Pak Sŏng-ch'ŏl of the North on October 12 at
Panmunjom and conferred on ceasing slander and denunciation,
along with such other matters as the details of the formation of
the South-North Coordinating Committee.[72] Yi Hu-rak had stated
on September 14 that he had been in touch with his North Korean
counterpart through both direct telephone lines and exchange of
messengers at Panmunjom.[73] Obviously these arrangements were
paying dividends.

Once the "culture shock" of encountering the opponents was
overcome, events began to move rather briskly. The Red Cross
teams held their third session in Pyongyang in late October
(beginning on October 24) and began to deal with concrete issues.
At the fourth session, held in late November, they agreed to
establish a permanent North-South Red Cross Joint Committee to
implement decisions reached at the Red Cross talks and to
establish a joint office at Panmunjom.[74]

More important, the cochairmen of the South-North
Coordinating Committee met at Pyongyang (November 2-4) and Seoul
(November 30-December 2) to operationalize that committee. A
joint statement issued in Pyongyang on November 4 said that
"both sides agreed that they must cooperate and work together in
various fields" and stated that both sides had reached a detailed
accord on the composition and function of the Coordinating
Committee, which would devise and implement concrete programs.
Both sides also agreed to end propaganda broadcasts and leaflet
distribution, as well as psychological-warfare programs
broadcast through loudspeakers in the demilitarized zone,
effective November 11.

An additional document signed in Pyongyang concerning the
composition and management of the Coordinating Committee
specified that the committee should have the functions of
1. Solving problems of "independent and peaceful unification" of
   Korea,
2. Realizing "wide-ranging political exchanges between political
   parties, social organizations, and individual persons,"
3. Arranging "economic, cultural, and social exchanges and joint
   cooperative projects,"
4. Easing tensions, preventing military clashes, and terminating
   a "state of military confrontation" between the two Koreas,
   and
5. "Taking joint steps in activities abroad in order to enhance
   the national pride as a homogeneous people."[75]

Yi Hu-rak's tone at the press conference after his return
from Pyongyang was optimistic, indeed exuberant. He
characterized his meeting with Premier Kim Il-sŏng as "very
warm." Elaborating on some of the future functions of the
Coordinating Committee, he referred to such possibilities as
forming joint sports teams or folk-music and dance troupes to be
sent abroad, promoting the common interest and arranging a
division of work in certain fields of industry, having South
Korean fishermen go to North Korean waters at certain seasons,
and developing resort and tourist facilities in the east coast
"Diamond Mountain" areas in the North.[76] The committee, he added
on December 2, would first undertake the easiest tasks, such as
economic, scholarly, and cultural exchanges. Joint political and
diplomatic ventures were definitely out for the immediate future,
as far as the South Korean leader was concerned.

This, however, was the South Korean position, not shared by
the North Koreans. While the South Koreans insisted on tackling
the easier problems first as a means of building trust, North
Korea insisted that tension could be eased and trust built only

if the state of military confrontation were terminated and that this could be achieved only if the United States forces were withdrawn from South Korea and armaments on both sides were reduced. As far as the Red Cross negotiations were concerned, North Korea proposed that all restrictions imposed by laws and regulations (the Law on State Security and the Anticommunist Law, cited earlier in this chapter) should be removed so that the reunited families and relatives might freely express themselves, have access to information, and conduct their activities freely.[77] The North Korean side also proposed that "Red Cross publicity workers" should be assigned to each ri (cluster of villages) and that their freedom of speech, publication, assembly, and travel, as well as the inviolability of their persons and belongings, should be guaranteed.[78]

When it became apparent that South Korea was unwilling to entertain these proposals, the North Korean attitude hardened. General O Chin-u, the chief of the General Staff of the (North) Korean People's Army, declared on February 7, 1973:

"[The South Koreans] refused even our proposal for discontinuing the arms race. . . , reducing munitions production, and curtailing the armed forces as an expression of mutual trust, calling it 'premature.' This shows that the South Koreans do not want to solve the problems, although they will engage in a dialogue with us, and do not want to put into practice any agreements with which they may concur.

"Diametrically opposed to our sincere efforts. . . , the South Korean authorities are taking the dangerous road of aggravating tensions, between the north and south and pursuing war by clamoring about 'confrontation' and 'prevailing over communism.'"[79]

Neither side was willing to yield, and the talks reached a stalemate. The second session of the South-North Coordinating Committee was held in Pyongyang on March 14 and 15 and the third on June 12, 1973, but without results. On August 28, in the aftermath of the Kim Dae-jung affair,* the North Korean

---

* On August 8, Kim Dai-jung, the principal opponent of President Pak in the 1971 election and the most acid critic of the president living outside Korea, was kidnapped by unidentified Koreans from a Tokyo hotel. A few days later, Kim turned up in Seoul where he told the story of the kidnapping, the last-minute instructions to his abductors not to dump him in the ocean, and

cochairman blamed the South Korean CIA headed by Yi Hu-rak for the incident and declared that the North Koreans would no longer sit with Yi Hu-rak, the South Korean cochairman, to discuss the affairs of the nation. This in effect signaled the end of the first phase of the negotiations that had aroused so much hope among the Korean people. Tension began to mount once more as each side denounced the other through broadcasts, leaflets, and other forms of propaganda.

Meanwhile, the two governments were locked in battle on the issue of whether the two states should join the United Nations as separate entities. On June 23, 1973, President Pak of South Korea took the initiative by announcing that he was ready to have the two Koreas simultaneously admitted to the United Nations. At the same time, he also called on North Korea to support some of the principles of Panchi Shila (the Five Principles of Coexistence), such as the maintenance of peace, noninterference in each other's domestic politics, and nonaggression. While the president denied that the new South Korean proposal meant recognition of North Korea as a state, there was no question that South Korea was moving in the direction of accepting the existence of the two states on the Korean peninsula as a basis for future negotiations.

On the same afternoon, the former premier and now president of North Korea, Kim Il-song, let it be known that the South Korean proposal was unacceptable. In the opinion of President Kim, the South Korean proposal would only perpetuate the division of Korea. Therefore, he argued, the two Koreas should first join in a confederation and then apply for UN membership as a single entity. Subsequently, North Korean editorials and broadcasts accused the South Korean president of taking a "treacherous stand" and of "concocting a criminal scheme to perpetuate the country's division."[80]

The stalemate continued even as 1973 ended. After Yi Hu-rak was ousted as the head of the South Korean CIA and as cochairman of the Coordinating Committee on December 3, the

---

his subsequent release. Although the South Korean government repeatedly denied any involvement in the incident, it later admitted the Japanese charge that a first secretary of the Korean embassy in Tokyo played a role in it. Kim was in Tokyo when President Pak declared martial law in October 1972 and decided to stay abroad as an exile. This incident severely strained Japanese-South Korean relations during the ensuing months.

deputy cochairmen of the committee met on December 5 for the
first time since June to discuss the resumption of talks, but
the two brief meetings (a third, scheduled for January 21, 1974,
was postponed by the North) did not mitigate differences.
Meanwhile, tension between the two Koreas rose sharply in early
December, as North Korea claimed territorial rights to waters
around five Yellow Sea islands held by the South, and as South
Korea placed its armed forces on special alert.[81]

In the spring of 1974, the prospect of agreement appeared as
dim as ever. The South-North Coordinating Committee no longer
served as an effective instrument of negotiation, let alone of
coordination. There was not even a faint trace of the spirit of
understanding so exuberantly displayed in July 1972.

President Pak's January 18, 1974, proposal that the two sides
conclude a nonaggression pact may have been intended to ease the
tension, but there was little hope for North Korean acceptance.
In the joint communiqué of July 4 the two states had already
renounced the use of force as a means of attaining unification,
but a number of armed skirmishes took place after the communiqué
was issued. Moreover, the signing of such a document would not
have altered any aspect of the confrontation because the pact
would have been nothing more than a declaration of intent by
both sides. Since North Korea had been arguing for a peace
treaty that entailed the withdrawal of foreign (i.e., American)
troops and reduction of armaments on both sides, as well as the
cessation of the arms race,[82] North Korea was expected to
denounce the latest proposal from Seoul as only a transparent
strategem to divert public attention from the "only solution"
proposed by the North. In proposing the nonaggression pact,
President Pak of South Korea rejected the earlier North Korean
proposal for a peace treaty as nothing but a communist scheme to
take over South Korea. The reasons behind these charges and
countercharges will be examined presently.

The International Impact on Domestic Politics
In the meantime, the South Korean president saw fit to tighten
his reign over South Korea. Evidently the measures he had taken
in December 1971 were inadequate for his purpose, although the
Law on National Emergency that had been rammed through the
National Assembly two days after Christmas had given him
complete power to control, regulate, and mobilize the people,
economy, and press. South Korea was still, in his view, in a
state of "national emergency" in late 1972, and nothing short of
fundamental change in the constitutional structure would be
adequate.

For this reason martial law was proclaimed on October 17. The National Assembly was dissolved, all universities and colleges were closed, press censorship was imposed, and political parties were suspended. The government then drafted a new constitution and on November 21 conducted a national referendum without lifting martial law. The constitution was easily ratified, and under it the 2,359-member National Conference on Unification was instituted. That body, serving as the electoral college, unanimously elected President Pak to a fourth term. He was the only candidate, and under the new constitution the National Conference was not permitted to debate before electing him. The other functions of the new organization were to deliberate on the president's policy on unification and to approve the president's slate of candidates for one-third of the National Assembly. The power of the National Assembly was thus greatly curtailed and that of the president expanded.

Most observers were unanimous in the opinion that the whole melodrama was played out in order that President Pak might stay in power. According to the old constitution, drafted under the leadership of a military junta that President Pak himself had headed from 1961 to 1963, the president was prohibited from succeeding himself after two four-year terms. This provision had then been amended to allow the president to serve a third term, which, in Pak's case, would have terminated in 1975. The new constitution of 1972 eliminated this provision altogether, thus permitting the president to serve any number of six-year terms.

While not denying that this was his purpose—except to announce publicly that the presidency was a cross for him to bear—President Pak and his followers strove to link the constitutional change with the North-South negotiations. The president stated at a press conference on January 12, 1973, for example, that many problems had emerged after the July 4 communiqué. He said he had "soon found out that a national consensus was unable to coalesce due to a divergence of public opinions." In addition, he went on, some politicians maintained that the South-North dialogue was unconstitutional and illegal. Others also made an issue of the legality of the high-level visits between Pyongyang and Seoul. In addition, he said,

"When we compared our system with North Korea's, we also found that our democratic institutions had many points vulnerable to the dialogue with the Communists and to exchanging mutual visits."[83]

Appropriately enough, the president likened the "October

Revitalizing Reforms" of 1972 to the coup d'état of May 16, 1961, because, according to him, both "stressed national identity."

Regardless of the validity of these arguments, and for that matter of the merit and legality of the actions taken, it is certain that the president now possesses the constitutional right and indeed the duty to continue the negotiations with North Korea, for Article 43 (3) of the new constitution specifies the sincere pursuit of "peaceful unification of the fatherland" as one of his duties. All the "points vulnerable to the dialogue" are presumably now eliminated, and he can pursue his goals in peace.*

Interestingly enough, North Korea also revised its constitution just a month after South Korea had done so. This gave rise to speculation that the leaders of the two Koreas had conferred on constitutional revisions to facilitate future unification, but the content of the new constitution does not substantiate such a theory. The North Koreans had begun the task of revising the constitution in 1960,[84] but for some reason the task was not completed until late 1972.

----

* It might be pointed out in passing, however, that whether a "national consensus" could "coalesce" through the National Conference for Unification is highly problematical. According to Article 38 (2) of the new constitution, "unification policy obtaining the concurrence of more than one-half of the delegates of the NCU. . . shall be regarded as the collective will of the people as a whole," but when one considers that most of the influential, knowledgeable, articulate, and vocal elements in South Korea were systematically excluded from that body by the circumstances of the election under martial law, one wonders whether the NCU will not be more divisive than cohesive.

In spite of, or because of, the strict restrictions placed on political activities, university students in Seoul began antigovernment demonstrations on October 3, 1973, and these spread rapidly throughout the country. The students demanded the dissolution of the South Korean Central Intelligence Agency, an end to the pervasive and severe suppression of freedoms, and restriction of the rapid inroads of Japanese capital into the Korean economy. By November, the government began to make concessions by replacing the CIA director, releasing the students arrested for participating in the demonstrations, and withdrawing CIA agents from the universites and newspaper offices. But after some of the intellectuals and religious leaders launched a nationwide campaign to restore the old (1973) constitution, President Pak declared a state of emergency (on January 8, 1974) and clamped down on all antigovernment activities.

The DPRK had badly needed a constitutional revision, not because Kim Il-sŏng lacked control over his opponents, but because the ideological assumptions embodied in the old constitution as well as the political structure it had instituted had become obsolete soon after the constitution was adopted in 1948. It had been a constitution framed for the "bourgeois democratic" stage in North Korea, while by 1958 the North Korean leadership was claiming to have entered the "socialist era."

Thus the new constitution was labeled the "socialist constitution," and the first four chapters of the eleven-chapter document (72 out of 149 articles) are devoted to the North Korean version of socialist principles of politics, economy, culture, and basic rights and duties of citizens. The new constitution also introduced a major structural change in the political system by creating the office of the president, with powers not very dissimilar from those of the ROK president under the new constitution. It also created the twenty-five member Central People's Committee, headed by the president, which was empowered to make all important decisions for the republic. Most of the major functions of the Supreme People's Assembly and its Presidium were given to either the president or the Central People's Committee.

These changes, however, did not basically alter the power distribution among the highest-ranking elites in North Korea beacuse the Korean Workers' party under the leadership of General Secretary Kim Il-sŏng had long since become a superstate and its control over the society was complete. The only new situation that might be relevant to future negotiations with South Korea was that the party leadership appoint (or, strictly speaking, elected) a number of individuals either in the cultural field or otherwise well known in South Korea to the now-emasculated Presidium of the Supreme People's Assembly. A more frequent use of the Presidium for propaganda purposes can therefore be anticipated. While ROK President Pak had come under attack from various quarters in South Korea for the manner in which he had conducted the negotiations with the North, there was no sign whatsoever from the North that would indicate any dissent against government policies. Given the nature of the totalitarian system built up by President Kim Il-sŏng during the last two and a half decades, it would have been highly surprising if any such indications had appeared.

Foreign Policy and Internal Goals. The foregoing outline of events brings up the question of whether rapid change in the

international environment, as well as the opening of
communication channels between the two parts of Korea, has
affected the outlook and internal goals and policies of the
leadership in each part of Korea. The assumption was advanced at
the beginning of this chapter that the leaders of each system in
Korea are intent on enhancing the interest of their own system
for either altruistic or selfish reasons. Do the events bear out
this assumption? Is there any sign that the leadership of either
side began to adjust their internal goals and policies for the
sake of a united Korea? Has the leaders' perception of one
another changed? Has the frame of reference changed to that of
the larger unit?

A cursory survey of the speeches and editorials of the
principal newspapers of each society does not reveal any change
in frame of reference, in perception of the other side, or in
goals and policies. The leadership on each side are still
absorbed by the security, stability, and prosperity of their
society, and neither side seems willing to take any risks that
might jeopardize previously established goals. As has been shown
earlier, tactical changes in foreign policies did take place and
hostile verbiage was greatly reduced, but basic aims did not
change.

The basic attitude of the South Korean leader can be seen
from the following statement made at his New Year's press
conference of January 12, 1973:

"It is true that all these changes gave rise to our worries and
concern in that they might directly or indirectly bring about a
great change in the existing international order and balance of
power. . . .

"The government has accurately grasped and analyzed the reality
of the situation, keeping a close eye on its process and,
thereby, we have steered our own course on the basis of a
situation corresponding with our own national interest and have
adapted ourselves to the rapidly changing international
situation. . . .

". . . The move to détente among the big powers has certainly
contributed to alleviating tension and improving relations among
themselves. . . .

"However, the question has arisen as to whether the rapprochement
movement between the big powers has brought about the same
achievements and progress in favor of the small countries. . . .
I don't think that has always been the case. . . .

"Then, what did the normalization of Japan and China bring
about? It culminated in the rupture of diplomatic relations
between Japan and the Republic of China. . . . We know well
about the great blow the Republic of China has suffered.

"Here we arrive at the conclusion that the small powers are
urgently required to be armed with discreet judgment and
behavior in pursuing their own survival, independence, and peace
and in shaping their own destiny amidst the whirlpool of
international developments."

What then were his goals? President Pak's first goal was
that all activity must be directly linked to production. "The
most important thing above all else in fostering national power"
was "economic strength." The second was to establish "correct
social discipline and national ethics." According to President
Pak:

"Only when every one of us is firmly equipped with a thorough
sense of obligation and duty for the nation; with a generous
sense of social service; with good manners and propensity to
follow law and order; and finally with a spirit of diligence,
independence and cooperation, then will we be able to
demonstrate righteous national morals and ethos."

What was the ultimate purpose of economic development and
national strength? His answer was that "in the final analysis
the purpose is to bring about welfare to the people and to build
a welfare state."[85]
     Thus the points President Pak Chŏng-hui emphasized in his
speech were national interest, survival, independence, economic
development, social discipline, and peace. He saw the need for
further consolidation and integration with South Korea, which
would enable the nation to "pursue peaceful unifciation and to
contribute positively with [its] own hands and achieving
national prosperity and stability." These are the themes that
President Pak had stressed ever since he took over governmental
power in 1961, except, perhaps, that the anticommunism of the
earlier period was replaced by concerns with peace.
     The perceptions that the leaders of North and South Korea had
of one another as of January 1973 can be best observed in a
North Korean broadcast of January 9 that bitterly denounced the
alleged "provocative outcries" on the part of South Korean
military leaders. While the broadcast was primarily aimed at
reproaching the South Korean leadership, its text also reveals
the North Korean attitude toward South Korea:

"According to a report from Seoul, the 'commander of the marine corps' of South Korea described on January 5 the situation today . . . as a 'trying period of confrontation' and hammered away at the poppycock that they should 'win' in this confrontation and that they should 'prepare themselves to play a leading role in reunification,' too, and the like.

"This blast lays bare the world design to extend by 'strength' the colonial rule of U.S. imperialism to the northern half of the republic and attain 'reunification by prevailing over communism,' opposed to the peaceful reunification through unity and collaboration between the north and the south.

"This treacherous intention was brought to daylight when he shouted himself hoarse before ROK Army soldiers that the 'anti-communist' education should be strengthened to equip them with 'anti-communist spirit more perfectly' and that they should establish 'predominance of strength' and must be on strict guard and get fully ready to go into action.

"Earler, the 'chiefs of the general staff' of the South Korean ground, naval and air forces, fanning up a war atmosphere, let out a torrent of power-reeking outcries, before officers and men of the 'ROK Army' that they should be 'armed spiritually' to attain 'reunification by prevailing over communism. . . .'

"These outpourings bespeak that this is not the personal view of some brass hats in the upper crust of the South Korean military but shows the stand and attitude of the South Korean authorities concerning the question of national reunification. We, therefore, cannot tolerate these provocative outcries of the upper crust of the South Korean military.

"We bitterly denounce this endless stream of outbursts. . . . Should the South Korean side persist in the acts of fostering antagonism and split and fanning up an atmosphere of 'confrontation' and fight betraying the cause of independent, peaceful reunification of the country, it will only bring the scourge of a fraticidal war. . . ."[86]

In brief, the Sino-American détente and the contacts between the two parts of Korea did not affect in any substantial way the leaders' image of their counterparts across the cease-fire line. An attitude of confrontation still prevailed in the Korean peninsula.

If the North Korean leaders found the pronouncements the South Korean leaders made to their soldiers so provocative, did they themselves modify any of their previous goals? The following excerpts from President Kim Il-sŏng's speech of December 27, 1972, on the occasion of the adoption of the new constitution, provide some clues:

". . . We can confidently say that we have the defense power
strong enough to repulse the invasion of any and all enemies,
defend our country and people and safeguard the revolutionary
gains. . . .

"[The] new constitution] is to protect by law the socialist
system and the dictatorship of the proletariat established in
the northern half of the republic and to serve the revolutionary
cause of the working class. . . .

"[I]t is the fundamental revolutionary task of the government
of the republic to attain the complete victory of socialism in
the northern half, reject foreign forces on the nation-wide
scale and achieve the reunification and independence of the
country on a democratic basis.

"For the successful implementation of this task we must,
first of all, strengthen the functions and role of our
government to intensify the struggle against the hostile
elements at home and abroad opposed to our socialist system and
powerfully accelerate the ideological revolution to
revolutionize and proletarianize all the members of society. . . .

"[O]ur state regards the steady improvement of the people's
material and cultural life as its primary duty, as the supreme
principal of its activity. . . .

"We must continue to thoroughly implement the party's
military line, the main content of which is to turn the entire
army into an army of cadres, modernize it from top to bottom,
arm all the people and fortify the whole country, and make the
nation's defense impregnable so as to promptly crush any
aggressive acts of the imperialists and firmly defend the
security of the country and the people and our socialist gains.
. . ."

In short, the victory of socialism, ideological revolution,
fortifications and militarization of the country, and
improvement of the people's livelihood are some of the themes
stressed by the president at the end of 1972. One should note
that these are the points the North Korean leadership had
stressed for over a decade, and in spite of his remarkable self-
restrait in not directly attacking the South Korean leadership—
a restraint later reciprocated by his South Korean counterpart—
the president's speech did not indicate any alterations in the
nation's internal goals.

The Nature, Problems, and Prospects of the Dialogue
From these statements coming at the end of some eighteen months
of negotiations, as well as from the actions taken by each side

in other areas, one can derive certain tentative conclusions as to the nature of the dialogue, problem areas, and future prospects.

It can be said, first of all, that the North-South dialogue was not begun on the initiative of the Korean leaders of either North or South. The animosity between the two Koreas had been so intense that such a development would have been totally unthinkable even as late as the spring of 1971. The most crucial factor that stimulated the leaders of the two Koreas to swallow their intense hostility and proceed to engage in the dialogue was the momentous change in the East Asian policy of the United States and the favorable reaction from the PRC. While doubts and suspicions remained in July 1969 when President Nixon announced his Guam Doctrine, the seriousness of his intent could no longer be doubted after he publicly staked the prestige of his office as well as the future of his career on his historic journey to Peking. The two Koreas, which had been closely tied to the United States and the PRC respectively, were therefore compelled to reassess their positions and seek the best alternatives possible.

Thus the dialogue in Korea began as a reaction to the dynamic changes occurring around the Korean peninsula. Herein lies one of the most important differences between the Korean and German situations. While the two German states initiated and maintained contacts with each other on their own initiative, in Korea the memory of the civil war and the character of the regimes had made it impossible for the two Koreas to engage in any meaningful dialogue before 1971. Not only were contacts across the truce line not maintained, but also neither of the regimes in Korea seems to have been prepared for such a possibility. This background explains the intermittent negotiating sessions interspersed with hostile pronouncements.

It is true, of course, that the North Korean leader had talked about the need for attaining peaceful unification ever since the end of active hostilities in 1953. But as Kim Il-sŏng himself had declared in November 1954, even his followers in North Korea were skeptical of such advocacy.[87] Since then North Korea had presented many proposals for contacts, exchanges, negotiations, joint commissions, reduction of forces, and mechanisms of confederation,[88] but all these fell on deaf ears in the South.

On the surface most of the North Korean proposals appeared reasonable. DPRK Foreign Minister Nam Il proposed at the 1954 Geneva Conference (1) to hold general elections for a united All-Korean National Assembly under the supervision of neutral nations,

(2) the organization of an all-Korean Commission composed of an
equal number of representatives from both sides, (3)
implementation of economic and cultural exchanges, (4) the
withdrawal of all foreign military forces from Korea, and (5) a
guarantee of the peaceful development of Korea by all interested
countries. In October 1954 North Korea again called for an
immediate meeting at either Seoul or Pyongyang to negotiate
unification. In March 1955 North Korea called for a
nonaggression pact with simultaneous reduction of armed forces.
In June 1956 another call was issued for an international
conference of the powers concerned, and in September 1957 and
again in February 1958 North Korea proposed a mutual reduction
of armed forces to 100,000 troops. In August 1960 the North
Korean premier called for the establishment of a confederation
as a transitional step toward a more complete unification. He
also demanded that the two governments conclude an agreement
that would expedite the speedy withdrawal of U.S. troops from
South Korea and would be accompanied by mutual renunciation of
the use of force. He also called for a Joint Economic Committee
to coordinate only economic and commercial matters in case the
confederation idea was unacceptable.

A glance at the agenda of the South-North Coordinating
Committee established in 1972 would reveal that much the same
agenda had been presented by the North Koreans one or two
decades before. Why was this delay then necessary? Why did South
Korean leaderships of different background and personality and
of different generations consistently brush aside the North
Korean proposals?

The first factor that had prevented the South Korean leaders
from any kind of contacts with the North has already been noted,
i.e., deep-seated distrust of the communists. It should be
recalled that the Supreme People's Assembly of the DPRK had
issued a call for peaceful unification through merger of the
legislative bodies of both Koreas on June 19, 1950, just a week
before the North Korean army launched the all-out invasion of
the South. While the North Korean regime still insists that
South Korea provoked the war, there is no doubt in the minds of
those in South Korea that the massive attack had been
prearranged and that the call for peaceful unification had been
issued only to lower the guard of the South Korean forces. The
same leader that launched the attack in 1950 still leads the
North, and hence any proclamation or proposal emanating from
Pyongyang was treated as a Trojan horse.

The second factor that militated against earlier North-
South contacts was the character of the monolithic political

system that President Kim Il-sŏng had built in North Korea since
the end of the Korean War. In addition, the incessant talk of
implementing the socialist revolution and building a "democratic
and revolutionary base" in the North gave no reason to the South
Korean leadership to change their perception of the communists
as aggressively dedicated to overthrowing the South Korean
political, social, and economic system. Until 1958 the top
elites in North Korea were engaged in fierce internecine
struggles for power, and after that the victorious faction under
Kim Il-sŏng allowed no dissent even among the highest-ranking
elites. The North Korean leadership manifested the utmost
rigidity in its pursuit of established goals, and there was no
sign that meaningful dialogue of any kind could take place.

In late 1962, a scant nine years after the cease-fire, the
North Korean regime reverted to a very bellicose policy, calling
for the fortification of the entire country and the arming of
every individual. It was impossible even to speculate on the
possibility of a dialogue in such an atmosphere. North Korea
continued to insist on peaceful unification, but the formula
called for the overthrow of the South Korean leadership by
revolutionary forces and the establishment of a regime willing
to toe the line established in Pyongyang. Under this formula,
unification was to be brought about peacefully only in the sense
that the regular armed forces of the DPRK would not be employed,
but nonetheless it presupposed the use of violence within South
Korea. The North Korean leadership expedited this process by
dispatching to the South a large number of armed agents.
Naturally, the South Korean leadership reacted vigorously
against this formula of "peaceful" unification.

Of course, the character of the South Korean leadership also
had its impact on the relationship between North and South Korea.
As is well known, President Syngman Rhee, who ruled South Korea
between 1948 and 1960, was strongly oriented against communism.
Even if ideology were not involved, however, Rhee could not
condone the idea of negotiating with the communists who not only
had defied his authority but had attacked him savagely as an
American imperialist lackey ever since 1946. The launching of
the civil war by the communists intensifed his hatred, of course,
and for him the only reasonable course of action against the
communists was to destroy them. One may recall that the Republic
of Korea government under President Rhee balked at the idea of
participating in the truce talks at Panmunjom and did not sign
the cease-fire agreement in 1953.

The leadership that succeeded President Rhee in 1960
contained some more pragmatically oriented elements, and had the

Democratic party been allowed to remain in power some form of
negotiation might have taken place. But a military junta quickly
replaced the Democrats in May 1961. The main forces that
constituted that junta still rule South Korea.

Even a cursory survey of the circumstances of the growth of
the officers' corps and the army in South Korea will reveal the
general attitude of the present leadership in South Korea toward
the North Korean communists. Under the United States military
government in South Korea, the security force, which eventually
developed into the ROK army, recruited anyone who had had even
the remotest experience in the military field. A large number of
leftist-oriented young men joined the security force, and the
Korean Communist party built a sizable underground organization
within it. By 1949, however, the army had rid itself of anyone
with the slightest taint of communism. After the outbreak of the
war, the army grew in size, and, through their bitter, personal
experience of combating the communist forces, its leaders
emotionally reinforced their previous anticommunist convictions.
Having commanded large armies at the front as well as at the
rear, these men became intimately acquainted with the potential
of the communist forces. Through personal experience and
otherwise, they also became well acquainted with the strategies
and tactics of communist revolution. Thus the junta leaders
could not easily accommodate the idea of a dialogue with the
communists. According to some sources, the North Korean leaders
sent an emissary to Seoul soon after the junta took power, but
he was promptly executed.

Another reason for South Korea's refusal in the past to
entertain any of the North Korean proposals—as well as for
North Korea's persistence in presenting them—was the South
Korean attempt to isolate and contain the communists and prevent
them from gaining international recognition. When the Republic
of Korea was established in 1948, it quickly obtained
recognition from the United Nations as the only legitimate
government in Korea, and since then diplomatic recognition has
been accorded it by many noncommunist nations. The DPRK, on the
other hand, was branded an aggressor by the United Nations in
1950 and was thus placed in a highly unfavorable position. It,
in turn, attacked the United Nations as an instrument of
American imperialism and denied that the UN had any authority
or legitimacy to deal with the Korean question.

Understandably, the ROK was not prepared to relinquish the
advantage it had gained from the favorable international
atmosphere since 1948. Establishment of any kind of nonhostile
relationship with the DPRK would have had the effect of

removing the stigma attached to North Korea and mitigating the
impact of its international condemnation. The ROK also found it
convenient to insist on general elections throughout Korea under
United Nations supervision while the DPRK initially insisted on
supervision by neutral nations and, later, on the solution of
the Korean problem by the Koreans themselves. It was only when
the situation in the UN became unfavorable for the ROK that the
latter stressed the importance of the Korean question not being
discussed at the United Nations General Assembly.

   Further, the ROK government refused to accord equal status to
the DPRK when the latter proposed a joint all-nation commission
with an equal number of representatives from both sides.
Granting equal status to the North Korean regime would have been
tantamount to recognizing its legitimacy, and South Korea was
not prepared to take such a step.

   These reasons, by and large, explain the adamant refusal of
the South Korean leadership to take up any of the earlier North
Korean proposals. But domestic and international pressures
directed against the policy of total negation of the communists
began to mount in the early 1960s. First, although the ROK's
position on the DPRK did have a strong effect on some of the
closer allies of South Korea, the DPRK gradually expanded its
diplomatic and commercial ties abroad, and the predominant
position of the ROK began to deteriorate. The changing
composition of the United Nations, climaxed by the admission of
the PRC, also affected the position of the ROK there. East and
West Germany began to improve their relations and by engaging in
commercial, postal, and personnel exchanges considerably
heightened the expectations of the South Korean populace. The
inevitable question posed in Korea was, if the Germans could do
it, why not Korea?

   The unrestrained outpouring of emotion after the downfall of
Syngman Rhee in 1960 was stopped by the junta in 1961, but
public clamor for rational solutions of unification problems led
to the establishment of a Special Committee for the Study of
National Unification within the National Assembly in 1966 and
the creation of the cabinet-level National Unification Board in
1969. Korean scholars also responded by holding a large
international conference on the problems of unification in
August 1970.

   If any kind of consensus developed out of all the public-
opinion polls, hearings, seminars, and conferences in South
Korea, it was the idea that some kind of contact should be
established with the North Korean regime at a proper time and
that limited functional contacts should be maintained. The

opposition parties openly supported the idea of facilitating
meetings and visits of divided families as early as 1966, and
many others talked of the possibility of exchanging reporters,
scholars, sports teams, artists, and so on. Possibilities for
commercial contacts as well as postal exchanges were also
discussed. But the breakthrough did not come until the summer of
1972.

The most important factor behind the reluctance of the South
Korean leadership before that was the fear that the
sociopolitical system in South Korea would provide too great an
advantage to North Korea in the event that exchanges with North
Korea were initiated. They feared that the initiation of
exchanges under existing conditions would open the floodgates to
communist propaganda over which the government would not be able
to exercise effective control.[89]

President Pak Chŏng-hui's repeated assertion that South Korea
must concentrate on economic development for the time being and
that discussions about unification should be postponed until the
second half of the 1970s also reveals another facet of the
problem. Was economic development in South Korea behind that of
North Korea? Or was the president hoping that the South Korean
economy would be so superior to that of North Korea by the
second half of the 1970s that the South would overwhelm the
North? These points call for closer scrutiny.

It does not require an elaborate analysis to see that the
North Korean leaders are in a far more advantageous position
than their South Korean counterparts in dealing with mutual
exchanges. The past policies of the South Korean leadership are
in part to blame for this situation, but there were factors
operating that transcended policy choices.

It should be noted, first of all, that the North Koreans have
built a tightly closed, mononlithic, and totally mobilized
society around President Kim Il-sŏng and the Korean Workers'
party. The party and the state apparatus have been used as a
mechanism of surveillance, control, indoctrination, and
education, reaching every aspect of individual lives in the
North. A society of some 15 million people has a party with 1.7
million members (the highest per capita membership in the
communist world). It also has the Socialist Working Youth
League (Komsomol), the Trade Union Federation, the Agricultural
Workers' League, and the Democratic Youth League, all auxiliary
organizations of the party. Every individual has been closely
screened, the extent of his or her loyalty to the regime has
been assessed, and necessary measures have been taken to prevent
potentially disloyal elements from treading the wrong path. The

mass media are entirely operated by the state and party
apparatus, and travel is closely regulated. Every individual in
the society interacts with the party and the state continuously
through daily work, where his work style and productivity are
closely evaluated by cadres of either the party or auxiliary
organizations, at interminable meetings or other "social"
occasions. It is an "open society" only in the sense that
individuals shun privacy and private thought, which can be
easily interpreted as antiparty and antistate behavior, and thus
spell danger for the individual.

Opening of contacts with South Korea, therefore, does not pose
much of a threat to the North Korean system. Even if any
information contrary to the established party line does reach an
individual, the party and the auxiliary organizations at the
lowest level can effectively blot it out. Only the very foolish
would refuse to cleanse themselves from all "falsehood"
propagated by the class enemy.

In South Korea, on the other hand, such thought control could
never be exercised. The government can, and in fact does, screen
out much "undesirable" information from the mass media, but even
here control is not perfect. Until 1971, when President Pak
declared the state of emergency, the opposition parties, the
press, the intellectuals, and the students openly criticized
government policies, and the government was often placed on the
defensive. Even under martial law, government control is limited
to control of speech, publication, and assembly, and the
government could not even hope to stop private channels of
communications, let alone to control private thoughts and
behavior.

Why, one may ask then, is the South Korean populace so
vulnerable to communist propaganda? A complete answer to this
question would require a separate essay, but some obvious
reasons, stemming from errors and imperfections of the South
Korean system, may be cited.

One of these reasons can be attributed to errors of judgment
on the part of successive governments in South Korea. In an
effort to inculcate strong anticommunist attitudes in the South
Korean populace, successive governments of the ROK imposed
strong censorship over matters pertaining to North Korea, and
only the worst aspects of that society were allowed to be
depicted in public. Until the latter part of the 1960s, even the
most trustworthy intellectuals were barred from free access to
North Korean publications, thus preventing all rational
discussions. As a result, a wide credibility gap developed
between the government and the public, which encouraged the

uninitiated to idealize the unknown. Very recently, within the last two or three years, some corrective measures have been taken in regard to certain segments of the intellectuals, but the public by and large is still kept in the dark.

Of course, the same phenomenon has taken place in the North with respect to news about the South, but as was stated above, North Korea has in the meantime developed an effective system to resist the possible inflow of counterinformation, while the very nature of the South Korean political system has not permitted such a development. Therefore, if and when extensive exchanges take place between the two parts of Korea, there is a strong likelihood that the masses in South Korea will be affected by North Korean propaganda.*

North Korean propaganda has concentrated on (1) the removal of United States armed forces from South Korea, (2) the solution of the Korean problem by the Koreans alone, and (3) the need for extensive exchanges in various areas. It also puts forward the claim that the communist system is inherently superior to that of capitalism and that President Kim Il-sŏng is an unparalleled leader of the Korean people. Let us briefly consider these points.

The first point, the removal of the United States forces from Korea, is without any doubt the core of North Korean efforts of the last several years. Ever since the cease-fire agreement was

----

* It is not assumed here that the exchange program would lead to the immediate exchange of publications from either side for the public at large. But how would a South Korean farmer, who had been inundated with reports that the North Korean populace was constantly suffering from semistarvation, react to a letter from his relative in the North reporting that he is well-fed and well-clothed and is living in a tile-roofed house? How would a South Korean official censor such a private letter? Would any one in the North, regardless of his actual condition, depict his life in less than glowing terms, particularly when he is likely to be "helped" by the cadres from the party, the agricultural cooperative, the Komsomol, the Agricultural Workers' League, or the Women's League? It should be noted in passing that while North Korea has these auxiliary organizations of the party to provide "help" and "guidance" to the letter-writers, and to ensure smooth processing of the letters, there is no such apparatus in the South. The "processing" of these letters in South Korea, particularly in Seoul, which has over five million people, would pose a serious problem.

signed at Panmunjom in 1953, the North Koreans have harped on
this point. Since the communists would have succeeded in their
attempt to unify the nation in 1950 had not the Americans
intervened, North Korea's anxiety on this score is
understandable.*

Pyongyang's advocacy of the removal of the American forces
from South Korea and of solving the Korean problem by the
Koreans themselves caters to the most deeply felt nationalistic
feelings of the Korean people. This advocacy therefore serves
the North Korean communists well. It also caters to powerful
forces in the United States that have been advocating the
withdrawal of all American forces from East Asia. As indicated
earlier, the North Koreans further reinforce their argument by
proposing the mutual reduction of armed forces and even
termination of all mutual defense pacts with foreign countries,
in order to realize the withdrawal of the United States forces.
The communists may ask, would it not be beneficial to the entire
Korean people if the wasteful defense expenditures were
curtailed and the human and material energies wasted on armament
were redirected to peaceful pursuits? Why does the ROK
government persist in degrading the integrity of the Korean
people by insisting on the continuation of American presence in
the Korean territory?

These are powerful arguments indeed, and perhaps no other
issue has caused more anxiety and trepidation to the South
Korean leadership since the announcement of the Guam Doctrine.
As tension declines in East Asia as a whole and as negotiations
among the Koreans progress, this line of argument will gather
further strength, increasing pressure on the South Korean
leadership.

South Korea's insistence on a continuing American presence on
the Korean peninsula is due to three interrelated factors: (1)
the geopolitics of the two Koreas, (2) the political systems of
their respective allies, and (3) continued suspicion of North
Korean intentions. The first two factors clearly place South

----

* The latest effort on this point was made by Foreign Minister
Hŏ Tam who flew to Peking in February 1973, just prior to the
arrival of Presidential Adviser Henry A. Kissinger. Hŏ is
believed to have asked the Chinese to convey to Dr. Kissinger
the North Korean desire to have the U.S. forces removed from
South Korea (The New York Times, Feb. 14, 1973). It is possible
that Hŏ Tam sought to see Kissinger personally in Peking.

Korea in a disadvantageous position even when military parity is
maintained between North and South Korea, and hence the South
Korean leaders are fearful that premature withdrawal of the U.S.
forces would place them in a dangerous position. Although
President Kim of the DPRK has repeatedly assured the world that
his regime never had any intention of provoking a war and that
the DPRK has never committed aggression against the South, the
leaders in Seoul have too fresh a memory of June 1950 to believe
Kim's words or to trust the fate of South Korea to his promises.

A glance at the map clearly shows the inherent geopolitical
advantage North Korea enjoys over South Korea. North Korea's two
principal allies, the Soviet Union and the PRC, border on the
DPRK to the north, while the principal South Korean ally, the
United States, is thousands of miles away. While entry of the
forces of North Korea's allies could occur on short notice, it
would take days for the U.S. to reestablish its military
presence in South Korea. Moreover, while the leaders of the
Soviet Union and the PRC can make decisions to assist the DPRK
with relative ease, the constitutional provisions of the United
States would require lengthy deliberation before the president
could act, even if he were inclined to keep treaty commitments.
A war in Korea could be over before the United States reached a
decision and sent help. Such a situation, of course, need not be
faced if the United States forces presently stationed in Korea
are not withdrawn completely. South Korean authorities believe
that as long as the United States displays a firm intention to
support South Korea's defense by continuing to station U.S.
troops in Korea, the contingency of war is not likely to occur,
while premature withdrawal might precipitate another conflict.
South Korean authorities frequently cite the historical
precedent of 1949-1950 in support of their argument. The United
States forces were withdrawn in 1949, and the invasion took
place in the following summer.

One could argue that modern warfare is not decided by
infantry and hence that the geographic proximity of one's allies
need not affect the outcome of a war. If this is indeed the
case, however, South Korea's dependence on its allies becomes
even greater because the DPRK is known to possess an air force
and a navy much superior to that of the ROK.

Certainly no one assumes that United States troops will be
stationed in Korea indefinitely. Both U.S. and ROK officials have
mentioned 1975, and later 1980, as the year when the American troops
will be completely withdrawn from Korea. In the meantime, efforts
are being made to modernize the ROK forces to enable them to
meet all contingencies.

The leadership of the DPRK, as expected, has taken exception
to this modernization policy and has attacked it as an imperialist
design to wreck the North-South dialogue. But until the dialogue
in other areas succeeds in allaying the deep-seated distrust, and
until the South Korean leaders feel secure in their position, even
in the inherently disadvantageous position, they are not likely to
yield on this most crucial issue. It is, of course, possible for
the two parties to negotiate on the means and procedures to bring
about the reduction of forces leading to complete U.S. withdrawal.
The ROK government, in the meantime, could effectively counter
whatever propaganda may be forthcoming from the North.

Finally, some mention should be made of the relative strength
of the economics of the two societies. Fierce competition has
taken place during the past two decades in this sector, and past
accomplishments as well as future prospects are likely to
determine the extent of personnel and commercial exchanges.
Discussion of these points may also reveal the areas in which
both sides are vulnerable to propaganda.

Lack of data and different statistical methods make detailed
comparisons impossible, but some broad generalizations can be
made. North Korea has approximately 120,000 square kilometers of
land while South Korea has approximately 100,000 square
kilometers. The North Korean population is estimated to be
approximately 15.5 million while South Korea has over 34 million
people. In terms of population density, therefore, the ratio is
1 to 3. In terms of natural resources, including energy, North
Korea is overwhelmingly superior. Potential hydroelectric power
sources are four times greater in North Korea than in the South,
and coal and iron reserves are nine times greater in the North.[90]

Because of these geographic factors, the Japanese colonial
administration that ruled Korea between 1910 and 1945
concentrated on industrial development in the North, leaving
much of the South to agriculture. As of 1940, the percentage
relationship of heavy industrial development between North and
South Korea was 79 to 21, while that of light industry was 53
to 47. Because of the difference in industrial structure,
however, industrial laborers represented 45.2 percent of the
population in the North and 54.8 percent in the South.[91]

Because of the Japanese emphasis on heavy industrial
development in the North, particularly toward the end of the
Japanese occupation period when Japan needed more war materials,
industrial production in Korea as a whole had begun to occupy a
more significant portion of total production, rising from 30.7
percent in 1936 to 37.4 percent in 1944, while agriculture
declined from 49.8 percent of the total production in 1936 to

37.4 per cent in 1944.[92] The proportion of industrial workers
among the total population was still minute, only 4.8 percent of
the people employed in industry, while agriculture employed 74.8
percent as of 1940.[93] As of 1945 Korea was still a predominantly
agricultural society with a very low living standard.

Since then, in spite of the devastating war between 1950 and
1953, substantial progress has been made in both North and South
Korea, and the economic structure of the society has undergone a
rapid change. By 1946 the North Korean communists had
nationalized all the major industrial, transportation,
communications, financial, and commercial establishments, and
had begun economic development in a socialist framework. By 1958,
when all the farmers were put in collectives, known as
cooperatives, all forms of private enterprise had ceased to exist
in the North. Meanwhile, South Korea adopted the market-oriented,
capitalist form of development, with, however, the state playing
a major role in the economy through fiscal policies and control
over the import and export of goods, capital, and services.

Through successive economic development plans (the three-year
plan, 1953-1956; the accelerated five-year plan, 1957-1960; the
extended seven-year plan, 1961-1970; and the six-year plan,
1971-1976), the North Korean leadership has concentrated on
industrial development, particularly in heavy industry and has
accomplished great results. Electric power generation, for
example, increased from 5.9 billion kilowatt hours in 1949 to
16.5 billion kilowatt hours in 1970. Coal production increased
from 4 million tons to 27.5 million tons in the same period,
cement production from half a million tons to 4 million, and
production of chemical fertilizers from 400,000 metric tons to
1,500,000 metric tons. Increase in grain production has been
much slower, but the North Koreans were able to increase
production from 2.6 million metric tons in 1949 to approximately
5.5 million tons in 1970.

South Korea's rate of growth has been no less phenomenal.
During the period immediately after the Korean War, South Korea
had very limited growth. The entire decade of the 1950s showed
an average annual growth rate of only 4.8 percent. Especially in
the late 1950s, when the North was engaged in its extraordinary
forced march, the South seemed close to stagnation. But
substantial economic growth in South Korea began with the first
five-year plan (1962-1966). During it, annual growth averaged
8.3 percent, with increases particularly marked in such basic
industries as power, petroleum, cement, and chemicals. The
industrial sector averaged 17.9 percent growth during those
years. Industrial growth accelerated in the course of the second

five-year plan. Overall growth averaged 12.7 percent for the
years 1967-1969, and industrial production grew 30.1 percent
annually in the 1965-1968 period, one of the highest increase
rates in the world. The rate of growth during the third five-
year plan, launched in 1972, is expected to decline. The
government aims at an average 8.5 percent annual overall growth
for 1972-1976, with the industrial sector scheduled to grow at
an average annual rate of 15 to 17 percent, a very respectable
showing for South Korea. Many inherent shortcomings have been
overcome. In electric power generation, for example, the ROK
government emphasized thermal power generation because the
sources of hydroelectric power were limited. By 1973 total
electric power generation reached 12 billion kilowatt hours, of
which 8.5 percent were from thermal sources. Coal production
reached 10 million metric tons in 1965, increased to 12
million in 1967, and 14.7 million metric tons in
1973. Urea fertilizer production was also started in 1960 and
reached 698,000 metric tons in 1973. Since the proportion of
active ingredients in urea fertilizer is far greater than that
of other fertilizers, South Korea enjoys a considerable
advantage in spite of the discrepancy in the gross weight of
fertilizer production. Cement production in the South reached
5.8 million metric tons in 1970 and 8.2 million in 1973. Food-
grain production in the South also registered a slower growth
rate; total production in 1973 was 7.16 million metric tons.[94]
    These developments also brought about very significant
changes in the social composition of the respective societies.
By 1960 North Korea was already claiming that the ratio of total
production in industry and agriculture was 71 to 29 while the
same ratio in 1954 was 42 to 58. The percentages of blue-collar
workers, white-collar workers, and farmers was reported to be
31.7, 14.4, and 53.0 in 1958, but there is no doubt that the
ratio of workers and farmers was reversed by the late 1960s. In
the South, agriculture made up 24.0 percent of the total GNP in
1971, while manufacturing, excluding construction,
transportation, and so on, make up 28.8 percent. Primary
industries, i.e., agriculture, forestry, and fishing, still
employ 61.3 percent of the total work force, while mining and
manufacturing employ a mere 10.7 percent (as of June 1970).
    While these statistics are important, particularly in
assessing the possibilities of establishing commercial
relations between North and South, propagandists of both sides
will be focusing on the problem areas of the other. What are
these features? In what particular areas are both sides
vulnerable?

The North Koreans have been advancing the highly political
theme that their phenomenal advance is the result of the policy
of self-reliance and that Pyongyang has attained self-
sufficiency in most sectors of the economy. They boast that the
DPRK is a highly industrialized society and that the security
of the workers is guaranteed in view of the fact that there are
no unemployed. (North Korea in fact suffers from a labor
shortage.) They claim, somewhat unjustifiably, that hardship is
a thing of the past and that the life of abundance has already
been achieved. The agricultural collectives, they declare, are
highly mechanized, irrigated, electrified, and the supply of
chemical fertilizers is adequate. The propagandists also boast
of superior education and welfare programs for the young, the
aged, and the sick.

South Korea also stresses its high rate of growth, the
increasing number of factories and high-rise buildings, and the
abundance of consumer goods and amenities of life.

Each society, however, has some serious shortcomings that are
likely to be highlighted if channels of communication become
more open. In spite of rapid industrial development, South Korea
has been plagued by a very high rate of unemployment. Although
the workers' life has been improving, a large number of
unskilled laborers are still poorly treated. The living
conditions of many city dwellers are very poor. The gap between
the rich and the poor and between the city and the country is
clearly visible. The scale of farming is too small, and many
farmers find it unprofitable to remain on the farms. The life of
the fisherman is also hard. Welfare measures, including medical
care, are virtually nonexistent.

Life in North Korea, on the other hand, is severely regimented
and the prolonged enforcement of the Stakhanovite movement
(known in North Korea as the "flying horse movement"),
accompanied by an extreme austerity policy, has pushed the
endurance of the masses to the extreme. Consumer goods are still
in short supply, with clothing constituting a special problem.
Highly nationalistic, even xenophobic economic policies have
demanded a high rate of forced domestic savings, and
gratification is postponed to an indefinite future.

Given these weaknesses, neither of the regimes is likely to
be sanguine about a very extensive exchange of persons in the
immediate future. Each side possesses a substantial number of
citizens susceptible to the other side's propaganda, and the
free flow of information or personnel would tend to erode each
system. The security system on each side would be severely taxed
if a large influx of persons from the other side were permitted.

For reasons discussed above, North Korea does enjoy some
advantages in this aspect, but it should be remembered that the
solidarity of the system has been brought about under conditions
of almost total isolation from the external world. Sudden
removal of the barriers might have too traumatic an effect on
the entire system, in spite of its relative strength.

In view of these facts, one can safely predict that the
current dialogue will not lead to very extensive exchanges in
either personnel or postal service, at least during the next
several years. Carefully selected reporters, scholars, artists,
politicians, economic personnel, sports teams, and others may
exchange visits, but their itineraries and activities are likely
to be strictly regulated in order not to disrupt the functioning
of each system. The leadership of both sides may also find it
mutually advantageous to cooperate on the establishment of joint
all-Korean groups in sports, arts, scholarship, and a few other
functional areas. Both sides will also find it advantageous to
engage in trade relationships. But it is doubtful that these
contacts and cooperation will soon spill over into the political
realm and thus encourage the process of national unification.

The political relationship between the two regimes is likely
to develop quite independent of these functional contacts.
Probably, the attitudes and actions of the major powers
surrounding the Korean peninsula will exert the greatest
influence on the dialogue in Korea, although the major powers
will in turn be affected by the attitudes and actions of the
two Koreas. For this reason, we must look briefly at the goals
and policies of the United States, Japan, China, and the Soviet
Union.

As has been mentioned before, United States policy in the
post-Vietnam era will be geared to bring about peace and
stability with minimal overseas involvement. Attainment of this
goal will require the "collaboration" of not only the Soviet
Union and the PRC but also both Koreas. Escalation of tension in
Korea would adversely affect the pursuit of the U.S. goals, and
hence the United States is likely to encourage the Korean
dialogue. Stability in Korea, of course, requires a firm U.S.
commitment to support the defense of South Korea, and therefore
the U.S. is not likely to depart from its present policies so
drastically as to disrupt the equilibrium, although its South
Korean ally will be asked to absorb more responsibilites as time
passes.

The following statement of Dr. Kissinger, published before
his appointment as presidential adviser, aptly summarizes the
United States policy toward the Korean dialogue:

"In the late sixties, the situation is more complex. The United
States is no longer in a position to operate programs globally;
it has to encourage them. It can no longer impose its preferred
solution; it must seek to evoke it. In the forties and fifties,
we offered remedies; in the late sixties and in the seventies
our role will have to be to contribute to a structure that will
foster the initiative of others. . . . We can continue to
contribute to defense and positive programs, but we must seek to
encourage and not stifle a sense of local responsibility. Our
contribution should not be the sole or principal effort, but it
should make the difference between success and failure."[95]

The United States created a "structure" that fostered the
initiative of the Koreans. The future efforts of the United
States are also likely to be concentrated on the reinforcement
of this structure through U.S. policies toward the PRC, Japan,
and the Soviet Union, rather than on intervention in the
negotiations in Korea.
    To a large extent, Japanese interests in the Korean
peninsula converge with those of the United States. Japan has a
large stake in peace and stability on the Korean peninsula for
security and economic reasons. Progress in the Korean dialogue
and an accompanying reduction of tension would not only minimize
the possibility of entangling Japan militarily but would also
increase the possibility of Japanese trade with both Koreas.
    The Japanese, however, may find the pace of progress in the
Korean dialogue too slow to suit their own interests. Some of
their economic giants are eagerly waiting for further
breakthroughs in the negotiations that would lessen the South
Korean objections to their investment in North Korea. A decline
in the strength of the Liberal Democratic party in either of the
two houses of the Diet will force the LDP to form a coalition
with the opposition parties, and as all the opposition parties
have been advocating closer ties with the DPRK, the LDP
leadership will find it necessary to accommodate them.
    Whether the establishment of closer ties between Japan and
the DPRK will have a marked effect on the process of
negotiation in Korea, however, remains to be seen. There is no
doubt that such a development would create further pressures on
the South Korean leaders. But would this development compel the
South Korean leaders to compromise and accelerate the North-
South rapprochement? Or would it have the effect of heightening
South Korean tension and therefore cause further retrenchment?
What would be the long-range effect of such a development on
peace and stability in East Asia and on Japan? These are some

of the hard questions that the Japanese leadership will be
forced to deal with in the very near future, and the answers to
them will determine Japan's course. It should be remembered,
however, that the Japanese have an overriding interest in South
Korea's political and economic stability and that this interest
is likely to govern Japan's basic policies in the next several
years.

As was made clear in the joint communiqués issued in
Shanghai and Moscow, both the PRC and the Soviet Union have
strongly supported the North Korean policies on Korean
unification, including the demand for the withdrawal of the
United States forces from the Korean peninsula. On the surface,
at least, both allies of the DPRK seem to share a common
interest in the Korean question. The PRC reportedly even
supplied a channel of communication between Foreign Minister Hŏ
Tam of the DPRK and Presidential Adviser Henry Kissinger. But to
what extent are Noth Korea's allies willing to exert their
influence on behalf of the DPRK? How committed are the Soviet
Union and the PRC to the withdrawal of the United States troops
from South Korea, for example?

On this and other crucial questions affecting the power
balance in East Asia as a whole, priorities and preferences are
likely to vary among the communist powers. Both the PRC and the
Soviet Union agree on the undesirability of the rise of Japanese
militarism and on the reduction of the American military
presence in East Asia. At the same time, neither the Soviet
Union nor the PRC would find the sudden withdrawal of U.S.
forces and commitments from East Asia advantageous, because the
vacuum might very well be filled by either the communist
adversary or by resurgent Japanese military might. Premier Chou
En-lai has been quoted as saying recently that Japan needs the
American nuclear umbrella against the Soviet Union and also
needs the defense treaty with the United States.[96] Liaison
offices were established in Peking and Washington before
American troops left Taiwan. In this situation the PRC would not
find it either desirable or necessary to press for the
withdrawal of American forces from Korea. The Soviet Union, on
the other hand, does not feel any threat from the skeleton
American forces in Korea and has never made any serious attempt
to press the United States on this matter.

In short, none of the four big powers surrounding Korea is
adversely affected by the recent developments in Korea, and
none would have an overriding interest in intervening on behalf
of its ally in the process of negotiation. It would be to the
interest of all the big powers to encourage the Korean

negotiations, even though none of them, except perhaps Japan, would be greatly affected by their outcome. Although the United States, the PRC, and the Soviet Union engaged in a war in Korea,[97] Korea is still a peripheral problem for these powers that are engaged in the struggle for survival, power, and hegemony, and they are not likely to alter their principal goals for the sake of their small ally. What Japan does in the next decade will significantly affect the balance between the DPRK and the ROK, but what impact this will have upon the course of negotiations is uncertain.

The impact of the major powers, however, should not be measured purely in terms of what they decide to do on the Korean question. As the Korean case clearly indicates, interactions among the major powers can often exert stronger and more decisive impacts on a smaller power than would their direct action toward it. In the case of Korea, the quadrangular relationship among the big powers will not fail to affect the future of the dialogue.

The future relationship between the two Koreas, in the final analysis, however, depends on the leaders of the two political systems. If the events of the three years since July 1972 proved anything at all, it was that a wide gap exists between the two sets of leaders in terms of ideologies, aims, and their visions of a unified Korea. But the frequent visits did have a salutary effect for the future of Korea in that the leaders—and to some extent the people—of both sides came to know their adversaries and became able to assess the conditions on the other side in a more realistic manner. While these developments may not contribute immediately to a better relationship between the two Koreas, at least the chances of miscalculation have been reduced. In time, when the leaders of both sides are ready, they may be able to arrive at a more realistic formula of negotiations rather than issuing highly idealized communiqués that contain many tantalizing but unrealistic promises. It is difficult to predict when each side will feel ready to face the other side in a realistic manner. But as each works toward the goal of reducing its vulnerability to the other side, chances for reopening negotiations will be improved.

Notes to Chapter 1

1. For an earlier, less extensive treatment of some of the themes of this chapter, see my Peking, Moscow and Beyond, The Washington Papers, no. 6 (Washington, D.C.: Georgetown University Center for Strategic and International Studies, 1973). See also Michel Tatu, Le triangle Washington-Moscou-Pékin et les deux Europe(s) (Paris: Casterman, 1972); his previous 1970 Atlantic Institute paper, The Great Power Triangles: Washington-Moscow-Peking: Winfried Böttcher et al., eds., Das grosse Dreieck: Washington-Moskau-Peking (Stuttgart: Deutsche Verlags-Anstalt, 1971); Robert L. Pfalzgraff, Jr., "Multipolarity, Alliances and U.S.-Soviet-Chinese Relations," Orbis, vol. 17, no. 3 (fall 1973), pp. 720-736; and the brilliant review of research on conflict limitation and arms control by Pierre Hassner, "On ne badine pas avec la force," Revue français de science politique (Dec. 1971).

2. For a thoughtful critique of orthodox and revisionist historiography on these issues, see John Lewis Gaddis, The United States and the Origins of the Cold War, 1941-1947 (New York: Columbia University Press, 1972).

3. The most authoritative published analysis of recent Sino-Soviet developments is Harold Hinton, The Bear at the Gate (Washington, D.C.: American Enterprise Institute, and Stanford, Calif.: The Hoover Institution, 1971), with full bibliography of previous studies. See also Geoffrey Jukes, The Soviet Union in Asia (Berkeley and Los Angeles: University of California Press, 1973).

4. Thomas W. Robinson, "The Sino-Soviet Border Dispute," American Political Science Review, vol. 66, no. 4 (Dec. 1972), pp. 1175-1202.

5. The Military Balance 1973-1974 (London: International Institute for Strategic Studies, 1973), p. 6.

6. Harry Gelber, Nuclear Weapons and Chinese Policy, Adelphi Paper, no. 99 (London: International Institute for Strategic Studies, 1973).

7. For authoritative Soviet expressions of this policy, see Konstantin Katushev [CPSU CC Secretary], "The World Socialist System: Main Development Trends," Kommunist, no. 5, March 1972, pp. 12-24 (JPRS 55961, May 10, 1972); V. V. Zagladin [CPSU CC

International Department], "Revolutionary Process and CPSU
International Policy," ibid., no. 13, Sept. 1972, pp. 14-26);
(JPRS 57306, Oct. 20, 1972); and Erich Glueckauf, "Common
Regularities and National Specifics in Building Socialism,"
World Marxist Review, vol. 15, no. 9 (Sept. 1972), pp. 133-140.
For regularized interparty expert consultative meetings, see
TANJUG English from Moscow, Jan. 22, 1974, 2100 GMT (FBIS/EE/
Jan. 23, 1974/I1).

8. I. Aleksandrov [an authoritative pseudonym], "On Certain
Principles Concerning the Chinese Leadership's Political Course,"
Pravda, Aug. 26, 1973 (CDSP, vol. 25, no. 34 [Sept. 19, 1973],
pp. 1-4); Konstantin Katushev, "The Main Direction," World
Marxist Review, vol. 16, no. 8 (Aug. 1973), pp. 3-14, and
"Strengthening the Unity among the Socialist Countries—a Law of
the Development of World Socialism," Kommunist, no. 16 (Nov.
1973), pp. 17-31 (JPRS 60882, Dec. 28, 1973, pp. 11-21); V. V.
Zagladin, "Proletarian Internationalism and the Communist
Movement Considered," Rabochiy Klass i Sovremennyy Mir, no. 4
(July-Aug. 1973), pp. 3-19 (JPRS 61045, Jan. 23, 1974, pp. 4-24);
Ryszard Frelek [Secretary and head of International Department,
PZPR CC], "Might and Dynamism," Izvestiya, Dec. 25, 1973 (FBIS/
SU/Jan. 9, 1974/A 1-2). Analysis: Kevin Devlin, "Back on the
Conference Trail," RFE Research, Dec. 7, 1973, and "Spanish CP
against International Conference," ibid., Dec. 14, 1973.

9. See the penetrating and comprehensive analysis by Heinz
Timmermann, "'Neue Einheit' in Weltkommunismus," Berichte des
Bundestinstituts für ostwissenschafliche und internationale
Studien (Cologne), no. 2, 1972.

10. lz [Louis Zanga], "The Albanian Way," RFE Research, Dec. 21,
1972; Kevin Devlin, "Discordant Notes in Marxist-Leninist Chorus,"
ibid., Feb. 19, 1973.

11. I have benefited greatly from talks on the state of the
international communist movement given by François Fejtö at the
Harvard Center for International Affairs on April 25, 1973, and
at the yearly conference of the Centre Québecois des affaires
internationales in Montréal, Sept. 23, 1972. For signs of renewed
Chinese interest in splinter parties, see. j.c.k. [Joseph C. Kun],
"China Revitalizes Its Ties with Splinter Parties," RFE Research,
Dec. 14, 1973.

12. See Viktor Meier's chapter in this volume and John C. Campbell, "Insecurity and Cooperation: Yugoslavia and the Balkans," Foreign Affairs, vol. 51, no. 4 (July 1973), pp. 778-793.

13. Dick Wilson, "China and the European Community," China Quarterly, no. 56 (Oct.-Dec. 1973), pp. 647-667; j.c.k. [Joseph C. Kun], "Sino-Soviet Polemics and European Security," RFE Research, April 4, 1973; Ernst Kux, "China and Europa," Neue Zürcher Zeitung, Dec. 6, 1972; "'Detente' Smokescreen Cannot Cover Up Military Ambitions in Europe," Peking Review, vol. 16, no. 51 (Dec. 21, 1973), pp. 4-5; "System for 'Security' or for Aggression and Expansion?" ibid., no. 52 (Dec. 28, 1973), pp. 7-9.

14. j.c.k. [Joseph C. Kun], "Peking Intensified Its Attacks on Soviet Leadership," RFE Research, Jan. 9, 1974.

15. See on Chou's Tenth CCP Congress speech Kx. [Ernst Kux], "China und der Konflikt mit Moskau," Neue Zürcher Zeitung, Sept. 11, 1973. For a recent authoritative Soviet view of China, see I. Aleksandrov [pseud.], "In the Interests of Peace and Socialism," Pravda, Aug. 7, 1973. For authoritative accounts of current official Chinese views on the Soviet Union, see Kx. [Ernst Kux] from Peking, "Relikte der chinesisch-sowjetischen Freundschaft," Neue Zürcher Zeitung, June 17, 1973, and "Chinas Nachbar im Norden," ibid., June 20, 1973. For India, see Bhabani Sen Gupta's chapter in this volume; Marcus F. Franda, "Indo-American Relations: A Year of Deterioration," American Universities Field Staff Reports, vol. 17, no. 3 (India), Jan. 1973; S. P. Seth, "India's New Role in the South Asian Context," Pacific Community, vol. 4, no. 3 (April 1973), pp. 471-484; Dieter Braun, Das Neue Kräftefeld in Südasien und seine aussenpolitische Aspekte (Ebenhausen: Stiftung Wissenschaft und Politik, SWP-S 212, June 1973); and articles by three American academics who visited China in January 1973: Robert A. Scalapino, "China and the Balance of Power," Foreign Affairs, vol. 52, no. 2 (Jan. 1974), pp. 349-386, and "China and the Road Ahead," Survey, vol. 19, no. 4(89) (Autumn 1973), pp. 1-22; A. Doak Barnett, "More Thoughts Out of China," New York Times Magazine, April 8 and May 6, 1973; Lucian W. Pye, China Revisited (Cambridge, Mass.: M.I.T. Center for International Studies monograph, C/73-5, April 1973.

16. For recent Chinese developments, see Philip Bridgham, "The Fall of Lin Piao," China Quarterly, no. 55 (July-Sept. 1973), pp. 427-449; Ellis Joffe, "The Chinese Army after the Cultural

Revolution: The Effects of Intervention," ibid., pp. 450–477;
Roderick MacFarquhar, "China after the 10th Congress," The World
Today, vol. 29, no. 12 (Dec. 1973), pp. 514–526.

17. John Burns from Peking in The New York Times, April 14, 1973;
j.c.k. [Joseph C. Kun], "Teng is Back--But What Next?" RFE
Research, April 16, 17, 1973; kx. [Ernst Kux], "Das
Wiederauftauchen von Teng Hsiao-ping," Neue Zürcher Zeitung,
April 26, 1973.

18. President Richard M. Nixon, U.S. Foreign Policy for the
1970s (Washington, D.C.: GPO, May 1973), pp. 232–233. For
critical views of Nixon's balance-of-power policy, see Stanley
Hoffman, "Weighing the Balance of Power," Foreign Affairs, vol.
50, no. 4 (July 1972), pp. 618–643; and Alastair Buchan, "A
World Restored?" ibid., pp. 644–659. For Chinese policy, see
William W. Whitson, "China's Quest for Technology," Problems of
Communism, vol. 22, no. 4 (July-Aug. 1973), pp. 16–30.

19. See Paul Langer's chapter in this volume; and also Ch. M.
[Christian Müller] from Tokyo in Neue Zürcher Zeitung, April 1,
1973; John P. Hardt, "West Siberia: The Quest for Energy,"
Problems of Communism, vol. 22, no. 3 (May-June 1973), pp. 25–36;
Kiichi Saeki, "Toward Japanese Cooperation in Siberian
Development," Problems of Communism, vol. 21, no. 3 (May-June
1972), pp. 1–12.

20. Ch.M. [Christian Müller] from Tokyo, "Kakuei Tanaka in
Japans Zwickmühle," Neue Zürcher Zeitung, March 28, 1973, "Japans
Lavierung zwischen Peking und Moskau," ibid., May 4, 1973, and
"Tanakas magere Reise-Erträge," ibid., Oct. 13, 1973. On Japan in
general, in addition to Paul Langer's chapter in this volume, see
also a series of articles in Survey, vol. 18, no. 4 (85) (Autumn
1972); Shinkichi Etō, "Japan and China—A New Stage?" Problems of
Communism, vol. 21, no. 6 (Nov.-Dec. 1972), pp. 1–17; Curt
Gasteyger, ed., Japan and the Atlantic World, The Atlantic
Papers, no. 3 (Paris: Saxon House for the Atlantic Institute for
International Affairs, 1972); Masataka Kosaka, Options for
Japan's Foreign Policy, Adelphi Paper, no. 97 (London:
International Institute for Strategic Studies, 1973); Kiichi
Saeki, "Toward Japanese Cooperation in Siberia;" Kenzo Kiga,
"Russo-Japanese Economic Cooperation and Its International
Environment," Pacific Community, vol. 4, no. 3 (April 1973), pp.
452–470.

21. Hans H. Baerwald, "Aspects of Sino-Japanese Normalization," Pacific Community, vol. 4, no. 2 (Jan. 1973), pp. 195-203; Geoffrey Hudson, "Japanese Attitudes and Policies Toward China in 1973," China Quarterly, no. 56 (Oct.-Dec. 1973), pp. 700-707; Derek Davies, "Will Japan's Accommodation with China Work?" Pacific Community, vol. 4, no. 3 (April 1973), pp. 340-355.

22. The Economist, Feb. 17, 1973; William Beecher in The New York Times, Dec. 14, 1972.

23. See Chong-Sik Lee's chapter in this volume.

24. Joseph S. Berliner, "Some International Aspects of Soviet Technological Progress," South Atlantic Quarterly, vol. 72, no. 3 (1973), pp. 340-350; Arnold Buchholz, "Wissenschaflich-technische Revolution und Wettbewerb der Systeme," Osteuropa, vol. 22, no. 5 (May 1972), pp. 329-390; Hans-Herman Höhmann, "Bestimmt die Wirtschaft die Aussenpolitik?" Berichte des Bundesinstituts für ostwissenschaftliche und internationale Studien (Cologne), no. 42, 1973; Jürgen Nötzold, Untersuchungen zur Durchsetzung des technischen Fortschritts in der sowjetischen Wirtschaft (Ebenhausen: Stiftung Wissenschaft und Politik, Dec. 1972).

25. Keith Bush, "Die Auswirkungen des sowjetischen Getreidedefizits," Osteuropäische Rundschau, vol. 18, no. 11 (Nov. 1972), pp. 1-4; Michael Kaser, "Comecon's Commerce," Problems of Communism, vol. 22, no. 4 (July-Aug. 1973), pp. 1-15.

26. For statements of the Soviet position justifying détente and emphasizing its advantage to the USSR because of U.S. weakness, see G. Arbatov [Director of the Institute on the U.S.A.], "On Soviet-U.S. Relations," Kommunist, no. 3 (Feb. 1973), pp. 101-113 (JPRS 58597, March 29, 1973); and N. Inozemtsev [Director of IMEMO], "At a New Stage in the Development of International Relations," Kommunist, no. 13 (Sept. 1973), pp. 89-103 (JPRS 60363, Oct. 25, 1973, pp. 112-128). See also Malcolm Mackintosh, "Moscow's View of the Balance of Power," The World Today, vol. 29, no. 3 (March 1973), pp. 108-118.

27. See Viktor Meier's chapter on the Balkans in this volume; for Poland, Robert W. Dean, "Ideological Pragmatism in People's Poland," RFE Research, Jan. 21, 1974; and Adam Bromke, "Polish Foreign Policy in the 1970s," Canadian Slavonic Papers, vol. 15, nos. 1-2 (Spring-Summer 1973), pp. 192-205; for Hungary, William Robinson, The Pattern of Reform Rule in Hungary (New York: Praeger, 1973).

28. Pierre Hassner, "Europe: Old Conflicts, New Rules," Orbis, vol. 17, no. 3 (Fall 1973), pp. 895-912.

29. See the sophisticated analysis by V. P. Lukin, "Sino-American Relations: Conceptions and Realities," SShA, no. 2 (Feb. 1973), pp. 12-23 (JPRS 58418, Mar. 8, 1973); and Gerhard Wettig, "Die amerikanisch-chinesische Annäherung aus sowjetischer Perspective," Osteuropa, vol. 22, no. 7 (July 1972), pp. 489-496.

30. In my view the best analyses of Ostpolitik have been by Wolfgang Wagner; see his "Voraussetzungen und Folgen der deutschen Ostpolitik. Der Vertrag von Moskau und seine Bedeutung für die internationale Lage," Europa Archiv, vol. 25, no. 17 (Sept. 10, 1970), pp. 627-628; "Ein neuer Anfang zwischen Polen und Deutschen. Der Vertrag von Warschau," ibid., no. 23 (Dec. 10, 1970), pp. 837-844; "Aussichten der Ostpolitik nach dem Abschluss der Berlin-Verhandlungen," ibid., vol. 27, no. 3 (Feb. 10, 1972), pp. 79-86; and "Ein Modus vivendi in Deutschland. Der Grundvertrag der beiden deutschen Staaten und seine Bedeutung für Europa," ibid., vol. 28, no. 1 (Jan. 10, 1973), pp. 1-6. See also Karl E. Birnbaum, Peace in Europe: East-West Relations 1966-1968 and the Prospects for a European Settlement (London and New York: Oxford, 1970), and East and West Germany: A Modus Vivendi (Lexington, Mass.: Lexington Books, and London: Saxon House, 1973); Lawrence Whetten, Germany's Ostpolitik (London: Oxford, 1971); Die aussenpolitische Perspektiven des westdeutschen Staates, 3 vols. (Munich: Oldenbourg, 1971, 1972); Dieter Mahncke, "The Berlin Agreement: Balance and Prospects," The World Today (Dec. 1971); Eberhard Schulz, "Die DDR als Element der sowjetischen Westeuropapolitik," Europa Archiv, vol. 27, no. 24 (Dec. 25, 1972), pp. 835-843; Josef Joffe, "Westverträge, Ostverträge und die Kontinuität der deutschen Aussenpolitik," ibid., vol. 28, no. 4 (Feb. 25, 1973), pp. 111-124; Peter Bender, "The Special Relationship of the Two German States," The World Today, vol. 29, no. 9 (Sept. 1973), pp. 389-397; Robert Bleimann, "Détente and the GDR: The Internal Implications," ibid., no. 6 (June 1973), pp. 257-265; Adam Bromke and Harald von Riekhoff, "The West German-Polish Treaty," ibid., vol. 27, no. 3 (March 1971), pp. 124-130. For the situation in early 1974, see the rather pessimistic analyses by F.L. [Fred Luchsinger], "Blickpunkt Deutschland," Neue Zürcher Zeitung, Jan. 13, 1974; and C.K. [Christian Kind], "Ein Jahr nach dem innerdeutschen Grundvertrag," ibid., Dec. 24, 1973; Robert W. Dean, "Bonn-Prague Relations: The Politics of Reconciliation," The World Today, vol. 29, no. 4 (April 1973), pp. 149-159.

31. See Michael Howard, "NATO and the Year of Europe," Round
Table (Oct. 1973), reprinted in Survival (Jan.-Feb. 1974), pp.
21-27.

32. For critical views, see Uwe Nerlich, "Westeuropa und die
Entwicklung des amerikanischen-sowjetischen Bilateralismus,"
Europa Archiv, vol. 27, no. 20 (Oct. 25, 1972), pp. 687-702;
Nerlich, "Die Einhegung des Nuklearkrieges. Zur politischen
Bedeutung des amerikanisch-sowjetischen Grundsatzabkommens über
die Verhütung von Nuklearkriegen," ibid., vol. 28, no. 19
(Oct. 10, 1973), pp. 669-678; Nerlich, Der NV-Vertrag in der
Politik der BRD (Ebenhausen: Stiftung Wissenschaft und Politik,
Sept. 1973); Leopold Labedz, "The Soviet Union and Western
Europe," Survey, vol. 19, no. 3(88) (Summer 1973), pp. 12-29;
Richard Pipes, "America, Russia and Europe in the Light of the
Nixon Doctrine," ibid., pp. 30-40; Pierre Hassner, Europe in the
Age of Negotiations, The Washington Papers, no. 8 (Beverly Hills
and London: Sage, 1973), and "Europe: Old Conflicts, New Rules";
Curt Gasteyger, "Weltmächte und Weltordnung. Die sowjetisch-
amerikanischen Beziehungen nach dem Treffen Breshnjew-Nixon,"
Europa Archiv, vol. 28, no. 16 (Aug. 25, 1973), pp. 541-548; for
a less critical view, see Kurt Birrenbach, "The United States and
Western Europe: Partners or Rivals?" Orbis, vol. 17, no. 2
(Summer 1973), pp. 405-414; Wolfgang Heisenberg, Die Politik zur
Verhütung eines Atomkrieges im Rahmen des amerikanischen-
sowjetischen Bilateralismus (Ebenhausen: Stiftung Wissenschaft
und Politik, SWP-AZ 2019, Nov. 1973). The most penetrating
European critical view of American policy is by Ernst-Otto
Czempiel, "Entwicklungslinien der amerikanisch-europäischen
Beziehungen," Europa Archiv, vol. 28, no. 22 (Nov. 25, 1973),
pp. 781-790. See also Karl Kaiser, Europe and the United States:
The Future of the Relationship (Washington, D.C.: Columbia Books,
1973); articles by Robert L. Pfalzgraff, Jr., Wilfrid L. Kohl and
William Taubman, Werner Kaltefleiter, Simon Serfaty, Paul C.
Davis, and J. I. Coffey in a special "Year of Europe" issue of
Orbis, vol. 17, no. 1 (Spring 1973); John Pinder, "America and
Europe: A Fair Bargain in the Coming Negotiations?" The World
Today, vol. 29, no. 7 (July 1973), pp. 291-299; James Chace,
"The Concert of Europe," Foreign Affairs, vol. 52, no. 1 (Oct.
1973), pp. 96-108; John W. Tuthill, The Decisive Years Ahead,
The Atlantic Papers, no. 4 (Paris: Saxon House for the Institute
for International Affairs, 1972); "Z," "The Year of Europe?"
Foreign Affairs, vol. 52, no. 2 (Jan. 1974), pp. 237-248. For a
recent official American view, see the speech by Secretary of
State Henry Kissinger in London on Dec. 12, 1973, in Department
of State Bulletin, vol. 69, no. 1801 (Dec. 31, 1973), pp. 777-782.

33. The formulation is Zbigniew Brzezinski's. I have profited from many discussions with him, from a seminar he gave at the Harvard Center for International Affairs on January 25, 1973, and from his "U.S. Foreign Policy: The Search for Focus," Foreign Affairs, vol. 51, no. 4 (July 1973), pp. 708-727. See also (for a relatively optimistic view of Soviet détente policy) Marshall Shulman, "Toward a Western Philosophy of Coexistence," ibid., vol. 52, no. 1 (Oct. 1973), pp. 35-58; and, for more pessimistic ones, Leopold Labedz, "The International Scene in the Seventies," Survey, vol. 19, no. 2(87) (Spring 1973), pp. 1-10; Richard Pipes, "Operational Principles of Soviet Foreign Policy," ibid., pp. 41-61. See also Vernon Aspaturian, "The USSR, the U.S.A. and China in the Seventies," ibid., pp. 102-122, and Hannes Adomeit, Soviet Risk-Taking and Crisis Behavior: From Consultation to Coexistence, Adelphi Paper, no. 101 (London: International Institute for Strategic Studies, Autumn 1973).

34. For the case for a mutual assured destruction (MAD) strategy, see J. H. Kahan, "Stable Deterrence: A Struggle Policy for the 1970s," Orbis, vol. 15, no. 2 (Summer 1971), pp. 528-543; and Wolfgang K. H. Panofsky, "The Mutual-Hostage Relationship between America and Russia," Foreign Affairs, vol. 52, no. 1 (Oct. 1973), pp. 109-118; for U.S. cases against it, see Martin J. Bailey, "Deterrence, Assured Destruction, and Defense," Orbis, vol. 16, no. 3 (Fall 1972), pp. 682-695; and Fred Charles Iklé, "Can Nuclear Deterrence Last Out the Century?" Foreign Affairs, vol. 51, no. 2 (Jan. 1973), pp. 267-285. On MIRV, see Herbert F. York, "Multiple-Warhead Missiles," Scientific American, vol. 229, no. 5 (Nov. 1973), pp. 18-27. For a relatively moderate Soviet view, see M. A. Mil'shtein and L. S. Semeyko, "SALT: Problems and Prospects," SShA, no. 12 (Dec. 1972), pp. 3-12 (JPRS 60933, Jan. 8, 1974, pp. 1-13). For SALT I, see Edward Luttwak, The Strategic Balance, 1972, The Washington Papers, no. 3 (Washington, D.C.: Georgetown University Center for Strategic and International Studies, 1972).

35. Juan Cameron, "The Rethinking of U.S. Defense," Fortune, vol. 88, no. 6 (Dec. 1973), pp. 83-87, 181-185; Michel Tatu, "L'U.R.S.S. démande le démantèlement des bases nucléaires américaines," Le Monde, Jan. 18, 1974 (which includes a report on the initial Soviet Salt II position); and the February 11, 1974 Time cover story on Secretary of Defense James Schlesinger. I am grateful to my colleague Professor W. W. Kaufmann for discussions of these matters.

36. Michael Palmer, The Prospects for a European Security Conference (London: Chatham House, European Series, no. 18, 1971), and "A European Security Conference: Preparation and Procedure," The World Today, vol. 28, no. 1 (Jan. 1972), pp. 36-46; Wolfgang Klaiber et al., Era of Negotiations (Lexington, Mass.: Lexington Books, 1973); Hans-Peter Schwarz, "Sicherheitskonferenz und westliche Sicherheitsgemeinschaft," Europa Archiv, vol. 27, no. 24 (Dec. 25, 1972); Christoph Bertram, "West German Perspectives on European Security: Continuity and Change," The World Today, vol. 27, no. 3 (March 1971), pp. 115-123; Andrew J. Pierre, "Can Europe's Security Be 'Decoupled' from America?" Foreign Affairs, vol. 51, no. 4 (July 1973), pp. 761-777; Jacques Freymond, "Welches Europa? Gedanken zur Konferenz über Sicherheit und Zusammenarbeit," Europa Archiv, vol. 28, no. 7 (April 10, 1973); Gerda Zellentin, "Institutions for Detente and Cooperation," The World Today, vol. 29, no. 1 (Jan. 1973), pp. 8-15; Gerhard Wettig, "Die Sowjetunion und die Europa-Konferenz," Osteuropa, vol. 23, no. 6 (June 1973), pp. 401-429, and Europäische Sicherheit. Das europäische Staatensystem in der sowjetischen Aussenpolitik 1966-1972 (Düsseldorf: Bertelsmann Universitätsverlag, 1972); Robert Legvold, "Soviet Policy in Western Europe and the Problem of European Security," Problems of Communism, vol. 23 (Jan.-Feb. 1974), pp. 13-33. See also Lilita Dzirkals and A. Ross Johnson, eds., Soviet and East European Forecasts of European Security: Papers from the 1972 Varna Conference, RAND R-1272-PR, June 1973; Adam Bromke, "The CSCE and Eastern Europe," The World Today, vol. 29, no. 5 (May 1973), pp. 196-205. For the Eastern position on the informational issue, see "Die 'ideologische Gefahr' der friedlichen Koexistenz," Osteuropäische Rundschau, no. 1/2 (Jan.-Feb. 1973), pp. 3-8; and Klaus Mehnert, "Ideologischer Krieg trotz Koexistenz--sagt Moskau," Osteuropa, vol. 23, no. 1 (Jan. 1973), pp. 1-8. See especially the analysis by Andreas Oplatka of the Helsinki preliminary phase, Neue Zürcher Zeitung, June 3, 1973. American Press coverage of CSCE and MBFR discussions was minimal. By far the best coverage of both CSCE and MBFR was in the Neue Zürcher Zeitung.

37. John Yochelson, "MBFR: The Search for an American Approach," Orbis, vol. 17, no. 1 (Spring 1973), pp. 155-175, reprinted in Survival, vol. 15, no. 6 (Nov.-Dec. 1973), pp. 275-283; J. I. Coffey, "Arms Control and the Military Balance in Europe," Orbis, vol. 17, no. 1 (Spring 1973), pp. 132-155; Klaiber et al., Era of Negotiations; Ian Smart, MBFR Assailed, Cornell University Peace Studies Program, no. 3 (mimeo.); Frederick S. Wyle, "European

Security: Beating the Numbers Game," Foreign Policy, no. 10
(Spring 1973), pp. 41-54; Christoph Bertram, "The Politics of
MBFR," The World Today, vol. 29, no. 1 (Jan. 1973), pp. 1-7, and
Mutual Force Reductions in Europe: The Political Aspects,
Adelphi Paper, no. 84 (London: International Institute for
Strategic Studies, Jan. 1972); Uwe Nerlich, "MBFR in der
europäischen Sicherheitspolitik," Europa Archiv, vol. 27, no. 5
(March 10, 1972), pp. 161-168; Lothar Ruehl, "Beiderseitige
Truppenverminderungen in Europa. Grundlagen, Möglichkeiten und
Grenzen von MBFR-Verhandlungen," ibid., vol. 28, no. 10 (May 25,
1973), pp. 325-339; Leslie H. Gelb, "East and West Far Apart in
Talks on Cuts in Force," New York Times, Feb. 8, 1974. See also
The Fletcher School, European Security and the Nixon Doctrine,
International Security Series, no. 1, 1972; Steven L. Canby,
"NATO Muscle: More Shadow than Substance," Foreign Policy, no. 8
(Fall 1972), pp. 38-49; R. W. Komer, "Treating NATO's Self-
Inflicted Wound," ibid., no. 13 (Winter 1973-1974), pp. 33-48;
Wolfgang Heisenberg, The Alliance and Europe. Part I: Crisis
Stability in Europe and Theater Nuclear Weapons, Adelphi Paper,
no. 96 (London: International Institute for Strategic Studies,
Summer 1973); Kenneth Hunt, The Alliance and Europe. Part II:
Defense with Fewer Men, Adelphi Paper, no. 98 (London:
International Institute for Strategic Studies, Summer 1973). The
best running documentation of CSCE and MBFR is in Europa Archiv.
See also Friedrich-Karl Schramm et al., Sicherheitskonferenz in
Europa. Dokumentation 1954-1972 (Frankfurt/M.: Metzner, 1972).
For a negative analysis of East-West détente in Europe, see
"It's Mostly Bubbles," The Economist, April 14, 1973. See also
the penetrating analysis by Miriam Camps, "Sources of Strain in
Transatlantic Relations," International Affairs, vol. 48, no. 4
(Oct. 1972), pp. 559-578. I have also profited from discussions
in the Harvard-M.I.T. Faculty Seminar on European Security,
1972-1973. For the official Soviet view, see V. I. Popov, ed.,
Sovetskaya vneshnaya politika i evropeiskaya bezopasnost'
(Moscow: Izdatelstvo Mezh. Otnosh., 1972) (JPRS 57815, Dec. 20,
1972), and its revised and expanded German version, Sowjetische
Aussenpolitik und europäische Sicherheit (Berlin: Staatsverlag
der DDR, 1973).

38. See Kissinger's speech re Europe in New York Times, April
24, 1973.

39. Legvold, "Soviet Policy in Western Europe."

40. Dennis J. Duncanson, "The Ceasefire in Vietnam," The World

Today, vol. 29, no. 3 (March 1973), pp. 89-87; James Markham
from Saigon in _New York Times_, Jan. 27, 1974; Allen Goodman,
"Leaving the Future Up for Grabs: The Political Consequences of
the Vietnam Cease-fire," _Asia Quarterly_ (Brussels), no. 2 (1973),
pp. 93-106; Jerry M. Silverman, "South Vietnam and the Return to
Political Struggle," _Asian Survey_, vol. 14, no. 1 (Jan. 1974),
pp. 65-77.

41. I have drawn for this section on my "The Fourth Middle
Eastern War, the Energy Crisis, and U.S. Policy," _Orbis_, vol. 17,
no. 4 (Winter 1974), pp. 1161-1188. See also Arnold Hottinger's
chapter in this volume; his "The Depth of Arab Radicalism,"
Foreign Affairs, vol. 51, no. 3 (April 1973), pp. 491-504; and
his "Heikals Interview mit Tschou En-lai," _Neue Zürcher Zeitung_,
March 30, 1973; for the "Islamization" of Mashrek politics, the
penetrating analysis by Udo Steinbach, _Ansätze zu regionaler
Zusammenarbeit im Nahen Osten. Islam und Erdöl als Faktoren
politischer Umgestaltung_ (Ebenhausen: Stiftung Wissenschaft und
Politik, SWP-S 220, Dec. 1973) (essential for the Islamization of
the Arab world); Lawrence L. Whetten, "Sadat's Strategic Options
in the Canal War," _The World Today_, vol. 29, no. 2 (Feb. 1973),
pp. 58-67. See also Lawrence L. Whetten, _The Canal War: Four
Power Conflict in the Middle East_ (Cambridge, Mass.: M.I.T.
Press, 1974), on the military aspects of Middle Eastern
developments, 1967-1974. For Soviet displeasure, see the
revealing communiqué of the July 1972 Plenum of the Sudanese CP
CC, in the (Soviet-sponsored) _Information Bulletin_ (Toronto),
vol. 10, no. 21-22 (229-230) (Jan. 1973), pp. 50-57. On Soviet
and Chinese policy in the Middle East, see the analyses by John
C. Campbell and W. A. C. Adie in _Problems of Communism_, vol. 21,
no. 5 (Sept.-Oct. 1972), pp. 40-68; and by John C. Campbell in
Survival, vol. 15, no. 5 (Sept.-Oct. 1973), pp. 210-217. See
also J. Bowyer Bell, "Bab el Mandeb: Strategic Troublespot,"
Orbis, vol. 16, no. 4 (Winter 1973), pp. 975-989. On the 1973
war, Griffith, "The Fourth Middle Eastern War"; Nadav Safran,
"The War and the Future of the Arab-Israeli Conflict," _Foreign
Affairs_, vol. 52, no. 2 (Jan. 1974), pp. 215-236; Arnold
Hottinger, "Der vierte arabisch-israelische Krieg und seine
politischen Folgen," _Europa Archiv_, vol. 29, no. 3 (Feb. 10,
1974), pp. 83-92.

42. For contrary views, stressing Soviet organization and
planning of the war, for which in my opinion there is no
convincing evidence, see Uri Ra'anan, "The USSR and the Middle
East: Some Reflections on the Soviet Decision-Making Process,"

Orbis, vol. 17, no. 3 (Fall 1973); and Eugene V. Rostow, "America, Europe and the Middle East," Commentary, vol. 57, no. 2 (Feb. 1974), pp. 40-55.

43. The extent of Iranian involvement in the Arabian peninsula was made clear by the involvement of Iranian helicopters, crews, and commando units in counterinsurgency operations in Dhofar (The Observer, March 3, 1974). See also Jean Gueyras in Le Monde, Feb. 17, 1973. For a general survey of Iranian hegemonic policy, see Arnaud de Borchgrave in Newsweek, May 21, 1973, and Griffith, "The Fourth Middle Eastern War." For Diego Garcia, see The Economist, Feb. 9, 1974, p. 38. See also Stephen Oren, "Bedrohliche Polarisierung im Mittleren Osten. Aussenpolitische Auswirkungen des afghanischen Umsturzes," Europa Archiv, vol. 29, no. 2 (Jan. 25, 1974), pp. 55-62.

44. For an authoritative analysis of repressive Soviet domestic policies, see Wolfgang Leonhard, "The Domestic Politics of the New Soviet Foreign Policy," Foreign Affairs, vol. 52, no. 1 (Oct. 1973), pp. 59-74. For domestic U.S. political factors in this context, see Stephen S. Rosenfeld, "Pluralism and Policy," Foreign Affairs, vol. 52, no. 2 (Jan. 1974), pp. 263-273; for Soviet-American trade, Raymond Vernon, "Apparatchiks and Entrepreneurs: U.S.-Soviet Economic Relations," ibid., pp. 249-263; for the case against barring MFN, see Theodore C. Sorensen, "Most-Favored Nation and Less Favorite Nations," ibid., pp. 273-286; Marshall I. Goldman, "Who Profits More from U.S.-Soviet Trade?" Harvard Business Review, vol. 51, no. 6 (Nov.-Dec. 1973), pp. 79-87. For American attitudes toward Israel, indicating breadth but lack of depth of popular support for it, see Earl Rabb, "Is Israel Losing Popular Support?" Commentary, vol. 57, no. 1 (Jan. 1974), pp. 26-29. For a pessimistic view of future Soviet-U.S. relations, see "If Gulliverisation Fails," The Economist, Dec. 29, 1973.

45. See the prophetic analysis of the decline in the U.S. foreign trade position by H. S. Houthakker and Stephen Magee, "Income and Price Elasticities in World Trade," Review of Economics and Statistics, vol. 51, no. 2 (May 1969), pp. 111-125; and Magee's "United States Trade and the New Economic Policy," University of California, Berkeley, Studies in International Business and Economics, no. 9 (Sept. 1971, mimeo.); Charles L. Schultze, "The Economic Content of National Security Policy," Foreign Affairs, vol. 51, no. 3 (April 1973), pp. 522-540; C. Fred Bergsten, "Future Directions for U.S. Trade,"

American Journal of Agricultural Economics, vol. 55, no. 2 (May
1973), pp. 280-288; Harold B. Malmgren, "Japan, the United
States, and the Pacific Economy," Pacific Community, vol. 4, no.
3 (April 1973), ,pp. 307-326. For monetary problems, see Richard
N. Cooper, "The Future of the Dollar," Foreign Policy, no. 11
(Summer 1973), pp. 3-23, and comments on it, pp. 23-32.

46. Lester R. Brown, "The Next Crisis? Food," Foreign Policy, no.
13 (Winter 1973), pp. 3-33.

47. See M. A. Adelman, "Is the Oil Shortage Real? Oil Companies
as OPEC Tax Collectors," Foreign Policy, no. 9 (Winter 1972),
pp. 69-107; Stephen D. Krasner, "The Great Oil Sheikdown," ibid.,
no. 13 (Winter 1973), pp. 123-138; James E. Akins, "The Oil
Crisis: This Time the Wolf Is Here," Foreign Affairs, vol. 51,
no. 3 (April 1973), pp. 462-490; Carroll L. Wilson, "A Plan for
Energy Independence," ibid., no. 4 (July 1973), pp. 657-675.;
Jahengir Amuzegar, "The Oil Story: Facts, Fiction and Fair Play,"
ibid., pp. 676-689; Linda Charlton, "Decades of Inaction Brought
Energy Gap," and Edith Penrose, "Building a Common Oil Policy,"
New York Times, Feb. 10, 1974, I, p. 1, and III, p. 1; Charles
Issawi, Oil, the Middle East and The World, The Washington
Papers, no. 4 (Washington, D.C.: Georgetown University Center for
Strategic and International Studies, 1972); Robert E. Hunter,
"Can the Arabs Really Blackmail Us?" New York Times Magazine,
Sept. 23, 1973; Walter J. Levy, "An Action Program for U.S.
Energy Policy During the Seventies," speech to the 1972 annual
meeting of the American Petroleum Institute, and "An Atlantic-
Japanese Energy Policy," Survey, vol. 19, no 3 (88) (Summer 1973),
pp. 50-73; J. E. Hartshorn, "Oil Diplomacy: The New Approach,"
The World Today, vol. 29, no. 7 (July 1973), pp. 281-290; John C.
Campbell, "Foreign Policy and the Future Supply of Energy,"
Hearings before the Subcommittee on Energy of the House of
Representatives Committee on Foreign Affairs, Oct. 3, 1972, and
"Middle East Oil: American Policy and Super-Power Interaction,"
Survival, vol. 15, no. 5 (Sept.-Oct. 1973), pp. 210-217; Melvin
A. Conant, "Oil: Cooperation or Conflict," ibid., no. 1 (Jan.-
Feb. 1973), pp. 8-14; Arnold Hottinger, "Die arabische Welt
zwischen der Israel-Frontund der 'Erdölwaffe,'" Europa Archiv,
vol. 28, no. 7 (April 10, 1973); "How the Arabs Plan to Spend
Their Riches," The Economist, May 5, 1973; Jean Riollot, "Moscow
and the Oil Crisis," Radio Liberty Research Bulletin, Jan. 16,
1974; Rufold Botzian et al., Zum Problem der Energieversorgung
in der BRD (Ebenhausen: Stiftung Wissenschaft und Politik, SWP-AP
2020, Oct. 1973). For alternative energy sources, U.S. Atomic

Energy Commission, The Nation's Energy Future (Washington, D.C.: GPO, Dec. 1, 1973); and the articles by White, Nephew, and Morrow in the M.I.T. Technology Review, vol. 76, no. 2 (Dec. 1973), pp. 10-43. I have also profited from a conference on the energy problems of Western Europe, held in Paris, March 9-10, 1973, sponsored by the Centre d'études de la politique étrangère and the IISS; from a seminar on OECD energy policy at M.I.T., Jan. 3-4, 1974; from a Columbia seminar by Professors Charles Issawi and J. C. Hurewitz, Jan. 23, 1974; from discussions with Professors M. A. Adelman, Sidney Alexander, Henry Jacoby, and Charles Kindleberger of M.I.T. and Professor A. J. Meyer and Dr. Thomas Stouffer of Harvard; from an energy seminar at M.I.T. conducted by Professors Sidney Alexander and Henry Jacoby; and from a discussion between Professor Adelman and Mr. William Tavoulareas, president of Mobil Oil, Inc., at the Harvard-M.I.T. Faculty Seminar on International Technology on May 10, 1973.

48. New York Times, Feb. 14, 15, 1973.

49. C. Fred Bergsten, "The World May Have to Live with 'Shortages,'" New York Times, Jan. 27, 1974, IV, p. 3, and his "The Threat from the Third World," Foreign Policy, no. 11 (Spring 1973); for a contrary view, Philip H. Trezise, "How Many OPEC's in Our Future?" New York Times, Feb. 10, 1974, III, p. 3; Brown, "The Next Crisis? Food" Yuan-li Wu, Raw Material Supply in a Multipolar World (New York: Crane, Russak, 1973).

50. Cf. "The American Comeback," The Economist, Feb. 2, 1974.

51. Cf. "The Unfriendly Friends," ibid., Feb. 9, 1974.

52. This critical view of EEC policy was well put by Secretary Kissinger in his speech, cited in note 38, supra.

53. Cf. the excellent analysis of Michel Tatu, "La hiérarchie des puissances," Le Monde, Jan. 1, 1974.

54. Ting Wang, "The Succession Problem," Problems of Communism, vol. 22, no. 3 (May-June 1973), pp. 13-24. See also note 16, supra.

55. For a perceptive early analysis of these developments, see Thomas W. Robinson, "China in 1973: Renewed Leftism Threatens the 'New Course,'" Asian Survey, vol. 14, no. 1 (Jan. 1974), pp. 1-21.

56. Cf. David Bonavia from Peking, "The Delicate Dance of the Three Powers," New York Times, Feb. 10, 1974, IV, p. 4.

57. For a convincing refutation of reports of factional struggle in Moscow, see Christian Duevel, "Suslov and Detente," Radio Liberty Research Bulletin, Dec. 26, 1973, and "Brezhnev and the Arms Lobby," ibid., Jan. 9, 1974.

58. Zbigniew Brzezinski, "U.S.-Soviet Relations," in Henry Owen, ed., The Next Phase in Foreign Policy (Washington, D.C.: The Brookings Institute, 1973), pp. 113-132.

59. Hassner, "Europe: Old Conflicts, New Rules," at pp. 896, 897.

Notes to Chapter 2

1. Tito's speech in Sarajevo, Dec. 22, 1971 (Politika [Belgrade], Dec. 23, 1971).

2. Quoted after Ceauşescu in "Rumäniens unabhaengigkeits-geladener Nationalkommunismus wird 25 Jahre alt," Tagesanzeiger (Zurich), Dec. 12, 1972.

3. Tito's speech in Ljubljana, Dec. 12, 1972 (Politika, Dec. 12, 1972).

4. Ibid.

5. Grigore Gafencu, Preliminari della Guerra all' Est (Milan: Mondadori, 1946), pp. 355ff.

6. Max Jakobson, Diplomatie im Finnischen Winterkrieg 1939/40 (Düsseldorf, 1970), pp. 127ff.

7. Nils Örvik, Sicherheit auf Finnisch (Stuttgart: Seewald, 1972), pp. 13ff.

8. Ghita Ionescu, Communism in Rumania: 1944-1962 (London: Oxford University Press, 1964), pp. 94ff.

9. For the best analysis of the Yugoslav case, see Ernst Halperin, The Triumphant Heretic (London: Heinemann, 1958).

10. Materials of the Congress of the United Polish Workers Party, Nov. 1968; Brezhnev's speech, Nov. 12, 1968. For analysis, see Boris Meissner, Die Breschnew-Doktrin (Cologne: Wissenschaft und Politik, 1969).

11. Brezhnev's toast, Politika, Sept. 27, 1971. For the political implications for the entire communist orbit, see Viktor Meier, "Die sowjetische Blockpolitik," in Sowjetpolitik der 70er Jahre, ed. Richard Löwenthal and Heinrich Vogel (Stuttgart, 1972).

12. Viaţa Economica (Bucharest), June 13, 1964.

13. Lucreţiu Patraşcanu, Sub trei dictaturi (Bucharest: Editura Politica, 1970).

14. See, for instance, Miron Constantinescu, Constantin Daicoviciu, and Stefan Pascu, Istoria Romaniei, Compendiu, 2nd ed. (Bucharest: Editura Didactică si Pedagogică, 1971), pp. 380, 382ff.

15. Ibid., p. 380.

16. Mihai Fata and Ion Spalatelu, Garda de Fier: Organizatie Terorista de tip Fascist (Bucharest, 1971), p. 10.

17. See, for example, Ceauşescu's speech at the Ninth Congress of the Communist Party of Rumania, English translation (Bucharest: Meridian, 1965).

18. Third Congress of the Communist Party of Rumania, Sept. 1924, in Ionescu, Communism in Rumania, p. 22.

19. Fata and Spalatelu, Garda de fier.

20. Herman Neubacher, Sonderauftrag Südost (Göttingen: Musterschmidt, 1957), p. 60.

21. Ibid., p. 126.

22. Paul Lendvai, Anti-Semitism Without Jews (New York: Doubleday, 1971).

23. Constantinescu, Daicoviciu, and Pascu, Istoria Romaniei, p. 453.

24. Ionescu, Communism in Rumania, pp. 209ff.

25. Paul Lendvai, Eagles in Cobwebs (Garden City, N.Y.: Doubleday, 1969), pp. 316ff.

26. Bernard Margueritte in Le Monde (Paris), July 18, 1972; and Viktor Meier in Tagesanzeiger, June 23, 1972.

27. Discussions at the Congress of Rumanian Writers, May 22-24, 1972 (Le Monde, May 21 and 22, 1972). In connection with this, see the affair of the writer Paul Goma.

28. Ceauşescu's speech before representatives of the German minority (Neuer Weg [Bucharest], Feb. 21, 1971).

29. Ceauşescu's speech before the Ninth Congress of the Communist Party of Rumania; and Rumanien: Kleine Enzyklopädie (Bucharest, 1965), pp. 96ff.

30. Tagesanzeiger, Dec. 29, 1972.

31. John Michael Montias, Economic Development in Communist Rumania (Cambridge, Mass.: M.I.T. Press, 1967), p. 247.

32. Ceauşescu's main speech at the National Party Conference, July 1972 (Scinteia [Bucharest], July 20, 1972); Resolutions (Scinteia, July 23, 1972).

33. For economic and administrative reforms, see "Ceauşescu rafft sich zu inneren Reformen auf," Tagesanzeiger, Feb. 16, 1971; and Ceauşescu's speech before the plenum of the Central Committee of the Communist Party of Rumania (Neuer Weg, Feb. 14, 1971). For discussion of reforms in the system of foreign trade, see Ceauşescu's speech in Neuer Weg, Feb. 7, 1971.

34. See poems, quoted in Rumanian newspapers, written for the National Party Conference in July 1972 and for the fifty-fifth anniversary of Nicolae Ceauşescu in January 1973; proceedings of the plenary session of the Rumanian Central Committee, Nov. 27, 1973; and Viktor Meier, "Ceauşescu's Plan setzt zu hohe Ziele," Tagesanzeiger, Dec. 29, 1973.

35. Paul Shoup, Communism and the Yugoslav National Question (New York and London: Columbia University Press, 1968), pp. 261ff.

36. Mil. Vukičević, "Program spoljne politike Ilije Garašanina" Delo (Belgrade), vol. 38 (1906), pp. 321ff.

37. Vaso Čubrilović, Istorija Političke Misli u Srbiji XIX veka (Belgrade: Prosveta, 1958), pp. 154ff.

38. Ante Starčević, Izabrani politički spisi (Zagreb: Znanje, 1971).

39. See, for example, Popijevke Slovinske, an old manuscript from Dubrovnik, 1758.

40. Mirjana Gross, Vladavina Hrvatsko-Srpske Koalicije (Belgrade: Institut Društvenih Nauka, 1960), pp. 11ff.

41. See Strossmayer's speech in the Sabor, 1861 (Bill 144); see bibliography in Strossmayer-Rački, Politički spisi (Zagreb: Znanje, 1971), p. 528.

42. "Drohen in Kroatien jetzt Hexenjagden?" Rheinische Post, Dec. 4, 1971.

43. Vladko Maček, In the Struggle for Freedom (University Park: Pennsylvania State University Press, 1957), p. 123.

44. Milan Stojadinović, Ni Rat ni Pakt (Buenos Aires: El Economista, 1963), pp. 512ff.

45. Shoup, Communism and the Yugoslav National Question, p. 263.

46. Svetozar Marković, Sabrini Spisi, vol. 3 (Belgrade: Kultura, 1965), p. 123.

47. Pregled Istorije Saveza Komunista Jugoslavije (Belgrade, Institut za izučavanje radničkog pokreta, 1963), p. 64.

48. Ibid., p. 193.

49. Ibid., p. 397.

50. See Materials from the Congress of Self-Management in Sarajevo, May 5-8, 1971.

51. Halperin, The Triumphant Heretic.

52. Charles Zalar, Yugoslav Communism: A Critical Study (U.S. Senate, Washington, D.C.: 87th Cong., 1961), pp. 181ff.

53. Kardelj's speech before the enlarged session of the Slovenian Central Committee, Ljubljana, Aug. 26, 1969 (Komunist [Belgrade], Oct. 2, 1969).

54. Andrej Marinc in <u>Delo</u> (Ljubljana), Nov. 5, 1972.

55. Tito's speech in Ljubljana (<u>Politika</u>, Dec. 13, 1972); and declarations of the Yugoslav secretary of defense, General Nikola Ljubičić (ibid., Dec. 18, 1972).

56. Speeches and Resolutions of the Eighth Congress of the League of Communists of Yugoslavia (Belgrade, 1964). Published in <u>FBIS</u>, <u>USSR and East Europe</u> (Dec. 14, 1964), pp. nn1-22.

57. <u>Politika</u>, July 2, 1966.

58. See Mika Tripalo before the Croatian Central Committee on May 14, 1971. <u>FBIS, Eastern Europe</u> (May 17, 1971), pp. I iiff.

59. For these arguments, see Hrvoje Šošić, <u>Za Čiste Račune</u> (Zagreb: Matica Hrvatska, 1970).

60. Tito's speech in Karadjordjevo (<u>Politika</u>, Dec. 3, 1971).

61. Ibid., Sep. 22, 1970.

62. Tito's speech at the Congress (ibid., May 6, 1971).

63. Ibid., May 3, 1971.

64. <u>Vjesnik</u> (Zagreb), Sept. 16, 1971.

65. See Salim Čerić, <u>Muslimani srpsko-hrvatskog jezika</u> (Sarajevo, Svjetlost, 1968).

66. An example of such an enterprise is "Energoinvest" in Sarajevo, with its general manager, Emerich Blum.

67. See NIN (<u>Nedeljne Ilustrovane Novine</u> [Belgrade]), Dec. 1972. From the beginning of 1973, General Mišković's role declined. In February 1973, the juridical commission of the Federal Assembly rejected a proposal for tightening pretrial investigations (Vjesnik u Sriedu [Zagreb], Feb. 7, 1973). In April, Mišković was transferred to the poisition of counselor for security of the State Presidency (<u>Politika</u>, April 6, 1973) and in June was sent on leave (<u>Tagesanzeiger</u>, June 20).

68. <u>Borba</u> (Belgrade and Zagreb), Dec. 23 and 24, 1971.

69. <u>Politika</u>, Sept. 22, 1972.

70. Ibid., Oct. 18, 1972. For Tito's Letter to all party organizations, see ibid., Oct. 19, 1972.

71. Delo, Dec. 30, 1972.

72. Draft constitution of the Yugoslav Socialist Federal Republic (Politika, June 9, 1973).

73. See Professor A. Bajt, "Napovedi ekonomistov za 1974," Delo, Jan. 9, 1974.

74. Tass and Agerpress (Bucharest), Feb. 21, 1973.

75. Lendvai, Eagles in Cobwebs, pp. 325ff.

76. Hansjakob Stehle, Nachbarn im Osten (Frankfurt am Main: S. Fischer, 1971), pp. 227ff.

77. "Ceauşescu sieht sich als nahöstlicher Briefträger," Tagesanzeiger, May 8, 1972.

78. President Johnson's speech in San Antonio, Texas (New York Times, Sept. 2, 1968), on Aug. 30, 1968.

79. Decree of December 15, 1972.

80. N. S. Stanescu, Gh. Marcu, and Tr. Silea, Romania in Economia Lumii (Bucharest, 1972), p. 20.

81. "La nouvelle Loi sur la Défense," Le Monde, Dec. 31, 1972.

82. Rumanian-Soviet Treaty of Friendship and Mutual Assistance, July 7, 1970; see Stehle, Nachbarn im Osten, p. 193.

83. Viaţa Economica, June 13, 1964.

84. "Rumänien bewährt nationale Selbstständigkeit," Rheinische Post, July 31, 1971.

85. "Rumänien hat eigene Pläne," ibid., Nov. 23, 1972.

86. Scinteia, March 3, 1973.

87. Stojadinović, Ni Rat ni Pakt, pp. 463ff.

88. Zalar, Yugoslav Communism, p. 275.

89. See Borba, July 4, 1957, after Khrushchev's victory over the "antiparty group."

90. Pravda (Moscow), June 4, 1958, for Khrushchev's speech in Sofia.

91. The Conference of the Heads of State or Government of Nonaligned Countries (Belgrade: Jugoslavija, 1961).

92. Tito's speech in Skoplje, Nov. 13, 1961.

93. Tito's press conference in Jajce, Nov. 30, 1968.

94. For Todor Zhivkov's attitude before the intervention in Czechoslovakia, see Erwin Weit, Ostblock intern (Hamburg: Hoffmann v. Campe, 1970), pp. 242ff. For Yugoslav's apprehensions afterward, see "Die Jugoslawen sprechen wieder von Bedrohung," Tagesanzeiger, Feb. 2, 1971.

95. Politika, June 9, 1971, and Wissenschaftlicher Dienst Südosteuropa (Munich: Sudost Institut), (June-July 1971), p. 96.

96. Ibid., p. 98.

97. For Yugoslav condemnation of the maneuvers, see Borba, Aug. 7, 1971.

98. For Foreign Minister Tepavać's trip to Peking, see Politika, June 11, 1971.

99. Yugoslav-Soviet communiqué, Sep. 30, 1971; for the main theses, see Wissenschaftlicher Dienst Südosteuropa (April 1972), p. 69.

100. Ibid.

101. Boris Hržić, on Radio Zagreb, June 10, 1972; and Barbieri in NIN, June 11, 1972.

102. Politika, Dec. 13, 1972.

103. These numbers are the official estimate; see Ivo Jerkić in Borba, Sept. 1, 1972.

104. Politika, Dec. 9, 1972.

105. Tanjug, Bulletin for Austria, Jan. 18, 1973.

106. "Susret na Jadranu," Politika, March 17, 1973.

107. "Tito unterstützt die sowjetische Nahostpolitik,"
Tagesanzeiger, Oct. 16, 1973; and "Enttäuscht," Weserkurier
(Bremen), Oct. 30, 1973.

108. TANJUG Bulletin, Nov. 13, 1973.

109. See Tito's toast to Nixon at the White House (Politika,
Oct. 30, 1971). For Tito's press conference in Québec, see ibid.,
Nov. 7, 1971.

110. Vladimir Dedijer, Josip Broz Tito: Prilozi za Biografiju
(Belgrade: Kultura, 1953), p. 466.

111. Weit, Ostblock intern, pp. 242ff.

112. See the declarations about "anti-Yugoslav political
activity" in Bulgaria, made by the speaker of the Federal
Secretariat for Information in Belgrade (Politika, Oct. 8, 1971).

113. Tagesanzeiger, March 16, 1973.

114. Zbigniew K. Brzezinski, The Soviet Bloc, rev. ed.
(Cambridge, Mass.: Harvard University Press, 1971), pp. 271ff.

115. William E. Griffith, The Sino-Soviet Rift (Cambridge,
Mass.: M.I.T. Press, 1964), and Albania and the Sino-Soviet
Rift (Cambridge, Mass.: M.I.T. Press, 1963).

116. For the foundation of Albania, see Stavro Skendi, The
Albania National Awakening (Princeton, N.J.: Princeton
University Press, 1967.

117. Politika, March 26, 1973.

118. "Bukarest—Peking—Moskau," Wissenschaftlicher Dienst
Südosteuropa (June-July 1971), pp. 89ff.

119. "Die jugoslawisch-chinesischen Beziehungen," ibid., pp. 94ff.

120. Vjesnik, Aug. 28, 1971.

121. Radio Tirana, Nov. 1, 2, and 4, 1971.

122. Tito's interview with the Washington Post, Oct. 25, 1971.

123. Hugh Seton-Watson, Eastern Europe Between the Wars (New York: Harper & Row, 1967), p. 373.

124. Chiru Stoica's proposal of Sept. 10, 1957. The first mention of transforming the Balkans into a nuclear-free zone was made June 8, 1959, when Stoica's suggestion was taken up again. See Ionescu, Communism in Rumania, pp. 291-292.

125. Ceaușescu's speech before the Central Committee of the Communist Party of Rumania, March 1973 (Scinteia, March 3, 1973).

126. See "Tito ist gegen das neue Balkankonsept aus Bukarest," Tagesanzeiger, Aug. 14, 1973.

Notes to Chapter 3

1. See Elie Kedourie, Nationalism in Asia and Africa (London: Weidenfeld and Nicolson, 1970), pp. 64, 68, 111.

2. For details of Nasser's military policy, see the following section of this chapter.

3. M. H. Heikal, Nasser and the World (in Arabic) (Beirut: Dar an-Nahar li-n-Nashr, 1972), pp. 76ff.

4. So in the Soviet reply of June 7, 1945; cf. Nuri Eren, Turkey Today and Tomorrow: An Experiment in Westernization (New York: Praeger, 1963), p. 233. For details, see F. C. Erkin, Les relations turco-soviétiques et la question des détroits (Ankara: Basnur Matbaasi, 1968), pp. 286ff, with documents.

5. For the connections between the CIA and the Free Officers, see the strange book by Miles Copeland, The Game of Nations (London: Weidenfeld and Nicolson, 1969). Jean Lacouture calls it "souvent vraisembable."

6. Jean Lacouture, Nasser (Paris: Seuil, 1971), p. 103.

7. Cf. Heikal, Nasser and the World, p. 77; for the evolution of Soviet appraisals, see Walter Z. Laqueur, The Soviet Union and the Middle East (London: Routledge and Kegan Paul, 1959), p. 151.

8. Heikal, Nasser and the World, p. 92.

9. Ibid., p. 90.

10. Ibid., p. 98.

11. Ibid., p. 165; cf. p. 205.

12. Ibid., p. 206: Nasser writing to Khrushchev in 1959, "Your warning had come nine days after the beginning of the battle."

13. Ibid., p. 185.

14. Ibid., p. 184.

15. Patrick Seale, The Struggle for Syria (London: Oxford University Press, 1965), pp. 184ff., 219ff., 315ff.

16. Laqueur, The Soviet Union and the Middle East, p. 259.

17. Nadav Safran, From War to War (New York: Pegasus, 1969), p. 117, citing al-Ahram of January 22, 1965; see also Heikal, Nasser and the World, p. 189.

18. Ibid., p. 198.

19. Ibid., p. 206.

20. Safran, From War to War, pp. 119ff.

21. Heikal, Nasser and the World, pp. 246-310.

22. Laqueur, The Soviet Union and the Middle East, p. 208 and the sources cited there.

23. Heikal, Nasser and the World, pp. 214-217.

24. Unpublished account by Dr. F. Büttner; see his forthcoming study on the revolutionary officers and their role in politics.

25. Laqueur, The Soviet Union and the Middle East, p. 96.

26. Safran, From War to War, pp. 271ff.

27. His version of events was given in a speech made in front of the Arab Socialist Union on July 23, 1970. See The New Middle East, no. 23 (Aug. 1970), pp. 47ff.: "We talked continuously for four days."

28. As was admitted much later by Heikal; see The New Middle East, no. 23 (Aug. 1970), p. 44: "500 to 2,000 soldiers killed during June"; and ibid., no. 24 (Sept. 1970), p. 17.

29. E.g., in his speech of May 1, 1970.

30. Heikal, Nasser and the World, p. 214.

31. Neue Zürcher Zeitung, Dec. 3, 1971.

32. Ibid., April 18, 1972.

33. A strong negative echo of this document is found in the so-called Organizational Declaration published by the ASU secretary-general in August 1972. Arabic text: Fuad Matar, Nasserite Russia and Egyptian Egypt (in Arabic)(Beirut: Dar an-Nahâr li-n-nashr, 1972), pp. 196-201.

34. Pravda, June 4, 1972.

35. Neue Zürcher Zeitung, Aug. 6 and 8, 1972, "Die Verstaatlichung der IPC im Lichte der sowjetischen Erdölstrategie."

36. Mahr, Die Baath Partei, p. 111.

37. Matar, Nasserite Russia, p. 54.

38. For the whole Ali Sabri affair, the book and documentary collection of Fuad Matar is the essential source: Where did Nasser Go in the Republic of Sadat? Secrets of the Fall of the Chiefs of the Nasserite Regime (in Arabic)(Beirut: Dar an-Nahâr li-n-Nashr, 1972). For Ali Sabri's previous career and setbacks, see p. 7.

39. Matar, Nasserite Russia, p. 54.

40. Ibid., p. 62.

41. Ibid., p. 72.

42. The Newsweek interview was published in Egypt on February 16, 1971, with some changes. Matar analyzes the differences.

43. Ibid., p. 89.

44. For details, see Matar, Where Did Nasser Go?, including documents and defense speeches of Ali Sabri and his group.

45. Ibid., p. 80. Matar's judgment, after having sifted all the evidence available, is,"It was a power struggle rather than a case of high treason."

46. Ibid., p. 17, for an explanation of the family relationships and ties of friendship among the members of the Ali Sabri group.

47. Speeches of July 24 and October 16, 1971; see al-Ahram of the following days.

48. Matar, Nasserite Russia, p. 91.

49. Ibid., p. 92.

50. Matar, The Communist Party in the Sudan: Did They Kill It or Did It Commit Suicide? (in Arabic)(Beirut: Dar an-Nahar li-n-nashr, 1971), p. 60. This collection of essays and documents is again fundamental to an understanding of the events in the Sudan.

51. Matar, Nasserite Russia, p. 95. Matar adds, "But this is not a verified story."

52. For documents about the party split, see Matar, The Communist Party in the Sudan, pp. 94-272.

53. Ibid., p. 96.

54. Ibid., p. 98.

55. A. McDermott in the Manchester Guardian Weekly, Nov. 25, 1972.

56. Matar, Nasserite Russia, p. 24ff. In theory, what he said was secret, but it filtered through.

57. An-Nahar, Jan. 21, 1972.

58. Matar, Nasserite Russia, pp. 108ff.

59. See Sadat's speech before the conference of the ASU as reported by the Le Monde correspondent, R. Delcour, July 26, 1972: "En octobre je revins en USSR pour expliquer notre position. Je dis aux Soviétiques que l'année 1971 devait être décisive, que c'était dans notre intérêt et dans le leur. Nous nous entendîmes

alors sur certaines affaires [M. Sadat fait allusion aux
livraisons d'armes]. L'accord prévoyait qu'elles seraient
réglées avant la fin de l'année 1971. Là encore rien ne vint. Je
dis aux Soviétiques que je me trouverais hors d'état de tenir ma
promesse à la nation Egyptienne. Les Soviétiques me dirent alors:
'Attendez février,' puis après février: 'Attendez le 18 mai, jour
de la rencontre Nixon-Brejnew.' Je retournai en URSS en février
puis en avril 1972, à la veille de la rencontre américaine-
soviétique. Je leur dis: 'J'ai fait tout cela pour garder votre
amitié.' Le Président Sadat rappelle alors les trois principes
qui'il fit valoir avant les Soviétiques: 'Pas de limitations aux
livraisons d'armes soviétiques à l'Egypte; pas d'accord sur
l'état de 'ni guerre ni paix'; pas de cession de territoire
arabe. Je leurs dis qu'il fallait une solution honorable.

"Il apparut alors une autre divergence. Je leur expliquai
qu'à notre sens l'appui des Etats Unis à Israel pour le
maintenir dans les territoires occupés allait plus loin que le
status quo, qu'Israel était l'agent des Etats Unis. Nous ne
sommes que des amis. Cependant si nous adoptons votre attitude
trop prudente, le problème ne sera pas réglé. 'Oui, oui,' et ils
ont essayé d'arranger les choses. Mais les divergences
subsistaient."

60. Matar, Nasserite Russia, p. 115.

61. Ibid., pp. 189-191. The memorandum has never been published
in the Egyptian press, but it filtered out and was published in
Beirut.

62. Interview with J. F. Chauvel, Le Figaro, Aug. 21, 1972: "Pas
du tout, pas du tout! Vous savez, toutes sortes de bruits sont
lancés par les pêcheurs en eau troublée."

63. Matar, Nasserite Russia, p. 162.

64. Ibid., p. 121.

65. Ibid., pp. 120ff.

66. Ibid., p. 118; al-Akhbar titled its edition of May 26: "We
have long-range jet planes."

67. Matar, Nasserite Russia, p. 27; Matar himself was the
interviewer. See also an-Nahar, June 4 and 5, 1972.

68. Matar, Nasserite Russia, p. 125.

69. Ibid., p. 120.

70. Ibid., p. 129; the seminar was published by al-Ahram on May 19, 1972, about two weeks after it had taken place.

71. Matar, Nasserite Russia, p. 31.

72. Ibid., p. 22.

73. Ibid., p. 24.

74. Ibid., p. 45.

75. McDermott, in the Manchester Guardian Weekly.

76. Le Monde, Nov. 23, 1972.

77. See Bernard Reich in The New Middle East, no. 1 (Oct. 1968), pp. 9ff.

78. Dan Margalit, "Politics of the Phantoms," Journal of Palestine Studies, vol. 2, no. 2 (Winter 1973), p. 151. This is the translation of an article by Margalit originally published in Haaretz, Sept. 8, 1972.

79. See The New Middle East, no. 14 (Nov. 1969), p. 6.

80. See Parker T. Hart, "The Go-Between: A Role the U.S. Can No Longer Play," ibid., no. 50 (Nov. 1972), esp. p. 8.

81. The military account is taken from Lawrence L. Whetten, "June 1967 to June 1971: Four Years of Canal War Reconsidered," ibid., no. 33 (June 1971), pp. 15-25. See also Lawrence L. Whetten, The Canal War: Four-Power Conflict in the Middle East (Cambridge, Mass.: M.I.T. Press, 1974).

82. Margalit, "Politics of the Phantoms."

83. N. Safran, "The Soviet-Egyptian Treaty as Seen From Washington," The New Middle East, no. 34 (June 1971).

84. Mrs. Meir's speech is reprinted in ibid., no. 29 (Feb. 1971), p. 45.

85. Margalit, "Politics of the Phantoms."

86. Reprinted in English in Journal of Palestine Studies, vol. 2, no. 4 (Summer 1973), pp. 125-126.

87. La deuxième session du congrès national général de l'Union Socialiste Arabe (July 23-26, 1972) (Cairo: Service de l'état pour l'information [1972]).

88. Ibid., p. 85.

89. Ministry of Information, State Information Service, "Speech by President Anwar el Sadat during the celebrations of the 21st anniversary of the July 23, 1952 Revolution, July 23, 1973" (Cairo, 1973, official English text), p. 47.

90. Ibid., p. 48.

91. Ministry of Information, State Information Service, "Speech by President A. el Sadat at Alexandria University, July 26, 1973" (Alexandria, 1973), p. 14.

92. La deuxième session du congrès national général, p. 80.

93. Cf. Nayef Hawatmeh as cited by Samir Franjié, "OLP-Une nouvelle stratégie diplomatique," Le Monde diplomatique, Jan. 1974.

94. Eric Rouleau, "La guerre d'Octobre ou la diplomatie du canon. I. La chance de ne pas être cru," Le Monde, Nov. 4, 1973.

95. See his interview with Eric Rouleau in Le Monde, Oct. 23, 1973: "Cette guerre n'est pas la mienne. . . . Sadat et Assad ont pris leur décision, ont arrêté leur plans sans mon agrément, sans me consulter, et sans même m'en informer. . . . Je leur avais soumis autrefois un plan stratégique mais leurs états majeurs en ont décidé autrement. . . . Mon projet est le meilleur, je ne peux donner ma caution à une guerre d'opérette. . . ."

96. For details and statistics see James E. Akins, "The Oil Crisis: This Time the Wolf Is Here," Foreign Affairs, vol. 51, no. 3 (April 1973), pp. 462-490.

97. See The Economist, Sept. 22, 1973, p. 64, for a reported Saudi "ultimatum" to the U.S.

98. Le Monde, April 22-23, 1973, cited in Eric Rouleau: "Les

dédales de l'opération 'Badr,' "Le Monde, Nov. 25-26, 1973.

99. Rouleau, "Les dédales de l'opération 'Badr.'" According to
others, the final date was set in August after the Israeli Labour
party had adopted a forward policy, the "Galili plan," in their
election platform.

100. Franjié, " OLP—Une nouvelle stratégie diplomatique."

101. Rouleau, "Les dédales de l'opération 'Badr.'"

102. H.E.T. [Hans E. Tutsch], "Amerikanische Luftbrücke nach
Israel," Neue Zürcher Zeitung, Oct. 17, 1973; also Neue Zürcher
Zeitung, Oct. 12 and 19, 1973.

103. Attempts to unravel the muddle of differing "clarifications"
given about the alert include the following: Michel Tatu, "Que
s'est-il passé le 25 octobre?," Le Monde, Nov. 3, 1973; André
Fontaine, "Business as Usual," ibid., Oct. 30, 1973; see also
[Général] Georges Buis, "Pour la sanctuairisation d'Israel,"
Le Monde diplomatique, Nov. 1973.

104. A.H. [Arnold Hottinger], "Sowjetische Offerte an die
Palästinenser," Neue Zürcher Zeitung, Nov. 13, 1973.

105. Egyptian Foreign Minister Fahmi had met a Palestinian
delegation and requested that they announce a Palestinian
government before the second round of talks in Geneva. The
Palestinians had replied that they would consult and answer
later (an-Nahar, Jan. 7, 1974).

106. An-Nahar, Dec. 20, 1972.

107. See the long interview given by Nimeiry in al-Hawadith
(Beirut) and republished in Al-Ayam (Khartoum) on June 8, 1972.
See also Matar, The Communist Party in the Sudan, p. 4.

108. See two long articles by Ali Hashem in an-Nahar, Sept. 16
and 23, 1972.

109. René Lefort, "Révolution au Sud-Yemen," Le Monde
Diplomatique, Feb. 2, 1971. Other sources of information are
G. Troeller and Claude Deffarge, "Sud-Yemen: Une révolution
menacée?" ibid., Apr. 5, 1972; Samir Franjié, "Yémen: Un accord
précaire," ibid., Dec. 1972; and an enthusiastic description by E
Rouleau, "L'Etoile sur le Yemen de Sud,"Le Monde, May 27-31, 1972. This

last-cited series of articles gives valid descriptions but is
insufficiently informed about the intricacies of the historical
evolution of the Yemen situation and its intrigues. See also Isam
Ghanem, "Will the Yemen Constitution hold?," The New Middle East,
nos. 52-53 (Jan. and Feb. 1973), Ali Hashem, writing from
San'a, in an-Nahar, Sept. 26 and 30, 1972.

110. Ray L. Cleveland, "Revolution in Dhofar, Sultanate of Oman,"
Middle East Forum, vol. 47, nos. 3 and 4 (Autumn and Winter 1971),
pp. 93-103, gives details of the geographic and linguistic
background of the people and of the general nature of the
rebellion.

111. Two articles by Jean-Pierre Viennot in Le Monde Diplomatique,
Jan. 4, 1970 and Aug. 1972, give deeper insight into motivations
and ideology.

112. Dhofar: Britain's Colonial War in the Gulf, a collection of
documents and articles edited by The Gulf Committee (London:
Crest Press, 1972), p. 14.

113. Viennot in Le Monde Diplomatique, Jan. 4, 1970.

114. Ibid.: "Tout récemment le front a obtenu l'autorisation
d'installer une représentation officielle à Alger et il est parvenu
à établir des relations avec l'URSS: des journalistes soviétiques
ont visité les régions libérées du Dhofar et, quoique indisposés
par l'abondance des portraits de Mao Tse-toung qu'on y rencontre,
ils ont publié au retour des articles favorables au mouvement."
Nasib Nimr, who is close to the PDFLP, wrote a book on the Sino-
Soviet differences and the refusal of the Arab "progressives" to
choose sides between them: Between Moscow and Peking (in Arabic)
(Beirut: Dar an-Nahar li-n-Nashr, n.d.).

115. Dhofar, pp. 17, 27.

116. Ibid., p. 68.

117. Ibid., p. 22.

118. Cleveland, "Revolution in Dhofar," p. 100.

119. Dhofar, p. 19.

120. Ibid., p. 23.

121. Cleveland, "Revolution in Dhofar," p. 101.

122. Dhofar, p. 70.

123. The Economist, April 1971, cited in Dhofar, p. 64.

124. R. Johns in Financial Times, May 9, 1973.

125. Neue Zürcher Zeitung, Jan. 6, 1973. The slogans contained such proposals as "serious military training for everyone; an army of all people capable of carrying arms; a militia; ending the isolation of the army from the people; democracy inside the army; training in guerrilla warfare; struggling against imperialist and reactionary thought; changing the programs of all schools and universities in order to bring them into agreement with the necessities of the battle and its principles; instruction in 'knowledge of the enemy'; the Egyptian war industry to stop fabricating expensive armament 'which only serves the interests of a certain class' and to concentrate on small arms and ammunition for the people."

126. Interview with Heikel in al-Ahram, Feb. 23, 1973.

Notes to Chapter 4

1. India's defense expenditure remained relatively low during the fifties. From Rs. 150.81 crore and 1.7 percent of GNP in 1949-1950, it rose to Rs. 266.98 crore and 2 percent of GNP in 1959-60 ("Indian Defense Budget 1972-1973," in the Institute for Defense Studies and Analyses Journal [New Delhi], vol. 4, no. 4 [April 1972], pp. 425-446.

2. India's defense expenditure began to spiral upward in 1960 and suddenly almost doubled in 1963-1964. In 1972 the defense budget was Rs. 1408.36 crore, nearly 4 percent of GNP; the growth rate of the economy for that year was also 4 percent (ibid).

3. New York Times, July 18, 1963. The Times correspondent added that this was the first Pakistani statement that China would assist Pakistan in case of aggression.

4. The China-Pakistan agreement was tentative, subject to revision after a settlement of the Kashmir dispute. For the text of the agreement, see China, India, Pakistan (Karachi: Pakistan Institute of International Relations, 1966).

5. Chester Bowles, "America and Russia in India," Foreign
Affairs, vol. 49, no. 4 (July, 1971), pp. 636-651.

6. For Pakistan's reaction to American military aid to India,
see Zulfikar Ali Bhutto, Foreign Policy of Pakistan (Karachi:
Pakistan Institute of International Relations, 1964).

7. For an informative report on India's defense infrastructure,
see Wayne Wilcox, "Strategic Reinsurance for India," Survival,
vol. 14, no. 4 (July-Aug., 1972, pp. 178-182); see also Annual
Reports of the Indian Defence Ministry (New Delhi: Government of
India, 1971 and 1972).

8. According to one report, Yahya Khan's refusal to support the
Soviet move was partly responsible for Moscow's anti-Pakistan
stance during the 1971 crisis. See Kishan Bhatia's report in the
Hindustan Times (New Delhi), July 22, 1971.

9. For Soviet thinking on an Asian collective security system,
see Bhabani Sen Gupta, "Soviet Thinking on Asian Security,"
Institute for Defense Studies and Analyses Journal, vol. 5, no.
2 (Oct. 1972), pp. 173-195.

10. Fred Crebbe, U.S. Policy and the Security of Asia (New York:
McGraw-Hill, 1968), p. 143. For further insight into South
Asia's security problems, see Alastair Buchan, "An Asian
Balance of Power," Encounter, vol. 27, no. 6 (Dec. 1966), pp.
62-71; Coral Bell, "Security in Asia: Reappraisal After Vietnam,"
International Journal, vol. 24, no. 1 (Winter, 1968-69); Richard
Butwell, "Asian Security—U.S. Style," Far Eastern Economic
Review, July 24, 1969; William Chapin, The Asian Balance of
Power (London: Institute of Strategic Studies, 1967); John R. D.
Cleland, "Chinese Rimland Strategy," Military Review, vol. 47,
no. 1 (Jan. 1967): B. Balasanov, "Peace and Security in Asia,"
United Asia (Bombay), vol. 22, no. 1 (Jan.-Feb. 1970), pp. 9-10;
Fred Gordon, Toward Disengagement in Asia (Englewood Cliffs,
N.J.: Prentice-Hall, 1969); "The Encirclement of China,"
Survival, vol. 8, no. 4 (April 1966); pp. 128-129; S. Gopal,
"India, China andthe Soviet Union," Australian Journal of
Politics and History, vol. 12, no. 2 (Aug.1966); and G. P.
Fitzerald, The Chinese View of Their Place in the World (London:
Oxford University Press, 1964).

11. One of the principal architects of the "arrangement," Lord
Mountbatten, reminisced to an Indian editor in October 1971, "I
told Jinnah that his moth-eaten Pakistan will not last more than

25 years" Kuldip Nayar, Distant Neighbours: A Tale of the
Subcontinent [New Delhi: Vikas, 1972], p. 1).

12. For a detailed account of the Sino-Indian encounter over
Tibet in 1950-1951 and the accord reached in 1954, see the
Bhabani Sen Gupta, Fulcrum of Asia: Relations Among China,
India, Pakistan and the USSR (New York: Pegasus, 1970), chap. 2.

13. Jawaharlal Nehru, "Changing India," Foreign Affairs, vol. 41,
no. 3 (April, 1963), pp. 453-465.

14. Sisir Gupta, "Break with the Past," in Seminar, no. 65, Jan.
1965), pp. 28-31.

15. For a perceptive appreciation of the dilemmas of Indian
nation-builders, see Barrington Moore, Jr., Social Origins of
Democracy and Dictatorship (Boston: Beacon Press, 1966), chap. 6.

16. Gunnar Myrdal, Asian Drama (New York: Pantheon, 1968). The
bulk of the work relates to India; see especially chapter 6.

17. V. M. Dandekar, "Poverty in India: I," Economic and
Political Weekly, Jan. 2, 1971.

18. Ashoka Mehta, "A Disappointing Profile," The Statesman,
Sept. 18, 1971. See also Sarwar Lateef, "The Economic Outlook,"
ibid., Oct. 9, 1971.

19. Ashok Mitra, "Myth of Green Revolution," The Times of India,
Nov. 27, 1972.

20. D. L. Seth, "Profiles of Party Support in 1967," Economic
and Political Weekly, special number, Jan. 1971; Ramashray Ray,
"Patterns of Political Instability," ibid.

21. Rajni Kothari, Politics in India (Delhi: Orient Longman,
1970), pp. 154-155.

22. Rajni Kothari, "Congress System in India," in Party System
and Election Studies, Occasional Papers No. 1, Center for the
Study of Developing Societies (Delhi: Allied Publishers, 1967);
also, Paul R. Brass, "Patronage Is the Cement of the Congress
Organization," in Brass, ed., Factional Politics in an Indian
State: The Congress Party in Uttar Pradesh (Berkeley: University
of California Press, 1965).

23. For a fuller account and analysis of this phase of Indian politics, see Bhabani Sen Gupta, Communism in Indian Politics (New York: Columbia University Press, 1972), esp. chap. 3.

24. M. R. Masani, "Poll Results in Perspective," The Statesman, April 14, 1971.

25. Rajni Kothari, "Toward a Political Perspective for the Seventies," Economic and Political Weekly, special number, Jan. 1970, pp. 101-116.

26. "Pakistan is not a nation and hardly a state. It has no justification in history, ethnic origin, civilization or in the consciousness of those who make up its population. They have no interests in common save one: fear of Hindu domination. It is to that fear and to nothing else that Pakistan owes its existence. . . ." (Hans J. Morgenthau, The Impasse of American Foreign Policy [Chicago: University of Chicago Press, 1962], pp. 260-262). See also Maulana Abul Kalam Azad , India Wins Freedom: An Autobiographical Narrative (Bombay: Asia Publishing House, 1959), p. 227.

27. That this was a result of American aid is borne out by the continued low level of Indian defense expenditures during the fifties; see notes 3, 4.

28. Mohammed Ayoob and K. Subrahmanyan, The Liberation War (New Delhi: S. Chand, 1972), pp. 62-64.

29. See Ayub Khan, Friends, Not Masters (Karachi: Oxford University Press, 1967), p. 275.

30. Ayoob and Subrahmanyan, Liberation War, pp. 71-72.

31. Tariq Ali, Pakistan: Military Rule or People's Power? (London: Morrow, 1970), p. 215.

32. "Why Bangladesh?" in Bangla Desh Documents (New Delhi: Ministry of External Affairs, 1971), pp. 15-22.

33. For the text of Yahya Khan's statement, see Dawn (Karachi), March 27, 1969.

34. For the text of the Legal Framework Order and related official explanations, clarifications, and assurances, see ibid., April 5 and 11, 1970.

35. Quoted in Anthony Mascarenhas, The Rape of Bangla Desh (New Delhi: Vikas, 1971), p. 57.

36. The Financial Times (London), Dec. 1, 1970.

37. Morning News (Dacca), Nov. 27, 1970.

38. The Pakistan People's Party captured 18 of the 27 national assembly seats from Sind; one of the 18 from the Northwest Frontier Province; and none of the four from Baluchistan. For details, see Bangla Desh Documents, p. 130.

39. Mohammed Ayoob, "Profile of a Party: PPP in Pakistan," Economic and Political Weekly, special number, Feb. 1972, pp. 215-219.

40. Bhutto persistently made the point that the Awami League had no mandate to govern West Pakistan. For Rahman's dilemma, see his statements in Pakistan Observer (Dacca), Jan. 4, 1971; Dawn, Jan. 4 and 12, 1971; Pakistan Times, Feb. 25, 1971.

41. Pakistan Observer, Dec. 10, 1970.

42. Bangla Desh Documents, pp. 142-187.

43. Dawn, Jan. 5, 1971.

44. Rahman said, "If the federating units of West Pakistan do not wish to have precisely the same degree of autonomy as Bangladesh or wish to cede certain additional powers to the Center or to establish certain regional institutions, the Six-Point formula does not at all stand in their way" (Pakistan Times, Feb. 25, 1971).

45. Ibid., Dec. 21, 1970; Dawn, Dec. 25 and 28, 1970; Pakistan Times, Jan. 14 and 31, 1971.

46. Pakistan Observer, Feb. 6, 1971.

47. Ibid. Rahman, in contrast to Bhutto, deplored the blowing up of the plane.

48. Dawn, Feb. 16, 1971.

49. Pakistan Times, March 1, 1971. Rahman's stand was this: "In this background, the insistence upon the retention of foreign

trade and aid in the Center appears too clearly to be designed
not to secure the interest of national integrity but to ensure
the retention in the hands of the Center of the principal
instruments required for the colonial exploitation of Bangladesh"
(Pakistan Times, Feb. 25, 1971).

50. Ibid., March 1, 1971.

51. Morning News (Karachi), March 2, 1971. The Pakistan president
did not consult Rahman before fixing the dates and places of the
national assembly session, nor before postponing announced
sessions.

52. Ibid., Nov. 28, 1970. Yahya Khan said in a broadcast that
East Pakistan, because of its geographical distance, must have
"maximum autonomy" within a united Pakistan. "After all, I do
not want five Pakistans."

53. Dawn, Jan. 12, 1971; Pakistan Observer, Jan. 15, 1971.

54. Mascarenhas, The Rape of Bangla Desh, p. 75.

55. Ibid., p. 85.

56. Ibid.

57. Ayoob and Subrahmanyan, Liberation War, p. 107. Rahman
claimed that several minority-party members of the national
assembly had already arrived in Dacca and others would have come
if they had not been threatened with "liquidation" The People
[Dacca], March 2, 1971).

58. David Loshak, The Pakistan Crisis (London: 1971), p. 59.

59. The People, March 3, 1971.

60. Dawn, March 4, 1971.

61. Ibid.

62. Ibid., March 5 and 6, 1971, Morning News (Dacca), March 7,
1971.

63. Dawn, March 6, 1971.

64. Ibid., March 7, 1971.

65. Loshak, The Pakistan Crisis, pp. 71-72; Rehman Sobhan, "Negotiating for Bangladesh: A Participant's View," South Asian Review, vol. 4, no. 4 (London) (July, 1971), pp. 315-326; also Sobhan, "Prelude to an Order for Genocide," The Guardian (London), June 5, 1971.

66. Dawn, March 8, 1971.

67. Ibid.

68. Ibid. The minority group, Rahman alleged, had "aligned itself with certain forces to obstruct the constitutional process and to deprive the majority of the people of their rights."

69. Bhutto said that there should be "a tripartite understanding" among the two "democratically elected majority parties" and the army which was to transfer power (Pakistan Times, March 23, 1971).

70. Dawn, March 16, 1971. Bhutto added, however, that he was not thinking in terms of two prime ministers, one for each wing.

71. Ibid., March 27, 1971.

72. The Sunday Times (London), July 11, 1971.

73. Bangla Desh Documents, pp. 349-351. This volume includes many primary and secondary reports of the systematic ruthlessness with which the Pakistani army sought to liquidate the autonomy movement. For the Pakistan government's version of the events leading to the military crackdown, see White Paper on the Crisis in East Pakistan (Karachi, 1971). See also Zulfikar Ali Bhutto, The Great Tragedy (Karachi: Pakistan People's Party Publications, 1971).

74. After Rahman's arrest his followers proclaimed an "Independent Bangladesh" on March 27. This was followed by the Proclamation of Independence Order on April 10. Text: Sunday Standard [New Delhi], April 18, 1971.) The formal inauguration of the republic took place, attended by a 10,000-strong crowd, on April 17 (The Statesman, April 18, 1971.

75. Ayoob and Subrahmanyan, Liberation War, pp. 156-157.

76. Ibid., pp. 161, 163.

77. "The Government of India, presumably after due deliberations, decided not to close the borders, but to allow the refugees to come in. In a sense the commitment of the Government of India to the liberation of Bangladesh was implicit in this decision" (ibid., p. 156).

78. The Statesman, April 1, 1971.

79. Ibid., May 25, 1971. Mrs. Gandhi apparently expected the great powers, especially the United States and the USSR, to press Pakistan for a solution of the crisis acceptable to the Awami League: "A political solution must be brought about by those who have the power to do so. . . . The great powers have a special responsibility."

80. See Foreign Minister Swaran Singh's statement in the Lok Sabha, reported in ibid., June 26, 1971.

81. For the text of chief of state Podgorny's message and other Soviet pronouncements during the 1971 crisis, see "The Soviet Union and the Struggle of the Bangladesh People," Soviet Review (Moscow), Supplement, Jan. 18, 1972.

82. The Times of India, April 13, 1971.

83. New York Times, Aug. 7, 1971. The Times report said, "American officials and foreign diplomats are now reported to believe that neither Moscow nor Peking wishes to see a war in which they might be forced into a direct confrontation." President Nixon in his foreign policy report to the Congress in February 1972 said, "To the Soviet Union we made the point repeatedly over the summer that it behooved the two superpowers to be forces for peace. We asked the Soviet Union for its ideas on possible joint action" (U.S. Foreign Policy for the 1970's: The Emerging Structure of Peace [Washington, D.C.: The White House, 1972], p. 50.

84. "Floating Pakistan Anew," editorial in Economic Times (Bombay), July 23, 1971; Amrita Bazar Patrika (Calcutta), July 24, 1971; Indian Express (New Delhi), July 31, 1971; The Times of India, Aug. 25, 1971.

85. New Delhi was reportedly included in Kissinger's itinerary at the insistence of the U.S. ambassador, Kenneth B. Keating (Nayar, Distant Neighbours, p. 163).

86. For a representative sample of Indian commentaries on the Sino-U.S. breakthrough, see Girilal Jain, "A Sino-U.S. Dialogue I, II," The Times of India, July 21 and 22, 1971; V. R. Bhatt, "The Great Powers and Pakistan," Hindustan Times, July 33, 1971; Pran Chopra, "Nixon's Pilgrimage to Peking," Tribune (Chandigarh), Aug. 6, 1971; "India and U.S. Drifting Apart," Motherland (New Delhi), Aug. 8, 1972.

87. Sisir Gupta, "The Great Powers and the Subcontinent," Institute for Defense Studies and Analyses Journal (April, 1972), p. 451.

88. K. Subrahmanyan, "Power Growing Out of the Barrel of a Gun," Tribune, July 27, 1971. Professor V. P. Dutt wrote in the same vein: "The first leg of our policy has to concern itself with our relations with the Soviet Union. Of all the Powers, the Soviet Union must be the most anxious and worried over the Sino-U.S. thaw; the Soviets have not many friends in Asia. The complementarity of Soviet and Indian interests is also unmistakably clear. Moscow would probably welcome a better and more meaningful dialogue with India and many other countries of the world. India can utilize this opportunity for a franker and healthier relationship to mutual advantage" ("Sino-U.S. Relations and India," Hindustan Times, July 31, 1971).

89. Pravda, August 10, 1971.

90. Among the spate of anti-China polemical writings in the Soviet Union, O. Vladimirov and V. Ryazanov, "Fiftieth Anniversary of the Communist Party of China," Kommunist, no. 10 (1971); Y. Nikolayev, "Sensation and Reality," Izvestia, July 28, 1971; I. Alexandrov, "Regarding Peking-Washington Contacts," Pravda, July 25, 1971; G. Yukubov "Conflict in Hindustan and the Provocative Role of Mao's Group," ibid., Dec. 28, 1971; and V. Vasiliev, "Increasing Militarization of Life in China Today," Soviet Review, no. 56 (1971). See also Pyotr N. Fedoseyev's 5,000-word article in Pravda, Dec. 5, 1971, which preceded a three day conference of Soviet scholars on China at which Fedoseyev delivered the keynote address.

91. The Hindu, August 10, 1971. "D. P. Dhar, former Ambassador to Russia, was sent to Moscow to receive the treaty proposal. His discussions and everything about the treaty were kept secret. Instead of coded cables, couriers were sent between New Delhi and Moscow to finalize the terms of the treaty. Mrs. Gandhi took even senior colleagues like Jagjivan Ram and Chavan

into her confidence only after the draft had been finalized in
Moscow. And the Cabinet was told about it only on the morning of
9 August, 1971" (Nayar, Distant Neighbours, p. 164).

92. Editorial, Aug. 10, 1971.

93. K. Subrahmanyan, "Where India Stands in Global Power
Equations," Motherland, Sept. 28, 1971. Subrahmanyan, then
director of the Institute for Defense Studies and Analyses, New
Delhi, wrote in another article (see note 88), "In this new
[Power] game, the U.S. and China have a shared incentive to come
together against the Soviet Union. The U.S. justifiably feels
that the primary challenge to its security and top position
comes not from China but from the Soviet Union. Consequently,
the compulsion is greater to curb the power and influence of the
Soviet Union. Similarly for China the Soviet Union is the next
power standing in its way to the top. Before it challenges the
U.S. in power terms, it must neutralize the Soviet Union to the
extent possible" ("Power Growing Out of the Barrel of a Gun").
    Most Indian commentators warned the government in September
and October 1971 not to subordinate Indian interests in South
Asia to the global interests of the USSR. A typical example:
"Consequently it is within the context of superpower rivalries
in the region that the significance of the treaty lies. If India
can, on the one hand, drive a wedge between the parallel
policies of the United States and the Soviet Union—which were
to keep India weak—and on the other hand deter China against
any adventurist enterprise, the treaty will have been a
diplomatic and political breakthrough. If, on the other hand, we
find ourselves shouldered into a subordinate role in our
relationship with Russia, we will have dealt a disastrous blow
to our sovereign right to make our own independent decisions"
(Patwant Singh, "Evolving Power Patterns," Hindustan Times, Aug.
22, 1971).
    For comment and analysis, mostly critical, see Indo-Soviet
Treaty: Reactions and Reflections (New Delhi: Deendayal Research
Institute, 1972); and A. P. Jain, Shadows of the Bear (New
Delhi: P. K. Deo, 1972).
    In Pakistan, the treaty was seen as primarily aimed at China
(Pakistan Times, Aug. 11, 1971). A Pakistani journal commented,
"If the Russians are real and genuine seekers of peace on the
continent, Mr. Gromyko should visit Pakistan and offer a similar
treaty to our country's Government" (The New Times [Rawalpindi],
Aug. 11, 1971. One report said that Pakistan immediately
approached Moscow for a similar treaty (Hindustan Times, Aug.
22, 1971).

94. Italics added. The advertisement appeared in Indian Express, Sept. 4, 1971. Curiously, it attracted little public notice in India. The Times of India was almost the only major newspaper to comment on it.

95. Kissinger reportedly said in the course of a background briefing for White House correspondents on December 7, 1971, "We established contact with the Bangladesh people in Calcutta, and during August, September and October of this year no fewer than eight such contacts took place. We approached President Yahya Khan three times in order to begin negotiations with the Bangladesh people in Calcutta. The Government of Pakistan accepted. We were told by our contacts in Calcutta that the Indian Government discouraged such negotiations. In other words, we attempted to promote a political settlement. . . . The difference may have been that the Government of India wanted things to happen so rapidly that it was no longer talking about political settlement, but about political collapse." (Congressional Record, U.S. Senate, Dec. 9, 1971, quoted in The Anderson Papers on U.S. Handling of Situation in Indian Sub-continent [New Delhi, Dec. 1971], pp. 119–120.

96. The Times of India, Oct. 5, 1971. In Washington, it may be noted, the main perception of the Soviet rule in the subcontinent was one of restraining India from military action. When the treaty was signed, the New York Times reported on August 13, "authoritative United States officials said that they understood the Soviet Union succeeded in dissuading India from formally recognizing East Pakistan as an independent country. . . . According to intelligence reports submitted to President Nixon . . . the Soviet Union had warned the Indian Government that recognition of Bangla Desh could precipitate a war between India and Pakistan." Even during the India–Pakistan war, when the Soviets vetoed three resolutions in the Security Council, there was no public criticism of Moscow by the U.S. government, although President Nixon "was reliably reported to be irked privately by what he regards as Soviet efforts to obtain unilateral advantages from the war. . ." (New York Times, Dec. 14, 1971).

97. Dev Murarka, "Two-fold Gain for India," Western Times (Ahmedabad), Oct. 16, 1971.

98. The Times of India, Nov. 16, 1971.

99. Ibid. (italics added).

100. See, for example, Oleg Orestov's article in Pravda, Nov. 9, 1971, replying to Joseph Alsop's charge that India was about to kick Pakistan in the groin at a time when the latter was "down."

101. Patriot (Delhi), Nov. 26, 1971, quoting an Associated Press report from Rawalpindi. The paper also carried a Press Trust of India report from Moscow that the Soviet Union had warned Pakistan against disastrous consequences should that country persist in its warlike course "in total disregard of international counsel for peaceful political means of resolving its problems."

This Soviet diplomatic pressure is to be seen in the context of what was happening along the India-East Pakistan border in the last weeks of November. On November 23 large numbers of Indian troops crossed into East Pakistan. Five days later, Indian Defense Minister Ram announced at a public meeting in Calcutta, "When the Pakistanis started creating trouble on the borders, I told my generals to take action. When it became worse, I told them to cross the borders to silence the guns. Now they've been told that if it becomes necessary, they can advance as many miles into Pakistan territory as the range of the Pakistani guns." Pakistan declared a state of national emergency. Some Indians expected the Pakistan president to declare war (New York Times, Nov. 24-29, 1971).

102. The Times of India, Dec. 1, 1971.

103. The Statesman, Dec. 2, 1971.

104. According to the U.S. and Chinese governments, the war actually began in the third week of November when Indian forces moved into East Pakistan. For reports of the fighting, see New York Times, Nov. 21-Dec. 14, 1971. Several books have been published in India on the war, most of them "quickies" and unworthy of serious consideration. Of some interest are Major D. K. Palit, The Lightning Campaign (New Delhi: Palit Publications, 1972), and Ayoob and Subrahmanyan, Liberation War. No study of the war was published in Pakistan until the beginning of 1973.

105. "The Soviet Union and the Struggle of the Bangladesh People," (see note 81), pp. 12-13.

106. Ibid., pp. 13-14.

107. According to the Economic Times, the cost of the war for India was probably in the region of Rs. 135-140 crore or about $200 million ("What the War Cost," editorial, Feb. 25, 1972).

108. J. D. Sethi, "Mrs. Gandhi's Political Strategies X-rayed," The Statesman, Aug. 27, 1972, and his "Prime Minister and States' Bosses," Northern India Patrika, Oct. 7, 1971. See also Rajni Kothari's analysis of the Indian federal system in The Times of India, March 24 and 25, 1972.

109. K. R. Narayanan, "Toward a New Equilibrium in Asia," Economic and Political Weekly, special number, Feb. 1972, p. 224.

110. Ibid., p. 221.

111. S. Viswam, "Back to Before the Split?" The Statesman, Sept. 15, 1972; Kuldip Nayar, "No Different from the Undivided Congress," ibid., June 16, 1971.

112. Ashoka Mehta, "The Next Power Structure, The Statesman, March 9, 1972.

113. Dilip Mukherjee, "The Politics of Succession: I, II," The Times of India, Oct. 2 and 3, 1971.

114. Inder Malhotra, "Have You Kept Your Promises?" Illustrated Weekly of India, Dec. 28, 1972.

115. See reports of the annual session of the Congress party in The Times of India, The Hindu, and the Hindustan Times, Dec. 30 and 31, 1972.

116. Peter Hazelhurst in The Times (London), April 6, 1972.

117. Peter Hazelhurst, "Emotion Delays Pakistan Recognition of Bangladesh," The Statesman, Aug. 27, 1972. See also Dilip Mukherjee's reports on Pakistan in The Times of India, March 11, 29, and 30, 1972, and News Review on South Asia (Jan. 1972).

118. Peter Hazelhurst, "Pakistani Provinces on Collision Course," The Statesman, Sept. 4, 1972; also his "Fresh Regional Tensions in Pakistan," ibid., Aug. 23, 1972.

119. Interview with Kuldip Nayar, News Review on South Asia (April 1972), pp. 69-79.

120. Ibid.

121. Nayar, Distant Neighbours, p. 212.

122. Rahman's interview with Kuldip Nayar, The Statesman, April 26, 1972. Rahman affirmed that India "will not and cannot" negotiate any settlement of the POW issue without the concurrence of Bangladesh: "Whatever the solution, it will have to be in consultation with us." He refused to take part in a tripartite meeting until Bangladesh had been recognized by Pakistan.

123. The Hindu, Jan. 11, 1972. For two very different versions of the Bhutto-Rahman "understanding" at the time of the Awami League leader's release from Pakistani prison, see Nayar, Distant Neighbours, pp. 196-197.

124. Sunanda Dutta-Ray, "Sheikh Mujib Returns to Crisis in Dacca," Daily Star (Beirut), Sept. 19, 1972.

125. Dilip Mukherjee, "Uncertainties in Bangladesh: I, II, III," The Times of India, April 27, 28, and 29, 1972.

126. Ibid.

127. Amalendu Das Gupta, "Outlook in Bangladesh: II," The Statesman, Jan. 24, 1972.

128. The People, Jan. 13 and 15, 1972; The Asian (Hong Kong), March 12, 1972; Hindustan Standard, Jan. 24, 1972.

129. Newsweek, March 9, 1972; The Asian, March 26, 1972; Straits Times (Singapore), April 5, 1972; The Times of India, May 17, 1972. The Soviets denied that they intended to build a naval base in Bangladesh (ibid., Sept. 8, 1972). The salvage operations were extended to December 1972.

130. For the text of the joint declaration, ibid., Feb. 9, 1972.

131. For text of the treaty, ibid., March 20, 1972.

132. Girilal Jain, "The Indo-Bangladesh Treaty," ibid., March 21, 1972.

133. Amalendu Das Gupta, "Outlook in Bangladesh." See also Dilip
Mukherjee, "Viability of Bangladesh," The Times of India, Feb.
28, 1972; Pran Chopra, "A Solid Basis for Hope," Hindustan Times,
June 5, 1972; Kirit Bhowmik, "Growing Unrest in Bangladesh," The
Times of India, May 9, 1972; "Steps Urged to Restore Bangladesh
Economy," ibid., Nov. 18, 1972; "Prices Still High in Bangladesh,"
ibid., Aug. 20, 1972; Sibdas Bannerji, "Problems Facing
Bangladesh," ibid., Feb. 5, 1972; Ajit Bhattacharjea, "In
Bangladesh Today: I, II," ibid., Nov. 2 and 3, 1972.

134. Indian Express, May 16, 1972.

135. Ibid., May 23, 1972.

136. Bangladesh Observer (Dacca), Aug. 3,4, and 15, and Sept. 4,
1972.

137. For the magnitude of the guerrilla arms problem, see Peter
Hazelhurst's report in The Times, March 27, 1972.

138. Girilal Jain, "Sharp Swing in U.S. Policy," The Times of
India, March 3, 1972. See also Amalendu Das Gupta, "Prospects in
Peking," The Statesman, Feb. 21, 1972; Ziaul Hasan, "Sino-U.S.
Aim to Block Peace in South Asia," Patriot, Sept. 12, 1972.

139. Indira Gandhi, "India and the World," Foreign Affairs, vol.
41, no. 1 (Oct. 1972), pp. 65-77.

140. M. V. Kamath, "Indo-U.S. Relations," The Times of India,
Sept. 8, 1972; Kishen Bhatia, "U.S. Fiscal Plan Has Disturbing
Notes for India," Hindustan Times, Sept. 28, 1972; "India May Not
Get U.S. Aid This Year Also," ibid., Oct. 24, 1972; M. V. Kamath,
"American Hostility to India," The Times of India, Oct. 19, 1972;
"USAID May Be Wound Up in India," Economic Times, Aug. 14, 1972.
USAID decided to lay off 78 percent of its Indian staff by
Juanuary 1973 (The Times of India, Sept. 27, 1972). See also
Sydney H. Schanberg, "U.S.-India Relations: A New Low," New York
Times, July 27, 1972.

141. Bowles, "America and Russia in India" (see note 5).

142. For the announcement of arms sales to Pakistan, see The New
York Times, March 15 and 16, 1973; for Indian reactions, The
Times of India, March 16 and 17, 1973); Hindustan Times, March
16, 1973; Patriot, March 17, 1973; for Soviet reaction, The Times
of India, March 17, 1973. For the release of U.S. economic aid to

India, The Times of India, March 17, 1973, and for agreement to discuss PL-480 rupee fund disposal, ibid., March 29, 1973.

143. Patriot, Aug. 26, 1971. Swaran Singh told the Rajya Sabha (upper house of parliament) that "India was ever prepared to create conditions" for talks with China if there were a favourable response" (ibid.).

144. The Times of India, April 13, 1971. This message upheld Pakistan's unity, characterized the events in East Pakistan as the country's internal affair, and promised to support Pakistan against aggression and to safeguard its sovereignty and independence. The timing of the message was interesting; it was delivered after it had become clear that there was not going to be any immediate Indian intervention in East Pakistan.

145. Indian Express, Sept. 5, 1971.

146. According to C. L. Sulzberger of the New York Times, the U.S. and China would have intervened if India carried the war into West Pakistan. "The Soviet Union understood the signal and then pressed India for a cease-fire. I know this is true. I have just been in Peking and Chou En-lai confirmed this to me" (International Herald Tribune, Feb. 14, 1972).

147. News Review on South Asia (Feb. 1972), pp. 59-66.

148. Ibid., pp. 59-61.

149. Bhutto's interview with R. K. Karanjia, the editor of Blitz (Bombay), published in Assam Tribune (Gauhati), November 12, 1972.

150. Chiao Kuan-hua implicitly blamed the Soviet Union for the dismemberment of Pakistan (The Guardian, Aug. 29, 1972). His visit to Pakistan seemed to confirm the belief in India that Peking would stand by Pakistan as long as Pakistan needed its help to block Bangladesh's entry into the UN.

151. Peking Review, vol. 15, no. 41 (Oct. 13, 1972), pp. 4-10, carried a commentary in which it said, "China's stand for postponing consideration [of Bangladesh's membership of the UN] does not mean that we are fundamentally opposed to the admission of 'Bangladesh' to the UN. . . . China cherishes friendly sentiments for the people of East Bengal and has no prejudice against Mujibur Rahman."

For the Indian perception of China's Bangladesh policy, see a series of articles in China Report (Delhi), special number on China and Bangladesh (Nov.-Dec., 1971).

152. The Hindu, April 1, 1972.

153. G. Yakubov, "Conflict on the Indian Subcontinent and the Provocative Role of Mao's Group," Pravda, Dec. 28, 1971.

154. The Times, Jan. 26, 1972.

155. The Statesman, March 24, 1972.

156. The Times of India, May 6, 1972; Economic Times, Sept. 1, 1972; Hindustan Times, Sept. 11 and 27, 1972; Patriot, Oct. 3 and 4, 1972.

157. The Statesman, Dec. 27, 1972.

158. Stockholm International Peace Research Institute, World Armaments and Disarmament: SIPRI Yearbook 1972, pp. 106-107.

159. Ibid., p. 105.

160. Ibid., p. 109.

161. For Mrs. Gandhi's statement, see The Statesman, Feb. 9, 1974. Earlier, on February 6, Foreign Minister Swaran Singh declared India's "total opposition" to the Anglo-U.S. accord on the ocean base (ibid., Feb. 7, 1974). For the Soviet perception of the American action, see the New York Times, Feb. 28, 1974.

162. The Times of India, Feb. 27 and March 1, 1974. For the likely impact of the energy crisis on the Indian economy, see the New York Times, Feb. 4, 1974; for Indian efforts to deal with the crisis, see The Statesman Overseas Weekly, Feb. 23, 1974.

163. For a perceptive summing up of Bangladesh's achievements since liberation and of the problems it faces in the task of nation-building, see the testimony of Professor Marcus Franda in Political Trends in India and Bangladesh, Hearing before the Subcommittee on the Near East and South Asia of the Committee on Foreign Affairs, U.S. House of Representatives, 93rd Congress, 1st session, October 31, 1973.

164. Swaran Singh dashed to Dacca to confer with Rahman on the
eve of the latter's flight to Lahore. His comment on
Bangladesh's participation in the Islamic conference was
distinctly lukewarm (The Statesman Overseas Weekly, Feb. 23,
1974). For India's subdued hope of getting the best out of a
tripartite or India-Pakistan summit, see The Statesman, Feb. 17,
1974.

165. Mujibur Rahman's declared objective is to make Bangladesh
the "Switzerland of the East."

Notes to Chapter 5

1. An excellent study of Japan's ruling party is Nathaniel B.
Thayer, How the Conservatives Rule Japan (Princeton: N.J.:
Princeton University Press, 1969).

2. For stimulating studies of the characteristics of Japanese
society and behavior relevant to decision-making, see the
classic, but not yet wholly dated, Ruth Benedict, The
Chrysanthemum and the Sword: Patterns of Japanese Culture
(Boston: Houghton Mifflin, 1946); the recent work of a Japanese
social anthropologist, (Ms.) Chie Nakane, Japanese Society
(Berkeley: University of California Press, 1970); Nyozekan
Hasegawa, The Japanese Character: A Cultural Profile (Tokyo:
Kodansha International, 1966); Takeshi Ishida, Japanese
Society (New York: Random House, 1971); and the recent best-
seller in Japan, attributed to a foreign Jewish author by the
name of Isaiah Ben-Dasan (supposedly born in Kobe, Japan, in
1918, and since 1941 a resident of the United States), who is
widely believed to be in actuality a Japanese author having some
familiarity with Jewish thought and practices. An English-
language version of that work appeared in 1972 under the title
The Japanese and the Jews (New York and Tokyo: Weatherhill),
translated rather freely by Richard L. Gage. One of the most
interesting and perceptive analyses of the cultural differences
between Japan and the West as reflected in diplomacy is the
brief essay by the political scientist Professor Kinhide
Mushakoji which appeared under the title "The Cultural Premises
of Japanese Diplomacy" in an outstanding translation by J.
Victor Koschmann in The Japan Interpreter: A Journal of Social
and Political Ideas, vol. 7 (Summer-Autumn 1972), pp. 282-292.
(This quarterly, published in Tokyo by the Japan Center for
International Exchange, is the best English-language publication
providing insights into the central concerns of Japanese society
and intellectual life.)

3. A useful discussion of the major dimensions—economic, political, and military—of the U.S.-Japanese relationship is Robert Scalapino, <u>American-Japanese Relations in a Changing Era</u>, issued as the second volume of the Washington Papers series by the Center for Strategic and International Studies of Georgetown University (New York: The Library Press, 1972).

4. For a brief account of the evolution of the Japanese communist movement in the period since World War II, see Paul F. Langer, <u>Communism in Japan: A Case of Political Neutralization</u> (Stanford, Calif.: Hoover Institution Press, 1972). An earlier and more extensive treatment is found in Robert A. Scalapino, <u>The Japanese Communist Movement, 1920-1966</u> (Berkeley, Calif.: University of California Press, 1967). The results of the conflicting Moscow and Peking pulls on the Japanese Communist Party are analyzed in Paul F. Langer, "The New Posture of the CPJ," <u>Problems of Communism</u>, vol. 20, nos. 1-2 (Jan.-April 1971), pp. 14-24.

Notes to Chapter 6

1. A measure of the effect of this announcement is that many newspapers in cities around the world, including New York, Washington, Tokyo, Paris, and even Philadelphia, greeted the news with large headlines. Television and radio commentators were equally enthusiastic.

2. For the text of the joint communiqué, see the <u>New York Times</u>, July 5, 1972, and the <u>Washington Post</u>, July 4, 1972.

3. Selig S. Harrison, writing from Pyongyang in the <u>Washington Post</u> of July 4, 1972, noted, however, that the "North Koreans are not talking about 'peaceful coexistence' when they forswear the use of force. Peaceful, yes, but coexistence, no, if this means placidly accepting the indefinite division of the Korean Peninsula."

4. For the text of the Shanghai communiqué, see the <u>New York Times</u>, March 1, 1972.

5. See Kenneth T. Young, <u>Negotiating with the Chinese Communists: The United States Experience, 1953-1957</u> (New York: McGraw-Hill, 1968), passim.

6. Republic of Korea, National Assembly, <u>T'ongil paeksŏ</u> [White Paper on Unification] (Seoul, 1967), p. 249.

7. Murakami Kaoru, Nihon to ajia no gunji jōsei [The Military Situation in Japan and Asia](Tokyo: Gōdō Shuppan, 1971), p. 188.

8. Cited in ibid., p. 189.

9. For the text of Premier Kim Il-sŏng's speech of July 22, as reported by the Korean Central News Agency (KCNA) International Service on July 23, 1971, see Foreign Broadcast Information Service (FBIS), Daily Report, July 23, 1971, Asia and Pacific, DC-9.

10. Kaoru, Nihon to ajia no gunji jōsei, p. 189.

11. The relationship between the DPRK and the PRC had deteriorated during the cultural revolution, but Premier Chou En-lai's visit to North Korea in April, 1970, signaled the restoration of the previous relationship. For details, see Robert A. Scalapino and Chong-Sik Lee, Communism in Korea (Berkeley and Los Angeles: University of California Press, 1972), pp. 620-639.

12. The complete text in English of this article can be found in FBIS, Daily Report, Aug. 6, 10, and 11, 1971, North Korea, IV. The English text runs to 35 single-spaced typed pages.

13. For Kim Il-sŏng's speech of August 6, 1971, see Kŭlloja [The Worker], the theoretical organ of the KWP, no. 8, (1971), pp. 2-11.

14. Nodong Sinmun [Worker's Daily], Sept. 9, 1971.

15. New China News Agency, Aug. 15, 1971. See FBIS, Daily Report, Aug. 16, 1971, I, A7.

16. Ibid., Aug. 10, 1971, I, A9, and Aug. 17, 1971, I, A2.

17. See Scalapino and Lee, Communism in Korea, vol. 1, pp. 670-671.

18. See FBIS, Daily Report, Sept. 8, 1971, I (PRC), A1. Nihon Keizai Shimbun [Japan Economic News] (Tokyo), Jan. 14, 1973, reported that "there were rumors to the effect that this agreement was not implemented after the fall of General Huang from power. Huang was implicated in the Lin Piao affair. The visit of Foreign Minister Chi Peng-fei in December 1972, however, is supposed to have 'revived' the agreement. We have no way of verifying this 'rumor' at this point."

19. Ibid., Jan. 14, 1973.

20. Asahi Shimbun (Tokyo), Nov. 29, 1972, citing "diplomatic sources" that "confirmed the top-secret visit."

21. For the English text of the interview, see Asahi Evening News (Tokyo), Sept. 28, 1971.

22. Ibid., Oct. 4, 1971.

23. Ibid., Dec. 10, 1971.

24. See Nodong Sinmun, Jan. 11, 1972, and Kŭlloja, No. 1 (1972), pp. 13-30.

25. Nihon Keizai Shimbun, Jan. 3, 1973. The actual trade figure between January and November 1972 was $125.2 million. Japanese exports to North Korea totaled $86.5 million and imports $33.9 million. The total trade volume in 1971 was $72.8 million.

26. Ibid., Dec. 28, 1972.

27. Tong-a Ilbo, May 11 and 18, 1972.

28. Asahi Shimbun, Mainichi Shimbun, and Yomiuri Shimbun, Sept. 8, 1972.

29. KCNA International Service, Feb. 27, 1972. A DPRK-Zambia joint communiqué issued on March 16 included the following paragraph: "The Zambian side supported and welcomed the new proposals of reunification advanced by His Excellency Kim Il-sŏng, the respected and beloved leader of the Korean people, on January 10, 1972, on concluding a peace agreement between the north and south and holding north-south political negotiations and other proposals for reunifying the country peacefully without any interference of outside forces" (KCNA, International Service, March 23, 1972).

30. UPI dispatch from Geneva, Philadephia Inquirer, July 5, 1972.

31. See, for example, the Pravda editorial of July 27, 1971, expressing Soviet views on the Nixon visit.

32. KCNA Domestic Service (in Korean), Feb. 26, 1972.

33. Soviet imports from North Korea in 1962 amounted to 79.4 million rubles. These declined to 79.3 million in 1963 and 72.6 million in 1964. For details, see Robert Own Freedman, Economic Warfare in the Communist Bloc (New York: Praeger, 1970), pp. 142-147.

34. For a more complete discussion, see Scalapino and Lee, Communism in Korea, Vol. 1, pp. 635-637.

35. Radio Moscow, March 31, 1965, cited in Freedman, Economic Warfare, p. 153.

36. Ibid., p. 153.

37. KCNA International Service (in English), Feb. 11, 1972.

38. KCNA Domestic Service, Feb. 21, 1972.

39. The commentary of Radio Pyongyang on February 29 (KCNA Domestic Service) was entitled "The 'Peace' Trumpet of the Nixon Clique is a Smokescreen for Further Intensifying Its Aggressive Maneuvers." On the same day, KCNA International Service (in English) broadcast the commentary of Minju Chosŏn [Democratic Korea], an organ of the DPRK, denouncing the passage of the U.S. aid bill, which was presented as a proof that "once again that the U.S. imperialists are bent on reinforcing the armed forces of Japanese militarism and the Asian satellite states and puppets to frantically drive them out to the maneuvers of aggression and war against the Asian revolutionary people." For the texts of these broadcasts, see FBIS, Daily Report, March 1, 1972, IV, D1-3, D6-7.

40. KCNA International Service (in English), March 4, 1972, in FBIS, Daily Report, March 6, 1972, Asia and Pacific, D3.

41. John M. Lee, "North Korea Acts to Ease Isolation," New York Times, March 12, 1972.

42. Selig S. Harrison, "The New Look of 1972 North Korea," Washington Post, May 26, 1972, p. 1.

43. Ibid., p. A16.

44. Republic of Korea, Ministry of Culture and Information, Unification: Goal of the '70s: An Address by President Pak Chung

Hee on the 25th Anniversary of National Liberation, August 15, 1970 (Seoul, 1970), pp. 6-8.

45. See Inaugural Speech by President Pak Chung Hee, July 1, 1971 (Seoul, 1971).

46. Tong-a Ilbo, July 1, 1971.

47. Ibid., July 6, 1971.

48. Ibid., Aug. 6, 1971.

49. See ibid., June 2 and 3, 1971.

50. Ibid., July 16, 1971.

51. Ibid., Aug. 6, 1971.

52. Ibid., July 17, 1971.

53. Ibid, Aug. 7, 1971.

54. Ibid., July 19, 1971.

55. Ibid., July 17, 1971.

56. For the text of Pak's speech, see ibid., Oct. 1, 1971.

57. Ibid., Nov. 2, 1971.

58. This was the official analysis of the military-political situation on the Korean peninsula presented at the time of the U.S.-ROK security conference held in mid-July 1971. U.S. Secretary of Defense Melvin Laird was in Seoul for the conference. See ibid., July 12, 1971.

59. Ibid.

60. See a reporter's analysis, ibid., Nov. 3, 1971.

61. For the text of Pak's proclamation as well as his statement accompanying the proclamation, see Special Statement by the President on the Declaration of a State of National Emergency (Seoul, 1971).

62. This bill was opposed by the New Democratic party, which staged a sit-in in the Assembly hall for five days and nights. Thereupon the government party convened a session at another location at three o-clock in the morning without notifying the opposition party members. The bill then passed very quickly.

63. See the statements of Foreign Minister Kim Yŏng-sik and Premier Kim Chŏng-p'il in Tong-a Ilbo, Feb. 28 and 29, 1972, respectively. The premier, however, was less than enthusiastic about the result of the Nixon trip. He expressed his concern that the trip may have ended up satisfying (or boosting) Chinese nationalism ("Chung-hua-ism") rather than conveying the true attitude of the peoples of the free world toward the Chiense people.

64. Ibid., Feb. 28, 1972.

65. Ibid., April 25, 1972.

66. Ibid., April 27, 1972.

67. For details of the conference results, see ibid., June 28, 1972.

68. Nodong Sinmun had issued strongly denunciatory statements aimed at the South Korean mass media and the "government behind them" for disparaging North Korea. See the issues of Sept. 14 and 22, 1972.

69. See the New York Times, Sept. 24, 1972, pp. 1 and 10.

70. Quoted in Korea Week (Washington, D.C.), Oct. 15, 1972.

71. Ibid.

72. Tong-a Ilbo, Oct. 13, 1972.

73. Ibid., Sept. 15, 1972.

74. Ibid., Nov. 23, 1972.

75. See the New York Times, Nov. 5, 1972.

76. Ibid.; see also Tong-a Ilbo, Nov. 6, 1972.

77. See the Nodong Sinmun editorials of March 18 and 20, 1973.

78. Public Relations Association of Korea, <u>South-North Dialogue in Korea: Where It Stands Now</u> (Seoul, 1973), pp. 38-39.

79. KCNA Domestic Service, Feb. 7, 1973, in FBIS, <u>Daily Report</u>, Feb. 13, 1973, IV, D6-21 (at D16).

80. For details, see various newspapers of both Koreas dated June 23 to June 26, 1973, as well as the <u>Christian Science Monitor</u>, June 25, 1973, and the <u>New York Times</u>, June 26 and 27, 1973. On October 28, President Kim Il-sŏng repeated some of the charges, using such words as "national traitors," "hired hands of foreign aggressors," and "national splitters." See <u>Nodong Sinmun</u>, Oct. 28, 1973.

81. <u>New York Times</u>, Dec. 2, 1973.

91. Ibid., Feb. 12, 1973.

83. <u>Korean News</u>, Korean Information Office, Washington, D.C., Jan. 13, 1973, p. 4.

84. See George Ginsburgs, "Soviet Sources on the Law of North Korea," <u>Journal of Korean Affairs</u> (January, 1972), p. 61, citing L. M. Gudoshnikov, "U yuristov Koreiskoi Narodno-Demokraticheskoi Respubliki" [Among the Lawyers of the Korean People's Democratic Republic], <u>Sovetskoe gosudarstvo i pravo</u> [Soviet State and Law], no. 10 (1960), p. 116.

85. All quotations are from <u>Korean News</u>, Jan. 13, 1973.

86. "Provocative Outcries From ROK Create Tension," FBIS, <u>Daily Report</u>, January 10, 1973, North Korea, IV, D1-2.

87. See Chong-Sik Lee, "Stalinism in the East: Communism in North Korea," in Robert A. Scalapino, ed., <u>Communist Revolution in Asia</u> (Englewood Cliffs, N.J.: Prentice-Hall, 1965), p. 126.

88. For an excellent summary and discussion of North Korean proposals, see Soon Sung Cho, "The Politics of North Korea's Unification Policies, 1950-1965," <u>World Politics</u>, vol. 19, no. 2 (Jan. 1967), pp. 218-241.

89. See ROK, National Assembly, <u>T'ongil paeksŏ</u>, 1971 edition, p. 387.

90. For a general discussion, see Chosen Shimbunsha, Tō-itsu
Chōsen Nanken, 1967-1968 [One Korea Year Book, 1967-1968]
(Tokyo, 1967), pp. 76-77.

91. From official Japanese sources, quoted in Chŏson kyŏngje
t'ongge yoram [Korean Economic Statistical Survey](Seoul, 1949),
pp. 72-73. The identity of the compiler of this very useful book
has not been established.

92. Ibid., p. 69.

93. Ibid., p. 4.

94. Statistical data cited above have been drawn from Scalapino
and Lee, Communism in Korea, chaps. 13 and 14.

95. Henry A. Kissinger, "Central Issues of American Foreign
Policy," in Kermit Gordon, ed., Agenda for the Nation
(Washington, D.C.: The Brookings Institution, 1968), p. 612,
reprinted in Kissinger, American Foreign Policy: Three Essays
(New York: Norton, 1969), pp. 93-94.

96. Daily Yomiuri, Jan. 19, 1973.

97. For an admission of the Russian involvement in the Korean
war, see O. B. Borisov and B. T. Koloskov, Sovetsko-Kitaiski
Otnosheniya 1945-1970; Kratkii Ocherk [Soviet-Chinese Relations
1945-1970: A Brief Essay](Moscow, 1971), pp. 55ff.